Handbook of Research on the Significance of Forensic Accounting Techniques in Corporate Governance

Suleman Sherali Kamwani
A'Sharqiyah University, Oman

Elisabete S. Vieira
University of Aveiro, Portugal

Mara Madaleno
University of Aveiro, Portugal

Graça Azevedo
University of Aveiro, Portugal

IGI Global
PUBLISHER of TIMELY KNOWLEDGE

A volume in the Advances in Finance, Accounting, and Economics (AFAE) Book Series

Published in the United States of America by
IGI Global
Business Science Reference (an imprint of IGI Global)
701 E. Chocolate Avenue
Hershey PA, USA 17033
Tel: 717-533-8845
Fax: 717-533-8661
E-mail: cust@igi-global.com
Web site: http://www.igi-global.com

Library of Congress Cataloging-in-Publication Data

Names: Kamwani, Suleman Sherali, 1974- editor. | Vieira, Elisabete S., editor. | Madaleno, Mara, 1981- editor.
Title: Handbook of research on the significance of forensic accounting techniques in corporate governance / Suleman Sherali Kamwani, Elisabete S. Vieira, Mara Madaleno, and Graca Azevedo, editors.
Description: Hershey, PA : Business Science Reference, [2022] | Includes bibliographical references and index. | Summary: "This book highlights the financial community's realization regarding the failure of corporate communication which is required for forensic skills/techniques professionals which helps to expose structural weakness in major areas such as flawed internal controls, poor corporate governance, and fraudulent financial statements"-- Provided by publisher.
Identifiers: LCCN 2021040461 (print) | LCCN 2021040462 (ebook) | ISBN 9781799887546 (hardcover) | ISBN 9781799887560 (ebook)
Subjects: LCSH: Forensic accounting. | Corporate governance. | Fraud.
Classification: LCC HV6768 .S554 2022 (print) | LCC HV6768 (ebook) | DDC 363.25/968--dc23/eng/20211007
LC record available at https://lccn.loc.gov/2021040461
LC ebook record available at https://lccn.loc.gov/2021040462

This book is published in the IGI Global book series Advances in Finance, Accounting, and Economics (AFAE) (ISSN: 2327-5677; eISSN: 2327-5685)

British Cataloguing in Publication Data
A Cataloguing in Publication record for this book is available from the British Library.

Advances in Finance, Accounting, and Economics (AFAE) Book Series

Ahmed Driouchi
Al Akhawayn University, Morocco

ISSN:2327-5677
EISSN:2327-5685

Mission

In our changing economic and business environment, it is important to consider the financial changes occurring internationally as well as within individual organizations and business environments. Understanding these changes as well as the factors that influence them is crucial in preparing for our financial future and ensuring economic sustainability and growth.

The **Advances in Finance, Accounting, and Economics (AFAE)** book series aims to publish comprehensive and informative titles in all areas of economics and economic theory, finance, and accounting to assist in advancing the available knowledge and providing for further research development in these dynamic fields.

Coverage

- Microeconomics
- Economics of Intellectual Property Rights
- Finance and Accounting in SMEs
- Banking
- Economics Geography
- Ethics in Accounting and Finance
- International Economics
- E-Accounting
- Economics of Risks, Uncertainty, Ambiguity, and Insurance
- Field Research

IGI Global is currently accepting manuscripts for publication within this series. To submit a proposal for a volume in this series, please contact our Acquisition Editors at Acquisitions@igi-global.com or visit: http://www.igi-global.com/publish/.

The Advances in Finance, Accounting, and Economics (AFAE) Book Series (ISSN 2327-5677) is published by IGI Global, 701 E. Chocolate Avenue, Hershey, PA 17033-1240, USA, www.igi-global.com. This series is composed of titles available for purchase individually; each title is edited to be contextually exclusive from any other title within the series. For pricing and ordering information please visit http://www.igi-global.com/book-series/advances-finance-accounting-economics/73685. Postmaster: Send all address changes to above address.

Titles in this Series

For a list of additional titles in this series, please visit: http://www.igi-global.com/book-series/advances-finance-accounting-economics/73685

Handbook of Research on Changing World Economic Order in the Post-Pandemic Period
Sushanta Kumar Mahapatra (IBS Hyderabad, The ICFAI Foundation for Higher Education, India) and Vishal Sarin (Lovely Professional University, India)
Business Science Reference • © 2022 • 470pp • H/C (ISBN: 9781799868965) • US $295.00

Cases on Applying Knowledge Economy Principles for Economic Growth in Developing Nations
Danilo Piaggesi (Knowledge for Development (K4D), USA) Helena Landazuri (Knowledge for Development (K4D), USA) and Bo Jia (Tsinghua University, China)
Business Science Reference • © 2022 • 327pp • H/C (ISBN: 9781799884170) • US $215.00

Economic Impact and Recovery Following a Global Health Crisis
Brian W. Sloboda (University of Maryland Global Campus, USA) and Yaya Sissoko (Indiana University of Pennsylvania, USA)
Business Science Reference • © 2022 • 253pp • H/C (ISBN: 9781799869009) • US $225.00

Handbook of Research on New Challenges and Global Outlooks in Financial Risk Management
Mara Madaleno (GOVCOPP, University of Aveiro, Portugal) Elisabete Vieira (GOVCOPP, University of Aveiro, Portugal) and Nicoleta Bărbuţă-Mişu (University of Galati, Romania)
Business Science Reference • © 2022 • 470pp • H/C (ISBN: 9781799886099) • US $285.00

Stabilizing Currency and Preserving Economic Sovereignty Using the Grondona System
Patrick Collins (Independent Researcher, Japan)
Business Science Reference • © 2022 • 244pp • H/C (ISBN: 9781799883029) • US $215.00

Transitioning From Globalized to Localized and Self-Reliant Economies
Ruchika Gupta (Amity University, India) Priyank Srivastava (Amity University, India) Shiv Ranjan (Amity University, India) and M. Affan Badar (Indiana State University, USA)
Business Science Reference • © 2022 • 256pp • H/C (ISBN: 9781799887058) • US $195.00

COVID-19 Pandemic Impact on New Economy Development and Societal Change
Cristina Raluca Gh. Popescu (University of Bucharest, Romania & The Bucharest University of Economic Studies, Romania & The National Institute for Research and Development in Environmental Protection (INCDPM), Romania & National Research and Development Institute for Gas Turbines (COMOTI), Romania)
Business Science Reference • © 2022 • 425pp • H/C (ISBN: 9781668433744) • US $195.00

IGI Global
PUBLISHER of TIMELY KNOWLEDGE

701 East Chocolate Avenue, Hershey, PA 17033, USA
Tel: 717-533-8845 x100 • Fax: 717-533-8661
E-Mail: cust@igi-global.com • www.igi-global.com

EDITORIAL ADVISORY BOARD

List of Contributors

Table of Contents

Detailed Table of Contents

evolutionary terms. Considering only the FA publications, the Scopus analysis led to a total database of 192 documents. However, this sudy focuses on the research that relates FA and corporate governance concentrating the bibliometric analysis in the Scopus database.

This chapter explores the role of forensic accounting in uncovering evidence for use in courts to litigate and arbitrate on financially related crimes. The chapter differentiates the operation of forensic accountants from external auditors and other accountants. It also provides examples of financial crimes and describes the role of forensic accounting in assisting courts deal with these crimes. Furthermore, the chapter outlines differences between forensic accounting and audit reports as well as discussing the admissibility of forensic accounting evidence in courts. Issues around forensic accounting are articulated. Recommendations include the convergence of all important stakeholders to agree on the appropriate curriculum for forensic accountants as well as guidelines and standards to shape the profession and prevent entry by incompetent and unqualified people. Future research should focus on the current inconsistencies on the profession's education mode of delivery, content, pedagogies, and empirical studies to establish specific skills required by forensic accountants.

Vietnam has been reforming its economy to be more market-oriented and globally integrated since 1986. Under the circumstances, the Vietnam accounting system has been developed to meet the practical needs of enterprises. Forensic accounting is a new field in Vietnam accounting, but it is emerging as a good prospect for preventing financial crime and accounting fraud. This chapter focuses on the existing conditions and demand for forensic accounting in Vietnam. It includes the technique and skill requirements of forensic accounting to provide advantages and disadvantages of applying forensic accounting in Vietnam. The chapter will also enrich the book titled Significance of Forensic Accounting Techniques in Corporate Governance by overviewing Vietnam's accounting system and helping Vietnam achieve sustainable economic growth.

The Fraud Triangle is the framework that regulators have chosen to assess fraud risk for auditors and practitioners. In this chapter, the authors will review the origins and each of the three elements of the Fraud Triangle and provide some tools for assessing whether each element is present in a fraud case. The chapter will distinguish between occupational and corporate fraud, as the authors believe that the drivers of each are slightly different. After defining each of the elements, the authors will apply the framework of analysis to some famous fraud cases in very different parts of the world so that the reader can see the differences and similarities of these cases.

The most popular frauds known in the early 21st century eroded investor and society confidence in the financial markets contributing to economic and social destruction. In response, the United States enacted the Sarbanes-Oxley Act (SOX) and the European Union issued several regulatory instruments, but the fraud cases have continued. Motivated by the idea that if we understand where the possible causes are, then the problem of fraud can be avoided or at least reduced in its dimensions and consequences. So, this study intends to understand the causes of fraud and its relevance, identifying their common points and also measuring if they changed in the post-SOX period. From the analysis carried out, it results that the lack of an ethical tone in top management is the cause that remains transversal to both sides of the Atlantic and to the two periods studied. In the post-SOX period, the fraudulent financial statements lost relevance, ceasing to be part of the most relevant causes, and internal control failures became one of the most relevant causes.

In the rise of digital transformation and big data, accounting and auditing professions are required to adopt advanced techniques that help detect irregularities and frauds. This chapter collects 1,112 documents from Scopus database published in 288 sources over the period 2008-2021. A bibliometric analysis is used to depict trends, and applicable methodologies are adopted to build a comprehensible base that will serve to instill a new fraud detection model. More specifically, RStudio through "biblioshiny package", VOSviewer, and Excel are the tools embraced to analyze the dataset information. The chapter explores the literature growth over time and addresses key aspects of the literature, such as most relevant documents, authors, countries, citation analysis. This chapter applies a network and content analysis using the bibliographical coupling, trend analysis, word cloud, and co-occurrence analysis. The theoretical model helps auditors, forensic accountants, top managements, analysts, and policy makers predict potential anomalies and misstatements.

In this chapter, the necessity for compliance and corporate governance is discussed. It is essential to shine the limelight on these practices, and they are considered important for economic growth. Corporate governance is, in theory, a rather straightforward process with pre-determined policies and procedures. However, it is becoming increasingly clear that there are plenty of deficiencies in the way these procedures are being implemented. In fact, fraud is becoming more difficult to detect as strategies to fight corruption continue to be loosely implemented. Implications of conventional theory and traditional practices are discussed with an emphasis on today's standards, along with the objectivity of the underlying pillars of ethics, social norms, and personal values. The chapter highlights the importance of corporate governance and its added value to professional and social settings.

Forensic accounting is a key emerging field for strengthening the corporate sector of any economy. Forensic accountants have to be well equipped with multiple skill competencies to act as catalysts for enhancing and leveraging on the best corporate practices in terms of minimizing the possibilities of fraud, damages, scams, and scandals all around the globe. Aspiring professional accountancy students are nowadays highly inspired and motivated to build their career in forensic accounting, and also there is an immense scarcity of talented people, specifically in the Indian context in this domain. Literature demonstrates the availability of a variety of skill competencies as required for proficiency in the same domain. The author in this chapter primarily explored the multiple skill competencies with the help of secondary data and further assesses them by reducing all skills to the most basic and relevant ones with the application of factor reduction technique through SPSS after collecting the primary data (survey method) from the chartered accountancy students in Meerut City, India.

The increasing sophistication of fraud has necessitated the use of forensic accounting tools to facilitate successful investigation. Perpetuation of fraud in the Nigerian public sector has reached alarming levels. This problem motivated the discussion on whether forensic accounting can facilitate detection and prevention of fraud in Nigeria. This chapter evaluates the relevance of forensic accounting on fraud detection in Nigerian public sector using a case study of Bayelsa state. This chapter finds that forensic accounting enhances fraud detection. The chapter consequently recommends that professional accounting bodies should constantly conduct forensic accounting training for accountants, and there is a need for the inclusion of forensic accounting in the syllabus of all the tertiary institutions offering accountancy in Nigeria. Further, the services of forensic accountants should be engaged more in Nigeria.

The necessity for forensic accounting has grown with the increased incidents of financial fraud. This is not unrelated to the inability of statutory audit to discover and prevent fraudulent acts. This chapter provides discussions on the need and prospects of forensic accounting in developing countries as it may address the prevalence of business failures and financial crimes resulting from audit failure and the growth of creative accounting. Although the chapter provides a general overview for developing countries, there is a specific focus on Nigeria, a developing country characterized by high level of corruption. The findings show that the use of forensic accounting is still at a very low level owing to the high cost of forensic accounting tools and the time and money involved in acquiring the requisite skills. The chapter recommends that forensic accountants nonetheless are suitable to eliminate economic crimes and corruption to improve growth in the economy in developing countries.

The purpose of this study is to determine artificial intelligence (AI)-supported Omani publicly listed organisations' attitudes towards fraud elimination and mitigation (FEM) concerns from the lens of agency theory with internal audit (IAF) serving as the mediator. A descriptive cross-sectional survey was conducted by involving Omani publicly listed companies as the unit of analysis. Data were gathered using an internet-based tool and analysed via PLS-SEM and SPSS. For results, AI displayed an insignificant but direct impact on FEM, whereas IAF exhibited a significant and direct effect on FEM. Apparently, AI exerted a significant and direct impact on IAF, while IAF mediated the correlation between AI and FEM. This study serves as a guidance to regulators, professional bodies, and organisations in amending their codes of corporate governance and organisational policies by initiating AI as a governance agent working for the principal, as well as operating towards eradicating fraud and fraudulent practices.

Corporate governance is considered the backbone of corporations. Audit committee is one of the factors that plays a pivotal role to guide and monitor business-related matters of firms while following the national and international audit standards. The chapter covers the involvement of the audit committee with respect to corporate governance. It ranges from audit committee formations to its importance, composition, significance, and the role in quality financial reporting according to international standards. The chapter generally focuses on the audit committee and not any particular country or firms. The importance of the audit committee has always been recognized, but due to some examples of bad corporate governance practices, it became an important variable of corporate governance.

In today's business environment, fraud is the main cause of organizational failure, which results in reputational damages and can also lead to the closure of the organizations. Forensic accounting with appropriate skills, knowledge, and mindset can perform proactive tasks towards mitigating fraud risk and can raise red flags even before the occurrence of fraudulent transactions or events. With the utilization of fraud triangle theory and forensic accounting theory, this chapter is focused on the preventive and detective role of forensic accounting which will highlight the importance of this function as a permanent feature in any organization. This chapter will also highlight the problems associated with the non-availability of forensic accounting in the current organizational culture and will also provide related recommendations. This chapter can be beneficial to regulators, organizational governance management, and standard-setting bodies towards drafting or amending the laws and regulations and inclusion of forensic accounting as a permanent element for all organizations.

Financial reporting fraud affects corporate organizations as stakeholders express lack of self-confidence in financial reports. The chapter assessed the effect of financial reporting fraud, improper expense recognition and fictitious revenue on the performance of firms in the Nigerian Exchange Group return on assets (ROA). Secondary data were collected from the firm annual accounts. Correlation and regression analysis were employed. The results revealed that improper expense recognition has a negative significant relationship with ROA. Also, fictitious revenue reflected a positive but insignificant relationship with ROA. The chapter concluded that financial reporting fraud somewhat affects the performance of firms as supported by a positive relationship reflected by fictitious revenue and negative relationships shown by improper expense recognition. The chapter recommended that financial reporting fraud needs to be investigated to reveal the fraud that affects the performance of firms to aid better and easier forensic accounting investigation.

This study aims to develop a proposed framework to explain the impact of disclosure of credit risks on financial reports to achieve bank stability in accordance with the requirements of the decisions of the Basel Committee. The results of the study showed there are specific criteria that can be relied upon in order to measure bank credit risk, create a provision, classify customers and creditworthiness. It is possible to incorrectly classify the merit of a customer to improve his image in front of investors and stakeholders and thus the value and the stability of the bank. The framework proposed by the researcher aids in the disclosure of bank credit risk of commercial banks to obtain more efficiency, competition, stability.

Internet-based payment methods in recent times are rapidly growing both in developing and developed economies. Credit card-based payment systems are among the prominent cashless payment methods in all economies. Credit card frauds by cyber-criminals are increasing in spite of several precautionary measures. Thus, fraud detection in real-time is a challenging task. Several machine learning tasks have

Preface

ABOUT THE SUBJECT

The topics of forensic accounting techniques have gained a huge international relevance.

The forensic accounting consists of a combination of accounting and the investigation about financial crimes, focusing on the research of whether companies are involved in financial reporting misbehavior. To this end, forensic accountants apply a variety of approaches and skills to control if there has been financial reporting transgression, trying to look beyond the numbers, understanding the real situation of businesses, and explaining the nature of a financial crime to the courts. Consequently, this field of accounting deals with fraud and misappropriation cases, trying to explain the nature of a financial crime and to establish damages from claims, namely by the insurance industry. Financial forensic activities can have various classes, such as bankruptcy, insolvency, and reorganization; business valuation; computer forensics; economic damages calculations; money laundering; post-acquisition disputes; and securities and tax fraud.

The forensic accounting market has grown dramatically especially since the last decade. In a survey of large Certified Public Accountant firms, 85% of the feedbacks directed about forensic accounting which is an enhancing portion of their work, and 100% of the feedback predictable demand is to enhance for the future. Accounting specifically is a growing profession. In the year 2008, there were 1,290,600 accountants' professionals working in the United States and was expected that to increase by 22% in 2018 with 279,400 extra jobs in the profession of accountancy.

Corporate governance can reduce the degree of fraud activities and financial reporting misbehavior. An institutional environment that provides efficient legal protection can control managers' self-interest. Board independence can improve the monitoring behaviors in managers, including the misappropriation of assets and some frauds. In the same vein, directors with financial expertise can provide additional control on financial reporting transgression. We believe in the continuity of expanding the growth of this field. It is realized that a vital need exists for the development of forensic accounting techniques, reduce external auditor deficiencies in fraud detection and its implications and benefiting from cloud forensic audit to enhance corporate efficiency in fraud detection.

It is fruitful to investigate and disseminate the results of theoretical and empirical studies that reveal different aspects of forensic accounting phenomenon, and the relation with corporate governance characteristics, namely to obtain insightful information in order to promote effectively financial decisions.

This book folds several coherent chapters which allow, on a scientific basis, to discuss at an international level the new directions in forensic account techniques, corporate governance, digital environment, fraud risk and firm's performance.

EXPECTATIONS

The editors intend this book to be a reference source that discusses the forensic accounting techniques and how forensic accountant add value while investigation claim and fraud. Moreover, this publication highlights the benefits of forensic accounting audit for corporate benefits and evidence acceptability in court of Law and point out external auditors lacking in fraud detection reasons and implications. We believed this publication emerge the significance of forensic accounting audits and attract new generation how they shape a research approach. This publication might allow to expand the network and communication with the international accounting and finance practitioners and forensic researcher to learn, development and research new techniques to minimize corporate damages which will benefit the society.

This book highlights the financial community realization regarding the failure of the corporate communication which is required for forensic skills and techniques which helps to expose structural weakness in major areas such as flawed internal controls, poor corporate governance, and fraudulent financial statements.

Through dissemination of the research findings on the rigor of finance, this publication could also be valuable to develop and inspire further studies by researchers and students in postgraduate courses, whose research interests are related to forensic accounting, corporate governance and economic value.

This book aims to achieve the following main objectives:

- Document the state of the art related to forensic accounting;
- Disseminate the methodologies that would ensure the quality of forensic accounting;
- Document the relationship between forensic accounting and corporate governance;
- Review governance models that improves the financial reporting;
- Document the state of the art related to corporate governance;
- Analyze the corporate governance effects on financial frauds;
- Document the relationship between forensic accounting and firm's performance;
- The influence of auditors on fraud detection.

ORGANIZATION OF THE BOOK

This book is organized by 17 chapters. The first three chapters are focused on the forensic accounting techniques. Thus:

- Chapter 1 – *Significance of Forensic Accounting Techniques in Corporate Governance Bibliometric Analysis* – offers a literature review on forensic accounting techniques based on the bibliometric analysis methodology.
- Chapter 2 – *What Are the Possible Methods and Techniques in Forensic Accounting Necessary to Comply With Corporate Governance in Portugal?* – investigates the possible forensic techniques and methods to improve the overall corporate governance in Portugal.
- Chapter 3 – *An Assessment of Forensic Accounting Skill Competencies Form Minimizing Corporate Frauds and Damages: Empirical Evidence From Chartered Accountancy Students of India* – analysis whether professional accountancy students are inspired and motivated to build their career in "Forensic Accounting" in the Indian context.

The next four chapters provide studies analyzing the issue of forensic accounting in specific situations, such as in developing countries, digital environment, and considering the court of law. In this way:

- Chapter 4 – *The Essence and Prospects of Forensic Accounting in Developing Countries: A Systematic Literature Review* – based on a systematic literature review, provides discussions on the need and prospects of forensic accounting in developing countries as it may address the prevalence of business failures and financial crimes resulting from audit failure and the growth of creative accounting.
- Chapter 5 – *Advantages and Disadvantages of Applying Forensic Accounting in the Developing Countries: The Case in Vietnam* – focuses on the existing conditions and demand for forensic accounting. It includes the technique and skill requirements of forensic accounting to provide advantages and disadvantages of applying forensic accounting in Vietnam.
- Chapter 6 – *Forensic Accounting in Digital Environment: A New Proposed Model* – uses the bibliometric analysis to depict trends and applicable methodologies to build a comprehensible base that will serve to instill a new fraud detection model in the rise of digital transformation and big data.
- Chapter 7 – *Financial Forensic Evidence and Acceptability in the Court of Law: Financial Forensics and the Courts* – explores the role of forensic accounting in uncovering evidence for use in courts to litigate and arbitrate on financially related crimes.

The following seven chapters provide studies analyzing the issue of forensic accounting, fraud risk and auditing, and the credit risk. Thus:

- Chapter 8 – *The Fraud Triangle: Assessing Fraud Risk* – reviews the origins and each of the three elements of the fraud triangle and provide some tools for assessing whether each element is present in a fraud case.
- Chapter 9 – *Forensic Accounting Is a Necessity in Today's Corporate World and Not an Extra Option: A Conceptual Framework* – considering the fraud triangle theory and forensic accounting theory, focuses on the preventive and detective role of forensic accounting which highlight the importance of this function as a permanent feature in any organization.
- Chapter 10 – *Qualitative Study of the Fraud Causes in the 21st Century: US and EU Cases* – analysis the causes of fraud and its relevance, identifying their common points and measuring if they change in the post-SOX period.
- Chapter 11 – *An Evaluation of the Relevance of Forensic Accounting on Fraud Detection in Nigerian Public Sector: A Case Study of Bayelsa State, Nigeria* – evaluates the relevance of forensic accounting on fraud detection in Nigerian public sector, which reached alarming levels as individuals at different levels and capacities all commit fraud and corrupt practices, using a case study of Bayelsa state.
- Chapter 12 – *With the Mediation of Internal Audit, Can Artificial Intelligence Eliminate and Mitigate Fraud?* – determines if artificial intelligence supported Omani public listed organizations towards fraud elimination and mitigation concerns from the lens of agency theory with internal audit serving as the mediator.
- Chapter 13 – *A Proposed Framework for the Disclosure of the Credit Risk, According to the Basel Agreement and Its Impact on the Financial Reports and the Stability Banks* – develops a proposed

framework to explain the impact of disclosure of credit risks on financial reports to achieve the bank's stability in accordance with the requirements of the decisions of the Basel committee.

- Chapter 14 – *Deep-Auto Encoders for Detecting the Credit Card Frauds* – proposes a two-step method to detect credit card fraud by coupling the deep learning- machine learning approaches.

Chapters 15 and 16 relate the forensic accounting and the audit committee with corporate governance. Thus:

- Chapter 15 – *Forensic Accounting and Corporate Governance* – discusses the necessity for compliance and corporate governance, discussing the implications of conventional theory and traditional practices, with an emphasis on today's standards, along with the objectivity of the underlying pillars of ethics, social norms, and personal values.
- Chapter 16 – *Significance of Audit Committee in Corporate Governance* – covers the involvement of audit committee with respect to corporate governance, considering that audit committee is one of the factors which plays a pivotal role to guide and monitor business related matters of firms while following the national and international audit standards.

Finally, the last chapter analyses the effect of financial reporting fraud on firm's performance. In this way:

- Chapter 17 – *Effect of Financial Reporting Fraud on the Performance of Firms in the Nigerian Exchange Group: Financial Reporting Fraud and Performance of Firms* – assesses the effect of financial reporting fraud, improper expense recognition and fictitious revenue on the performance of firms in the Nigerian Exchange Group.

Suleman Sherali Kamwani
A'Sharqiyah University, Oman

Elisabete Vieira
University of Aveiro, Portugal

Mara Madaleno
University of Aveiro, Portugal

Graça Azevedo
University of Aveiro, Portugal

Chapter 1

What Are the Possible Methods and Techniques in Forensic Accounting Necessary to Comply With Corporate Governance in Portugal?

Suleman Sherali Kamwani
https://orcid.org/0000-0002-2558-1388
A'Sharqiyah University, Oman

Mara Madaleno Madaleno
https://orcid.org/0000-0002-4905-2771
University of Aveiro, Portugal

Elisabete S. Vieira
https://orcid.org/0000-0003-3593-368X
University of Aveiro, Portugal

Graça Azevedo
https://orcid.org/0000-0002-6346-4035
University of Aveiro, Portugal

ABSTRACT

The forensic accountant profession has been highly established around the world due to world-renowned financial scams that occurred from Malaysian to Europe and leading to closures and to failures like Adelphia and many more. Forensic accounting techniques are a consortium of investigation and interrogation attempts by corrupt financial gurus. The sole rationale of this study is to investigate the possible forensic techniques and methods to improve the overall corporate governance in Portugal. The outcome of this study guides the Portuguese universities and colleges to set the syllabus of integrated forensic accounting techniques and to comply with corporate governance policies. The study found the necessity to highlight possible forensic accounting techniques. The methods proposed are to align the corporate communication structure via rectifying their corporate governance weaknesses, particularly in the areas of internal control and fraud financial reporting.

DOI: 10.4018/978-1-7998-8754-6.ch001

INTRODUCTION

The forensic accounting market has grown dramatically during, especially, the last decade. In a survey of large Certified Public Accountant (CPA) firms, 85% of the feedbacks is directed about forensic accounting which is an enhancing portion of their work, and 100% of the feedback predictable demand is to enhance for the future. Accounting, specifically, is a growing profession with high relevance for a firm's growth and market survival. According to the US Bureau of labor statistic, the employment opportunities of auditors and accountants speculated to enhance by seven percent from the year 2020 to 2030 that means 135,000 more job opportunities will be available for the auditors and accountant each year. The reason behind attracting this profession is to replace workers those transfer to another occupation or get retirement from their job tenure (US Statistic, 2020).

In the year 2008, there were 1,290,600 accountants' professionals working in the United States, and that number was expected to increase by 22% in 2018, with 279,400 extra jobs in the profession of accountancy (Schiavone, 2012). The Statista website presents the numbers more recently (Statista, 2021). In Portugal, the Institute of Statutory Auditors (OROC) (http://www.oroc.pt/) and the Association of Certified Accountants of Portugal (OCC) non-Accountancy Europe member (https://www.occ.pt/pt/) point that in total, the structure and organization of the profession in 2020, counts with 1,504 (OROC) and 71,260 (OCC) accountants, with numbers as well growing.

The accountants' and auditors' role is of extreme importance for companies, institutions, and organizations. They are responsible for preparing financial records, examining these records to ensure their accuracy and compliance, and ensuring that the correct amount of tax is paid. Most companies employ in-house accountants to maintain financial records. However, to ensure independence, audits are generally conducted by third-party consultancy firms. By far, the largest external accountancy and audit firms Worldwide (true for the USA and Portugal as well) are the Big Four – PwC, Deloitte, EY, and KPMG (Statista, 2021).

The authors highlight the financial community realization regarding the failure of corporate communication which is required for forensic skills/techniques professionals to expose structural weakness in major areas such as flawed internal controls, poor corporate governance, and fraudulent financial statements. Integrating accounting, auditing, and investigation skills lead to the role of forensic accounting. Recent, and even older, white-collar crimes and financial frauds called the need for forensic accounting worldwide (Subash, 2015; Jain and Lamba, 2020). Due to its strict relationship with corporate governance, forensic accounting is becoming crucial nowadays (Subash, 2015; Kljajić et al., 2017). As argued by Rehman and Hashim (2020), corporate governance maturity would be reached by controlling and mitigating fraud within organizations. This is due to the two major roles of forensic accounting for corporate governance, namely, preventive and detective (Rehman and Hashim, 2020).

This new skill in accounting practice arose due to corporate and accounting scandals (Gligorić et al., 2017). Corporate governance corresponds to the system of direction and control that dictates how will the board of directors rule and govern within an organization. So, effective control should take place to prevent fraud (subash, 2015; Jain and Lamba, 2020; Wahyuni-TD et al., 2021). Nandini and Ajay's (2021) study starts with theoretical research about the role of forensic auditors in the fight against corruption. They found that forensic audit decreases the number of fraud cases, improving corporate governance. Baten (2021), in Bangladesh, states that creative accounting and the high level of political corruption lead to a deep change and flexibility in accounting. This has allowed managers to select the most beneficial strategies in their favor, delivering the profit figure that serves their interests.

The objective of this study is to find out the possible accounting methods and techniques for strengthening Portugal's corporate governance practices. In the accomplishment of the study objectives, the authors intend to develop a framework to reduce corporate financial frauds and also identify the areas of improvement in Portuguese corporate governance practices. The continuity of expanding the growth of this field realized that a vital need exists for the development of forensic accounting techniques, reduce external auditor deficiencies in fraud detection and its implications, and benefiting from cloud forensic audit to enhance corporate efficiency in fraud detection.

BACKGROUND

The Emergence of Forensic Accounting

Initially, the expression in forensic accounting was introduced by Maurice Ein in 1946. He had worked in the role of partnership in Peloubet & Coin New York, The USA. Auditors shifted their concentration from fraud discovery to public financial statement reporting after the American stock market crashed in 1929 which resulted in a decline of confidence between the users of financial statements and auditors, which is exposed while corporate failure. Therefore, auditors carrying on high pressure through regulatory bodies and the public as well. The outcome of this situation enhances the role of forensic accountants in corporate governance all over the world.

Forensic accountants examine financial information to examine possible financial fraud (Ramaswamy, 2007). There is a list of these crimes such as passing investors 'incorrect information, securities fraud, etc.

According to George Manning, "Forensic Accounting is defined as the science of congregation and presenting financial information in the shape at will be acknowledged by a court of law against the executor economic crimes. (Manning, 2011)". According to Terry Chilvers "Forensic accounting is the use of analytical techniques, incorporate with accounting and business skills, to develop information and estimation for evidence in court and used by specialist witnesses (Omondi, 2013)".

What are the Responsibilities of Forensic Accountants?

The forensic accountant is responsible for the verification of financial events and improves the financial reporting processes which is an integral part of the job to achieve objectivity and sustain reliability. Most importantly, a forensic accountant is responsible for gathered fraudulent evidence which is always acceptable in the court of law.

Forensic accountants are quite knowledgeable in legal matters and capable to apply specialized skills about collecting evidence material, evaluation, and expertise in authoring a legal report along with the interpretation of key areas of frauds such as corruption, money laundering, forgery, and distortion of information (Perduv, 2018).

Significance of Forensic Audit Part in Corporate Governance

As a part of corporate governance; forensic audit can make a significant difference in financial fraud prevention. Forensic audits put into effect by the official proclamation into the company's corporate governance not only enhance the shareholder confidence but also the firewall for the corrupted practices.

External auditors are declined to detect, reduce and prevent financial frauds and are not considered as a part of auditor statutory responsibility during the financial audit. Therefore, a gap is created among the accounting profession and users of financial statements, which is known as the audit expectation gap and it creates adverse effects on corporate governance practices (Eyisi, 2014).

The corporate governance mechanism failure created serious threats for the stakeholder, creditors, and government legal departments. Therefore, the corporate sectors are uncertain about to trust on unqualified audit report which is released by the audit firm and after some time it's revealed; such as Enron and WorldCom companies have had serious financial crises and they are leading to bankruptcy (Enofe, 2016).

Portugal Corporate Governance and Firm Performance

As a pioneer of Portugal's investigative research, Alves and Menes (2004) concentrated on the corporate governance mechanisms, to research these effects for the Portuguese corporate sector. These researcher findings revealed that there is a positive relationship between a few of the recommended Portuguese corporate governance codes and company performance. There are several financial market issues and misuse of Information technology that exist around the world and these cannot be ignored by the Portuguese companies as a part of their corporate governance. These circumstances result in the Portuguese Securities Market Commission implementing a set of structures regarding the exercise span of authority and supervision at almost all the companies. These should be considered as a part of their corporate governance practices and should resemble the management and shareholder's rules of conduct appropriately. Therefore, in the year 2018, the Portuguese Institute of Corporate Governance disclosed its updated corporate governance code which has been promulgating the transparency in the capital market and corporate governance by the management which is the outcome. Firms in Portugal should promote good corporate governance practices and enhance corporate performances appropriately.-(Vieira and Neiva, 2019)The objective of the updated corporate governance code is to set the proportion of independent directors in a firm, where executive directors should be less than non-executive directors and independent directors must be part of the nomination committee (Teodósio, 2021).

The first-time formal structure of the corporate governance regulation was published in the year 2001. This document states that all Portuguese listed companies should reveal rules and policies information to the stock market. The only purpose to release corporate information regulations is to explain and comply with the stock market with Portugal legislation-(Teodósi, 2021).

The Role of Forensic Auditors Techniques in Corporate Governance

According to the Institute of Forensic Auditors (IFA), forensic auditors are responsible for setting financial investigations and find out the facts and pieces of evidence for filing the lawsuit against illegal practices and disputes, along with suggested preventive measures appropriately. Moreover, forensic auditors are fully commendable in their expert forensic accounting techniques. They have the criminal phycology to identify the flows in financial systems practices and such mal-practices always legitimize under the umbrella of a firm's corporate governance policies (Ezuwore, 2014).

The auditing standards and financial reporting always establish a threshold for corporate governance. Nevertheless, corporate governance principles set the line of direction for the accounting profession to perform. Particularly rights and responsibilities that are an essential part of management. According to the OECD (Organisation for Economic Co-operation and Development), the accounting profession is responsible for providing entire pertinent accounting information to shelter equity among foreign and domestic stakeholders (minority and majority) and importantly is to timely notify the entire corporate governance entities (OECD, 1993).

A reliable corporate governance practice contributes to justifiable economic development by (Vedrana, 2018):

Adding the value inside the company's intangible and tangible assets such as raising capital and the value of assets makes an effort for reducing the cost of companies.

Attract foreign investment in capital markets.

Reducing financial crises and bad business performance, creating positive effects on economic and social consequences.

Regardless, the financial forensic auditors are hired by the company's management or belong to print media financial news agencies. They can even be appointed by the courts of law. Still, they all are experts in nontraditional audits procedures for investigating specific allegations which are beyond the international audit standards criteria for fraudulent financial practices. Besides, the entire parameters adopted by the forensic financial auditors, these forensic techniques targeting an eye-opener for the settlers of corporate governance policies via suggested several tools to the audit committee for strengthening accountability of management practices, enhancement in firm's financial reporting systems, and improve overall audit functions for reducing the deficiencies of auditors detection of frauds as well (Ezuwore, 2014). Those constantly endorse the state of the art of a business and fulfill with an efficient market theory-(Imoniana, 2013).

LITERATURE REVIEW

The Significance of Financial Forensic Analytics Skills

To evaluate the fraud risk assessments, the forensic analytical skills used to find out the pattern of fraud practices and then extracting that useful information related to the subject matter to whom forensic auditors assign to perform their task via regression modeling, visualization and critically analyze the diversified aspects of the fraud components. According to AICPA (American Institute of Certified Public Accountants) in the year 2017, the Guide to Audit Data analytics defined it to be (AICP, 2017): "The science and art of discovering and analyzing patterns, identifying anomalies, and extracting other useful information in data underlying or related to the subject matter of an audit through analysis, modeling, and visualization to plan or perform the audit".

In the context of traditional analytical review by financial ratios, (Kaminski, 2004), has selected a matched sample for seven years and investigate the analytical strength of 21 financial ratios. The results show that non were consistently significant throughout the sample period examined. And also discriminate analysis resulted from 58 to 98 percent misclassification for fraud companies. From here it is concluded that ratio analysis is not a reliable tool in detecting financial fraud.-(Hogan, 2008). This study uses the chaos theory which is used to estimate prices of the stocks by using the information of trader sentiment and trading stock volume (Juárez, 2016). Therefore, Chaos theory was also used in longitudinal examination by Kaminsk and Wetzel in the year 2004. Kaminsk selected 10 financial ratios on 30 companies (match pair) (Hoga, 2008) . Results in none of the ratios show steady differences in dynamics nor periodic behavior. Eventually, this result stresses rare benefits for the companies to rely on to detect frauds (Abdullah, 2015).

Brief Bibliometric Search for "Forensic Accounting" and "Corporate Governance"

As part of this chapter analysis, we present in this section a brief bibliometric search. In the Scopus bibliographic database, searching in title, abstract, and keywords for "forensic accounting" and "corporate governance" in July 2021, we have retrieved solely 12 document results that we will analyze next. This proves that the research topic is still in its infancy, opening room for deeper research needs.

From these 12 documents, the first was published in 2006. In the years 2009, 2011, 2013, 2014, and 2016-2020, only one article per year was published while up to July 2021 we already have 2 published articles. Table 1 presents the list of the 12 articles found and the citations per year. From these 12 documents, only one refers to a book chapter (8.3%) being the others scientific peer-reviewed published articles (91.7%). As to the documents per affiliation, the USA is the country with the highest number of publications (5) followed by Malaysia (3) and the University Utara Malaysia counts with 2 of these documents published (considering the authors' affiliations).

Akkeren and Buckby (2017) qualitative inductive study, analyze perceptions and experiences of forensic accountants concluding that inadequate corporate governance leads to fraud occurrence. These fraudulent activities executed often remain undetected. Mustafa and Meier (2006) investigate the role of corporate governance structure in reducing misappropriation incidence. Results point that the percentage of independent members in audit committees and the average tenure of its members negatively lead to the incidence of misappropriation of assets in publicly held companies. Bhasin (2016) points that poor corporate governance leads to dismal performance, manipulated financial reports, and unhappy stakeholders in India. Owojori and Asaolu (2009) discuss the concept, need, and role of forensic accounting in solving the vexing problems of the corporate world.

Yang and Lee (2020) develop a strategy map of forensic accounting as to the key priorities indicators' to reach effective strategy planning and control fraud risk management in Taiwan. Dutta et al. (2014) present a case study of accounting topics that are necessary to learn in curricula such as to prevent corporate governance from fraudulent actions. Assad (2011) also presents a case study that consolidates techniques and methodologies of special investigations and evidence weaknesses in governance and internal controls, which are relevant for teaching aspects of corporate governance. Abdul Malak and Wan Hussin (2019) presented a case study focusing o the accounting policy choices of the foreign associates of AirAsia Berhad. Rehman and Hashim (2021) try to measure forensic accounting's impact on sustainable corporate governance of Omani public listed companies. Williams (2018) presents a review of board composition characteristics (the ratio of corporate boards) and company fraud reported in 2012. Concludes that emphasis on legislation within financial reporting is crucial. Yale et al. (2013) present a countrywide report of risk management lessons learned. Recently, Yu and Rha (2021) conduct a network text and cluster analysis to conclude that literature on accounting fraud was developed based on fraud detection techniques, executive compensation, assessment of fraud risks in audit processes, forensic accounting, corporate governance, and top management.

From this quick analysis of the 12 documents listed in Table 1, it is evident the interesting research topics that still emerge from here. Just to point a few, i) the need to identify the factors able to explain the relationship between forensic accounting and corporate governance; ii) the characteristics of the board

Table 1. List of the 12 articles and citations

				≤2017	2018	2019	2020	2021	total
Publ. Year	**Document Title**	**Authors**	**Journal Title**	**10**	**3**	**9**	**19**	**11**	**52**
2021	Research trends in accounting fraud using network analysis	Yu S.-J., Rha J.-S.	Sustainability (Switzerland)	0	0	0	0	0	0
2021	Can forensic accounting impact sustainable corporate governance?	Rehman A., Hashim F.	Corporate Governance (Bingley)	0	0	0	0	1	1
2020	Developing a strategy map for forensic accounting with fraud risk management: An integrated balanced scorecard-based decision model	Yang C.-H., Lee K.-C.	Evaluation and Program Planning	0	0	0	1	4	5
2019	AirAsia Berhad's accounting in the spotlight	Abdul Malak S.S.D., Wan Hussin W.N.B.	Emerald Emerging Markets Case Studies	0	0	0	0	0	0
2018	Role of Management, Corporate Governance, and Sarbanes-Oxley in Fraud: A Focus on the Precious Metals Industry	Williams T.	Accounting, Finance, Sustainability, Governance and Fraud	0	1	0	0	0	1
2017	Perceptions on the Causes of Individual and Fraudulent Co-offending: Views of Forensic Accountants	Van Akkeren J., Buckby S.	Journal of Business Ethics	0	0	1	9	3	13
2016	Contribution of forensic accounting to corporate governance: An exploratory study of an Asian country	Bhasin M.L.	International Business Management	0	0	1	3	2	6
2014	Blurred vision, perilous future: Management fraud at Olympus	Dutta S.K., Caplan D.H., Marcinko D.J.	Issues in Accounting Education	1	1	1	1	0	4
2013	Risk management lessons learned: Countrywide report	Yale G., Grove H., Clouse M.	Corporate Ownership and Control	0	0	0	1	0	1
2011	Fraud at the Central Bank of Tanzania (A)	Assad M.J.	Emerald Emerging Markets Case Studies	0	0	2	2	0	4
2009	The role of forensic accounting in solving the vexed problem of the corporate world	Owojori A.A., Asaolu T.O.	European Journal of Scientific Research	3	0	1	1	1	6
2006	[CAP forum on forensic accounting in the post-enron world audit committees and misappropriation of assets: Publicly held companies in the United States, Les comités de vérification et le détournement de biens: les sociétés ouvertes aux États-Unis]	Mustafa S.T., Meier H.H.	Canadian Accounting Perspectives	6	1	3	1	0	11

Source: Own elaboration based on Bibliometric Scopus analysis.

of directors and the audit committee members such as to prevent frauds are still lacking research; iii) highlight the key political regulations/policies necessary for control by country and economic activity sector; iv) the need to explore this relationship in countries like Portugal, where some recent scandals appeared; v) identify the possible methods and techniques in forensic accounting, able to comply with corporate governance.

Escalation of Financial Fraud in a Covid-19 World

The president and CEO (Mr. Bruce Dorris) of ACFE - Association of Certified Fraud Examiners, identified the nature of frauds that have been committing during the recession time since the pandemic started around the world. It is evident the impact of COVID-19 spread on our individual lives, global economy, and government. The authors speculate that the looming economic downturn left long-lasting implications and one of them is financial frauds in the upcoming years; therefore organization needs to support themselves to avoid repeated fraud cases which were occurred during the time of recession in the year 2008. Therefore, its highly encourage that organizations protect employees and themselves against fraud.

During the great recession that occurred from 2007 to 2008, the ACFE surveyed and 80% of the respondents said that financial fraud appreciates during economic downturn circumstances. These frauds prevail due to enormous pressures on employees and companies to meet their earning targets and struggle to acquire finance from financial or government institutions. According to a Global Fraud survey in 2019, on average, $8.7 million costs were incurred due to fraud in firms' financial statements. It is evident from the past and present, Covid-19 languish the economies development which is advantageous for existing manipulators and discovered new techniques as to how to cook the books as well. The prevalent areas of fraud are dry-up cash flows position and eventually unable to cover up what they have filched. One of the similar examples of financial fraud occurred in the year 2008 recession time; that is Bernie Madoff's Ponzi scheme. In this case, the only man Madoff played a major role in dry up the company's cash flow position. He has caused catastrophic damage not only to the company's financial position but also to thousands of people who were adversely affected. That is to say, which has led to people lost their jobs and also attempted suicides as well. Eventually, the company moved toward bankruptcy and destabilized significant parts of industries. As we can observe nowadays several companies tied up their cash flow positions due to the after-effects of the corona pandemic, therefore we may expect many more discoveries of financial frauds coming up until the world becomes a safer place (free of coronavirus) to live (Bruce, 2020).

Nowadays it is inevitable for any organization to maintain anti-fraud staff and resources. According to a report issued by ACFE's a possible organization reduces 5% revenue due to abusive and fraud practices, and if firms vanishing the anti-fraud programs, this percentage escalates to cost more money than it saves (ACFE, 2020).

There was a survey conducted by ACFE in the year 2019 and published in 2020 named "Report to the nations", also revealing that organizations declined to invest significantly in the area of internal control which is the outcome where firms bear higher fraud losses. Due to this, it expedites the period to detect frauds those can find out before attempting by anti-fraud measures. It is also evident more than 50% of occupational frauds are incurred due to failure in the execution or usefulness of internal controls. It is a time for organizations to bolstering their internal control (ACFE, 2020). The brief literature analysis presented previously also exposes the need to explore the effects of the crisis and the recent pandemic in the relationship between forensic accounting and corporate governance. Therefore, we leave as a suggestion for future work the analysis of this relationship by the country for comparison purposes, but as well considering economic activity sectors where little is known in this respect.

EFFICIENCY OF FRAUD AUDIT STANDARDS AND IMPACT ON PORTUGAL CORPORATE GOVERNANCE

The position of forensic auditors is unlike accepting clarification and documents at face value (Cole, 2009). Therefore, the role of forensic auditors just goes beyond the firewalls for search the frauds to report the statutory authority or company's management. Academic researchers have been played a major role in find-out the impact of fraud audit standards while auditing practices. During the year 2001 Shelton recognized that to raise the audit performance about the detection of financial frauds, the fraud task force introduced a new standard which is SAS No. 82 applied on or after December 15, 1997 (Board, 1997). Regardless of the introduction of the SAS No. 82 audit standard, the fraud task force missed quite a few imminent areas of the auditor's domain of investigations such as timing and method of fraud risk assessment. It is suggested by the academicians rather integrate all of the firm's risk assessments better to treated separately each financial risk assessment (Shelton, 2001). Shelton (2001) examines the significant areas regarding time, method, and separately assessment of financial fraud risk assessment; these are missed inside SAS No, 82 standards. The outcome suggests by the auditors, the separate fraud risk assessments will consume more time of auditors and budgeted hours to perform audit procedures and that will influence the method of audit planning as well.

Nevertheless, the standard SAS No. 82 enhances the domain of auditors for detecting financial fraud materiality. This argument was investigated via a survey by Glover and Prawit (2003), whereas before introducing the SAS No. 82 audit standard, he did not find the evidence to change in audit planned test but after the implication of this standard. The auditors are more cautious of changes in their audit plans and enhanced their audit tests due to the spread of malpractices of financial obligations (Glover & Prawit, 2003). In the year 2001, Apostolou et al. also evaluated what are the risk factors possibly faced during the fraud risk assessment while applying to audit standard SAS No. 82. This audit standard furnished 25 significant management fraud risk factors that should be part of audit risk assessments, conducted by the auditors. The authors found that financial and operating stability frauds are less significant in comparison to management control over the environment and misgovernance practices (Apostolou, 2001).

Due to the deficiencies in fraud audit standards and practices, the authors analyze the Portuguese corporate governance disclosure according to Euronext Lisbon stock exchange policies and also considering the timeliness and relevance of corporate governance. Largely Portuguese companies are strongly controlled by the ownership and acquainted with the fragile legal system for the investors which is working under the civil law legal system. Therefore, it is inevitable the improvement of Portuguese firm's corporate governance disclosure and also better for enhancing both empirical and theoretical research about to companies' governance. Moreover, one of the intergovernmental economic organizations also watching Portuguese corporate governance practices, the regulator of the organization for economic co-operation and development (OECD) monitoring all 37 countries, reveals corporate governance structure and practices of information disclosure as a sign to safeguard the organization and investors, needed to ensure performance improvements of the capital market (Cunhal, 2018).

How to Detect and Prevent Fraud

Initially, forensic auditors set the process of investigative tasks and adopted several procedures which are helpful to find out the high-risk areas of possible financial frauds, gather evidence, verifying the credibility of documentation and conclude about the effects of tricky transactions on the financial statements. By using these processes, forensic skills are used to analyze interconnected business segments and that helps to identify the low poles of the system.

Over the next step, the following are the drivers of occupational frauds for detection and prevention of misuse of employer resources for personal benefits, which is a crime against any organization (Nigrini, 2011). The data accumulated in the year 2019 surveyed that 42% of occupational fraudulent maintains a standard of living beyond that which is commensurate with his/her sources of income and 26% fraudulent snip from an employer due to struggling in financial difficulties (Bruce, 2020).

People's self believes that they are above the law;
People competency to override a firm's internal control;
People get the opportunity to do the fraud on responsible positions;
People greediness to commit fraud;
People justify their frauds;
People carefree the size of penalty which can be imposed from the court of law.

Lack of Frequent Forensic Accounting Practices in Portugal

This study examines the Portuguese educational institutions and companies that are still far behind to realize the frequent practices of forensic accounting techniques for preventing and detecting frauds, although Portuguese followed the standards called Norma de Contabilidade e de Relato Financeiro (NCRF). This standard set the line of direction for the accounting rules in terms of recognition of NCRF 7, which speaks about the treatment of tangible fixed assets (TFA), and NCRF 6 regarding recognition of intangible assets (IA). The Portuguese conceptual framework "Estrutura Conceptual (EC)" also helps to better understand NCRF and also further explain the accounting concepts appropriately (Terziev, 2020).

NCRF standards and EC framework didn't much help to stop a mega scandal case in Portugal named Grupo Banco Espirito Santo company. In the year 2014, the company decided to go under the forensic audit to identify the illegal practices. Therefore, contact one of the 4 big-tier audit firms, Deloitte Portugal. The Portuguese Securities Market Commission was also requested to become part of this process to perform its areas of fiduciary duty. The outcome of the forensic audit found a failure of corporate governance and integrity of financial reporting. Moreover, the company extensively invested in non-financial companies and used his family powers in the board of directors for used fraudulent financial reporting and adopted related party transactions (Banco, 2014).

The Financial Fraud Triangle

The fraud triangular theory established in the year 1953 by Donald R. Cressey has revealed the three reasons in every instance of fraud which are rationalization, opportunity, and pressure. Moreover, according to Cressey theory (Hadian, 2013): "People are believed to be violators of confidence when he sees himself as a person who has financial problems that cannot be told to someone else, be aware that

Figure 1. The financial fraud triangle remains in existence for decades as a symbolic diagram to guide us in analyzing and understand frauds.

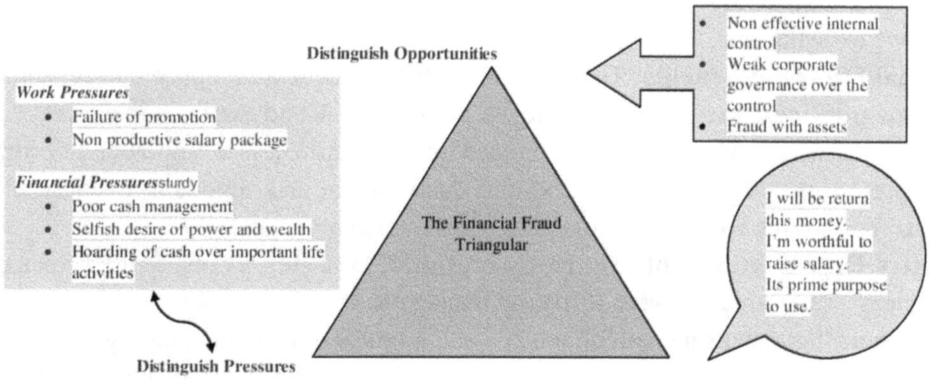

this problem can be overcome secretly by abusing his authority as the holder of the trust in the financial sector, and the doings of the day enable-day views on himself as someone who can be trusted in the use of funds or property entrusted."

Fraud is considered an intentional attempt which is occurred by an organization or staff for their benefits such as opportunity which is an element of the fraud triangle that can also be intensified during pandemic circumstances. As the matter of fact, during this economic crushing time, organizations found ways out to cut costs, therefore, targeted non-revenue generating departments. The fallout by taken this step is an organization becoming more susceptible to the enhancing likelihood of financial frauds. This step can find themselves caught in a perfect tornado for fraud and at the same time, it pressures the employees to safeguard themselves against fraudulent transactions (Bruce, 2020). There are several reasons given below surface, constructed by the fraud triangular framework (CFI, 2016).

- **Noneffective Internal Control**: Internal controls of an organization has always a strong grip over the company's procedures and processes to verify the transparency of financial information. There are several examples of weak internal controls that exist and enhance the chances of financial frauds or IT frauds, such as non-sufficient documentations, reduce delegation of power, and missing appropriate work and activities supervision.
- **Weak Corporate Governance Over the Control:** The directors and leadership of an organization set the direction to run the company affairs. The areas of fraud become more vulnerable due to the lack of ethical corporate governance issues by the top management and that is reflecting a company unable to control operational affairs and compromising on the corporate and ethical values.
- **Don't Follow Sufficient Accounting Policies/Methods:** without following IFRS and GAAP accounting standards, it's quite easy for a company to fudge the number in many other ways such as management can shift the accounting methods in the way it is the best fit for them.
- **Employees Bonuses and Financial Performance:** Bonuses enhance employee performance when it measures its key area's performance and if it is unable to meet the targets it may commit fraud to achieve the objective.

- **Meet the Investor Expectations:** it is a market phenomenon that share prices keep change due to demand and supply. If more investors demand a course of particular shares then it is obvious the price move up. Due to meet this expectation the portfolio managers commit frauds to achieve the investor's expectations.
- **Personal Financial Benefits:** Two incentives that motivate an employee to do something wrong or create greediness to earn more money such as intrinsic and extrinsic incentives.
- **Unfair Treatment:** The possible workplace unfair treatment is a hindrance in promotion, favoritism, prefer juniors over seniority, politics, harassment, and nepotism. Because of one of these reasons' employees committing financial fraud to take revenge.
- **Negative Organization Culture:** Every organization having its own culture that influences the employees' work ethics as well. If the top management decline to follow an honest culture within departments that means it created the gaps to commit frauds by the employees.
- **Fear of Losing a Job:** It is a hard feeling for an individual to lose the job. This fear (such as stress, threat, increase unemployment, felt powerless) also forces an employee to commit fraud in an organization.

RESULTS OF THE EMPIRICAL RESEARCH

To understand the negatively affected reasons on the firm's corporate governance, find the following outcomes in the result of the conducted survey by Prof. Vedrana from the ministry of science and technology of the Republic of Srpska Bosnia (Vedrana, 2018):

1. Noncompetent & nonexperience of that particular industry auditors assign for taken up responsibilities to do the audit
2. Firms manipulate financial results and nonsufficient disclosure part of the information regarding financial & nonfinancial matters in the company's annual reports.
3. Regardless of the company act rule & sustain the good relationship, the company's directors use their influence with the audit firm; over a long period (more than 5 years) fix it same audit partner, to do the company's financial audit each year.
4. The macro economical changes and enhancement in the level of tax rate also created difficulties to follow corporate governance.
5. Organizations non appropriately comply with the IFRS standards, such as missing related party transactions and earning management disclosures.
6. Absence in corporate governance regarding forensic audit procedures for detecting and preventing financial frauds appropriately.

The second survey conducted to identify the benefits of forensic accounting practices; resulted from the following outcomes:

1. Investigate unlawful financial practices
2. Verifying the organization compliment with policies and laws
3. Performance evaluation of existing accounting system
4. Make sure to prepare timely & reliable financial statements

Beneish Model Application and Detecting for Financial Frauds in Portugal

Beneish M-Score Model is one of the best models developed in the Kelley School of Business at Indiana University—Bloomington for the detection of financial fraud.

During the process of building this Model in 1999 by Professor Messod D. Beneish; considered the following meters before the set of eight and five factors based Beneish model. The model foundation was laid down in 1982 when the US securities and exchange commission gathered several companies' data for detecting financial frauds and find out that 74 companies cook the books and the remaining (2332) declared non-manipulators organocations (Beneish, 1997).

- Is it related to cash flow?
- Is it related to accrual differences?
- Is it the manager depict to manipulates data?
- Is it an indication of future effectiveness?

Beneish M score is an empirical application which is describing the level of possible manipulation in earning management such as covering misappropriation or fraudulent activities (Beneish, 2012).

Initially, the M-score value above -2.22 indicated that financials could be manipulated. In the year 2004 the score of the M-score level moved to -1.99 due to the research on companies' financials evaluations from the year 1986 to 2001, 67,366 companies exist non-manipulator and 120 firms nominated manipulators. Eventually, in the year 2012 set the final threshold which is -1.78 M score for the manipulation of financial statements (Beneish, 2013).

The Beneish M Score model formula used both factors models which is consist of five and eight criteria/standard equations given below (Hołda, 2020):

M_8 factor = -4.840 + 0,920XDSRI + 0,528XGMI + 0,0404XAQI + 0,892XSGI + 0,115XDEPI-0,172XSGAI + 4,679X \ TATA- 0,327XLVGI

M_5 factor = -6.065 + 0.823DSRI + 0.906GMI + 0.593AQI + 0.717SGI + 0.107DEPI

Where:

DSRI = Day Sales in Receivables Index. The objective of this formula is to check out whether sales (revenue) and receivables are in the balance till two repeated years. Therefore, if an increase in the volume of sales is disproportionate with the increase in receivable accounts; which means the company shows high revenues due to the artificially inflated sales growth towards pretended a high-performance ratio analysis. Another scenario, increase in sales growth due to increase in receivables also shows deviate from company's credit policy that could be considered a reaction to surge in competitiveness on the market.

Formula: (DSRI = [net receivables(t) / sales(t)]/ / [net receivables (t–1) / sales (t–1)) (Hołda, 2020)

GMI = Gross Margin Index. Under this formula, the higher possibility of manipulation can be traced in a situation when the financial market perceived corrosion in sales margin and that is the decline in the efficacy of invested capital. (Hołda, 2020)

Formula: GMI = {[sales (t – 1) – cost of goods sold (t – 1)]/ sales (t – 1)} / {[sales (t) – cost of goods sold (t) / sales (t)}. (Hołda, 2020)

AQI =Asset Quality Index. This formula refers to the fundamental practices of financial frauds by transfer a part of operating cost toward balance sheet, firstly its bypass the accounting standard and deliberate attempt to depreciate the company's profits to avail the tax benefits.

Formula: AQI = {1 – [(current assets(t) + net fixed assets(t)) / total assets (t)]}/ {1 – [(current assets(t – 1) + net fixed assets(t – 1)) / total assets (t – 1)]} (Hołda, 2020)

SGI = Sales Growth Index. The gross margin result in this formula gives conducive hope to the capital market investors which is created pressure on the company's management to accomplish expected results. Therefore, it emerges some doubts in case of an increase in the company sales that's may not be manipulated practice by the managers.

Formula: SGI = [sales(t)] / [sales (t – 1)]. (Hołda, 2020)

DEPI = Depreciation Index. The outcome of this formula investigates whether firms have intentional attempts to achieve incremental financial results or enhance the depreciation period by reducing the operating cost in their financial statements; justified through set the lower depreciation rate (below 1).

Formula: DEPI = [depreciation (t – 1) / (depreciation (t – 1) + net assets (t – 1))] / [depreciation (t) / (depreciation (t) + net assets (t))] (Hołda, 2020)

SGAI = Sales and General Administration Expenses Index. This segment of the formula also does its assessments regarding disproportionate deviations in sales revenue. Here, the evaluation carries forward to find out the link between selling expenses and administrative costs. That's mainly focused on manager interference in reporting processes due to disproportioned changes in sales volume. It gives further indicators toward auditor's investigation to find out fraudulent financial activities of managers.

Formula: SGAI = [(selling, general & administrative expense (t) + sales (t)) / sales (t)] / [(selling, general & administrative expense (t – 1) + sales (t – 1)) / sales (t – 1)] (Hołda, 2020)

TATA = Total Accruals to Total Assets. Within this indicator, the high-level results reveal that managers possibly can do financial manipulation by look at the big difference between cash flow from operating activities and net profit of the company.

Formula: TATA = (Δnet working capital– Δcash and equivalents– Δincome tax – depreciation) / total assets (t) (Hołda, 2020)

LVGI = Leverage Index. This index results in signaling the red flags as if a company increases in debt during the financial risk assessment just to portray a progressive image centered on the market.

Formula: LVGI = [current liabilities (t) / total assets (t)] / [current liabilities (t – 1) / total assets (t – 1)] (Hołda, 2020)

The Beneish model was applied to test earnings management of Portuguese listed companies based on their financial statement data from 2003 till 2014 to find out manipulators and non-manipulator performers (Kacharava, 2016). According to Beneish financial ratios analysis, it reveals that financial crisis leaving an adverse impact on the firm's financial positions which is increase the tendency to perform financial manipulation in Portugal. The authors find out the main results from the data analysis conducted by Aleksandre Kacharava in the year 2016 ((Kacharava, 2016) confirms that Portuguese companies are involved in receivable manipulation rather than other manipulations such as administrative and sales expenses, asses quality indexes, and depreciation indexes. Eventually, the main highlights of Aleksandre data analysis revealed that Portuguese firms are determined to do manipulation to influence financial investors' perception instead of manipulating the cost of obtained funds for tax benefits. Different regions and cultures have diverse laws and legal forces; exist around the world. According to La Porta et al 1998 (Rafael, 1998) "common law countries generally have the strongest, and French civil law countries the weakest, legal protections of investors, with German and Scandinavian civil law countries located in the middle". Therefore, the UK quality of accounting is possibly better than the Portuguese sample collection. According to Kacharava (Kacharava, 2016) financial data samples analysis from 2003 till 2014, selected 56 Portuguese companies and find out 618 observations. The outcome showed that 8 Portuguese companies (14.29%) were involved in manipulating. The data also revealed that 41 out of 56 Portuguese companies were involved in manipulation during the financial crisis time that is also suggested by George Iatridis and Augustinos I. Dimitras in the year 2013 (Dimitras, 2013); states financial crises resulted from more listed companies involved in manipulations. There are 16% and 5% manipulator companies determined after and before crises in Portugal that means a 200% increase in manipulation in Portugal companies. The earning management has been increased at a particular rate due to the world was passing through the financial crises; began in the year 2006 followed by the downfall of a US bank named Lehman brothers bank in 2008 due to enormous default in mortgages. During the year December 2008 Banco Privado Português and in November 2008 Banco 30 Português de Negócios were also warped due to crises. Eventually, Portugal suffered in public deficit in the year 2010, and later on, Portugal requested Troika's to deal with this issue in the year 2011. It was a non ended financial crisis around the world, therefore another bank collapsed in Portugal named Banco Espírito Santo in the year 2014 as well.

FUTURE RESEARCH DIRECTIONS

In our chapter, we produce prevailing research and recognize the gaps for the areas of future research that reduce external auditors' deficiencies in fraud detection & the importance of forensic audit efficiency for fraud detection to benefiting the overall companies' corporate governance. This precise research encompasses our findings and would advantage from being investigated includes the following examples.

- Include the importance of the top-down and risk-based approach in detecting fraud.
- Scrutinize the role of the auditor in recognizing and possibly justifying incentives and opportunities for management to involve in financial statement fraud

Forensic Accounting is a vastly significant area of interest that is undergoing incredible growth. Altogether accounting students can greatly advantage from the development of technical skills in forensic accounting classes irrespective of future employment in the audit or tax profession.

Due to high growth in forensic accounting education, it would also be recommended by the practitioners for developing future academic research areas of fields that are cybercrime and security, interviewing & interrogations, and digital forensics; all these are more significant to include in forensic accounting education for the future academic research. Nevertheless, these are distinct areas of traditional accounting. However, it is the responsibility of the universities to find out their key shareholders' expectations of competencies/skills/knowledge by their employers. This data set the line of direction regarding which department to collaborate to whom for structuring their forensic accounting research education.

Finally, the author identified that regulatory bodies (such as the Portuguese securities market commission) should release adequate guidelines for proper financial disclosure practices in the company"s financial statements plus auditing firms those taken independent audit assignments from Portugees stock exchange-listed companies should also help at improving firms corporate governance about reporting practices and eventually regulatory bodies and corporate firms recommended to engage in active dialogues and related activities to encourage alertness by identifying potential solutions.

CONCLUSION

Forensic accountants, existence in the role of professional members of the audit and corporate governance committees, can play a significant role in managing companies' exertions to establish a consistent policy of ethical and professional behavior within an organization. The presence of forensic accountants helping companies to set proactive strategies to timely prevent & detect frauds, and also workout with the internal auditors for strengthening the firm's internal controls system which shows a vigilant corporate governance policy and establishes an effective line of communication & evolvement between the forensic accountant and corporate governance system. The empirical results also highlight, which factors negatively affected the firm's corporate governance and positive effects for the practicing of forensic accounting techniques & methods.

The contribution of this research study is to differentiating between lack of auditor's domain to detect fraud and financial irregularities in their audit plan and shows eminence of forensic auditors/accountants' skills & methods, and document controls, and link controls to assertions, and audit evidence, and their investigative abilities to understand, and competencies to deal with corporate governance, and knowledge of statuary requirements which is accepted by the court of law. All such features of the forensic accountants/auditors suggested during the research are to complying with Portugal's corporate governance mechanism for carrying out their responsibilities of accomplishing corporate goals and depreciate financial frauds. Nevertheless, forensic accountants/auditors leave great effects on firms' corporate governance by improving the financial reporting system and management accountability and put enormous pressure on external auditors to perform their statutory duties with greater responsibilities. The results of this study also shed light on numerous features of fraudulent financial reporting such as characteristics of fraud firms that pressurize to meet analyst forecast rapid growth targets in cooked financial reporting to satisfy both internal and external stakeholders.

According to A.O. Enofe, Michael Sunday Olorunnuho & American Duke Okporua survey in 2016 Nigeria, a bachelor's degree is necessary to qualify for the CFA (chartered financial analyst) professional certification. This may have consequences for the higher educational institutions when designing their curriculum. Therefore, the majority of respondents revealed, they observe that demand for forensic accountants continuing to grow in the future (Enofe, 2016). Eventually, this chapter highlights the importance for the Portugal universities should design curricula according to the forensic accounting investigation techniques & methods as discussed in the above literature. The outcome of this study also emphasizes the students should familiarize themselves with information technology in the digital environment and exclusively learn the application of technology and anti-fraud programs those helpful for fraud investigation for an effective forensic accountant/auditor.

REFERENCES

Abdul Malak, S. S. D., & Wan Hussin, W. N. B. (2019). AirAsia Berhad's accounting in the spotlight. *Emerald Emerging Markets Case Studies*, *9*(1), 1–26. doi:10.1108/EEMCS-06-2018-0115

Abdullah. (2015). Transparency and Reliability in Financial Statement: Do They Exist? Evidence from Malaysia. *Open Journal of Accounting, 4*, 29-43.

ACFE. (2020). *Report to the nation.* Retrieved from https://www.acfe.com/surveys-and-statistics.aspx

ACFE. (n.d.). *Membership and Certification.* Retrieved from https://www.acfe.com/

AICP. (2017). *Audit Data Analytics Guide.* Retrieved from AICPA: https://www.aicpa.org/interestareas/frc/assuranceadvisoryservices/auditdataanalyticsguide.html

Apostolou, Hassell, J. M., Webber, S. A., & Sumners, G. E. (2001). The relative importance of management fraud risk factors. *Behavioral Research in Accounting, 13*(1), 1–24. doi:10.2308/bria.2001.13.1.1

Assad, M. J. (2011). Fraud at the central bank of tanzania (A). *Emerald Emerging Markets Case Studies, 1*(1), 1–12. doi:10.1108/20450621111110492

Baten, M. A. (2021). Corporate Governance And Creative Accounting From Bangladesh Experience. *Accounting, Organization & Economics, 1*(1), 12-25. Retrieved from https://fortunepublishing.org/index.php/aoe/article/view/43

Beneish, M. (1997). Detecting GAAP violation: Implications for assessing earnings management among firms with extreme financial performance. *Journal of Accounting and Public Policy, 16*(3), 271–309.

Beneish. (2012). Fraud Detection and Expected Returns. *SRRN*, 53.

Beneish. (2013, March). Earnings Manipulation and Expected Returns. *Financial Analysts Journal.*

Bhasin, D. M. (2017, January). Integrating Corporate Governance and Forensic Accounting: A Study of an Asian Country. *International Journal of Management Sciences and Business Research, 6*(1), 31–52.

Bhasin, M. L. (2016). Contribution of forensic accounting to corporate governance: An exploratory study of an asian country. *International Business Management, 10*(4), 479–492. doi:10.3923/ibm.2016.479.492

Board, A. S. (1997). *Recently Issued Statement of Auditing Standards (SAS) No. 82 and Its Potential Effect on Fidelity Claims.* The Fraud Task Force.

Bruce. (2020). *Coronavirus Pandemic Is a Perfect Storm for Fraud.* Retrieved from Associate of certified fraud examiners: https://www.acfe.com/press-release.aspx?id=4295010491

CFI. (2016). *Fraud Triangle A framework used to explain the motivation behind an individual's decision to commit fraud.* Retrieved from Corporate financial institute: https://corporatefinanceinstitute.com/resources/knowledge/accounting/fraud-triangle/

Chris, E., & Hogan, Z. R. (2008, November). Financial Statement Fraud: Insights from the Academic Literature. *Auditing, 27*(2), 231–252.

Cole, S. (2009). *Suspect identities: A history of fingerprinting and criminal identification.* Harvard University Press.

Cunhal. (2018). Determinants of Structure of Corporate Governance Disclosure in Portugal. *RBGN*, 338.

Dimitras, G. I. (2013). Financial crisis and accounting quality: Evidence from five European countries. *Elsevier, 29*(1), 154-160.

Dutta, S. K., Caplan, D. H., & Marcinko, D. J. (2014). Blurred vision, perilous future: Management fraud at olympus. *Issues in Accounting Education, 29*(3), 459–480. doi:10.2308/iace-50787

Enofe, Ao, M. O. (2016). Forensic accounting and fraudulent financial reporting in Nigeria. *Journal of Accounting and Financial Management, 2*(1), 21–34.

Enofe. (2016). Forensic Accounting and Fraudulent Financial Reporting in Nigeria. *Journal of Accounting and Financial Management, 2*(1), 21-34.

Eyisi, E. (2014). The Impact of Forensic Auditors in Corporate Governance. *Research Journal of Finance and Accounting, 5*(8), 31–39.

Ezuwore, E. a. (2014). The Impact of Forensic Auditors in Corporate Governance. *Research Journal of Finance and Accounting, 5*(8).

Glover & Prawit. (2003). A Test of Changes in Auditors' Fraud-Related Planning Judgments since the Issuance of SAS No. 82. *Auditing: A Journal of Practice & Theory, 22*(2), 237–251.

Hadian, D. T. (2013). Detection fraud of financial statement with fraud triangle. *Proceeding of 23rd International Business Research Conference.*

Hogan. (2008, November). Financial Statement Fraud: Insights from the Academic Literature. *Auditing: A Journal of Practice & Theory, 27*(2), 231–252.

Hołda, A. (2020, December 22). Using the Beneish M-score model: Evidence from non-financial. *Investment Management and Financial Innovations.*

Imoniana, J. O. (2013). The forensic accounting and corporate fraud. *Journal of Information Systems and Technology Management, 10*(1), 119–144.

Jain, D. E., & Lamba, J. (2020). Forensic Accounting: A Way To Fight, Deter And Detect Fraud. *International Research Journal. Vic. Australia, 10*(1). Advance online publication. doi:10.51611/iars.irj.v10i1.2020.106

Juárez, F. (2016). Chaos theory and financial statements. Nova Science Publishers, Inc.

Kacharava, A. (2016, June). *O IC-online é o Repositório Institucional de Informação Científica do Instituto Politécnico de Leiria.* Retrieved from Instituto Politécnico de Leiria: https://iconline.ipleiria.pt/bitstream/10400.8/2139/1/Aleksandre%20Kacharava.pdf

Kaminski. (2004, Jan 1). Can financial ratios detect fraudulent financial reporting? *Managerial Auditing Journal.*

Kljajić, M., Đurić, L., & Arežina, N. (2017). The purpose of forensic accounting in detecting occupational fraud in contemporary corporate governance. *FINIZ, 78-82.* Advance online publication. doi:10.15308/finiz-2017-78-82

Manning, G. A. (2011). Financial Investigation and Forensic Accounting (3rd ed.). Routledge.

Mustafa, S. T., & Meier, H. H. (2006). CAP forum on forensic accounting in the post-enron world audit committees and misappropriation of assets: Publicly held companies in the United States [Les comités de vérification et le détournement de biens: les sociétés ouvertes aux États-Unis]. *Canadian Accounting Perspectives*, *5*(2), 307–333. doi:10.1506/CCWW-JRWB-ECUE-YMM

N, E. A. (2014). The Impact of Forensic Auditors in Corporate Governance. *Research Journal of Finance and Accounting, 5*(8).

Nandini, N. S., & Ajay, R. (2021). A Study on impact of Forensic Audit towards Investigation and Prevention of Frauds. *Asian Journal of Management, 12*(2), 186–2. doi:10.52711/2321-5763.2021.00028

Nigrini, M. J. (2011). Forensic Analytics. In Forensic Analytics: Methods and Techniques for Forensic Accounting Investigations (2nd ed.). John Wiley & Sons.

OECD. (1993). Accounting reform in Estonia, Latvia and Lithuania. Paris: OECD.

Omondi, E. O. (2013, November). *The impact of forensic accounting services on fraud detection and prevention among Commercial Banks in Kenya.* University of Nairobi.

Owojori, A. A., & Asaolu, T. O. (2009). The role of forensic accounting in solving the vexed problem of corporate world. *European Journal of Scientific Research*, *29*(2), 183–187. www.scopus.com

Perduv. (2018). The role of forensic accounting in corporate governance for economic societies. *Poslovnestudije.com, 10*(19-20), 119-131.

Rafael. (1998, December). Law and Finance. *Journal of Political Economy, 106*(6), 1113-1155.

Ramaswamy, V. (2007, September 1). New frontiers: Training forensic accountants within the accounting program. *Journal of College Teaching and Learning*, *4*(9), 31–38.

Rehman, A., & Hashim, F. (2020). A Conceptual Framework: Forensic Accounting and Corporate Governance Maturity. *International Journal of Accounting Finance and Business*, *5*(30), 52–63.

Rehman, A., & Hashim, F. (2021). Can forensic accounting impact sustainable corporate governance? *Corporate Governance (Bingley)*, *21*(1), 212–227. doi:10.1108/CG-06-2020-0269

Schiavone, A.-J. (2012). *And The Survey Says... Increasing Demand for Forensic Accounting*. AICPA.

Shelton. (2001, March). Auditing Firms' Fraud Risk Assessment Practices. *Accounting Horizon, 15*(1).

Statista. (2021). *Number of accountants and auditors employed in the U.S. 2012-2020.* Statista Research Department. https://www.statista.com/statistics/317587/number-of-accountants-and-auditors-employed-us/

Statistic, U. S. B. (2020). *Occupational outlook handbook.* Retrieved from Accountant and Auditors: https://www.bls.gov/ooh/business-and-financial/accountants-and-auditors.htm

Subash, T. (2015). Forensic accounting and Corporate Governance. *EXCEL International Journal of Multidisciplinary Management Studies*, *5*(11), 49–54.

Teodósi. (2021). Corporate Governance in Portugal: A Literature Review. In *Comparative Research on Earnings Management, Corporate Governance, and Economic Value* (p. 21). IGI Global.

Terziev. (2020, October). *Libraries and tourism – possibilities for integration and new directions for sustainable social development.* Academic Press.

Van Akkeren, J., & Buckby, S. (2017). Perceptions on the causes of individual and fraudulent co-offending: Views of forensic accountants. *Journal of Business Ethics, 146*(2), 383–404. doi:10.100710551-015-2881-0

Vedrana. (2018). The role of forensic accounting in corporate governance for economic socieites. *Poslovne studije/Business Studies, 10*(19-20), 119-131.

Vieira & Neiva. (2019). Corporate governance board of directors and firm performance in Portugal. In *Board of Directors and Company Performance: An International Outlook* (p. 121). Virtus Interpress.

Wahyuni-TD, I. S., Haron, H., & Fernando, Y. (2021). The effects of good governance and fraud prevention on performance of the zakat institutions in Indonesia: A Sharīʿah forensic accounting perspective. *International Journal of Islamic and Middle Eastern Finance and Management, 14*(4), 692–712. https://doi.org/10.1108/IMEFM-03-2019-0089

Williams, T. (2018). *Role of management, corporate governance, and sarbanes-oxley in fraud: A focus on the precious metals industry.* Retrieved from www.scopus.com

Yale, G., Grove, H., & Clouse, M. (2013). Risk management lessons learned: Countrywide report. *Corporate Ownership and Control, 11*(1H), 33-46. doi:10.22495/cocv11i1conf1p4

Yang, C., & Lee, K. (2020). Developing a strategy map for forensic accounting with fraud risk management: An integrated balanced scorecard-based decision model. *Evaluation and Program Planning, 80.* Advance online publication. doi:10.1016/j.evalprogplan.2020.101780

Yu, S., & Rha, J. (2021). Research trends in accounting fraud using network analysis. *Sustainability (Switzerland), 13*(10). Advance online publication. doi:10.3390u13105579

ADDITIONAL READING

Hube, J. A. (2015). Topics and methods in forensic accounting research. *Accounting Research Journal, 28*(1), 98–114. doi:10.1108/ARJ-08-2014-0071

Mary-Jo Kranacher, R. R. (2019). Forensic Accounting And Fraud (2nd ed.). Wiley.

KEY TERMS AND DEFINITIONS

Corporate Communication: A set of professional activities channeling to manage and compose the entire external and internal communication specifically between middle to top-level management.

Corrupt Financial Gurus: The financial professionals are involved in dishonest behavior by using illegitimate positions and power for corruption.

Financial Frauds: It happens when somebody misleads regarding companies or government money with the help of illegal practices.

Financial Scam: It is a deliberate attempt to falsification financial information or illegal practices to enhance a company's profits and deceive public opinion.

Fraud Financial Reporting: It occurs via materiality misleading amounts in financial statements to deceive investors or government officials.

Internal Control: This is a process of interlocking the entire activities of an organization that are layered onto the normal operating procedures for safeguard assets & management policy.

Interrogation Skills: An interviewer provoking to get honest information from a candidate specifically information regarding crime suspected.

Investigation: This is the act of analysis and gathering facts that are to be used in a court of law.

Chapter 2
Significance of Forensic Accounting Techniques in Corporate Governance:
Bibliometric Analysis

Suleman Sherali Kamwani
https://orcid.org/0000-0002-2558-1388
A'Sharqiyah University, Oman

Mara Madaleno
https://orcid.org/0000-0002-4905-2771
University of Aveiro, Portugal

Elisabete Vieira
https://orcid.org/0000-0003-3593-368X
University of Aveiro, Portugal

Graça Azevedo
https://orcid.org/0000-0002-6346-4035
University of Aveiro, Portugal

ABSTRACT

This chapter intends to contribute to the analysis of forensic acounting (FA) techniques through a bibliometric review of the existent literature in order to understand the current state of FA research as well as to contribute to the analysis of the influence of FA on corporate governance. Although FA is a modern discipline, in recent years its relevance has been growing very quickly, with the aim to study the use of accounting skills to investigate fraud, embezzlement, and other irregularities hidden as financial transactions. However, no recent study tries to update the current state of the research over this topic. To do so, the authors conduct a bibliometric analysis. The study describes the evolutional research studies published in the digital library Scopus between 2005 and 2020 and compares the results obtained in evolutionary terms. Considering only the FA publications, the Scopus analysis led to a total database of 192 documents. However, this sudy focuses on the research that relates FA and corporate governance concentrating the bibliometric analysis in the Scopus database.

INTRODUCTION

No bibliometric research should start without previously defining what the main subject under analysis

DOI: 10.4018/978-1-7998-8754-6.ch002

is. The study concentrate on FA articles published in the recent years of 2005-2020. As well, what is FA? Forensic accounting consists of the use of accounting skills to investigate fraud, embezzlement, and other irregularities hidden as financial transactions, being related to the process of presenting and interpreting financial issues (Howard & Sheetz, 2006). The demand for FA is related to the emergence of entrepreneurs and business professionals establishing their own companies. With the current reliance on internet technologies, the role of forensic accountants has expanded for that reason. Lawbreakers may have a false sense of security, as they believe that they can easily hide their tracks because financial transactions are made online. Besides, more sophisticated individuals can use the internet to obfuscate illegal transactions, so forensic accountants are increasingly required, in an attempt, to detect these situations. According to Golden et al. (2006), an audit answers to the risk of fraud, and the FA research replies to suspicions, allegations, or evidence of fraud.

This chapter intends to analyze the FA techiques, by trying to understand how the literature has researched the topic in recent years. By doing this through a bibliometric analysis, the authors are able to find the main reported conclusions in differenty studies and among different fields of analysis.

According to Shah (2018), the development of FA techniques benefits the detection of financial fraud, as well as the promotion of audit effectiveness. Indeed, there are several studies finding evidence that the application of FA services on corporate organizations was effective in determining fraudulent activities (Adegbie&Fakile, 2012; Ahmadu et al., 2013; Enofe et al., 2013; Gbegi&Adebisi, 2014; Ehioghiren&Atu, 2016). This effect of FA on fraud detection leads to an improvement in corporate governance. Consequently, FA work is essential to encourage corporate governance practices. Thus, it is expected that forensic accounting has some influence on corporate governance practices.

The authors do not intend to present a literature review, but yes a bibliometric analysis stating clearly what are the relevant topics being analyzed in more recent years (2005-2020) and the current state of research.

As will be evidenced in the next section, these results report different findings that could lead us to other research fields. As such, it is intended to present the state of the current literature regarding research on FA and its relation to corporate governance practices. The rest of this chapter develops as follows. Section two presents a brief literature review on the FA topic and its relationship with corporate governance. Section three presents the general status of FA and corporate governanceresearch from 2005 to 2020, first in global terms and then concentrating on the top seven articles, considerind the number os citations, while Section four concludes the chapter and provides some insights for possible future research regarding FA and corporate governance.

BRIEF LITERATURE REVIEW ON FORENSIC ACCOUNTING

The interest of FA research is based on some reasons, such as to identify fraud, embezzlement, and other irregularities hidden as financial transactions. According to Akinbowale et al. (2020), the FA aims to identify and review fraudulent transactions in order to understand what the author's true intention is. Pamungkas et al. (2018) report that accounting fraud results from inadequate supervision of systems. Thus, firms must implement efficient monitoring mechanisms, seeking to standardize the adopted procedures. To put into practice FA, it is needed that accountants possess accounting, auditing, and forensic abilities to deal with fraudulent cases (Grubor et al., 2013). Yang and Lee (2020) argue that associate FA technology with fraud detection is a noteworthy accounting and management issue. Indeed, Bhasin

(2016a, 2016b) indicates that applications of analytic technology are crucial for the effectiveness of FA, anti-fraud programs, and fraud investigation.

Some commonly used techniques in the FA approach are the structured interview and the data mining technique (Golden & Dyer, 2006). More recently, some authors develop digital frameworks for the FA implementation, such as Prayudi et al. (2015) and Jadhap and Agarwal (2016). According to Shah (2018), the development of FA techniques benefits the detection of financial fraud, as well as the promotion of audit effectiveness. Indeed, there are several studies finding evidence that the application of FA services on corporate organizations was effective in determining fraudulent activities (Adegbie&Fakile, 2012; Ahmadu et al., 2013; Enofe et al., 2013; Gbegi&Adebisi, 2014; Ehioghiren&Atu, 2016). This effect of forensic accounting on fraud detection leads to an improvement in corporate governance. Consequently, forensic accountant work is essential to encourage corporate governance practices.

As a modern discipline, FA is beginning to see many avenues for additional skills that go beyond accounting and finance. Recent reforms in FA technology have opened up new opportunities for corporate governance and internal control mechanism implementation, through corporate fraud risk management (Yang & Lee, 2020). Some authors established that poor corporate governance leads to fraud, misappropriation of assets, and dissatisfied shareholders (Ramaswamy, 2005; Bhasin, 2013). In the same vein, Vinita (2005) notes that when firms have poor corporate governance practices, they may end up in bankruptcy or incorporate losses into their financial statements. Besides, controlling ownership and minority shareholders' protection is difficult through conventional corporate control mechanisms. Thus, it can be facilitated through forensic accounting (Fan & Wong, 2005). To sum, forensic accounting is useful to prevent fraud, which, in turn, improves corporate governance efficiency. Consequently, it is expected that FAhas some influence on corporate governance practices.

Corporate governance rules and recommendations are crucial to defend stakeholder's interests, including the ones of investors from managerial misconduct and potential financial risk (Soltani&Maupetit, 2015), namely because it suggests a group of practices that results in a reduction of conflicts between managers and shareholders (Vieira & Neiva, 2019). Thus, corporate governance is a system that provides directions for organizations to be beneficial to all stakeholders.According to Olaoye and Olanipekun (2018), corporate governance consists of a set of rules that define the relationship among stakeholders, management, and the board of directors of a firm, as well as their influence on the operations of the companies. Consequently, it deals with matters that are derived from the separation of ownership and control, related to the agency theory (Jensen &Meckling, 1976). In this sense, the OECD (2004) argues that it is necessary to provide a reliable structure, through which objectives must be defined and achieved, as well as to monitor the performance of managers, which depends on good corporate governance practices.An inefficient system of corporate governance has a significant effect on performance, fraud, misappropriation of assets, and dissatisfied shareholders (Bhasin, 2013). Ali and Oseni (2010) and Bhasin (2013) state that forensic accounting is positioned to explore the restructuring of corporate governance because of its skills and knowledge. Several empirical research concludes that FA affects corporate governance effectiveness, such as Enofe et al. (2013), Ehioghiren and Atu (2016), Bachin (2017), Olaoye, and Olanipekun (2018), and Yang and Lee (2020). Bachin (2013) considers that forensic accounting can help to formulate an inclusive governance policy that ensures an appropriate mix of management and independent directors on the board, and that guarantees the stakeholder's interests. He concludes that forensic accounting makes significant contributions to corporate governance, fraud prevention, and investigation, leading to transparency and honesty in corporate governance and corporate reporting. Bachin (2017) examines how the expertise of FA can be integrated to improve corporate governance practices in India, surveying 120 practicing chartered accountants, accounting academics, and potential users of forensic accounting services, during the years 2011 and 2012. According to Bachin, forensic accountants are valuable to help the improvement of the corporate governance system. However, this is still a work-in-progress process. Olaoye and Olanipekun (2018) explore the relationship between forensic accounting and corporate governance in the state of Nigeria (Ekiti State). The results show a significant relationship between forensic accounting and corporate governance. The evidence suggests that fraud detection and internal control system contributed significantly to corporate governance. The authors conclude that FA and investigation influence corporate governance, improving the management accountability, internal control system, and financial reporting system. The authors conclude that FA significantly influences fraud detection and control, which would lead to improved corporate governance. This conclusion is following previous ones, such as the studies of Enofe et al. (2013) and Ehioghiren and Atu (2016).

Rehman and Hashim (2018) intend to enhance the value of forensic accounting as part of governance management where fraud can be prevented before it occurs. The authors intend to identify the role of forensic accounting as a preventive measure rather than a detective control, proposing that internal audit has a mediate role between forensic accounting and corporate governance by connecting professional theory and agency theory in its relationship. The authors also conclude that forensic accounting is only requested once the fraud is detected, which is in line with Adrian et al. (2009) and Singleton and Singleton (2010), among others.Yang and Lee (2020) analyze the forensic accounting decision-making process in Taiwan, finding evidence that corporate decision-makers effectively fulfill corporate governance quality assurance and anti-fraud through a forensic accounting strategy. Recently, there is an intensifying apprehension for the sustainability in corporate governance (Crifo et al., 2019) and FA is the most appropriate action that can help to eliminate and mitigate frauds (Rehman & Hashim, 2019).

GENERAL BIBLIOMETRIC ANALYSIS ON FORENSIC ACCOUNTING AND CORPORATE GOVERNANCE: 2005-2020

Bibliometric analysis is a method that turns easier the research of the relationship between research criteria and variables related to the research and environment of that research. During this research, it was applied the exploratory, descriptive, and bibliographic research methodology, performing a content analysis through the keyword earnings management. The search was performed at the end of April 2021 and as such the authors excluded from it articles published after 2020. Provided the authors wanted a recent analysis period, they concentrate the chapter research during the period 2005-2020. Even so, just by searching for the keyword "Forensic Accounting"in the Scopus database, it was found192 documents (from all types) published from 2005 until 2020. The last year of the sample (2020), was the one with more documents published (25), and the 2015-2020 represents about 50% of the publiucations (105), suggesting yhis is a recent topic of research. The acquired data has on its basis several sources which are found in Scopus (https://www.scopus.com/search/), a database with a huge quantity of articles. The process of data collection in this platform is divided into several parameters: the choice of the database, the definition of keywords, the identification of the article, the journal identification, and the classification of the articles. The study performed and presented next will follow over some of these parameters.

Figure 1 presents the evolution of the documents collected for the period between 2005 and 2020, after applying the parameters defined in the Scopus database, and looking for the keywords "Forensic

Figure 1. Number of documents published during 2005-2020, by year
Source: Scopus

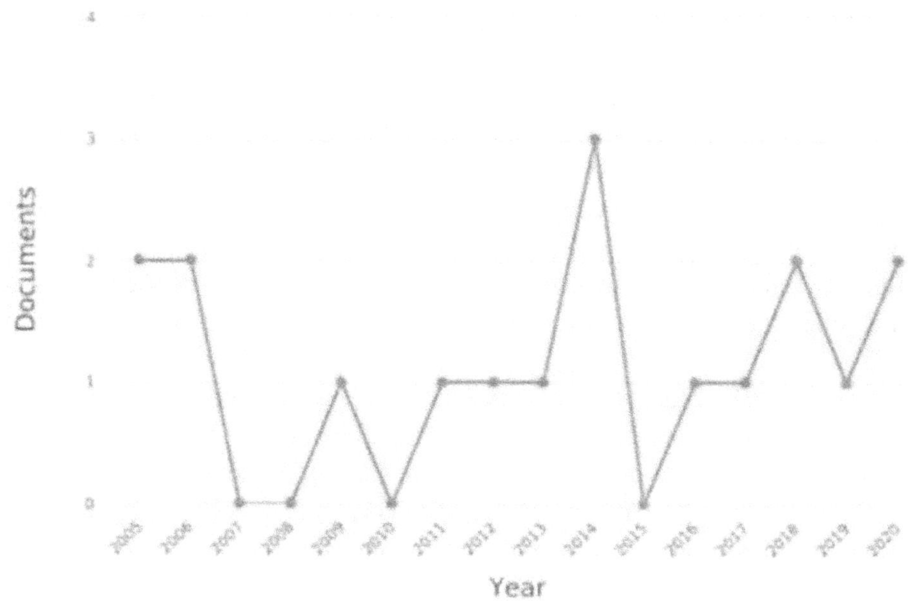

Accounting" and "Corporate Governance, which relation we want to analyse, leading us to a total database of 18 documents, proving that this is a new topic in the accounting research.

It is visible an instability of publications durinhg the period in analysis, ranging bwteen zero and three, being the year of 2014 with the highest number of documents published (three).It is even denotedthat in four years (2007, 2008 and 2015) there are no publications on this subjects, which may be due to the lack of a deeper exploration of the subject by researchers.

Figure 2 shows the documents published by source title.

As it can be seen in Figure 2, the journal tht registered the higher number of publications about the relation between FA and Corporate Governance is the Emerald Emerging Markets Case Studies, following by the

Wit Transactions on Information and Communication Technologies. There are several journals with just one paper published during the period of the study, namely the British Journal of Criminology, the Canadian Accounting Perspectives and the Corporate Governance Bingley.

The peak of published documents ocuured in the Emerald Emerging Markets Case Studies, but just on one year, whereas the Emerald Emerging Markets Case Studies published documents during more years whose keywords included FA and Corporate Governance.

Figure 3 highlights the authors which most published in the field of FA and Corporate Governance during the 2005-2020 period. With three documents during this period, there is the author Williams, J.W., followed by a list of several authors with a publication each one, such as Abdul Malak, S.S.D., Asaolu, T.O, Assad, M.J.,Bhasin, M.L., Buckby, S., Caplan, D.H., Clouse, M., Dhamija, S., and Dutta, S.K..

The authors want to highlight that up to this phase they are considering all kinds of published documents under the FA and Corporate Governance keywords for the period of analysis.

Figure 2. Documents published in 2005-2020period, by source title
Source: Scopus

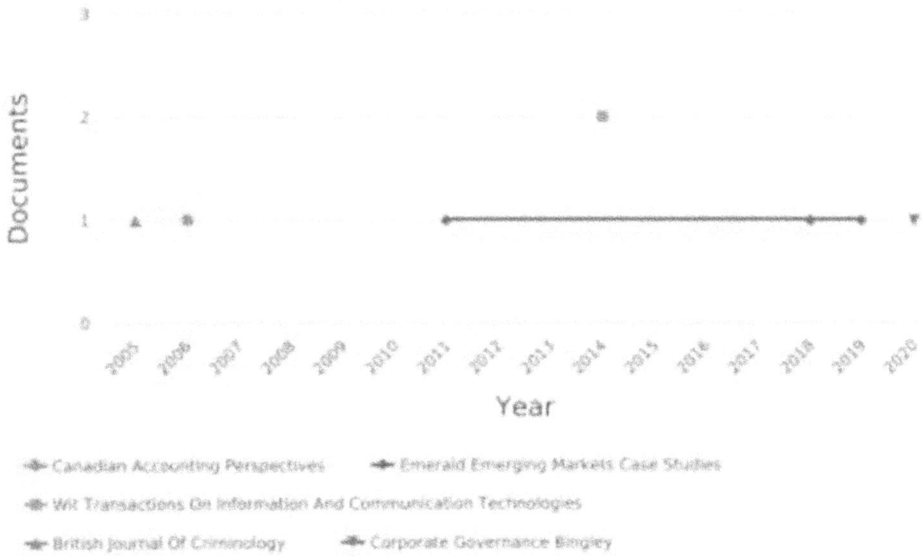

Figure 4 shows the documents published by affiliation under the keywords FA and Corporate Governance, for the period between 2005 and 2020.

Regarding the affiliation of the authors, the University of Utara Malaysia and the University of Windsor are the two with the highest number of affiliated authors and co-authors publishing during 2005 and 2020. This is followed by the Baker College of Flint, the Yale, the University Sains Malaysia, the State University of New York System, the London School of Economics and Political Science, the Cleveland State University, the Queensland University of Technology and the Obafemi Awolowo University in the lowest top ten of affiliations.

Figure 5 displays the documents by country or territory during 2005 and 2020.

In what concerns the number of documents published by country or territory, it can be seen that research on FA and Corporate Governance are focused on Canada and onthe United States, followed by Malasya. The rest of the countries in the top ten documents by counry are Australia, Asian countries (India, Oman and Taiwan), Africa (Nigeria and Tanzania), and only one European country (United Kingdom). The low number of published papers on this subject shows that the research on the relationship between FA and Corporate Governance is still on its initial stage, with a high potential of research. In addition, more research is needed on countries within Europe, where there is still a scarcity of research under the FA and corporate governance subject.Moreover, a comparative analysis of FA and Corporate Governance is necessary within regions and among regions in order to compare results and conclusions.

As it can be seen in Figure 6, the most published documents during this period were made in the form of Scientific Articles (72.2%). Conference Reviews and Book Chapters represent both 11.1%, while Review represent only 5.6% of the published documents.

Figure 7 shows the documents by subject area published during the period in analysis.

Regarding the main subject areas of publication,it can be seen that mostly are within the Business, Management and Accounting area (31.0%), followed by the area of Social Sciences with 23.8% and

Figure 3. Documents published during 2005-2020 by author
Source: Scopus

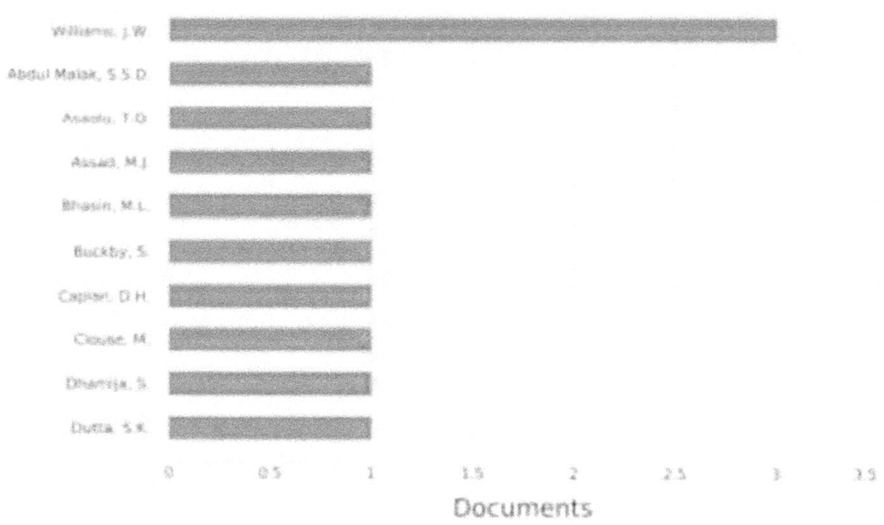

Economics, Econometrics and Finance (11.9%). However, it is visible that FA and Corporate Governance research is being explored in other knowledge areas such as Computer Science, Arts and Humanities, Medicine and Psychology.

The most cited articles are those described in Table 1.

Figure 4. Documents published by affiliation during 2005-2020 under the keywords FA and corporate governance
Source: Scopus

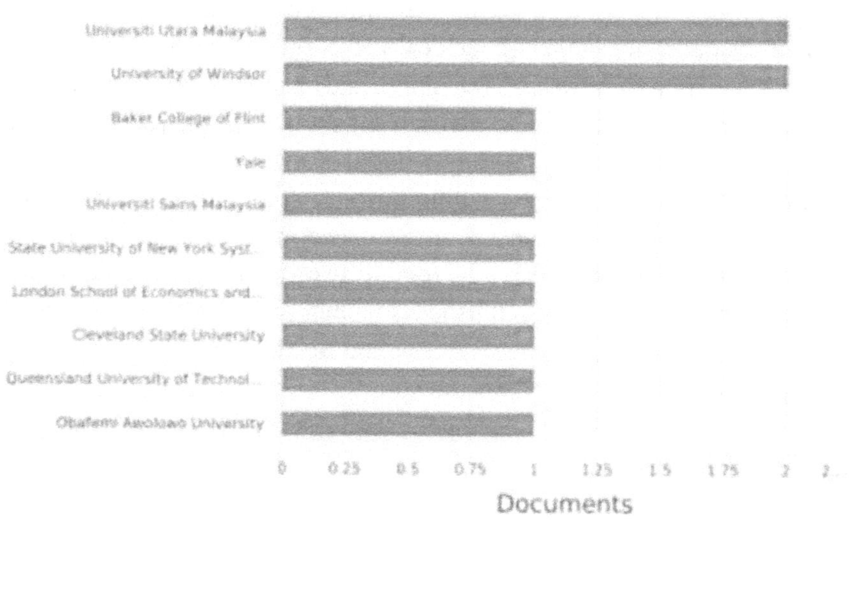

Figure 5. Documents by country or territory during 2005-2020
Source: Scopus

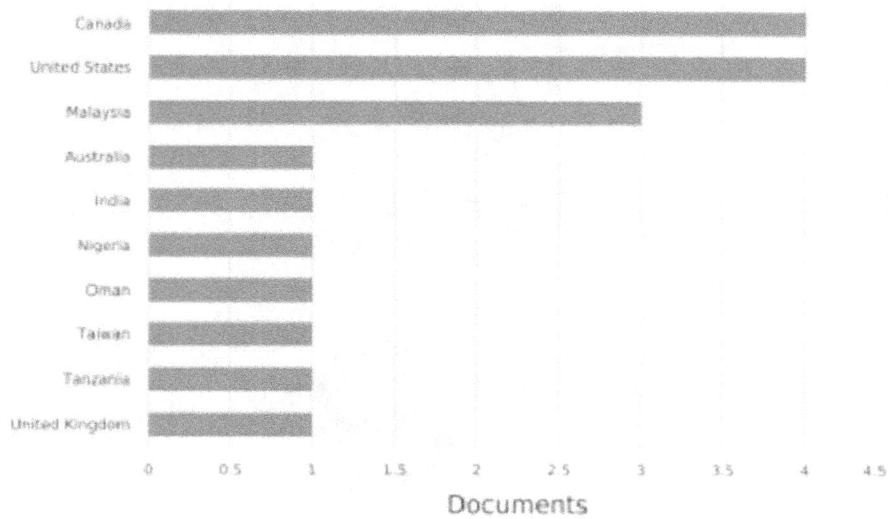

The top 3 articles are published by the same author (Williams, J.W.). The article gathering more citations was published in 2005 in the British Journal of Criminology, with 52 citations at the moment of this chapter writing, with a cientific paper that make some reflections on the private versus public policing of economic crime, analyzing the role of private agencies in the governance of neo-liberal market economies. It documents the growth and evolution of the FA and Corporate investigation indus-

Figure 6. Documents published by type during 2005-2020
Source: Scopus

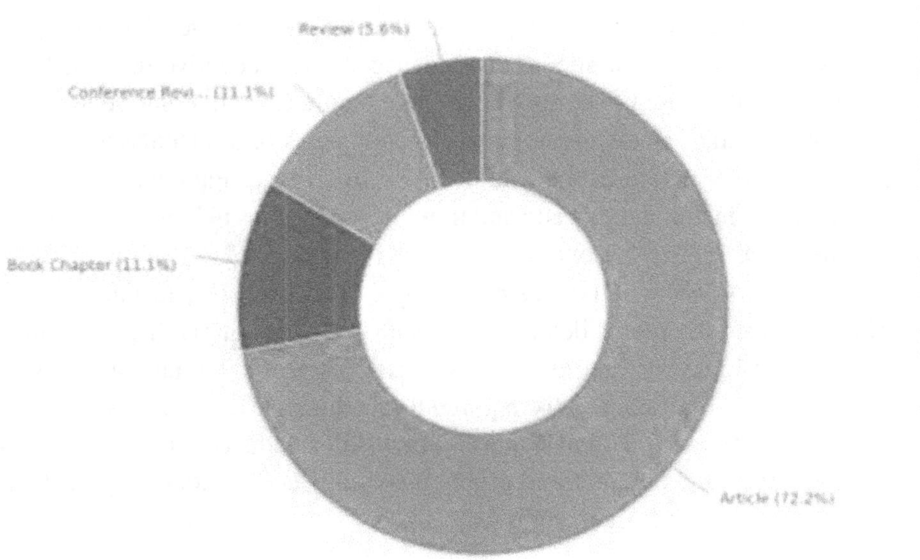

Figure 7. Documents by subject area published during 2005-2020
Source: Scopus

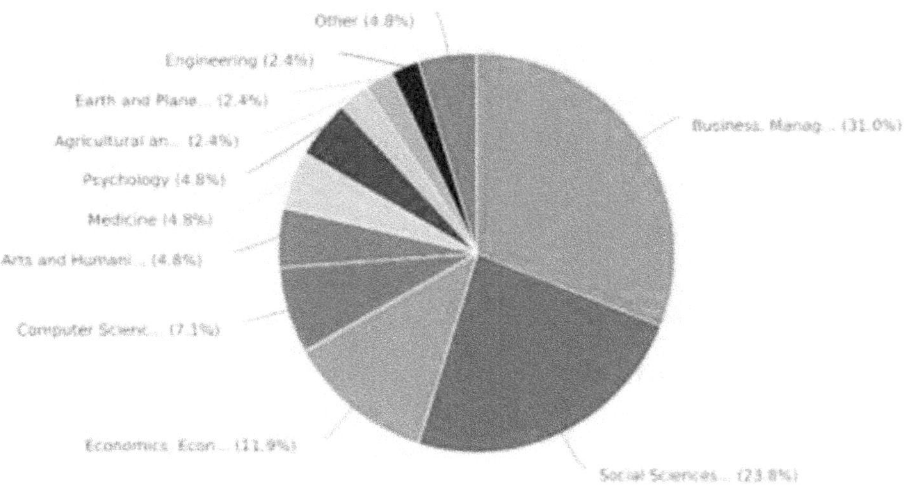

tries in cases of economic crime. From the same author, and also published in 2005, the second paper with more citations (39) was published in the international journal entitled Policing and Society. This study extend the research on governance and accountability to the field of financial security and the activities of the FA and corporate investigation industry, drawing on documentary research and semi-structured interviews. The authors conclude that the unique characteristics of this industry and the legal environment in which it operates conspire to problematize and limit its amenability to external forms of governance and control. He continues his research on FA and corporate investigation industry, focusing on the regulation as a state function to governance (Williams, 2006).

Mustafa and Meier (2006) focused on financial fraud and corporate governance structure, studying the relationship between the incidence of misappropriation of assets by employees, including management, and the effectiveness of the audit committee. The evidence shows a negative relationship between the independent members in audit committees and the average tenure of audit committee members and the incidence of misappropriation of assets in publicly held companies of the United States.

Owojori and Asaolu (2009) explores the role of FA in fraud investigations and litigation support, concluding that the increase in number of fraud and fraudulent activities in Nigeria and around the world hasemphasized the need for forensic accountants.

Bhasin (2016) conducts a survey in India using a sample of accountants, accounting academics, and potential users of FA services, in order to determine what are the necessary skills, education and training requirements for the professional community. The results suggest that potential practitioners, academics and users agree that the most significant skills required for the forensic accountants are critical thinking, written and oral communication, legal knowledge, auditing skills, deductive analysis, investigative flexibility, analytical proficiency and unstructured problem-solving. The authors suggests thar these skills should be used as a guide to desig FA curriculums.

Table 1. Top 7cited articles during 2005-2020

	Document title	Authors	Year	Source	Cited by
1	Reflections on the private versus public policing of economic crime	Williams, J.W.	2005	British Journal of Criminology, 45(3), 316-339	52
2	Governability matters: The private policing of economic crime and the challenge of democratic governance	Williams, J.W.	2005	Policing and Society, 15(2), 187-211	39
3	Private legal orders: Professional markets and the commodification of financial governance	Williams, J.W.	2006	Social and Legal Studies, 15(2), 209-235	12
4	Perceptions on the Causes of Individual and Fraudulent Co-offending: Views of Forensic Accountants	Van Akkeren, J. Buckby, S.	2017	Journal of Business Ethics, 146(2), 383-404	11
5	CAP forum on forensic accounting in the post-enron world audit committees and misappropriation of assets: Publicly held companies in the United States | [Les comités de vérification et le détournement de biens: les sociétésouvertes aux États-Unis]	Mustafa, S.T. Meier, H.H.	2006	Canadian Accounting Perspectives, 5(2), 307-333	11
6	Contribution of forensic accounting to corporate governance: An exploratory study of an Asian country	Bhasin, M.L.	2016	International Business Management, 10(4), 479-492	5
7	The role of forensic accounting in solving the vexed problem of corporate world	Owojori, A.A. Asaolu, T.O.	2009	European Journal of Scientific Research, 29(2), 183-187	5

Source: Own Development

Van Akkeren and Buckby (2017) examineperceptions and experiences of forensic accountants in order to get knowledge into individual fraud and co-offending, determining whether the conceptual framework developed from literature correctlyrepresents the causes of fraud committed by individuals and groups. The findings support the conceptual framework, showing that tension and anomie can result in fraud, that deviant sub-groups recruit and coerce members by providing relief from strain. The authors also conclude that inadequate corporate governance devicescontribute to fraud occurrences that, frequently, are not detected.

Looking for the subjetcs addressed on the 7 papers, it can be seen that FA and corporate governance are related with each other.

In terms of citations made by other authors of these same 7 articles, it can be seen in Table 2 the total number and by year of citation, by article. Since the citations are concentrated on last years, and the toral number are not very high durung the first years, the authors consider the total citations for the 2005-2011 period, 2012-2018 years, and the last two years are presented separately, since they are more recent, and have a concentration of citations. Indeed, the years with more citations are the last two years of the analysis.

Although the period with more citations for the top 2 papers is the 2012-2018 period (the first with more citations in 2013 and the second in 2017), 2019 was the year with more citations made by other articles to the most cited articles. The citations done to the Van Akkeren and Buckby (2017) paper (n.º

Table 2. Total citations made by other articles to the most cited articles

	Documents	Citations	2005-2011	2012-2018	2019	2020	Total
	Total		**34**	**61**	**21**	**19**	**135**
1	Reflections on the private versus public policing of economic crime	2005	21	24	1	6	52
2	Governability matters: The private policing of economic crime and the challenge of democratic governance	2005	7	23	4	5	39
3	Private legal orders: Professional markets and the commodification of financial governance	2006	5	5	1	1	12
4	Perceptions on the Causes of Individual and Fraudulent Co-offending: Views of Forensic Accountants	2017			10	1	11
5	CAP forum on forensic accounting in the post-enron world audit committees and misappropriation of assets: Publicly held companies in the United States I [Les comités de vérification et le détournement de biens: les sociétésouvertes aux États-Unis]	2006	1	6	3	1	11
6	Contribution of forensic accounting to corporate governance: An exploratory study of an Asian country	2016			1	4	5
7	The role of forensic accounting in solving the vexed problem of corporate world	2009		3	1	1	5

Source: Own Development

4) was concentrated on 2019. During the analysis period, there was been done 135 citations to the most cited articles.

Table 3 shows the research activity and some facts for the authors, such as the number of documents done by each one, the total citations considering each author, and the h-index of each one, considering the most cited articles in the period between 2005 and 2020, considering data of 2019.

The author with the highest number of published documents, number of citations, and h-index is Williams, J.W., the author of the top 3 articles by citations, identified in Table 1. It should be as well noticed that the author with the lowest numbers in these components is Owojori, A.A., maybe because it is a junior researcher, which will clearly be reflected in these lowest numbers identified at date.

Table 4 shows the number of authors for the top 7 cited articles during 2005-2020. It is easily perceived that most of these articles are composed by only one author, three of them with the same author (Williams, J.W., as it have been said before). The other papers were written by two authors. The top 3 papers were written by a sole author.

Table 5presents some stylized facts related to the journals of the most cited articles during 2019.

The authors want to emphazise the fact that 3 of the 7 reviews have no score, which shows the need for improve the publications in reviews with higher score. The review that published more articles on the analysed domain was the Emerald Emerging Markets Case Studies. However, this review is the one that shows lower levels of Score Indexes.

For all of the indexes (CiteScore, SJR and SNIP), the review that presents the highest score was the British Journal of Criminology. It was also the one that shows the higher number of citations.

Table 3. Research activity and facts for the authors of the most cited articles during 2005-2020 (data from 2019)

	Author	Documents by author	Total citation	h-index
1-3	Williams, J.W.	231	7872	46
4	Van Akkeren, J.	9	97	6
	Buckby, S.	13	168	9
5	Mustafa, S.T.	2	31	2
	Meier, H.H.	6	86	4
6	Bhasin, M.L.	2	5	1
7	Owojori, A.A.	1	5	1
	Asaolu, T.O.	10	19	3

Source: Own Development

To conclude, Table 6 summarizes the 18 articles that results from the research in this section, considering the keywords "Forensic Accounting" and "Corporate Governance" in the Scopus database, for the period between 2005 and 2020.

There has been a total of 18 documents, resulting in 150 citations. From the 18 articles, 5 have no citations, and two of them are papers presented in international conferences, with no name available. The highly cited articles were published in 2005, followed by papers published in 2006 and 2017. These articles were published in the British Journal of Criminology, Policing and Society, Social and Legal Studies, Journal of Business Ethics and Canadian Accounting Perspectives. Considering the most recent publications, for the 2018-2020 period, there is one articles published in 2018 and another in 2019. However, none of them were been cited. The year of 2020 counts with 2 articles published, but only one has citations (3), which authors are Yang, C.-H. and Lee, K.-C.

Table 4. Articles collaboration for the top 7 cited articles during 2005-2020: number of authors

	Documents	Number of authors
1	Reflections on the private versus public policing of economic crime	1
2	Governability matters: The private policing of economic crime and the challenge of democratic governance	1
3	Private legal orders: Professional markets and the commodification of financial governance	1
4	Perceptions on the Causes of Individual and Fraudulent Co-offending: Views of Forensic Accountants	2
5	CAP forum on forensic accounting in the post-enron world audit committees and misappropriation of assets: Publicly held companies in the United States I [Les comités de vérification et le détournement de biens: les sociétésouvertes aux États-Unis]	2
6	Contribution of forensic accounting to corporate governance: An exploratory study of an Asian country	1
7	The role of forensic accounting in solving the vexed problem of corporate world	2

Source: Own Development

Table 5. Facts related to the journals of the most cited articles in FA and corporate governance during 2019

	Review	CiteScore 2019	SJR 2019	SNIP 2019	Citations 2016-2019	Documents 2016-2019
1	Emerald Emerging Markets Case Studies	0.1	0.166	0.048	31	366
2	Wit Transactions on Information and Communication Technologies					
3	British Journal of Criminology	5.3	1.416	2.573	1.397	266
4	Canadian Accounting Perspectives					
5	Corporate Governance Bingley	3.3	0.574	1.396	810	242
6	Corporate Ownership and Control		0.148	0.268		
7	European Journal of Scientific Research					

Source: Own Development

FUTURE RESEARCH DIRECTIONS

The publications on these subjects are still in its infancy, leaving space for new developments in research terms. In addition, European markets exploration is still in deeper need of analysis.

Corporate governance can be used as a tool for frauds control. A deeper understanding of corporate governance beyong the audit committees, the institutional and market pressures, legal environments, macroeconomic conditions, and many others are still in need of research or deserve more understanding. For instance, sustainable corporate governance and fraud control activities are two main supports for organizational successful business growth and sustainability, which needs further research. The regulators and the responsible authorities can adjust the codes of corporate governance, including sustainable corporate governance and FA limitations in order to contribute to to achieve sustainable corporate governance and fraud-free organizations (Rehman & Hashim, 2020). Relating these two themes with the economic value of the firm is still in its infancy even though much research has emerged in recent years.

CONCLUSION

Forensic accounting consists of the use of accounting skills to investigate fraud, embezzlement, and other irregularities hidden as financial transactions, being related to the process of presenting and interpreting financial issues. The demand for FA is related to the emergence of entrepreneurs and business professionals establishing their own companies.

Corporate governance is a system that provides instructions in order to protect all the firms' stakeholders. According to the literature, an inefficient system of corporate governance has a significant effect on performance, fraud, misappropriation of assets, and dissatisfied shareholders. In addition, there are evidence that forensic accounting affects corporate governance effectiveness, leading to transparency and honesty in corporate governance and corporate reporting.

Table 6. Summary of articles exploring simultaneously forensic accounting and corporate governance for the period 2005-2020

	Document Title	Authors	Year	Source	Cited by
1	Reflections on the private versus public policing of economic crime	Williams, J.W.	2005	British Journal of Criminology, 45(3), 316-339	52
2	Governability matters: The private policing of economic crime and the challenge of democratic governance	Williams, J.W.	2005	Policing and Society, 15(2), 187-211	39
3	Private legal orders: Professional markets and the commodification of financial governance	Williams, J.W.	2006	Social and Legal Studies, 15(2), 209-235	12
4	Perceptions on the Causes of Individual and Fraudulent Co-offending: Views of Forensic Accountants	Van Akkeren, J., Buckby, S.	2017	Journal of Business Ethics, 146(2), 383-404	11
5	CAP forum on forensic accounting in the post-enron world audit committees and misappropriation of assets: Publicly held companies in the United States I [Les comités de vérification et le détournement de biens: les sociétésouvertes aux États-Unis]	Mustafa, S.T., Meier, H.H.	2006	Canadian Accounting Perspectives, 5(2), 307-333	11
6	Contribution of forensic accounting to corporate governance: An exploratory study of an Asian country	Bhasin, M.L.	2016	International Business Management, 10(4), 479-492	5
7	The role of forensic accounting in solving the vexed problem of corporate world	Owojori, A.A., Asaolu, T.O.	2009	European Journal of Scientific Research, 29(2), 183-187	5
8	Blurred vision, perilous future: Management fraud at Olympus	Dutta, S.K., Caplan, D.H., Marcinko, D.J.	2014	Issues in Accounting Education, 29(3), 459-480	4
9	Fraud at the Central Bank of Tanzania (A) Open Access	Assad, M.J.	2011	Emerald Emerging Markets Case Studies, 1(1), 1-12	4
10	Developing a strategy map for forensic accounting with fraud risk management: An integrated balanced scorecard-based decision model	Yang, C.-H., Lee, K.-C.	2020	Evaluation and Program Planning, 80,101780	3
11	The managerialization of security (Book Chapter)	Power, M.	2012	Securitization, Accountability and Risk Management: Transforming the Public Security Domain, 70-87	2
12	Role of Management, Corporate Governance, and Sarbanes-Oxley in Fraud: A Focus on the Precious Metals Industry	Williams, T.	2018	Accounting, Finance, Sustainability, Governance and Fraud, 391-409	1
13	Risk management lessons learned: Countrywide report Open Access	Yale, G., Grove, H., Clouse, M.	2013	Corporate Ownership and Control, 11(1 H), 33-46	1
14	Can forensic accounting impact sustainable corporate governance?	Rehman, A., Hashim, F.	2020	Corporate Governance (Bingley), 21(1), 212-227	0
15	AirAsia Berhad's accounting in the spotlight Open Access	Abdul Malak, S.S.D., Wan Hussin, W.N.B.	2019	Emerald Emerging Markets Case Studies, 9(1), 1-26	0
16	Corporate governance failure at Ricoh India: rebuilding lost trust	Goyal, S., Dhamija, S.	2018	Emerald Emerging Markets Case Studies, 8(4), 1-20	0
17	2013 International Conference of Information Science and Management Engineering, ISME 2013, Volume 3	[No author name available]	2014	WIT Transactions on Information and Communication Technologies, 46(3)	0
18	2013 International Conference of Information Science and Management Engineering, ISME 2013, Volume 2	[No author name available]	2014	WIT Transactions on Information and Communication Technologies, 46(2)	0
	Total				150

Source: Own Development

Based on the evidence that fraud detection and internal control system contributed significantly to corporate governance, this study proposes to contribute to the analysis of the influence of forensic accounting on corporate governance, by conducting a bibliometric analysis focused on forensic accountingand corporate governance for the period between 2005 and 2020, making a point of situation in what concerns the current state-of-the-art.

REFERENCES

Abdul Malak, S. S. D., & Wan Hussin, W. N. B. (2019). Air Asia Berhad's accounting in the spotlight. *Emerald Emerging Markets Case Studies*, *9*(1), 1–26. doi:10.1108/EEMCS-06-2018-0115

Adegbie, F. F., & Fakile, A. S. (2012). Economic and financial crime in Nigeria: Forensic accounting as an antidote. *British Journal of Arts and Social Sciences*, *6*(1), 37–50.

Adrian, N. K., Lawrence, A., & Cristal Lee, A. S. (2009). Forensic Accounting: Public Acceptance towards Occurrence of Fraud Detection. *International Journal of Business and Management*, *4*(11), 145–150.

Ahmadu, B. U., Zayyad, A. B., & Rasak, A. I. (2013). An empirical examination of the role of forensic audit in enhancing financial investigations in Nigeria. *ICAN Journal of Accounting and Finance*, *2*(1), 145–159.

Akinbowale, O. E., Klingelhöfer, E. H., & Zerihun, M. F. (2020). An innovative approach in combating economic crime using forensic accounting techniques. *Combating Economic Crime*, *27*(4), 1253–1271. doi:10.1108/JFC-04-2020-0053

Ali, M., & Oseni, A. (2010). Corporate Governance, Transparency and Shareholders' Rights: The Role of The Forensic Accountants in Propelling Economic Growth. *Multidisciplinary Journal of Research Development*, *15*(1), 1–9.

Assad, M. J. (2011). Fraud at the Central Bank of Tanzania. *Emerald Emerging Markets Case Studies*, *1*(1), 1–12. doi:10.1108/20450621111110492

Bhasin, M. L. (2013). Corporate governance and forensic accountant: An exploratory study. *Journal Accounting Business and Management-International*, *20*(2), 55–83.

Bhasin, M. L. (2016a). Forensic accounting in Asia: Perspectives and prospects. *International Journal of Management and Social Sciences Research*, *5*(7), 25–38.

Bhasin, M. L. (2016b). Contribution of forensic accounting to corporate governance: An exploratory study of an Asian country. *International Business Management*, *10*(4), 479–492.

Bhasin, M. L. (2017). Integrating Corporate Governance and Forensic Accounting: A Study of an Asian Country. *International Journal of Management Sciences and Business Research*, *6*(1), 31–52.

Crifo, P., Escrig-Olmedo, E., & Mottis, N. (2019). Corporate governance as a key driver of corporate sustainability in France: The role of board members and investor relations. *Journal of Business Ethics*, *159*(4), 1127–1146. doi:10.100710551-018-3866-6

Dutta, S. K., Caplan, D. H., & Marcinko, D. J. (2014). Blurred vision, perilous future: Management fraud at Olympus. *Issues in Accounting Education, 29*(3), 459–480. doi:10.2308/iace-50787

Ehioghiren, E. E., & Atu, O. O. K. (2016). Forensic accounting and fraud management: Evidence from Nigeria. *Igbinedion University Journal of Accounting, 2*, 245–308.

Enofe, A. O., Mgbame, C. O., Ayodele, F. O., & Okunbo, O. (2013). Forensic accounting: A tool for detecting fraud in Nigeria's business environment. *ESUT Journal of Accountancy, 4*(1), 194–199.

Fan, J. P., & Wong, T. J. (2005). Do External Auditors Perform a Corporate Governance Role in Emerging Markets? Evidence from East Asia. *Journal of Accounting Research, 43*(1), 35–72. doi:10.1111/j.1475-679x.2004.00162.x

Gbegi, D. O., & Adebisi, J. F. (2014). Forensic Accounting Skills and Techniques in Fraud Investigation in the Nigerian Public Sector. *Mediterranean Journal of Social Sciences, 5*(3), 243–252. doi:10.5901/mjss.2014.v5n3p243

Golden, T. H., Skalak, S. L., & Clayton, M. M. (2006). *A Guide to forensic accounting investigation.* John Wiley & Sons, Inc.

Golden, T. W., & Dyer, M. T. (2006). In T. W. Golden, S. L. Skalak, & M. M. Clayton (Eds.), *The art of the interview, A Guide to Forensic Accounting Investigation* (pp. 349–364). John Wiley and Sons.

Goyal, S., & Dhamija, S. (2018). Corporate governance failure at Ricoh India: Rebuilding lost trust. *Emerald Emerging Markets Case Studies, 8*(4), 1–20. doi:10.1108/EEMCS-06-2017-0166

Grubor, G., Ristić, N., & Simeunović, N. (2013). Integrated forensic accounting investigative process model in the digital environment. *International Journal of Scientific and Research Publications, 3*(12), 1–9.

Howard, S., & Sheetz, M. (2006). *Forensic accounting and fraud investigation for non-experts.* John Wiley and Sons Inc.

International Conference of Information Science and Management Engineering, ISME 2013, Volume 2. (2014). *WIT Transactions on Information and Communication Technologies, 46*(2).

International Conference of Information Science and Management Engineering, ISME 2013, Volume 3. (2014). *WIT Transactions on Information and Communication Technologies, 46*(3).

Jadhap, A., & Agarwal, A. (2016). Digital forensics investigation model for social networking site. *Proceedings of the Second International Conference on Information and Communication Technology for Competitive Strategies.*

Jensen, M. C., & Meckling, W. H. (1976). Theory of Firm – Managerial behavior, agency costs, and ownership structure. *Journal of Financial Economics, 3*(4), 305–360. doi:10.1016/0304-405X(76)90026-X

Mustafa, S. T., & Meier, H. H. (2006). CAP forum on forensic accounting in the post-enron world audit committees and misappropriation of assets: Publicly held companies in the United States [Les comités de vérificationet le détournement de biens: les sociétésouvertes aux États-Unis]. *Canadian Accounting Perspectives, 5*(2), 307–333. doi:10.1506/CCWW-JRWB-ECUE-YMMN

OECD. (2004). *White paper on corporate governance in Latin America*. Organization for Economic Co-operation and Development. Retrieved from www.oecd.org

Olaoye, C. O., & Olanipekun, C. T. (2018). Impact of Forensic Accounting and Investigation on Corporate Governance in Ekiti State. *Journal of Accounting, Business and Finance Research, 4*(1), 28–36.

Owojori, A. A., & Asaolu, T. O. (2009). The role of forensic accounting in solving the vexed problem of corporate world. *European Journal of Scientific Research, 29*(2), 183–187.

Pamungkas, I. D., Ghozali, I., & Achmad, T. (2018). A pilot study of corporate governance and accounting fraud: The fraud diamond model. *The Journal of Business and Retail Management Research, 12*(2), 253–261. doi:10.24052/JBRMR/V12IS02/APSOCGAAFTFDM

Power, M. (2012). The managerialization of security. *Securitization, Accountability and Risk Management: Transforming the Public Security Domain*, 70-87.

Prayudi, Y., Ashari, A., & Priyambodo, T. (2015). A proposed digital forensic business model to support cybercrime investigation in Indonesia. *International Journal of Computer Network and Information Security, 7*(11), 1–8. doi:10.5815/ijcnis.2015.11.01

Ramaswamy, V. (2005). Corporate governance and the forensic accountant. *The CPA Journal*. http://archives.cpajournal.com/2005/305/essentials/p68.htm

Rehman, A., & Hashim, F. (2018). Forensic Accounting on Corporate Governance Maturity mediated by Internal Audit: A Conceptual Overview. *Advances in Economics, Business and Management Research, 46*, 161–168.

Rehman, A., & Hashim, F. (2019). Impact of mature corporate governance on detective role of forensic accounting: case of public listed companies in Oman. *FGIC 2nd Conference on Governance and Integrity 2019, KnE Social Sciences*, 637-665. 10.18502/kss.v3i22.5080

Rehman, A., & Hashim, F. (2020). Can forensic accounting impact sustainable corporate governance? *Corporate Governance, 21*(1), 212–227. doi:10.1108/CG-06-2020-0269

Shah, M. K. (2018). Will implementation of forensic accounting identify the sense of financial fraud? *Journal of Commerce & Accounting Research, 7*(4), 47–50.

Singleton, T., & Singleton, A. (2010). *Fraud Auditing and Forensic Accounting* (4th ed.). John Wiley & Sons. doi:10.1002/9781118269183

Soltani, B., & Maupetit, C. (2015). Importance of core values of ethics, integrity, and accountability in the European corporate governance codes. *The Journal of Management and Governance, 19*(2), 259–284. doi:10.100710997-013-9259-4

Van Akkeren, J., & Buckby, S. (2017). Perceptions on the Causes of Individual and Fraudulent Co-offending: Views of Forensic Accountants. *Journal of Business Ethics, 146*(2), 383–404. doi:10.100710551-015-2881-0

Vieira, E., & Neiva, J. (2019). Corporate Governance Board of Directors and Firm Performance in Portugal. In Handbook of Board of Directors and Company Performance: An International Outlook. VirtusInterpress.

Vinita, R. (2005). Corporate governance and the forensic accountant. *The CPA Journal*, *75*(3), 68–78.

Williams, J. W. (2005). Reflections on the private versus public policing of economic crime. *British Journal of Criminology*, *45*(3), 316–339. doi:10.1093/bjc/azh083

Williams, J. W. (2005). Governability matters: The private policing of economic crime and the challenge of democratic governance. *Policing and Society*, *15*(2), 187–211. doi:10.1080/10439460500071671

Williams, J. W. (2006). Private legal orders: Professional markets and the commodification of financial governance. *Social & Legal Studies*, *15*(2), 209–235. doi:10.1177/0964663906063575

Williams, T. (2018). Role of Management, Corporate Governance, and Sarbanes-Oxley in Fraud: A Focus on the Precious Metals Industry. *Accounting, Finance, Sustainability, Governance and Fraud*, 391-409.

Yale, G., Grove, H., & Clouse, M. (2013). Risk management lessons learned: Countrywide report. *Corporate Ownership and Control*, *11*(1H), 33-46.

Yang, C.-H., & Lee, K.-C. (2020). Developing a strategy map for forensic accounting with fraud risk management: An integrated balanced scorecard-based decision model. *Evaluation and Program Planning*, *80*, 101780. doi:10.1016/j.evalprogplan.2020.101780 PMID:32044113

ADDITIONAL READING

Akinbowale, O. E., Klingelhöfer, H. E., & Zerihun, M. F. (2020). An innovative approach in combating economic crime using forensic accounting techniques. *Journal of Financial Crime*, *27*(4), 1253–1271. doi:10.1108/JFC-04-2020-0053

Crifo, P., Escrig-Olmedo, E., & Mottis, N. (2019). Corporate Governance as a Key Driver of Corporate Sustainability in France: The Role of Board Members and Investor Relations. *Journal of Business Ethics*, *159*(4), 1127–1146. doi:10.100710551-018-3866-6

Effiok, S. O., & Eton, O. E. (2013). Ensuring quality control of forensic accounting for efficient and effective corporate management. *Global Journal of Social Sciences*, *12*(1), 27–33.

Enofe, A., Ekpulu, G., & Ajala, T. O. (2015). Forensic accounting and corporate crime mitigation. *European Scientific Journal Edition*, *11*(7), 167–185.

GuptaD. K. (2020). *Growing Needs of Forensic Audit in Corporate and Banking Frauds in India*. https://ssrn.com/abstract=3624001 doi:10.2139/ssrn.3624001

Olaoye, C., & Olanipekun, C. (2018). Impact of Forensic Accounting and Investigation on Corporate Governance in Ekiti State. *Journal of Accounting, Business and Finance Research*, *4*(1), 28-36.

Rehman, A., & Hashim, F. (2021). Can forensic accounting impact sustainable corporate governance? *Corporate Governance*, *21*(1), 212–227. doi:10.1108/CG-06-2020-0269

Wahyuni-TD, I. S., Haron, H., & Fernando, Y. (2021). The effects of good governance and fraud prevention on performance of the zakat institutions in Indonesia: A Sharīʿah forensic accounting perspective. *International Journal of Islamic and Middle Eastern Finance and Management*, *14*(4), 692–712. doi:10.1108/IMEFM-03-2019-0089

KEY TERMS AND DEFINITION

Bibliometric Analysis: Is the attempt to quantitatively assess the academic quality of journals or authors by statistical methods such as citation rates.

Case Study: Is an in-depth, detailed examination of a particular case (or cases) within a real-world context.

Content Analysis: Is the study of documents and communication artifacts, which might be texts of various formats, pictures, audio or video. Social scientists use content analysis to examine patterns in communication in a replicable and systematic manner.

Corporate Governance: Is the system of rules, practices, and processes by which a firm is directed and controlled. Corporate governance essentially involves balancing the interests of a company's many stakeholders, such as shareholders, senior management executives, customers, suppliers, financiers, the government, and the community. Since corporate governance also provides the framework for attaining a company's objectives, it encompasses practically every sphere of management, from action plans and internal controls to performance measurement and corporate disclosure.

Forensic Accounting: Is a specialty practice area of accounting that investigates whether firms engage in financial reporting misconduct, in order to aplly practices of fraud or embezzlement. It is usedto analyse financial information for use in legal proceedings, such as to toexlain the nature of a financial crime in court.

Fraud: Is intentional deception to secure unfair or unlawful gain, or to deprive a victim of a legal right. Fraud can violate civil law or criminal law or it may cause no loss of money, property, or legal right. The purpose of fraud may be monetary gain or other benefits, where the perpetrator may attempt to qualify for a mortgage by way of false statements.

Measurement: Is the numerical quantitation of the attributes of an object or event, which can be used to compare with other objects or events. The scope and application of measurement are dependent on the context and discipline.

Risk: Is the possibility of something bad happening. Risk involves uncertainty about the effects/implications of an activity with respect to something that humans value, often focusing on negative, undesirable consequences. The international standard definition of risk for common understanding in different applications is "effect of uncertainty on objectives."

Chapter 3
Financial Forensic Evidence and Acceptability in the Court of Law

Varaidzo Denhere
https://orcid.org/0000-0003-1249-1591
University of Johannesburg, South Africa

ABSTRACT

This chapter explores the role of forensic accounting in uncovering evidence for use in courts to litigate and arbitrate on financially related crimes. The chapter differentiates the operation of forensic accountants from external auditors and other accountants. It also provides examples of financial crimes and describes the role of forensic accounting in assisting courts deal with these crimes. Furthermore, the chapter outlines differences between forensic accounting and audit reports as well as discussing the admissibility of forensic accounting evidence in courts. Issues around forensic accounting are articulated. Recommendations include the convergence of all important stakeholders to agree on the appropriate curriculum for forensic accountants as well as guidelines and standards to shape the profession and prevent entry by incompetent and unqualified people. Future research should focus on the current inconsistencies on the profession's education mode of delivery, content, pedagogies, and empirical studies to establish specific skills required by forensic accountants.

INTRODUCTION

The increased number of corporate scandals that eroded investor confidence globally on financial markets created the necessity for forensic accounting. Examples of such scandals include the Enron, World.Com and Parmalat in the 2000's. The aftermath of these scandals was the enactment of legislation such as the Sarbanes-Oxley Act in 2002, as efforts to minimise or totally eliminate corporate scandals (Wijerathna & Perera, 2020). However Prabowo (2013) noted that despite the standards instituted to eliminate fraud, new kinds of fraud keep surfacing each day due to growing complexities of business and legal procedures, as well as inefficiencies in the system. Therefore the current epoch in business is associated with

DOI: 10.4018/978-1-7998-8754-6.ch003

increasing change, which has come with increased threats. Some of the threats might result in litigation. This increasingly justifies the need for financial forensics, which is often related to financial criminal investigations with all the associated legal proceedings. The indicators globally demonstrate that the demand for financial forensics is growing with time as business technological development is also on the rise (Al-Abbadi, Alrawashdeh, Dabaghia & Darwazeh, 2021b). According to Dreyer (2014), those countries with intricate economies established specialised foundations to gather experience in forensic accounting. For example in the mid-nineteenth century, the United States of America's FBI employed more than 700 forensic accountants in the financial crime section to handle fraud crimes (Dreyer, 2014). The Institute of Forensic Commercial Practitioners (2016) indicated that financial crime has become more sophisticated, resulting in increased business and reputational risk, thereby calling for a unified approach to deal with the increasing risk of financial crime. Financial forensics have therefore become an integral component of risk management process, particularly when assessing fraud and conduct risk (Shapiro, 2015). Against this backdrop, the chapter focuses on financial forensic evidence and how it is used in the courts of law. The chapter objectives are to: define financial forensics and financial crimes; identify key financial crimes; describe the function of forensic accounting in courts; explore the admissibility of forensic accountants' expertise in the courts; and identify issues with the forensic accounting profession and suggest possible solutions.

BACKGROUND

Oftentimes lawyers and their clients need advice from experts on financial matters crucial to the outcome of litigation. They get this through financial forensics, also called forensic accounting. According to Sinha (2020) the word 'forensic' came from a Latin word 'forensis' which means 'in open court'. This shows that forensics have something to do with the courts of law. Shapiro (2015) defines financial forensics as a skill set that employs accepted knowledge and empirical data to come up with an expert opinion useful in settling issues with the potential of an adverse impact on business performance objectives. Examples of accepted knowledge include laws of evidence, customary practices, as well as professional ethics, while empirical data includes financial statements and non-financial measures among others. Renzhou (2011) also described forensic accounting as a composite discipline that integrates accounting, audit, and law, whilst targeting maintaining and adding value to a legal subject matter, treating the legal system as the criterion, and the economic business facts as the foundation. Furthermore, it is invariably considered that forensic accounting sees the court as its operating objective, and criminal or civil lawsuits as its primary service inclination (Renzhou, 2011). The eventual goal of forensic accounting is to provide expert advice in form of an expert report as well as expert evidence resulting from investigations. In courts, the expert evidence is embraced as adjudicator evidence to prove legal liability by a defendant who has committed a financial crime.

The main reason why forensic accounting has emerged is to provide evidence in courts of law to address financial crimes, a role that audit procedures and reports have failed to do. This has been prompted by the alarming escalation and prevalence of financial crimes. Despite financial crime being one of the prominently established illegal activities, the term 'financial crime,' which is also known as white collar crime, has no precise universally accepted definition but constitutes economically motivated crime, and covers expansive illegal activities and regulatory violations (Institute of Forensic Commercial Practitioners, 2016). Jung and Lee (2017) indicated that while there are a number of definitions, the

International Monetary Fund (2001) defined financial crime as any non-violent crime that normally results in a financial loss. Also, according to the Financial Services and Markets Act 2000 in the United Kingdom, financial crime includes "any offence involving fraud or dishonesty; misconduct in, or misuse of information relating to a financial market; or handling the proceeds of crime." Further, Pickett and Pickett (2002:3) defined the term as "the use of deception for illegal gain, normally involving breach of trust, and some concealment of the true nature of the activities." The definitions outlined above all tie up with the elements constituting financial crime as indicated by the Institute of Forensic Commercial Practitioners (2016). Some examples of financial crimes include money laundering, insider trading, fraud, and manipulation of the market (Jung & Lee, 2017).

Financial forensics is an emerging area meant to detect the fraudulent transactions occurring in businesses (Wijerathna & Perera, 2020; Bhasin, 2007). The concept of forensic accounting was first coined by Maurice Peloubet in 1946 (Alshurafat, Al Shbail & Mansour, 2021; Brown, 2008). To date forensic accounting has become a fully-fledged profession having evolved and progressed in tandem with the business world globally (Rechtman, 2020). In the past, detection and prevention of fraud was recognised as one of the accounting functions, and consequently auditors, both internal and external were expected to root out and avert fraud (Bhasin, 2007). This notion however later shifted after the realization that auditors were not responsible for the detection and prevention of fraud but could only examine and ascertain whether the financial statements of businesses were compliant with the accounting regulatory standards for financial reporting (Wijerathna & Perera, 2020). This notion led to the emergence of the new accounting category, named Forensic Accounting, which is performed by Forensic Accountants.

The forensic accountants are specialists in seeing beyond the figures in financial statements and addressing the realities of business situations. Consequently they play a crucial role of reducing risk through crafting and executing extended procedures, advising audit committees, as well as participating in research for investment analysis (Bhasin, 2007). They are also considered as financial investigators who audit, investigate and establish the accuracy of financial-related reporting records, usually concerning expected or continual legal proceedings. Forensic accountants act as the interface linking the financial and legal domains with their skills employed to identify, analyse and examine financial evidence as well as to evaluate claims (Institute of Forensic Commercial Practitioners, 2016). According to Shapiro (2015), forensic accountants' analytical approaches go beyond the ordinary procedures that are frequently employed for conventional audits, and are applied to other management issues, among them financial crime risk, operational auditing, as well as performance auditing. They also challenge operative estimates and assumptions which can be effectual, vigorous, and unbiased correctives to defective presumptions (Shapiro, 2015). Wijerathna and Perera (2020) and Bhasin, (2007) concur that for the forensic accountants to perform their work they require comprehension of information for the business, financial reporting systems, standards and procedures for accounting and auditing, gathering of evidence, techniques for investigation, as well as litigation processes.

Alshurafat et al. (2021) and Hegazy, Sangster and Kotb (2017) acknowledge the broadness of forensic accounting services, hence they describe it as a multidisciplinary specialization. Consequently forensic accountants can work in various entities, among them insurance companies, public organisations, the police forces, and banks, as well as government agencies (Tiwari & Debnath, 2017; Prabowo, 2013). There are various types of forensic accounting that can be performed by forensic accountants, and they are categorized according to the types of legal proceedings that they belong to (Corporate Finance Institute, 2021). The most common examples include: stealing of money by customers, employees, or outsiders; fraud of securities; bankruptcy; debt defaulting; economic damages; and evasion of tax, among others

(Corporate Finance Institute, 2021). Whilst forensic accounting could be providing some overlapping services, most research in the area has categorized the services into the following four major categories: litigation services; fraud investigation; computer forensic analysis; and business valuation (Alshurafat et al., 2021).

MAIN FOCUS OF THE CHAPTER

Key Financial Crimes

The occurrence of financial crimes varies and in light of this, Jung and Lee (2017) posited that some financial crimes happen on their own while some might involve either financial or non-financial crimes. Brown and Smith (2018) identified the key crime enablers which frequently constitute crimes on their own, as well as promoting other categories of crime. Among these crimes are money laundering, cyber-crime, public sector corruption, identity crime, and manipulation of business structures.

Money Laundering

Money laundering is defined by the Financial Sector Conduct Authority (2021) as "the process used by criminals to disguise the nature, source, location, disposition or movement of the proceeds of unlawful activities or any interest which anyone has in such proceeds." For money laundering to be acknowledged, the money involved should be recognised as criminal proceeds, implying that there should be a base crime prior to pursuing money laundering (Jung & Lee, 2017). The International Monetary Fund (2001) suggests that the predicated crimes are often financial crimes, with the argument that generally most financial crimes necessitate money laundering for them to be disclosed by law enforcing agencies.

Cyber and Technology-Enabled Crime

Whilst cybercrime is known to be closely related to numerous financial crimes, the internet is also perceived to be a hotbed for financial crimes (Jung & Lee, 2017; Wall, 2007). This is because cybercrime occurs on or through the internet. Most financial crimes can be categorized as cyber-enabled, since criminals tend to manipulate the networked ICTs to commit these crimes (Jung & Lee, 2017). The magnitude and extent of financial crimes is heightened by the increased use of computers and networks. It is important to note that the majority of the cyber-enabled crimes are fraud and theft (McGuire & Dowling, 2013). Lately the use of the internet has been on the rise, thereby increasing the rate of cybercrime, and ongoing rapid technological advances also come with the increased complexity of these crimes. Jung and Lee (2017) identified the following major types of cyber-enabled fraud: internet banking fraud, fraudulent sales occurring through online shopping platforms, mass-marketing frauds, and consumer scams.

Public Sector Corruption

Both financial and non-financial crimes are accelerated by public sector corruption. This occurs when organised criminals try to corrupt public officials so as to access information, or public funds, as well as to influence future investigations on the crimes. Examples of crimes in this category include bribes that lead to money-laundering, embezzlement, tax evasion, and illicit enrichment.

Identity Crime

Cassim (2015) highlights that identity crime as a form of financial crime is also rapidly increasing globally. This type of crime involves identity theft which is committed as a base to facilitate other crimes, either physically or online. Culprits who commit this crime steal personal information from individuals, for example names, date of birth or banking details, and this stolen information is used by fraudsters to impersonate someone and defraud targeted victims (Gottschalk & Benson, 2020). Just like cyber and technology-based crimes, the rapid growth of internet use for business financial transactions, as well as social networking and storage of personal information is a conducive environment for identity thieves (Cassim, 2015).

Exploitation of Business Structures

Complicated business structures as well as sophisticated company networks can be exploited to conceal real legatees in the background through engaging numerous foreign jurisdictions. Frequently global corporations as well as financial institutions utilise this crime strategy to avoid paying corporate tax or to draw off illicit funds (Jung & Lee, 2017). Crimes associated with this strategy include money laundering, investment and premium fraud, illegal commodities, and tax evasion.

Empirical Studies on Forensic Accounting and Financial Crimes

Various empirical studies were conducted in the field of forensic accounting and financial crimes. Among them is Ernest & Young's EMEIA Fraud Survey in 2017. This survey was conducted in Africa, Europe, India and the Middle East (Kumar & Venkataraman, 2019). The survey was conducted in response to the increase in financial crime particularly against the background that these crimes are committed by experts in accounting who are capable of covering up and leaving no traces to suspect any fraud incident (Kumar & Venkataraman, 2019). This has become so prevalent and well supported by the rapid technological changes which just require a click on a technological device and the financial crime is committed. Commission of financial crime seems to be now deep-rooted even within the top management including Board members as well as other employees of companies. To substantiate the deep-rootedness of financial crimes amongst businesses, findings from Ernst & Young (2017) Fraud survey indicated that one out of three Board members and senior managers, as well as one out of five employees find it justifiable to exchange cash for retaining business. Further findings from this study indicated that 12% of Board members and senior managers, as well as 24% of the rest of employees had the audacity to falsify their career or remuneration information. Furthermore, another Ernst & Young Global Fraud survey conducted in 2016 established that many Finance employees holding key roles, among them CFOs readily justified unethical behaviour. The above statistics are a clear testimony of the prevalence and how justifiable committing financial crimes has become. The findings attest to the fact that audit on its own could no longer keep in check nor detect these financial crimes but needed assistance from more diverse tools and expertise which can be provided by forensic accounting.

Another empirical study was conducted by Dada & Jimoh (2020). The study sought to examine the relationship existing between forensic accounting and financial crimes in the Nigerian public sector. This was achieved by evaluating the measures emplaced to warrant reduction of the Nigerian public sector financial crimes as well as assessing the consequence of litigation support service on the same. This was a quantitative research which employed a survey to collect data through questionnaires and interviews, with linear regression employed to analyze the collected empirical data. Basing on hypothesis testing, the findings at 5% significance level indicated that litigation support service had significant negative effect on financial crimes in the Nigerian public sector. This implies that litigation support through courts of law had an effect of reducing financial crimes in the Nigerian public sector. Literature has also indicated that public sectors are also known for notoriety in financial crimes.

Execution of Forensic Accounting: Investigation and Evidence Generation

Literature has indicated that there is no consensus on a number of issues surrounding forensic accounting, and many as points of views and perceptions are available on this, the same applies to the execution of forensic accounting. However Driskell (2019) identified the best practices that should be followed when executing forensic accounting. The procedures include initiating the engagement, planning and liaising during the progress of the engagement, conducting the engagement, and reporting the discovery. In most instances it takes an interested party to engage the forensic accountant to get assistance on finding out what happened, and who was responsible for their case. The interested party could be an individual, a company or a government agency. The engaged forensic accountant considers relevant and applicable professional standards in executing a particular engagement. These standards address ethical issues, reporting procedures, and conflict of interest declarations among other things.

The practical procedures of forensic accounting involve conducting a preliminary assessment in order to understand the internal controls and processes of a company, analysing company records, and hold discussions with company executives who are not part of the investigation targets. After preliminary assessments, necessary adjustments are made to the approach memorandum with considerations to team changes if necessary. It is crucial to keep all the working papers put together during the investigation since they can always be referred to when necessary. The working papers include among others notes, schedules, and any other documents that can be put together to form a memorandum that could be used for interviews or providing evidence in courts. Preservation of these evidence is also crucial and calls for the forensic accountant to maintain the correct sequence of custody if they take responsibility to keep the original documents such as signed original documents, cancelled cheques and computer hard drives.

Communication is also an important component of the forensic accounting procedure. The forensic accountant directs this to the client who should preferably be a legal counsel. During the investigation, the forensic accountant and the client together agree on the form of communicating a conclusion from the engagement and basically it could be in form of either a written report or oral presentation. The cost of preparing a written report in terms of both time and money is high because it is highly detailed. It is noted that despite its high cost, it still remains the most preferable by clients for reference purposes or evidence before the courts in the event that they want to seek reimbursement of costs from their insurance. Execution of the engagement immediately begins after the client approves the work plan. The first step is to collect relevant documents both hard and soft copies. Generally the soft copy documents are processed and loaded into a review environmental tool. The next step depends on the type of engagement but basically involves the use of analytical procedures in order to identify trends as well as uncommon transactions that would help the forensic accountant. Examples of these analytical procedures include: comparing company data against operational data; comparing present company data against historical times; comparing actual financial results against company budgets; comparing company data against data from competitors within the industry; and comparing data from all types of financial statements analysis. The third step involves quick scheduling of interviews that may involve external legal counsel, whistle-blowers, and company employees. An additional person could be in attendance during the interview but out of direct eyesight to be taking notes.

When all the collection of data and analysis is done with, the findings should be reported. Findings can be documented either as written or oral form to the client or to a court of law or a law enforcing agency. Driskell (2019) highlights the basic elements of an investigative report, and these are outlined as follows: client identity; qualifications and background of the forensic accountant; description of the forecast; broad terms of the forensic accountant's task; time period and scope of the engagement; information on restrictions if any to the distribution and use of the report if any; identification of any professional standards that guided conducting of the engagement; identification of exclusions in the dependence on the forensic accountant's report; a statement that the work should not be depended upon for fraud detection; a list of the reviewed documents that were relied upon during the investigation; the names, titles or organizations, and dates of the engagement interviewees; procedures performed and the technical pronouncements relied upon; and a description of the observations and the findings.

When summing up the report, the forensic accountant should not categorically state conclusions of fraud but may conclude that there were indications of fraud and also indicate that the subject of investigation admitted to some allegations. The act of fraud remains a legal conclusion hence should be left to courts, judges, arbitrators, and juries.

The Forensic Accounting Report

The forensic accounting report aims at presenting evidence both professionally and concisely (Slot, 2012; Zysman, 2006). This report differs from one produced by an auditor, since the intended objectives are also different. The following are characteristics of the forensic accounting report: does not stand alone; the objective is to present evidence in an accurate and professional way; preparation is not guided by uniform international standards but varies according to jurisdictions and client requirements; encapsulates all the evidence from the investigation; and focuses on proving beyond doubt that fraud has occurred; and focuses on specific purpose and targeted end-user. There could be some similarities between the forensic accounting and audit reports, but it is their differences that create the wide gap between the audit and the forensic accounting professions. Cantoria (2010) also posited that the users of the two reports also show the key difference between the goals of a financial audit vis-à-vis a forensic evaluation.

Whilst the forensic report is not controlled by any common international standards, there are general international standards provided for accounting engagements. Whilst the term 'forensic accounting' was first coined in 1946, ever since that time there have not been common standards for the profession (Slot, 2012). There were fragmented pieces of legislation guiding forensic accountants across the globe. It is only in 2019 that the American Institute of Certified Public Accountants (AICPA) promulgated a set of new professional standards to guide members who perform forensic accounting (Gallagher & Schiavone, 2019). These were to be effective starting from 2020. These standards provide authoritative guidance for practitioners who conduct litigation and investigative engagements. Notably, the standards elucidate definitions of the terms 'litigation' and 'investigation' for forensic accounting purposes, outline principal considerations for clients and service provider relationships, as well as delimiting the services that can be provided by practicing members. Gallagher and Schiavone (2019) highlighted that the newly-enacted forensic standards bring with them the first codification of best practices for litigation and investigation engagements. Professional standards are enacted to safeguard the public interests as they ensure uniformity in the execution of forensic accounting engagements as well as giving assurance that minimum standards of practice are met (American Institute of Certified Public Accountants, 2016). Furthermore, the standards give a framework for the implementation of professional judgment in discharging forensic accounting engagements.

Function of Forensic Accounting in Courts

Renzhou (2011) points out that the initial stage of bringing financial criminals to account is to conduct an investigation into the criminal responsibility. This is where the forensic accountants with their complicated knowledge and expertise can point out and form an opinion on financial crimes, hence assisting investigators to establish the accounting reality involving the crimes from both perspectives of accounting and law. In light of this the forensic accountants will assist investigators through the following functions: lawsuit assessment functions; preservation of evidence function; and loss measurement function (Renzhou, 2011).

Lawsuit Assessment Functions

1. Assessing Litigation Risks

   Litigation risks are the probability of unfavourable outcomes resulting from legal action such as criminal, civil, and administrative lawsuit risks, among others.

   a. Criminal lawsuit risks: After the defendant and his lawyer participate in court in the first instance, possible outcomes in the process include adverse criminal judgements to the accused, adverse related civil judgments to the accused, and weak or no imposition of judgements. Furthermore, the innocent accused could be convicted; the accused who committed a misdemeanour could be sentenced heavily; the defendant could be wrongly accused; a penalty could be too heavy for the defendant; the plaintiff could request for too heavy a sentence, but the accused instead gets a lighter sentence; the plaintiff might request for the conviction of the accused, but the accused could be deemed innocent; and the civil compensation could be too small. All these possible outcomes could be addressed by engaging a forensic accountant.

   b. (ii) Civil litigation risks: After the plaintiffs and their lawyer make the first appearance in court, they might face possible risk factors inapplicable to argued facts which might determine the court proceedings outcome and imposition of cases rendering legal rights and interests unable to be safeguarded. Risks included in this category are the risk of inappropriate claims; risk of incapacity to avail adequate evidence; risk of incapacity to furnish original evidence; risk of failure to appear in court on time or withdrawing of the case; and risk of litigation interests being below the litigation costs (Renzhou, 2011).

   c. (iii) Administrative litigation risks: After the plaintiffs and their lawyer make the first appearance in the court, they might face some risk factors inapplicable to disputed facts which might determine the trial and imposition of cases rendering legal rights and interests unable to be safeguarded. Specific risks in this category include the risk of inappropriate claims; risk of ineligible litigation; and risk of litigation being unfeasible (Renzhou, 2011).

2. Risk prevention

Forensic accountants might also assist the plaintiffs and their lawyer by providing plans to avert litigation risk and strategies to increase the chances of a successful lawsuit and give assurance for the worthiness of a lawsuit.

Function of Preserving Evidence

Evidence is deemed the critical element of litigation and arbitration, hence cases involving accounting facts require that evidence be provided (Renzhou, 2011; Slot, 2012). Furthermore, inappropriate forensic accounting evidence or lack of forensic accounting evidence amounts to the greatest risk of litigation and arbitration (Slot, 2012). This calls for the need to correctly determine the loss items as well as amounts of the losses. In the event of inappropriate practices like false accounting and fraud, technology and sophisticated forensic accounting methods and procedures should be employed to gather and preserve forensic accounting evidence. This evidence, which could be in form of accounting information, audit documents, and evaluation in accordance with rules that guide evidence, should be provided to the plaintiffs and their lawyer, in a court of law but in a legal way a layman can easily comprehend (Renzhou, 2011; Institute of Forensic Commercial Practitioners, 2016).

Loss Measurement Function

Forensic accountants do quantify loss and damages resulting from some event such as premature cancellation of a contract or halting supply of a key product by a supplier leading to loss of profit (Institute of Forensic Commercial Practitioners, 2016). In this case the lawyer proves the breach of contract while the forensic accountant quantifies the damage resulting from the breach thereby showing the financial position the plaintiff could have been in had the event not occurred. Various problems might arise in the plaintiff's damages and among them are: a vast disparity from the plaintiff's claim and the confirmed amount by the judge; wrong understanding of loss-determining item by the plaintiff causing loss of support for the compensation request items; and the plaintiff's poor understanding of the stipulated loss standard by the legal system, resulting in the disparity between the claim measurement standard and the judgment (Renzhou, 2011). Forensic accountants are capable of professional addressing these problems and predicting conceivable litigation interests, determining the worthiness of a lawsuit, evaluating numerous risks in the court processes, assisting the plaintiff in decision-making, and managing blind litigation. The forensic accountants' expertise enables them to address the above problems.

In addition to the above functions, the Institute of Forensic Commercial Practitioners (2016) identified other litigation support functions offered by forensic accountants, among which are: disputes over amounts owed between parties; share value disagreements between shareholders and directors; disputes that could occur after transactions; and negative financial impact on employees if employment conditions change.

Furthermore, Dolmanbateman Chartered Accountants Australia, (2019) also identified the following functions of forensic accounting in courts: helping legal practitioners in initial discovery where they ask for the right information the first time; translating and interpreting client financial and tax returns applying commercial knowledge and expertise; and providing independent, objective and unbiased expert evidence which gives undoubted grounds for acceptance by the court of law.

Real Cases Where Accounting Evidence was Applied in Courts

There are so many real cases where accounting evidence was applied in the courts of law to bring perpetrators to account. Because there are so many of these the author focused on the most recent ones, in the period from 2015 to date. Literature has highlighted cases based on lost money, impacted lives, and relevance to the forensic accounting profession. However, for the purpose of this section, only those cases relevant to the forensic accounting will be discussed. One example of such cases is the '80 indicted in Nigerian online fraud, money laundering scheme'. Primeaux (2020) reported that the United States Department of Justice opened a 252-count federal indictment in 2019, charging 80 defendants. Most of these defendants were Nigerian nationals. They were charged for conspiracy to steal millions of dollars through online frauds. The defendants targeted businesses, women and the elderly. This was one of the largest internet fraud unearthed by an FBI investigation which took almost three years. The FBI indicated that the schemes involved in this case resulted in the fraudulent transfer of at least $6 million.

Another case involves the Fake 28 year old German heiress by the name Anna Sorokin. According to Helmore (2019), she was sentenced in May 2019 to serve 12 years in prison for defrauding hotels, restaurants, a private jet operator and banks out of more than $200,000. She masqueraded as a German heiress operating a $60 million trust fund. Sorokin lured the most exclusive hotels, clubs and parties in New York City and in the process overdrew a bank account and manipulated financial records to promote her ploy that she sustained under the name Anna Delvey. The court convicted her of grand larceny and theft of services.

The last example in this discussion involves Steinhoff, a South African International retail holding company mainly dealing in furniture and household goods. The company operates in Europe, Africa, Asia, the United States of America, Australia and New Zealand. According to Motsoeneng & Rumney (2019), the company for a number of years overstated profits amounting to $7.4 billion accounting fraud which involved a small group of top executives and outsiders as indicated by the PwC independent report. Steinhoff first disclosed irregularities in its accounting books in December 2017, but only had its accounting fraud revealed in 2019 when PwC conducted and completed its investigation. The PwC investigation revealed that the company recorded fictitious transactions amounting to $7.4 billion between 2009 and 2017.

The above are just but a few examples of a rampant practice by companies and individuals in committing financial crimes which will require the application of accounting evidence in courts to bring the perpetrators to account for their undesirable business actions.

Admissibility of Forensic Accountants' Expertise in the Courts

The Forensic Accountant's Role in Testimony

The evidence of financial crime provided by the forensic accountant for court proceedings should be of such quality that it is valid or acceptable. The admissibility of poor quality evidence can be challenged by lawyers (Slot, 2012). While in some cases the forensic accountant might be called to testify before the court as a witness of fact, in other cases he might be requested to testify as to the findings, as well giving an opinion (Golden, Skalak & Clayton, 2006). This means that the forensic accountants can provide two categories of expertise which were identified by Matson (1999) as consulting and testifying. The role of the consulting expert is to provide facts and the backdrop, while the role of the testifying expert is to give an opinion based on facts. The forensic accountant can also provide testimony to help the court interpret and comprehend the facts with ease so as to come up with a resolution (Slot, 2012). When asked to testify as to findings as well as to give an opinion, a forensic accountant is referred to as an expert witness in court. Matson (1999, p. 17) defines an expert witness "as a person who, by reason of education or special training, possesses knowledge of some particular subject area in greater depth than the public at large and assists the court to understand complicated subjects outside the knowledge of the average person."

Slot (2012) and Pagano and Buckhoff (2005) share the view that there is an increasing importance of being an expert witness because a number of sophisticated financial cases will only be resolved after the expert witnesses have provided comprehensive reports. However, when appearing as an expert for certain facts, it is encouraged that a forensic accountant should be objective and not support the client's position, but instead assist the court to understand the complex issue (Wecht, 2006; Pagano & Buckhoff, 2005; Slot, 2012). It should be noted that what differentiates the ordinary witness from the expert witness is that an expert witness is permitted to provide an opinion to the court, while an ordinary witness is not permitted to give an opinion (Slot, 2012). However the decision on whether the expert witness' opinion is just, lies with the court. Furthermore, the expert's opinion must be regarded as inadmissible if its basis is some hypothetical situation that is totally at odds with the facts (Schwikkard & Van der Merwe, 2016). In some cases, after the court examines and weighs the expert opinion, it can still deem the opinion admissible, but places no reliance on the pinion. This implies that the facts on which such an opinion was based were not deemed inadmissible and the expert's credibility was not disputed by the court, but the court could not just rely on it.

Slot (2012) pointed out that for any opinion expressed, whether by an expert or non-expert, if the court can give a decision without requiring such opinion it will be rendered inadmissible. This implies that the point of view of an expert will be admissible if the court can obtain considerable assistance from the witness (Schwikkard & Van der Merwe, 2016; Slot, 2012). Further, Schmidt and Rademeyer (2000) argued that one of the considerations to be made when assessing an expert opinion is whether the expert's experience and knowledge qualifies him to be more capable than the court in giving an opinion in his area of expertise. In the event that the expertise of an expert witness is questioned in the court of law, the lawyer for the plaintiff must exhibit the requisite backdrop through questions in court, wherein the judge uses his circumspection to qualify the witness and decide whether they are an expert or only an expert on restricted subjects (Slot, 2012; Hill & Hill, 2009). It can therefore be concluded that the expert's testimony as a witness will only be admissible in the court of law as an expert because of their specialty and when they are more equipped than the court to make a deduction from a certain point (Slot, 2012). Any deviations from these conditions will render the expert's testimony as a witness inadmissible.

Relevance and Admissibility of Expert Evidence

There is a general rule that irrelevant evidence is inadmissible, and when the judge is passing a ruling on admissibility concerning a matter of relevance, he must decide on whether the provided evidence will increase or decrease the possibility of the existence of a fact in issue (Slot, 2012). All facts of any case before the courts must be considered when analysing expert evidence for relevance. Meintjes-Van der Walt (2003) and Slot (2012) share the view that in the face of dramatic development of emerging scientific, technological and social scientific approaches and policies, judges will encounter the development of definite criteria and standards to try out the admissibility and dependability of evidence presented in the courts.

Some standards can be used to ascertain the admissibility of a testimony from an expert witness, and one example is the United States of America's Frye standard (Slot, 2012). According to Pagano and Buckhoff (2005, p. 49) the Frye standard employs the following tests to determine the admissibility of expert testimony if: the testimony from an expert witness will help the court to ascertain a fact; the witness relies upon the theory as well as techniques that have support from the pertinent professional community; and if the expert who is giving expert testimony on a certain topic is qualified.

The Frye standard was replaced by the Daubert standard, which is based on the fact that the moderator executes the position of gatekeeper in presenting expert testimony (Pagano & Buckhoff, 2005). Furthermore, Pagano and Buckhoff (2005, p. 51) indicated that the standard instituted the following to guide the court in determining the dependability of the expert witness if: the employed theory and approaches could be verified or had been verified; the employed theory and approaches had also been employed in the past by others; there is a possibility that the employed theory and approaches could have been wrong; and if the theory and approaches are generally acceptable to the community.

Issues, Controversies, Problems

Forensic accounting as an emerging profession is surrounded by some issues. The increasing challenges befalling this profession are attributed to the technological developments which promote creativity in ways of committing crimes of fraud. According to Al-Abbadi, Alrawashdeh, Dabaghia & Darwazeh, (2021a), the challenges that are faced by forensic accounting emanate from the obtainable information pertaining to the profession in the global sources to the obtainable information pertaining to the localized fraud crimes, and the essential knowledge to combat these crimes. The type of challenge also vary from developed to developing economies, with those economies that pay attention to fraud crimes as well as employing forensic accounting experiencing fewer difficulties in alleviating the challenges to the use of forensic accounting (Al-Abbadi et al., 2021a). A study by Alshurafat et al. (2021) revealed some issues with forensic accounting as a practice, and among them are the scarcity of regulations, absence of control over the entry requirements of the profession, absence of consensus on the teaching pedagogies of forensic accounting, the dearth of specialized research journals, misconstruction of the innate goal of forensic accounting, the scarcity of exceptionally qualified forensic accounting practitioners and educators, and absence of recognition of the profession by the public as well as the absence of occupational reputation. These issues interfere with the successful accomplishments of forensic accounting engagements and admissibility of forensic accounting expertise in courts. This definitely comes with its own share of negative impacts on corporate governance in different organisations that should rely on this expertise as well.

Scarcity of Professional Regulations

Literature has shown that different countries have their own forensic accounting regulations that guide the engagements (Hegazy et al., 2017; Louwers, 2015; Slot, 2012). These differences are potential sources of inconsistencies in terms of forensic accounting guidelines locally and globally. Furthermore, this might lead to forensic accounting being strictly regulated in some countries and less regulated in others. An example is an observable difference between regulations in the United Kingdom and the United States of America, with the profession significantly less regulated in Ireland than in the United States of America, and most likely similar to countries such as Canada, United Kingdom and Australia (Brennan, 2014; Alshurafat et al., 2021). According to Slot (2012) and Alshurafat et al. (2021), the first professional forensic accounting body, called the Association of Certified Fraud Examiners (ACFE), was established in 1989 in the United States of America. The body published its first standards in 1991 with the aim to facilitate certified fraud examiners in their professional work, as well as related to independence and objectivity, qualifications, due professional care in fraud investigation, and confidentiality. After this body, several other forensic accounting bodies emerged in the United States of America, with each of these having the liberty to issue out certificates and put in place their membership benchmark (Huber, 2014; Alshurafat et al., 2021). This state of affairs promotes distortion in the forensic accounting profession globally.

Absence of Control over Entry Requirements to the Profession

There is no uniformity within countries regarding the mandatory qualifications for forensic accountants, as there is no specific universal law that regulates the entry requirements and qualifications into the forensic accounting profession. There is also no uniformity with regards to the required qualifications for the professional forensic accountants in various jurisdictions (Howieson, 2018; Hegazy et al., 2017; Alshurafat et al., 2021). This inconsistency results in numerous practitioners professing that they are forensic accountants without any validated qualifications. This opens the doors to anyone claiming to be a forensic accountant, exposing the profession to entry by non-accounting-based experts (Alshurafat et al., 2021; Van Akkeren, Buckby & MacKenzie, 2013). The problem of lack of standards regulating forensic accounting went for too long without being addressed, considering the fact that the term forensic accounting was conceived in 1946.

Inconsistency in Forensic Accounting Education Content

There is currently no consensus amongst academics, practitioners and service consumers on various issues regarding the forensic accounting education mode of delivery, content of the knowledge, and pedagogies (Wang, Lee & Crumbley, 2016; Alshurafat et al., 2021). There is an ongoing argument that auditing, and accounting courses are inadequate when it comes to offering relevant knowledge to the learners in terms of combining accounting knowledge with other interdisciplinary content, such as fraud investigation and litigation support (Alshurafat et al., 2021; Kresse, 2008). The argument has been supported by an observation of notable differences of perceptions of forensic accounting content matter and preferred pedagogies between the educators and practitioners (Kramer, Seda & Bobashev, 2017). It was observed that educators paid more attention than practitioners did to the notion of including fraud examination, as well as types of fraud, elements of fraud, red flags of business, as well as measures of anti-fraud, while practitioners focused on the significance of combining fraud education, emphasizing more on issues associated with locating concealed assets, conflicts of interest, effective report writing, expert testimony, expert witness techniques, complying with legislation as well as litigation consulting techniques (Alshurafat et al., 2021). These differences in focus by the important stakeholders in the provision of forensic accounting education cause discord in the whole profession. This calls for more discussion by all stakeholders and reaching a consensus on what should be the core focus areas of education and curriculum of the forensic accounting profession.

Scarcity of Research

Alshurafat et al. (2021) and Howieson (2018) concur that focus by most forensic researchers has been narrowed to fraud investigation topics, a scenario which hampers the evolution of forensic accounting as a specialty and profession. In this field there is need to increase research in both the theoretical and methodological contributions, as indicated by DiGabriele and Huber (2015). DiGabriele and Huber (2015) and Alshurafat et al. (2021) observed that the quantitative methodology contributes the largest portion of research methods published in forensic accounting journals. This consequently leads to the scarcity of journals which are exclusive to forensic accounting. It has also been observed that presently there are few forensic accounting research journals as well as research journals that might be concerned with publishing forensic accounting studies (Alshurafat et al., 2021). Since research is vital in providing both theoretical and practical contributions in any field of study, scarcity of research journals in forensic accounting cripples the evolving process of forensic accounting. This has a ripple effect of rendering forensic accounting topics unattractive to both researchers and practitioners.

Misconstruction of the Innate Goal of Forensic Accounting

Contrary to traditional accounting and auditing, the inherent goal of forensic accounting is to offer arbitration, evaluation and investigative services that potentially end as an attestation in a court of law on financial misconduct (Muehlmann, Burnaby & Howe, 2012). Literature has indicated that forensic accounting is defined from both a narrow and a broad perspective, with the narrow perspective showing the role of forensic accountants in the courts, while the broad one shows the adversarial, evaluation and investigative duties of forensic accountants (Botes & Saadeh, 2018; Alshurafat et al., 2021). In analysing the extent of use of these two definition perspectives, Botes and Saadeh (2018) concluded that the narrow perspective prevails. Further, Huber (2013) observed the variations in forensic accounting definitions with some contradictions, specifically concerning the inclusion of fraud. Conceptual dissimilarities between fraud examination and forensic accounting have also been noted by Smith and Crumbley (2009) indicating that forensic accounting is extensive. Consequently there is a call on accounting syllabus instructors to decide on to building forensic accounting degrees on a fraud framework, a more extensive forensics framework or an integration of the two frameworks. Failure by the two perspectives to provide a comprehensive definition of forensic accounting resulted in the threat of misconstruction of the innate goal of forensic accounting (Botes & Saadeh, 2018; Alshurafat et al., 2021).

Need For Highly Qualified Practitioners and Educators

Research on precursory skills, education, and training that are required by forensic accountants established that analytical skills, legal roles, investigative skills and computer skills are critical (Alshurafat et al., 2021). It is therefore important that instructors consider these skills for a valuable forensic accounting curriculum. Alshurafat et al. (2021) and Souza (2017) concur that finding qualified forensic accounting instructors is a challenge because the field is extensive and covers a variety of services that require specialised instructors, which could also be costly for many organisations.

Absence of Recognition by the Public and Lack of Professional Reputation

Williams (2006) posited that forensic accounting lacks public recognition because it is fairly new to both the public and businesses. Furthermore, the lack of recognition by the public leads to confusion about the roles of forensic accountants by the public, which then ignores the importance of this profession. The instructors need to take the initiative to inculcate public confidence and recognition of forensic accounting. Equally it is the responsibility of the forensic accountants to also safeguard their occupational reputation.

The above issues have opened doors to unqualified people to practice as forensic accountants, due to lack of standards, regulators and bodies with stern rules that control entry requirements to the profession. This ultimately costs the reputation and public recognition of forensic accounting.

SOLUTIONS AND RECOMMENDATIONS

The above outline of issues surrounding forensic accounting showed that forensic accounting is faced with various hindrances that need to be addressed. It will take the involvement of all stakeholders, among them instructors, universities, professional bodies and the courts to establish the perfect curriculum content for forensic accountants as well as guidelines and standards to shape the profession. If the current state of affairs goes unattended, the profession will be inundated by incompetent people claiming to be qualified for the profession. There is need for harmonization of all aspects of the profession as well as improving both the education and profession.

Alshurafat et al. (2021) suggested the following ways to improve forensic accounting tuition and profession: Enhancing the degree of professionalism by setting up extemporary accounting associations; Controlling the entry requirements to the forensic accounting profession in order to preserve a high quality of services from the practicing members; Developing consistent education that corresponds to the genuine work of forensic accounting practitioners in order to enhance the quality of the profession; Encouraging researchers to take part in forensic accounting and introduce new forensic accounting research journals in order to promote the research output that is relevant to the profession; and Increasing the public recognition for the profession through offering public awareness workshops of fraud and its repercussions on the society, and how forensic accountants could assist to put off the risk of fraud as a way of increasing the reputation of forensic accounting as a profession.

In addition to the above suggested ways of improving forensic accounting, Ocansey (2017) posited that governance of information technology and risk management tools are also critical in attaining effectual systems of forensic accounting. This is crucial because information technology is used as a means or platform for committing fraud crimes. Conclusively, the author also proposes that a global summit be held to deliberate on issues of forensic accounting and financial crimes since they continue to ravage the globe indiscriminately affecting all nations. The proposed summit should come up with binding solutions on how to deal with forensic accounting and financial crimes. All nations will be expected to become signatories to the proposed global summit resolutions.

FUTURE RESEARCH DIRECTIONS

This chapter explored the role of forensic accounting in uncovering evidence that could be employed in a court of law. The chapter established that there is a dearth of research on forensic accounting, to an extent that there is scarcity of research journals in the field. It has also been indicated that most forensic researchers have been focusing on fraud investigation topics, yet the forensic accounting field is vast, and this slows down the evolution of forensic accounting as a profession. The chapter has also established that the quantitative methodology contributes the largest portion of research methods published in forensic accounting journals. Based on these findings, the author suggests future research to focus more on qualitative methodology in forensic accounting. Future research should also broaden the focus on forensic accounting other than fraud investigation, only because this field is so vast, as it encompasses other topics outside fraud. The author also suggests future research on the current inconsistencies on the forensic accounting education mode of delivery, content of the knowledge, and pedagogies to promote consensus amongst academics, practitioners and service users on various issues regarding the profession. In addition, future research in forensic accounting should also focus on empirical studies to establish specific skills required by forensic accountants to enable them to deliver in the rapidly changing technological environment which also promotes the committing of forensic crimes. This will contribute towards the education and training of forensic accountants.

CONCLUSION

The chapter explored the role of forensic accounting in uncovering evidence that could be employed in a court of law to litigate and arbitrate on financially related criminal cases. This has been achieved through identifying the differences between forensic accountants and external auditors, as well as other accountants, in terms of the way they perform their work. The chapter also provided examples of financial crimes and described the role of forensic accounting to provide assistance in courts. Furthermore, the chapter outlined the differences between a forensic accounting report and an audit report, as well as discussing the admissibility of financial forensics as evidence in courts. Issues, controversies and problems around forensics accounting were also articulated. The chapter also provided recommendations and future research directions. Some issues hampering the evolution of forensic accounting as a profession were also identified, and amongst the issues is the current lack of consensus among stakeholders on the forensic accounting education mode of delivery, content of the knowledge, and pedagogies. Another issue raised was the lack of common entry requirements into the profession, thereby opening a door to unqualified people to practice as forensic accountants. The admissibility of expert evidence in courts was also discussed in this chapter. Finally, this chapter provided a general overview of forensic accounting and its role in a court of law.

REFERENCES

Al-Abbadi, H., Alrawashdeh, B., Dabaghia, M. N., & Darwazeh, R. (2021b). The Role of Courts and Universities in Activating the Forensic Accounting to Discover Financial Fraud. *Academy of Accounting and Financial Studies Journal*, *25*(2), 1–9.

Al-Abbadi, H. M., Alrawashdeh, B., Dabaghia, M. N., & Darwazeh, R. N. (2021a). The challenges of application of forensic accounting in Jordan. *Academy of Strategic Management Journal*, *20*(2), 1–10.

Alshurafat, H., Al Shbail, M. O., & Mansour, E. (2021). Strengths and weaknesses of forensic accounting: An implication on the socio-economic development. *Journal of Business and Socio-economic Development*, *1*(2), 135–148. doi:10.1108/JBSED-03-2021-0026

Bhasin, M. (2007). Forensic Accounting: A New Paradigm For Niche Consulting. *The Chartered Accountant*, (January), 1000-1010.

Botes, V., & Saadeh, A. (2018). Exploring evidence to develop a nomenclature for forensic accounting. *Pacific Accounting Review*, *30*(2), 135–154. doi:10.1108/PAR-12-2016-0117

Brennan, N. M. (2014). Forensic accounting in a constitutional parliamentary democracy: the case of Ireland. *Journal of Forensic and Investigative Accounting*, *6*(3), 62-97.

Brown, M. (2008). *Forensic Accounting-Past, Present, & Future. It's All About Money*. http://www.envoynews.com/rwcpas/e_article001108198.cfm

Brown, R., & Smith, R. G. (2018). Exploring the relationship between organised crime and volume crime. *Trends and Issues in Crime and Criminal Justice*, *565*, 1–14.

Cantoria, C. S. (2010). *Financial Statement Audit vs. Forensic Accounting*. https://www.brighthub.com/office/finance/articles/81471.aspx

Cassim, F. (2015). Protecting personal information in the era of identity theft: Just how safe is our personal information from identity thieves? *Potchefstroom Electronic Law Journal*, *18*(2), 69–110. doi:10.4314/pelj.v18i2.02

Corporate Finance Institute (CFI). (2021). *Forensic Accounting*. https://corporatefinanceinstitute.com/resources/knowledge/accounting/forensic-accounting-litigation/

Dada, S. O., & Jimoh, F. B. (2020). Forensic accounting and financial crimes in Nigerian public sector. *Journal of Accounting and Taxation*, *12*(4), 118–125. doi:10.5897/JAT2020.0417

DiGabriele, J. A., & Huber, W. (2015). Topics and methods in forensic accounting research. *Accounting Research Journal*, *28*(1), 98–114. doi:10.1108/ARJ-08-2014-0071

Dolmanbateman Chartered Accountants Australia. (2019). *The Role of Forensic Accountants*. https://dolmanbateman.com.au/the-role-of-forensic-accountants/

Dreyer, K. (2014). *A History of Forensic Accounting* [Honours Project, Grand Valley State University]. https://scholarworks.gvsu.edu/honorsprojects/296

Driskell, F. D. (2019, Autumn). Conducting Forensic Accounting and Internal Investigations. Forensic Accounting and Special Investigations Thought Leadership. *Insights*, 3-10. http://www.willamette.com/insights_journal/19/autumn_2019_1.pdf

Ernst & Young. (2016). *Corporate Misconduct - Individual Consequences*. 14th Global Fraud Survey.

Ernst & Young. (2017). *Human instinct, Machine logic. Which do you trust most in the fight against fraud and corruption?* Europe, Middle East, India and Africa Fraud Survey.

Financial Sector Conduct Authority (FSCA). (2021). *Anti-Money Laundering and Counter-Terrorism.* https://www.fsca.co.za/Regulatory%20Frameworks/Pages/AMLCFT.aspx#:~:text=Money%20Laundering%20is%20the%20process,anyone%20has%20in%20such%20proceeds

Financial Services and Markets Act. (2000). https://www.legislation.gov.uk/ukpga/2000/8/contents

Forensic Accounting Standards. (n.d.). *Forensic Accounting Demystified.* https://www.forensicaccounting.com/standards.html#:~:text=1%20provides%20standards%20in%20professional,to%20the%20ultimate%20conclusion%20of

Gallagher, J., & Schiavone, J. (2019, July 10). *AICPA Issues New Professional Standards for Forensic Accounting Service Providers.* https://www.aicpa.org/news/article/aicpa-issues-new-professional-standards-for-forensic-accounting-service

Golden, T. W., Skalak, S. L., & Clayton, M. M. (2006). *A guide to forensic accounting investigation.* Wiley.

Gottschalk, P., & Benson, M. L. (2020). *The Evolution of Corporate Accounts of Scandals From Exposure to Investigation.* Oxford University Press. doi:10.1093/bjc/azaa001

Hegazy, S., Sangster, A., & Kotb, A. (2017). Mapping forensic accounting in the UK. *Journal of International Accounting, Auditing & Taxation, 28*, 43–56. doi:10.1016/j.intaccaudtax.2016.12.004

Helmore, E. (2019). Anna Sorokin: fake German heiress sentenced to up to 12 years in prison. *New York and Agencies.* https://www.theguardian.com/us-news/2019/may/09/anna-sorokin-sentence-fake-heiress-scammer-delvey-jail-time-latest-news-new-york-trial

Hill, G. N., & Hill, K. T. (2009). *Expert witness.* http://legaldictionary.thefreedictionary.com/Expert+witnesses

Howieson, B. (2018). What is the 'good' forensic accountant? A virtue ethics perspective. *Pacific Accounting Review, 30*(2), 155–167. doi:10.1108/PAR-01-2017-0005

Huber, W. (2014). What is the value of multiple certifications in forensic accounting? *Journal of Forensic and Investigative Accounting, 7*(2), 113–143.

Institute of Forensic Commercial Practitioners. (2016). Everything you should know about South Africa's commercial forensic industry. *The Forensic Practitioner*, (3). https://www.icfp.co.za/sites/default/files/articles/2714_icfp_ezine_issue_3_nov_2016.pdf

International Monetary Fund. (2001). *Financial System Abuse, Financial Crime and Money Laundering-Background Paper.* https://www.imf.org/external/np/ml/2001/eng/021201.htm

Jung, J., & Lee, J. (2017). Contemporary Financial Crime. *Journal of Public Administration and Governance, 7*(2), 88–97. doi:10.5296/jpag.v7i2.11219

Kramer, B., Seda, M., & Bobashev, G. (2017). Current opinions on forensic accounting education. *Accounting Research Journal, 30*(3), 249–264. doi:10.1108/ARJ-06-2015-0082

Kresse, W. J. (2008). The Saint Xavier University graduate program in financial fraud examination and management. *Issues in Accounting Education, 23*(4), 601–608. doi:10.2308/iace.2008.23.4.601

Kumar, S., & Venkataraman, R. (2019). An Empirical Study on Forensic Accounting for Corporate Fraud Management. *Adalya Journal.*

Louwers, T. J. (2015). The past, present, and future (?) of crime-related forensic accounting methodology. *Accounting Research Journal, 28*(1), 4–9. doi:10.1108/ARJ-04-2015-0047

Matson, J. V. (1999). *Effective expert witnessing* (3rd ed.). CRC Press.

McGuire, M., & Dowling, S. (2013). *Cybercrime: A review of the evidence. Summary of key findings and implications* (Home Office Research Report, 75). Home Office. https://assets.publishing.service.gov.uk/government/uploads/system/uploads/attachment_data/file/246754/horr75-chap3.pdf

Meintjes-Van Der Walt, L. (2003). The proof of the pudding: The presentation and proof of expert evidence in South Africa. *Journal of African Law, 47*(1), 88–106. doi:10.1017/S0221855303001998

Motsoeneng, T., & Rumney, E. (2019). *PwC investigation finds $7.4 billion accounting fraud at Steinhoff, company says.* https://www.reuters.com/article/us-steinhoff-intln-accounts/pwc-investigation-finds-74-billion-accounting-fraud-at-steinhoff-company-says-idUSKCN1QW2C2

Muehlmann, B. W., Burnaby, P. A., & Howe, M. A. (2012). The use of forensic accounting experts in tax cases as identified in court opinions. *Journal of Forensic and Investigative Accounting, 4*(2), 1–34.

Ocansey, E. O. N. D. (2017). Forensic Accounting and the Combating of Economic and Financial Crimes in Ghana. *European Scientific Journal, 13*(31), 379. doi:10.19044/esj.2017.v13n31p379

Pagano, W. J., & Buckhoff, T. A. (2005). Expert witnessing in forensic accounting. Academic Press.

Pickett, K. H. S., & Pickett, J. M. (2002). *Financial Crime Investigation and Control.* Wiley.

Prabowo, H. Y. (2013). Better, faster, smarter: Developing a blueprint for creating forensic accountants. *Journal of Money Laundering Control, 16*(4), 353–378. doi:10.1108/JMLC-05-2013-0017

Primeaux, E. (2020). *5 most scandalous fraud cases of 2019.* https://www.fraud-magazine.com/recap-article19.aspx?id=4295009428

Rechtman, Y. (2020). The Past, Present, and Future of Forensic Accounting. *The CPA Journal.* https://www.cpajournal.com/2020/04/10/the-past-present-and-future-of-forensic-accounting/

Renzhou, D. (2011). Research on Legal Procedural Functions of Forensic Accounting. *Energy Procedia, 5*, 2147–2151. doi:10.1016/j.egypro.2011.03.371

Schmidt, C. W. H., & Rademeyer, H. (2000). *Law of evidence.* LexisNexis.

Schwikkard, P. J., & Van Der Merwe, S. E. (2016). *Principles of evidence* (4th ed.). Juta Legal and Academic Publishers.

Shapiro, D. M. (2015, September 2). *Forensic Accounting: Beyond the Courtroom.* https://sfmagazine.com/post-entry/september-2015-forensic-accounting-beyond-the-courtroom/

Sinha, R. (2020). *Financial Forensics-An overview*. Preprint. doi:10.2139srn.3599703

Slot, J. (2012). *An evaluation of the forensic accountant's role in criminal law proceedings* [Master's Dissertation, North-West University, South Africa]. https://repository.nwu.ac.za/bitstream/handle/10394/9839/Slot_J.pdf?sequence=1

Smith, G. S., & Crumbley, D. L. (2009). How divergent are pedagogical views toward the fraud/ forensic accounting curriculum? *Global Perspectives on Accounting Education, 6*, 1–24.

Souza, J. L. (2017). Using the classroom to assist students to find their fit in the forensic accounting profession. *Journal of Forensic and Investigative Accounting, 9*(1), 724–735.

Tiwari, R. K. & Debnath, J. (2017). Forensic Accounting: A blend of knowledge. *Journal of financial Regulation and Compliance, 25*(1), 73-85.

Van Akkeren, J., Buckby, S., & MacKenzie, K. (2013). A metamorphosis of the traditional accountant: An insight into forensic accounting services in Australia. *Pacific Accounting Review, 25*(2), 188–216. doi:10.1108/PAR-06-2012-0023

Wall, D. (2007). Cybercrime: The Transformation of Crime in the Information Age. Cambridge University Press.

Wang, J., Lee, G., & Crumbley, D. L. (2016). Current availability of forensic accounting education and state of forensic accounting services in Hong Kong and mainland China. *Journal of Forensic and Investigative Accounting, 8*(3), 515–534.

Wecht, B. E. (2006). *Forensic science and law: Investigative applications in criminal, civil and family justice*. CRC Press.

Wijerathna, A. G. H. S. K., & Perera, H. A. P. L. (2020). A Systematic Literature Review on Forensic Accounting. *Proceedings of the 11th International Conference on Business and Information (ICBI 2020)*. https://www.researchgate.net/publication/351710923_A_Systematic_Literature_Review_on_Forensic_Accounting

Williams, J. W. (2006). Private legal orders: Professional markets and the commodification of financial governance. *Social & Legal Studies, 15*(2), 209–235. doi:10.1177/0964663906063575

Zysman, A. (2006). *Forensic accounting demystified*. http://www.forensicaccounting.com/home.html#one

ADDITIONAL READING

Crumbley, D. L., Heitger, L. E., & Smith, G. S. (2007). *Forensic and investigative accounting*. CCH.

Eliezer, O., & Emmanuel, B. (2015). Relevance of forensic accounting in the detection and prevention of fraud in Nigeria. *International Journal of Accounting Research, 2*(7), 67–77. doi:10.12816/0017351

Kranacher, M. (2010). *Forensic Accounting and Fraud Examination*. John Willey and Sons Inc.

Lama, P., & Chaudhuri, B. (2018). Forensic accounting: A study of its role in investigating corporate frauds and scams in India. *Proceedings of the 11th International Conference on Science, Technology and Management (ICSTM-18).* www.conferenceworld.in

Nunn, L., Brian, L., McGuire, B. L., Whitcomb, C., & Jost, E. (2006). Forensic Accountants: Financial Investigators. *Journal of Business & Economics Research*, *4*(2), 1–6.

Olaoye, C. O., & Olanipekun, C. T. (2018). Impact of Forensic Accounting and Investigation on Corporate Governance in Ekiti State. *Journal of Accounting. Business and Finance Research*, *4*(1), 28–36. doi:10.20448/2002.41.28.36

Ozili, P. K. (2015). Forensic accounting and fraud. A review of literature and policy implications. *International Journal of Accounting and Economics Studies*, *3*(1), 63–68. doi:10.14419/ijaes.v3i1.4541

Rufus, R. (2015). *Forensic Accounting* (Global Edition). Education Limited Pearson.

KEY TERMS AND DEFINITIONS

Admissibility: Refers to the acceptability or validity of evidence in a court of law based on its quality.

Arbitration: Refers to making a binding decision by an arbitrator agreed to by both parties involved in a dispute.

Cyber Crime: Refers to criminal activities committed by means of computers or the internet.

Defendant: Is an individual, company, or institution sued or accused in a court of law.

Expert Advice: This is advice given by someone who has studied a subject thoroughly.

Expert Opinion: Is a belief or judgment about something given by an expert on the subject.

Litigation: Is the process of taking legal action.

Plaintiff: Refers to a litigant or an individual who institutes a case against another individual in a court of law.

Witness: Refers to a person who provides evidence in a court of law as a result of having seen an event or a crime taking place.

Chapter 4
Advantages and Disadvantages of Applying Forensic Accounting in the Developing Countries:
The Case in Vietnam

Phi Thi Diem Hong
Vietnam National University of Agriculture, Vietnam

Do Quang Giam
Vietnam National University of Agriculture, Vietnam

Lai Phuong Thao
Vietnam National University of Agriculture, Vietnam

ABSTRACT

Vietnam has been reforming its economy to be more market-oriented and globally integrated since 1986. Under the circumstances, the Vietnam accounting system has been developed to meet the practical needs of enterprises. Forensic accounting is a new field in Vietnam accounting, but it is emerging as a good prospect for preventing financial crime and accounting fraud. This chapter focuses on the existing conditions and demand for forensic accounting in Vietnam. It includes the technique and skill requirements of forensic accounting to provide advantages and disadvantages of applying forensic accounting in Vietnam. The chapter will also enrich the book titled Significance of Forensic Accounting Techniques in Corporate Governance by overviewing Vietnam's accounting system and helping Vietnam achieve sustainable economic growth.

DOI: 10.4018/978-1-7998-8754-6.ch004

INTRODUCTION

Vietnam is an independent nation after passing a long time in the war of colony and empire from 1945–1975. Since 1986, Vietnam has been reforming its economy to be more market-oriented and globally integrated. The success of this reformation pushes Vietnam into a situation of stable growth economy recently. From a poor and backward economy before 1986, Vietnam nowadays is rapid developing country towards a market oriented and greatly integrated economy (World Bank & Ministry of Planning and Investment of Vietnam, 2016). Vietnam economy has been forecasted as the fastest-growing one in the world and possibly become the 20th greatest economy by 2050 (Maruichi & Abe, 2019). Following the economic freedom index by the Heritage Foundation (2021), Vietnam's economic freedom score is 61.7, ranks as the world's 90th freest, and is 17th among 40 countries in the Asia–Pacific region in 2021. Under the circumstances, Vietnam accounting has been developed to meet the practical needs of enterprises.

Unfortunately, some foreign organizations in the business community do not fully support the Vietnam business environment (Maruichi & Abe, 2019). According to World Bank (2020), the ease of Vietnam doing business ranking in 2020 was 115 among 190 countries. The GDP per capita of Vietnam 2020 was still low at US$3,609, which is far from the world average at US$12,152 (International Monetary Fund [IMF], 2021). The research by Maruichi & Abe (2019) reported that corruption in Vietnam still occurs and is the most impactful business obstacle. In 2020, according to Trading Economics, the Corruption Index in Vietnam was at 36 points in the survey of 196 countries with 20 million different indicators. According to results of a survey conducted in 2018 by PricewaterhouseCoopers (PWC) from 7,228 respondents in 123 territories in 24 months of 2016-2018 period, the rate of frauds in Vietnamese companies reached 52%, which is higher than that of global level at 49%. In which, accounting fraud is 22%, ranking at 6th top of the most common types of economic crime, while the highest level is belonging to assets misappropriation at 40%. In this survey, 53% of respondents in Vietnam estimated that they lost less than US$100,000, while 32% of them reported the losses of more than US$100,000 for economic crimes (PWC, 2018).

One scandal was about false accounting information on Audiovisual Vietnam Global (AVG). Actually, AVG had a accumulated losses of US$ 68 million, approximately VND1,563.7 billion in 2010-2015, however, the fair value of appraisal report was published without this information. In January 2016, Vietnam Mobifone still acquired 95% of AVG's shares for more US$370.4 million, around VND 8,445.324 billion (Bac Van, 2019). These company accounting frauds put multiple ministries and high-ranking officials at risk of punishment (Luong, 2018). Another typical situation was found during 2011–2012 when the Vinashin executives had intentionally broken national economic regulations, which led to severely consequences. It is not the whole cause, but part of these consequences is investigations, thefts, or fraud cases. In which, the financial fraud and white-collar crimes were not prevented.

As part of the governance in business, forensic accounting can contribute to fraud prevention and investigation (Bhasin, 2013a). However, forensic accounting in Vietnam is still a new term (Diep, 2018, 2020). In the legislature, academic research about forensic accounting seems to be not mentioned or is rarely studied. Only few forensic accounting researchers or accountants, or auditors considered while almost of them never heard this term before (Diep, 2020). Their knowledge and identification of the term forensic accounting are still low, while business governance always requires many flexible ways to prevent the tendency of increasing and various financial frauds. Therefore, research on the advantages and disadvantages of applying forensic accounting in developing countries, especially in Vietnam, is essential. This research is to review the scope of forensic accounting in developing countries with the special description of corporate governance and accounting reformation in Vietnam to provide the advantages and disadvantages of applying forensic accounting. These findings are evidences for proposing solutions and recommendations for improving forensic accounting in Vietnam. The remainder of the chapter contains the research background, the main focus of study, solutions and recommendations, and conclusion.

BACKGROUND

Many researchers worldwide have defined forensic accounting in various ways. A formal mention by the court decision was in 1817 and by an accountant in 1824 relevant to the expertise in the arbitration sector (Apostolou & Crumbley, 2005; Bhasin, 2013a; Crumbley, 2001; Ocansey, 2017). The expert witnesses evolved forensic accounting (Okoye & Akenbor, 2009). The meaning of 'forensic' is fit for use in a court of law, while 'accounting' mentions to a system of recording, summarizing, and analyzing business transactions and communicating financial information (Oseni, 2017). Bhasin (2013a) considers Sherlock Homes to be the first forensic accountant. However, until 1946 the term forensic accounting was mentioned in business by Peloubet in New York (Bhasin, 2013b; Okoye & Akenbor, 2009; Oseni, 2017). Forensic accounting is the process that accounting works are strong in purposes of investigating, gathering evidence of fraud, determining the damage caused by fraud, and explaining the results in court. Bologna and Lindquist (1995) explained that forensic accounting is conducted to explain the regulations, evidence, and the application of financial skills and an investigative mentality to unresolved issues. Forensic accounting often strongly involves an investigation to collect evidence to answer the questions: 'Did the labors or managers commit fraud?' or 'What are the losses by fraud or a financial scandal?' (Okoye & Akenbor, 2009).

The forensic accounting definition changes in response to the growing requirements of corporations (Bhasin, 2013b), however, it is gaining prominence since the massive accounting scandals and the increasing wave of crime, including the Enron and WorldCom scandals that occurred around the 2000s (Pedneault et al., 2012) as well as recent wrong doing of Luckin Coffee in 2019, Wells Fargo and Wirecard in 2020 (Fortune, 2020; Minh An, 2021). The increasing fraud allegations and earnings restatement of business always affect on benefits of shareholders and investors. The need for evidence, information and standards for corporate investigation, litigation, or dispute resolution also increases as the primary motivation of forensic accounting. As a profession, forensic accounting requires investigative and analytical skills to resolve financial issues in complying the standards requirements within the context of the rules of evidence (Okoye & Akenbor, 2009; Pedneault et al., 2012; Sule et al., 2019; Ozili, 2020; Alaoubi & Almomani, 2021). In theory, forensic accounting includes financial appraisal, fraud understanding, business environment and legal system compliance. According to Pedneault et al. (2012), forensic accounting is a series of actions not only collecting, recognizing, extracting, classifying, reporting but also affirming past or current financial data by accounting activities or prospective legal arguments or applying historical financial data to realize future financial situations.

Paradoxically, in Vietnam, not many people are familiar with accounting forensic, and very few articles and research focus on this issue. One of the first academic studies by the Vietnamese is a project from the State Auditing Office in 2005 by Huu (2005). After that, Van (2015), Diep (2018), and Phuoc (2020) continued this line of research on deep information functioning, comparisons to auditing, and foreign experiences to learn about forensic accounting. Recently, a research by Diep (2020) mentioned

Figure 1. Analysis framework

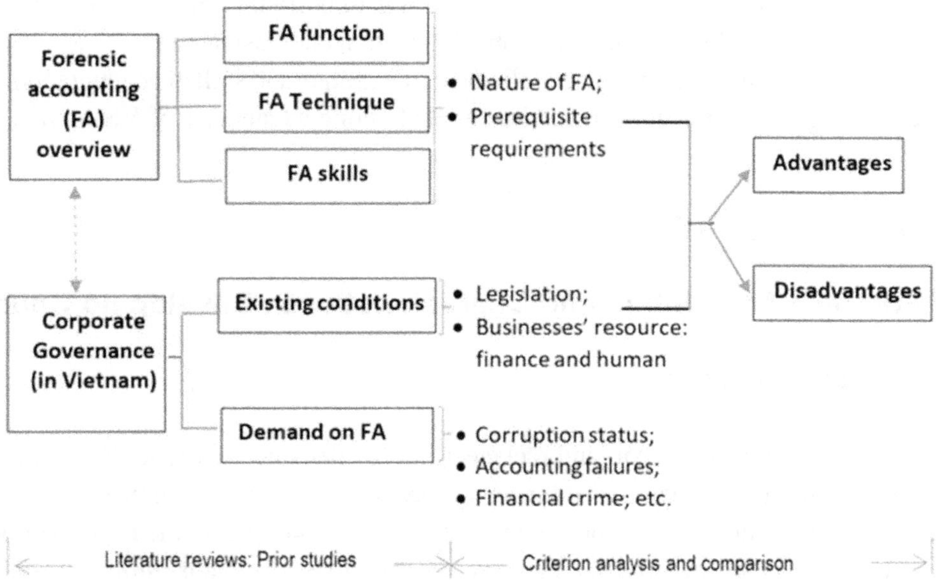

to the status of forensic accounting in Vietnam with purpose answering two questions: Does forensic accounting exist in Vietnam? and What is the application and research demand on forensic accounting in Vietnam? Through a survey of 150 interviewees who work as accountants, lawyers, investigators, auditors, and justices, her research results showed that there is still not any existing legal document about forensic accounting, about 79.33% of responses said "don't know" or "never heard before" about this term. However, the research also concluded that forensic accounting did exist in different ways, mainly in the investigative sector in Vietnam, with 54.64% of interviewees agreeing. In fact, forensic accounting was applied to collect evidence about financial fraud of the district inspection offices in Ho Chi Minh city (Lan & Phong, 2021).

Analysis Models

The analysis models were constructed based on literature review from the library, the internet, and the researchers' networks to provide relevant materials for review. In which, indicator statistics relevant to fraud and corruption were collected mainly from reputably global organizations. Additionally, references on fraud and corruption of Vietnam's case were obtained and reviewed from accounting and auditing agencies. The study divides the research documents into two groups. The first is "forensic accounting overview" which considers the nature and characteristics of the field. The other is "corporate governance in Vietnam" to find all available Vietnam conditions to apply to forensic accounting. For the first group, the concepts of forensic accounting are reviewed to understand its functions and application requirements, including skills and techniques. The second group focused on discovering the status of Vietnam on forensic accounting and available application conditions. Then, the comparison between Vietnam's existing conditions and the requirements of forensic accounting is conducted to get the advantages and disadvantages in Vietnam (Figure 1).

The analysis purpose is to identify criteria to measure the existing conditions for forensic accounting in Vietnam. Given the demand for forensic accounting, it is important to make these comparisons. The disadvantages incurred including a lack of available legislation and business resources (i.e., finance and human), support for developing forensic accounting (i.e., technique and skill of accountants). Other cases of forensic accounting development occurred that are belonging advantages of Vietnam.

MAIN FOCUS OF CHAPTER

Scope of Forensic Accounting and Characteristics in Developing Countries

Scope of Forensic Accounting

As a result of recent corruption, terror, and racketeering, the demand for accountants in fraud prevention and detection is high. However, the information provided by accountants has several limitations. First, the decision-makers are usually not the ones who collect and process the information rather they use the information provided by others. Therefore, in the process of transmitting information, there can be intentional or invisible information distortion. The second is the conflict of interests between information providers and users of the information for decision-making as cause of financial information misrepresentation (for instance: providing different information to the tax authorities, banks, and creditors). Third, accountants record economic transactions arising under the guidance of very complex laws and accounting standards related to accounting estimates and professional judgments (Ladda, 2014; Randal et al., 2019).

Actually, many accounting scandals have shown that even though the information has been audited, serious fraud still occurs. According to Gray (2008), a significant number of auditors, as independent and competent experts, collect and audit pieces of evidence verify and express their opinions on the auditee with still misstatements on materiality. Normally, the auditor stops at the discovery of a misstatement and does not investigate whether the misstatement is indeed fraud or error. Thus, frauds that are identified as free of material misstatements can be ignored by the auditor when selecting the audit sample, which may distort the nature of the audited information.

To ensure transparent financial information and improve the accountability of each business and the whole economy, especially in preventing financial crime as well as accounting frauds, the requirement of a new accounting module to overcome the limitations of traditional accounting and auditing appearances can occur with forensic accounting (Bhasin, 2013a; Oseni, 2017; West Virginia University [WVU], 2007). Forensic accounting is a type of accounting that combines accounting, auditing, and fraud investigation to form a new accounting module. This means the scope of forensic accounting needs to cover two broad areas of practice (i.e., litigation matters and investigation accounting; Okoye & Akenbor, 2009; WVU, 2007). The litigation often provides the necessary expert witnesses for both liability and civil claims. The investigation involves gathering and determining the existence of financial crimes and accounting fraud (Figure 2).

Figure 2. The main functions, scope, and goals of forensic accounting

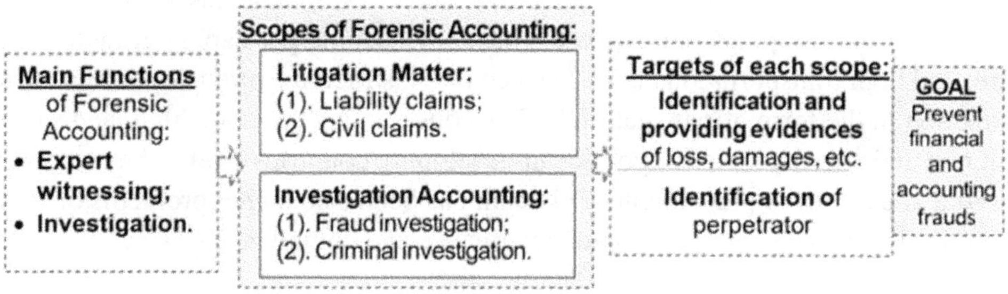

Characteristics of Developing Countries

The classification system based on a country's development was proposed by Nielen (2011), but depending on different purposes this issue is very differently. Regarding the choice of terminology, international organizations such as The United Nations Development Program (UNDP), the World Bank (WB), and the International Monetary Fund (IMF) showed about 20–25 percent of countries marked as developed. In which, the WB does not clarify the threshold between developed and developing countries as per capita income level of US$12,535 in 2019. The UNDP does not give any basis for why the ratio between the developed and developing countries is at 20%. There is not any clear answer on what limit is utilized by the IMF's classification system.

Table 1. Country classification systems in selected international organizations

Criteria	IMF	UNDP	WB
Name of developed countries	Advanced countries	Developed countries	High-income countries
Name of developing countries	Emerging and developing countries	Developing countries	Low- and middle-income countries
Development threshold	Not explicit	75 percentiles in the human development index distribution	$12,535 gross national income per capita in 2019
Type of development threshold	Most likely absolute	Relative	Absolute
Share of developed countries in 2019	20 percent	20 percent	37 percent
Subcategories	(1) Low-income (2) Emerging and others	(1) Low human development (2) Medium human development (3) High human development	(1) Low-income (2) Middle-income

Source: Nielsen (2011), p. 9; Umar & Nada (2020); IMF (2020); UNDP (2020).

Commonly, a developing country has low national income and application of technology, poor living standard, high level of indiscipline and, a high rate of corruption and fraud (Okoye & Akenbor, 2009). For the social aspect, developing countries often fail to ensure income equality among economic sectors. A large gap between the rich and the poor existed. The social structure of developing countries is often accompanied by a lack of orientation and management of the legal system. This has led to an increased population structure, high rates of corruption and risks, and increased social evils. In terms of economy and politics, developing countries often have low income-per-capital growth due to the weak infrastructure, and high transportation costs. The economic structures often depend on agriculture and resource extraction in the form of raw materials. The consumption costs are high, and savings are low. Due to economic and social problems, politics in developing countries tend to be unstable. The PWC (2018) showed that as a developing country, Vietnam has been also facing problems of frauds, bribery and corruption in risk management, corporate governance and compliance of legal.

Corporate Governance and Accounting Reformation in Vietnam

Poor Corporate Governance

According to ICAEW (2021), corporate governance is directed and controlled system of companies is to encourage compelling, entrepreneurial, judicious administration that can convey the long-term methodology of the company. The poor corporate governance is the leading cause of inefficiencies in production and business activities. Fraud still exists in the activities of organizations and businesses without depending on governance, and is not so easy to detect, however the volume and damage of fraud often tend to be less in case of good corporate governance. ACFE (2020) showed that different types of fraud cause different average losses to organizations. The biggest damage to organizations is financial reporting fraud, up to US$954,000 for only 10% of cases. However, 26% of fraudsters engaged in both misappropriations of assets and corruption, while these figures for both misappropriations of assets and financial reporting fraud is 3%, for both corruption and financial reporting fraud is 1%, and for all 3 categories above is 5%. In Vietnam, many people support that non-transparent finance will lead to negative consequences, fraud, and damage to the state and business-related entities. Recently, Vietnam has witnessed fraud in many areas such as maritime (Communist Party of Vietnam, 2013; Trang, 2017), pharmaceutics (Nam-Anh, 2011; Vinh-Duong, 2011), banks (Huy, 2018), commercial business (Ha, 2018), land acquisition (Quan, 2019; Tuyen, 2021), and smuggling and money laundering (Phuc, 2020).

Thus, the violations took place in almost all areas of the economy with very sophisticated fraud and involved many objects in society. The system with two accounting books effectively assisted the subjects in committing fraudulent acts. One book reflects the arising economic transactions that took place and are stored internally in the enterprise, and the other book recorded the enterprise, which only records economic transactions that bring benefits to the business and are issued to the outside. Thao & Hang (2014) showed that up to 82% of small and medium enterprises in Vietnam currently implement the double-book system for two reasons.

First, many businesses want high actual revenue but low tax declarations. This causes revenue evasion and increases the cost to reduce profits, thereby reducing corporate income tax expenses payable to the state budget. When the company wants to raise capital from investors, the company tends to form short contracts to increase revenue to beautify financial statements. The corollary of this problem has led to compromises between businesses and tax officials or businesses with securities companies, making the business environment not transparent. The financial image of the business is distorted, and shareholders are not fully informed about the value and profitability of the business.

Second, in the current business environment of Vietnam, there are still hidden and pre-emptive costs to get projects and contracts. These expenses cannot be recorded on the books. Therefore, to offset the

Table 2. Economic scandals or cases regarding forensic accounting in Vietnam

Scandals /Cases	Year of detecting errors	Lost/ damage value	Main object	Summary
Price collusion	2011	More than VND 6,000 billion	Duong Chi Dung- Chairman of the Director Board of Vinashine, Mai Van Phuc- General Director and associates, and some customs officers	Violated the provisions of the law on investment, bidding, import conditions, depositing the purchase price, chartering, leaving the accounting books; 4 death sentences, 1 life imprisonment, and many other sentences maritime (Communist Party of Vietnam, 2013; Trang, 2017).
Making stock prices (manipulating stock prices)	2010	One pharmaceutical company went bankrupt, 1702 shareholders lost everything	Le Van Dung and his accomplices	The transaction of buying and selling goods goes around in a closed-loop (i.e., the seller is also the person who buys the goods at the end of the circle) to beautify the financial statements. Also manipulating competitor's stock prices; 1 sentence of 4 years in prison and many other penalties.
Interest rate scam	2011	VND 1,085 billion	Huynh Thi Huyen Nhu, former Deputy Department and associates	Fraudulent appropriation of assets, forging seals the bank's poor management of customer deposits, etc.; one life sentence and many other sentences.
Fraud on personal income tax	2017	VND 104.5 billion	Leaders and accountants of Nguyen Kim Trading Joint Stock Company	It is illegal to convert wages and bonuses into overtime to evade personal income tax (Quan, 2019;Tuyen, 2021) .
Acquiring land, giving bribes	2018	More than VND 22,000 billion	Phan Van Anh Vu and many senior leaders	Placed bribes to receive a lot of project land, buying state-owned houses at low prices. The case is still under investigation.
Smuggling, money laundering	2019	Not fully calculated yet	General Director of Nhat Cuong Trading and Technical Services Co. Ltd., his staff, and some leaders of departments and branches	Smuggled electronic devices, using a 2-book system to hide illegal information; violated regulations on bidding to provide services to state agencies to launder money. The case is still under investigation (Phuc, 2020).

hidden costs spent, many businesses falsely declare costs and fabricate false accounting vouchers. When the business is big enough, they understand that the damage from the two-book system is huge. In the context of strong global economic integration, more businesses are moving toward transparency to attract investment capital from domestic and international investors.

International Accounting Integration and Accounting Reforms in Vietnam

Intending to become a developed country by 2045, Vietnam has made drastic moves to upgrade the quality of enterprises instead of focusing on developing the number of enterprises. The Enterprise Law No. 59/2020/QH14 passed by the National Assembly of Vietnam on June 17, 2020, officially went into effect on January 1, 2021, and has made breakthrough innovations in the legal framework for governance enterprises according to international standards, attracting capital and resources into production and business, and improving information transparency and corporate accountability. The objectives set by Government in Resolution 02/NQ-CP dated January 1, 2021, has four objectives. First, it will create more favorable conditions for business establishment and registration, reduce costs and time to start a business, and improve the rank from the World Bank's starting a business index by at least 25 places in 2021. Second, it will improve the mechanism to effectively protect the legitimate rights and interests of investors, shareholders, and members of the enterprise; it will also bring corporate governance up to standards by following good and common practices regionally and internationally and upgrade the rating of the investor protection index to 14 to 19 by 2021 (according to the rating of the World Bank). Third, it will improve the effectiveness of governance, publicity, transparency, and accountability for enterprises in which the State has a controlling stake, create favorable conditions for business households to maximize their potential and benefits, contribute to economic development, and raise the ranking of the corruption control index to 5 to 10 in 2021. Finally, it will improve the stock market capitalization index ranking by at least 10 to 15 steps by 2021 and integrate into the global economy.

Besides perfecting institutions and policies on corporate governance, Vietnam needs international accounting integration and accounting development. The first Vietnamese accounting standards (VAS) were promulgated in 2001 based on the international accounting standard system and adjusted to the socio-economic characteristics of Vietnam. In addition to completing legal system, Vietnam has made accounting as a useful tool for managing business activities, and providing timely and transparent information to state management agencies, business leaders, and those who use accounting information to make decisions.

Since economic relationships change, accounting standards must also change. On March 16, 2020, the Minister of Finance issued Decision No. 345/QD-BTC to approve the project of applying international financial reporting standards (IFRS) in Vietnam. The plan's preparation phase is from 2020 to the end of 2021, followed by a period of voluntary application of IFRS from 2022 to the end of 2025. This means a number of specific enterprises such as State-owned economic groups, listed companies, large-scale public companies, and other large-scale companies would transition to consolidated financial statements. The mandatory application period is after 2025 and will apply at the level of consolidated financial statements for enterprises in the voluntary application group. This confirms Vietnam's efforts to innovate accounting policies to help businesses actively integrate into the world economy.

Advantages and Disadvantages of Applying Forensic Accounting in Vietnam

Required Competencies in Forensic Accounting

The primary objective of forensic accounting is to investigate alleged fraud (Dabor et al., 2017). This purpose is only successful in supplying evidence of fraud. Unfortunately, fraud always exists, and it is necessary to have the knowledge and skills to effectively collect relevant evidence. Ozili (2020) indicates that the knowledge or skills provide tools relevant to accounting and non-accounting. Ozili explained the considerations of accounting and non-accounting decisions by forensic investigators and presented the skills and competencies required for a forensic accountant compared to a normal accountant.

The main requirements of a forensic accountant are core knowledge and personal skills (Bahasin, 2013b). The core in which the accounting, auditing, legal and investigative skills are always special skills. Harris & Brown (2000) identified five areas to be qualified as one forensic accountant. The first area is education qualification, which requires a basic background of accounting, financial evaluation, law, computer science, information technology, and other relevant fields. The second area is working experience of forensic accountant that shows his/her competence (Mohd & Mazni, 2007). Because forensic accounting work often must find evidence of criminal behaviors or fraud, the background of an accountant who has

Figure 3. Required competencies in forensic accounting
Source: Authors' compilation based on Okyoye & AkenBor (2009), DiGabriele (2008, 2009a), Bhasin (2013a), and Oseni (2017).

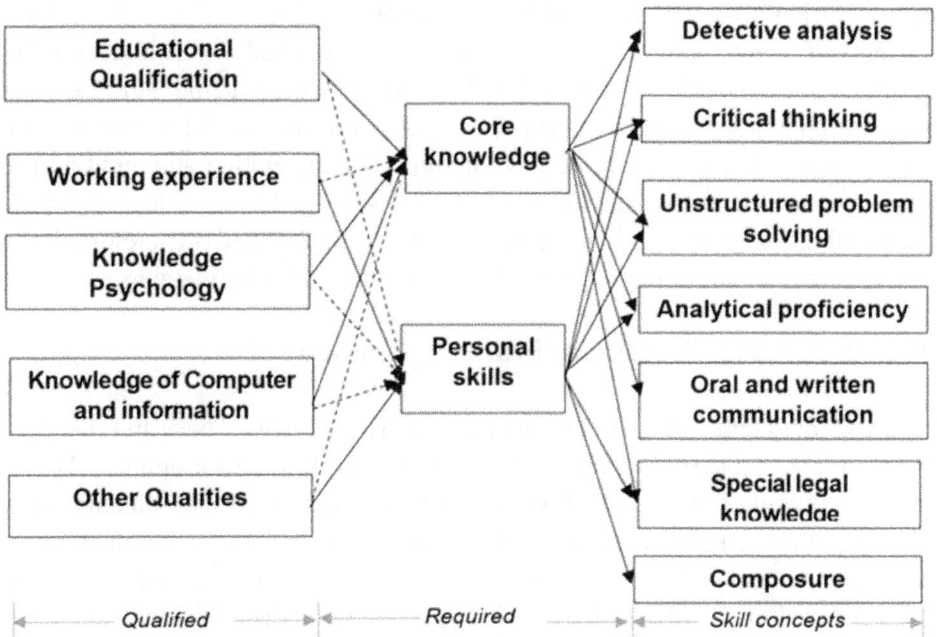

only graduated is not enough to be successful; at least three years in working experience is required be a good forensic accountant. The third area is knowledge of psychology. This requirement enhances the ability to interrogate suspects or witnesses, which is a primary task of forensic accountants. The fourth area is knowledge of computer and information technology (IT). Following Okyoye & Akenbor (2009), a good forensic accountant needs to have knowledge of computing and information technology alongside the requirements for education, experience, or psychology. The main reason is that crimes facilitated in cyberspace are common, and it is more difficult for forensic investigators to track without an IT background. The last area includes other qualities, such as analytical skills, communication, interpretation, logical thinking, critical thinking, or knowledge of relevant laws and the legal system. Singleton et al. (2006) noted that this area is important to become a forensic accountant

DiGabriele (2008, 2009a) identified a set of skills for forensic accountants that included seven prominent criteria such as (i) analytical proficiency, (ii) deductive analysis, (iii) critical thinking, (iv) unstructured problem solving, (v) oral and written communication, (vi) specific legal knowledge, and (vii) composure. From this, Bhasin (2013a) developed nine items by separating oral and written communication into two different skills, and by adding investigative flexibility. Figure 3 aggregates prior researches on competency skills for forensic accounting.

The center of Figure 3 shows two competency requirements for forensic accountants, including core knowledge and personal skills. On the right, the seven skills detail the required competencies. On the left, the five main groups of forensic accountants' qualities are the fundamental criteria to measure the competencies of forensic accountants. For all, the forensic accountant needs to have specific skills in financial accounting and in the internal control system (i.e., detective analysis or critical thinking), the law, other institutional requirements, investigation proficiency (i.e., special legal knowledge, unstructured problem solving, and analytical proficiency), and interpersonal skills (i.e., oral and written communication, and composure).

Surveys by the World Bank (2016) and by the World Economic Forum (2016) showed that two major business constraints of Vietnam are a skilled shortage of laborers and financial access. In which, the low labor demand is not incurred in Vietnam but the employers cannot find workers that match their skill needs because job applicants have inadequate skills (World Bank, 2014). For accounting sector, accounting education is still focused on the medium-term for accounting and auditing profession. In fact, the accounting education in Vietnam focuses more on theory and national legal compliance but less and practice and adaptation of international standards (World Bank, 2016). Therefore, it is difficult for forensic accountants to learn all of the required skills to be successful in Vietnam.

Corruption and Complex Financial Fraud or Crimes

Economic crime and fraud remain a hard control for enterprises globally. The term fraud is often applied to express deception or dishonesty for personal gain, or a loss creation for another (Bahasin, 2013c). Fraud is commonly the result of unexpected activities or not following formal standards or legal regulations such as bribery, money laundering, corruption, conspiracy, embezzlement, and extortion. At the national level, corruption and financial crimes are great obstacles to development efforts and harm the economy (Adegbie & Fakile, 2012). At the firm level, corruption is one of three main groups of fraud that strongly affect business achievements in a number of ways (Maruichi &Abe, 2019). First, corruption makes high cost of providing public goods and services through providing low-quality goods therefore the investment and economic growth rates reduce (Bardhan, 1997; Campos et al., 1999). Second, corruption prevents development from using resources ineffectively in human capital and productive sectors (Lambsdorff, 2003). For instance, research has shown that corruption results from the lack of transparency, accountability, oversights in government, undermines fair competition or foreign aid effectiveness, and stifles the economy (Maruichi & Abe, 2019). Third, corruption with inefficient bureaucracies such as multi-step administrative procedures creates more chance for corrupt public official. Fourth, corruption firms normally report higher costs and uncertainly, which damages their plan, investment decisions, and other business activities. This means corruption is an increasingly pervasive obstacle to improve surplus and run businesses.

Corruption and financial fraud cannot be correctly recognized but can be depicted and observed. It is popular under artificial cost, bribes, individualism, nepotism, fake donation, kickbacks, and others, namely financial crime such as surprises, tricks, cunning or misleading, and any unjust way used to cheat a person. Financial crimes involve property speculation by unlawful transformation of properties' ownership by another for their use and benefit. Under the rapidly developing information technology, financial fraud can use smart technology and accounting tricks to conduct complex financial affair. According to Bahasin (2013c), the modern digital environment often brings new opportunities for creating criminals or fraud. Nowadays, the computer is a common tool used in white-collar crimes. Through computer hardware or specialized software, people can crack encryption or codes or exact and sort data. This comes up when globalization has to a large extent, been facilitated. As a natural trend and out of human expectation, the spread of financial and economic crimes is continuously increasing globally.

Martini (2012) found that rampant corruption has been a great challenge to improving the business environment in Vietnam. It occurs in the relationship between enterprises and state, among businesses or exclusive service providers, between sellers and normal customers, etc. In which, the land management, banking and finance, capital construction investment, using funds or natural resources and minerals, state-owned assets in enterprises and the area of justice often have corruption rather than other sector (Thuong, 2017). In the field of land management, fraud mainly takes place in the planning and converting land use purpose and is typical in moving agricultural land acquisition for the construction of economic zones, industrial parks, and urban areas. In the banking and finance sector, the violations, particularly in commercial banks, tend to increase rapidly and the fraud occurs in all stages. In state-owned enterprises, financial crimes and fraud lower the value of assets, which then need to be equitized, sold, exchanged, or leased. There is no different corruption level between small and big enterprises or among business sizes. The bribery is still the most popular form of corruption (Thuong, 2017).

Accounting Failures and Financial Transparency Mechanisms

During the last several decades, much of corporate fraudulent financial reporting occurred (such as big corporations in the US during the 2000s) has prompted global actions to reform financial reporting. There are various reasons for these frauds, but accounting failure emerges as one of the main causes (Bhasin, 2013b).

Accounting information has been applied to give a true and fair picture of the accounts as a fair presentation that serves the interests of users. Accounting is influenced by personal judgment in respect of various terms. Although most countries use national or even international accounting standards, accounting limitations exist. For example, under the accounting principles, the accountant measures only those events that are of financial nature in terms of money. This means the non-monetary items or events that cannot be measured are not recorded in accounting. Paradoxically, many business activities cannot be precisely measured monetarily. For example, provision and labor competency accounting data are based on estimates and may be inaccurate. Moreover, depending on the accounting, one asset or financial transaction can be measured differently by different entities. These natural differences push accountants, even the accountancy profession, to easily break the principles by attempting to mislead, make mistakes, and abstract the truth, such as the accounting scandals of the early 2000s in the US.

To understand the purpose of each accounting information user, it is necessary to distinguish among misleading, fraud, and mistakes. Taking advantages of flexibility in accounting principle, many preparers do accounting works for their own benefits. Unfortunately, misleading causes presenting un-true and unfair view of business transactions by accountants or preparers (Jones, n.d.). The flexibility to give "true and fair accounting information" within or outside the regulatory framework is relevant to financial fraud, as shown in Figure 4.

The true and fair views directly influence the quality of financial statements as an output of accounting work; however, the existing accounting system consists of audited reports and statement procedures, which has not often ensured the prevention and exploration of fraud in financial statements (Awolowo, 2016). In alignment with this conclusion, other research also agreed that using audited financial statements may not be enough to promulgate reliable financial reporting without fraud (Bhasin, 2013b). Each type of fraud can be l occurred at a certain stage. The income smoothing or exaggeration and over net worth occur on the financial report.

For Vietnam accounting requirements, prudent is prevailing over VAS when the different accounting treatment and disclosure methods are applied to prepare the financial statements. Several VAS financial statements contain warnings about deviations from international standards and practices (World Bank,

Figure 4. Flexibility of giving a "true and fair view" in fraud accounting
Source: Jones (n.d.)

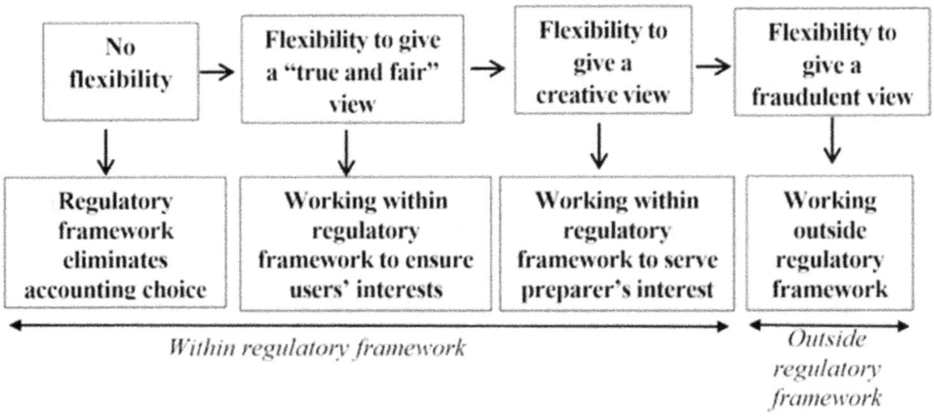

2016). This has led to apply inconsistently VAS and accounting regulations for financial institutions. The transparency and comparability of information on financial reports are not available.

Advantages and Disadvantages for Vietnam

Frauds and financial crimes have an extremely negative effect on the human capital development and infrastructure in developing countries. Forensic accounting considers solutions to prevent fraud and financial crimes (Oseni, 2017). Emeh & Obi (2013) found that having forensic accountants with forensic accounting skills can reduce employee theft, financial fraud, and top management fraud. Globalization has facilitated the spread of corruption or fraud globally as a natural trend and out of human expectation. Vietnam, in terms of international integration, and with the rapid development of the economy, spreading false accounting information is increasing. When false accounting information develops, society and the economy could severely suffer from large losses. Nevertheless, under the conditions of a developing country, are still positive and negative points to introduce and practice forensic accounting in Vietnam.

Efforts in Anti-Corruption and Legal Sector Reform

Maruichi & Abe (2019) stressed that the most influent business problem for operation is corruption. Therefore, prevention and anti-corruption play an important role in Vietnam. As the Government's anti-corruption strategy in 2009 indicates, Vietnam improved the quality of public service, enhanced economic management, and improved capacity building in inspections, and strengthened audits and public awareness (Norwegian Agency for Development Cooperation [NORAD], 2011). Under the cause of economic reformation, Vietnam economic environment has changed remarkably such as anti-corruption policies, training, raising awareness, and other administrative measures. Thuong (2017) indicated five measures in fighting corruption. First, publicity and transparency were prioritized in policymaking, lawmaking, and compliance. Second, it was to improve the quality of civil public services, and servant mechanisms. Next, equality and transparency in business environment were established and improved. Then, corruption detection and dealing were conducted to enhance effectiveness and efficiency of inspections, examinations, supervisions, audits, investigations, prosecutions. Last, it was spreading the Law on Anti-Corruption and public role.

Legal sector reform is gradually establishing the rule of law with many new laws that aim to reduce the scope of administrative abuse and corrupt behavior. However, there has been little focus on possible corruption within the sector. Effective and credible legal processes and administrative complaint procedures that individuals or organizations can access to constrain corrupt behavior remain underdeveloped in Vietnam, as many believe that reducing corruption is meaningless. Nowadays, block chain has been applied widely in many sectors for preventing financial crime, therefore this is considered as a tool to combat accounting frauds.

In the accounting sector, Vietnam is trying to improve its current accounting standards (VAS) to align more closely with international accounting standards by creating a system to prevent accounting fraud. Under prudential regulation, VAS and VFRS should be applied to prepare financial statements, however, the disclosure form of accounting profit following VFRS is more detail than that of VAS. This is more helpful for accounting information users.

Government Support for National Accounting Orientation

In accordance to Decision No. 480/QD-TTG was enacted by Prime Minister on March 18, 2013 a strategy on accounting and auditing in 2020, with a vision to be approved by the government by 2030, Vietnam will develop domestic and international accounting and auditing services. This includes rapidly increasing the number of service enterprises and quantity of auditors and practicing accountants, improving the quality of accounting (i.e., auditing services), and diversifying products and services of accounting and auditing to meet the national economy requirements. Therefore, forensic accounting, as a part of the accounting system, is being developed.

Recently, the Minister of Finance issued Decision No. 345/QD-BTC, dated March 16th, 2020. Vietnam has also announced the roadmap for applying international financial reporting standards for formal legal for accountants and auditors to improve their knowledge about international skills and competency requirements. There is no doubt that accountants with adequate technical knowledge in the academic curriculum are at a great advantage for developing forensic accounting in Vietnam.

Laws and Accounting Limitations

In Vietnam, there are a lot of specific regulations for business entities. Directly relevant to financial crime and accounting fraud, the Law on Enterprise enacted first time in 2005 and amendments in 2015 and 2020, however the Law on Anti-Corruption was enacted in 2018. Under the law, various regulations are issued as guidance for implementation documents for enterprises. But corruption situation has remained high and regulations under the law have not been suitable development of business practice.

Vietnam's legal accounting system covers accounting, auditing, and corporate financial reporting. The accounting law details the requirements for the accounting profession. Beside the Independent Audit Law has promulgated. The Government improved in the institutional framework for corporate financial statements, but audited financial statements complying with Vietnam's accounting standards were at low quality (World Bank, 2016). IFRSs require the fair value in full for accounting while VASs apply quantitative factors i.e., aging or time of useful life for recognizing impairment or deprecation value.

No Strong Professional Institution to Provide Forensic Accounting Services

Although growth of Vietnam economy has been stable and rapid for long period as an emerging economy in Asian region, in order to enhance economic competitiveness, the World Bank (2016, 2019) suggested that the reliable financial information of corporation needs to be assessed. Forensic accounting has strongly contributed to financial reporting quality and transparency through detecting fraud or preventing financial crimes but it is a new area in Vietnam because of lacking many requirements for development. The professional accountancy organizations including Association of Certified Public Accountants (VACPA) and accounting universities have a significant role in qualification of professional accountants and auditors, however, their programs or operations have limited in improving the knowledge, competencies, and skills of future accounting professional. Actually, the VACPA takes part currently in the International Federation of Accountants (IFAC) but not a full member (World Bank, 2019).

Over the 35 years since the economic reform in 1986, the Government conducted significant efforts to develop education system of accounting based on outcome. Unfortunately, these efforts are not enough to create a shift from traditional education to a significantly appreciated one. Many universities did not train on principles-based financial reporting standards instead of doing strongly following the accounting curricula based on the government regulations. Current accounting education is still too much emphasis on knowledge to record transactions and memory rules and procedures rather than develop the accountants' competencies and judgments (World Bank, 2019). Almost all university programs do not have enough curricula content on professional ethics, values, and attitudes in the curricula and have an uneven quality of examinations. Although the lecturers are generally qualified, information technologies (IT) are introduced on an overly simple basis or not at all into the teaching process.

Lack of Conditions to Quickly Adapt the Full Forensic Accounting Competency Requirements

The key solution for successful transition of Vietnam's economy and society is skilled workforce (World Bank, 2013b). In accounting sector, skilled accountants are also the most important point. Following accounting and auditing vision for 2030 by Government, three main national goals includes: (i) develop the profession of accounting and auditing, (ii) improve corporate financial statements to high quality, and (iii) improve transparency and accountability. However, many prior studies show employers are seeking accountants who match their skill needs (Anh, 2016). The case of "over quantity but lack of quality" is popular in the supply of accounting and auditing as a human resource. This reflects that the competency of existing accountant resources does not fit the requirements for forensic accountants in terms of knowledge, investigation, accounting, or auditing. Since a forensic accountant often requires more specific skills than a normal accountant, these skills are not only in accounting and auditing but also in investigation.

Given the disadvantages, in the next five years, the preparation of human resources to fully adapt the required skills for forensic accountants seems to be far from successful. This is also a key advantage of Vietnam on the road to developing forensic accounting.

SOLUTIONS AND RECOMMENDATIONS

Regulatory Framework: Accounting Bases, Financial Information Transparency, Professional Accounting Body, and Other Relevant Laws

In order to develop a successful forensic accounting program, it is necessary to have a effective framework of accounting and auditing with updated knowledge and special skills support by a national legal. The two main laws on accounting and independent audit in Vietnam still cover specific obligations in complementation, these laws should be amended (World Bank, 2016). Moreover, most of these laws do not mention anything relevant to forensic accounting. Therefore, the Accounting Law should be revised toward a general regulation of proper books and records and should add articles for forensic accounting as the formal legislating basis in Vietnam.

Moreover, the existing accounting base should also change quickly to fair value to harmonize with international accounting standards and to minimize fraud in the revaluation of business assets or equitization of state-owned enterprises. Under the law, the statutory frameworks, including standards, circulars, or implementing guidance, help combat financial fraud. The regulating body of accounting practitioners can verify that accountants are trained to use forensic accounting techniques.

Aside from improving the accounting body, relevant national laws should reform forensic accounting. To apply forensic accounting techniques effectively, it is essential to create a skillful workforce to discovery the truth and easily prosecute financial crimes or accounting fraud. On the other hand, the strict punishment of corrupt offenders should apply to all entities, and those who behave with integrity need to be awarded. Additionally, it is necessary to publish organization and individual corruption by stating the name and title of them, including people in positions of power.

Role of Forensic Accountants: National, Local, and Business

As a developing country, Vietnam has an increasing demand for professional accounting practitioners to detect and prevent fraud. At the firm level, any fraud involves an intentional deception to informally obtain money or other assets. Therefore, corporations are responsible for setting up and doing internal controls to prevent and detect financial fraud. At the national level, in terms of economic transformation, accounting information is more important in the whole economy. The amount of accounting scandals in recent decades has increased, the economy suffers from large losses, and benefits of investors are also considerably losses. The harm increases when these scandals or frauds develop. In many situations, when completion integration cannot happen, single accounting and legal knowledge could be a problem (Hao, 2010). It is necessary to combine closely theories and practices to deal problems effectively. This means the functions of forensic accounting are accepted. The enterprises should use forensic accounting as an important measurement to examine the quality of their financial statements and accounting information before issuing or using them.

Forensic Accounting Education: Concept, Skills, and Techniques

The combination of knowledge, skills, and abilities of the professional performing the work contributes strongly to success of entity (West Virginia University, 2007). Forensic accountants have special skills not only in accounting, auditing, finance, quantitative methods but also in certain areas of the law, research, and investigation to collect, analyze, and evaluate evidential matter and to interpret and communicate findings. Consequently, the demand for education in forensic accounting has grown, at least case of Vietnam, since forensic accounting is still new.

Bahasin (2013b) showed that universities should consider forensic accounting at the bachelor's and master's levels. Following this, universities need to design relevant academic curriculum in forensic accounting to build the concept, skills, and techniques as the background or benchmarks for beginners in the position of forensic accounting. Moreover, a national competency framework needs to be established for accounting and auditing training in universities and colleges. According to the World Bank (2019), a preparation of national competency framework for accounting curricula based on international benchmarks and standards, and adaptation of newly curricula by lecturers will require further assistance.

FUTURE RESEARCH DIRECTIONS

Actually, the topic of forensic accounting not only in Vietnam but also in many developing countries has been still new aspect in both academic and practice. In order to reduce financial crime and fraud as well as improve business environment, in-depth researches of forensic accounting i.e., relevant to merger business transaction, plant asset transformation, impairment loss assessment should be conducted continuously. Moreover, the reformation of legal system and improvement of accounting skilled workforce have been studied. For legal system, it needs to study how and what new articles should be added; or how and what existing regulations should be amended. Meanwhile, for accounting skilled workforce, the essential researches should be related to training and certifying criteria of a good forensic accountant.

CONCLUSION

Under International integration trends, the financial crime and accounting fraud are also growing, especially with current events after the bankruptcy of a series of leading companies in the world. This has raised concerns about the truthfulness and reasonableness of financial statements and concerns about the quality of audit and accounting works (Diep, 2020; Okoye & Akenbor, 2009). Therefore, the widespread demand for accounting and auditing reformation is going up on a global scale. These reformations examine whether financial statements and their public disclosures properly report balances, results, and publicly required disclosures such as omissions, overstatements, improper accounting treatments, understatements, and the calculation of the identified issues on the financial statements. Forensic accounting has bright prospects in preventing financial crimes and accounting fraud and is a good way for developing countries to harmonize international accounting, at least in Vietnam.

This study is one of a few references to forensic accounting in Vietnam, and it presented an overview of the concept as well as the role and skill requirements for forensic accountants. It also described and analyzed the conditions for developing countries to find out the advantages and disadvantages of forensic accounting development. The findings show that significant obstacles exist in the process of developing forensic accounting in Vietnam, including limited laws and accounting limits, a lack of a professional institution to provide forensic accounting, and a lack of conditions to quickly adapt to the competency requirements of forensic accounting. To overcome these obstacles, three dimensions including regulatory framework, the role of a forensic accountant, and education, are urgent requirements for finding appropriate solutions.

REFERENCES

ACFE. (2020). *Report to the nations – 2020 global study on occupational fraud and abuse.* https://acfepublic.s3-us-west-2.amazonaws.com/2020-Report-to-the-Nations.pdf

Adegbie, F. E., & Fakile, A. S. (2012). Economic and financial crime in Nigeria: Forensic accounting as antidote. *British Journal of Arts and Social Science, 6*(10), 37–50.

Alaoubi, A., & Almomani, M. A. (2021). The Moderating Effect for Forensic Accounting on the Relationship between corporate Governance and Quality of Accounting Information in The Jordanian Public Shareholding Companies. *International Journal of Academic Research in Accounting Finance and Management Sciences, 11*(2), 47–61.

Anh, V. D. (2016, August 3). *Integration of Vietnam human resources for accounting in the AEC* [Conference presentation]. National Conference for Brexit and the Asean Economic Community from a perspective of integration, Van Hien University.

Apostolou, N., & Crumbley, D. L. (2005). Fraud survey: Lessons for forensic accountants. *Journal of Forensic Accounting, 6*(1), 103–118.

Awolowo, I. F. (2016). Financial statement fraud: The need for a paradigm shift to forensic accounting. World Academy of Science, Engineering and Technology. *International Journal of Economics and Management Engineering, 10*(3), 987–991.

Bac Van. (2019). *Lesson from acquiring AVG's shares.* https://nhandan.vn/tin-tuc-su-kien/bai-hoc-tu-vu-an-mua-co-phan-avg-445948

Bardhan, P. (1997). Corruption and development: A review of issues. *Journal of Economic Literature, 35*(3), 1320–1346. https://www.jstor.org/stable/2729979

Bhasin, M. L. (2013a). Corporate governance and forensic accountants' role: Global regulatory action scenario. *International Journal of Accounting Research, 1*(1), 1–19. doi:10.12816/0001124

Bhasin, M. L. (2013b). Corporate governance and forensic accountants: An exploratory study. *Journal of Accounting – Business and Management, 20*(2), 55–83.

Bhasin, M. L. (2013c). An empirical investigation of the relevant skills of forensic accountants: Experience of a developing economy. *European Journal of Accounting Auditing and Finance Research, 1*(2), 11–52.

Bologna, G. J., & Lindquist, R. J. (1995). *Fraud auditing and forensic accounting: New tools and techniques* (2nd ed.). John Wiley and Sons, Inc.

Campos, J. E., Lien, D. & Pradhan, S. (1999). The impact of corruption on investment: Predictability matters. *World Development, 27*(6), 1059–1067. doi:10.1016/s0305-750x(99)00040-6

Communist Party of Vietnam. (2013). *End of a trial of Vinalines case: Duong Chi Dung and Mai Van Phuc were sentenced to death.* Communist Party of Vietnam Newspapers Online. https://dangcongsan.vn/thoi-su/ket-thuc-xet-xu-vu-vinalines-duong-chi-dung-va-mai-van-phuc-linh-an-tu-hinh-222936.html

Crumbley, D. L. (2001). Forensic accounting: Older than you think. *Journal of Forensic Accounting*, *2*(2), 181–202.

Dabor, A. O., Aggreh, M., & Eruse, U. (2017). Forensic accounting and fraud control in the Nigerian banking sectors. *Journal of Global Accounting*, *5*(1), 165–174.

Diep, T. N. (2018). An overview of forensic accounting and the need for research on forensic accounting. *Journal of Accounting and Auditing, 9*. https://www.hoiketoanhcm.org.vn/vn/trao-doi/khai-quat-ve-ke-toan-dieu-tra-va-su-can-thiet-nghien-cuu-ve-ke-toan-dieu-tra/

Diep, T. N. (2020). Theoretical concepts of forensic accounting in Vietnam. *Finance Journal, 2*(9). https://tapchitaichinh.vn/tai-chinh-kinh-doanh/mot-so-van-de-ly-luan-ve-ke-toan-dieu-tra-tai-viet-nam-330750.html

DiGabriele, J. (2008). An empirical investigation of the relevant skills of forensic accountants. *Journal of Education for Business*, *83*(6), 331–340. doi:10.3200/JOEB.83.6.331-338

DiGabriele, J. (2009a). Fishbowl the forensic accountant: A closer look at the skills forensic accounting education should emphasize. *Forensic Examiner*, *18*(2), 77–79.

DiGabriele, J. (2009b). Implications of regulatory prescriptions and audit standards on the evolution of forensic accounting in the audit process. *Journal of Applied Accounting Research*, *10*(2), 109–121. doi:10.1108/09675420910984673

Emeh, Y., & Obi, J. O. (2013). An empirical analysis of forensic accounting and financial fraud in Nigeria. *African Journal of Social Sciences*, *4*, 112–121.

Fortune. (2020). *The biggest business scandals of 2020*. https://fortune.com/2020/12/27/biggest-business-scandals-of-2020-nikola-wirecard-luckin-coffee-twitter-security-hack-tesla-spx-mcdonalds-ceo-ppp-fraud-wells-fargo-ebay-carlos-ghosn/

Gray, D. (2008). Forensic accounting and auditing: Compared and contrasted to traditional accounting and auditing. *American Journal of Business Education-Fourth Quarter*, *1*(2), 115–126. doi:10.19030/ajbe.v1i2.4630

Ha, T. (2018). *Around Nguyen Kim Company's arrears of personal income tax*. Public Security News Online. https://cand.com.vn/Kinh-te/Xung-quanh-viec-Cong-ty-Nguyen-Kim-bi-truy-thu-thue-thu-nhap-ca-nhan-501809/

Hao, X. (2010). Analysis of the necessity to develop the forensic accounting in China. *International Journal of Business and Management*, *5*(5), 185–188. doi:10.5539/ijbm.v5n5p185

Harris, C. K., & Brown, A. M. (2000). The qualities of a forensic accountant. *Pennsylvania CPA Journal*, *71*(1), 6–8.

Heritage Foundation. (2021). 2021 Index of Economic Freedom. *Vietnam Section*, 436–437. https://www.heritage.org/index/pdf/2021/countries/2021_IndexofEconomicFreedom-Vietnam.pdf

Huu, N. D. (2005). *Theory and practice of applying forensic audit in current status of State Audit* [Research project]. Vietnam State Audit.

Huy, A. (2018). *Huynh Thi Huyen Nhu was sentenced to life in prison*. Public Security News Online. https://cand.com.vn/Phap-luat/Huynh-Thi-Huyen-Nhu-bi-tuyen-an-chung-than-478435/

ICAEW. (2021). *What is corporate governance?* https://www.icaew.com/technical/corporate-governance/principles/principles-articles/does-corporate-governance-matter

IMF. (2021). *Index 2021: Vietnam section*. https://www.imf.org/en/Countries/VNM

Jones, M. (n.d.). *Creative accounting, fraud and international accounting standards*. University of Bristol. https://pdfs.semanticscholar.org/1c0b/be6f34709bb824586ee3b0b79bfb3105ef65.pdf

Ladda, R. L. (2014). *Introduction: Basic concepts of accounting* (1st ed.). Laxmi Book Publication. https://books.google.com.vn/books?id=q5q2BgAAQBAJ&printsec=frontcover#v=onepage&q&f=false

Lambsdorff, J. G. (2003). How corruption affects productivity. *Kyklos*, *56*(4), 457–474. doi:10.1046/j.0023-5962.2003.00233.x

Lan, D. T., & Phong, P. T. (2021). *Application of forensic accounting techniques at the District 10 Inspection Office*. Vietnam Club of Chief Accountants. https://www.clbketoantruong.com/ung-dung-ky-thuat-ke-toan-dieu-tra-tai-phong-thanh-tra-quan-10-tphcm/

Luong, S. (2018). *Company in US$392 million investment scandal in Vietnam had profile doctored: State inspector.* Tuoi Tre News Online. https://tuoitrenews.vn/news/business/20180316/company-in-362mn-investment-scandal-in-vietnam-had-profile-doctored-state-inspector/44564.html

Martini, M. (2012). *Overview of corruption and anti-corruption in Vietnam. U4 expert answer*. A4 - Anti-Corruption Resources Centre. https://www.transparency.org/files/content/corruptionqas/315_Overview_of_corruption_and_anti-corruption_in_Vietnam.pdf

Maruichi, D., & Abe, M. (2019). Corruption and the business environment in Vietnam: Implications from an empirical study. *Asian and the Pacific Policies Studies*, *6*(2), 222–245. doi:10.1002/app5.275

Minh, An. (2021). *The scandals that "evaporate" billions of USD in 2020*. https://laodong.vn/kinh-te/nhung-vu-gian-lan-lam-boc-hoi-hang-ti-usd-trong-nam-2020-875852.ldo

Mohd, S. I., & Mazni, A. (2007, July 10–13). *An overview of forensic accounting in Malaysia* [Conference presentation]. International Conference on Business and Information, Tokyo, Japan. http://eprints.um.edu.my/8616/1/All.pdf

Nam-Anh. (2011). *Former General Director of Vien Dong Pharmaceutical, Le Van Dung was sentenced to 4 years in prison*. Cafef.vn News Online. https://s.cafef.vn/dvd-73453/cuu-tong-giam-doc-duoc-vien-dong-le-van-dung-linh-an-4-nam-tu.chn

Nielsen, L. (2011). *Classifications of countries based on their level of development: How it is done and how it could be done*. IMF Working Paper. https://www.imf.org/external/pubs/ft/wp/2011/wp1131.pdf

Norad. (2011). *Joint evaluation of support to anti-corruption efforts Viet Nam country report*. Evaluation Department of the Norwegian Agency for Development Cooperation. https://www.oecd.org/countries/tanzania/48912883.pdf

Ocansey, E. O. N. D. (2017). Forensic accounting and the combating of economic and financial crime in Ghana. *European Scientific Journal, 13*(31), 379–393. doi:10.19044/esj.2017.v13n31p379

Okoye, E. I., & Akenbor, C. O. (2009). Forensic accounting in developing economies - problems and prospects. *The University Advanced Research Journal, 1*, 1–13.

Oseni, A. I. (2017). Forensic accounting and financial fraud in Nigeria: Problems and prospects. *Journal of Accounting and Financial Management, 3*(1), 23–33.

Ozili, P. K. (2020). Forensic accounting theory. *Finance, Insurance and Risk Management Theory and Practices* (Vol. 1). Emerald. https://mpra.ub.uni-muenchen.de/102566/

Pedneault, S., Rudewicz, F., Sheetz, M., & Slilverstone, H. (2012). *Forensic accounting and fraud investigation* (CPE Edition). John Wiley & Sons. www.cpestore.com

Phuc, L. (2020). *The 5 crimes and 26 defendants prosecuted in Nhat Cuong case*. Doanh Tri Newspaper Online. http://www.doanhtri.net/tin-5-toi-danh-va-26-bi-can-bi-khoi-to-trong-vu-an-nhat-cuong-d66510.html

Phuoc, N. T. (2020). Forensic audit – A new type of auditing. *Industry and Trade Magazine Online*. https://tapchicongthuong.vn/bai-viet/kiem-toan-dieu-tra-mot-loai-hinh-kiem-toan-moi-71273.htm

PWC. (2018). *Pulling fraud out of the shadows -Global Economic Crime and Fraud Survey 2018: Vietnam Perspectives*. https://www.pwc.com/vn/en/publications/vietnam-publications/economic-crime-fraud-survey-2018.html

Quan, H. (2019). *How did the two former presidents of Da Nang and Phan Van Anh Vu caused a loss of 22,000 billion VND?* Ho Chi Minh City Police Newspaper Online. https://congan.com.vn/an-ninh-kinh-te/cuu-chu-tich-da-nang-va-vu-nhom-gay-that-thoat-22000-ty-dong-ra-sao_84392.html

Randal, J. E., Mark, S. B., Chris, E. H., & Alvin, A. A. (2019). *Auditing and Assurance Services - International Perspective*. Pearson.

Singleton, T. W., Singleton, A. J., Bologna, G. J., & Lindquist, R. J. (2006). *Fraud Auditing and Forensic Accounting*. John Wiley and Sons, Inc.

Sule, S., Ibrahim, S., & Sani, A. (2019). The Effect of Forensic Accounting Investigation in Detecting Financial Fraud: A Study in Nigeria. *International Journal of Academic Research in Business and Social Sciences, 9*(2), 545–553. doi:10.6007/IJARBSS/v9-i2/5590

Thao, L.P. & Hang, N.T.T. (2014). *Factors that Affect Accounting Information System Quality in Small Medium Enterprises in Vietnam.* Summary report of research funded by Vietnam National University of Agriculture.

Thuong, N. T. (2017). Corruption in Vietnam: The current situation and proposed solutions. In *The changing face of corruption in the Asia Pacific: Current perspectives and future challenges* (pp. 221–230). Elsevier. https://www.researchgate.net/publication/319310522_Corruption_in_Vietnam_the_current_situation_and_proposed_solutions

Trang, B. T. (2017). *The death sentences with Giang Kim Dat and Tran Van Liem*. Vietnam Investment Reviews Online. https://tinnhanhchungkhoan.vn/y-an-tu-hinh-voi-giang-kim-dat-va-tran-van-liem-post166006.html

Tuyen, P. (2021). *Who did Phan Van Anh Vu give bribes to?* Ho Chinh Minh City Legal Newspaper Online. https://plo.vn/phap-luat/phan-van-anh-vu-dua-hoi-lo-cho-ai-980489.html

Umar, S., & Nada, H. (2020). *New World Bank country classifications by income level: 2020-2021*. https://blogs.worldbank.org/opendata/new-world-bank-country-classifications-income-level-2020-2021

UNDP. (2020). *Human development reports*. http://hdr.undp.org/en/content/latest-human-development-index-ranking, http://hdr.undp.org/en/content/developing-regions

Van, N. T. H. (2015). *Developing orientation of forensic accounting in Vietnam* [Master thesis, Ho Chi Minh Economic University]. https://digital.lib.ueh.edu.vn/handle/UEH/44025

Vinh-Duong. (2011). *Nearly 2,000 shareholders of Vien Dong Pharmaceutical are at risk of losing their hands*. Dan Tri News Online. https://dantri.com.vn/kinh-doanh/gan-2000-co-dong-duoc-vien-dong-nguy-co-trang-tay-1316301396.htm

West Virginia University. (2007). *NIJ special report: Education and training in fraud and forensic accounting: A guide for educational institutions, stakeholder organizations, Faculty and Students*. West Virginia University - Forensic Science Initiative Cooperative Argument. https://www.ojp.gov/pdffiles1/nij/grants/217589.pdf

World Bank. (2014). *Skilling up Vietnam: Preparing the workforce for a modern market economy*. Vietnam Development Report. https://documents1.worldbank.org/curated/en/283651468321297015/pdf/888950PUB0Box30lso0829400June172014.pdf

World Bank. (2016). *Vietnam report on the observance of standards and codes (ROSC) – Accounting and auditing module*. https://documents1.worldbank.org/curated/en/220021512482581847/pdf/121901-ROSC-PUBLIC-FinalROSCEN.pdf

World Bank. (2019). *Vietnam corporate accounting education in universities*. https://openknowledge.worldbank.org/bitstream/handle/10986/33469/Vietnam-Corporate-Accounting-Education-in-Universities.pdf?sequence=1&isAllowed=y

World Bank. (2020). *Economic profile of Vietnam: Doing business 2020, comparing business regulations in 190 countries*. https://openknowledge.worldbank.org/handle/10986/32436#:~:text=Doing%20Business%202020%20is%20the,business%20environment%20in%20190%20economies

World Bank and Ministry of Planning and Investment of Vietnam. (2016). *Vietnam 2035: Toward prosperity, creativity, equity, and democracy*. The World Bank Group. https://openknowledge.worldbank.org/handle/10986/23724

World Economic Forum. (2016). *Insight Report: The Global Competitiveness Report 2016 - 2017*. Geneva: World Economic Forum. https://www3.weforum.org/docs/GCR2016-2017/05FullReport/TheGlobalCompetitivenessReport2016-2017_FINAL.pdf

KEY TERMS AND DEFINITIONS

Accounting Fraud: A kind of fraud involves to deception or dishonesty for personal gain, or a loss creation for another in accounting work.

Core Knowledge: All prerequisite knowledge that individual needs to get for normal certain position.

Corporate Governance: A directed and controlled system of companies is to encourage compelling, entrepreneurial, judicious administration that can convey the long-term methodology of the company.

Developing Country: A nation has low national income and application of technology, poor living standard, high level of indiscipline and a high rate of corruption and frauds.

Financial Crime: Any person involves property speculation by unlawful transformation of properties' ownership by another for their use and benefit.

Forensic Accountant: An accountants have special skills not only in accounting, auditing, finance, quantitative methods but also in certain areas of the law, research, and investigation to collect, analyze, and evaluate evidential matter and to interpret and communicate findings.

Forensic Accounting: A process that accounting works are strong in purposes of investigating and gathering evidence of fraud, determining the damage caused by fraud, and explaining the results in court.

Investigative Skills: The ability to interrogate suspects or witnesses that forensic accountant needs to determine the damage by frauds.

Chapter 5
The Fraud Triangle:
Assessing Fraud Risk

Núria Villaescusa
https://orcid.org/0000-0002-6412-9642
Universitat Internacional de Catalunya, Spain

ABSTRACT

The Fraud Triangle is the framework that regulators have chosen to assess fraud risk for auditors and practitioners. In this chapter, the authors will review the origins and each of the three elements of the Fraud Triangle and provide some tools for assessing whether each element is present in a fraud case. The chapter will distinguish between occupational and corporate fraud, as the authors believe that the drivers of each are slightly different. After defining each of the elements, the authors will apply the framework of analysis to some famous fraud cases in very different parts of the world so that the reader can see the differences and similarities of these cases.

INTRODUCTION

Why does a company commit financial statement fraud? Could it have been detected before the stock plummeted and lost thousands of investors' money? These are some questions that investors, auditors, financial analysts and regulators wonder about every time a financial scandal is made public.

Academics have done a great deal of research on this topic, aiming to identify what causes managers to commit fraud, the most common ways to do so and what circumstances increase the likelihood of committing fraud. (See Hogan et al., 2008; Trompeter et al., 2012 for literature reviews on this topic).

One of the most used models used to analyse, explain and detect fraud is the Fraud Triangle, first developed by Donald Cressey in 1950. This model states that embezzlement has three elements in common: a perceived pressure or incentive, a perceived opportunity and the subsequent rationalisation of the fraudster behaviour. Other authors have reshaped the geometric figure with the capability and creating The Fraud Diamond (Wolfe & Hermanson, 2004) or with competence and arrogance creating the Crowe's fraud pentagon (developed by Crowe Horwath in 2010).

DOI: 10.4018/978-1-7998-8754-6.ch005

However, none of these extended geometric models has had the same impact as the original. The most relevant accounting regulators have taken the fraud triangle as the model for establishing fraud audit guidelines. For example, the *International Standards on Auditing 240 (The auditor's responsibility to consider fraud in an Audit of Financial Statements* and its equivalent SAS No 99 in the US states something very similar) states explicitly that the auditor should analyze the risk of fraud as follows: *"Fraud, whether it consists of fraudulent financial information or misappropriation of assets entails the existence of an incentive or an element of pressure to commit fraud, as well as the perception of an opportunity to carry it out and some rationalization of the act."*

The objective of this chapter is twofold: to develop the different elements of the fraud triangle into parameters that one can apply to a case of study and analyse how these elements were present in two cases of convicted accounting fraud in different parts of the world. The authors have chosen two highly mediatised companies. Therefore, there is a lot of public information available intending to apply a theory to a case study, which is not generalisable in any case.

The first study case is Enron. At the beginning of the 21st century, some famous accounting scandals, and Enron at the top cause that the Sarbanes-Oxley Act in the US was put into place, setting new standards for auditing firms, corporate management and board of directors. Ten years later, in Europe, another scandal was made public. Although both cases happened in different countries and industries, they had some things in common; they overstated revenues and understated debt through companies outside the consolidation perimeter.

BACKGROUND

In December of 1950, Donald Cressey published "The Criminal Violation of Financial Trust" in the American Sociological Review. The paper was the product of his research searching for generalisations in the criminology field, which was not very common. He thought that a better understanding of why managers commit fraud would reduce its incidence in the same way that research into the causes of some diseases had reduced its mortality rate. Some research has ignored this first approach of Cressey to the three elements of the later called fraud triangle as the publication of his book Other people's money in 1953 and re-edited in 1971 has usually been considered the starting point of this theory.

Cressey's primary concern was explaining embezzlement by defining a sequence of events always present in any case of trust violation. He interviewed around 130 inmates convicted for white-collar crime in three different prisons in the US. After redesigning his research questions and hypotheses several times, he came up with three characteristics: (i) the existence of a financial problem that is non-shareable (Incentive), (ii) the knowledge that they can secretly resolve this problem through trust violation (Opportunity) and (iii) the application to their conduct verbalisations which enable them to adjust their conceptions of themselves as trusted persons (Rationalisation).

These three elements were later called The Fraud Triangle (See Figure 1). This framework has been widely used to study any occupational and corporate fraud, and audit standard setters have also used it to set a basis for analyzing the likelihood of fraud in a financial statement audit.

Some authors consider fraud a multi-faceted phenomenon that one can not explain using a single framework (Lokanan, 2015). Using a single framework to analyse one specific phenomenon does not mean

Figure 1. The fraud triangle
Source: Cressey (1953)

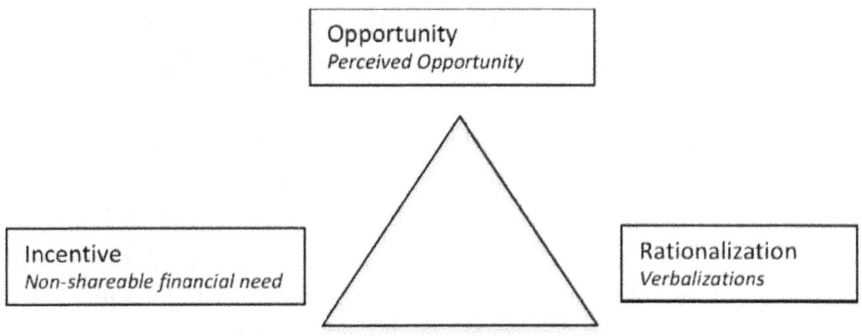

that every case can fit into it but may be the first proxy to explain a particular fraud instead. However, we can use it to compare fraud cases in different countries and analyse their similarities despite cultural or social-environmental differences. Using the fraud triangle to study a particular fraud case and assess the likelihood can help homogenise the analysis of this phenomenon worldwide.

The main characteristic of this model and why it has become so relevant is that Cressey found that all three elements must be present simultaneously in any case of embezzlement. Therefore, if an auditor or any other agent wants to assess the likelihood of fraud, it would be enough to determine that only one of the three elements is not present. For example, suppose I can have a reasonable assurance that the company have enough internal controls so the employees have the perception that perpetrating a fraud would be easily detected. In that case, we can say that there is no perceived opportunity for fraud, so the likelihood of fraud in that company is less than in another with fewer internal controls. In the next part of the present chapter, we will discover what can be considered a perceived pressure, opportunity and rationalisation and how can we use this information to assess fraud risk.

THE THREE ELEMENTS OF THE FRAUD TRIANGLE

Assessing Incentive/Pressure

In the study of accounting fraud, incentive and pressure are treated as synonymous, although there might be some differences in the meaning. However, we should distinguish between personal incentives/pressure of management or any other type of employee and business incentives/pressure.

It is often difficult, if not impossible, to know whether the employees may have some personal financial pressure. These problems could be in the form of a gambling problem, alcohol, drugs or any other addiction, a sudden personal expense or financial shortfall, an unexpected medical expenditure or any other cause that exerts tremendous pressure on the individual to obtain additional money. As Cressey stated since the beginning, the main characteristic of this pressure is that it is non-shareable, so it is unlikely that the employee has explained their problems to any other member of the organization. Therefore, unless we observe some alteration in the employee's behaviour, It is complicated to detect g these issues that can turn into an incentive to commit fraud.

When employees perpetrate these frauds, the most common form of fraud is asset misappropriation. Employees may charge false expenses; they can authorize payments to inexistent suppliers or fake employees, or they can steal inventories to sell them. According to the ACFE Report of the Nations, in 2020 the occupational fraud comes from the operations department (15%), the accounting department (14%) and the sales department (11%).

Following with the case of personal incentives, when perpetrators are the managers, they may have additional incentives such as showing themselves as particularly good at their positions (arrogance and overconfidence) or meeting the requirements for a salary bonus. In these cases, they will opt for other forms of fraud that modify the company's performance indicators and, therefore, their performance indicators.

But when the incentive is not personal but a **business incentive**, the whole fraud scheme changes completely. Employees and managers do not seek a personal benefit as a primary goal but the company's survival or reputation. In this case, common elements of pressure are: to achieve analysts' predictions, the need for external financing, because the company is not doing well (reputation), meet debt covenants, show the company as particularly attractive because they are issuing or equity.

It may also happen that the company does not have an incentive to commit fraud. Instead, it is the product of an initial manipulation in a legal manner, hoping to reverse it shortly after. But manipulation of accounting profit cannot be done without limit as manipulated accruals will leave a trace on the balance sheet that the company must undo in the future. In this case, the need to report good results in the face of the impossibility of reversing manipulations exerts a high pressure to commit fraud. In January 2009, Ramalinga Raju, the founder and chairman of an Indian IT company named Satyam, wrote a letter to the board of directors. In this letter, he recognized that he had inflated sales (by 6 billion the last quarter), assets (cash and debtors) as a consequence of the fake sales, the operating margin (by almost 6 billion) and understated liabilities. He explained that *"what started as a marginal gap between real operating profit and the one reflected in the books of accounts continued to grow over the years"* Clearly, he started manipulating the accounts with the hope of a soon reversal. However, he could not do it as he described the situation as *"It was like riding a tiger, not knowing how to get off without being eaten."*

In conclusion, incentives can be presented in many forms depending on whether they are personal or business-related incentives, even though some of them are very difficult to assess or predict. A summary of the different types of incentives is in table 1.

Assessing Opportunity

Once the fraudster has perceived a non-shareable pressure or an incentive to commit fraud, they have to have the capability and the way to do it, which constitutes the opportunity. So we will consider an opportunity as the perception that (1) The fraudster has the technical skills to commit fraud, (2) There is a weak control system and (3) The possibility of being caught is remote. The fraudster has to believe that s/he has the skills needed to commit fraud and s/he is not going to be detected. In occupational fraud, the non-existence, insufficiency, or ability to override the company's internal controls are considered the primary sources of opportunity. In the case of corporate fraud, weak corporate structures have been considered the main drivers of opportunity.

Opportunity is a broad concept that can appear through many different faces. Suppose an employee falsely charges expenses, for example. The opportunity can come because of poor segregation of duties (s/he is the same person that approves the expenditures). It may also come because the person in charge is not checking their reasonableness correctly (e.g., an employee applies much more distance between

Table 1. Type of incentives

Type of Incentive	Examples	Type of fraud Most common
Personal financial pressure. Employees and Managers	Gambling Addictions like alcohol and drugs Sudden financial shortfall Unexpected medical expenditures Living beyond one's means Greed	Asset misappropriation False expense claims Payroll fraud (non-existent employees) Inexistent suppliers invoices Inventory shrinkages
Personal financial pressure. Managers	Arrogance Overconfidence Bonus	Financial indicators fraud Show the personal performance as a manager is above expectations.
Business Financial Pressure	Initial Public Offering Risk of a hostile takeover Debt/Equity issue Meet analysts' forecasts Need of external financing Meet debt covenants Obtain continued support from an investor/supplier Initial legal manipulation that can not be reversed	Financial Statement Fraud Overstated sales Understated debt Understated expenses Overstated assets

Source: Own elaboration

two different cities than the real one). If an employee detects weak internal controls or any vulnerability in the system, this will constitute an opportunity for misbehaviour.

In the case of corporate fraud, poor management control through weak corporate governance structures constitutes the most significant opportunity to commit fraud. We usually consider the board of directors and the audit committee when looking at these corporate governance structures. Dechow et al. (1995) were one of the first authors to examine the governance structures in the case of accounting manipulation. They found that Firms that manipulate their financial statements are more likely to (i) have a management-dominated board of directors, (ii) have the CEO as a board member, (iii) have the CEO as the founder of the company, and less likely to (iv) have an audit committee and (v) have independent board members.

The board of directors' mission is to exercise specific control over the managers of the company. One of the most potent elements of a board of directors in exercising control over management is having some independent members, as they have no direct economic or any other interest in the company. However, the CEO's influence over the appointment of these directors is often substantial, which does not guarantee one hundred per cent independence. On the contrary, if all or a large part of the directors are members of the board, the power that this body must exercise will diminish, if not eliminated.

The complexity of a corporation may increase the opportunity when it is composed of many companies in a large number of countries. The complexity of the corporation may facilitate the commission of accounting fraud in the form of related party transactions, especially the ones not related to the ordinary course of the business. Suppose the group has some of these subsidiaries in countries with poor legal control. In that case, it will not be difficult to hide some companies controlled by the parent company and not include them in the consolidation perimeter. So the activity between these companies and the group is not eliminated in the consolidated financial statements allowing the group to increase revenues and decrease expenses artificially.

Table 2. Examples of opportunities

Type of opportunity	Examples	Use of the opportunity
Occupational fraud. Lack or ineffective internal controls.	Segregation of duties	False expenses claims Payroll fraud (non-existent employees) Inexistent suppliers invoices Inventory shrinkages
Corporate Fraud. Lack of control of the management by the board of directors and the audit committee	Managers are members of the board. CEO is the founder and chairman of the board Lack or insufficient independent members Non-independent members of the audit-committee. Appointment made by the CEO (Dechow et al., 1996)	No control over the decisions made by managers.
Group Structure	Large groups formed by many companies in different countries with different legal requirements	Related party transactions Existence of companies controlled by the parent company and not included in the consolidation perimeter

Source: Own elaboration

The 2020-2021 pandemic has also increased the opportunities to commit occupational fraud. According to KPMG COVID-19 Fraud survey 2020, remote working has increased the chance for occupational fraud. Financial controls are not adapting well to the mass remote working environment, and internal controls are under tremendous pressure. According to the companies participating in the survey, segregation of functions is vulnerable to override. The ability to verify the integrity of the operations and hasty system workarounds to get things done is becoming more common. The sudden change of the working environment has forced companies to improvise new ways of working and interacting among the organisation members, and internal controls have passed into the background. During the pandemic, the companies' priority has been survival. Once they achieved this goal, then they would have to rethink all internal controls. Otherwise, all the work done before the pandemic would have been useless to ensure the company had the proper control environment to avoid occupational fraud..

Assessing Rationalisation

In Cressey's (1950, 1953) original theory, fraud perpetrators need verbalizations to mitigate the conflict between their actions and social norms. He stated that a morally acceptable rationalisation is necessary before the crime occurs because the fraudster does not see himself as a criminal. Fraudsters need to internally justify what they are doing, not because they do not know it is illegal but because "they" are not unlawful. White-collar offenders try to find a way to show the fraud as less wrongful and somehow justified for many different reasons that may vary from one fraudster to another. Cohen et al. (2010) found that managers of the fraud cases they analyzed have certain attitudes/rationalisations in common. For example, they found that a typical attitude in managers that have committed fraud is an excessive interest in maintaining or increasing the entity's stock price or earnings trend. Another common trait was to achieve aggressive or unrealistic forecasts because of the management commitment to analysts, creditors and other third parties. In 2016 the Wells Fargo scandal was made public. The employees had created around 3,5 million fake savings and checking accounts on behalf of existing customers without their consent. The company, which considered itself "The king of cross-selling", set a very aggressive sales target of averaging eight products per customer. Cross-selling was the driver for rewarding performance; the bank failed to see that being so unrealistic could boost fraudulent practices (Wells-Fargo cross-selling ratio was 6.3 products per customer while the industry average cross-selling ratio was 2.7)

Even though it gives us a wide range of possible rationalisations, the most relevant research in this field is based on interviews with convicted white-collar criminals. According to their processes of rationalising the criminal act, Free (2015) found different categories of rationalisation in previous research. The most common are described in table 3

Table 3. Some examples of rationalisations

Type of rationalisation	Explanation	Example
Moral justification	Reconstructing the act as socially worthy or having moral purpose. Some people consider themselves Robin Hoods, so deceiving the rich is an act of justice.	*"I am protecting the company."*
Advantageous comparison	Comparing the wrongful act to a much more flagrant act.	*"There is nothing compared to..."*
Euphemistic labelling	Using convoluted rethoric to make a wrongful act sound better.	*"I am trying to level the playing field."*
Ignore or misconstrue consequences	Minimizing, ignoring or misconstruing any consequences of the act. Sometimes fraudsters underestimate the consequences of their acts as no personal injury is involved. This usually happens with corporate fraud as fraudsters do not see the real consequences of misreporting.	*"I can't see that anyone is hurt."*
Denial of the victim	Placing blame onto the victim, arguing the victim is physically absent or unknown.	"It all ends up cutting covered by insurance anyway."
Displacing responsibility	Placing responsibility for the fraudulent act into someone else. Sometimes, employees may argue that they are only obeying a superior order and that the illegality is therefore not their responsibility.	*"I was just part of the team that was doing it."*
Diffusing responsibility	Sharing responsibility with others.	*"Everybody else was doing it."*
Entitlement	Deserving of more, regardless of anything else	*" I deserved more money."*
Disbelief	Claiming disbelief of how the rules work	*"What we are doing isn't illegal"*
Temporary loan	The perpetrator argues that s/he plans to pay it back or fix the fraud	*" I fully intended to pay back the money that I took"*

Source: Adapted from Free (2015) based on previous research done by Murphy (2012), Mayhew and Murphy (2014) and Free et al., (2017)

AN APPLICATION OF THE FRAUD TRIANGLE

Even though fraud has existed since the very beginning of accounting, we have witnessed some accounting scandals that have shaken the foundations of what we thought was a relatively stable system in the last decades. Famous accounting scandals like Enron, Worldcom, Tyco, Parmalat, Satyam, Pescanova and many others have made us realise that we were doing something wrong, and they have completely changed the rules of the game. Because of those scandals, accounting practitioners and auditors have a lot more regulatory requirements. The Sarbanes-Oxley Act of 2002 issued right after the Enron scandal is a clear example of that. But Could it have been avoided? Of course, we don't know the answer to that question, but we can apply some techniques to assess the likelihood of fraud or analyse it.

This part of the chapter will analyse notorious frauds according to the frame proposed, the Fraud Triangle. We will set how the three elements are present in every case, following the pattern described in the previous sections. There might be more reasons in some cases than the ones stated as an incentive or an opportunity. Still, we will consider the most relevant based on the public information available of each case.

Enron (US)

In December 2001, Enron, the energy giant and one of the largest ten companies in the US, went bankrupt. It was a huge company that employed more than 20,000 people, with a $100 billion income, $979 million profits and $65 billion assets. It is the most famous accounting fraud in the last two decades, as it was a starting point in the field of fraud research and analysis, and it was the case that changed the rules of the game. It was one of the biggest bankruptcies ever.

Enron was founded in 1985 in the initial years of the deregulation of the energy market due to the merger of Houston Natural Gas and InterNorth, a gas company based in Nebraska. In the beginning, Enron was a traditional gas company that delivered gas to customers. In 1986, Kenneth Lay, the CEO of Houston Natural Gas, was appointed chairman and CEO of Enron's newly formed company.

Under the lead of Kenneth Lay, Enron transformed itself into a commodities-trading company, buying and selling natural gas. In 1990 Kenneth Lay hired the consulting company Mckinsey to design the business plan for the following years. The consultant assigned in charge of the project was Jeffrey Skilling. As a consultant, he was in charge of leading the transformation of Enron from a traditional gas business into an energy-trading business. He created a "gas bank" where the gas producers, which had lots of gas available due to the deregulation, could sell the gas to the consumers. The producers would deposit the gas in a "bank" that was Enron, selling it to the final customers. The gas producers liked that idea as they could get long-term contracts to predict their future cash-flows easily, and so did the consumers as they could buy long-term gas at a specific price.

In 1990, Kenneth Lay was impressed by the work done by Jeffrey Skilling as a McKinsey consultant, and he hired him as Executive director of Enron Finance Corp. In the following years, Enron expanded the trading to other commodities: steel, oil, paper pulp, plastic and broadband capacity. The vision of Enron changed from a gas transporter to a future and other derivatives trader. The complexity of these long-term contacts increased over time as customers could get insurance for all sorts of risks related to energy and commodity prices. Moreover, as Enron realized that oil and gas producers had enormous reserves that they could not exploit because of a lack of financing, Enron decided to act as a bank with the producers themselves.

Their business strategy needed enormous liquidity, so they had to rely on credit facilities provided by the lenders as they needed to borrow massive amounts of money. They had to keep the rating of the company high to be attractive to the market. In 1998, they mentioned that fact in the annual report as their senior unsecured long-term debt was rated BBB+ by Standard & Poor's. To maintain an attractive profile for rating agencies and, therefore, investors, they had to maintain a certain level of growth. As those markets matured and competition grew, trading margins declined, and this growing strategy became unsustainable. So, to fix that, they pushed accounting practices to the limit of ethics and legality and, in the end, crossed the line.

Enron was the first company to use mark-to-market accounting in 1991. This accounting technique allowed them to report the contracts at market value. Under the mark-to-market accounting, they could account for the total value of the long-term contract when they signed the agreement. In doing so, they had to make a lot of assumptions: (i) they had to estimate all the revenues and costs of the contract, (ii) compute the net present value and (iii) recognize as profits the whole amount upfront instead of doing it over the lifetime of the contract (which could be of 20 years or more), as it was with the traditional system. The employees who closed a new contract were rewarded based on those net present value of the contracts, so they tended to use the most optimistic assumptions to get a higher net present value and, consequently, a higher bonus.

The other big hole in the accounting practices of Enron was the Special Purpose Entities (SPE). The SPE were companies created with a lawful purpose. Explained very simply, they were independent business partnerships that they do not have to consolidate if a third (non-related) party owned an equity investment at risk in the SPE equals at least 3% of total assets. They failed to fulfil the 3% condition. Still, they did not consolidate these SPE entities as they were supposed to do, allowing ENRON to use these non-consolidated SPE to hide the losses and debt off Enron's main business.

If we analyze the Enron case from a Fraud Triangle perspective, we can see how the different elements are present:

Incentives/Pressure

- From a corporate perspective, there was a high pressure to increase revenues year after year to improve the rating to get the liquidity they needed for their business strategy.
- They rewarded only profits. Although Enron's corporate values were said to be: Communication, Respect, Integrity and Excellence, some former employees declared that there were no rewards for saving the company from a potential loss; there were only rewards for doing a deal that could increase profits.
- Following this culture of rewarding only profit-makers, the employees had the incentive of the bonus, so they made unrealistic assumptions when calculating the net present value of the long-term contracts as they got higher pay.
- These unrealistic assumptions turned to be losses in the years right after they signed the agreement. This fact increased the losses, so they had to hide them from the official financial information.

Opportunities

- The accounting practices, mark-to-market accounting and SPE allowed Enron to inflate the profits and hide the debt and losses.
- The board of directors did not effectively exercise control over the activities of the firm. The business of Enron was complex, and many of the board members failed to correctly understand the nature of the transactions. In a report issued in February 2002 and commissioned by the board, they concluded that the board overestimated the effectiveness of internal controls.

- The board of directors was found to lack independence as some of their members had some financial interest in Enron. This fact represented a conflict of interest of some of the members of Enron's management.
- Although it was said to be more accounting experts than other companies' committees, the audit committee failed to understand the complexity of the business of Enron and how the company designed their operations.
- The audit company also lacked independence as Andersen was billing Enron for consulting and tax services.

Rationalisation

- Both Lay and Skilling said few executives who stole money through secret deals perpetrated the fraud. They attribute Enron's bankruptcy to a combination of bad publicity and loss of shareholder confidence.
- Jeffrey Skilling declared in the trial that Enron's collapse was *"the most painful thing in my life" "I did everything I could humanly do during this time. Did I make mistakes? I'm sure I did, Mr Hueston. I had to make real-time decisions based on the information I had at the time."*

Pescanova (Spain)

On February 28, 2013, Pescanova communicated to the Spanish regulator that it could not formulate the annual accounts for the 2012 financial year under the going concern accounting principle. They argued they could not ensure the company's continuity unless they could favourably resolve one of the following two situations: (1) the sale of assets related to salmon farming or (2) The renegotiation of bank debt.

Several companies that had no commercial relationship with Pescanova, others that were indeed clients and some subsidiaries of Pescanova had received notifications from financial institutions claiming debts that they did not know existed. A few days later, the company declared that "they have detected discrepancies between its accounting and the bank debt figure and that these discrepancies could be significant".

The forensic audit carried out by KPMG concluded that the company had understated its liabilities, mainly bank debt, by 2.2 billion euros concerning the accounts initially presented to the board for approval. In addition, they estimated the company's net worth as -927 million euros compared to the 653 million euros proposed to the board. On April 25, 2013, Pescanova filed for the equivalent of Chapter 11. The forensic auditors found evidence of different irregular accounting practices. They were aimed mainly at two objectives: (1) To provide biased information about the evolution of the company's business and (2) To hide a significant part of the liabilities, mainly with credit institutions, to counteract the poor results obtained.

Pescanova was founded in Vigo in 1960 due to the innovative vision of one of its founders. He realised that nobody was taking advantage of the more distant fishing grounds due to the lack of boats suitable for long trips and the conservation problems for the fish that this represented. In 1961, shortly after its foundation, Pescanova built the first freezer vessel in the world (the "Lemos"), which allowed freezing the fish in the same place where they caught it and later processing the already frozen fish for its commercialisation. The freezer vessels made it possible to discover the largest fisheries, especially in the southern hemisphere, by allowing longer campaigns once they solved the problem of fish preservation.

The "Lemos "At the end of the 1960s, and after several innovations that revolutionised the fishing industry worldwide (such as stern trawling), Pescanova had 100 vessels operating in various parts of the world.

During the 1970s and 1980s, the company developed the leading frozen food logistics network in Spain with more than 150 refrigerated and isothermal trucks, which allowed them to distribute their products throughout the peninsula. Internationally, it extended its activity by creating companies in the southern hemisphere, mainly in Australia, Chile and Argentina, which gave it access to fishing and aquaculture rights in those places. In the 1990s, the company made an extraordinary commitment to aquaculture, with the cultivation of salmon in Chile, shrimp in southern Spain and turbot in northern Spain. Because of the introduction of aquaculture, Pescanova became a fully vertically integrated company.

In the management report of Pescanova's 2011 annual report, the company defined itself as follows: "a unique business proposition, which differentiated itself from its competitors by being a large company in the top 10 list of the seafood industry, vertically integrated, with strong brands, with three aquaculture projects with excellent returns, the largest European fishing fleet, with risk reduction through diversification by species and geography and 50 years of uninterrupted organic growth."

For two decades, the company dedicated its efforts to consolidating the vertical integration model. Through heavy investments, €766 million in fixed assets and acquisitions of other companies between 2008 and 2012, the company expanded its production capacity in shrimp aquaculture in Nicaragua, Honduras, Guatemala and Ecuador, salmon in Chile and turbot in northern Spain and Portugal. In September 2005, the company obtained a 5-year syndicated loan for 100 million euros. In 2009, there was a capital increase of approximately €96 million. Subsequently, in 2010, 2011 and 2012, the company issued three convertible bond issues of €110 million, €180 million, and €160 million, respectively. In 2012, they carried out the last capital increase of 120 million.

From 2008 onwards, access to credit, easy and cheap until then, became more complicated due to the global financial crisis. Pescanova, like many other companies, saw its long-term credit availability restricted under advantageous conditions and had to replace it with short-term credit under worse conditions, much more expensive. A large part of the investments in aquaculture (salmon and turbot) were in species with a long production cycle, around 24 months, so they were in an initial production phase and did not yet produce returns. Moreover, one of the most significant investments during this period, a turbot aquaculture plant, had a problem with the seawater supply, apparently due to a design problem. Consequently, unusually high fish mortality rates occurred during the breeding process, causing an estimated 70 million euros losses. Pescanova never recognised these losses but, on the contrary, recorded a contingent asset amounting to 37 million euros for the possible indemnities that they could collect from the insurance companies.

They designed a fraud scheme to obtain financing, so they created some companies (fourteen) controlled by them but not included in the consolidation perimeter. They used these "fake" companies (they failed to have a real activity) to increase sales fictitiously and, at the same time, obtain short term financing by factoring of trade receivables. They also failed to consolidate some companies by selling the shares before the closing date and repurchasing shares afterwards.c

Incentives/Pressure

- Because of the significant investments the company was involved in, there was high pressure to obtain financing. Getting it from banks had become very difficult due to the financial crisis. That forced the company to issue debt, with the pressure of the absolute necessity to obtain it at a reasonable price, so they had to show the company as unrealistically profitable.

Opportunities

- The Board of Directors and the Audit Committee did not exercise any control over the management decisions. Only two out of 13 members of the board were independent directors. Both had been directors for many years (more than 20 years, one of them), and they were previously linked to shareholder companies.
- The CEO was the board chairman, and the rest of the members were proprietary directors, stable for years until 2011. Although it was a listed company, the founding families, together with the two most relevant local banks, controlled the company as they had more than fifty per cent of the shares and voting rights.
- The corporate structure was large and complex. The group included many associated companies consolidated by the equity method, so they did not include their assets and liabilities in their consolidated balance sheet.
- Due to the forced exit of the local banks from the shareholders, the entry of new shareholders and the appointment of two new board members with no previous relationship with the existing ones discovered the lack of control and the misstatement of the financial statements.
- The auditor's independence was questionable as the firm was billing more for consulting services than for the annual accounts audit.

Rationalisation

- In his final statement during the trial, the chairman of the company declared that *"everything was in the accounting books, there was no concealment. It is just that the way they expressed it was not the appropriate"*
- According to the press releases during the trial, the company's chairman relied on two arguments for his defence: 1) everything was in the accounting, there was no concealment, only misstatement, and 2) The auditor and the regulator never said it was wrong.
- The chairman and member of the founding family also argued that as he was one of the major shareholders, he was the main victim of the fraud, so he considered himself a victim and not a fraudster. He argued that he was one of the biggest losers of the company's bankruptcy as he had lost everything.
- He also argued about the concealment of information of some of the group companies that they could not reveal their competitors where they were making money in the fishing industry as they would come after them.
- The auditor was also convicted. In his defence, he said that he was cheated and misled by the company and only knew about the hidden accounting when it went bankrupt.
- He also argued about the concealment of information of some of the group companies that they could not reveal their competitors where they were making money fishing as they would come after them.

SOME LIMITATIONS OF THE FRAUD TRIANGLE AND FUTURE RESEARCH DIRECTIONS

The examples we have analysed in this chapter would not have been possible without the connivance of many people involved, not only employees and managers but also auditors and bankers. When multiple parties work together for corporate or organisational fraud, the damage caused can be a lot more devastating. Some authors (Dorminey et al., 2012, Villaescusa & Amat, 2021) consider that the Fraud Triangle does not adequately explain the better-organised fraudsters, as these types of criminals have better concealment schemes. The framework analysed does not provide a suitable framework for assessing the likelihood of fraud under conditions of collaboration.

The 2020 Association of Certified Fraud Examiners (ACFE) Report to the Nations show that 51% of the fraud cases examined were perpetrated by two or more fraudsters working in collusion, and 33% by more than three. The study also shows that collusive fraud exponentially multiplies the losses. If the average loss is 90 thousand dollars for a single perpetrator fraud, it raises to 350 thousand when three or more people are involved. Corporate accounting and organisational schemes designed to commit fraud are rarely the work of a single errant executive, as they require coordinated efforts of networks of organisations or individuals because of their complexity. Sometimes, the members of this "fraud consortium" are not only members of the company but also outside members such as bankers, suppliers, customers, and even auditors. Although later found not guilty, Arthur Andersen, Enron's auditor, disappeared as an audit firm after this scandal. Pescanova's auditing firm was ordered to pay millions of euros, and the partner in charge of the audit was sentenced to prison.

When we analyse a case of accounting fraud in collusion, or we suspect it may be in collusion, we must consider that the company may have internal controls that may seem adequate. Fraudsters design procedures that may look like they are efficient and that they work, but the truth is that they don't, basically because the designers are the fraud perpetrators

The Fraud Triangle is not a helpful framework in the case of predator fraudsters. The predator fraudster is an individual who is continuously seeking the opportunity to commit fraud. They don't need a financial non-shareable problem and don't need to rationalise their behaviour. A predator fraudster does not require an incentive nor a rationalisation. They only need the opportunity.

In the last two decades, there has been a vast production in fraud research. However, as we discover new cases, new questions are raised regarding the effectiveness of internal controls and fraudsters profiles.

Some researchers have shown that fraud in collusion is a lot more difficult to detect, as different fraudster profiles are involved. They design internal controls to provide a false image of control. Further research should focus on this characteristic of fraud: what do fraudsters have in common when fraud is in collaboration, and how are corporate governance structures modified or adapted in these cases.

CONCLUSION

Assessing fraud is not an easy task. Historically, audit procedures are not designed for this purpose. However, it seems that the famous accounting scandals over the last decades have changed the game's rules. The auditing standards have included the obligation to determine the risk of fraud as part of the audit procedure.

The Fraud Triangle is the framework that regulators have chosen to assess fraud risk by the audit firms. It offers a helpful framework for analysing and evaluating fraud. However, it also has its limitations, especially in fraud cases with the cooperation of many people. In these cases, although adequately designed, internal controls and corporate governance structures are ineffective as the creators are the same people interested in overriding them. It also proves ineffective when the fraudster is a predator fraudster since they do not need an incentive or rationalisation. They only seek constantly an opportunity to commit fraud.

Charlie Munger, Berkshire Hathaway vice-president, once said: "Show me the incentive, and I will show you the outcome". Sometimes managers do not realize the effect of specific policies adopted by the company regarding compensation schemes or procedures. Opportunities may create incentives and vice versa.

The most powerful characteristic of the fraud triangle is that if only one of the three elements is not present, the likelihood of fraud decreases considerably. For this reason, auditors focus on corporate governance structures as the leading indicator for assessing fraud risk. Strong corporate governance structures, with a board of directors and audit committees independent from management that can exercise a robust control on the company, are among the best indicators of low fraud risk.

The two cases analyzed are Enron in the US and Pescanova in Spain. In the analysis, the authors look at both companies' stories and explain how the three elements were present when the frauds were detected. Although the companies were from very different industries and established in other parts of the world, some characteristics are common. Enron was an energy and commodity trader company, and Pescanova was a fishing company vertically integrated. The main similitudes in both frauds found are

- Both felt high pressure to show the company as particularly profitable and attractive when it was not.
- Both had a high pressure to obtain financing and conceal debt.
- The lack of control that the board exerted over the management, although for different reasons. In the Enron case, the board did not understand the complex business practices and in the case of Pescanova because the managers controlled the committees and the board of directors.
- In both cases, there was a lack of independence of the audit firm that was billing for other consulting services.
- The existence of controlled companies outside the consolidation perimeter, where they deviate debt and losses
- The managers' explanations about their behaviour, considering that nothing illicit was their responsibility and either other people did the illegal act or no illegality.

The main difference in both cases is regarding the accounting practices. Pescanova was a traditional company that used non-permitted accounting techniques, like offsetting assets and liabilities. Enron took some legal accounting practices and pushed them to the limit until they crossed the line of legality.

REFERENCES

Association of Certified Fraud Examiners. (2020). *Report to the Nations. Global Study of occupational fraud and abuse.* Author.

Cohen, J., Ding, Y., Lesage, C., & Stolowy, H. (2010). Corporate Fraud and Managers' Behavior: Evidence from the Press. *Journal of Business Ethics, 95*(S2), 271–315. doi:10.100710551-011-0857-2

Cressey, D. R. (1950). The Criminal Violation of Financial Trust. *American Sociological Review, 15*(6), 738–743. doi:10.2307/2086606

Cressey, D. R. (1953). *Other people's money; a study of the social psychology of embezzlement.* Academic Press.

Dechow, P. M., & Sloan, R. G. (1995). Detecting Earnings Management. *The Accounting Review, 70*(2), 193–225.

Dechow, P. M., Sloan, R. G., & Sweeney, A. P. (1996). Causes and Consequences of Earnings Manipulation: An Analysis of Firms Subject to Enforcement Actions by the SEC. *Contemporary Accounting Research, 13*(1), 1–36. doi:10.1111/j.1911-3846.1996.tb00489.x

Dorminey, J., Fleming, A. S., Kranacher, M.-J., & Jr, R. A. R. (2012). The Evolution of Fraud Theory. *Issues in Accounting Education, 27*(2), 555–579. doi:10.2308/iace-50131

Free, C. (2015). Looking Through the Fraud Triangle: A Review and Call for New Directions. SSRN *Electronic Journal.* doi:10.2139/ssrn.2590952

Free, C., Macintosh, N., & Stein, M. (2007). The organizational fraud triangle: Leadership, culture and control within Enron. *Ivey Business Journal, 32*(1), 18–54.

Hogan, C. E., Rezaee, Z., Riley, R. A. Jr, & Velury, U. K. (2008). Financial Statement Fraud: Insights from the Academic Literature. *Auditing, 27*(2), 231–252. doi:10.2308/aud.2008.27.2.231

Lokanan, M. E. (2015). Challenges to the fraud triangle: Questions on its usefulness. *Accounting Forum, 39*(3), 201–224. doi:10.1016/j.accfor.2015.05.002

Mayhew, B. W., & Murphy, P. R. (2014). The impact of authority on reporting behavior, rationalization and affect. *Contemporary Accounting Research, 31*(2), 420–443. doi:10.1111/1911-3846.12037

Murphy, P. R. (2012). Attitude, Machiavellianism and the rationalization of misreporting. *Accounting, Organizations and Society, 37*(4), 242–259. doi:10.1016/j.aos.2012.04.002

Trompeter, G. M., Carpenter, T. D., Desai, N., Jones, K. L., & Jr, R. A. R. (2012). A synthesis of fraud-related research. *Auditing, 32*(sp1), 287–321. doi:10.2308/ajpt-50360

Villaescusa, N., & Amat, O. (2021). When collusion meets the fraud triangle: A case study approach. *Journal of Financial Crime.* Advance online publication. doi:10.1108/JFC-05-2021-0111

Wolfe, D. T., & Hermanson, D. R. (2004). The Fraud Diamond: Considering the Four Elements of Fraud: Certified Public Accountant. *The CPA Journal, 74*(12), 38–42.

ADDITIONAL READING

Cohen, J., Ding, Y., Lesage, C., & Stolowy, H. (2010). Corporate Fraud and Managers' Behavior: Evidence from the Press. *Journal of Business Ethics*, *95*(S2), 271–315. doi:10.100710551-011-0857-2

Dechow, P. M., & Sloan, R. G. (1995). Detecting Earnings Management. *The Accounting Review*, *70*(2), 193–225.

Dorminey, J. W., Fleming, A. S., Kranacher, M.-J., & Riley, R. A. Jr. (2010). Beyond the Fraud Triangle: Certified Public Accountant. *The CPA Journal*, *80*(7), 3, 17–23.

Free, C., Macintosh, N., & Stein, M. (2007). The organizational fraud triangle: Leadership, culture and control within Enron. *Ivey Business Journal*, *32*(1), 18–54.

Marquardt, C. A., & Wiedman, C. (2004). How Are Earnings Managed? An Examination of Specific Accruals. *Contemporary Accounting Research*, *21*(2), 461–491. doi:10.1506/G4YR-43K8-LGG2-F0XK

Morales, J., Gendron, Y., & Guénin-Paracini, H. (2014). The construction of the risky individual and vigilant organization: A genealogy of the fraud triangle. *Accounting, Organizations and Society*, *39*(3), 170–194. doi:10.1016/j.aos.2014.01.006

Murphy, P. R., & Dacin, M. T. (2011). Psychological Pathways to Fraud: Understanding and Preventing Fraud in Organizations. *Journal of Business Ethics*, *101*(4), 601–618. doi:10.100710551-011-0741-0

Schnatterly, K., Gangloff, K. A., & Tuschke, A. (2018). CEO Wrongdoing: A Review of Pressure, Opportunity, and Rationalization. *Journal of Management*, *44*(6), 2405–2432. doi:10.1177/0149206318771177

Schuchter, A., & Levi, M. (2016). The Fraud Triangle revisited. *Security Journal*, *29*(2), 107–121. doi:10.1057j.2013.1

KEY TERMS AND DEFINITIONS

Collusion: Agreement of people to acttogether secretly or illegally in order to deceive or cheat someone.

Control System: A means of gathering and using information to aid and coordinate the process of making planning and control decisions through- out the organisation and to guide the behaviour of its managers and employees.

Embezzlement: The crime of secretly taking money that is in your care or that belongs to the organisation or business you work for.

Financial Statement Fraud: Delliberate attempt by corporations to deceive or mislead users of published financial statements; especially investors and creditors, by preparing and disseminating materially misstated financial statements.

Incentive: Something that encourages a person to do something.

Misappropriation: The act of stealing something that you have been trusted to take care of and using it for yourself.

Non-Shareable Financial Need: A financial problem that cannot be resolved by seeking the help of another person due to their fear that they will lose status and/or forfeit the respect of others

Pressure: The act of trying to make someone else do something by arguing, persuading, etc.:

Rationalisation: an attempt to find reasons for behaviour, decisions, etc., especially your own

Sarbanes-Oxley Act: A law the U.S. Congress passed on July 30, 2002 of that year to help protect investors from fraudulent financial reporting by corporations.

Chapter 6
Qualitative Study of Fraud Causes in the 21st Century:
US and EU Cases

Fábio dos Santos
University of Aveiro, Portugal

Helena Inácio
https://orcid.org/0000-0003-1281-2156
GOVCOPP, University of Aveiro, Portugal

Maria Anunciação Bastos
https://orcid.org/0000-0002-3825-9304
GOVCOPP, University of Aveiro, Portugal

ABSTRACT

The most popular frauds known in the early 21st century eroded investor and society confidence in the financial markets contributing to economic and social destruction. In response, the United States enacted the Sarbanes-Oxley Act (SOX) and the European Union issued several regulatory instruments, but the fraud cases have continued. Motivated by the idea that if we understand where the possible causes are, then the problem of fraud can be avoided or at least reduced in its dimensions and consequences. So, this study intends to understand the causes of fraud and its relevance, identifying their common points and also measuring if they changed in the post-SOX period. From the analysis carried out, it results that the lack of an ethical tone in top management is the cause that remains transversal to both sides of the Atlantic and to the two periods studied. In the post-SOX period, the fraudulent financial statements lost relevance, ceasing to be part of the most relevant causes, and internal control failures became one of the most relevant causes.

DOI: 10.4018/978-1-7998-8754-6.ch006

INTRODUCTION

In 2001, with the Enron case, a phase of financial scandals broke out, such as WorldCom, Adelphia, and Tyco, in America, followed by others in Europe (Ex.: Parmalat and Vivendi) and elsewhere in the globe. These cases have shaken investor confidence in the capital market worldwide. The United States (US) government responded by legislating, namely by issuing in 2002 the Sarbanes-Oxley Act (SOX) so that such cases would not be repeated. On the European side, instead of a single response, the European Union (EU) created several regulatory instruments to also respond to fraud. Despite all the efforts, it did not take many years for new large-scale fraud cases to reappear (remember the cases of Siemens, Société General or Banco Espírito Santo (BES)). Which begs the question: how did this happen?

This study focuses on understanding the most relevant causes that led to the fraud cases, motivated by the idea that the understanding of the probable causes, the problem of fraud can be avoided or at least reduced in its dimension and consequences. Thus, this study aims to understand if there are common points between the various frauds before and after SOX in US and EU and seeks to know whether the effort made resulted in a change in the relevance of the causes of fraud in the post-SOX period.

To meet its objectives, this chapter compares the relevance of each cause to the outbreak of fraud in a sample of US and EU cases, in the periods before and after the implementation of SOX, analyzing common causes and identifying their relevance changed after the entry into force of the different responses.

The present work is structured in five parts: introduction, background, methodology, multiple fraud case study and conclusions.

BACKGROUND

Fraud and Audit Role

Fraud Concept and Determinants

The concept of fraud is complex and without a single consensual definition. Considering the International Standard on Auditing (ISA) 240, fraud is defined as being "an intentional act by one or more individuals among management, those charged with governance, employees, or third parties, involving the use of deception to obtain an unjust or illegal advantage" (International Auditing and Assurance Standards Board [IAASB], 2020, p. 168).

The issue of the act intentionality on the part of the individual is of particular importance given that ISA 240 (IAASB, 2020) distinguishes fraud from error based on the intention of the act: if it is intentionally intended to distort financial reports, it is considered fraud, otherwise it will be considered an error.

At the business level, frauds are so diverse that they can be divided from financial to commercial, including real estate, accounting, technological and other types of fraud (Bonotto, 2010; Parodi, 2008).

Throughout this work, within the broad concept of fraud, greater relevance is given to what the Association of Certified Fraud Examiners (ACFE, 2020, p. 6) defines as occupational fraud - "the use of one's occupation for personal enrichment through the deliberate misuse or misapplication of the employing organization's resources or assets". The concept of occupational fraud includes corruption, misappropriation of assets and fraudulent financial reporting.

Corruption occurs when an individual misuses their influence in a business, infringing on their obligations to their employer and thereby obtaining direct or indirect advantages.

Asset misappropriation results from the individual stealing or misusing the organization's assets.

Fraudulent financial reporting occurs when an individual intentionally misrepresents or omits important data in the organization's financial reports. It is this type of occupational fraud that is the object of study in this chapter.

From the 2,504 cases of occupational fraud that were investigated between January 2018 and September 2019 by ACFE, fraudulent financial reporting represents the lowest percentage of cases (10%), but in terms of average losses it is the type of occupational fraud that represents the highest values, namely, 954,000$ per case against the 100,000$ of misappropriation of assets that represents 86% of the cases that occurred (ACFE, 2020).

It should be noted that, despite the measures taken, namely SOX and community regulation, cases of fraudulent financial reporting increased from 4.8% in 2010 to 9.6% in 2016 and 10% in 2020 (ACFE, 2014, 2016, 2020). Thus, they doubled from 2010 to 2016 and from 2016 to 2020 were maintained, but also did not decrease, which may indicate that the measures adopted may not be the most adequate to combat this type of fraud.

The importance of this type of fraud led, in 2016, the president of the US Securities and Exchange Commission (SEC) to confirm that they will continue to increase the scrutiny of financial reporting and its gatekeepers (Ernst & Young, 2016). Also, according to the ACFE study (2020), the executive/upper management department is the department that most commits financial reporting fraud, which is associated with the fact that owners/executives are the ones who cause the highest average losses in cases of fraud, it follows that top executives and owners are one of the main culprits in this type of fraud. ACFE (2016) reports that since 1996, when this type of reporting on fraud began, a strong correlation has always been noted between the level of authority of the perpetrator and the dimension of the fraud committed by him.

Cressey, a well-known North American criminologist, made a fundamental contribution to the understanding of fraud by presenting, in 1953, the Fraud Triangle, an explanatory model of the factors that lead an individual to commit fraud, consisting of 3 components that, together, result in fraudulent behavior. The components are incentive/pressures, opportunity, and attitude/rationalization (M. Almeida, 2015).

The incentive/pressure is what motivates the individual to commit fraud. This point is usually related to financial problems that the individual cannot solve by legitimate means, thus turning to fraud as a solution to their problem (ACFE, 2018; M. Almeida, 2015). At the level of top management, it is often associated with the pressure to increase/reduce (depending, for example, on the tax burden of a given country) the company's results, achieving performance goals or showing a better situation of the company to stakeholders (ACFE, 2018; M. Almeida, 2015). According to Albrecht, Holland, Malagueño, Dolan and Tzafrir (2015), in cases of fraudulent financial reporting, the motivation felt by the individual is often related to the potential negative result of disclosing the company's true performance, since the financial results have an enormous influence on the company's market value. This market value often influences the professional stability and financial rewards of individuals who serve as top executives in these companies. According to Ernst & Young (2016), 36% of Chief Financial Officers (CFO) and 46% of other members of the finance team may opt for unethical conduct when subjected to pressure.

The opportunity is the gateway for fraud to be committed. The individual understands that there is a way or a method that they can take advantage of to solve their problem with a minimal risk of being discovered (ACFE, 2018). Weak or non-existent controls are usually examples of this type of opportunity

(M. Almeida, 2015; Bernardo, Lima, Medeiros, & Miranda, 2017). According to PricewaterhouseCoopers (2018), 59% of companies consider that the main factor for the fraud or economic crime to have happened was the opportunity.

The attitude/rationalization is related to the individual's moral and ethical attitudes and refers to the justification he presents for carrying out the fraud (M. Almeida, 2015). It is common for the individual to find as justifications the fact that it is a temporary situation, that they are only borrowing money or that other companies adopt the same behaviors (ACFE, 2018; Bernardo et al., 2017). When rationalizing, the individual also considers that the advantages of fraudulent behavior outweigh the risk he is taking (Wolfe & Hermanson, 2004). According to Ernst & Young (2016), 42% of CFOs can justify unethical behavior to achieve financial goals.

In the 21st century, considering the increase in the regularity and severity of fraud cases, the Fraud Triangle evolved to the Fraud Diamond, through the addition of another vertex, capacity. According to Wolfe and Hermanson (2004), capacity is understood as the individual's personal characteristics and abilities so that fraud can effectively occur.

In continuation of these studies, Dorminey, Scott, Kranacher and Riley (2012) present an evolution from the Diamond of Fraud to the Pentagon of Fraud, with 5 vertices, having as a common point the element of opportunity and highlighting the difference between the accidental criminal and the predator that is recurrent in crime. However, the Fraud Triangle remains the most accepted and used theory as shown in several of the articles and publications (C. Albrecht et al., 2015; W. Albrecht, C. Albrecht, & C. C. Albrecht, 2008; PricewaterhouseCoopers, 2018; Soltani, 2014). It should also be noted that Appendix 1 of ISA 240 (IAASB, 2020) identifies several examples of risk factors for the occurrence of fraudulent financial reporting associated with the components of the fraud triangle.

The Role of the Auditor in Relation to Fraud

Since, according to ISA 200 §3, the audit objective is "enhance the degree of confidence of intended users in the financial statements" (IAASB, 2020, p. 81), the auditor must obtain "reasonable assurance about whether the financial statements are free from material misstatement, whether due to fraud or error" (IAASB, 2020, p. 83). Thus, the auditor obviously has an important relationship with the phenomenon of fraud, presenting ISA 240 (IAASB, 2020) several points of the relationship between the auditor and fraud, and clarifying several issues, such as the fact of those in charge of governance and the management are those primarily responsible for preventing and discovering fraud. ISA 240 (IAASB, 2020) refers that the possibility of not detecting a materially relevant misstatement is higher when there is fraud than when there is an error, because the efficient audit procedures for error detection may not be when it comes to fraud. The detection of fraud can become even more complicated for the auditor when there is collusion between several parties to perpetrate this fraud and conceal it (IAASB, 2020) since, from this pact between several individuals, results more elaborate and complex schemes of fraud. C. Albrecht et al. (2015) report that there are studies indicating that the majority of fraudulent financial reporting cases are carried out in collusion by several individuals within an organization. The more elements that participate in the fraud, the greater the average loss associated with that fraud (ACFE, 2016, 2020; KPMG International, 2016). However, despite the increase in complexity and costs for the company, ACFE (2016, 2020) states that collusive frauds do not last much longer than those committed by only one individual, from which it is drawn that they are not necessarily harder to detect.

Thus, fraud detection is not an audit objective in itself, but it is one of the risks to be considered throughout the audit process. Ismajli, Perjuci, and Prenaj (2019) concluded that external auditors consider a high potential risk of errors and fraud, have adverse attitudes against errors and fraud, and that there is a negative relationship between errors, fraud, and financial reporting. They also concluded that the audit quality positively affects the detection of the financial statements' fraud or errors.

Linking the auditor's role with the fraud triangle, we can say that the external auditor, while also having a role in reducing the opportunity for the appearance of fraud, focuses its attention and relationship on the attitude/rationalization element, since it is a deterrent to the individual who intends to commit fraud. It should be noted that, in the case of the internal auditor, whose action involves the assessment and improvement of internal control, the focus will be on reducing opportunity as a necessary element for the occurrence of fraud.

Fraud Answers

The Sarbanes-Oxley Act in the US

The Public Company Accounting Reform and Investor Protection Act of 2002 or, as it is commonly known, the Sarbanes-Oxley Act (SOX), signed in July 2002, applied to listed companies in the US, aimed to achieve through regulation and the creation of the Public Company Accounting Oversight Board (PCAOB) to oversee audit activities (SEC, nd), the restoring of shareholder confidence that their investments are protected, and similar scandals will not be repeated.

According to Anand (2007), to achieve this goal, SOX considered 3 principles:

- Integrity: companies with high ethical and moral behavior, present complete, relevant, and representative financial information.
- Accuracy: the information disclosed must be reliable and accurate, in the sense of exact, hence the reinforcement of controls.
- Accountability: make management and financial reporting executives accountable and make the entire process more transparent. As they are the last to analyze the final financial reports to be published, this responsibility normally falls to the Chief Executive Officer (CEO) and CFO of the companies (F. Almeida, 2014).

In brief, and according to Morales (2005), it is possible to condense the main contents of SOX into the following points: i) Improvement of the quality of public information and its details; ii) Increased responsibilities for corporate governance of companies; iii) Improvement of ethical conduct and behavior with increased responsibility on issues such as improper management of confidential information; iv) Strengthening supervision; v) Increased sanctions for non-compliance; and, vi) Increased demand and pressure on the effective independence of auditors.

The studies carried out on the effects of SOX are numerous, however, the results obtained are not always consensual.

As regards the positive consequences of SOX, there are: a positive image in the eyes of the public (Alkhafaji, 2007) and increased confidence in capital markets (Coates, 2007); the creation by companies of measures to combat fraudulent behavior (Ahmed, McAnally, Rasmussen, & Weaver, 2010); strengthening internal control (Patterson, Smith & Patterson, 2007); the large decrease in fraud (Patterson, Smith &

Patterson, 2007; Jahmani & Dowling, 2008); the increase in public scrutiny of companies (F. Almeida, 2014; Leuz, 2007); increasing the quality of financial reporting (Coates & Srinivasan, 2014).

With regard to the negative consequences of SOX, it should be noted that they are essentially related to the increase in costs, on the one hand, of the external audit itself, which now has to comment on the assessment of key internal controls and, therefore, auditing internal controls (F. Almeida, 2014), on the other hand, by the companies audited due to the need to hire new employees in order to respond to SOX requirements (Carney, 2006); increased number of Audit Committee meetings (Linck, Netter & Yang, 2009); increased costs with company directors as a result of the greater responsibility that these professionals had to assume with the new legislation (Linck, Netter & Yang, 2009).

Finally, it should be noted that SOX, affecting companies at a global level, have also influenced legislation in other parts of the planet (Elbling, 2015). An example of this is Japan, with the so-called "J-SOX", or even the EU, with amendments to directives and other regulations that adopted various points of SOX (Coates & Srinivasan, 2014).

European Regulatory Instruments

In Europe, since the 1990s, with the Commission's Green Paper (1996) on the role, status and responsibility of the auditor, various reflection measures and recommendations were taken on the issues of fraud, corporate governance, and auditing.

In 2002, Recommendation 2002/590/EC on the independence of auditors was issued and, in July, Regulation (EC) No 1606/2002 of the European Parliament and of the Council was published, which requires the adoption of the international accounting standards adopted by the EU to the consolidated accounts of listed entities, and for individual accounts of listed entities was left to the discretion of member states. According to Fernandes (2010), this regulation has similarities with SOX in targeting listed companies and aiming to increase the transparency of financial information, to restore investor confidence, reinforce public confidence in audit professionals and increase sustainability of organizations. In November 2002, the report of the High-Level Group of Company Law Experts was published, entitled "A Modern Regulatory Framework for Company Law in Europe".

In January 2003, Directive 2003/6/EC of the European Parliament and of the Council on insider dealing and market manipulation (market abuse) was issued. In May of the same year, the Commission of the European Communities issues a communication to the Council and the European Parliament on company law and corporate governance (Commission of the European Communities, 2003), as well as a communication on strengthening the audit of accounts in the EU (European Commission, 2003).

In 2005, the European Commission created the European Group of Auditor's Oversight Bodies, a body to ensure effective coordination of new systems for oversight of auditors in the EU (CMVM, nd), having supervisory powers like those of the PCAOB (M. Almeida, 2015). In the same year, the Committee draws up a recommendation on the role of non-executive directors or members of the supervisory board of listed companies and the committees of the board of directors or supervisory board, addressing issues such as conflict of interest at management level.

With the revision of the VIII Directive carried out by Directive 2006/43/EC of the European Parliament and of the Council, greater focus is given to the auditor's independence and to improving the quality of their work, to recover the society trust in financial markets (C. B. Costa, 2019). This directive was amended in 2014 by Directive 2014/56/EU of the European Parliament and of the Council, together with the publication of Regulation (EU) No 537/2014 of the European Parliament and of the Council on specific requirements for the review legal accounts of public interest entities. This regulation is intended, among other things, to strengthen the auditor's independence and objectivity, establish the use of international auditing standards in the EU and improve the understanding of the audit report (Elbling, 2015), being that this reinforcement is much greater in entities of public interest.

From the analysis of the various documents issued by the EU at the end of the 1990s of the last century and the beginning of the new century, it is understood that the EU did not only react when the financial scandals started to emerge in the US and Europe, but that it was discussing for some time several issues such as the independence of auditors, their quality control, or areas such as corporate governance. Unlike the US, the EU has not produced only a major response to early 21st century fraud, as US has done with SOX.

Empirical Research in the Area

Several studies have been carried out on the common points that exist between the different frauds (Silveira, 2013, 2015; Soltani, 2014).

Silveira (2013) identifies 14 causes that he considers to be common to 11 large global financial and media frauds from the beginning of the 21st century, in a pre-SOX era, but also in the period 2007-2009, a time after the approval of this legislation. The causes identified are: i) Excessive concentration of power; ii) Ineffective Board of Directors; iii) Passivity of investors; iv) Failure of gatekeepers; v) Weak regulation; vi) Illusion of business success; vii) Inner atmosphere of greed and arrogance; viii) Lack of ethical tone in top management; ix) Corporate governance seen as a marketing tool; x) Over-expansion of the business; xi) Bad strategic decisions; xii) Corrupted financial statements; xiii) Weak internal controls; and, xiv) Inadequate compensation system. The author concludes that several of the lessons that could have been learned from the Enron scandal have not been learned, although he highlights positive aspects that have resulted from the Enron scandal, and others, at the beginning of the 21st century. Two years later, the author publishes a working paper which extends from 11 to 23 the number of frauds analyzed in relation to the 14 causes identified in the previous study, this time focusing on the need for a new behavioral approach to the theme of corporate governance (Silveira, 2015).

The Organization for Economic Co-operation and Development (OECD), after the financial crisis of the beginning of the 21st century, issued a report on what corporate governance lessons can be learned from that crisis. According to the OECD (2009), there are 4 common areas related to companies, but also related to each other, that triggered this crisis and that need to be improved: the incentive and remuneration system, which is inadequate; risk management practices that are inefficient; the performance of boards of directors, which is weak; and the exercise of shareholder rights, which tends to be reactive rather than proactive.

Hamilton and Micklethwait (2006) analyze 9 media cases of company failures at the end of the last century and beginning of the 21st century, all of them North American and European cases. During this analysis, the authors conclude that the common causes among the various cases are: poor strategic decisions; over-expansion and miscalculated acquisitions; dominant CEOs; greed, arrogance, and desire for power; failure of internal controls; and ineffective boards of directors.

Coffee (2005) mentions as causes for fraud an inadequate remuneration/compensation system and the failure of gatekeepers in their functions. Regarding the inadequate remuneration/compensation system, the author gives an example of financial statement restatement: companies in which CEOs are compensated with greater facilities to buy shares of the company itself (typical in the US) they are also more likely to change the financial statements presented due to earnings management. In the European case, the focus is on the majority shareholders who withdraw private benefits from companies, emptying them of value, as a form of remuneration. Regarding gatekeepers, the author refers to their failure to predict and avoid or, at least, report situations such as earnings management or the "expropriation of private benefits", which later results in the loss of market value, by companies when correcting their financial statements.

Soltani (2014) compares a total of six frauds (three North American and three European) using a theoretical framework that includes six areas: i) Corporate ethical climate and management misconduct; ii) Tone at the top and executive leadership; iii) Environmental factors including bubble economy and market pressure; iv) Accountability, control mechanisms, auditing, and corporate governance; v) Executive personal interest, compensation package and bonus; and, vi) Fraud, fraudulent financial reporting and earnings. The author concluded that common features of the European and American Corporate failures are poor ethical climate; greed; corruption; fraud; misconduct management; lack of effective control and governance mechanisms; and impaired auditor independence within these groups. He also concluded with the analysis from the fraud triangle perspective on the evidence of the existence of some incentives. Finally, he concluded that the conditions were favorable to fraudulent actions, as the control mechanisms and corporate governance policies were ineffective. Additionally, the regulation was soft and flexible.

Rezaee (2005) found 7 common causes of fraud: i) Lack of vigilance on the part of those who would have this function (as in the case of boards of directors and audit committees); ii) Arrogant and greedy management; iii) Business misconduct by top management; iv) Ineffective auditing functions; v) Weak laws; vi) Inadequate and non-transparent financial statements; and vii) Inattentive shareholders.

Castellano and Lightle (2005) indicate ethics (or lack thereof) in top management as a crucial factor in triggering fraud, suggesting an audit of the company culture to avoid negative consequences for companies. The same authors refer to the issue of compensation and incentive plans that, if inadequate, can act as a factor for illegal and unethical behavior in earnings management.

Coenen (2008) identifies the following reasons as the primary causes of fraud at the corporate level: pressure from investors and the market on managers to achieve short-term goals in terms of company results; compensation for managers often linked to the value of the company's shares; and, the greed, inherent to human nature, and that corrupts managers.

Grant and Visconti (2006) analyzed 12 listed companies, both in the US and in Europe, which in the period 2001 to 2003 were involved in major accounting scandals. Not disregarding other works with different views, these authors argue that the failures in the process of building strategic decisions by the companies involved in these scandals should also be considered as causes of accounting scandals.

KPMG International (2016) highlights weak internal controls as the biggest contributor to facilitating fraud and points to personal gain and greed as the initial motive of most people who committed fraud in the different cases they examined.

Dowd (2016) examines a total of 4 fraud cases, considering those that happened before and after the implementation of SOX, analyzing the similarities and differences between pre- and post-SOX cases, with the conclusions focused on the benefits of SOX, in particular, the reduction of fraud cases.

W. Albrecht et al. (2008), in an analysis of the frauds of the 90s and the beginning of the 21st century, consider that there were 9 reasons why frauds occurred on such a large scale. In the same article, the authors relate these 9 reasons to the 3 elements of the Fraud Triangle: inadequate incentives for executives, unrealistic Wall Street expectations, enormous amounts of debt, greed – incentives/pressures; economic results concealed several problems, selective interpretation of accounting rules, behavior of audit firms – opportunity; and moral decay of society, failures in educators – attitude/rationalization.

Dewi and Anisykurlillah (2021) analyzed the effect of fraud pentagon on fraudulent financial statements with audit committee as moderating variable using data from 52 companies in the property, real estate and construction sectors of companies listed on the Indonesia Stock Exchange during the period 2016 to 2018. The authors have concluded that company growth has a positive effect on fraudulent financial statements, being that the audit committee weakens this effect. Factors such as the effectiveness of supervision, the quality of external auditors, the experience of directors, and CEO duality do not affect fraudulent financial statements. The authors have also concluded that audit committee weakens too the effect of the effectiveness of supervision, and the experience of the directors on fraudulent financial statements.

As we have seen, there are several studies carried out on the causes of large frauds, however they focus only on different geographies, or in the pre and post sox period, but there are no studies that relate these two aspects to understand if the implemented measures produced any it is made.

METHODOLOGY

Objectives, Questions, and Research Method

Despite the various initiatives, at the beginning of the 21st century, to reduce the occurrence of fraud, new frauds of high dimension and media coverage re-emerged on both sides of the Atlantic. Thus, it is of particular interest to understand the regularity and relevance of the causes that led to the frauds in the two periods, pre and post-SOX. Thus, this study's main objective is to understand if there are common points in the causes that triggered some cases of fraud in the two geographic spaces (US and EU) and in the two-time horizons (pre and post-SOX). The secondary objective is to assess whether the causes of fraud in the second period have changed, considering the regulations created after the first period of fraud.

Consequently, the research questions are:

- Are there commonalities in the causes that triggered public fraud in the 21st century in the US and the EU?
- Are the most relevant causes for the outbreak of fraud in the pre-SOX period keep in the post-SOX period in the North American and European reality?

To answer these questions, the case study method is used, which is based on the study of singular and unique situations to better understand a phenomenon of interest (Oliveira & Ferreira, 2014) – in this study, particular cases of fraud are analyzed with a view to a global understanding of the phenomenon of fraud. According to Oliveira and Ferreira (2014), this study is considered an exploratory case study since it aims to understand a phenomenon (the various causes of fraud) in a specific temporal and geographic context and is still little discussed. According to Yin (1994) it is a multiple case study since several fraud cases are studied that are later compared.

The approach used is qualitative, which argues that phenomena can be better understood if they are framed in the context in which they happen (Oliveira & Ferreira, 2014). This approach is interpretive and subjective, using induction to clarify phenomena and understand the global phenomenon - the relevance of various fraud causes is defined based on qualitative data converted into a value, which definition, although justified, has an interpretive nature and a degree of subjectivity.

Sample and Data Processing

The selection of the frauds object of study is based on studies carried out by Silveira (2013, 2015) but considering the geographic and temporal comparison that is intended to be made. In this study, as sample selection criteria, are considered only those fraud cases that meet, cumulatively, the following points:

- Fraud occurred in US companies or companies from EU countries (criterion 1);
- Fraud occurred in companies with securities admitted to trading on a regulated market (criterion 2);
- Fraud with a large scale and economic impact (criterion 3);
- Duly proven fraud, excluding those where there was a media scandal due to the bankruptcy/fall of the company, but there was no conviction in the courts (criterion 4); and,
- Fraud with information available in quantity and quality that allows a reasoned analysis of the relevance of its causes (criterion 5).

Considering these criteria, of the 23 fraud cases studied by Silveira (2015) 12 were used. Although the author considers the case of the French multinational Vivendi as "uncertain" in relation to fraud, it was identified as such by several authors (SEC, nd; Raymond, 2016; Soltani, 2014; Gates, Prachyl, & Sullivan, 2016; Grant & Visconti, 2006; Umar, Sitorus, Surya, Shauki, & Diyanti, 2017). The remaining North American and European post-SOX fraud cases present in Silveira's study are not considered in this study because the companies did not meet the criteria. Additionally, at European level, the case of BES is considered, which shook the Portuguese economy. On this particular case, although it is not yet concluded, as several court cases are still underway and there is no confirmation at the criminal level that it was a fraud, the intense debate that was held and still continues in the public square, the publication of several journalistic and scientific articles and the report of a parliamentary commission of inquiry, the size of the case, as well as the various dissertations on the subject, lead to the BES case being considered as a fraud of special interest in the post-SOX for the purposes of this study. At the North American level, despite the research carried out, it was not possible to find frauds in the post-SOX period (apart from the initial group studied by Silveira in 2015) that fulfilled the aforementioned criteria, so only this initial group will be considered.

Table 1 presents the fraud cases that make up the sample, identifying the geographic area to which they belong (US or EU) and the time period to which they are involved (before or after the implementation of SOX).

A total of 13 fraud cases are considered in this study, of which 6 are related to the US and 7 to the EU. At the temporal level, 9 cases take place in the period before the implementation of SOX and 4 take places after that period.

In the case of this study, content analysis is used, one of the techniques most frequently used in qualitative research in social and human sciences (Vilelas, 2009).

Based on the causes considered by Silveira (2015) and considering the numerous studies presented above, the causes to be used in this study (twelve) are those presented in Table 2.

Based on W. Albrecht et al. (2008), in conjunction with other authors, it is possible to relate the causes previously considered for the outbreak of fraud with the 3 elements of the Fraud Triangle. Table 3 presents this relationship.

Table 1. Fraud cases used as a sample by geographic area and time period

Fraud	Geographic area	Time period
ENRON	US	Pre-SOX
Worldcom	US	Pre-SOX
XEROX	US	Pre-SOX
Adelphia	US	Pre-SOX
Tyco	US	Pre-SOX
Refco	US	Pos-SOX
Vivendi	EU	Pre-SOX
Parmalat	EU	Pre-SOX
Royal Ahold	EU	Pre-SOX
Royal Dutch Shell	EU	Pre-SOX
Siemens	EU	Pos-SOX
Société Générale	EU	Pos-SOX
BES	EU	Pos-SOX

Although not mentioned by other authors, it is considered that the passiveness of investors is interconnected with the vertex of opportunity because when investors do not play their role actively and reward unsustainable practices, they create conditions for fraud to be committed. Likewise, distorted financial statements only exist when there is an opportunity for this to happen.

In establishing a relationship between the common causes of fraud and the cases under analysis, the methodology used by Silveira (2013, 2015) is followed, classifying the causes into 4 levels of relevance: "0" when the cause was not relevant to the case in question, "1" when the cause was relevant to the initiation of the fraud; "2" when the cause was highly relevant; and "3" when the cause was critical for triggering the fraud.

As this is a subjective criterion and the aim is to compare the results with those obtained by Silveira (2013, 2015), two of the fraud cases studied by the author were analyzed, to conclude whether with the information available on the cases, it results in evaluations of causes close to those of Silveira (2013, 2015). The criteria for choosing these cases were: valid information that is easy to obtain, scientific data about the frauds in analysis, and the existence of a representative fraud from each of the 2 geographies (US and EU). In this way, the cases of Enron (US) and Parmalat (EU) were analyzed, resulting in 20 classifications of causes like the 24 of Silveira (2015), so the same logical-deductive reasoning was followed in the classification of the different causes for the case BES added in this study and whose analysis is presented in Table 4.

To outline the investigation sequence, Figure 1 presents the various steps taken.

Table 2. Common causes for the outbreak of fraud used in the chapter and authors who address them

Common causes for the outbreak of fraud		Studies that address specified causes
Designation	**Meaning**	
Excessive concentration of power	Business decisions usually reflect the vision of an individual or a small number of them, and there is no counterbalance to this vision	Hamilton and Micklethwaith (2006), IAASB (2020), Silveira (2013, 2015), Soltani (2014)
Ineffective Board of Directors	The Board of Directors does not properly supervise the management, nor does it provide appropriate strategic management.	Hamilton and Micklethwaith (2006), OECD (2009), Rezaee (2005), Silveira (2013, 2015), Soltani (2014), W. Albrecht et al. (2008)
Investor passivity	Shareholders do not have an active role, but rather a reactive one, therefore attributing too much importance to companies that have unsustainable practices that only aim to increase market value	OECD (2009), Rezaee (2005), Silveira (2013, 2015), Soltani (2014)
Gatekeepers' failures	They do not fulfill their functions, hiding behind the reputation they have	Coffee (2004, 2005), Rezaee (2005), Silveira (2013, 2015), Soltani (2014), W. Albrecht et al. (2008)
Weak regulation	Lack of regulation or defective regulation allow for problems at the level of corporate governance	Rezaee (2005), Silveira (2013, 2015), Soltani (2014), W. Albrecht et al. (2008)
Business over-expansion	The excessive growth of the company, with a special focus on the acquisition of other companies, in the years prior to the management problems	Grant and Visconti (2006), Hamilton e Micklethwaith (2006), Silveira (2013, 2015), W. Albrecht et al. (2008)
Bad strategic decisions	Management adopts strategic decisions that are harmful to the company due to overconfidence or irrational obedience to authority, and the objective of affecting the company is not intentional.	Grant and Visconti (2006), Hamilton e Micklethwaith (2006), Silveira (2013, 2015), W. Albrecht et al. (2008)
Biased financial statements	The published financial statements are intentionally altered not reflecting a correct image of the company	Rezaee (2005), Silveira (2013, 2015), Soltani (2014),
Weak internal controls	Basic elements of effective internal control are lacking namely an adequate control environment, control activities or effective risk management	Hamilton and Micklethwaith (2006), IAASB (2020), KPMG International (2016), OECD (2009), Silveira (2013, 2015), Soltani (2014), W. Albrecht et al. (2008)
Inadequate compensation system	The payment of remuneration and incentives based on short-term goals, with highly aggressive goals, leading to problems at the level of the company's management	Castellano and Lightle (2005), Coenen (2008), Coffee (2004, 2005), IAASB (2020), OECD (2009), Silveira (2013, 2015), Soltani (2014), W. Albrecht et al. (2008),
Inner atmosphere of greed and arrogance	An internal environment of euphoria and arrogance creates the feeling that those who are inside the company are superior to those who are not part of it.	Coenen (2008), Hamilton and Micklethwaith (2006), KPMG International (2016), Rezaee (2005), Silveira (2013, 2015), Soltani (2014), W. Albrecht et al. (2008)
Lack of ethical tone in top management	Company leaders do not promote high ethical values and principles disregarding this theme	Castellano and Lightle (2005), Coenen (2008), IAASB (2020), Rezaee (2005), Silveira (2013, 2015), Soltani (2014), W. Albrecht et al. (2008)

STUDY OF MULTIPLE FRAUD CASES

Relevance of Common Causes to Trigger Fraud

Table 3. Relationship between the elements of the Fraud Triangle and the 12 common causes for the outbreak of fraud

Elements of the Fraud Triangle	12 common causes for the outbreak of fraud
Incentives/Pressures	Inadequate compensation system (W. Albrecht et al., 2008; IAASB, 2020)
	Inner atmosphere of greed and arrogance (W. Albrecht et al., 2008)
Opportunity	Excessive concentration of power (IAASB, 2020; Soltani, 2014)
	Ineffective Board of Directors (W. Albrecht et al., 2008; IAASB, 2020; Soltani, 2014)
	Weak internal controls (W. Albrecht et al., 2008; IAASB, 2020; Soltani, 2014)
	Bad strategic decisions (W. Albrecht et al., 2008)
	Business over-expansion (W. Albrecht et al., 2008)
	Gatekeepers' failures (W. Albrecht et al., 2008)
	Weak regulation (W. Albrecht et al., 2008)
	Investor passivity
	Biased financial statements
Attitude/rationalization	Lack of ethical tone in top management (W. Albrecht et al., 2008; IAASB, 2020; Soltani, 2014)

Pre-SOX Cases

Table 5 shows the relevance of common causes of pre-SOX fraud, both in the US and in the EU. For the purposes of comparative analysis, mean and mode were also calculated.

Comparing the 2 geographic realities, the most relevant common causes are, on average, the lack of ethical tone in top management and biased financial statements. Regarding the less relevant causes identified, these are, on average, the investors' passivity, and weak regulation.

The difference in the degree of relevance of some causes between the 2 geographies stands out. Even though it is one of the causes with the lowest mean and mode both in the US and in the EU, weak regulation is considered truly relevant in the US, but only relevant in the EU, which indicates that the latter already had stronger regulatory mechanisms than the US during the pre-SOX period frauds (as mentioned in the EU Fraud Responses topic). It is interesting to note that the answer to mitigate the scourge of fraud and prevent similar cases to those analyzed came through the strengthening of regulation, namely, in the maintenance of adequate key controls, although this cause was considered one of the least relevant in the pre-SOX period.

Gatekeeper failures also have a substantial difference in relevance between the US and the EU. With an average of 2.4, this cause has an almost critical relevance in the US, but in the EU the relevance is, on average, 1.5. It is possible to assume that the strong link between US fraud and inefficient gatekeepers, such as auditors and financial analysts, had an influence on the creation of the PCAOB or Title V (on analysts' conflicts of interest) in the SOX.

The inadequate compensation system has the 3rd biggest difference between the relevance of causes in the US and EU (2.2 in the US and 1.5 in the EU). As the North American market is more focused on market capitalization and stock market gains than the European market, it is natural to find this difference.

Table 4. Common causes for the outbreak of BES fraud

Common causes for the outbreak of fraud	Relevance	Interpretation of available information
Excessive concentration of power	3	- The CEO took on several presidency positions in different bodies, concentrating a lot of information and decisions that were not always communicated to other responsible (CPI, 2015; Gomes, 2017; Morais, 2014)
Ineffective Board of Directors	3	- Passivity of some management members (CPI, 2015) - Dispersion and complexity under the control of the CEO, allowing assets to be disposed of in his own way (CPI, 2015) - Lack of formal meetings of the Board of Directors of one of the group's top companies (CPI, 2015) - Regarding BES's Board of Directors: - it was numerous and 3 of the 7 independent members were not truly so (Gomes, 2017) - until 2007, the chairman was the uncle of the CEO (Gomes, 2017) - it was seen as not having a real supervisory action (Simões, 2014) - BES' majority shareholder was withdrawing funds from the bank in order to finance other non-financial businesses (Morais, 2014)
Investor passivity	0	- Capital increase even with high risks that were already identified, but were not known by investors (Morais, 2014) - Large investors sold an abnormal number of shares on the last day before the BES resolution (Coelho, 2014; CPI, 2015) - There were requests for clarification on various matters at the end of 2013 from the shareholder Crédit Agricole
Gatekeepers' failures	3	- In the transfer of testimony to KPMG, PwC warned, in 2002, about the group's various structural problems. However, the KPMG reports do not mention any alerts (CPI, 2015) - BES Angola's audit reports, despite some reservations and emphases, did not warn of the poor situation of the credit portfolio (CPI, 2015; Morais, 2014) - The CPI (2015) concluded that the various external audits of BES and other group companies were not effective in identifying and alerting on existing problems
Weak regulation	3	- In the passing of witness- Following the BES scandal, Banco de Portugal issued recommendations with specific suggestions to regulate the accumulation of functions, exercise of certain positions or its relationship with the banking entities external auditors (Banco de Portugal, 2015) - After the BES scandal, legal changes emerged to strengthen the Bank of Portugal's effective intervention skills and capacities (CPI, 2015) - The CPI report (2015) listed several recommendations to be implemented in order to avoid other cases - The CPI (2015) concluded that the level of collaboration and articulation between the various BES supervisors was below expectations - The lack of adequate regulation at the time of the fraud is demonstrated
Business over-expansion	0	- In the research carried out, no direct references were found to an over-expansion of BES's business that was relevant in the outbreak of fraud
Bad strategic decisions	2	- There were contradictory decisions regarding the good principles of financial management in the case of BES, namely, to use short-term instruments to support medium or long-term investments (CPI, 2015) - According to Fialho (2015), the figure of the CEO was taken by employees as a reference, denoting an irrational obedience to his authority - Employees had the illusion of invulnerability, tending to devalue negative indicators about the bank (Fialho, 2015) - The non-use of state support by BES after the arrival of the Troika, unlike other national banks, harmed shareholders (Morais, 2014)
Biased financial statements	3	- As of 2008 there was, according to the CPI (2015, p. 264) "a systematic concealment of liabilities and/or overvaluation of assets" in one of the group companies - From 2008 to 2012 there was a great increase in the distortion of accounts (CPI, 2015; Morais, 2014) - It were identified distortions in the order of 759 million overvalued real estate assets (CPI, 2015)
Weak internal controls	3	- The need to improve internal controls was pointed out, on several occasions, by its auditors over the years and by Banco de Portugal, and was later identified by the forensic audit, namely, the segregation of functions (CPI, 2015) - BES' audit committee and remuneration committee included members who were not effectively independent (Gomes, 2017) - Several BES administrators had credits granted by the bank itself, without respecting internal procedures and regulations (CPI, 2015) - Large loans were granted, without guarantees, to group companies controlled by the CEO's family (C. A. Costa, 2017)
Inadequate compensation system	0	- Several BES employees received undisclosed commissions (CPI, 2015). However, given the values in question, it is not considered relevant to the collapse of BES.
Inner atmosphere of greed and arrogance	1	- The CEO and other shareholder family members received money from various businesses, through complex schemes to minimize taxation (CPI, 2015) - BES maintained a salary and bonus payment scheme to senior management through an off-shore company (Rosa & Porto, 2018)
Lack of ethical tone in top management	3	- In PwC reports in the early 2000s, there are references to the need to implement codes of conduct and promote ethical behavior (CPI, 2015) - There are records of non-compliance with what was stipulated by the regulators (CPI, 2015) - The handling of accounts was known by top managers (CPI, 2015) - The forensic audit, after the collapse of BES, identified 21 infractions and 4 possible malicious acts of ruinous management (Silva, 2015) - The main shareholder used the bank as a source of financing for its own benefit (Morais, 2014) - The opinion of the BES Liquidation Committee indicates that thinsolvency must be considered culpable, with 13 BES responsible persons accused of intent or gross negligence (Santos, 2017)

Figure 1.

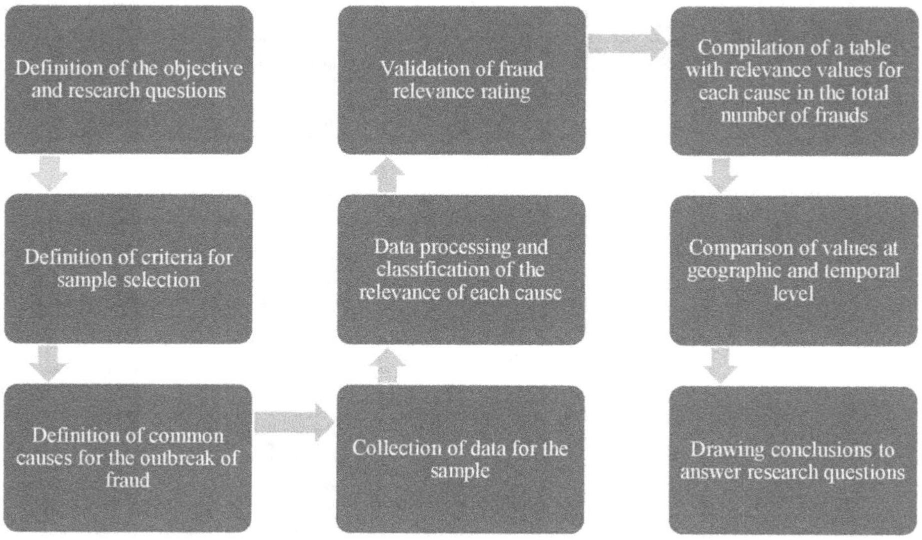

Table 5. Relevance of common causes for the outbreak of pre-SOX fraud in the US and EU

	Companies												
	US							EU					
Common causes for the outbreak of fraud	**Enron (2001)**	**Xerox (2001)**	**Adelphia (2002)**	**Tyco (2002)**	**Worldcom (2002)**	**Mean**	**Mode**	**Vivendi (2002)**	**Royal Ahold (2003)**	**Parmalat (2003)**	**Royal Dutch Shell (2004)**	**Mean**	**Mode**
Excessive concentration of power	2	1	3	3	3	2.4	3	3	2	3	1	2.25	3
Ineffective Board of Directors	3	2	3	3	3	2.8	3	2	2	3	2	2.25	2
Investor passivity	3	1	2	2	2	2	2	2	2	2	0	1.5	2
Gatekeepers' failures	3	3	2	1	3	2.4	3	1	1	3	1	1.5	1
Weak regulation	3	2	2	1	2	2	2	1	1	2	1	1.25	1
Business over-expansion	3	1	2	3	3	2.4	3	2	3	3	0	2	3
Bad strategic decisions	3	0	3	3	3	2.4	3	3	3	3	0	2.25	3
Biased financial statements	3	3	3	2	3	2.8	3	3	3	3	3	3	3
Weak internal controls	2	3	2	2	2	2.2	2	1	3	3	2	2.25	3
Inadequate compensation system	3	2	0	3	3	2.2	3	2	2	1	1	1.5	2
Inner atmosphere of greed and arrogance	3	1	2	3	3	2.4	3	3	2	2	1	2	2
Lack of ethical tone in top management	3	2	3	3	3	2.8	3	3	2	3	2	2.5	3

Table 6. Relevance of common causes for the outbreak of post-SOX fraud in the US and EU

	Companies					
	US	EU				
Common causes for the outbreak of fraud	**Refco (2005)**	**Siemens (2007)**	**Société Générale (2008)**	**BES (2014)**	**Mean**	**Mode**
Excessive concentration of power	3	0	2	3	1.7	---
Ineffective Board of Directors	2	3	2	3	2.7	3
Investor passivity	1	1	0	0	0.3	0
Gatekeepers' failures	1	2	1	3	2	
Weak regulation	1	3	1	3	2.3	3
Business over-expansion	1	0	0	0	0	0
Bad strategic decisions	1	0	0	2	0.7	0
Biased financial statements	3	1	0	3	1.3	---
Weak internal controls	3	2	3	3	2.8	3
Inadequate compensation system	1	1	2	0	1	---
Inner atmosphere of greed and arrogance	1	0	3	1	1.3	---
Lack of ethical tone in top management	3	3	3	3	3	3

Managers tend to manipulate results (with a view to greater personal gains) while majority shareholders tend to benefit from their control (Coffee, 2005).

The analysis through mode corroborates what was presented above, also highlighting bad strategic decisions as one of the most relevant causes.

Post-SOX Cases

As indicated in the methodology, Siemens, Société Générale and BES are included in the European post-SOX fraud cases. In relation to the North American frauds, the case of Refco is considered.

Table 6 shows the relevance of common causes for the post-SOX fraud, both North American and European.

Regarding the fraud cases under analysis in the post-SOX period, given their small number, it was decided to analyze and compare the values of relevance of North American fraud with the average of European frauds (the mode was not possible to determine in several of the causes).

After the implementation of SOX, the lack of ethical tone in top management proved to be the most relevant cause for the triggering of fraud in the set of all frauds, both in Europe and in North America. This cause was considered critical in all analyzed cases. Weak internal controls also stand out for their relevance, being considered a critical cause at Refco (US), Société Générale (EU) and BES (EU), and truly relevant at Siemens (EU).

Among the less relevant causes, the over-expansion of the business stands out, which has no relevance in the 3 European cases (average 0) and is only considered as relevant in the North American case. The investors' passivity is also of minor importance, with an average of 0.3 in the EU and relevant in the case of Refco (US).

Table 7. Summary of the most relevant causes and least relevant causes in the pre and post-SOX periods, in the US and EU (The mean was used to define the most relevant and least relevant causes in the pre-SOX period)

	Pre-SOX		Pos-SOX	
	US	EU	US	EU
Most relevant causes	Ineffective Board of Directors (opportunity) Lack of ethical tone in top management (attitude/rationalization)	Lack of ethical tone in top management (attitude/rationalization)	Lack of ethical tone in top management (attitude/rationalization)	Lack of ethical tone in top management (attitude/rationalization)
Most relevant causes	Biased financial statements (opportunity)	Biased financial statements (opportunity)	Weak internal controls (opportunity)	Weak internal controls (opportunity)
Least relevant causes	Investor passivity (opportunity)	Investor passivity (opportunity) Gatekeepers' failures (opportunity)	Investor passivity (opportunity)	Investor passivity (opportunity)
Least relevant causes	Weak regulation (opportunity)	Weak regulation (opportunity) Inadequate compensation system (incentives/pressures)	Business over-expansion (opportunity)	Business over-expansion (opportunity)

Comparative Analysis of Common Causes

Table 7 incorporates a summary of the most relevant and least relevant causes in the two periods and geographies analyzed. In this way, it is possible to carry out a better analysis of the transversality of certain causes.

From the analysis of Table 7 it is possible to see that the lack of ethical tone in top management remains one of the most relevant causes for the triggering of fraud, even after the implementation of SOX and all the EU regulations, denoting that the measures adopted were not sufficient to combat this cause. These results corroborate the review of the literature carried out by Montesdeoca, Medina and Santana (2019) that also highlights the importance of responsible corporate governance and good accounting practices, as well as the importance of certain psychological characteristics of managers and employees as enhancers of the lack of ethics.

On the other hand, investors' passivity remains one of the least relevant causes.

Biased financial statements are no longer one of the main causes for the triggering of fraud after the implementation of SOX, their relevance varying depending on the cases of fraud. On the US side, although there is only one case of fraud under analysis, it should be questioned whether SOX's responses to this cause (increasing accountability for management positions in the integrity of company accounts (section 302), need not to be omitted material information (section 401) or heavier penalties for non-compliant (SOX section 906)) had an impact on decreasing its relevance. In the European case, the adoption of International Accounting Standards with Regulation (EC) No. 1606/2002 may have been one of the reasons for the decrease in relevance, together with other European regulatory instruments.

The failures in internal control, in turn, became more relevant in the second period under analysis, being one of the most relevant causes, despite the regulation that was implemented to strengthen this area in companies. One of the main criticisms of SOX included section 404 and the costs involved in developing adequate internal control, so it is surprising to see that this area has become one of the most relevant for triggering fraud. Also, at European level, the Directive 2006/43/EC had as one of the objectives to improve internal control in organizations. However, the report by KPMG International (2016) indicates that, in 2016, internal control failures contributed to the occurrence of 3/5 of frauds, although it should be noted that these data refer to the total types of fraud in the report (misappropriation of assets, corruption and fraudulent financial reporting). The same report indicates that 72% of European and 59% of North American offenders consider that weak internal controls were the factor that gave them the opportunity to develop fraud (KPMG International, 2016).

Weak regulation is no longer one of the least relevant causes in the post-SOX period, with the business over-expansion being considered in this group. This change in the relevance of weak regulation is strange since the answer to mitigate fraud and prevent similar cases to those analyzed came through the strengthening of regulation such as SOX and the various European regulatory instruments, therefore, one would expect that its relevance remained low (indicating the achievement of the regulation's intended objective).

Considering the relationship between the elements of the Fraud Triangle and the 12 common causes for the triggering of fraud, it is observed in Table 7 that the elements of the most relevant causes in the two periods and in both geographies are opportunity (Ineffective Board of Directors, biased financial statements, and weak internal controls) and attitude/rationalization (lack of ethical tone in top management). Observing the elements of the less relevant causes, it is possible to distinguish that opportunity is dominant in all periods on both sides of the Atlantic, except in the pre-SOX period in the EU where the incentive/pressure element is also present (inadequate compensation system). Another interesting observation from Tables 5 and 6, it is visible that all fraud cases considered in the sample have causes considered relevant, truly relevant, or critical of all 3 elements of the Fraud Triangle.

The presence of opportunity as one of the most relevant elements to trigger the analyzed frauds is in line with the PwC 2018 report which indicates that companies consider opportunity (59%) as the main factor for fraud or economic crime has occurred (although it should be considered that the data refer to the 3 types of fraud considered by ACFE). These are followed by incentives/pressures (21%) and finally attitude/rationalization (11%). So, it is not surprising that anti-fraud efforts focus on opportunity. By not betting so much on attitude/rationalization, considering that it is an element with less influence, organizations make room for less ethical environments, giving greater propensity to the appearance of fraud and as verified, the cause of "lack of ethical tone in top management" related to the attitude/rationalization component, is one of the most relevant in the two periods and geographic spaces.

FUTURE RESEARCH DIRECTIONS

In future works, it would be of special interest to increase the number of frauds under analysis, either through frauds of different dimensions or considering the analysis of frauds from other countries or regions.

The subprime crisis has brought a new wave of scandals that have multiplied around the world, and it will be interesting to broaden the sample selection criteria to include, for example, Lehman Brothers (which has not yet been charged with fraud to date) or Bernard Madoff (not subject to SOX) and study the commonalities between the various cases.

A line of study development might be understanding the reasons for the relevance of certain common causes. In the post-SOX period, weak internal controls were one of the most relevant causes, despite SOX and European regulatory instruments focusing on improving internal control. It will be relevant to understand which areas have failed in internal control in cases of fraud following the entry into force of the legislation.

Finally, it would be interesting to see what impact new technological tools, namely artificial intelligence, can have in preventing the occurrence of some of the identified fraud causes, as well as in their detection.

CONCLUSION

Fraud at the corporate level is a phenomenon that impacts not only organizations, but also the societies in which they operate. At the beginning of this century, the triggering of fraudulent scandals in the US and the EU gave rise to responses by governments to prevent this from happening again. The greatest example of this response is SOX, built with the goal of preventing new "Enron or WorldCom" from happening again. However, a few years later, new fraudulent scandals emerged and, therefore, it makes perfect sense to try to understand the causes behind this phenomenon, especially regarding fraudulent financial reporting.

Aiming to find commonalities in the causes that triggered the frauds that were made public in the early 2000s in the US and EU and to understand whether the most relevant causes remained in the post-SOX period, this study helps to identify whether the different responses to frauds given by the US and the EU had the expected effects. Thus, 12 causes defined as common to trigger fraud were examined in a sample of 13 fraudulent cases, comparing the causes through a classification of 4 levels of relevance.

With the analysis carried out, it is possible to observe as a tendency that the lack of ethical tone in top management is the cause that remains transversal to both sides of the Atlantic and to the two periods studied. It must, therefore, be the cause to given special attention to prevent the appearance of fraud. This is not a current reminder, given that as far back as 1987 the Treadway Commission report indicated that there would have to be concern for the ethical tone of top management to prevent and deter fraud (National Commission on Fraudulent Financial Reporting, 1987). SOX itself has a considerable number of sections that relate to this common cause. ISA 240 (IAASB, 2020) also indicates that it is management's responsibility to have primary responsibility for fraud prevention and detection. Also, in common points between the US and the EU in the period before the implementation of SOX, it was observed that biased financial statements were one of the most relevant causes.

In the post-SOX period, there was a tendency for internal control failures to become one of the most relevant causes. Bearing in mind that regulation, in both geographies, has given more focus to internal control, this propensity for internal control failures to assume a greater role as a cause for the outbreak of fraud is of particular interest. On the other hand, biased financial statements lost relevance in the post-SOX period, no longer being part of the most relevant causes.

This work corroborates what was already observed in the ACFE report (2016) which indicated that the lack of internal controls (23.9%) and the weak ethical tone of the management (22.9%) were the main responsible for the fraudulent financial reporting.

This chapter has the contribution of deepening the knowledge of the causes of fraud considering its geographical area and exploring the effect of certain measures introduced. This fact helps to better choose the measures to be implemented to avoid the occurrence of similar frauds in the future.

The small number of frauds under analysis, especially in the post-SOX period in the US, is one of the main limitations, and it is therefore not possible to generalize the conclusions drawn to all fraud cases. This number of cases also influenced the criteria for analyzing the relevance values of common causes. Regarding the fraud cases used, it is also possible to question whether they can be comparable given the uniqueness of each one and the different dimensions of the frauds. However, it is understood that it becomes exceedingly difficult to find a sample of similar fraud cases, either respecting the same conditions, or having available information in sufficient quantity and quality for analysis.

The subjectivity of the scale that assesses the relevance of each cause is also evident, even if based on Silveira (2015).

REFERENCES

ACFE. (2014). *Report To the Nations on Occupational Fraud and Abuse. Global Fraud Study* (Vol. 15). Association of Certified Fraud Examiners.

ACFE. (2016). *Report to the nations on Ocupational Fraud and Abuse*. Association of Certified Fraud Examiners. Retrieved from https://www.acfe.com

ACFE. (2018). *Portal da Association of Certified Fraud Examiners*. http://www.acfe.com

ACFE. (2020). *Report to the nations on Ocupational - 2020 Global Study on Occupational Fraud and Abuse*. Association of Certified Fraud Examiners. https://www.acfe.com

Ahmed, A., McAnally, M., Rasmussen, S., & Weaver, C. (2010). How costly is the Sarbanes Oxley Act? Evidence on the effects of the Act on corporate profitability. *Journal of Corporate Finance, 16*(3), 352–369. doi:10.1016/j.jcorpfin.2009.11.003

Albrecht, C., Holland, D., Malagueño, R., Dolan, S., & Tzafrir, S. (2015). The Role of Power in Financial Statement Fraud Schemes. *Journal of Business Ethics, 131*(4), 803–813. doi:10.100710551-013-2019-1

Albrecht, W., Albrecht, C., & Albrecht, C. C. (2008). Current Trends in Fraud and its Detection. *Information Security Journal: A Global Perspective, 17*(1), 2–12.

Alkhafaji, A. (2007). Corporate governance: The evolution of the Sarbanes- Oxley Act and its impact on corporate America. *Competitiveness Review, 17*(3), 193–202. doi:10.1108/10595420710833598

Almeida, F. (2014). *Custos e Benefícios da Lei Sarbanes-Oxley O Caso BPN* [Unpublished master dissertation] Universidade Católica Portuguesa, Portugal.

Almeida, M. (2015). *A fraude de relato financeiro e a indepenência dos auditores* [Unpublished master dissertation] Universidade Autónoma de Lisboa, Portugal.

Anand, S. (2007). *Essentials of Sarbanes-Oxley*. John Wiley & Sons. doi:10.1002/9781118384596

Banco de Portugal. (2015). *Comunicado do Banco de Portugal: Recomendações do Grupo de Trabalho sobre os Modelos e as Práticas de Governo, de Controlo e de Auditoria das Instituições Financeiras*. Banco de Portugal Eurosistema.

Bernardo, R., Lima, N., Medeiros, C., & Miranda, G. (2017). Fraudes corporativas e a formação de contadores: Uma análise dos currículos dos cursos de ciências contábeis. *Revista Ambiente Contábil*, *9*(1), 97–116.

Bonotto, P. (2010). *As Fraudes Contábeis da Enron e Worldcom e seus efeitos nos Estados Unidos* [Unpublished final academic course work]. Universidade Federal do Rio Grande do Sul.

Carney, W. (2006). The cost of being public after Sarbanes-Oxley: The irony of "going private." *Emory Law Journal*, 51.

Castellano, J., & Lightle, S. (2005). Using Cultural Audits to Assess Tone at the Top. *The CPA Journal*, *75*(2).

CMVM. (n.d.). *Portal da Comissão do Mercado de Valores Mobiliários*. http://www.cmvm.pt

Coates, J. IV. (2007). The goals and promise of the Sarbanes–Oxley Act. *The Journal of Economic Perspectives*, *21*(1), 91–116. doi:10.1257/jep.21.1.91

Coates, J., & Srinivasan, S. (2014). SOX after ten years: A multidisciplinary review. *Accounting Horizons*, *28*(3), 627–671. doi:10.2308/acch-50759

Coelho, S. (2014). CMVM investiga venda de ações do BES no último dia: grandes investidores venderam a correr. *Observador*. http://observador.pt

Coenen, T. (2008). *Essentials of Corporate Fraud*. Wiley. doi:10.1002/9781118386156

Coffee, J. (2004). What Caused Enron-A Capsule Social and Economic History of the 1990s. *Cornell Law Review*, *89*(2), 269–309.

Coffee, J. (2005). A Theory of Corporate Scandals: Why the USA and Europe Differ. *Oxford Review of Economic Policy*, *21*(2), 198–211. doi:10.1093/oxrep/gri012

Comissão das Comunidades Europeias. (1996). *Livro verde: Papel, estatuto responsabilidade do revisor oficial de contas na União Europeia*. Bruxelas: Comissão das Comunidades Europeias.

Comissão das Comunidades Europeias. (2003). *Comunicação da Comissão ao Conselho e ao Parlamento Europeu: Modernizar o direito das sociedades e reforçar o governo das sociedades na União Europeia - Uma estratégia para o futuro*. https://eur-lex.europa.eu/

Comissão Europeia. (2003). *Comunicação da Comissão ao Conselho e ao Parlamento Europeu sobre reforçar a revisão oficial de contas na UE*. https://eur-lex.europa.eu

Comissão Parlamentar de Inquérito à Gestão do BES e do GES (CPI). (2015). *Relatório Final da Comissão Parlamentar de Inquérito à gestão do BES e do GES*. Lisboa: Assembleia da República. http://app.parlamento.pt

Costa, C. A. (2017). *Salgado permitiu empréstimos de 463 milhões a empresa da família. Sem garantias.* https://www.sabado.pt/

Costa, C. B. (2019). Auditoria Financeira - Teoria & Prática (12.a ed.). Lisboa: Rei dos Livros.

Dewi, K., & Anisykurlillah, I. (2021). Analysis of the Effect of Fraud Pentagon Factors on Fraudulent Financial Statement with Audit Committee as Moderating Variable. *Accounting Analysis Journal.*, *10*(1), 39–46. doi:10.15294/aaj.v10i1.44520

Directiva 2003/6/CE do Parlamento Europeu e do Conselho de 28 de Janeiro de 2003 relativa ao abuso de informação privilegiada e à manipulação de mercado (abuso de mercado) (2003). https://eur-lex.europa.eu

Directiva 2006/43/CE do Parlamento Europeu e do Conselho de 17 de Maio de 2006 relativa à revisão legal das contas anuais e consolidadas (2006). https://eur-lex.europa.eu

Diretiva 2014/56/UE do Parlamento Europeu e do Conselho de 16 de abril de 2014 que altera a Diretiva 2006/43/CE relativa à revisão legal das contas anuais e consolidadas (2014). https://eur-lex.europa.eu

Dorminey, J., Scott Fleming, A., Kranacher, M., & Riley, R. (2012). The evolution of fraud theory. *Issues in Accounting Education*, *27*(2), 555–579. doi:10.2308/iace-50131

Dowd, K. (2016). *A Comparison of Accounting Fraud Before and After Sarbanes-Oxley* (Bridgewater State University Honors Program Theses and Projects). https://vc.bridgew.edu/honors_proj/165

Elbling, P. (2015). *Fraude e suas implicações em auditoria* [Unpublished master dissertation] Instituto Superior de Contabilidade e Adminsitração de Lisboa, Portugal.

Ernst & Young. (2016). *14th Global Fraud Survey: Corporate misconduct — individual consequences: Global enforcement focuses the spotlight on executive integrity*. EY. https://www.ey.com/

Fernandes, L. (2010). *Alterações normativas na auditoria após SOX: efeitos na opinião do auditor* [Unpublished master dissertation] Instituto Superior de Contabilidade e Administração da Universidade de Aveiro, Portugal.

Fialho, V. (2015). *(Un)Ethical Leadership, Organizational Identification and Sensemaking: the BES case and its impact on employees* [Unpublished work project as part of the requirements for the Award of a Masters Degree in Management]. NOVA School of Business and Economics.

Gates, S., Prachyl, C., & Sullivan, C. (2016). Using Report To the Nations on Occupational Fraud and Abuse To Stimulate Discussion of Fraud in Accounting and Business Classes. *Journal of Business and Behavior Sciences*, *28*(1), 106–115.

Gomes, M. (2017). *Corporate Governance at BES: Would new recommendations have avoided the failure?* [Unpublished work project as part of the requirements for the Award of a Masters Degree in Finance]. NOVA – School of Business and Economics.

Grant, R., & Visconti, M. (2006). The Strategic Background to Corporate Accounting Scandals. *Long Range Planning*, *39*(4), 361–383. doi:10.1016/j.lrp.2006.09.003

Hamilton, S., & Micklethwait, A. (2006). *Greed and Corporate Failure: The Lessons from Recent Disasters*. Palgrave Macmillan UK. doi:10.1057/9780230502758

International Auditing and Assurance Standards Board (IAASB). (2020). *Handbook of International Quality Control, Auditing, Review, Other Assurance, and Related Services Pronouncements*. Academic Press.

Ismajli, H., Perjuci, E., Prenaj, V., & Braha, M. (2019). The Importance of External Audit in Detecting Abnormalities and Fraud in the Financial Statements of Public Enterprises in Kosovo. *Ekonomika (Nis)*, *98*(1), 124–134. doi:10.15388/Ekon.2019.1.8

Jahmani, Y., & Dowling, W. (2008). The Impact Of Sarbanes-Oxley Act. *Journal of Business & Economics Research*, *6*(10), 57–66.

KPMG International. (2016). *Global profiles of the fraudster: technology enables and weak controls fuel the fraud*. KPMG International.

Leuz, C. (2007). Was the Sarbanes–Oxley Act of 2002 really this costly? A discussion of evidence from event returns and going-private decisions. *Journal of Accounting and Economics*, *44*(1–2), 146–145. doi:10.1016/j.jacceco.2007.06.001

Linck, J., Netter, J., & Yang, T. (2009). The effects and unintended consequences of the sarbanes-oxley act on the supply and demand for directors. *Review of Financial Studies*, *22*(8), 3287–3328. doi:10.1093/rfs/hhn084

Montesdeoca, M., Medina, A., & Santana, F. (2019). Research Topics in Accounting Fraud in the 21st Century: A State of the Art. *Sustainability*, *11*(6), 1570. doi:10.3390u11061570

Morais, L. (2014). *The Good, the Bad and the Ugly - The fall and resolution of Banco Espírito Santo* [Unpublished work project as part of the requirements for the Award of a Masters Degree in Finance]. NOVA School of Business and Economics.

Morales, J. (2005). La Ley Sarbanes-Oxley y la auditoria. *Partida Doble*, *169*, 105–109.

National Commission on Fraudulent Financial Reporting. (1987). *Report of the National Commission on Fraudulent Financial Reporting*.

OECD. (2009). *Corporate Governance and the Financial Crisis: Key Findings and Main Messages*. OECD Steering Group on Corporate Governance. https://www.oecd.org/

Oliveira, E., & Ferreira, P. (2014). *Métodos de Investigação - Da Interrogação à Descoberta Científica*. Vida Económica.

Parodi, L. (2008). Manual das fraudes (2.ª edição). Rio de Janeiro: Brasport.

Patterson, E., Smith, J., & Patterson, R. (2007). The Effects of Sarbanes-Oxley on and Internal Control Auditing Strength. *The Accounting Review*, *82*(2), 427–455. doi:10.2308/accr.2007.82.2.427

PricewaterhouseCoopers (PwC). (2018). *Global Economic Crime and Fraud Survey: Pulling fraud out of the shadows*. PwC. https://www.pwc.com

Raymond, N. (2016). *Vivendi loses U.S. appeal in long-running investor lawsuit*. Reuters. https://www.reuters.com

Regulamento (CE) n.º 1606/2002 do Parlamento Europeu e do Conselho de 19 de Julho de 2002 relativo à aplicação das normas internacionais de contabilidade (2002). https://eur-lex.europa.eu

Regulamento (UE) n.º 537/2014 do Parlamento Europeu e do Conselho de 16 de abril de 2014 relativo aos requisitos específicos para a revisão legal de contas das entidades de interesse público (2014). https://publications.europa.eu

Rezaee, Z. (2005). Causes, consequences, and deterence of financial statement fraud. *Critical Perspectives on Accounting, 16*(3), 277–298. doi:10.1016/S1045-2354(03)00072-8

Rosa, L., & Porto, R. (2018). *Os documentos do 'saco azul' do GES: 20 milhões a mais de 50 altos funcionários. Observador.* https://observador.pt/

Santos, C. (2017). *Ex-administradores do BES arrasados. Jornal I.* https://ionline.sapo.pt/

Sarbanes-Oxley Act of 2002. (2002). *Exchange Organizational Behavior Teaching Journal.* https://news.findlaw.com/

SEC. (n.d.). *Portal da U.S. Securities and Exchange Comission.* http://www.sec.gov

Silva, T. (2015). *As 21 infrações detetadas na auditoria da Deloitte ao BES. Dinheiro Vivo.* https://www.dinheirovivo.pt

Silveira, A. (2013). The Enron Scandal a decade later: Lessons Learned? *Homo Oeconomicus, 30*(3), 315–347.

Silveira, A. (2015). *Corporate Scandals of the 21st Century: limitations of mainstream corporate governance literature and the need for a new behavioral approach.* Working paper. doi:10.2139/ssrn.2181705

Simões, S. (2014). *Ex-administrador do BES: "Eu sabia tanto de bancos como de calceteiro."* Observador. https://observador.pt/

Soltani, B. (2014). The Anatomy of Corporate Fraud: A Comparative Analysis of High Profile American and European Corporate Scandals. *Journal of Business Ethics, 120*(2), 251–274. doi:10.100710551-013-1660-z

Umar, M., Sitorus, S., Surya, R., Shauki, E., & Diyanti, V. (2017). Pressure, Dysfunctional Behavior, Fraud Detection and Role of Information Technology in the Audit Process. *Australasian Accounting. Business and Finance Journal, 11*(4), 102–115.

Vilelas, J. (2009). *Investigação: O Processo de Construção do Conhecimento.* Edições Sílabo, Lda.

Wolfe, D., & Hermanson, D. (2004). The Fraud Diamond : Considering the Four Elements of Fraud. *The CPA Journal, 74*(12), 38–42.

Yin, R. (1994). *Case Study Research: Design and Methods* (2nd ed.). Sage Publications, Lda.

ADDITIONAL READING

Abu-Tapanjeh, A. M., & Al-Sarairah, T. M. K. (2021). The Availability of Forensic Accounting Application Factors to Enhance the Auditors Efficiency in Jordan. *Journal of Asian Finance, Economics and Business*, *8*(3), 807–819.

Akinbowale, O. E., Klingelhöfer, H. E., & Zerihun, M. F. (2021). The integration of forensic accounting and the management control system as tools for combating cyberfraud. Academy of Accounting and Financial Studies Journal, 25(2).

Al-Shattarat, B. (2021). The consequence of earnings management through discretionary accruals on the value relevance in Saudi Arabia. *Cogent Business and Management*, *8*(1), 1–16. doi:10.1080/23311975.2021.1886473

Albanese, J. S., Artello, K., & Nguyen, L. T. (2019). Distinguishing Corruption in Law and Practice: Empirically Separating Conviction Charges from Underlying Behaviors. *Public Integrity*, *21*(1), 22–37. doi:10.1080/10999922.2018.1423859

Kassem, R. (2019). Understanding financial reporting fraud in Egypt: Evidence from the audit field. *Third World Quarterly*, *40*(11), 1996–2015. doi:10.1080/01436597.2019.1626709

Kızıl, C., Muzır, E., & Yılmaz, V. (2021). Auditing Techniques to Minimize Accounting Related Fraud and Errors: A Qualitative Analysis with the Interview Method. *Emerging Markets Journal*, *11*(1), 95–103. doi:10.5195/emaj.2021.232

Malau, W., Ohalehi, P., Badr, E., & Yekini, K. (2021). Fraud interpretation and disclaimer audit opinion: Evidence from the Solomon Islands public sector (SIPS). *Managerial Auditing Journal*, *36*(2), 240–260. doi:10.1108/MAJ-04-2018-1867

McAllister, M., Blay, A., & Kadous, K. (2021). Fraud Brainstorming Group Composition in Auditing: The Persuasive Power of a Skeptical Minority. *The Accounting Review*, *96*(3), 431–448. doi:10.2308/TAR-2018-0027

KEY TERMS AND DEFINITIONS

Case Study: A research method that involves a detailed examination of a subject of study (the case), considering its related contextual conditions. The case to be studied can be an organization, an action, or an event, existing at a specific time and place.

Cause Relevance: Is the classification of the causes into 4 levels of relevance: "0" when the cause was not relevant to the case in question, "1" when the cause was relevant to the initiation of the fraud; "2" when the cause was highly relevant; and "3" when the cause was critical for triggering the fraud.

Fraud Triangle: Is a framework developed by Cressey that tends to explain the reason behind an individual's decision to commit fraud. It considers three components that contribute to increasing the risk of fraud: (1) opportunity, (2) incentive, and (3) rationalization.

Fraudulent Financial Reporting: Intentionally altered financial information containing distortions and/or omissions of important data in the organization's financial reports.

Multiple Case Study: When it is studied two or more cases allowing to do a comparative analysis among cases, identifying similarities, differences, benefits and tries to understand and explain a phenomenon in its context.

Chapter 7
Forensic Accounting in a Digital Environment:
A New Proposed Model

Nohade Hanna Nasrallah
Conservatoire National des Arts & Métiers, France

Rim El Khoury
https://orcid.org/0000-0003-4359-7591
Notre Dame University, Louaize, Lebanon

Etienne Harb
https://orcid.org/0000-0002-4222-1173
ESSCA School of Management, France

ABSTRACT

In the rise of digital transformation and big data, accounting and auditing professions are required to adopt advanced techniques that help detect irregularities and frauds. This chapter collects 1,112 documents from Scopus database published in 288 sources over the period 2008-2021. A bibliometric analysis is used to depict trends, and applicable methodologies are adopted to build a comprehensible base that will serve to instill a new fraud detection model. More specifically, RStudio through "biblioshiny package", VOSviewer, and Excel are the tools embraced to analyze the dataset information. The chapter explores the literature growth over time and addresses key aspects of the literature, such as most relevant documents, authors, countries, citation analysis. This chapter applies a network and content analysis using the bibliographical coupling, trend analysis, word cloud, and co-occurrence analysis. The theoretical model helps auditors, forensic accountants, top managements, analysts, and policy makers predict potential anomalies and misstatements.

DOI: 10.4018/978-1-7998-8754-6.ch007

INTRODUCTION

The Association of Certified Fraud Examiners (ACFE) recently released the "Report to the Nations: 2020 Global study on Occupational Fraud and Abuse" which covers 2,504 fraud cases from 125 countries that caused total loss of more than $ 3.6 billion. Organizations worldwide lose about five percent of their annual revenue to fraud with a median loss of $125,000 per case and an average loss of $1,509,000 per case (ACFE, 2020). The report concludes that the corruption is the most common scheme in every global region. On the other hand, 86% of fraud cases are due to the misappropriation of assets which appears to be the least costly ($100,000 median loss) while 10% are due to financial statement manipulation that appears to be the costliest ($954,000 median loss).

In parallel, a rising trend highlights the emergence of forensic accounting that includes a wide range of activities such as litigation support, expert witness, and fraud investigation. Forensic accounting is "the science of gathering and presenting financial information in a form that will be accepted by a court of jurisprudence against perpetrators of economic crimes" (Manning & CFE, 1999). According to the American Institute of Certified Public Accountants (AICPA), "Forensic accounting is the application of accounting principles, theories and discipline to facts or hypotheses at issues in a legal dispute and encompasses every branch of accounting knowledge."

In the present study, the authors collect 1,112 previous publications related to the said topic from Scopus Database. The authors conduct the analysis using RStudio, VOSviewer, and Excel. The analysis will serve to derive important conclusions such as: similarities in fraud circumstances, main reasons, methodologies to depict and prevent frauds, technological advances in fraud detection, and qualitative variables such as CEO behavioral patterns, ethics, gender, and compensation biases along with whistle-blowing incentives and employees' training programs that aim at signaling early fraud stages.

Deep data analysis, clustering methods, data mining, artificial intelligence and expert system application are expected to shift the knowledge base. Some common techniques such as Beneish Model, Benford's Law and other sampling techniques are used in the forensic accounting investigations. Foremost, trend analysis, horizontal and vertical analysis, regression analysis, ratio analysis and Markov chain are applied. Computer-based programs are managed to analyze quantitative and qualitative data that have a significant association with financial information manipulation. But what is the optimal model to depict a fraud? Can forensic auditors generalize a unique model? In fact, such models remain inconsistent and dissatisfactory randomized. Concomitantly, some techniques suffer from major drawbacks. To tackle the problem, one should address the topic from an aggregate perspective where auditors and researchers gather data from fraudulent companies, perform analytical procedures and approach their similarities based on clustering techniques that account for country-industry-firm levels. The objective is to generate a new model that combines classical techniques with digital ones which will help depict anomalies and provide valuable insights to deter potential frauds.

The authors contribute to the literature by attempting to introduce a new model based on previous literature in the studied field. It addresses a basic and essential question: What major role would be played by forensic accountants? Are they able to reduce fraud attempts? How would the analysis of the previous literature lead to find the best model to predict and early detect fraud?

In fact, to detect anomalies, most of the previous discern the different facets of the audit process. This study conducts a bibliometric analysis that constitutes a framework to generalize results and methods. It aims at contributing to the knowledge of auditors and forensic accountants. It provides stakeholders with a window of credible information free from earnings manipulations and sheds light on the quality of firms' financial reporting. The study is novel as it suggests recommendations to further test the model and gradually refine it to suit all case scenarios.

The remainder of the chapter is structured as follows: Section 2 discusses the background with relevant literature review. Section 3 describes the research methodology, while Section 4 presents the bibliometric findings and presents a proposed fraud detection model. Section 5 concludes, while section 6 suggests solutions, recommendations, and future research directions.

BACKGROUND

The turbulence of the business world and the openness of the global economies surcharged the scientific research with a variety of fraud schemes and fueled database with plenty of publications, analyses, and interpretations. Many scholars investigated the root of frauds, well-tailored scenarios, and main motives while others innovated in introducing methodologies and techniques to detect and early deter frauds and misstatements.

In fact, earnings management topic was extensively explored but findings remain inconclusive. Nowadays, forensic accounting emerges as a new field where accountants are expected to apply quantitative and qualitative techniques (Nasrallah & El Khoury, 2021), acquire deep knowledge of investigation and strive to uncover fraudsters and perpetrators. For instance, the science of criminology provides common techniques such as the fraud triangle which helps forensic accountant profile fraudsters and depict anomalies or fraud activities (Rahim et al., 2017; Reinstein & Taylor, 2017). The fraud triangle fundamentally relies on three main areas: opportunity, motivation, and rationalization (Ramos-Rodrígue & Ruíz-Navarro, 2004).Governmental and institutional reforms took place to center the problem and avoid its occurrence. Nevertheless, the last era witnessed a myriad of unethical and corrupted practices whereas attempts to counteract them are not yet conclusive. Entities such the International Federation of Accountants (IFAC), the American Institute of Public Accountants (AICPA), the International Financial Reporting Standard Foundation, the Association of Chartered Certified Accountants (ACCA), and the International Auditing and Assurance standards Boards (IAASB) held forums to lessen the extent of creative accounting and frauds, but facts tell other stories and a perfect business world free of frauds and misstatements would imaginary exist.

Some studies enumerate the main actors: managers, analysts, regulators, auditors, investment banks, merchant banks and legal authorities. Others tackle methods to reduce the likelihood of creative accounting and frauds that fall under the spectrum of effective corporate governance such as: effective internal controls (Handayani & Kawedar, 2021; Albanese et al., 2019), segregation of duties (Kouki et al., 2011; Moche Halman, 2013), audit committee (Gebrayel et al., 2018; Khatwani & Goyal, 2019), and independent board of directors . Some of them list favorable instances and circumstances to commit frauds such as competition (Guo et al., 2015; Kao et al., 2018; Liao et al., 2019; Schoenefeld, 2020), reputational incentives (Muzurura, 2019), corporate conduct on capital markets and inclination to magnify their values (Cole et al., 2021), distressed companies (Shayan-Nia et al., 2017; Xu et al., 2019), higher operating costs (Ahlin et al., 2021), tax avoidance (Haruna Abubakar et al., 2021; Madrueño & Tezanos, 2018) and on a broader level less favorable economic conditions (Dichev et al., 2012) and major disruptive events.

The present bibliometric analysis retraces the methods employed to analyze the evaluation of risk management and the probability of frauds detection. There are two distinct streams in the literature debate that tackle the detection of earning managements (EM) and fraudulent practices. The first one resonates on exogeneous factors such as political, economic, and societal environment while the second one delves into endogenous factors that surround the daily activities of the business and evaluate its long-term strategies. Accordingly, the role of governments to reinforce rules and regulations and to pursue reforms is essential to curb frauds and EM (Almutairi, 2021; Lassou et al., 2021). Moreover, the role of courts to activate the forensic accounting system and to establish new division to record the investigation of frauds cases and styles is necessary (Taminiau et al., 2019). Such records serve as a strong base from which accountants, auditors and scientists can instill valuable information and build on it to derive appropriate solutions. In this regard, the digital transformation and the development in information and communication technology play a key role where algorithmic models mimic past scenarios and offer consequential results (Akinbowale et al., 2021). Correspondingly, the integration of forensic accounting and management control as tools for combating fraud should be implemented to ensure reputation and regulatory compliance (Abbasi et al., 2012; Todd Dezoort et al., 2012). These factors improve the efficiency of auditors due to their increased responsibility in the face of various fraud scenarios and due to their appearance in the courts as financial experts who are expected to adjudicate financial cases (Abu-Tapanjeh & Al-Sarairah, 2021). Forensic accounting techniques are also employed in reducing cloud-based accounting risks (Hashem, 2021) to cope with the nature of computer crime and the urgency to conduct cloud investigations. Environmental, social and governance (ESG) practices along with corporate social responsibility (CSR) compliance proved to have an important effect on corporate frauds and earning management tentative (Giese et al., 2021; Hickman et al., 2021).

On another echelon, external auditors play a critical role in this subject. Some scholars explore the mediating effect of audit price on the link between the audit committee and financial reporting quality (Bala et al., 2019). They find that audit committee curtails artificial manipulation and enhances financial reporting quality. Moreover, an increase in the price of auditing services is negatively correlated with EM practices (Chakrabarty et al., 2020) and audit effort reduces the likelihood of misconduct where auditor resignations are more likely for delinquent clients (Chakrabarty, 2015). Furthermore, the audit firm size (Comprix & Huang, 2015; Yasser & Mamun, 2015) affects EM as, for instance, small audit firms are less able to constrain managers' opportunistic use of discretionary accruals. The relationship of the quality of internal audit team on audit fees, audit quality, audit choice, audit opinion (Dzikrullah et al., 2020) and audit team size, as a corporate oversight mechanism, has a positive and significant relationship to the magnitude of external auditor fees, audit quality, and the tendency of companies to choose auditors with big names (the Big Four). In addition, this study finds that internal audit also has a negative and significant influence on the tendency of companies to accept going concern audit opinions. This research provides support on the benefit of having a good quality of internal auditors for the company as adequate internal audit function tends to hire auditors with big names (Big Four) to produce high audit quality. In addition, the existence of adequate internal auditors also reduces the probability of the firms on receiving the going concern audit opinions. The whistleblowing within the audit firms/ professional commitment and independence commitment was also assessed as a tool to detect frauds (Latan et al., 2019; Tuan Mansor et al., 2020).

The other streams focus on endogenous factors and business context status that are segregated into two main groups qualitative and quantitative. The impact of qualitative factors on frauds was investigated in the prior literature under many aspects like: corporate geographical attributes (Yamada et al., 2020), management cognitions and CFO/CEO demography such as age, education and gender (Sun et al., 2019; Binashour et al., 2021), religion (Alsaadi, 2021), corporate values (ALQIREM et al., 2020), CEO narcissistic trait (Taleatu et al., 2020), and employees' ethical attitudes (Kountur et al., 2021; Meiryani et al., 2019), timing effect such as year-end to boost earnings (Makarem & Roberts, 2020), managerial comments within annual reports (Craja et al., 2020), and quality of voluntary disclosure (quantity, spread and usefulness of the information) (Salem et al., 2020). The quantitative factors to depict frauds stand as well, namely the ratio analysis, trend analysis and past performance indicators with free cash flow as moderator (Sari et al., 2021), book value and earnings (Al-Shattarat, 2021), and differential role of R&D versus selling, general, and administrative expenses (E. Y. Sun, 2021).

METHODOLOGY

The authors aim to study previous literature and analyze their contents to aggregate methods and findings. Studies related to forensic accounting or forensic audit are not conclusive. Findings are conflicting and fraud detection methods are still inefficient. Though many papers are innovative and offer new advanced techniques, financial reporting quality and earnings managements remain timely topics. A bibliometric analysis was applied to depict trends and applicable methodologies to build a comprehensible base (Dhiaf et al., 2021) that will serve to instill a new model that can help auditors, accountants, top managements, analysts, and policy makers predict potential anomalies and misstatements in published financial statements.

A query was constructed (see Appendix A) through Scopus database to extract publications related to the topic. 1,844 articles were collected between 1982 and 2021 and apply two refinements: the first excludes studies prior to 2008 and restricts the period to 2008-2021 which represents 84% of total publications. The second excludes publications related to online frauds, cybercrime, supply chain and purchases fraud, high frequency trading frauds and academic frauds. 1,112 documents published in 288 sources were retained for the analysis. The average citation per document is 15.75 whereas the yearly average citation per document is 1.99. 221 documents are single authored, and the collaboration index (CI) is 2.43 which indicates that each paper is developed by a minimum 2 authors. CI is an indicator of high and wealthy contribution which is one of the research pillars stone.

The authors rely on the following analysis tools: RStudio, VOSviewer, and Excel. For further statistical insights, they implement RStudio through "biblioshiny package". They sequentially run the analysis. First, they perform an analysis for the dataset information and for the literature growth over time. They also address key aspects of the literature, such as most relevant documents, authors, and countries. Second, they conduct a citation analysis to gather the most cited documents, references, sources, and to account for authors' impact. Third, they apply a network and content analysis using the bibliographical coupling, trend analysis, word cloud, and co-occurrence analysis.

RESULTS

In this section, the authors first present the findings of the bibliometric. The bibliometric analysis serves to infer trends over time, themes researched, identify shifts in the boundaries of the disciplines, and detect most of the prolific scholars and institutions. Second, the authors conclude this section by proposing a top-down model to detect fraud.

Figure 1. Yearly publication trend

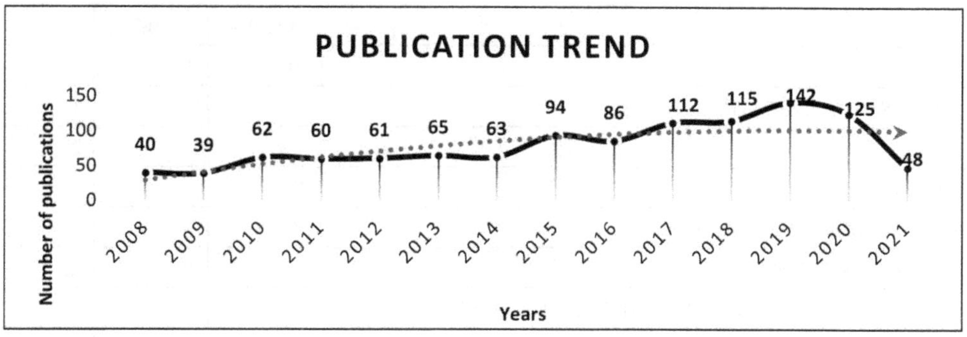

Bibliometric Analysis

Figure 1 depicts the yearly trend of publications related to the topic. It highlights a rising trend over the years that reflects scholars' growing interest to explore areas of forensic audit, frauds, internal control, earnings management, CEO gender and behavioral impacts on frauds and financial reporting manipulation, whistleblowing, and new techniques to detect and prevent frauds. More distinctly, publications became abundant since 2015 with a peak in 2019 (142 publications).

The declining trend in 2021 is insignificant since it only includes the first quarter.

Out of 288 sources, the top 20 sources are listed in Table 1. The Journal of Business Ethics contributes to 70 documents, followed by Issues in Accounting Education with 32 documents. The journals of Auditing and Managerial Auditing are ranked third with 28 publications each. The Journal of Business Ethics has the highest h-index (26). Remarkably, while Accounting Review ranks third in terms of h-index (13), it is the first in terms of total number of citations over the studied period (2163).

The study also investigates the most influential authors and publications. As such, in Table 2, Zhang J. ranks first in terms of total publications. He has published 8 articles, earned 168 citations and his h-index is 6 which indicates that at least 6 of his articles are cited at least 6 times since 2009. Kaplan SE ranks second with 8 papers, 151 citations, and an h-index of 6. Chen Y. is the most influential author with 493 citations since 2011.

Moreover, Table 3 shows that the most influential paper is "Accrual-based and real earnings management activities around seasoned equity offerings" (Cohen & Zarowin, 2010) published in the journal of Accounting and Economics with 712 citations. The paper tackles the problem of real activity management prior to Seasoned Equity Offering (SEO) and analyzes post-SEO operating underperformance. Real versus accrual-based earnings management activities around SEOs are also analyzed and findings relate the firm's choice to two main criteria: costs and ability to use accrual management. The second top cited paper is titled "Evidence on the trade-off between real activities manipulation and accrual-based earnings management" (Zang, 2012) published in the journal of "Accounting Review" with 668 citations. The paper uses large-sample to discover managers' discretion to apply real activities manipulation versus accrual-based earnings management. The main findings indicate the trade-off between real and accrual earnings management methods based on their relative costs.

Based on Table 4 and Figure 2, words cloud dynamics present a complete picture about the keywords' frequency in the studied sample. Mainly, the word "Crime" is the most frequent word (39), followed by "Finance" (20), Fraud (18), "Fraud detection" (14), and "Financial fraud" (10). Keyword analysis ensures

Table 1. Top 20 sources

Sources	Articles	h_index	g_index	TC
JOURNAL OF BUSINESS ETHICS	70	26	41	1992
ISSUES IN ACCOUNTING EDUCATION	32	7	14	251
AUDITING	28	16	28	790
MANAGERIAL AUDITING JOURNAL	28	11	18	359
CORPORATE OWNERSHIP AND CONTROL	26	3	3	23
JOURNAL OF CORPORATE FINANCE	21	12	21	577
ACADEMY OF ACCOUNTING AND FINANCIAL STUDIES JOURNAL	19	3	4	23
ACCOUNTING REVIEW	19	13	19	2163
REVIEW OF ACCOUNTING STUDIES	18	8	16	279
ADVANCES IN ACCOUNTING	17	8	14	198
INTERNATIONAL JOURNAL OF SCIENTIFIC AND TECHNOLOGY RESEARCH	15	0	0	0
DECISION SUPPORT SYSTEMS	14	12	14	1164
JOURNAL OF ACCOUNTING AND ECONOMICS	14	11	14	1783
JOURNAL OF BUSINESS FINANCE AND ACCOUNTING	14	9	14	230
INTERNATIONAL JOURNAL OF ACCOUNTING INFORMATION SYSTEMS	13	8	13	217
INTERNATIONAL JOURNAL OF ACCOUNTING AND INFORMATION MANAGEMENT	12	3	6	51
ACCOUNTING HORIZONS	11	6	9	90
ACCOUNTING RESEARCH JOURNAL	11	5	8	75
INTERNATIONAL JOURNAL OF AUDITING	11	5	7	60
INTERNATIONAL JOURNAL OF FINANCIAL RESEARCH	11	1	1	2

Table 2. Top 10 influential and productive authors

Author	h_index	g_index	m_index	TC	NP	PY_start
ZHANG J	6	8	0.462	168	8	2009
KAPLAN SE	6	8	0.429	151	8	2008
HABIB A	5	7	0.5	110	7	2012
CARPENTER TD	6	6	0.5	228	6	2010
SAMUELS JA	5	6	0.385	123	6	2009
SALIN ASAP	3	6	0.6	53	6	2017
NAWAWI A	3	6	0.6	53	6	2017
JR	2	4	0.25	22	6	2014
CHEN Y	3	5	0.273	493	5	2011
BRAZEL JF	4	5	0.333	86	5	2010

Table 3. Top 15 most cited papers

Paper	Total Citations	TC per Year
COHEN DA, 2010, J ACCOUNT ECON	712	59.33
ZANG AY, 2012, ACCOUNT REV	668	66.80
KIM Y, 2012, ACCOUNT REV	587	58.70
NGAI EWT, 2011, DECIS SUPPORT SYST	481	43.73
GUNNY KA, 2010, CONTEMP ACCOUNT RES	419	34.92
KARPOFF JM, 2008, J FINANC ECON	300	21.43
DICHEV ID, 2012, J ACCOUNT ECON	296	29.60
SCHRAND CM, 2012, J ACCOUNT ECON	281	28.10
MCGUIRE ST, 2012, ACCOUNT REV	274	27.40
CHIH H-L, 2008, J BUS ETHICS	223	15.93
RAVISANKAR P, 2011, DECIS SUPPORT SYST	200	18.18
HAZARIKA S, 2012, J FINANC ECON	159	15.90
KEDIA S, 2011, J ACCOUNT ECON	158	14.36
LENNOX C, 2010, CONTEMP ACCOUNT RES	149	12.42
HOGAN CE, 2008, AUDITING	146	10.43

capturing very similar themes and covers nearly identical topics. Such analysis sheds light on the most frequent themes studied and analyzed in the literature and depicts areas of similarity in research topics.

Table 4. Keywords' frequency

Terms	*Frequency*
Crime	***39***
Finance	***20***
Fraud	***18***
Fraud detection	***14***
Financial fraud	***10***
commerce	***9***
Risk assessment	***9***
Data mining	***8***
Decision making	***8***
Laws and legislation	***8***

To advance the analysis, the authors perform two distinct bibliometric measures: keywords thematic trend and clustering groups. In Figure 3, keywords thematic map generates a co-word analysis that draws density and centrality in order to classify themes and map them in a two-dimensional diagram. Both median and mean values for density and centrality can be used in classifying themes into four groups

Figure 2. Keywords cloud and dynamics

(Cahlik, 2000; Callon et al., 1991; Coulter et al., 1998): (1) upper-right quadrant: motor-themes; (2) lower-right quadrant: basic themes; (3) lower-left quadrant: emerging or disappearing themes; (4) upper-left quadrant: very specialized/niche themes.

- Themes in the upper-right quadrant, mostly "crime" are both well developed and important for the structuring of a research field. The "crime" theme is known as the motor-themes of the specialty, given that it presents strong centrality and high density.
- Themes in the upper-left quadrant such as "Fraud", "Decision making", and "Laws and legislation" have well developed internal ties but unimportant external ties and so are of only marginal importance for the field.
- Themes in the lower-left quadrant are both weakly developed and marginal. In this chapter, no themes belong to this quadrant.
- Themes in the lower-right quadrant such as "Corporate governance", "Commerce", and "Risk assessment" are important for a research field but are not developed. So, this quadrant groups transversal and general basic themes.

Furthermore, the authors follow the process of clustering to locate subgroups of keywords that are strongly linked to each other (Callon et al., 1991). Different clustering algorithms can be used to create a partition of the keywords network or graph: streemer (Kandylas et al., 2010), spectral clustering (X. Chen & Cai, 2011), modularity maximization (P. Chen & Redner, 2010) and a bootstrap resampling with a significance clustering (Rosvall & Bergstrom, 2010). In the present study, the clustering algorithm was performed based on the similarity matrix that returns labelled groups. Apparently, keywords are grouped in 6 clusters:

Figure 3. Keywords thematic map

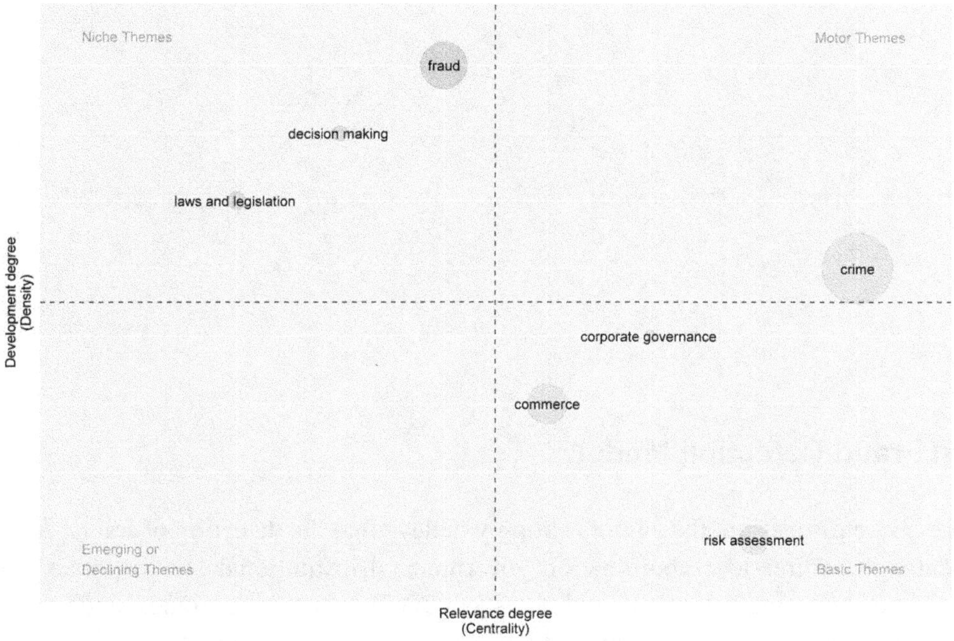

- First cluster (red) titled "Fraud" includes accounting, accounting fraud, audit, auditors, ethics, financial reporting, forensic accounting, frauds, internal control, regulation, Sarbanes-Oxley, and United States of America.
- Second cluster (green) titled "Corporate Governance" includes board independence, boards of directors, corporate governance, corporate social responsibility, discretionary accrual, earning management, financial reporting quality, real activity manipulation and real earnings management.
- Third cluster (dark blue) titled "Fraud triangle" includes corruption, financial statements fraud, fraud triangle, fraudulent financial reporting, internal control, rationalization, and whistleblowing.
- Fourth cluster (yellow) titled "Fraud detection" includes audit, audit committee, audit quality, fraud detection, fraud risk, governance, and professional skepticism.
- Fifth cluster (purple) titled "Corporate fraud" includes accountability, corporate fraud, fraud prevention, reputation, restatements, and trust.
- Sixth title (clear blue) titled "Earning manipulation" includes agency theory, earning manipulation, executives' compensation, and internal audit.

When depicting the yearly trend, it is noticeable that in 2014, 2015 and 2016, the bulk of publication addresses fraud, earning managements and corporate governance topics. The trend changed thereafter to tackle related topics such as whistleblowing, forensic accounting, real activities manipulation and audit quality.

Figure 4. Keywords co-occurrence network and keywords co-occurrence network by time

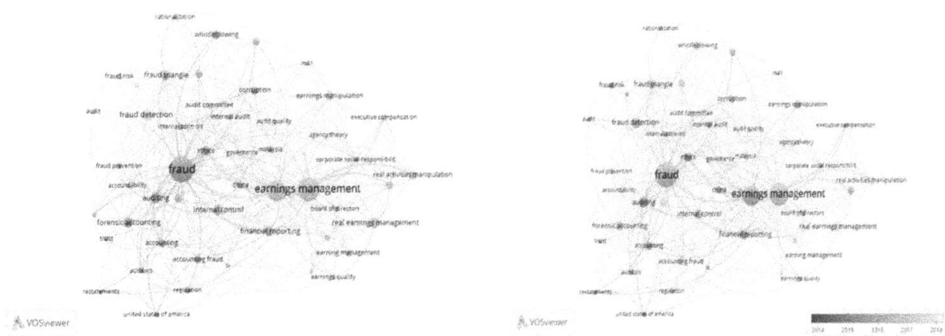

Proposed Fraud Detection Model

Based on the above discussion, the authors strongly believe that the detection of frauds is a joint-effort task which entangles a three-level coordination: governmental, institutional, and corporate. Governments play a vital role in enforcing rules and regulations, combating corruption, frauds, and tax evasion. The role of courts and forensic accounting and the intervention of the department of justice on Companies' frauds can alleviate the risk of frauds. In addition, government requirements to adopt specific accounting and auditing standards interact with the probability of committing or not committing frauds.

From institutional perspectives, many players can influence the risk of corporate frauds. Capital market authorities act as watchdog and monitor companies conduct whereby stock returns are assessed and analyzed to deduce fraud risk. In addition, global entities that grade companies based on environment, social and governance practices (ESG/CSR/GRI) are key players in monitoring and controlling corporate behavior and compliance. Analysts and media also affect companies' reputation by criticizing their behavior and scrutinizing their day-to-day activities. External auditors (Big Four) also contribute to reduce fraud risks. The audit choice, tenure, price, size, and quality are key metrics to analyze fraud probability. Auditors express their opinion and provide an assurance about the financial statements' quality.

On corporate level, there are two distinct components that describe the internal environment and reflect companies' qualitative and quantitative traits. The first group encompasses the board of directors (BOD) structure, corporate governance framework, audit committee, geography, CEO/CFO demographic traits, internal control and segregation of duties, code of ethics, quality control, IT and cloud-based accounting system, companies' media coverage and advertising, performance management and assessment of going concern. All these factors contribute to increase/decrease fraud risk. The second group covers financial data such as ratio, trend, and benchmarking analyses.

Thus, a three-level risk assessment and fraud detection model is built based on integrating the above metric while assigning weights to each one of them (Table 5). The weight assigned can be derived based on simulations and algorithms that account for all variables in all case scenarios. In this regard, the digital transformation and the development in information and communication technology play a key role where algorithmic models mimic past scenarios and offer consequential results (Akinbowale et al., 2021). A data bank should be created for all former manipulators from which a fraud detection threshold should be derived based on the three levels mentioned above.

Table 5. Three-level risk assessment and fraud detection model

	Level	Risk metric type	Risk metric %
Exogeneous	Country	Societal, political, and economic environment	C1
		Country risk level	C2
		Rules & Regulations	C3
		Courts& Forensic accounting	C4
		Department of justice intervention on Companies 'frauds	C5
		E-government system/ Tax revenues	C6
		Accounting standards requirements	C7
		Audit standards requirements	C8
		Reputation & Regulatory compliance	C9
	Institutional	Capital markets monitoring & compliance	I1
		ESG/GRI/CSR monitoring	I2
		Analysts monitoring	I3
		Media monitoring	I4
		Audit price/audit choice/audit quality/Audit firm size	I5
		Whistleblowing within the audit firms	I6
		Industry risk level	I7
Endogenous	Corporate/ qualitative	BOD structure	CQ1
		Audit committee/Corporate Governance framework	CQ2
		CEO demographics (gender/education/religion)	CQ3
		Code of ethics	CQ4
		Quality control framework	CQ5
		IT/cloud-based accounting risks	CQ6
		Segregation of duties	CQ7
		Internal control environment	CQ8
		Performance management system	CQ9
		Company media coverage & advertisement Bias	CQ10
		Assessment of going concern	CQ11
	Corporate/ quantitative	Financial ratios	CT1
		Trend analysis	CT2
		Peer benchmarking analysis	CT3
		Industry benchmarking analysis	CT4

Source: Prepared by authors

CONCLUSION

As the business world is surcharged with a myriad of forensic audit debates and fraud schemes, many scholars have explored the root of frauds, well-tailored scenarios, and main motives while others innovated in introducing methodologies and techniques to detect and early deter frauds and misstatements. In this chapter, the authors seek to help the body of auditors, forensic accountants, and regulators to learn from past fraudulent cases, explain the advantages and disadvantages of existing models and theoretically illustrate a new proposed model.

Thus, a bibliometric was conducted covering 1,112 documents from Scopus database published in 288 sources over the period 2008-Q1 of 2021 using RStudio, VOSviewer, and Excel. The average citation per document is 15.75 whereas the yearly average citation per document is 1.99. The Journal of Business Ethics contributes to 70 documents, followed by Issues in Accounting Education with 32 documents. In the third place are Auditing and Managerial Auditing journals with 28 publications each. Accounting review receives the highest number of citations over the studied period. On the level of authors, Zhang J. ranks first in terms of publications, with 8 articles, 168 citations and an h-index of 6. Kaplan SE ranks second with 8 papers, 151 citations, and an h- index of 6. The most influential author is Chen Y. with 493 citations. The most influential paper is "Accrual-based and real earnings management activities around seasoned equity offerings" (Cohen & Zarowin, 2010) published in the journal of Accounting and Economics with 712 citations.

From a deeper perspective, keyword analysis concluded with the word "crime" as the most frequent word (39), followed by "finance" (20), fraud (18), "fraud detection" (14), and "financial fraud" (10). The keywords thematic map pinpointed three quandrants: the first quandrant "crime" included the motor-themes of the specialty; the second quadrant "Fraud; Decision making; and Laws & legislation" included well developed internal ties but unimportant external ties, and the third quadrant "Corporate Governance; Commerce; and Risk assessment" included transversal and general basic themes. The clustering algorithm performed with a similarity matrix grouped the keywords in 6 clusters: "Fraud", "Corporate Governance", "Fraud triangle", "Fraud detection", "Corporate fraud", and "Earning manipulation".

In light of the above, the authors proposed a three-level model built based on 31 metrics to be integrated with weights assigned to each metric. The theoretical model helps auditors, forensic accountants, top managements, analysts, and policy makers predict potential anomalies and misstatements.

Solutions, Recommendations, and Future Research direction

A joint-effort harmonization and full coordination are recommended among accountants, auditors, IT developers and data analysts to concretize the model to benefit from digital techniques, handle a huge volume of accounting data and efficiently use them in the investigation process. The weight assigned to each metrics in the suggested model can be derived from simulations and algorithms that account for all variables in all case scenarios. In this regard, the digital transformation and the development in information and communication technology play a key role where algorithmic models mimic past scenarios and offer consequential results (Akinbowale et al., 2021). To concretize the model and test its accuracy, future research must approach its real application and apply it to a set of companies. A data bank should be created for all former manipulators from which a fraud detection threshold should be derived based on the three levels mentioned above.

This research received no specific grant from any funding agency in the public, commercial, or not-for-profit sectors.

REFERENCES

Abbasi, A., Albrecht, C., Vance, A., & Hansen, J. (2012). Metafraud: A meta-learning framework for detecting financial fraud. *MIS Quarterly: Management Information Systems, 36*(4), 1293-1327. doi:10.2307/41703508

Abu-Tapanjeh, A. M., & Al-Sarairah, T. M. K. (2021). The Availability of Forensic Accounting Application Factors to Enhance the Auditors Efficiency in Jordan. *Journal of Asian Finance, Economics and Business*, *8*(3), 807–819. doi:10.13106/jafeb.2021.vol8.no3.0807

ACFE. (2020). *Report to the Nations 2020 Global Study on Occupational Fraud and Abuse*. ACFE.

Ahlin, C., Kim, I. K., & Kim, K. I. (2021). Who commits fraud? evidence from korean gas stations. *International Journal of Industrial Organization*. https://www.scopus.com/inward/record.uri?eid=2-s2.0-85102045798&doi=10.1016%2Fj.ijindorg.2021.102719&partnerID=40&md5=21cfbb2fc7e1a1465354e13078ca68f0

Akinbowale, O. E., Klingelhöfer, H. E., & Zerihun, M. F. (2021). The integration of forensic accounting and the management control system as tools for combating cyberfraud. *Academy of Accounting and Financial Studies Journal*. https://www.scopus.com/inward/record.uri?eid=2-s2.0-85104067180&partnerID=40&md5=8b7e6a6124bc8e0c7ac0a7f06f8185ce

Al-Shattarat, B. (2021). The consequence of earnings management through discretionary accruals on the value relevance in Saudi Arabia. *Cogent Business and Management*. https://www.scopus.com/inward/record.uri?eid=2-s2.0-85101147598&doi=10.1080%2F23311975.2021.1886473&partnerID=40&md5=367058ea5b81f0eaead97587cbe97118

Albanese, J. S., Artello, K., & Nguyen, L. T. (2019). Distinguishing Corruption in Law and Practice: Empirically Separating Conviction Charges from Underlying Behaviors. *Public Integrity*. https://www.scopus.com/inward/record.uri?eid=2-s2.0-85052105879&doi=10.1080%2F10999922.2018.1423859&partnerID=40&md5=76d67089fff4e497f0c92633e0c304af

Almutairi, A. R. (2021). Earnings management and the role of MOSAL in co-ops. *Journal of Co-Operative Organization and Management*. https://www.scopus.com/inward/record.uri?eid=2-s2.0-85103615322&doi=10.1016%2Fj.jcom.2021.100131&partnerID=40&md5=6f69ee5f8e318dd4217e6fec547050ce

Alqirem, R., Abu Afifa, M., Saleh, I., & Haniah, F. (2020). Ownership Structure, Earnings Manipulation, and Organizational Performance: The Case of Jordanian Insurance Organizations. *Journal of Asian Finance, Economics and Business*. https://www.scopus.com/inward/record.uri?eid=2-s2.0-85098487789&doi=10.13106%2FJAFEB.2020.VOL7.NO12.293&partnerID=40&md5=3ac142432343b9a5574a8608f21622ff

Alsaadi, A. (2021). Can Inclusion in Religious Index Membership Mitigate Earnings Management? *Journal of Business Ethics*. https://www.scopus.com/inward/record.uri?eid=2-s2.0-85073994888&doi=10.1007%2Fs10551-019-04280-y&partnerID=40&md5=b3464c5aa65ec0dbce2ff8dc2c55b036

Attig, N., Chen, R., El Ghoul, S., Guedhami, O., Kwok, C., & Pittman, J. (2020). Are insiders equal? Evidence from earnings management in closely held East Asian firms. *Research in International Business and Finance*. https://www.scopus.com/inward/record.uri?eid=2-s2.0-85087213864&doi=10.1016%2Fj.ribaf.2020.101243&partnerID=40&md5=cbcb35eb6565e98a11fe507d582b3b7d

Bala, H., Amran, N. A., & Shaari, H. (2019). Audit committee attributes and cosmetic accounting in Nigeria: The moderating effect of audit price. *Managerial Auditing Journal*. https://www.scopus.com/inward/record.uri?eid=2-s2.0-85076140390&doi=10.1108%2FMAJ-06-2018-1897&partnerID=40&md5=a5f5e05da4e89e826d69570874e90dfa

Cahlik, T. (2000). Comparison of the maps of science. *Scientometrics*, *49*(3), 373–387. doi:10.1023/A:1010581421990

Callon, M., Courtial, J.-P., & Laville, F. (1991). Co-word analysis as a tool for describing the network of interactions between basic and technological research: The case of polymer chemsitry. *Scientometrics*, *22*(1), 155–205. doi:10.1007/BF02019280

Callon, M., Courtial, J. P., Turner, W. A., & Bauin, S. (1983). *From translations to problematic networks an introduction to co-word analysis.pdf*. Academic Press.

Chakrabarty, B., Duellman, S., & Hyman, M. A. (2020). A new approach to estimating the relation between audit fees and financial misconduct. *Accounting Horizons*, *34*(2), 41–61. doi:10.2308/horizons-19-042

Chakrabarty, S. (2015). The Influence of Unrelated and Related Diversification on Fraudulent Reporting. *Journal of Business Ethics*. https://www.scopus.com/inward/record.uri?eid=2-s2.0-84948387956&doi=10.1007%2Fs10551-013-2023-5&partnerID=40&md5=a7316538ac4117d860cbc0fdd3d640df

Chen, P., & Redner, S. (2010). Community structure of the physical review citation network. *Journal of Informetrics*, *4*(3), 278–290. doi:10.1016/j.joi.2010.01.001

Chen, X., & Cai, D. (2011). Large scale spectral clustering with landmark-based representation. *Twenty-Fifth AAAI Conference on Artificial Intelligence*.

Cohen, D. A., & Zarowin, P. (2010). Accrual-based and real earnings management activities around seasoned equity offerings. *Journal of Accounting and Economics*. https://www.scopus.com/inward/record.uri?eid=2-s2.0-77950950399&doi=10.1016%2Fj.jacceco.2010.01.002&partnerID=40&md5=4e52610cd23c687d0091eceda8f72f75

Cole, R., Johan, S., & Schweizer, D. (2021). Corporate failures: Declines, collapses, and scandals. *Journal of Corporate Finance*. https://www.scopus.com/inward/record.uri?eid=2-s2.0-85099838795&doi=10.1016%2Fj.jcorpfin.2020.101872&partnerID=40&md5=81aa80e1e264fd7314ae354d07079bef

Comprix, J., & Huang, H. (2015). Does auditor size matter? Evidence from small audit firms. *Advances in Accounting*. https://www.scopus.com/inward/record.uri?eid=2-s2.0-84929953630&doi=10.1016%2Fj.adiac.2015.03.007&partnerID=40&md5=e5dd2da87aca3a47bba08305181b1572

Coulter, N., Monarch, I., & Konda, S. (1998). Software engineering as seen through its research literature: A study in co-word analysis. *Journal of the American Society for Information Science*, *49*(13), 1206–1223. doi:10.1002/(SICI)1097-4571(1998)49:13<1206::AID-ASI7>3.0.CO;2-F

Craja, P., Kim, A., & Lessmann, S. (2020). Deep learning for detecting financial statement fraud. *Decision Support Systems*, *139*, 113421. Advance online publication. doi:10.1016/j.dss.2020.113421

Dhiaf, M. M., Atayah, O. F., Nasrallah, N., & Frederico, G. F. (2021). *Thirteen years of Operations Management Research (OMR) journal: a bibliometric analysis and future research directions.* Operations Management Research. doi:10.100712063-021-00199-8

Dichev, I. D., Graham, J. R., Harvey, C. R., & Rajgopal, S. (2012). Earnings quality: Evidence from the field. *Journal of Accounting and Economics.* https://www.scopus.com/inward/record.uri?eid=2-s2.0-84890151024&doi=10.1016%2Fj.jacceco.2013.05.004&partnerID=40&md5=3d337b47fd462c1a8d90c73ab0aae393

Dzikrullah, A. D., Harymawan, I., & Ratri, M. C. (2020). Internal audit functions and audit outcomes: Evidence from Indonesia. *Cogent Business and Management*, *7*(1), 1750331. Advance online publication. doi:10.1080/23311975.2020.1750331

Gebrayel, E., Jarrar, H., Salloum, C., & Lefebvre, Q. (2018). Effective association between audit committees and the internal audit function and its impact on financial reporting quality: Empirical evidence from Omani listed firms. *International Journal of Auditing.* https://www.scopus.com/inward/record.uri?eid=2-s2.0-85043695901&doi=10.1111%2Fijau.12113&partnerID=40&md5=99cff6d3411d5b36cc6237eca6c86167

Giese, G., Nagy, Z., & Lee, L.-E. (2021). Deconstructing ESG ratings performance: Risk and return for E, S, and G by time horizon, sector, and weighting. *Journal of Portfolio Management.* https://www.scopus.com/inward/record.uri?eid=2-s2.0-85101927608&doi=10.3905%2FJPM.2020.1.198&partnerID=40&md5=5d4227b8dc01f23e2e0ccb4c32d145bc

Guo, J., Huang, P., Zhang, Y., & Zhou, N. (2015). Foreign ownership and real earnings management: Evidence from Japan. *Journal of International Accounting Research.* https://www.scopus.com/inward/record.uri?eid=2-s2.0-84956875166&doi=10.2308%2Fjiar-51274&partnerID=40&md5=31fcd005420bda14068534b400cf9649

Handayani, S., & Kawedar, W. (2021). Could the minimization of opportunity prevent fraud? An empirical study in the auditors' perspective. *Accounting*, *7*(5), 1157–1166. doi:10.5267/j.ac.2021.2.023

Haruna Abubakar, A., Mansor, N., & Adilah Wan-Mohamad, W. I. (2021). Corporate tax avoidance, free cash flow and real earnings management: Evidence from Nigeria. *Universal Journal of Accounting and Finance.* https://www.scopus.com/inward/record.uri?eid=2-s2.0-85101872498&doi=10.13189%2Fujaf.2021.090109&partnerID=40&md5=4321320ced3149ba01c0556e4e69cf1f

Hashem, F. (2021). The role of forensic accounting techniques in reducing cloud based accounting risks in the Jordanian five stars hotels. *WSEAS Transactions on Business and Economics*, *18*, 434–443. doi:10.37394/23207.2021.18.44

Hickman, L. E., Iyer, S. R., & Jadiyappa, N. (2021). The effect of voluntary and mandatory corporate social responsibility on earnings management: Evidence from India and the 2% rule. *Emerging Markets Review*. https://www.scopus.com/inward/record.uri?eid=2-s2.0-85095772108&doi=10.1016%2Fj.ememar.2020.100750&partnerID=40&md5=7584a931ef7ab0c2247f2fc5c4bec42b

Kandylas, V., Upham, S. P., & Ungar, L. H. (2010). Analyzing knowledge communities using foreground and background clusters. *ACM Transactions on Knowledge Discovery from Data*, *4*(2), 1–35. doi:10.1145/1754428.1754430

Kao, L., Chen, A., & Lu, C.-S. (2018). Ex ante and ex post overvalued equities: The roles of corporate governance and product market competition. *Asia Pacific Management Review*. https://www.scopus.com/inward/record.uri?eid=2-s2.0-85026657065&doi=10.1016%2Fj.apmrv.2017.07.002&partnerID=40&md5=dfde7f1eaad43e8fb8da6a616e13c35d

Khatwani, R. K., & Goyal, V. (2019). Predictor of financial dishonesty: Self control, opportunity, attitudes. *Academy of Accounting and Financial Studies Journal*. https://www.scopus.com/inward/record.uri?eid=2-s2.0-85081894874&partnerID=40&md5=9ce60b2912d6ed1525cc0126f0d35015

Kouki, M., Elkhaldi, A., Atri, H., & Souid, S. (2011). Does corporate governance constrain earnings management? Evidence from U.S. firms. *European Journal of Economics, Finance and Administrative Sciences*. https://www.scopus.com/inward/record.uri?eid=2-s2.0-84860420479&partnerID=40&md5=e7947bb7f8010d890ea7e2faccf2a5fa

Kountur, R., Djohanputro, B., & Sari, M. R. (2021). Past performance and earning management: The moderating effect of employee relative earning. *Accounting*. https://www.scopus.com/inward/record.uri?eid=2-s2.0-85097960334&doi=10.5267%2Fj.ac.2020.11.018&partnerID=40&md5=67cbd80897fa6c1407250365e1abac79

Lassou, P. J. C., Hopper, T., & Soobaroyen, T. (2021). Financial controls to control corruption in an African country: Insider experts within an enabling environment. *Financial Accountability and Management*. https://www.scopus.com/inward/record.uri?eid=2-s2.0-85082423108&doi=10.1111%2Ffaam.12240&partnerID=40&md5=8627825723b9c3629471b9584fc6f752

Latan, H., Chiappetta Jabbour, C. J., & de Sousa Jabbour, A. B. (2019). 'Whistleblowing Triangle': Framework and Empirical Evidence. *Journal of Business Ethics*, *160*(1), 189–204. doi:10.100710551-018-3862-x

Liao, P., Wan, Y., Tang, P., Wu, C., Hu, Y., & Zhang, S. (2019). Applying crowdsourcing techniques in urban planning: A bibliometric analysis of research and practice prospects. *Cities (London, England)*, *94*, 33–43. doi:10.1016/j.cities.2019.05.024

Madrueño, R., & Tezanos, S. (2018). The contemporary development discourse: Analysing the influence of development studies' journals. *World Development*, *109*, 334–345. doi:10.1016/j.worlddev.2018.05.005

Makarem, N., & Roberts, C. (2020). Earnings management to avoid earnings boosts. *Journal of Applied Accounting Research*. https://www.scopus.com/inward/record.uri?eid=2-s2.0-85091466628&doi=10.1108%2FJAAR-01-2019-0012&partnerID=40&md5=b6a4f42012afb7f2aab28201c8f2e4c3

Manning, G. A., & CFE, E. A. (1999). *Financial investigation and forensic accounting*. CRC Press.

Meiryani, F., Susanto, A., & Warganegara, D. L. (2019). The effect of accounting information systems performance and unthetic behavior on accounting fraud. *International Journal of Recent Technology and Engineering*. https://www.scopus.com/inward/record.uri?eid=2-s2.0-85073496595&doi=10.35940%2Fijrte.C4966.098319&partnerID=40&md5=3ed88275c72684e024ea89ef098bebf3

Moche Halman, R. (2013). Equity agency costs in payouts, pension plan manipulation and firm performance. *Managerial Finance*. https://www.scopus.com/inward/record.uri?eid=2-s2.0-85015645884&doi=10.1108%2FMF-09-2011-0218&partnerID=40&md5=e4774675540dc5aed39b6673584d2b19

Muzurura, J. (2019). Causes, dissemination channels, and consequences of corruption in Zimbabwe: Searching for a kryptonite solution. *Humanities and Social Sciences Letters*. https://www.scopus.com/inward/record.uri?eid=2-s2.0-85071653198&doi=10.18488%2Fjournal.73.2019.72.105.122&partnerID=40&md5=254654870a65d9f071761ed04a63bce8

Nasrallah, N., & El Khoury, R. (2021). Is corporate governance a good predictor of SMEs financial performance? Evidence from developing countries (the case of Lebanon). *Journal of Sustainable Finance and Investment*, *0*(0), 1–31. doi:10.1080/20430795.2021.1874213

Rahim, S. A. A., Nawawi, A., & Salin, A. S. A. P. (2017). Internal control weaknesses in a cooperative body: Malaysian experience. *International Journal of Management Practice*. https://www.scopus.com/inward/record.uri?eid=2-s2.0-85015886071&doi=10.1504%2FIJMP.2017.083082&partnerID=40&md5=4c5b97c0acf352ee760e64874fea6d1a

Ramos-Rodrígue, A.-R., & Ruíz-Navarro, J. (2004). Changes in the intellectual structure of strategic management research: A bibliometric study of the Strategic Management Journal, 1980-2000. *Strategic Management Journal*, *25*(10), 981–1004. doi:10.1002mj.397

Reinstein, A., Moehrle, S. R., & Reynolds-Moehrle, J. (2006). Crime and punishment in the marketplace: Accountants and business executives repeating history. *Managerial Auditing Journal*, *21*(4), 420–435. doi:10.1108/02686900610661423

Reinstein, A., & Taylor, E. Z. (2017). Fences as Controls to Reduce Accountants' Rationalization. *Journal of Business Ethics*. https://www.scopus.com/inward/record.uri?eid=2-s2.0-84930157585&doi=10.1007%2Fs10551-015-2701-6&partnerID=40&md5=8d4292750a411f3f29d8be9a256e33bc

Rosvall, M., & Bergstrom, C. T. (2010). Mapping change in large networks. *PLoS One*, *5*(1), e8694. doi:10.1371/journal.pone.0008694 PMID:20111700

Salem, R. I. A., Ezeani, E., Gerged, A. M., Usman, M., & Alqatamin, R. M. (2020). Does the quality of voluntary disclosure constrain earnings management in emerging economies? Evidence from Middle Eastern and North African banks. *International Journal of Accounting and Information Management*. https://www.scopus.com/inward/record.uri?eid=2-s2.0-85090935141&doi=10.1108%2FIJAIM-07-2020-0109&partnerID=40&md5=73f58289a72c2b79d8fa4d3161bc255f

Sari, M. R., Djohanputro, B., & Kountur, R. (2021). Past Performance and Earnings Management: The Effect of Free Cash Flow. *Journal of Asian Finance, Economics and Business*. https://www.scopus.com/inward/record.uri?eid=2-s2.0-85099637578&doi=10.13106%2Fjafeb.2021.vol8.no1.037&partnerID=40&md5=a11c09379fc61ada4780f669773e12e5

Schoenefeld, J. J. (2020). Interest Groups, NGOs or Civil Society Organisations? The Framing of Non-State Actors in the EU. *Voluntas*. Advance online publication. doi:10.100711266-020-00283-w

Shayan-Nia, M., Sinnadurai, P., Mohd-Sanusi, Z., & Hermawan, A.-N. A. (2017). How efficient ownership structure monitors income manipulation? Evidence of real earnings management among Malaysian firms. *Research in International Business and Finance*. https://www.scopus.com/inward/record.uri?eid=2-s2.0-85018729713&doi=10.1016%2Fj.ribaf.2017.04.013&partnerID=40&md5=858da065c490e22a3c1e8a734d564353

Sun, E. Y. (2021). The Differential Role of R&D and SG&A for Earnings Management and Stock Price Manipulation. *Contemporary Accounting Research*. https://www.scopus.com/inward/record.uri?eid=2-s2.0-85099405498&doi=10.1111%2F1911-3846.12634&partnerID=40&md5=977fef5faee3f0d38cec19be8623b3e3

Sun, J., Kent, P., Qi, B., & Wang, J. (2019). Chief financial officer demographic characteristics and fraudulent financial reporting in China. *Accounting and Finance*. https://www.scopus.com/inward/record.uri?eid=2-s2.0-85026315834&doi=10.1111%2Facfi.12286&partnerID=40&md5=c9962c7814b0a9c2aa2bf8cd3e010630

Taleatu, T. A., Adetula, D. T., & Iyoha, F. O. (2020). Moderating effect of governance quality on the relationship between CFOs' narcissism and corporate earnings management in Nigeria. *Journal of Management Information and Decision Science*. https://www.scopus.com/inward/record.uri?eid=2-s2.0-85099143260&partnerID=40&md5=ca2f8249beb76a5b11ab5cf73e3be5f5

Taminiau, Y., Heusinkveld, S., & Cramer, L. (2019). Colonization contests: How both accounting and law firms gain legitimacy in the market for forensic accounting. *Journal of Professions and Organization*. https://www.scopus.com/inward/record.uri?eid=2-s2.0-85070185712&doi=10.1093%2Fjpo%2Fjoz001&partnerID=40&md5=81c8178d9c0e5aeacc0f3c8f9b3568e2

Todd Dezoort, F., Harrison, P. D., & Schnee, E. J. (2012). Tax professionals' responsibility for fraud detection: The effects of engagement type and audit status. *Accounting Horizons*, *26*(2), 289–306. doi:10.2308/acch-50137

Tuan Mansor, T. M., Mohamad Ariff, A., & Hashim, H. A. (2020). Whistleblowing by auditors: The role of professional commitment and independence commitment. *Managerial Auditing Journal*, *35*(8), 1033–1055. doi:10.1108/MAJ-11-2019-2484

Xu, H., Dao, M., & Wu, J. (2019). The effect of local political corruption on earnings quality. *Review of Quantitative Finance and Accounting*. https://www.scopus.com/inward/record.uri?eid=2-s2.0-85053195338&doi=10.1007%2Fs11156-018-0758-x&partnerID=40&md5=048b681de68277ce67d67e14d2c8f407

Yamada, A., Sakurai, Y., & Ishida, R. (2020). Influence of geographic distribution on real activities manipulation within consolidated companies: Evidence from Japan. *Research in International Business and Finance*. https://www.scopus.com/inward/record.uri?eid=2-s2.0-85089901554&doi=10.1016%2Fj.ribaf.2020.101306&partnerID=40&md5=64a2b8249def4ae41d06a4271c1f2dbf

Yasser, Q. R., & Mamun, A. A. (2015). The impact of CEO duality attributes on earnings management in the East. *Corporate Governance (Bingley)*. https://www.scopus.com/inward/record.uri?eid=2-s2.0-84942770012&doi=10.1108%2FCG-04-2015-0041&partnerID=40&md5=dee41da152434b8c74c812876115c772

Zang, A. Y. (2012). Evidence on the trade-off between real activities manipulation and accrual-based earnings management. *Accounting Review*. https://www.scopus.com/inward/record.uri?eid=2-s2.0-80155175155&doi=10.2308%2Faccr-10196&partnerID=40&md5=36a3f07a5e0186426d834341805eb3fb

APPENDIX 1

TITLE-ABS-KEY ("forensic account*" OR " forensic audit*" OR " earning management" OR " manipulation" OR "financial crime*" OR "fraud*") AND (LIMIT-TO (PUBSTAGE, "final")) AND (LIMIT-TO (DOCTYPE, "ar")) AND (LIMIT-TO (SUBJAREA, "BUSI")) AND (LIMIT-TO (EXACTKEYWORD, "Fraud") OR LIMIT-TO (EXACTKEYWORD, "Earnings Management") OR LIMIT-TO (EXACTKEYWORD, "Corporate Governance") OR LIMIT-TO (EXACTKEYWORD, "Fraud Detection") OR LIMIT-TO (EXACTKEYWORD, "Manipulation") OR LIMIT-TO (EXACTKEYWORD, "Auditing") OR LIMIT-TO (EXACTKEYWORD, "Corruption") OR LIMIT-TO (EXACTKEYWORD, "Internal Control") OR LIMIT-TO (EXACTKEYWORD, "Fraud Triangle") OR LIMIT-TO (EXACTKEYWORD, "Financial Fraud") OR LIMIT-TO (EXACTKEYWORD, "Forensic Accounting") OR LIMIT-TO (EXACTKEYWORD, "Laws And Legislation") OR LIMIT-TO (EXACTKEYWORD, "Risk Management") OR LIMIT-TO (EXACTKEYWORD, "Whistleblowing") OR LIMIT-TO (EXACTKEYWORD, "Real Earnings Management") OR LIMIT-TO (EXACTKEYWORD, "Accounting") OR LIMIT-TO (EXACTKEYWORD, "Earnings Manipulation") OR LIMIT-TO (EXACTKEYWORD, "Corporate Fraud") OR LIMIT-TO (EXACTKEYWORD, "Forgery") OR LIMIT-TO (EXACTKEYWORD, "Risk Assessment") OR LIMIT-TO (EXACTKEYWORD, "Financial Statement Fraud") OR LIMIT-TO (EXACTKEYWORD, "Fraudulent Financial Reporting") OR LIMIT-TO (EXACTKEYWORD, "Internal Audit") OR LIMIT-TO (EXACTKEYWORD, "Real Activities Manipulation") OR LIMIT-TO (EXACTKEYWORD, "Accounting Fraud") OR LIMIT-TO (EXACTKEYWORD, "Market Manipulation") OR LIMIT-TO (EXACTKEYWORD, "Earning Management") OR LIMIT-TO (EXACTKEYWORD, "Fraud Risk") OR LIMIT-TO (EXACTKEYWORD, "Audit Committee") OR LIMIT-TO (EXACTKEYWORD, "Fraud Prevention") OR LIMIT-TO (EXACTKEYWORD, "Information Asymmetry") OR LIMIT-TO (EXACTKEYWORD, "Benford's Law") OR LIMIT-TO (EXACTKEYWORD, "Financial Reporting Quality")) AND (LIMIT-TO (LANGUAGE, "English"))

APPENDIX 2

The Institute of Museum and Library Services has collected some interesting statistics indicating that despite the sharp decline in library usage over the last ten years, libraries have actually seen an *increase* in the number of people who come through their doors annually since the beginning of the current recessionary period in 2008. Was this a contradiction, or some kind of error? Table 1 shows the data in question.

Table 6. Visits to public libraries

Year	Per Capita Visit to Public Library	Year	Per Capita Visit to Public Library
1998	4.2	2003	4.6
1999	4.3	2004	4.6
2000	4.3	2005	4.7
2001	4.4	2006	4.8
2002	4.4	2007	5.0

(Data Source: National Center for Education Statistics, 1998-2007)

Chapter 8
Forensic Accounting and Corporate Governance

Randa Diab-Bahman
Kuwait College of Science and Technology, Kuwait

Talal Abdullah Bahman
Kuwait Union of Exchange Companies, Kuwait

ABSTRACT

In this chapter, the necessity for compliance and corporate governance is discussed. It is essential to shine the limelight on these practices, and they are considered important for economic growth. Corporate governance is, in theory, a rather straightforward process with pre-determined policies and procedures. However, it is becoming increasingly clear that there are plenty of deficiencies in the way these procedures are being implemented. In fact, fraud is becoming more difficult to detect as strategies to fight corruption continue to be loosely implemented. Implications of conventional theory and traditional practices are discussed with an emphasis on today's standards, along with the objectivity of the underlying pillars of ethics, social norms, and personal values. The chapter highlights the importance of corporate governance and its added value to professional and social settings.

DEFINITION AND HISTORY

The issues of poor corporate governance in organizations have pushed for the functions of forensic accounting. Organizations value forensic accounting in the current world as intangible assets that trace to the vital role of effective corporate governance. In its definition, corporate governance is a system of regulations, rules, and accepted practices that define the way an organization is controlled and directed. It aims at balancing stakeholders' interests to achieve a balance of interests and attainment of the corporate objectives and performance measures. Forensic accounting includes the investigative and accounting techniques used by organizations to identify instances of financial crime (Ocansey, 2017). It entails identifying assets, conducting due diligence to recover lost assets, and tracing funds that have been illegally assigned to diverse segments, some of which end up being pocketed by the corporate

DOI: 10.4018/978-1-7998-8754-6.ch008

leaders and employees. Forensic accounting, including auditing and accounting practices,is used to examine how finances are utilized by business holders and individual operators. The analysis helps in legal proceedings, especially when there is embezzlement or fraud involved.

Forensic accounting dates back to ancient times in Egypt, where the pharaohs used scribes to help them in tracking valuable items like grain and gold. They could record independent transactions, an aspect that included internal control checks, and thorough record-keeping, which helped them to solve disputes regarding financial damages. Such accounts were merely informal, until 1817 when the first case of forensic accounting was documented. In the case of Meyer vs Sefton, the case of bankruptcy required them to identify the estate's value. The court issued an order for accountants to examine the accounts before testifying. The process of identifying litigation matters required expertise in accounting for the involved parties to identify flaws in the case and present their findings before courts.

Smith (2015) explains that based on the accounting standards, the renowned superhero forensic accountant is Frank Wilson, who was used to identify theft patterns and bring down Al Capone, a notorious gangster. Al Capone had been documented as a criminal with a history of organized crimes, and there were several attempts to prosecute him that had failed. Capone could buy his freedom by issuing threats to witnesses and bribing officials. When the US government decided to build a case of tax evasion in 1930 against Capone, Frank Wilson took the responsibility to investigate his tax evasion claims and extravagant lifestyle. Wilson worked with other members to trace Capone's incomes, yet he had claimed he did not have a source of income. He was eventually arrested, convicted, and prosecuted for the crime of tax evasion, leading to his eleven years in prison.

The incidents of white-collar crimes relating to the embezzlement of funds led to the rise of forensic accounting. The fraud triangle, a concept developed in the 1950s by criminologist Donald Cressey, introduced three aspects of fraudsters' motives to steal; rationalization, motivation, and opportunity. Donald established findings that helped in forensic accounting, including how fraud is conducted and ways to detect and prevent its occurrence. For instance, Donald claims that a business can have little control over rational elements or motives in the fraud triangle. However, they need to hold internal control systems to help in tracking and eliminating possible opportunities that spur fraud. The 20th century has seen financial complexities and accounting rules evolve (Gray & Moussalli, 2006). In the same way, there was a growing demand for forensic accountants due to the increasing accounting scandals. One of the known cases is that of Enron, which took place in 2001. When the firm was declared bankruptcy, the firm's auditor, Arthur Andersen, passed on. Other scandals emerged, including WorldCom's bankruptcy. The discoveries included manipulated financial statements amounting to millions of funds. This resulted in regulations to enhance financial reporting and transparency among firms. The Sarbanes-Oxley Act was developed to enhance the role of forensic accounting for all publicly traded firms. Forensic accountants have since become essential for investors and corporations that want to avoid financial scandals relating to fraud and embezzlement (Yadav & Yadav, 2013). As the number of accounting crimes continues to increase, organizations are relying on forensic accountants to track illegal transactions, manipulate financial statements, and other motives and opportunities for fraudulent activities.

Forensic Accounting and Transparency in Corporate Governance

The current global economy is characterized by increasing financial corruption, which presents an adverse phenomenon in terms of financial reporting and control. The poor governance systems and lack of implementation of financial control regulations have seen public finance crimes increasing especially within the public sector. The laws and legislations passed are not sufficient to hold firms accountable for the financial budgets and allocation of funds. Brennan (2011) argues that because of poor corporate governance, most firms are subjected to a lack of information disclosure as contained within the financial statements. Others operate on manipulated systems that favour the interests of minority groups that control the financial operations. To achieve transparency and promote accountability, firms are investing in forensic accounting to achieve relevant and efficient representation in their financial data and statements. They are working towards understanding the diverse operations, allocation of resources, and funds to achieve organizational growth instead of misuse of funds, fraudulent allocations, and other forms of embezzlement (Herbert et al., 2017). Through forensic accounting, firms are engaging professional and legal actions to deal with problems in accounting and events that present manipulated reports and financial information. The concept of transparency relates to the clarity of presented data in the financial statements and other forms of auditing reports. Forensic accountants are working towards handling any discrepancies in the corporate financial statements and accounting reports. They help to achieve transparency by evaluating the statements and reports, identifying any flaws in accounting, and presenting the findings for judicial review (Brennan, 2011). In cases where a firm engages in fraud and embezzlement, the forensic accountant helps to identify instances of lack of transparency and accountability.

Current Mandates in the Middle East and North Africa (MENA)

According to OECD (2017), governments in MENA regions are assigning forensic accounting experts with responsibilities of assessing risks and promoting effective internal controls. The economies operating under fraud and related uncertainties call for policies that counter the growing economic challenges of the embezzlement of funds. Within the MENA states, there are international standards involved in promoting auditing, risk management, and internal control processes, although most of them required advanced control and management. The functions of internal auditing in forensic accounting extend beyond just the budgetary expenditures. Forensic accountants have been involved in setting investigations to identify inherent risks of wrong allocations in diverse professional areas. They integrate diverse procedures that help in reducing risks of embezzlement and promote effective allocation of resources and funds to the correct accounts. For instance, there are cases involving entities that assign resources and funds to family members, allocate tenders and other government subsidies to imaginary accounts, and pocket funds for personal growth. MENA nations have responded by introducing forensic accounting within the public and private spheres to track illegal allocations and identify flaws in performance that can result in embezzlement. The forensic experts ensure that there are functional responsibilities assigned to the public office holders, and the senior management remains accountable for the corporate governance and budgetary allocations (Digabriele, 2008). The mandates introduced by MENA nations include financial inspections through auditing and carrying out verification processes to investigate instances of corruption and fraud. With these programs instituted for forensic experts, most officeholders have been arrested and prosecuted for wrongful allocation and embezzlement.

The forensic accountants in MENA nations have also built on professional capacity from the audit practitioners and internal control systems. The regional hinges surrounding improper auditing by internal accountants subject most public and private resources to illegal allocations, with the dominating few members taking advantage of their powers to control and use the resources for personal growth. As indicated by Brennan (2011), the weak corporate governance systems have become a challenging concept, and forensic accounting has grown in these nations to ensure that they introduce actions that hold corporate leaders accountable for misappropriations. Firms no longer rely on internal systems solely to conduct auditing and establish closing financial statements. Apart from the internal auditors, the forensic accountants keep track of the developing allocations and standards of practice following the established code of performance. In promoting professional practice, they are crucial in evaluating the performance of a company about the economy and evaluating whether government policies such as taxation have been adhered to. In instances where there are tax evaders in the economy, forensic accountants come in to track them and record the deviations that result from their corrupt operations.

The forensic accounting mandates in the MENA nations have also incorporated the impacts of information technology in forensic accounting for internal controls. The information technology procedures and tools are becoming essential in modern accounting systems, and they are inseparable from organizational activities and control procedures. Incorporate governance, information technology has been integrated to influence performance and data analytics. Information technology has become important in promoting risk management, monitoring processes to ascertain compliance, and providing data analytics that governs corporate decisions. Just like auditors, forensic accountants in the MENA economies understand the impact of information technology in promoting fraud and corruption. By incorporating the IT tools into their performance structures, forensic accountants get to track analytics linked to corruption and fraud cases. They easily identify behavioral patterns such as online transactions made to private accounts and other instances that affect the interoperability within the corporate offices. Information technology is becoming central to their accounting decisions, and most nations are promoting IT infrastructures that help in addressing control practices and creating a platform for better forensic accounting.

Forensic accounting in Africa has been used to develop and implement policies and procedures geared towards addressing corruption and fraud. Despite corporate governance insisting on effective internal controls, the forensic accountants provide special procedures for risk assessment, tracking illegal transactions, and recording corrupt incidents within the organization. Most public offices across Africa, have been subjected to adverse corporate governance, and most officials, including presidents, are engaged in embezzlement of public resources and funds. Forensic accounting has become an add-on element for management practices through the specific approaches to separate risk analysis and determination of the overall accountability in the organization. The forensic accountants help to raise concerns on areas where senior management needs to act to protect resources and funds for effective allocation. The gradual processes in forensic accounting growth in Africa have seen most leaders finding financial gaps that have been existing since the previous leadership governances. Some corporate officials even duplicate events and transactions to take control of resources, but forensic accounting brings out the policies that identify such patterns.

Being a forensic accountant/fraud examiner in Africa requires a background of multidisciplinary skills and expertise that helps to identify international trajectories of fraud and corruption crimes. According to Digabriele (2008), the majority of cases of embezzlement of public funds are based on international links, which makes it challenging for accountants and auditors to evaluate the patterns and bring out trends that help in risk assessment. For fraud examiners or forensic accountants, the financial crimes relating to abuse of office and corruption are interlinked, and these professionals have to possess effective background skills in handling international crimes. The complex patterns in Africa, for instance, call for specialized skills in electronic commerce, globalization patterns, and the growth of Internet fraud (Bhasin, 2015). In essence, forensic accountants in Africa are required to be Certified in Financial Forensics (CFF). The current society has seen the increasing demand for these forensic accountants, a call for most of them to get efficient training and expertise to handle the international cases of fraud and embezzlement (Bhasin,

2015). Nations in Africa have diverse bodies that certify forensic accountants. For instance, Nigeria has the Association of National Accountants in Nigeria, and the Chartered Accountants of Nigeria (Dada, Owolabi & Okwu, 2013). The forensic accountants acquire specialized training and certification to help them in fighting financial crimes and enforcing regulations that fight over capital crimes.

These developments in Africa illustrate how the growth of financial crimes and accounting fraud has affected the areas of corporate governance. They illustrate a call for research, education,and certification, and professional practice for more forensic accountants to enhance the practical application of forensic expertise in protecting resources. The mandates relating to the control of financial crimes also indicate how Africa is suffering from weak corporate governance, and how most leaders are using power and their political positions to control public resources and subject the public to turmoil. There have been several cases of public funds embezzlement from the politicians and holders of public office, and some of them are presented before the International Criminal Courts to answer fraud and financial corruption allegations. Though the problem of embezzlement continues to persist, and this calls for better reforms to counter the growing greed from public officials (Subash, 2015). Even in the private sector, several firms are suffering from bankruptcy due to embezzlement and improper accounting. The philosophy of exploiting the moment has led to most holders of the office taking advantage of the moment to exploit the resources for personal gains before they leave office. For this reason, Africans are on the verge of giving up because even the political agendas and reforms do not protect public resources.

Forensic Accounting Mandates in Europe

The EU has introduced several actions in response to the growing cases of fraud and corruption across the globe. The fraudulent financial reports and incidents of firms and states violating the corporate governance codes have led to the growing need for forensic accounting. The EU recognizes that there are growing scandals in Europe, which are inevitable, and call for new regulations and corporate governance reforms that enhance transparency, accountability, and responsibility of the outcomes of forensic auditing. With the established code of professional ethics, firms in Europe have to deal with guidelines established to promote roles of corporate governance. The EU has also established a code of conduct that guides the performance of independent auditors and the roles of forensic accountants in tracking and ensuring that the auditors promote the requirements of financial recording and documentation as per the corporate laws (Okpako & Atube, 2013). The EU has a statutory audit requirement that helps in documenting financial transactions, an aspect that helps to certify that the preparation of financial records and statements are valid and contain appropriate data and analytics. The shareholders and stakeholders rely on the statutory audit to determine the accuracy of accounts and the effectiveness of corporate governance. The statutory audit requirements have become essential in promoting independence among firms, individuals, and public offices. They allow investors to evaluate the audited reports and validate their projections before choosing the investment options. They are also important in promoting audit supervision and the development of the EU audit market. Overall, these statutory audit mandates are essential in promoting cooperation among EU nations.

The EU forensic accounting mandates cover several requirements. One of them is insolvency, bankruptcy, and reorganization of corporate governance. For instance, forensic accountants come in to analyze and document debts that lead to bankruptcy, the creditors that require payment, and validate entities that legally required reimbursement after a firm goes bankrupt. Through their analysis and auditing, the forensic accountants help corporate officials in Europe to manage financial affairs, identify transfers before a corporation goes bankrupt, recover assets and funds that can be used to reimburse creditors, and determine the payments that can be used to protect a firm from going bankrupt. Since bankruptcy fraud is a common issue that results in closure for many firms, forensic accountants focus on scientific and analytical research to make claims and disclosures that help to understand the sources of bankruptcy for firms. In public offices, the forensic accountants track instances of insolvency and help in creating the need for reorganization and development of new programs and agendas that counter the increasing public office fraud.

According to Ozili (2015), there are also mandates covering computer forensic analysis, which include recovery and preservation of electronic pieces of evidence for litigation. The current society is characterized by the growth of social networks, and the Internet becoming a source of online transactions. With electronic forms of payments and transactions, the valuable information stored in the computers can help forensic accountants to identify manipulated files and hard drives containing fraud and corruption information. Cloud computing is a growing part of Europe, and digital information is becoming useful for forensic accountants just like the traditional paperwork systems. Through mandates allowing forensic accountants to engage computer forensic in their investigations, they can track physical locations of suspects and data sets that can help them to identify fraud-related issues. These laptops, iPhones, and notebooks among other gadgets can track information and help in conducting a forensic evaluation to identify prevailing patterns of litigation and help to prove that an individual or entity is engaging in financial fraud.

Finally, the EU mandates are also applicable in calculating economic damages and filing lawsuits. When a party feels that a wrong has been conducted against him or her, the prevailing litigation may not be sufficient. The same case applies to corporate governance, where the causation of damages pushes a firm to evaluate economic losses from events such as floods, theft, fire, and other instances of property loss. Forensic accountants are engaged to inspect the property, evaluate historical information relating to the loss case, interviews individuals around to evaluate whether there are insights that can guide the investigation process, and ensure that they present findings that can help to address the existing issue. Although the forensic accountant can advise the parties, he or she has to remain objective when engaging the parties and ensure that the damage calculations do not refute justice.

Identifying Fraud

According to McMullen & Sanchez (2010), the process of identifying fraud can be challenging. Though, forensic accountants evaluate existing data to determine the performance gaps that could lead to loss of resources and funds. Typically, a financial accountant will gather the information that helps in tracking down a suspect, after which the accountant uses available findings and reports to present evidence for the hearing. Most of them track down irregular patterns that can affect corporate governance, such as cases where scammers use fake identity to embezzle resources and funds. When the firm's corporate governance structures are weak, the accountants come in to evaluate the probability of certain corporates exploiting others and achieving personal benefits at the expense of the firm. Because they are responsible for the provision of financial security, forensic accountants use their skills and expertise to track patterns that can lead to fraud.

Evidence and Credibility

Forensic accountants are required to quantify a loss and present claims of negligence to ascertain that they are credible in their operations. For instance, if there is an accountant who has breached the duty to care, resulting in the company losing a client, then the forensic accountant comes in to quantify the loss and show how the duty to care was breached. Through the accountancy services, the forensic accountant will present considerations that need to be followed or addressed to achieve credibility and effective accountancy. Forensic accountants also require witnesses of fact to provide pieces of evidence to help in investigations. Since most fraud cases are capital, these witnesses might feel threatened. For this reason, forensic accountants call on governments to protect witnesses of facts. Sometimes, they require accountants in a corporation to become a professional witness to achieve accountancy through the evidence provided.

DEFICIENCIES IN AUDITING METHODS

Compliance in an organization is a mindset that starts from the top down in an organization. The main point of an audit is to see that there are no material mistakes in the record-keeping process -according to the accounting standards that the country follows rather than operational methods or techniques. However, external audit typically does not take into account the ethical standards or understandings of the board members and their tolerance level. This section will examine the possible flaws in conventional auditing methods which may impact governance.

Financial Record Keeping

In an organization, all the transactions have to be recorded and summarized in an organized form by the accounting department. These records are essential to provide evidence of the financial transaction to the relevant party. Financial record keeping is a process that starts from the identification of the transaction, recording it, and classifying it according to its nature. After the classification transactions are posted and then balanced out for the preparation of the financial statement. This information is used by policymakers and managerswhen making financial decisions at the organization. Moreover, the auditing process in an organization is based on the cross-check that all the financial records are present in the financial statements and that standard is being followed by the organization while compiling the financial record. Proper record keeping will ensure that, at the time of audit or in case of any employee issue, these records will be available and will be used as evidence (Skills, 2021). While keeping financial records, the operational methods and techniques should be avoided as the accounting department is adhering to the rules and regulations to follow the standard method of record-keeping in that country. Auditing checks that there is no deviance to the standard of accounting being accepted and practiced in that country by the other organizations.

Efficiency in the Digital World

With the advancement in information technology, there is a shift in the method by which conventional audits are being done. As there are new techniques available through which the audit is performed, it could be done in lesser time and with more reliable data. Also, there is more automation in the auditing process by the introduction of artificial intelligence (AI) systems that are being used by the organization. Yet, one of the key issues that have been faced by many companies is how to mitigate the risk associated with the introduction of a new information technology system in accounting and finance. One of the real challenges that have been associated with the use of new digital technology in auditing and finance is the risk of data that maybe lost due to cybercrime and issues of confidentiality. Moreover, with digitalization, there is more need for security of the data that is exposed to the outer world and high costs associated with these issues when it comes to the expected regulations. Many companies and organizations are now moving toward the development of more secured solutions that will help to reduce the risk of data loss due to privacy issues (Hobeika, 2017).

Geopolitical Factors and Government Interference

Auditing may sometimes be affected by the interference of government and the other political factors that are affecting the whole process. At times, it happens becauseauthoritiesdo not wish to publish any negative information about the standards of accountancy and the organizing of the data for the financial statements that are applied in their country (Beasley, 2021). For this purpose, some authorities try to hide the factual data from the public, and thus this lack of transparency deems any audit report incompetent. Even within a country, different political parties may modify audit reports for personal interest because it helps them keep their assets away from the public eye. This is surely against the code of accounting ethics that is being applied across the globe but is, unfortunately, a possible situation in any part of the world. Therefore, it is essential to propose both punishment and reward when such cases arise and to consistently impose them.

Weakness in the Global Framework

Across the globe, a major weakness in the framework of auditing is the expectations of the numerous stakeholders involved. Independent externalauditors are often appointed by shareholders due to a lack of transparencyfrom management as some may believe that auditors will give more reliable information about the credence of the financial record that is kept by the management. This perception has been becoming increasinglypopular to such an extent that these external firms are usually accused of exaggeratingreporting errors and mismanagement by the appointed auditors (Olojede, 2020). Even though national governance is important, this could very well provide grounds for the potential of a conflict of interest. This, there is a need to make an integrated system where the auditing and accounting would be taken as two separate departments and they work independently without the interference of the government in the compliance of the accounting standards and the guidelines. There may be a difference in the financial record-keeping method across the nations but one has to completely follow the rules and regulation that has been set in the country of operation regardless of the operational techniques and methods.

CORPORATE GOVERNANCE IN THE 21st CENTURY

With the digital race in full swing, the need to make the process of forensic accounting and corporate governance efficient is essential for its existence. In this section, the current tactics of implementation are discussed alongside a few recommendations for future success.

Need for Change

In a world where people are frequently exchanging information and data within a fraction of a second, it is important to introduce the concept of forensic accounting and corporate governance. The number of frauds related to accounting has increased over time with the introduction of new technologies and there is a constant need to identify scams thatare happening in societies and industriesaround the globe. Financial crime has led to a decrease in trust of investors worldwide and shareholders on the financial statement provided by the company's as it has become easier now to change and manipulate the financial information (Vedrana, 2018). Moreover, to build organizations in which the investors have trust and good relationships with the company, the credibility and the reliability of the data provided in the financial statement are necessary. Forensic accounting & governance thus reduce the number of unethical practices and operations at the organization and provides data that is more reliable to the shareholders, managers, investors, and other stakeholders. This will enable a company to regain the trust of the investors that may avoid investing activity in that organization because of the perception that the company has lost its credibility in terms of accounting and auditing as falsified facts are compiled in the financial statements. Specialized skills in the field of accounting should be acquired to perform forensic accounting tasks whereas the end goal of forensic accounting is to issue a credible credit report on the financial statement of the organization.

Mechanisms of Impact

The mechanism of impact is a combination of the policies that are being initiated by the organization to reduce the inefficacy and manage the organization in a better way. For corporate finance, the mechanism can be internal control or by the balancing power. The mechanism of internal control is based on the guidelines that are set for each employee in that organization. This way, the financial information of the company is kept intact. Furthermore, there should be a continuous internal and external audit. These audits identify whether there is any kind of deviance or the guideline is overruled by a corporate member. This mechanism helps the organization in dealing with the risks associated with the accounting measures at the organization because the assets are being protected by the internal control measure and areas of risk are identified early (Vitez, 2021).

Another method involves the balancing of power. In an organization,many departmentsare interlinked and are working together. Instead of the one department being responsible for all the functions and duties, there should be a separation of the duties within the organization and even within the departments. This will help to limit the resources that a single employee can use. Overextended resources of the organization by a single person or department may result in compromising the balance of power, which in turn may affect governance procedures. By balancing the power through duty segregations, organizations are in a better position to implement corporate governance mechanisms to increase their credibility and reliability.

Future Measures and Control

Audits play a crucial role in providing security to financial markets. There have been vast improvements in audit technology and the advances are only expected to grow in the future. One of the transformative fragments of this technology is 'Artificial Intelligence (AI) which is comprised of computer software that mimics human interaction. The modern tools and technologies are allowing industries to transform audit processes and techniques and are likely to broaden the conventional audit methods beyond the ordinary sample-based testing techniques. These advances are expected to aid auditors to analyze whole data sets and populations like never before to obtain quality audits, meet stakeholder expectations and strengthen capabilities to identify frauds or risks related to financing.

The introduction of such splendid technologies into the profession furnishes amazing opportunities for providing superior customer service to all the present and upcoming clients. To keep up with advanced technology, audit training is frequently required. The continuous advancement in technology is leading the way towards superior assessment of audit evidence and will continue to be an integral part of the audit process. But,the judgment given by audit experts will continue to be fundamental as it is an inherent procedure in the audit process. According to experts, traditional audit needs to undergo various changes to fashion it in a more relevant form to conform and meet the needs of the present economy. There must be a focus on the key risk areas and areas which can provide benefit to all stakeholders.

Global Financial Governance

The fragility and weakness of afinancial governance systemhave a strong impact on both companies and economies as a whole. When governance strategies are flawed, they cause a huge risk to the financial systems, across the globe. In all the countries of the world, people from all walks of life experience the effects of financial turbulence. Societies have been going through financial insecurities as a consequence of many failed schemes of corporate governance. The relationship between corporate governance with that of the stakeholders has never been vivid enough. The problem does not lie in the strategies, themselves. Rather, the issue is with the improper implementation and maintenance of the policies. Risk management has been another major factor that has contributed to the financial upheavals at the global level. To avoid the related concerns and circumstances, policymakers must have the capability to ask for suggestions from the various points of view and stakeholders. To conclude, it can be said that it is the quality and not the quantity of the governance that matters. The hallmark of any business is to be profitable and reputable at the same time.

CASE STUDY

Corporate Governance and Economic Growth in Kuwait

Setting the stage: In the grand scheme of things, Kuwait is considered one of the richest countries in the world. However, the country hasrecently been suffering from internal issues such as strategic planning and liquidity. These issues have caused it to fall back on many global indices – particularly financial ones. This case gives a brief overview of the situation and aims to analyze the reasons for these unfortunate outcomes. It represents a mere opinion-based analysis from a local perspective and ties it to the macro elements of corporate governance. At the end of the case study, there are discussion questions that apply to the situation discussed.

With the unfortunate corruption reputation which plagues the country, it is crucial to highlight the importance of corporate governance. After all, they are the driving forces behind our economy and the ones who can also impede its growth. It is meant to be a reflection of shareholders' values, in line with the expectations and considerations of all stakeholders, including customers and society. However, the issue of whose interests should be considered is particularly contentious in this matter. Good corporate governance can strengthen the "good" and weaken the "bad". So what elements can be enhanced to continue our journey on the path to sustainable economic development?

Defining Corporate Governance

The umbrella of corporate governance is very vague and is inclusive of both written and unwritten rules and policies throughout an organization. In theory, it is a piece of paper with best-practice scenarios and step-by-step instructions. However, the desire and intention to follow certain ways of working are not always accompanied by the ability or willingness of others to do so. In the reality of its practice, it is a mindset of "corporate culture" which steps from the local culture. If we were to break it down to its very essence, it is the pillars on which we individually place our decisions, which is better known as 'ethics'.

Ethics and Business Sustainability

When academics define a culture, they look for what it does not tolerate. But also, and more importantly, one must look at what is being tolerated. Similarly, in any given institute, corporate governance will rely heavily on the type of leadership displayed – what it does not tolerate, but also what it allows without punishment. From past research, there have been many findings that support the notion that there is a strong and positive relationship between corporate governance and overall profits. It has been found that Implementation of corporate governance standards improves the financial performance of the company as well as positively impacts the internal efficiency of the firms. Governance quality presents diminishing marginal returns, which means that the high-speed economic growth effect becomes less and less, while the high-quality economic development effect becomes more and more and could bring a high-quality economic development effect.

Legal Compliance vs. Moral Compliance

Legal compliance, in part, is also an investment in the human capital. Therefore, it is essential to have a reasonable approach as often times it takes more than intelligence to act intelligently. For example, to fight financial corruption, entities should be offsetting the potential for malice with reasonable compensation for those involved as an incentive to offset bribery. That is not to say that people who work in the financial field are more likely to be corrupt, but rather it is to highlight the importance of a holistic view of a workplace problem and take the appropriate measures to ensure the best outcomes. Furthermore, an investment in diversity and inclusion is also likely to be fruitful. It has often been found that boards with more women in them have been found to commit less fraud. Also, investing in a proper roll-out of corporate governance has been proven to increase innovation amongst employees as they feel safe to share their ideas and are confident that they will be rewarded for their ideas.

To promote the sustainable development of Kuwait's economy, policymakers should improve local governance quality by stressing ethics and responsibility as well as promote the diversity and adoption of organizational culture amongst the human capital.

FUTURE RESEARCH DIRECTIONS

Analyses about corporate governance in the current century focus on the growth aspects of globalization, the influx of technology, and international trade prospects that have seen firms enhance their operations to occupy global spheres. Such changes have impacts on corporate boards and governance systems. There are issues that corporate leaders ought to address and manage before they escalate to become adverse for corporate governance. For instance, the financial performance of institutions in the current world can impact consumer perceptions. Corporate management is determined by the ability of the management to handle its financial performance, track down its finances, and remain accountable. The radical changes in global markets have pushed 21st-century market operators to rely on forensic accountants for improved corporate governance, support systems, and the development of regulatory frameworks that encourage credibility and accountability. Therefore, future research in this field is expected to be ongoing to keep up with the generic fast-paced nature of the field. With many ambiguous, moving pieces involved including personal ethics and social norms, the field is expected to grow with complexities over time. Thus, it is essential to keep a pragmatic and proactive approach to engaging in this field and embrace all of its aspects.

CONCLUSION

In conclusion, there are many benefits and challenges to embrace when it comes to forensic accounting and corporate governance. The chapter highlights the key points to consider when planning an efficient and sustainable strategy. Increasingly, boards are waking up to the importance of a corporate financial strategy and governance and acknowledging their role in addressing and overseeing such issues within the company. A key reason why investors are asking boards to pay attention to these issues is that they are considered to be material financial risks that can have an impact on the bottom line. If a company has implemented a positive corporate governance framework, it allows them to effectively allocate their resources in their decision-making process. Also, it increases the level of confidence in the financial markets of the accuracy and transparency of their information and allows the firms to be able to develop more viable strategic objectives by having accurate information (Stanwick, 2008). As we move into the future, the challenges facing corporate boards have grown dramatically who face a growing range of complex issues. From stakeholder and shareholder demand to local and global indices, the continuous need for adapting and reporting requires a great deal of time and attention. To benefit and reach optimal results, it is essential to ensure that there are complementary layers and sufficient collaborations between forensic accounting and corporate governance. After all, they both function best in synergy.

REFERENCES

Beasley, J. V. (2021). Top 10 Audit Deficiencies. *Journal of Accountancy.*

BhasinM. L. (2015). An empirical investigation of the relevant skills of forensic accountants: experience of a developing economy. *Available at* SSRN 2676519.

Brennan, D. (2011). *Corporate social responsibility: The corporate governance of the 21st century.* Kluwer Law International BV.

Dada, S. O., Owolabi, S. A., & Okwu, A. T. (2013). Forensic accounting is a panacea to the alleviation of fraudulent practices in Nigeria. *International Journal of Business Management and Economic Research, 4*(5), 787–792.

Digabriele, J. A. (2008). An empirical investigation of the relevant skills of forensic accountants. *Journal of Education for Business, 83*(6), 331–338. doi:10.3200/JOEB.83.6.331-338

Gray, O. R., & Moussalli, S. D. (2006). Forensic accounting and auditing united again: A historical perspective. *Journal of Business Issues*, (2), 15–25.

Herbert, W. E., Tsegba, I. N., Ene, E. E., & Onyilo, F. (2017). The rise of fraud examination and forensic accounting in Africa: The Nigerian experience. *Archives of Business Research, 5*(4). Advance online publication. doi:10.14738/abr.54.3013

Hobeika, A. (2017). *Understanding the impact of technology in audit and finance.* ICAEW and DFSA.

McMullen, D. A., & Sanchez, M. H. (2010). A preliminary investigation of the necessary skills, education requirements, and training requirements for forensic accountants. *Journal of Forensic & Investigative Accounting, 2*(2), 30–48.

Ocansey, E. O. N. D. (2017). Forensic accounting and the combating of economic and financial crimes in Ghana. *European Scientific Journal, 13*(31), 379–393. doi:10.19044/esj.2017.v13n31p379

OECD. (2017). *Internal Control and Risk Management for Public Integrity in the Middle East and North Africa.* OECD.

Okpako, A. E. P., & Atube, E. N. (2013). The impact of forensic accounting on fraud detection. *European Journal of Business and Management, 5*(26), 61–70.

Olojede, P. (2020). *Audit expectation gap: an empirical analysis.* Future Business Journal.

Ozili, P. K. (2015). Forensic Accounting and Fraud: A Review of Literature and Policy Implications. *International Journal of Accounting and Economics Studies, 3*(1), 63–68. doi:10.14419/ijaes.v3i1.4541

Skills, P. B. (2021). *Managing a Business.* Retrieved from Practical Business Skills: https://www.practicalbusinessskills.com/managing-a-business/record-keeping

Smith, G. S. (2015). The past, present, and future of forensic accounting. *The CPA Journal, 85*(3), 16.

Subash, T. (2015). Forensic accounting and Corporate Governance. *EXCEL International Journal of Multidisciplinary Management Studies, 5*(11), 49–54.

Vedrana, J. (2018). The role of forensic accounting in corporate governance for economic societies. *Business Studies*, 119-131.

Vitez, O. (2021). *What are the Different Kinds of Corporate Governance Mechanisms?* Retrieved from wise-geek.com: https://www.wise-geek.com/what-are-the-different-kinds-of-corporate-governance-mechanisms.htm

Yadav, S., & Yadav, S. (2013). Forensic accounting: A new dynamic approach to investigate fraud cases. *Excel International Journal of Multidisciplinary Management Studies, 3*(7), 1-9.

ADDITIONAL READING

Becht, M., Bolton, P., & Röell, A. (2003). Corporate governance and control. In *Handbook of the Economics of Finance* (Vol. 1, pp. 1–109). Elsevier.

Freeman, R. E., & Reed, D. L. (1983). Stockholders and stakeholders: A new perspective on corporate governance. *California Management Review*, *25*(3), 88–106. doi:10.2307/41165018

Frydman, R., Gray, C. W., & Rapaczynski, A. (1996). *Corporate Governance in Central Europe and Russia*. Central European University Press.

Hermalin, B., & Weisbach, M. (Eds.). (2017). *The handbook of the economics of corporate governance* (Vol. 1). Elsevier.

Keasey, K., Thompson, S., & Wright, M. (Eds.). (2005). *Corporate governance: accountability, enterprise, and international comparisons*. John Wiley & Sons.

Kranacher, M. J., & Riley, R. (2019). *Forensic accounting and fraud examination*. John Wiley & Sons.

Rezaee, Z., Crumbley, D. L., & Elmore, R. C. (2004). (Forthcoming). Forensic accounting education: A survey of academicians and practitioners. *Advances in Accounting Education*.

Shleifer, A., & Vishny, R. W. (1997). A survey of corporate governance. *The Journal of Finance*, *52*(2), 737–783. doi:10.1111/j.1540-6261.1997.tb04820.x

Singleton, T. W. (2010). *Fraud auditing and forensic accounting* (Vol. 11). John Wiley & Sons. doi:10.1002/9781118269183

Stapledon, G. P., & Stapledon, G. P. (1997). *Institutional shareholders and corporate governance*. Oxford University Press.

Sternberg, E. (1998). Corporate governance. *Accountability in the Market*.

Williamson, O. E. (1988). Corporate finance and corporate governance. *The Journal of Finance*, *43*(3), 567–591. doi:10.1111/j.1540-6261.1988.tb04592.x

KEY TERMS AND DEFINITIONS

Accounting Ethics: To record and report accounting information with the intent of reflecting the actual information available following the generally accepted accounting principles of the jurisdiction where the institution is based.

Audit: An inspection of the institution's records and activities usually by an internal or independent body.

Compliance: The act of complying with the regulatory bodies of a given institution in all aspects of the organization.

Corporate Governance: A system of regulations, rules, and accepted practices that define the way an organization is controlled and directed.

Embezzlement: Theft, misuse, or misappropriation of assets usually under one's care or their employer/institution.

Forensic Accounting: Analyzing and documenting debts that lead to bankruptcy, the creditors that require payment, and validating entities that legally require reimbursement after a firm goes bankrupt.

Fraud: Irregular patterns that can affect corporate governance, such as cases where scammers use fake identity to embezzle resources and funds.

Transparency: Relates to the clarity of presented data in the financial statements and other forms of auditing reports.

APPENDIX

Case Study: Questions and Answers

- 1. What are the main issues presented?
  Answer: *The main issues which are present in this case include corporate governance and the mediums associated with delivering it. As global rates of corruption rise, countries are careful to fulfill the required elements as per international standards. Kuwait is suffering not only from a lack of a transparent system but also methods of enforcement which have caused many economic disruptions and corruption.*
- 2. Does the overall issue discussed only involve/affect the country in question? Please explain.
  Answer: *No, the issues of corporate governance are international about all aspects of society and involve many stakeholders. The case describes the need for building a sustainable environment including common standards of reporting worldwide.*
- 3. Discuss the managerial obligations involved in issues like corporate governance.
  Answer: *Some of the managerial obligations may go far beyond the walls of an organization. When implementing such a system, it is important to consider logistical and legal issues to name a few as they may complicate other aspects of the overall reporting mechanisms involved.*
- 4. What are the advantages and disadvantages of implementing a full-on corporate governance system?
  Answer: *Advantages may include more cooperation and inclusion from international entities which could lead to more profitable opportunities. Yet, some disadvantages may arise from this as many will be hesitant to take part and provide the necessary transparency.*
- 5. To what extent do you think decision-makers' cooperation will make this project a success?
  Answer: *The cooperation of decision-makers in cases of building a sustainable corporate governance system is crucial as they are the main stakeholders involved. Institutes should be careful to pursue their constant feedback and allow room for some flexibility.*

EPILOGUE AND LESSONS LEARNED

The history and events that help shape the current understanding of forensic accounting and its relation to corporate governance are discussed. Current structures and standards required of organizations to meet the basics of corporate governance are explained with their repercussions. Because it is highly embedded in ethics and personal values, there are countless varying points of view and ethical dilemmas regarding info-sharing and reporting are highlighted. Moreover, identifying and reporting, alongside simple adherence to policies, are essentially examined. Also, challenges of finding common grounds of understanding reporting concepts and mechanisms are explained due to social pressures and the use of punishment. Moreover, the pillars of which accounting firms are established are vulnerable to corruption as partners around the globe race to perform. In many cases, governments do not tolerate negative news or information regarding operational standards or ethics as it detracts international investors. Thus, the outcome is not favorable to auditors as they are coerced into showing a positive report or omitting any damaging material. The dilemmas and efficiency of these implications are highlighted and discussed. The ever-changing world is in dire need of corporate governance and transparency. In this day and age where global connectivity continues to grow exponentially, it is important to shed the light on the importance of ethical and documentable practice.

Lessons to take away from the chapter:

- *Corporate Governance is multi-dimensional* – Turning to a full-blown strategy is not as simple as adopting a new framework and making a few changes. An entire system should be reconsidered to create a sustainable online model.
- *Every stakeholder involved is important* – It is important to consider all parties involved and encourage their feedback. It is also wise to consider rewards and recognition for those who are committed to transparency and governance in a sustainable way.
- *Institutes & policy-makers should work collaboratively* – Because governance has many layers, it can be beneficial for those who are proactively implementing it to learn from methodologies and experiences from other case studies around the world.

Chapter 9
An Assessment of Forensic Accounting Skill Competencies for Minimizing Corporate Fraud and Damages:
Empirical Evidence From Chartered Accountancy Students of India

Ankur Goel
Dewan VS Group of Institutions, India

ABSTRACT

Forensic accounting is a key emerging field for strengthening the corporate sector of any economy. Forensic accountants have to be well equipped with multiple skill competencies to act as catalysts for enhancing and leveraging on the best corporate practices in terms of minimizing the possibilities of fraud, damages, scams, and scandals all around the globe. Aspiring professional accountancy students are nowadays highly inspired and motivated to build their career in forensic accounting, and also there is an immense scarcity of talented people, specifically in the Indian context in this domain. Literature demonstrates the availability of a variety of skill competencies as required for proficiency in the same domain. The author in this chapter primarily explored the multiple skill competencies with the help of secondary data and further assesses them by reducing all skills to the most basic and relevant ones with the application of factor reduction technique through SPSS after collecting the primary data (survey method) from the chartered accountancy students in Meerut City, India.

INTRODUCTION

Forensic accounting integrates the accounting, auditing, and investigative techniques, procedures, and skills all around the world to identify, detect and investigate financial reporting frauds (Bhasin, 2013)

DOI: 10.4018/978-1-7998-8754-6.ch009

especially in the corporate world wherein 'Forensic Accounting' is considered a catalyst for smoothing, strengthening, enhancing and overall uplifting the corporate world of any nation. Forensic Accounting is the study and interpretation of accounting evidence. It examines individual and company financial records as an investigative measure that attempts to derive evidence suitable for use in litigation. In the times of recent financial and cyber frauds in the corporate sector, there is an intense need for expertise in this emerging field of study, especially in the Indian context. The 'Institute of Chartered Accountancy of India' which is the prime institution of accountancy study in India has recognized this need and has started offering various specialized certificate courses in 'Forensic Accounting. There is also a scarcity or rather a deficiency of professional forensic accountants in a country like India (Gupta & Viz, 2021) where a large pool of students of accounting, auditing, finance, and corporate law are available. For the result-oriented application and efficient practice of 'Forensic Accounting' diverse skill competencies are required and these need to be addressed and assessed from the point of view of professional chartered accountancy students opting for 'Forensic Accounting' as a career option and that too in the corporate sector of India. These students are already 'Commerce Graduates' and are on a verge of securing membership in 'Institute of Chartered Accountancy of India' and many of them are undergoing their training or internship under-qualified and practicing 'Chartered Accountants'.

In accordance with the fundamental objective of this research study, there is also an intense need for the development of a specialized youth and talented pool in the field of forensic accounting embedded with resourceful competencies. Hence, this study intends to answer the research questions as:

- What are the fundamental skill competencies required for an emerging efficient and effective 'Forensic Accountant'?
- What are the exact resourceful competencies in the Indian context which consequently support minimizing the frauds and scams in the corporate world?

Hence, the above research questions lead to the specific research objective of this chapter as to extract the specific and resourceful skill competencies required by the proficient 'Forensic Accountant' for enhancing the 'Corporate Sector'. For the accomplishment of said objective, the author has explored a total of twenty key skill competencies required for 'Forensic Accounting' (Sources) in general, and a survey has been conducted to collect the primary data which is subjected to the 'Component Extraction Method' applied through SPSS. The subsequent sections of this chapter portray the "Background of the study majorly stressing on the 'Literature Review'", "Main focus of the chapter emphasizing 'Research Methodology' used in this study", "Solutions and Recommendations depicting the 'Results of SPSS with its interpretation'", "Future Research Directions with specific limitations" and finally ended up with concrete "Conclusion of the entire study".

BACKGROUND OF THE STUDY (LITERATURE REVIEW)

A brief background with the relevant literature review of the past ten years regarding the theme of the study has been presented by the author in this section.

Kumar (2012) explained that the task performed by forensic accountants was handled either by 'Chartered Accountants' or by 'Cost or Work Accountants' in India and there was an urgent need for forensic accounting services due to an increase in the number of frauds continuously as various law enforcement agencies of India did not have sufficient expertise required to prevent from these frauds. This study supported the need for skilled 'Forensic Accountants' in India.

Biswas et. al. (2013) studied to understand the significance of forensic accounting in the wake of recent financial scams in India and to highlight the problems of forensic accounting in India. He indicated that in India due to the complex and traditional judicial system with stressful political compulsion, forensic accountants were facing the challenge of gathering evidence against the big criminals that were admissible in the court of law. He suggested that the appointment of forensic accountants should be made mandatory in the public sector and large-scale companies. Forensic accounting was used for fraud examination and it covers all aspects of the same from inception to disposition including obtaining evidence, interviewing, writing reports, and testifying the same.

Lohana (2013)highlighted the meaning, nature, validation, and prospects of 'Forensic Accounting' in India. Forensic accounting as a new area of accounting in India had come into the limelight recently due to the rapid increase in white-collar crimes, financial crimes, cybercrimes, and the growing complexities of the corporate environment. Forensic accounting is a tripartite practice that integrates accounting, auditing, and investigative skills to examine a company's financial statements. Though forensic accounting was an untapped area in India, prospects were growing fast in public as well as private organizations.

Sharma (2014)discussed that forensic accounting was still at an early stage in India and its practice had been very minimal, whereas in developed countries like USA and UK, 'Forensic Accounting' was not new and they were very advanced in this field. In Indian 'Forensic Accounting' was not treated as a separate specialized tool for combating frauds, but it was considered as an extension of investigation auditing, which adds to the misery of its less awareness and practice in India.

Nena (2015) studied to know the detailed conceptual clarity regarding the term 'Forensic Accounting. The study covered the necessary information regarding knowing the term 'Forensic Accounting', its definition, characteristics, and objectives. It also covered differentiating points among accounting, audit & forensic accounting. Moreover, the well-known case of Satyam Computers' fraud had also been taken in the study.

Bhasin (2016) in his study concluded that the 'Forensic Accounting' in India had arrived late due to the occurrence of severe financial crimes, scams, and frauds and the legal framework of the country was not sufficient to investigate the same in all desired aspects. He furthermore forecasted greater demand for a widespread talent pool in the field of 'Forensic Accounting' which had overall supported the need of the present study as well.

Shair (2017) examined the scope and modus operandi of 'Forensic Accounting' in the backdrop of rising corporate frauds in India. This research largely made use of secondary sources of data to capture the experts' opinions and views on the same. In a nutshell, the research suggested that there were immense possibilities for 'Forensic Accounting' to be assumed as a separate field of expertise and provides numerous opportunities for forensic experts to offer litigation support, investigative accounting, and consulting services. There was an urgent need to regularize the 'Forensic Accounting' movement by the government and recognized accounting bodies in India. There was much scope for advancements in the 'Forensic Accounting' techniques and legislation in the wake of the unrelenting number and complexity of corporate frauds and economic crimes.

Jugurnath et. al. (2017) explained that a 'Forensic Accountant' was an expert in accounting, auditing, and financial frameworks. Being the transformation in corporate size and growth, the 'Forensic Accountant' must be capable of a wide range of expert abilities and skills. These skills were the composition of dealing with financial statements, dealing with frauds and scams, risk management and evaluation, investigative skills, psychological skills, computing skills, interpersonal and relational abilities, complete knowledge of organizations policies and governance, and comprehensive skills.

Bhasin (2017) conducted an empirical study in Delhi & NCR on one hundred and twenty (120) accounting professionals, practitioners, and prospective users of forensic accounting services and found that all these accounting practitioners had agreed that financial and economic fraud in India had reached up to that level that there had been an intense need of specific skill competencies in the field of forensic accounting beyond the accounting, auditing, and investigative skills. His results further revealed that the potential practitioners and academics agreed that critical thinking, unstructured problem-solving, investigative flexibility, analytical proficiency, and legal knowledge are more important skills of CFA's. Potential practitioners of forensic accounting services rated analysis more important than did the academic staff. These results show that ——some skills are relevant and important to the outcome of forensic accounting education. This study was the most prominent and significant to frame the foundation of the current research work.

Lama and Chaudhuri (2018) highlighted the conceptual framework, various provisions, and applicability of 'Forensic Accounting' in investigating corporate frauds and scams in India. With the growing complexities of business and commercial operations, the financial irregularities had also increased. Just because of the mindless obsession with profit maximization at any cost when carried to any extreme could lead to failures like Enron, Worldcom, Satyam which had an extremely negative impact on the survival and growth of any economic entity. But there were no appropriate conventional accounting and auditing procedures that can provide absolute assurance in preventing and detecting all fraudulent financial reporting. As a mechanism to detect and prevent corporate frauds and scams, 'Forensic Accounting' had emerged as a relatively new and effective tool in the hands of accountants to find out the mistakes and malpractices in the accounting world.

Kumar et. al. (2018) studied the basics of 'Forensic Accounting' and provided an overview of various forensic accounting techniques. One of the techniques, 'Beneish M-Score model', had been used for finding earnings manipulation in 10 foreign companies and 10 Indian companies in the past five years which had been selected on the assumption that the companies were involved in manipulative activities in any particular financial year. The results from such analysis had been categorized between manipulative and non-manipulative companies. For proving the manipulative results, complaints and enforcements against the companies had been collected and provided as evidence for such manipulative results. The paper concluded by stating the necessity of incorporating 'Forensic Accounting' into the internal and statutory audit functions and procedures to avoid frauds or manipulations.

Venkataraman & Kumar (2019) revealed that there had been a strong impact of incorporating the 'Forensic Accounting' which gives an edge in fighting corporate frauds. He added further that 'Forensic Accountants' face interference from management, but clearing those barriers would help the forensic accountants and auditors to perform the task with their fashion and potential. Regulating bodies and accounting professionals should change their perception of 'Forensic Accounting' not only as an investigation tool but as a preventive mechanism. The regulating bodies should also create awareness and training on forensic accounting, which would lay its path to better corporate governance and a healthy society.

Naik (2019)studied the elaborative scope and role of 'Forensic Accounting' in the detections and investigation of company fraud. In India, forensic accounting had come into the limelight due to the increase in scams or white-collar crimes and there was a huge requirement for forensic accountants in India. The secondary data were collected to understand the objectives of 'Forensic Accounting' and the challenges faced by forensic investigators while examining various cases. She also confirmed that organizations like ICAI, India were offering specialized courses in 'Forensic Accounting' being a shortage in forensic accountants in India.

All the above studies had supported the requirement of forensic accountants in India with specific skill competencies and 'Forensic Accounting' is beyond the routine accounting and auditing practices. Especially for the detection and investigation of corporate crimes and frauds, professional accountancy institutions like ICAI, India had designed specialized courses in 'Forensic Accounting' for the accounting and auditing professionals. However, very few empirical studies were available in the field of 'Forensic Accounting. The author had tried to eliminate this gap by surveying the 'Chartered Accountancy' students aspiring for a proficient corporate career in 'Forensic Accounting.

MAIN FOCUS OF THE CHAPTER (RESEARCH METHODOLOGY)

This part of the chapter focused on the major issues, needs, and relevance in support of this study. Predominantly it stated the research methodology used to undergo this study. Forensic accounting emerged due to the growth in 'Fraud' which could be a bank, insurance, corporate, healthcare, cyber, securities, consumer, and even more about the corporate sector. The existence of forensic accounting in India is minimal and this calls upon the need to make suggestions on how to promote it. Being a country of rich political culture and governmental framework, the government must play an active role in promoting its need. Like the Chartered Accountants Act, 1949, legislation must be passed to make forensic accounting mandatory in companies (Kumar, 2018). The major issue which had been noticed after the literature study was that very little empirical research till to date had been conducted in forensic accounting and its application in the corporate sector, even after so many corporate frauds and scandals in India. Therefore this study had been conducted with the help of primary data after exploring the data related to key skill competencies required for 'Forensic Accounting. The author had surveyed the chartered accountancy students who are highly inclined for boosting the corporate sector of India by opting for 'Forensic Accounting' as a career option. This study is highly significant as it directly strengthens 'Corporate Governance' by developing the youth generation for 'Forensic Accounting' careers.

At an initial stage, the secondary data had been explored with the help of standard websites through 'Google' specifically by entering the keywords and phrases like forensic accounting skills, skill competencies for forensic auditor, skills to enhance corporate sector through forensic accounting, forensic auditing skills, etc. The assistance of online literature available in the form of research papers, articles, e-books, book chapters, and websites had been also considered in this aspect. As an outcome, the totals of twenty (20) key skill competencies were identified for the study and subjected to further analysis. These competencies were considered as key attributes/variables/factors of the study and named as A1 to A20. Eventually, the empirical data had been gathered from one hundred and twenty-five (125) professional chartered accountancy (CA) students of Meerut City, Uttar Pradesh opting for 'Forensic Accounting' as a career option. These students are already 'Commerce Graduates' and are onthe verge of securing membership of 'Institute of Chartered Accountancy of India' and many of them are undergoing their training or internship under qualified 'Chartered Accountants'. The sample size is arbitrarily selected without the application of any scientific calculation being there is a limitation of time. Convenience with Snowball Sampling Technique was applied for selecting the sample units for the research purpose. A structured questionnaire was designed using the five-point scale (Skill Competencies were written in statement form, 5- Most important, 4- Important, 3- Not Sure, 2- Not important, 1- Least Important).

There were in total twenty-five (25) questions in the questionnaire as the first four were related to the respondent's Name, Contact Number (not mandatory), Stage of their Course, Awareness of 'Forensic Accounting' with its relevance in 'Corporate sector' and Opting 'Forensic Accounting' as a career for enhancing 'Corporate sector'. The next twenty (20) were directly related to the explored key competencies. Respondents were contacted personally for collecting the data speedily and accurately with the assistance of management students (MBA final year of DVSGI, Meerut (UP)). Reliability analysis was not conducted scientifically, but pilot testing was ensured among the fifteen (15) known 'Chartered Accountancy Interns', and minor modifications regarding the skill competencies were commenced. Complete data were collected in 35-40 and then the data was entered in an excel sheet with proper coding. It was found that due to the availability of missing and improper values, the valid responses were finally selected to be one hundred (100). Also, the respondents who were not willing to opt for their career in 'Forensic Accounting' to detect 'Corporate Frauds' were not considered, though all the respondents were fully aware of the same. The 'Factor Analysis Technique (Extraction Method: Principal Component Analysis)' was applied as a part of multivariate analysis with the help of SPSS for portraying the main solutions and recommendations to the underlying problem of multiplicity of skill competencies among the upcoming and aspiring youth talent in the domain of 'Forensic Accounting.

SOLUTIONS AND RECOMMENDATIONS (DATA ANALYSIS AND INTERPRETATION)

This part of the chapter was the most dominated one being this chapter was fundamentally based on the analysis of primary data which was collected through a survey conducted among the accountancy students. Therefore after the exploration/ identification of twenty (20) skill competencies with their assigned names as the key variables of the study (A1…A20), the author demonstrated the data analysis with interpretation in three aspects in this part as follows:

- Survey Analysis with interpretation
- Descriptive Statistics of Skill Competencies with interpretation
- Results of multivariate analysis technique – Factor Analysis or Dimension Reduction Method to arrive at the concrete solution for the problem concerned.

Total Attributes/Variables Explored through Secondary Data

Interpretation: It was clear from Table 1 that a total of twenty (20) skill competencies were identified as required by the professionals in the field of 'Forensic Accounting' especially for strengthening the 'Corporate sector' by preventing and detecting frauds and scams in the same domain being corporate world being the most vulnerable sector.

Survey Analysis

- Mathematical and Statistical Skills

Table 1. Skill competencies explored

S. No	Key Variables	Key Skill Competencies
1	A1	Accounting & Business Reporting Practices
2	A2	Auditing Standards & Techniques
3	A3	Information Technology Skills
4	A4	Data Analytics Ability
5	A5	Knowledge of Criminology
6	A6	Legal Framework & Methods
7	A7	Litigation Process & Procedures
8	A8	Investigative Techniques
9	A9	Evidence Collection & Gathering
10	A10	Versatile Professional Network
11	A11	Critical & Strategic Thinking Skills
12	A12	Effective Oral/Written Communication
13	A13	Research Oriented Skills
14	A14	Solving Unstructured Problems
15	A15	Synthesize Result of Discovery & Analysis
16	A16	Questioning & Probing Skills
17	A17	Psychological Skills
18	A18	Identifying Key issues
19	A19	Storytelling & Thinking like a Wrongdoer
20	A20	Mathematical & Statistical Skills

Source: Author's tabulation based on exploratory research.

Table 2. Mathematical and statistical skills (A1)

		Frequency	Percent	Valid Percent	Cumulative Percent
Valid	Not Important	20	20.0	20.0	20.0
	Not Sure	12	12.0	12.0	32.0
	Important	50	50.0	50.0	82.0
	Most Important	18	18.0	18.0	100.0
	Total	100	100.0	100.0	

Source: SPSS output based on Primary data.

Interpretation: The output of Table 2 indicated that 50% of the respondents felt that 'A1' skill competency was 'important' for the professionals of forensic accountancy however 20% of the respondents marked it as 'not important at all.

- Versatile Professional Network

Table 3. Versatile professional network (A2)

		Frequency	Percent	Valid Percent	Cumulative Percent
Valid	Least Important	3	3.0	3.0	3.0
	Not Important	6	6.0	6.0	9.0
	Not Sure	17	17.0	17.0	26.0
	Important	58	58.0	58.0	84.0
	Most Important	16	16.0	16.0	100.0
	Total	100	100.0	100.0	

Source: SPSS output based on Primary data.

Interpretation: The output of Table 3, indicated that 58% of the respondents felt that 'A2' skill competency was 'important' for the professionals of 'Forensic Accounting' however only 6% of the respondents marked it as a 'not important' at all being large and versatile professional network did not make a much difference.

- Knowledge of Criminology

Table 4. Knowledge of criminology (A3)

		Frequency	Percent	Valid Percent	Cumulative Percent
Valid	Least Important	3	3.0	3.0	3.0
	Not Important	6	6.0	6.0	9.0
	Not Sure	15	15.0	15.0	24.0
	Important	52	52.0	52.0	76.0
	Most Important	24	24.0	24.0	100.0
	Total	100	100.0	100.0	

Source: SPSS output based on Primary data.

Interpretation: The output of Table 4, indicated that 52% of the respondents felt that 'A3' skill competency was 'important' for the professionals of forensic accountancy though 24% of the respondents marked it as a 'most important' being knowledge of criminology is significantly important while dealing with fraud cases.

- Identifying Key Issues

Interpretation: The output of Table 5, indicated that 67% of the respondents felt that 'A4' skill competency was 'important' for the professionals of forensic accountancy though 11% of the respondents marked it as a 'most important and 22% of the respondents were not able to decide on the same as they marked it as 'Not Sure'.

Table 5. Identifying key issues (A4)

		Frequency	Percent	Valid Percent	Cumulative Percent
Valid	Not Sure	22	22.0	22.0	22.0
	Important	67	67.0	67.0	89.0
	Most Important	11	11.0	11.0	100.0
	Total	100	100.0	100.0	

Source: SPSS output based on Primary data.

- Litigation process and procedures

Table 6. Litigation process and procedures (A5)

		Frequency	Percent	Valid Percent	Cumulative Percent
Valid	Not Important	5	5.0	5.0	5.0
	Not Sure	18	18.0	18.0	23.0
	Important	51	51.0	51.0	74.0
	Most Important	26	26.0	26.0	100.0
	Total	100	100.0	100.0	

Source: SPSS output based on Primary data.

Interpretation: The output of Table 6, indicated that 51% of the respondents felt that 'A5' skill competency was 'important' for the professionals of forensic accountancy though 26% of the respondents marked it as a 'most important' being forensic accountant deal with the evidence to be presented in the 'court of law' hence this skill competency is highly significant.

- Synthesize Results of Discovery and Analysis

Table 7. Synthesize result of discovery and analysis (A6)

		Frequency	Percent	Valid Percent	Cumulative Percent
Valid	Not Sure	15	15.0	15.0	15.0
	Important	71	71.0	71.0	86.0
	Most Important	14	14.0	14.0	100.0
	Total	100	100.0	100.0	

Source: SPSS output based on Primary data.

Interpretation: The output of Table 7, indicated that 71% of the respondents (majority) felt that 'A6' skill competency was 'important' for the professionals of forensic accountancy though 14% of the

Table 8. Psychological skills (A7)

		Frequency	Percent	Valid Percent	Cumulative Percent
Valid	Not Sure	16	16.0	16.0	16.0
	Important	61	61.0	61.0	77.0
	Most Important	23	23.0	23.0	100.0
	Total	100	100.0	100.0	

Source: SPSS output based on Primary data.

respondents marked it as a 'most important being as a true investigator, the forensic accountant had to synthesize the results of discovery attained and analyze it from a multidimensional perspective.

- Psychological Skills

Interpretation: The output of Table 8, indicated that 61% of the respondents felt that 'A7' skill competency was 'important' for the professionals of forensic accountancy though 23% of the respondents marked it as 'most important.

- Data Analytics Capability

Table 9. Data analytics ability (A8)

		Frequency	Percent	Valid Percent	Cumulative Percent
Valid	Least Important	2	2.0	2.0	2.0
	Not Important	4	4.0	4.0	6.0
	Not Sure	13	13.0	13.0	19.0
	Important	46	46.0	46.0	65.0
	Most Important	35	35.0	35.0	100.0
	Total	100	100.0	100.0	

Source: SPSS output based on Primary data

Interpretation: The output of Table 9, indicated that 46% of the respondents felt that 'A8' skill competency was 'important' for the professionals of forensic accountancy though 35% of the respondents marked it as 'most important. Only 2% of respondents felt it as a 'least important' followed by 4% who marked it as 'Not important.

- Investigative Techniques

Interpretation: The output of Table 10, indicated that 79% of the respondents (majority) felt that 'A9' skill competency was 'important' for the professionals of forensic accountancy though 15% of the respondents marked it as 'most important. Only 6% of respondents were not able to decide its significance and marked it as 'Not Sure'.

Table 10. Investigative techniques (A9)

		Frequency	Percent	Valid Percent	Cumulative Percent
Valid	Not Sure	6	6.0	6.0	6.0
	Important	79	79.0	79.0	85.0
	Most Important	15	15.0	15.0	100.0
	Total	100	100.0	100.0	

Source: SPSS output based on Primary data.

Table 11. Information technology skills (A10)

		Frequency	Percent	Valid Percent	Cumulative Percent
Valid	Not Important	2	2.0	2.0	2.0
	Not Sure	10	10.0	10.0	12.0
	Important	62	62.0	62.0	74.0
	Most Important	26	26.0	26.0	100.0
	Total	100	100.0	100.0	

Source: SPSS output based on Primary data.

- Information Technology Skills

Interpretation: The output of Table 11, indicated that 62% of the respondents (majority) felt that 'A10' skill competency was 'important' for the professionals of forensic accountancy though 26% of the respondents marked it as 'most important. Only 10% of respondents were not able to decide its significance and marked it as 'Not Sure'.

- Solving Unstructured Problems

Table 12. Solving unstructured problems (A11)

		Frequency	Percent	Valid Percent	Cumulative Percent
Valid	Not Important	1	1.0	1.0	1.0
	Not Sure	13	13.0	13.0	14.0
	Important	56	56.0	56.0	70.0
	Most Important	30	30.0	30.0	100.0
	Total	100	100.0	100.0	

Source: SPSS output based on Primary data.

Interpretation: The output of Table 12, indicated that 56% of the respondents felt that 'A11' skill competency was 'important' for the professionals of forensic accountancy though 30% of the respondents marked it as 'most important.

Table 13. Evidence collection and gathering (A12)

		Frequency	Percent	Valid Percent	Cumulative Percent
Valid	Not Important	1	1.0	1.0	1.0
	Not Sure	11	11.0	11.0	12.0
	Important	59	59.0	59.0	71.0
	Most Important	29	29.0	29.0	100.0
	Total	100	100.0	100.0	

Source: SPSS output based on Primary data.

Table 14. Effective oral/written communication (A13)

		Frequency	Percent	Valid Percent	Cumulative Percent
Valid	Not Important	2	2.0	2.0	2.0
	Not Sure	11	11.0	11.0	13.0
	Important	55	55.0	55.0	68.0
	Most Important	32	32.0	32.0	100.0
	Total	100	100.0	100.0	

Source: SPSS output based on Primary data.

- Evidence Collection & Gathering

Interpretation: The output of Table 13, indicated that 59% of the respondents (majority) felt that 'A12' skill competency was 'important' for the professionals of forensic accountancy though 29% of the respondents marked it as 'most important. Only 1% of the respondents, which means that only a single respondent was marked as 'not important at all.

- Effective Oral/Written Communication

Interpretation: The output of Table 14 indicated that 55% of the respondents felt that 'A13' skill competency was 'important' for the professionals of forensic accountancy though 32% of the respondents marked it as 'most important.

Table 15. Auditing standards and techniques (A14)

		Frequency	Percent	Valid Percent	Cumulative Percent
Valid	Not Sure	6	6.0	6.0	6.0
	Important	70	70.0	70.0	76.0
	Most Important	24	24.0	24.0	100.0
	Total	100	100.0	100.0	

Source: SPSS output based on Primary data.

- Auditing Standards & Techniques

Interpretation: The output of Table 14 indicated that 70% of the respondents (majority) felt that 'A14' skill competency was 'important' for the professionals of forensic accountancy though 24% of the respondents marked it as 'most important.Only 6% of the respondents were not able to decide regarding the same.

- Critical and Strategic Thinking Skills

Table 16. Critical and strategic thinking skills (A15)

		Frequency	Percent	Valid Percent	Cumulative Percent
Valid	Not Important	1	1.0	1.0	1.0
	Not Sure	8	8.0	8.0	9.0
	Important	61	61.0	61.0	70.0
	Most Important	30	30.0	30.0	100.0
	Total	100	100.0	100.0	

Source: SPSS output based on Primary data.

Interpretation: The output of Table 16 indicated that 61% of the respondents (majority) felt that 'A15' skill competency was 'important' for the professionals of forensic accountancy though 30% of the respondents marked it as 'most important.Only 1 respondent felt that there was no requirement for critical and strategic thinking skills for forensic accountants.

- Research Oriented Skills

Table 17. Research oriented skills (A16)

		Frequency	Percent	Valid Percent	Cumulative Percent
Valid	Not Sure	12	12.0	12.0	12.0
	Important	53	53.0	53.0	65.0
	Most Important	35	35.0	35.0	100.0
	Total	100	100.0	100.0	

Source: SPSS output based on Primary data.

Interpretation: The output of Table 17 indicated that 53% of the respondents felt that 'A16' skill competency was 'important' for the professionals of forensic accountancy though 35% of the respondents marked it as 'most important.Only 12% of the respondents were not able to decide regarding the same.

- Questioning & Probing Skills

Table 18. Questioning and probing skills (A17)

		Frequency	Percent	Valid Percent	Cumulative Percent
Valid	Not Sure	11	11.0	11.0	11.0
	Important	54	54.0	54.0	65.0
	Most Important	35	35.0	35.0	100.0
	Total	100	100.0	100.0	

Source: SPSS output based on Primary data.

Table 19. Legal framework and methods (A18)

		Frequency	Percent	Valid Percent	Cumulative Percent
Valid	Not Sure	13	13.0	13.0	13.0
	Important	48	48.0	48.0	61.0
	Most Important	39	39.0	39.0	100.0
	Total	100	100.0	100.0	

Source: SPSS output based on Primary data.

Interpretation: The output of Table 18 indicated that 54% of the respondents felt that 'A17' skill competency was 'important' for the professionals of forensic accountancy though 35% of the respondents marked it as 'most important.Not a single respondent was available who marked it as 'least important' or 'not important.

- Legal Framework and Methods

Interpretation: The output of Table 19 indicated that 48% of the respondents felt that 'A18' skill competency was 'important' for the professionals of forensic accountancy though 39% of the respondents marked it as 'most important.Only 13% of the respondents were not able to decide regarding the same. However, not a single respondent was available who marked it as 'least important' or 'not important.

- Storytelling and Thinking like a Wrongdoer

Table 20. Storytelling and thinking like a wrongdoer (A19)

		Frequency	Percent	Valid Percent	Cumulative Percent
Valid	Not Sure	9	9.0	9.0	9.0
	Important	53	53.0	53.0	62.0
	Most Important	38	38.0	38.0	100.0
	Total	100	100.0	100.0	

Source: SPSS output based on Primary data.

Interpretation: The output of Table 20 indicated that 53% of the respondents felt that 'A19' skill competency was 'important' for the professionals of forensic accountancy though 38% of the respondents marked it as 'most important.Only 9% of the respondents were not able to decide regarding the same.Again, not a single respondent was available who marked it as 'least important' or 'not important. While investigating the financial crimes among the people concerned and involved, 'A19' was one of the most prominent aspects.

- Accounting and Business Reporting Practices

Table 21. Accounting and business reporting practices (A20)

		Frequency	Percent	Valid Percent	Cumulative Percent
Valid	Important	60	60.0	60.0	60.0
	Most Important	40	40.0	40.0	100.0
	Total	100	100.0	100.0	

Source: SPSS output based on Primary data.

Interpretation: The output of Table 21 indicated that 60% of the respondents felt that 'A20' skill competency was 'important' for the professionals of forensic accountancy though 40% of the respondents marked it as 'most important.Not a single respondent was available who marked it as a 'least important' or 'not important or 'Not Sure'. The most important reason for the same was all the respondents were professional accountancy students only aspiring to build their career in forensic accounting.

Descriptive Statistics of Skill Competencies

Interpretation: The output of SPSS, Table 22 indicated the maximum mean value more than important for 'Accounting & Business Reporting Practices' being respondents were all professional accountancy students and with the lowest mean to the 'Mathematical & Statistical Skills' as they moreover considered as an integrated element of accounting studies only.

KMO and Barlett's Test

Interpretation: The output of SPSS, as indicated in Table 23, the value of KMO statistics was more than 0.5 and the p-value is 0.000, which was less than 0.5. It showed that 'Factor Analysis' was an appropriate method for this study. Also, the numbers of respondents were exactly five (5) times the total number of variables identified.

Extraction of Communalities

Interpretation: It was evident from above Table 24 that almost all the variable's communality values were high, resulting in the maximum variation explained by the extracted components.

Table 22. Descriptive statistics

	Mean	Std. Deviation	Variance
	Statistic	Statistic	Statistic
Mathematical & Statistical Skills	3.66	.997	.994
Versatile Professional Network	3.78	.894	.800
Knowledge of Criminology	3.88	.946	.895
Identifying Key issues	3.89	.567	.321
Litigation Process & Procedures	3.98	.804	.646
Synthesize Result of Discovery & Analysis	3.99	.541	.293
Psychological Skills	4.07	.624	.389
Data Analytics Ability	4.08	.907	.822
Investigative Techniques	4.09	.452	.204
Information Technology Skills	4.12	.656	.430
Solving Unstructured Problems	4.15	.672	.452
Evidence Collection & Gathering	4.16	.647	.419
Effective Oral/Written Communication	4.17	.697	.486
Auditing Standards & Techniques	4.18	.520	.270
Critical & Strategic Thinking Skills	4.20	.620	.384
Research Oriented Skills	4.23	.649	.421
Questioning & Probing Skills	4.24	.638	.406
Legal Framework & Methods	4.26	.676	.457
Storytelling & Thinking like a Wrongdoer	4.29	.624	.390
Accounting & Business Reporting Practices	4.40	.492	.242

Source: SPSS output based on Primary data.

Component Matrix

Interpretation: The data in Table 25 presented the correlation coefficient between the variable and the corresponding component. These values were used to compute the Eigen values for each factor.

Table 23. KMO and Bartlett's test

Kaiser-Meyer-Olkin Measure of Sampling Adequacy.		.721
Bartlett's Test of Sphericity	Approx. Chi-Square	1196.238
	Df	190
	Sig.	.000

Source: SPSS output based on Primary data.

Table 24. Communalities

	Initial	Extraction
Accounting & Business Reporting Practices	1.000	.843
Auditing Standards & Techniques	1.000	.784
Information Technology Skills	1.000	.807
Data Analytics Ability	1.000	.651
Knowledge of Criminology	1.000	.506
Legal Framework & Methods	1.000	.808
Litigation Process & Procedures	1.000	.598
Investigative Techniques	1.000	.491
Evidence Collection & Gathering	1.000	.794
Versatile Professional Network	1.000	.561
Critical & Strategic Thinking Skills	1.000	.705
Effective Oral/Written Communication	1.000	.774
Research Oriented Skills	1.000	.784
Solving Unstructured Problems	1.000	.853
Synthesize Result of Discovery & Analysis	1.000	.852
Questioning & Probing Skills	1.000	.923
Psychological Skills	1.000	.762
Identifying Key issues	1.000	.806
Storytelling & Thinking like a Wrongdoer	1.000	.879
Mathematical & Statistical Skills	1.000	.564
Extraction Method: Principal Component Analysis. *Source: SPSS output based on Primary data.*		

Total Variance Explained

Interpretation: It was evident from Table 26 that six (6) components were available whose Eigen values were more than 1; hence a total of six (6) factors were extracted and the total variance explained by these factors was 73.725%.

Component Score Covariance Matrix

Interpretation: Table 227 indicated the covariance between the corresponding components as a diagonal matrix demonstrating absolute significance among the extracted features.

Rotated Component Matrix

Interpretation: From Table 28, the cut-off point was taken as 0.679, and finally, 10 variables were highlighted under four extracted components. All the variables which were appearing under one component had not been repeated in the subsequent component.

Table 25. Component matrix

	Component					
	1	2	3	4	5	6
Accounting & Business Reporting Practices	.321	.081	-.593	-.474	.011	.395
Auditing Standards & Techniques	-.604	.606	-.072	.017	.205	.068
Information Technology Skills	-.557	.656	.189	.023	.157	-.074
Data Analytics Ability	-.565	.294	-.343	.099	-.062	-.340
Knowledge of Criminology	.406	.251	-.195	-.210	.442	-.040
Legal Framework & Methods	.017	-.052	.632	-.544	-.303	-.133
Litigation Process & Procedures	.627	.320	-.136	-.033	.267	-.110
Investigative Techniques	-.243	-.102	.149	.170	.119	.597
Evidence Collection & Gathering	.671	.440	-.037	-.106	.193	-.316
Versatile Professional Network	-.378	.445	.075	-.330	.119	.301
Critical & Strategic Thinking Skills	-.674	.285	-.314	.149	-.170	-.142
Effective Oral/Written Communication	.442	.544	.143	.393	-.287	.162
Research Oriented Skills	-.665	.467	.261	-.197	-.081	-.096
Solving Unstructured Problems	.753	.448	-.039	-.089	.119	-.250
Synthesize Result of Discovery & Analysis	-.162	-.303	.140	.802	.200	-.176
Questioning & Probing Skills	.576	.613	.099	.385	-.212	.108
Psychological Skills	-.518	.574	.327	-.020	.227	.069
Identifying Key issues	.323	-.182	.781	-.196	.105	-.093
Storytelling & Thinking like a Wrongdoer	.576	.549	.144	.230	-.322	.262
Mathematical & Statistical Skills	.113	-.168	.265	.219	.608	.187
Extraction Method: Principal Component Analysis.						
a. 6 components extracted.						

Source: SPSS output based on Primary data.

As an outcome, it could be stated as follows:

- Component 1 was a combination of 'Auditing Standards & Techniques', 'Information Technology Skills' 'Research-Oriented Skills', and 'Psychological Skills'.

Labeled as "Digital & Research enabled Auditing Skills with Psychological Attitude".

- Component 2 was related to 'Litigation Process & Procedures', 'Evidence Collection & Gathering', and 'Solving Unstructured Problems'.

Labeled as "Intensive Investigation with Litigation Process".

- Component 3 was related to 'Effective Oral/Written Communication', 'Questioning and Probing Skills', and 'Storytelling & Thinking like a Wrongdoer'.

Table 26. Total variance explained

Component	Initial Eigenvalues			Extraction Sums of Squared Loadings			Rotation Sums of Squared Loadings		
	Total	% of Variance	Cumulative %	Total	% of Variance	Cumulative %	Total	% of Variance	Cumulative %
1	5.042	25.210	25.210	5.042	25.210	25.210	3.871	19.354	19.354
2	3.416	17.081	42.291	3.416	17.081	42.291	2.846	14.230	33.584
3	2.022	10.108	52.399	2.022	10.108	52.399	2.805	14.026	47.610
4	1.881	9.407	61.807	1.881	9.407	61.807	2.104	10.518	58.128
5	1.247	6.235	68.042	1.247	6.235	68.042	1.742	8.712	66.840
6	1.137	5.683	73.725	1.137	5.683	73.725	1.377	6.885	73.725
7	.937	4.687	78.412						
8	.843	4.217	82.629						
9	.710	3.550	86.179						
10	.541	2.704	88.883						
11	.462	2.309	91.192						
12	.358	1.788	92.980						
13	.286	1.429	94.409						
14	.233	1.167	95.576						
15	.227	1.136	96.711						
16	.207	1.034	97.746						
17	.139	.693	98.439						
18	.132	.661	99.100						
19	.106	.529	99.629						
20	.074	.371	100.000						
Extraction Method: Principal Component Analysis.									

Source: SPSS output based on Primary data.

Table 27. Component covariance matrix

Component	1	2	3	4	5	6
1	1.000	.0000	.0000	.0000	.0000	.0000
2	.0000	1.000	.0000	.0000	.0000	.0000
3	.0000	.0000	1.000	.0000	.0000	.0000
4	.0000	.0000	.0000	1.000	.0000	.0000
5	.0000	.0000	.0000	.0000	1.000	.0000
6	.0000	.0000	.0000	.0000	.0000	1.000
	Rotation Method: Varimax with Kaiser Normalization. Component Scores.					

Source: SPSS output based on Primary data.

Table 28. Rotated component matrix

	Component					
	1	2	3	4	5	6
Accounting & Business Reporting Practices	-.211	.233	-.002	-.262	.821	.027
Auditing Standards & Techniques	.834	-.036	-.017	-.295	.032	.007
Information Technology Skills	.885	.004	.058	-.054	-.125	-.048
Data Analytics Ability	.461	-.067	-.191	-.434	-.153	-.432
Knowledge of Criminology	-.001	.648	-.007	-.071	.220	.180
Legal Framework & Methods	.090	-.109	-.052	.848	.124	-.224
Litigation Process & Procedures	-.136	.699	.272	-.037	.098	.082
Investigative Techniques	.120	-.430	.064	-.072	.090	.523
Evidence Collection & Gathering	-.065	.818	.313	.107	.034	-.101
Versatile Professional Network	.634	-.070	-.016	.041	.372	.114
Critical & Strategic Thinking Skills	.502	-.290	-.112	-.460	-.089	-.371
Effective Oral/Written Communication	.033	.144	.865	-.019	-.065	-.011
Research Oriented Skills	.810	-.215	-.079	.145	-.013	-.230
Solving Unstructured Problems	-.128	.798	.413	.116	.082	-.098
Synthesize Result of Discovery & Analysis	-.137	-.197	-.010	-.265	-.812	.254
Questioning & Probing Skills	.005	.318	.904	-.038	-.057	-.004
Psychological Skills	.853	-.043	.051	.073	-.083	.134
Identifying Key issues	-.116	.127	.028	.824	-.197	.238
Storytelling & Thinking like a Wrongdoer	-.035	.192	.904	.079	.129	.009
Mathematical & Statistical Skills	-.030	.158	-.105	.056	-.250	.679
Extraction Method: Principal Component Analysis. *Rotation Method: Varimax with Kaiser Normalization.*						

Source: SPSS output based on Primary data.

Labeled as "Efficient Evaluative Communicator".

- Component 4 was a combination of 'Legal Framework' and 'Identifying Key Issues'.

Labeled as "Identifier of key issues within Legal framework'.

- Component 5 was a single extracted factor as 'Accounting & Business Reporting Practices'.
- Component 6 was 'Mathematical & Statistical Skills'.

Labeled as "Quantitative Aptitude".

However surprisingly, some major skill competencies like criminology, data analytics, critical thinking, and synthesizing results had not been extracted though considered to be most prominent for forensic accounting reason being the major elements of the same had already submerged in the fourteen (14) extracted skill competencies by all means and level of understanding.

FUTURE RESEARCH DIRECTIONS

Although this study is accompanied by some of the major limitations like the limited survey of past literature, time constraints, Covid-19 restrictions, and precautions and wave-3 are on upsurge, reluctant (due to time disturbance) and hesitant (as not planned till yet to pursue a career in forensic accounting) attitude of respondents, selection of convenience sampling method which is not a true representation of the entire population. Also, the sample size of 125 'Chartered Accountancy' students has been selected arbitrarily without any scientific and research-based technique. However, it can be stated that there is a vast scope for future research in this domain of forensic accounting and the corporate sector specifically in the Indian context. This is one of the most prominent and emerging fields of study in the current scenario. The upcoming youth and accountancy students are attracted to the latest insights and new paradigms of learning in this field. In a country like India, forensic accountants will be high in demand due to an increase in employee and management-related fraud, theft, embezzlement, tax evasions, and other financial crimes. Hence future research opportunities are also immense in this field being new technologies and methodologies are consistently required to solve the most critical and challenging inquiries with intense investigations.

CONCLUSION

The study concluded that a specialized branch of accounting termed 'Forensic Accounting' is one of the most lucrative and aspiring career options as far as professional chartered accountancy students of India are concerned. They are moving towards this career alternative as they feel that this specialized branch of accounting will act as a catalyst for strengthening and enhancing the corporate sector which results in boosting the economy of the country as a whole. Although there is an existence and further requirement of multiple skills for 'Professional Forensic Accounting Practices' but the major ones are 'Digital & Research enabled Auditing Skills with Psychological Attitude', 'Intensive Investigation with Litigation Process', 'Efficient Evaluative Communicator', 'Identifier of key issues within Legal framework', 'Accounting & Business Reporting Practices' and 'Quantitative Aptitude'. These major skill competencies have been extracted after the analysis of primary data which has been collected from the professional chartered accountancy students of Meerut City, Uttar Pradesh in India. Forensic Accounting is one of the most sought careers among accountancy and auditing students in the current economic scenario.

REFERENCES

Bansal, N., & Sharma, A. K. (2016). Audit Committee, Corporate sector and Firm Performance: Empirical Evidence from India. *International Journal of Economics and Finance*, *8*(13), 103–116. doi:10.5539/ijef.v8n3p103

Biswas, M., Hiremath, K. G., & Shalini, R. (2013). *Forensic Accounting In Indian Perspective* [Paper presentation]. The 5th International Conference on Financial Criminology (ICFC) 2013 on 'Global Trends in Financial Crimes in the New Economies.

Bhasin, M. L. (2013). Corporate Governance and Forensic Accounting Role: Global Regulatory Action Scenario. *International Journal of Accounting Research, 1*(1), 1–19. doi:10.12816/0001124

Bhasin, M. L. (2016). Contribution of Forensic Accounting to Corporate sector: An Exploratory Study of an Asian Country. *International Business Management Journal, 10*(4), 479–492.

Bhasin, M. L. (2017). Integrating corporate sector & Forensic Accounting: A Study of an Asian Country. *International Journal of Management Sciences & Business Research, 6*(1), 32–52.

Gupta, R., & Vij, S. (2021). Financial Frauds and Forensic Accounting: Empirical Evidence from the Indian Corporate Sector. *International Journal of Creative Research Thoughts, 9*(2), 1611–1619.

Jugurnath, B., Bissessur, R., Ramjattan, Y., Soondrum, H., & Seedoyal, A. (2017). Forensic Accounting and Fraud Investigation: An Empirical Study from Malaysia. *International Journal of Management and Applied Science, 3*(7), 20–24.

Kumar, A. A. (2018). Forensic Accounting – A Vision for Fraud Detection. *International Journal of Engineering Technology Science and Research, 5*(1), 694–707.

Kumar, D. S. (2012). Forensic Accounting: A Tool of Detecting White Collar Crimes in Corporate World. *Indian Journal of Research, 1*(2), 1–3.

Kumar, M. B., Nandeesh, G., Ayyappa, R., & Jayakumar, K. (2018). Role of Forensic Accounting - An Analysis. *International Journal of Research and Analytical Reviews, 5*(4).

Lama, P., & Chaudhari, B. (2018). *Forensic Accounting: A Study of its role in Investigating Corporate Frauds and Scams in India* [Paper presentation]. 11th international conference on Science, Technology and Management (ICSTM-18).

Lohana, P. M. (2013). Forensic Accounting at Nascent Stage in India. *Voice of Research, 2*(1).

Naik, M. (2019). Challenges and Scope of Forensic Accounting in India. *International Journal for Research in Engineering Application & Management*, (Special issue), 24–25.

Nena, S. (2015). An Overview of Forensic Accounting. *International Journal of Advance Research in Computer Science and Management Studies, 3*(8), 170–175.

Shair, P. (2017). Prospects and Techniques of Forensic Accounting in India. *International Journal of Research in Economics and Social Sciences, 7*(8), 604–614.

Sharma, A. (2014). Frauds in India and Forensic Accounting. *International Journal of Research & Development in Technology and Management Science, 21*(5).

Venkataraman, R., & Kumar, S. (2019). An Empirical Study on Forensic Accounting for Corporate Fraud Management. *Adalya Journal, 8*(10), 20–35.

KEY TERMS AND DEFINITIONS

Accounting: It is the process of identification, recording, classifying, summarizing, reporting, and analyzing business transactions with the preparation of the final results of an organization.

Auditing Practices: It is a collection of checking and authorizing financial statements and records in an organization.

Chartered Accountancy: It refers to the body of knowledge or the field of study which integrates disciplines like accounting, auditing, taxation, finance, business, corporate laws, etc.

Corporate Sector/Corporate World: It is a part of any economy that is composed of companies.

Forensic Accounting: It is a field of study which is a combination of accounting, auditing, and investigative techniques to detect frauds and scandals.

Investigation: The practice, procedure, and process to detect fraud, crimes, or scandals.

Skill Competencies: It refers to an array of those specific knowledge domains that are required for any particular field of study.

Chapter 10
An Evaluation of the Relevance of Forensic Accounting on Fraud Detection in the Nigerian Public Sector:
A Case Study of Bayelsa State, Nigeria

Hawal Olayiwola Dalegan
American Trinity University, USA

Abdullahi Omogbolahan Ishola
https://orcid.org/0000-0002-7651-6850
University of Essex, UK

ABSTRACT

The increasing sophistication of fraud has necessitated the use of forensic accounting tools to facilitate successful investigation. Perpetuation of fraud in the Nigerian public sector has reached alarming levels. This problem motivated the discussion on whether forensic accounting can facilitate detection and prevention of fraud in Nigeria. This chapter evaluates the relevance of forensic accounting on fraud detection in Nigerian public sector using a case study of Bayelsa state. This chapter finds that forensic accounting enhances fraud detection. The chapter consequently recommends that professional accounting bodies should constantly conduct forensic accounting training for accountants, and there is a need for the inclusion of forensic accounting in the syllabus of all the tertiary institutions offering accountancy in Nigeria. Further, the services of forensic accountants should be engaged more in Nigeria.

INTRODUCTION

Government spending has always been of significance but more so in current times where the government budget runs in to trillions of naira (or hundreds of billions of USD) (Akinlo, 2013; Aregbeyen &

DOI: 10.4018/978-1-7998-8754-6.ch010

Kolawole, 2015). This spend is so massive today and largely being funded by debts that the Nigerian public through its legislators is demanding to know whether the huge outlays of funds are being judiciously spent or whether they should be spent at all. Officials and employees who manage public sector activities are by virtue of that duty, required to render accounts of their activities to the public. Despite this, the incidence of fraud continues to increase across public sector organizations and across nations. Although fraud is a universal problem that no nation is immune to, developing countries such as Nigeria however tend to suffer more from fraud in the public sector as it directly hampers the growth of the economy (Okoye & Gbegi, 2013; Abdullahi & Mansour, 2018).

Fraudulent practices and corruption have resulted in poor infrastructural development, poor investment in security, poor development of health and education, weak citizen empowerment and job creation which all contribute to the state of insecurity present in Nigeria currently (Adebisi & Gbegi, 2015; Nwankwo, 2014; Page, 2018). The menace of fraud in the Nigerian public sector dates back to the colonial era when administrators were deployed to govern different areas of the country and they instead used their newfound powers to enrich themselves (Abdullahi & Mansor, 2015; Owolabi, 2007). The problem however continued to persist after the country gained independence due to different corrupt military regime ruling one after the other (Abdullahi & Mansor, 2015; Owolabi, 2007). The first democratic administration took over in 1999 under the leadership of General Olusegun Obasanjo (a retired army general and former head of state during the military regime) and marked the beginning of Nigeria's fight against fraud and corruption.

The Nigerian government has since taken several steps to address the evil of fraud and corruption in the society for example the enactment of legislations to criminalize all corrupt conducts including unjust enrichment. Several laws were enacted including Independence corrupt practices commission (ICPC) Act, 2000, Economic and Financial Crimes Commission (EFCC) Act, 2004, Money laundering (Prohibition) Act, 2004, Public Procurement Act, 2007, Fiscal Responsibility Act, 2007. The ICPC Act 2000 and the EFCC Act 2004 formed these respective bodies who are charged with the investigation and prosecution of fraud in Nigeria. Although they have enjoyed some success, the menace of fraud nonetheless prevails (Ngwube & Okoli, 2013).

Forensic accounting evolved in response to growing fraud related cases as a brief of all other investigation related areas in uncovering fraud. The increasing sophistication of fraud requires that forensic accounting be added to the tools necessary to bring about the successful investigation and prosecution of those individuals involved in criminal activities (Moduga & Anyaduba, 2013). For instance, the scandals that recently rocked the corporate world with classical examples being the oft cited Enron and WorldCom cases have highlighted the need for forensic accounting. The extent of the incidence of fraud has made traditional auditing and investigation inefficient and ineffective in detecting fraud (Oyerogba, 2021). Forensic accounting is a rapidly growing field of accounting that describes the engagement that results from actual or anticipated dispute or litigations (Amake & Ikhatua, 2016). The word forensic translates to being suitable for use in a court of law, and accountants generally operate to that standard (Crumbley, Heitger, & Smith, 2005). Forensic Accounting therefore is an investigative style of accounting used to uncover the incidence of illegal financial activities.

Forensic accounting involves the use of accounting, auditing, and investigative skills to assist in legal matters (Abdulrahman, 2019; Ozuomba, Ofor & Okoye, 2016). It consists of two major components; litigations services that recognize the role of an accountant as an expert consultant, and investigative service that uses a forensic accountant's skills and may require possible court room testimony. According to the definition developed by the Association of Institute of Certified Public Accountants (AICPA's) forensic and litigation services committee, forensic accounting may involve the application of special skills in accounting, auditing, finance, quantitative methods, the law and research. It also involves quantitative skill to collect, analyze, and evaluate financial evidence, as well as the ability to interpret and communicate findings.

Extant studies on forensic accounting have highlighted its potential to facilitate significant improvement in the quality of fraud detection and prevention (Dada & Jimoh, 2020; Owojori & Asaolu, 2009). This chapter is motivated by the understanding of the growing menace of fraud in the Nigerian public sector (Kasum, 2009) as well as extant literature on the suitability of forensic accounting to address fraud in the public sector (Dada & Jimoh, 2020; Owojori & Asaolu, 2009) and seeks to investigate the relevance of forensic accounting to fraud detection and prevention in the Nigerian public sector.

The general objective of this study is therefore to determine the effect of Forensic Accounting techniques in detecting the various categories of fraud in the Nigeria's Public Sector using a case study of Bayelsa state of Nigeria. Specifically, the chapter focuses on two major categories of fraud prevalent in the Nigerian public sector which are asset misappropriation and financial statement fraud (Abdullahi & Mansor, 2018). Beyond the main objective, the chapter further considers specific techniques associated with forensic accounting and their effectiveness in addressing the fraud in the Nigerian public sector. Specifically, the following questions are posed:

1. Is the application of computer assisted auditing tools (CAATs) effective in detecting asset misappropriation fraud in Nigeria's public sector?
2. Does ratio analysis technique of forensic accounting affect detection of financial statement fraud in Nigeria's public sector?

The chapter contributes evidence to the discussion on the relevance of forensic accounting technique to fraud detection and prevention. The chapter findings show that forensic accounting tools are suitable for use in detecting and thereby preventing fraud in the Nigerian public sector. Although the chapter conclusions are similar to that of extant studies (Dada & Jimoh, 2020; Owojori & Asaolu, 2009), the study focused on Bayelsa state of Nigeria which is one of the most insolvent and underdeveloped states in Nigeria despite the state being an oil producing one. This state has been significantly hampered by the incidence of corruption and fraudulent practices in its public sector leading to it being one of the most poorly developed states in Nigeria and therefore a unique setting to better understand how forensic accounting can contribute to addressing incidence of fraud.

Subsequent parts of this chapter are structured thus: the second section presents a discussion of the key literature on forensic accounting as well as highlight our theoretical framework, the third section discusses the research methodology and highlights the research questions, the fourth section presents the analysis and results of the research, and the last section concludes the chapter and provides recommendations.

LITERATURE REVIEW

The Conceptual Review

This section provides discussions of the key terms and concepts relevant to the chapter. These discussions facilitate a better understanding of what forensic accounting involves and how it relates to fraud.

Forensic Accounting

Forensic refers to suitability for use in a court of law (Crumbley et al, 2005). Forensic accounting is therefore the use of accounting, auditing, and investigative skills to obtain and present evidence suitable for use in a court of law to resolve issues of financial nature (Arokiasamy & Cristal-Lee, 2009; Stanbury & Paley-Menzies, 2010) Baird and Zelin (2009) view forensic accounting as an important investigative tool for detection of fraud. Gray (2008) meanwhile opined that forensic accounting is the combination of auditing and investigating skills to assist in effective internal control and prevention of fraud in organization. Simply put, it is the process of interpreting, summarizing and presenting complex financial issues, clearly, succinctly and factually often in a court of law as an expert witness. Degboro and Olofinsola (2009) viewed forensic accounting as the application of criminalities methods and integration of accounting investigative activities and law procedures to detect and investigate financial crime and economic misdeal.

From the definitions provided, forensic accounting can therefore be understood as a discipline involving the use of a wide range of skills including accounting, investigation and communication skills to obtain and communicate evidence on a subject matter relating to financial fraud or misconduct usually in a court of law or up to a standard acceptable in a court of law.

Fraud

Defining fraud is as difficult as identifying it. No definite and invariable rule can be laid down as a general proposition in defining fraud as it includes surprise, trick, cunning and unfair ways by which one party cheats another (Abduullahi & Mansor, 2018). Fraud is a legal term that refers to the intentional misrepresentation of the truth by one party to manipulate or deceive another party usually to obtain financial gains (Adebisi & Gbegi, 2015; Abdulrahman, 2019). Okafor (2004) described fraud as a broad term which encompasses all the multifarious means which human ingenuity can devise, which are resorted to by one individual to get advantage over another in false representation. According to Anyanwu (1993), fraud is an act or course of deception, deliberately practiced to obtain unlawful or unfair advantage; such deception directed to the detriment of another. David (2005) stating that fraud is not a possibility but a probability, explained that fraud can be better prevented if decisions are made by a group and not an individual. However, this control may not be effective where the interest of the group is aligned.

Accounting fraud is an act of knowingly falsifying accounting records, such as sales or cost records, in order to boost the net income or sales figures; accounting fraud is illegal and subjects the company and the executives involved to civil lawsuits (Koh, Arokiasamy & Suat, 2009). Company officials may resort to accounting fraud to reverse loss or to ensure that they meet earning expectations from shareholders or the public. According to Karwai, (2002); Okafor, (2004) and Adeniji, (2004) some of the most common types of fraud on the basis of methods of perpetration include the following (note this is not an exhaustive list as the methods are devised day in-day out): defalcation, suppression, outright theft and embezzlement, tampering with reserves, insider abuses and forgeries, fraudulent substitutions, unauthorized, unauthorized lending, lending to ghost borrowers, kite flying and cross firing, unofficial borrowing, impersonation, teeming and lading, fake payment, fraudulent use of the firms documents, fictitious accounts, false proceeds of collection, manipulation of vouchers, dry posting, over invoicing, inflation of statistical data, ledger accounts manipulation, fictitious contracts, duplication cheque books, computer fraud, misuse of suspense accounts, and false declaration of cash shortages.

Fraud Triangle

Fraud triangle is an oft employed theory in fraud literature that provides explanation on why people commit fraud (Abdulrahman, 2019; Abdullahi & Mansor, 2015; 2018; Adebisi & Gbegi, 2015; Cressey, 1953; Kassem & Higsion, 2012). Fraud triangle developed form the work of Cressey (1953) and describes three elements that results in fraud; pressure, opportunities and rationalization as discussed below:

1. Pressure: This refers to sources of needs that an individual or group require to achieve which incentivise them to fraudulently achieve the needs. They may include personal needs, social needs, economic needs, and the need to meet compensation-based targets. For example, the use of incentive systems to compensate managers for achievement of performance targets has been found to increase the likelihood of managers to commit fraud. Likewise, personal financial needs in relation to health or lifestyle issues as well may prompt people to commit fraud.
2. Opportunities: When the incentive to commit fraud exist, the perpetuator will seek an opportunity to perform the fraudulent act. Opportunity thus refer to the possibility and chance of successfully committing the fraud without being caught. An example could be legal or illegal access to cash or bank account of another individual, company, or government. Although opportunities for fraud can be reduced by implementing effective monitoring and control systems, the imperfection in the systems often present an avenue for the fraud minded individual to take advantage of.
3. Rationalization: When fraud perpetrators have some incentive and find an opportunity to commit fraud, the perpetrator will seek explanations to justify their actions. Rationalization thus refers to actions or beliefs that the fraud perpetrator believes in to convince themselves of going through with the action. Some examples of justifications include claiming that: 'I borrowed the money', 'I would pay back', or 'nobody has suffered as a result of this'.

Forensic Accounting and Fraud Detection

It is agreeable that an auditor does not have the absolute duty to uncover fraud but is expected to practice fair and true reporting to ensure that the interests of the public as well as the employees are protected (Enofe, Okpako, & Atube, 2013). Companies should look towards new approaches rather than follow the traditional approach as forensic accounting may be the next best alternative in resolving financial problems. Buckhoff and Schrader (2000) observed that the inclusion of forensic accounting as a course to the accounting curriculum can greatly benefit the three major stakeholders in accounting education namely, the academic institutions, students, and employers of accounting graduates.

A study by Boritz, Kotchetova and Robinson (2008) found that forensic accountants detect significantly higher incidences of fraud relative to the traditional auditors. Similarly, Srivastava, Mock and Turner (2003) found that forensic accounting processes significantly reduced fraud risks. Furthermore, Brown, Aiken, and Visser, (2007) show that proactive forensic analysis of data with the aid of computer-based sophisticated analytical tests can detect fraud that otherwise may remain undetected for years.

Basic Skills of Forensic Accountants

There are numerous opinions on the skills a forensic accountant should have. Harris and Brown (2000) while investigating the qualities of a forensic accountant identifies specialized skills and abilities that should be possessed by experts of their nature. They discovered that a forensic accountant should be conversant with civil and criminal law. Also, the need for understanding of court room procedures and expectations, investigative skills, creative thinking as well as clear and precise communication skills.

A forensic accountant must possess the characteristics/qualities of curiosity, persistence, creativity, discretion, organization, confidence, and sound professional judgement. A forensic accountant must also be open to consider all alternatives, scrutinize the fine details and at the same time see the big picture. In addition, a forensic accountant must be able to listen effectively and communicate clearly and concisely.

Forensic accountants apply accounting, auditing and investigating skills in detecting fraud and present litigation support service in the court (Bolgna & Liquist, 1995) and therefore forensic accountants are trained to look beyond mere numbers and deals with business reality (Bhasin, 2007). According to Zysman (2004), forensic accountants are usually geared towards finding where money went, how it got there and who was responsible.

In a study conducted by Davis, Farrell and Ogilby (2010), on the features and skills of a forensic accountant; the results showed that a forensic accountant should be analytical, detail–oriented, ethical, responsive, insightful, persistent and sceptic. The skills and knowledge required of a forensic accountant can be structured across 5 core skills that encompass other skills and attributes as discussed below (DiGabriele, 2009).

1. Deductive analysis: The ability to identify financial contradictions that do not fit in the normal pattern of assignment. In consideration of the barrage of recent financial reporting scandals this skill appears to be necessary and essential for a forensic accountant to meet the objective of uncovering a potential financial fraud.
2. Creative thinking: The ability to differentiate between opinion and fact. The essence of being an expert witness is to be able to perform the task of discerning fact from fiction to maintain a credible testimony. Courses developed in this area should emphasize the ability to remove any non-corroborated opinions from expert reports and testimony.
3. Unstructured problem solving: The ability to treat each situation as inherently unique and preparedness to solve problems with an unstructured approach. Accounting education has been based around concentrating on compliance with rules and procedures. This skill is a direct contradiction to this concept.
4. Analytical proficiency: The ability to look out for what should be provided rather than what was provided. Considering the post financial fraud regulatory environment, solving a financial puzzle with less than a complete set of pieces appears to be the direction the current business environment is heading.
5. Specific legal knowledge: The ability to understand basic legal processes and legal issues including the rule of evidence.

The Role of Forensic Accountant

The principal role of a forensic accountant as an expert witness is to analyse, interpret, summarize, and present complex business and financial deals in a logical, understandable manner supported with facts. An expert witness is a witness, who by virtue of education, training, skill, or experience, is believed to have knowledge in a particular subject beyond that of the average person, sufficient that others may officially (and legally) rely upon the witness's specialized (scientific, technical, or other) opinion about an evidence or fact issued within the scope of their expertise, referred to as the expert opinion, as an assistance to the fact-finder.

Challenges of Forensic Accounting Application

With an upsurge in financial accounting fraud in the current economic scenario experienced, financial accounting fraud detection has become an emerging topic of great importance for researchers and practitioners alike. The failure of the traditional auditing function including both internal and external auditing systems in identifying the accounting frauds has motivated the use of specialized procedures termed forensic accounting to detect financial accounting fraud, (Modugu & Anyaduba, 2013).

Following Rezaee, Crumbley, and Elmore (2006), the following are some of the major challenges to the application of forensic accounting:

1. The task of collecting evidence admissible in a court of law. This challenge is particularly relevant in the Nigerian public sector which is infamous for poor record keeping.
2. Globalization of the economy and the fact that a fraudster can be based anywhere in the world has led to the problem of inter-jurisdiction.
3. The law is not always up to date with the latest advancements in technology. This therefore might lead to evidence collected through recent technological developments being inadmissible in court.
4. Forensic accounting is seen as an expensive service that only big companies can afford.
5. The relative newness of forensic accounting particularly in developing countries mean that there is limited availability of accountants with adequate technical know-how on forensic issues.

Theoretical Framework

White-Collar Crime theory serves as the theoretical foundation of this chapter. The emergence of white-collar crime can be traced to sociology when Edward Ross addressed the concept white-collar offenses in 1896 by adapting the term criminaloid. A criminaloid makes use of the vulnerabilities in society through exploitation and does not fit the stereotype of a typical offender (Ross, 1907). Similar to white-collar crime offenders, a criminaloid is not viewed as culpable by the public as well as in their own perception of self. Sutherland (1940, p.1) further supports this notion when he defines white-collar crime as "crime in the upper or white-collar class; composed of respectable or at least respected business and professional men". White-collar offenses are typically organized, rational, as well as deliberate and its' offenders do not perceive themselves as law violators for they do not fit the stereotype of a common criminal (Sutherland, 1949; 1983).

Although, Sutherland is often hallmarked as the father of white-collar crime theory, he did not make a clear distinction between the different types of white-collar crimes and the structural forces (Geis, 2007; Meier, 2001). A simple definition is hard to come by, for there are opposing views as to what constitutes these acts. For instance, some acts that could be defined as white-collar crimes are codified in the criminal law, while other acts are administrative violations. Also, discrepancies arise when deciding if a corporate entity or rather an individual is responsible for the commission of white-collar crime. White-collar crime therefore fits the perspective of fraud in the public sector whereby perpetrators do not perceive themselves as criminals since they do not directly defraud or steal from others but rather from the governments' endless pockets.

Conclusively, based on White-Collar Crime theory argument, the perceived effect is that forensic accounting is expected to affect and help in curbing fraud in the public sector and also have a positive effect. This stems from the understanding that forensic accounting is able to identify fraud even where they appear inconspicuous as is often the case in white-collar crimes.

Literature Discussion

Emeh and Obi (2013) carried out an empirical analysis on forensic accounting and financial fraud in Nigeria examining the relationship between the presence of forensic accountants, the number of accountants with forensic accounting skills, extent of forensic accounting practices and extent of financial fraud. They found that all three factors have a significant negative effect on the extent of financial fraud. Similarly, Dada, Owolabi and Okwu (2013) examined the relevance of forensic accounting in the effective reduction of fraudulent practices in Nigeria. The results of their study reveal that fraud reduction is significantly and positively related to fraud investigation and detection through forensic accounting thus implying that forensic accounting is effective as a tool for managing and reducing the incidence of fraud in Nigeria.

Boritz, Kotchetova and Robinson (2008) found that forensic accountants could detect significantly higher number of fraud than auditors, meanwhile, Srivastava, Mock and Turner (2003) found that forensic audit procedures significantly lowered the risk of fraud. Likeiwse, Brown, Aiken and Visser (2007) observe that proactive forensic data analysis using computer based sophisticated analytical tests can better detect fraud that may otherwise go unnoticed. A study by Anuolam, Onyema, and Ekeke, (2016) examines the significance of forensic accounting in the face of increasing fraudulent practices in Nigeria with a view to advancing some solution. The findings of the study show that forensic accounting can play a significant role in the fight against the increasing fraudulent practices in Nigeria. Ogundana, Okere, Ogunleye and Oladapo (2018) examined the role of the forensic accountant in the prevention and detection of fraud in the Nigeria banking sector and found that forensic accounting has a significant impact on fraud prevention and detection. In addition, the findings of this study also revealed that there is a low level of the awareness of forensic accounting in the Nigeria banking industry.

A study by Bassey (2018) focused on forensic accounting as it affects the management of fraud in microfinance institutions in Cross River State, Nigeria and discovered that the active engagement of forensic investigation and litigation support reduces fraud in microfinance banks. Sule, Ibrahim, and Sani, (2019) as well discuss whether the use and application of forensic accounting investigation have an effect in detecting financial fraud in Nigeria. The study synthesizes the discussions in extant literature on forensic accounting and its application techniques. This study shows that forensic accounting service has a significant effect in detecting financial fraud. The review also indicated that forensic accounting investigation is a step forward on the discovery of financial fraud and other fraudulent exercises in Nigeria.

The discussion above therefore provides empirical basis to anticipate a significant impact of forensic accounting on fraud detection and prevention in Nigeria.

RESEARCH DESIGN

The research is a case study research carried out mainly at the government ministries, department, and agencies in Bayelsa state, Nigeria. The chapter adopts the survey research method in the process of data collection. The method entails identifying population of study and collection of data. This gives credence to the use of this methodology. The research relies on primary data solely collected through the administration of questionnaires to a sample of accounting and audit professionals who are staff members of the Bayelsa state government. The choice of a the research design is in line with extant studies in this line of research such as Adebisi and Gbegi (2015), Ademola, Ch-Ahmad and Popoola (2017), Amake and Ikhatua (2016), Gbegi and Adebisi (2014) and Oyerogba (2021). Also, the use of primary data facilitates firsthand data collection about the issue being investigated, particularly in the context of Nigeria where there is limited availability of secondary data on the use of forensic accounting in the public sector.

The research population refers to the total members of a defined class of people, objects, places, or events selected because they are relevant to one's research questions (Binford, 1964; Sharma, 2017). The population for the purpose of this research is the Bayelsa State public sector accounting and auditing professionals amounting to one thousand two hundred and seventy (1,270) staff. The population is made up of professionals in the Bayelsa State Ministry of Finance (400 staff), Office of the Accountant General of Bayelsa state (500 staff), Bayelsa State Ministry of Commerce, Trade and Investment, (150 staff), Office of Auditor General of Bayelsa State (state – 100 staff) and (Local Governments – 120 staff).

From this large population, a sample is randomly selected to participate in the study and based on the findings, generalizations can be made about the population. The decision to use random sampling technique is because it is the simplest probability sampling in term of conception and application which affords every member of the population an equal chance of being selected as part of the sample (Binford, 1964; Sharma, 2017). The random sampling technique presents the benefit of avoiding any bias in the sample selection process and thus improving the validity of the findings.

The final sample size used in this study is 93 staff derived using the Taro Yamane formula for determining the sample size from populations as shown below:

$$n = \frac{N}{1+N(e)^2}$$

Where: n = sample size

N = population size

e = Level of significance

$$n= \frac{1270}{1+1270(0.10)^2} . n = \frac{1270}{1+12.7} . n = \underline{93}$$

The required data was then collected by administering questionnaires to 93 members of staff of the Bayelsa state government. The questions contained in the questionnaire were structured in a manner that motivated the respondents to provide the necessary information regarding the suitability of forensic accounting for addressing frauds in the public sector. The questionnaire was structured into sections A and B with close ended questions. Section A generated information on respondents' bio-data while, section B, elicited information on respondents' perception on the relevance of forensic accounting on fraud detection in Nigerian public sector, case study of Bayelsa state. The questionnaire was in a close ended format which allowed the respondents to offer their views according to the 5-point Likert scale of responses ranging from strongly disagree to strongly agree. A sample of the questionnaire is provided in the appendix.

DATA PRESENTATION AND ANALYSIS

This section presents the data collected through responses to questionnaire administered. The analysis was executed through the use of simple statistics to extract the opinions and views of the respondents. As shown in table 1 below, 75 of the 93 questionnaires administered were returned thus yielding a response rate of about 81% which is a high rate for studies of this nature employing questionnaires.

Table 1. The distribution of questionnaires

Questionnaires distribution	N	Percentage
No. of questionnaires returned	75	80.6
No. of questionnaires not returned	18	19.4
Total No. of questionnaires distributed	93	100

Source: Authors' computation (2021)

Analysis of Respondents' Bio-Data

Following extant studies, bio-data of the respondents was collected to facilitate understanding of the characteristics of the respondents. These descriptions of the bio-data are presented in this section and in table 2 As shown in panel A, 48 respondents identified as male gender representing 64% of the sample while 27 respondents identified as female gender representing 36% of the sample. In panel B, we observe that 20% of the respondents were single, 72% were married, 2.6% were divorced and 5.3% were widowed. Both of these statistics help indicate that the sample is identical to the population whereby the majority identified as the male gender and in terms of marital status majority were married.

In panel C, it can be observed that 36% of the sample were early career professionals with less than 5 years of working experience, 44% were within 6-10 years of working experience, 13% were within 11-15 years of working experience, and 7% had the working experience of 15 years and above. This suggests that majority of the sample were well experienced professionals in the system of the Bayelsa state government and therefore suitably qualified to provide insights into how forensic accounting might assist the government in combating the incidence of fraud.

Finally, panel D shows that 7% of the respondents were educated up to high school level with a West African School Certificate (WASC), 33% held a diploma level qualification such as Higher School Certificate (HSC) and National Certificate of Education (NCE), 40% held a higher education institution level degree such as B.Sc., HND and BA., and 20% held further higher degrees at postgraduate level such as Postgraduate Diplomas (PGD), MSC, MA, MBA, and professional qualifications. This shows the level of education of the sample was dominated by professionals qualified beyond at least the university level.

Table 2. Bio-data of respondents

Panel A. The distribution of respondents by gender		
GENDER	**FREQUENCY**	**PERCENTAGE (%)**
MALE	48	64
FEMALE	27	36
TOTAL	75	100
Panel B. The distribution of respondents by marital status		
MARITAL STATUS	**FREQUENCY**	**PERCENTAGE (%)**
SINGLE	15	20
MARRIED	54	72
DIVORCED	2	2.7
WIDOWED	4	5.3
TOTAL	75	100
Panel C. The distribution of respondents by working experience		
EXPERIENCE	**FREQUENCY**	**PERCENTAGE (%)**
LESS THAN 5 YEARS	27	36
6 TO 10 YEARS	33	44
11 TO 15 YREAS	10	13
15 AND ABOVE	5	7
TOTAL	75	100
Panel D. The distribution of respondents by educational qualification		
QUALIFICATION	**FREQUENCY**	**PERCENTAGE (%)**
WASC	5	7
HSC/NCE	25	33
B.Sc./HND/BA	30	40
PGD/MSC/MA/MBA	15	20
TOTAL	75	100

Source: Authors' computation (2021)

Analysis of Research Questions

This section presents the discussions of the section B of the questionnaire where responses were solicited regarding the key questions based on which conclusions can be reached on whether forensic accounting plays a role in the detection and prevention of fraud in Bayelsa State public sector. The responses to each of the questions were firstly analyzed and then synthesized to provide a conclusive discussion achieving the research objectives. A total of 6 questions split into 4 categories were asked. The first category contained two questions that clarified whether forensic accounting aids in fraud detection in relation to asset misappropriation, and the second category featured two questions that ask similar questions but in relation to financial statement fraud. The last two categories contained questions that directly assess the further research questions on specific forensic accounting techniques of computer assisted audit tools (CAATS) and ratio analysis as they relate to addressing asset misappropriation and financial statement

Table 3. Is forensic accounting effective in detecting skimming and larceny fraud?

Response Option	Frequency	Percentage
Strongly Agree	14	19
Agree	48	64
Undecided	5	7
Strongly Disagree	2	2
Disagree	6	8
Total	75	100

Source: Authors' computation (2021)

fraud respectively. The design of the questions allows the chapter to directly answer questions pertaining to the most prevalent forms of fraud in the Nigerian public sector.

As shown in table 3, 14 respondents representing 19% strongly agreed that forensic accounting is effective in detecting fraud pertaining to skimming and larceny, while 48 respondents representing 64% also agreed to this. This shows that 83% of the respondents were in agreement with the effectiveness of forensic accounting in the detection of larceny and fraud. Meanwhile 5 respondents representing 7% were undecided, and 10% of the respondents either disagreed or strongly disagreed. Based on this, it can therefore conclude that forensic accounting is effective in detecting skimming and larceny fraud in the Bayelsa state public sector.

In table 4, 38 respondents representing 50% of the total respondents strongly agreed that the application of forensic accounting is effective in detecting payroll scheme and cheque tampering fraud, and 25 respondents representing 33% also agreed. Thus, 83% of the respondents found that forensic accounting is suitable for use and effective in addressing payroll and cheque tampering fraud. 8 respondents were undecided, while 4 respondents representing 6% did not share the view that forensic accounting might be effective in addressing cheque tampering and payroll scheme frauds. Therefore, it can be concluded that forensic accounting is effective in detecting payroll scheme and cheque tampering fraud in Bayelsa state public sector.

Table 4. Is the application of forensic accounting effective in detecting payroll scheme and cheque tampering fraud?

Response Option	Frequency	Percentage
Strongly Agree	38	50
Agree	25	33
Undecided	8	11
Strongly Disagree	2	3
Disagree	2	3
Total	75	100

Source: Authors' computation (2021)

Table 5. Is computer assisted auditing tools (CAATs) effective in detecting asset misappropriation fraud in Nigeria's public sector?

Response Option	Frequency	Percentage
Strongly Agree	22	29
Agree	28	37
Undecided	17	23
Strongly Disagree	2	3
Disagree	6	8
Total	75	100

Source: Authors' computation (2021)

Based on the findings from the first two questions put together, the chapter can conclude that forensic accounting is effective in detection of fraud relating to asset misappropriation in the Bayelsa state case study. Information presented in table 5 answers the first additional research question and shows that 22 respondents representing 29% strongly agreed that computer assisted auditing tools (CAATs) is effective in detecting Asset Misappropriation fraud, similarly, 28 respondents representing 37% agreed. Meanwhile 17 respondents representing 23% were undecided, while 3% and 6% of the respondents disagreed and strongly disagreed respectively. This implies that computer assisted auditing tools (CAATs) is effective in detecting Asset Misappropriation fraud in Bayelsa state public sector. The high rate of undecided responses could also be a pointer to the relatively low level of familiarity of the respondents with computer assisted auditing tools (CAATS).

In table 6, 10 respondents representing 14% strongly agreed and 28 respondents representing 37% agreed that forensic accounting is effective in detection of fraud on fictitious revenue and misapplication of accounting rules. 25 respondents representing 33% were undecided while 7 respondents strongly disagreed and 5 respondents disagreed. As the majority of the respondents (51%) of the respondents agreed that forensic accounting is effective in fraud detection on fictitious revenue and misapplication of accounting rules in Nigerian public sector, the chapter therefore concludes that forensic accounting is effective in detection of fraud relating to fictitious revenue and misapplication of accounting rules in Bayelsa state public sector.

Table 6. Is forensic accounting effective in fraud detection of fictitious revenue and misapplication of accounting rules in Nigeria's public sector?

Response Option	Frequency	Percentage
Strongly Agree	10	14
Agree	28	37
Undecided	25	33
Strongly Disagree	7	9
Disagree	5	7
Total	75	100

Source: Authors' computation (2021)

Table 7. Is forensic accounting effective in fraud detection of concealing liabilities, expense and overstating of asset?

Response Option	Frequency	Percentage
Strongly Agree	40	53
Agree	21	28
Undecided	9	12
Strongly Disagree	2	3
Disagree	3	4
Total	75	100

Source: Authors' computation (2021)

Table 7 above shows that 61 respondents representing 91% either strongly agreed or agreed that forensic accounting is effective in fraud detection of concealing liabilities, expense, and overstating of asset. 9 respondents were undecided, 5 disagreed or disagreed strongly. It is therefore concluded that forensic accounting is indeed effective in detection of frauds relating to concealing liabilities, expense and overstating of asset in the Bayelsa state public sector.

The two findings above put together shows the effectiveness of forensic accounting in addressing financial statement fraud in the Bayelsa state public sector. Furthermore, table 8 shows that about 83% of the respondents were in support of ratio analysis technique of forensic accounting being effective in detection of financial statement fraud. Although, about 11% were undecided and another 7% in disagreement, it can be concluded that ratio analysis technique of forensic accounting is deemed effective in detection of financial statement fraud in the Bayelsa state public sector.

Table 8. Is ratio analysis technique of forensic accounting effective in detection of financial statement fraud in Nigeria's public sector?

Response Option	Frequency	Percentage
Strongly Agree	14	18.7
Agree	48	64
Undecided	8	10.7
Strongly Disagree	2	2.7
Disagree	3	4
Total	75	100

Source: Authors' computation (2021)

Summary of Findings

Based on the analysis presented above, a number of findings emanated from the research. Firstly, the chapter finds that the use of forensic accounting significantly improves the detection of fraud in the Bayelsa state of Nigeria public sector. This could consequently serve as a deterrent to fraud perpetrators and effectively prevent fraud or at least reduce it significantly. This finding is similar to those of previous studies such as Abdulrahman (2019), Amake and Ikhatua (2016), Gbegi and Adebisi (2014) who all found that forensic accounting techniques are useful in prevention and detection of fraud in the Nigerian public sector.

Secondly, the findings show that Computer assisted audit tools (CAATS) is an effective method of carrying out forensic analysis to determine the occurrence of fraud. This finding supports the proposition of Bassey (2018) as well as the findings of Amahalu, Ezechukwu and Obi (2017) regarding the effectiveness of CAATS in combating incidence of fraud. Third, the chapter found that ratio analysis is an effective method of determining fraud relating to financial statement fraud. This is similar to the findings of Amahalu et al (2017) although the authors focused on the the private sector, in particular banks in Anambra state of Nigeria.

Fourth, the chapter observed that there is a good level of awareness and knowledge about forensic accounting and its implications. Finally, it was also found that the services of professional forensic accountants are needed more in the public sector. This echoes the findings of numerous other studies on the use of forensic accounting in the Nigerian public sector such as Abdulrahman (2019), Adebisi and Gbegi (2015), Amake and Ikhatua (2016), Gbegi and Adebisi (2014).

FUTURE RESEARCH DIRECTIONS

This study has evaluated the relevance of forensic accounting on fraud detection and prevention in the Nigerian Public sector using a case study of Bayelsa state. The findings here although may be an indicator of what can be expected in other states of Nigeria, the findings may however not be generalized. It is therefore important that future studies build on this chapter to investigate the extent of usage of forensic accounting for the whole Nigerian public sector by covering more states of the country and the outcomes in such cases. Secondly, this study has engaged with accounting and audit professionals in Bayelsa state, future studies may also engage with Universities, Professional bodies and associations to investigate how forensic accounting knowledge and skills are being disseminated. Finally, future studies may also carry out case studies documenting instances of either successful or failed usage of forensic accounting to investigate and prosecute high profile fraud cases in Nigeria.

CONCLUSION AND RECOMMENDATIONS

This chapter has analyzed how forensic accounting may be helpful in enhancing fraud detection in the Nigerian public sector. To do this, the chapter utilized a case study of Bayelsa State of Nigeria where data was collected via the administration of close-ended questionnaires that posed questions to accounting and audit professionals regarding the effectiveness of forensic accounting in the Nigerian public sector. The study has found that there is a good level of awareness about forensic accounting and that forensic accounting is suitable for the detection of incidences of fraud in the Bayelsa state of Nigeria public sector. Despite these findings, it should be emphasized that both in the business world and in the public sector, the ultimate responsibility for discouraging, mitigating, and detecting fraud rests with management. Therefore, the ultimate effectiveness of forensic accounting is limited to the management allowing professionals to work and investigate incidences of fraud. This however cannot be assured when the said leadership is also culpable of fraud.

It is recommended that firstly professional accounting bodies should constantly conduct forensic accounting training for accountants in order to improve the awareness, education, and knowledge of accountants with forensic accounting techniques. Similarly, forensic accounting should be included in the syllabi of all higher education institutions offering accounting programs in Nigeria as well as professional accountancy bodies. Secondly, the government of Nigeria should enact a law which will make forensic accounting a practice in Nigeria such that forensic accountants will have a practicing license as is obtainable in developed countries like USA, United Kingdom and Canada where they work tirelessly and professionally to eradicate fraud. Finally, lawyers and courts should employ the services of forensic accountants to assist in understanding the technicalities of some cases by serving as expert witness to facilitate the quick dissemination of judgment. They may also employ or collaborate with forensic accountants for professional discovery of evidence which will support litigation in the courts.

REFERENCES

Abdullahi, R., & Mansor, N. (2015). Concomitant debacle of fraud incidences in the Nigeria public sector: Understanding the power of fraud triangle theory. *International Journal of Academic Research in Business & Social Sciences*, *5*(9), 2222–6990. doi:10.6007/IJARBSS/v5-i9/1833

Abdullahi, R., & Mansor, N. (2018). Fraud prevention initiatives in the Nigerian public sector: Understanding the relationship of fraud incidences and the elements of fraud triangle theory. *Journal of Financial Crime*, *25*(2), 527–544. doi:10.1108/JFC-02-2015-0008

Abdulrahman, S. (2019). Forensic accounting and fraud prevention in Nigerian public sector: A conceptual paper. *International Journal of Accounting & Finance Review*, *4*(2), 13–21. doi:10.46281/ijafr.v4i2.389

Adebisi, J. F., & Gbegi, D. O. (2015). Fraud and the Nigerian public sector performance: The need for forensic accounting. *International Journal of Business Human Technology*, *5*(5), 67–78.

Ademola, L. S., Ch-Ahmad, A. B., & Popoola, O. J. M. (2017). The forensic accountants' skills and ethics on fraud prevention in the Nigerian public sector. *Academic Journal of Economic Studies*, *3*(4), 77–85.

Adeniyi, A. A. (2004). *Auditing and Investigation*. El-Toda Ventures Limited.

Akinlo, A. E. (2013). Government spending and national income nexus for Nigeria. *Global Journal of Business Research*, *7*(1), 33–41.

Amahalu, N. (2017). Effect of Forensic Accounting Application on Financial Crime Detection in Deposit Money Banks in Anambra State. *International Journal of Advanced Engineering and Management Research*, *2*(6).

Amake, C. C., & Ikhatua, J. O. (2016). Forensic accounting and fraud detection in Nigerian public sector. *Igbinedion University Journal of Accounting*, *2*, 148–173.

Anuolam, O. M., Onyema, T. E., & Ekeke, U. (2016). Forensic Accounting and Financial Crisis in Nigeria. *West African Journal of Industrial and Academic Research*, *17*(1), 120–125.

Anyanwu, J. C. (1993). *Monetary economics: Theory, policy and institution*. Hybrid.

Aregbeyen, O., & Kolawole, B. O. (2015). Oil revenue, public spending and economic growth relationships in Nigeria. *Journal of Sustainable Development*, *8*(3), 113. doi:10.5539/jsd.v8n3p113

Arokiasamy, L., & Cristal-Lee, S. (2009). Forensic accounting: Public acceptance towards occurrence of fraud detection. *International Journal of Business and Management*, 145–160.

Baird, J. E., & Zelin, R. C. (2009). An examination of the impact of obedience pressure on perceptions of fraudulent acts and the likelihood of committing occupational fraud. *Journal of Forensic Studies, Accounting Business, 1*(1).

Bassey, E. B., (2018) Effect of Forensic Accounting on the Management of Fraud in Micro-Finance Institutions in Cross River State. *IOSR Journal of Economics and Finance*, *9*(4), 79-89.

Bhasin, M. (2007). Forensic Accounting: A New Paradigm Niche Consulting. *The Chartered Accountant Country*, 1000.

Bologna, J., & Lindquist, R. (1995). *Fraud Auditing and Forensic Accounting*. Wiley and Sons.

Boritz, J. E., Kotchetova, N., & Robinson, L. A. (2008). Planning fraud detection procedures: Forensic accountants vs auditors. IFA Conference.

Brown, A., Aiken, P., & Visser, L. (2007). Reducing Fraud: A Programme that will Deliver Benefits on the Bottom Line. *Accountancy Ireland*, *39*(6), 28–30.

Buckhoff, T. A., & Schrader, R. W. (2000). The Teaching of Forensic Accounting. *Journal of Forensic Accounting*, *1*(1), 135–146.

Cressey, D. (1953). *Other People's Money: A Study in the Social Psychology of Embezzlement*. Free press.

Crumbley, D. L., Heitger, L. E., & Smith, G. S. (2005). *Forensic and Investigative Accounting*. CCH Group.

Dada, S. O., & Jimoh, F. B. (2020). Forensic accounting and financial crimes in Nigerian public sector. *Journal of Accounting and Taxation*, *12*(4), 118–125. doi:10.5897/JAT2020.0417

Dada, S. O., Owolabi, S. A., & Okwu, A. T. (2013). Forensic accounting a Panacea to alleviation of fraudulent practices in Nigeria. *International Journal of Business Management and Economic Research*, *4*(5), 787–792.

David, A. (2005). *Low level fraud is a high level issue, supply management*. Retrieved from: http://www.highbeam.com/doc/1P3-821992191.html

Davis, C., Farrell, R., & Ogilby, S. (2010). *Characteristics and Skills of the Forensic Accountant*. American Institute of Certified Public Accountants.

Degboro, D. & Olofinsola. (2007). Forensic accountant and litigate support engagement. *The Nigerian Accountant*, *40*(2), 49–52.

DiGabriele, J. A. (2009). Fishbowl the Forensic Accountant: A Closer Look at the Skills of Forensic Accounting Education should emphasize. *Forensic Examiner*, *18*(2), 77–79.

Emeh, Y., & Obi, J. O. (2013). An empirical analysis of forensic accounting and financial fraud in Nigeria. *African Journal of Social Sciences, 3*(4), 112–121.

Enofe, A. O., Okpako, P. O., & Atube, E. N. (2013). The Impact of Forensic Accounting on Fraud Detection. *European Journal of Business and Management, 5*(26), 61–72.

Gbegi, D. O., & Adebisi, J. F. (2014). Forensic accounting skills and techniques in fraud investigation in the Nigerian public sector. *Mediterranean Journal of Social Sciences, 5*(3), 243–243. doi:10.5901/mjss.2014.v5n3p243

Geis, G. (2007). *White-Collar and Corporate Crime*. Pearson.

Gray, D. (2008). Forensic accounting and auditing: Compared and contrasted to traditional accounting and auditing. *American Journal of Business Education, 1*(2), 115–126. doi:10.19030/ajbe.v1i2.4630

Harris, C. K., & Brown, A. M. (2000). The Qualities of a Forensic Accountant. Pennsylvania. *The CPA Journal, 71*, 2–3.

Karwai, S. A. (2002). Bank Fraud: Can Shari'ah prevent it? *Journal of Business Administration, 2*(1), 62–78.

Kassem, R., & Higson, A. (2012). The new fraud triangle model. *Journal of Emerging Trends in Economics and Management Science, 3*(3), 191–195.

Kasum, A. S. (2009, June). The Relevance of Forensic Accounting to Financial Crimes in Private and Public Sectors of Third World Economies: A Study from Nigeria. *Proceedings of the 1st International Conference on Governance Fraud Ethics and Social Responsibility*. 10.2139srn.1384242

Koh, A. N., Arokiasamy, L., & Suat, C. L. A. (2009). Forensic accounting: Public acceptance towards occurrence of fraud detection. *International Journal of Business and Management, 11*(11), 145–160. doi:10.5539/ijbm.v4n11p145

Meier, R. F. (2001). Geis, Sutherland and white-collar crime. In H. N. Pontell & D. Shichor (Eds.), *contemporary issues in crime and criminal justice*. Prentice Hall.

Modugu, K. P., & Anyaduba, J. O. (2013). Forensic Accounting and Financial Fraud in Nigeria. An Empirical Approach. *International Journal of Business and Social Science, 4*(7), 281–289.

Ngwube, A., & Okoli, C. (2013). The role of the economic financial crime commission in the fight against corruption in Nigeria. *Journal of Studies in Social Sciences, 4*(1), 92–107.

Nwankwo, O. F. (2014). Impact of corruption on economic growth in Nigeria. *Mediterranean Journal of Social Sciences, 5*(6), 41–41. doi:10.5901/mjss.2014.v5n6p41

Ogundana, O., Okere, W., Ogunleye, O., & Oladapo, I. (2018). Forensic Accounting and Fraud Prevention and Detection in Nigerian Banking Industry. *COJ Reviews & Research, 1*(1), 1–8.

Okafor, B. (2004). Strategic approach to reduction of employee, theft fraud and embezzlement. *Nigerian Accountant, 37*(4), 3–5.

Okoye, E. I., & Gbegi, D. O. (2013). Forensic accounting: A tool for fraud detection and prevention in the public sector (A study of selected ministries in Kogi state). *International Journal of Academic Research in Business & Social Sciences*, *3*(3), 1–19.

Owojori, A. A., & Asaolu, T. O. (2009). The Role of Forensic Accounting in Solving the Vexed Problem of Corporate World. *European Journal of Scientific Research*, *29*(2), 183–187.

Oyerogba, E. O. (2021). Forensic auditing mechanism and fraud detection: The case of Nigerian public sector. *Journal of Accounting in Emerging Economies*, *11*(5), 752–755. doi:10.1108/JAEE-04-2020-0072

Ozuomba, C.N., Ofor, T.N., & Okoye, P.V.C. (2016). Forensic Accounting and Fraud in the Public Sector (A Case of Imo State Ministry of Finance). *Research Journal of Management Science,* 1-6.

Page, M. T. (2018). *A new taxonomy for corruption in Nigeria*. Carnegie Endowment for International Peace.

Rezaee, Z., Crumbley, D. L., & Elmore, R. C. (2006). Forensic accounting education; A survey of academicians & practitioners. *Journal of Forensic Accounting*, *10*(3), 48–59.

Ross, E. A. (1907). *Sine and Society*. Houghton Mifflin.

Srivastava, R. P., Mock, T. J., & Turner, J. L. (2003). *The Effects of Integrity, Opportunity, Incentives, Militating factors and Forensic Audit Procedures on Fraud Risk* [paper presentation]. *Business and Information Management Auditing Research Workshop, Australian National Universities.*

Stanbury, J., & Paley-Menzies, C. (2010). *Forensic Futurama: Why Forensic Accounting Is Evolving*. Retrieved from: http://www.aicpa.org/Publications/Newsletters/AICPACPAInsider/2010/jun28/Pages/ForensicFuturmaWhyForensicAccountingIsEvolving.aspx

Sule, S., Ibrahim, S. S., & Sani, A. A. (2019). The Effect of Forensic Accounting Investigation in Detecting Financial Fraud: A Study in Nigeria. *International Journal of Academic Research in Business & Social Sciences*, *9*(2), 545–553. doi:10.6007/IJARBSS/v9-i2/5590

Sutherland, E. H. (1940). White-Collar Criminality. *The Sociological Review*, *5*(1), 1–12.

Sutherland, E. H. (1949). *White-Collar Crime*. Holt, Rirehart and Winston.

Sutherland, E. H. (1983). *White collar crime*. Yale University Press.

Zysman, A. (2004), Forensic accounting demystified. *World Investigation Network Standard Practice for Investigative and Forensic Accounting*, 1-28.

ADDITIONAL READING

Golden, T. W. (2011). *A guide to forensic accounting investigation* (2nd ed.). Wiley.

Hopwood, W. S., Leiner, J. J., & Young, G. R. D. (2012). Forensic accounting and fraud examination (2nd ed.). McGraw-Hill.

Kranacher, M. J., & Riley, R. (2019). *Forensic accounting and fraud examination*. John Wiley & Sons.

Manning, G. A. (2000). *Financial investigation and forensic accounting*. CRC Press.

Nigrini, M. J. (2020). *Forensic analytics: Methods and techniques for forensic accounting investigations*. John Wiley & Sons.

Silverstone, H., & Sheetz, M. (2011). *Forensic accounting and fraud investigation for non-experts*. John Wiley & Sons.

Singleton, T. W., & Singleton, A. J. (2010). *Fraud auditing and forensic accounting* (Vol. 11). John Wiley & Sons. doi:10.1002/9781118269183

Skalak, S. L., Golden, T. W., Clayton, M. M., & Pill, J. S. (2011). *A guide to forensic accounting investigation*. John Wiley & Sons.

Taylor, J. F. (2011). *Forensic accounting*. Financial Times/ Prentice Hall.

KEY TERMS AND DEFINITION

Asset Misappropriation: The diversion of funds kept in one's care to purposes beyond what they were allocated for.

Cheque Tampering: The forging or altering of a cheque drawn on the account of another party.

Computer-Assisted Audit Tools (CAATs): The use of computer technology to aid the execution of audit exercise. It facilitates efficient and effective processing of large volume of data.

Financial Statement Fraud: The deliberate misrepresentation of the financial statement of an entity to show a different picture from the reality.

Larceny: The unlawful possession or taking of something that belongs to another party. This can be likened to theft albeit without the use of forceful actions against the victim.

Payroll Scheming: The manipulation of the payroll to derive benefits for oneself. One of the most common examples is the creation of fictitious staff (ghost workers).

Ratio Analysis: The measurement of the relationship between two items of the financial statements using ratios.

Skimming: The removal of physical cash belonging to another party before it is recorded. For example, if an employee sells an item for $100 but only record $80 and keep $20 then they have committed skimming.

APPENDIX: QUESTIONNAIRE

Instruction:

Please tick in boxes where choice options are provided

SECTION A: BIO-DATA

1. Sex: Male ( ), Female ( )
2. Marital status: Single ( ), Married ( ), Divorced ( ) Widow ( )
3. Working Experience: Less than 5 years ( ), 6 to 10 years ( ), 11 to 15 years ( ), Over 15 years ( )
4. Educational Qualification: WASC ( ), HSC/NCE ( ), B.SC/HND/BA ( ), PGD/MSC/MA/MBA ( )

SECTION B: OPERATIONAL DATA

	CLASSIFICATION OF FRAUD					
S\n	**ASSET MISAPPROPRIATION**	**SA**	**A**	**UD**	**SD**	**D**
1	Forensic Accounting is effective in detecting skimming and larceny fraud					
2	The application of Forensic Accounting is effective in detecting payroll scheme and cheque tampering fraud					
S\n	**FINANCIAL STATEMENT FRAUD**	**SA**	**A**	**UD**	**SD**	**D**
1	Forensic Accounting is effective in fraud detection of fictitious revenue and misapplication of accounting rules in Nigeria's public sector					
2	Forensic Accounting is effective in fraud detection of concealing liabilities, expense and overstating of asset					
S\n	**FORENSIC ACCOUNTING TECHNIQUE**	**SA**	**A**	**UD**	**SD**	**D**
1	Computer Assisted auditing tools (CAATs) is effective in detecting asset misappropriation fraud in Nigeria's public sector					
S\n	**TECHNIQUE**	**SA**	**A**	**UD**	**SD**	**D**
1	Ratio Analysis technique of Forensic Accounting is effective in detection of financial statement fraud in Nigeria's public sector					

Chapter 11
The Essence and Prospects of Forensic Accounting in Developing Countries:
A Systematic Literature Review

Abdulkadri Toyin Alabi
https://orcid.org/0000-0002-3103-5367
Kwara State University, Nigeria

Abdullahi Omogbolahan Ishola
https://orcid.org/0000-0002-7651-6850
University of Essex, UK

ABSTRACT

The necessity for forensic accounting has grown with the increased incidents of financial fraud. This is not unrelated to the inability of statutory audit to discover and prevent fraudulent acts. This chapter provides discussions on the need and prospects of forensic accounting in developing countries as it may address the prevalence of business failures and financial crimes resulting from audit failure and the growth of creative accounting. Although the chapter provides a general overview for developing countries, there is a specific focus on Nigeria, a developing country characterized by high level of corruption. The findings show that the use of forensic accounting is still at a very low level owing to the high cost of forensic accounting tools and the time and money involved in acquiring the requisite skills. The chapter recommends that forensic accountants nonetheless are suitable to eliminate economic crimes and corruption to improve growth in the economy in developing countries.

INTRODUCTION

Forensic accounting is a branch of the accounting profession that deals with engagements emerging from or connected to actual or prospective litigation or disputes. The word forensic implies suitable for use

DOI: 10.4018/978-1-7998-8754-6.ch011

in a court of law and forensic accountants must typically work to that standard and possible resolution (Crumbley, Heitger, & Smith, 2005). Forensic accounting is a form of accounting that is acceptable for legal examination and gives the greatest degree of credibility (Apostolou, Hassell, & Webber, 2000). Specifically, forensic accounting is the use of financial skills and investigative attitude to unresolved matters, undertaken within the framework of the norms of evidence (Arokiasamy & Cristal, 2009).

The rising need for forensic accounting is widely acknowledged. The burning need for forensic accounting stems from the prevalence and consequence of fraud and blunders. In developing nations, especially in Nigeria, forensic accounting is still very recent and in its embryonic stages as organizations have just begun to discover the necessity of forensic accountants in combating the growing number of fraud cases. According to Bologna and Lindquist (1987), forensic accounting comprises fraud knowledge, financial skill, and a thorough awareness of corporate realities and the legal system's operation. Therefore, one of the most effective and efficient ways to reduce and check accounting fraud is through forensic accounting. Consequently, forensic accounting is now gaining popularity across the globe and is being introduced to curriculums at educational institutions across the world.

As a result of the recent spates of company failures, forensic accountants now have a larger responsibility to equip themselves with the abilities to recognize and act on signs of weak governance, mismanagement, frauds, and other wrongdoings. Professional forensic accountants must be well-versed in the strategies for recognizing, finding, and preserving the evidence of all types of financial misdeeds. Though accounting processes have vastly improved, contemporary electronic scams have grown so intricate and sophisticated that they may go unnoticed (Joshi, 2008). This necessitates figuring out how to overcome new obstacles to match the capabilities of financial crime. The inability of statutory audit to identify, prevent, and decrease corporate fraud and embezzlement, as well as the rise in corporate crime, has placed pressure on forensic accounting professionals and legal practitioners to devise a better method of exposing fraud in the business sector. As a result, this chapter examines the notion and necessity for forensic accounting, as well as the effects of financial corruption and crime on the economy in a developing country.

Forensic Accounting in Developing Countries

A succession of events over the past two decades has pushed accounting procedures to the forefront of the worldwide society and international financial institutions' agendas. The accountant's job is to act in the public interest, which is regarded as the overall pleasure of a group of stakeholders or institutions (Sheetz, 2006). The auditors' certification is unique and important since it lends credibility to financial statements by certifying them as legitimate for a range of actions that should purportedly benefit users. For example, a result of any violation of the core ethical norms of integrity and competence has extensive ramifications, it taints and contaminates accounting figures, making them of dubious validity (Joshi, 2008; Coenen, 2008). This was clearly observed in various heavily published cases of fraud or corporate scandals, including Enron, Worldcom, Xeror, Tyco and Global Crossing in the United States of America, Parmalat in Italy and in Nigeria, Cadbury, Lever Brothers now UniLever, Union Dicon Salt and the incident of Central Bank of Nigeria (CBN) sacking of the management and board of financial institutions resulting from fraud and financial abuses (Owojori & Asaolu 2009; Kapmag 2008). Corruption, fraud, money laundering, resource mismanagement, and other associated crimes have reached worrisome proportions in Nigeria and have become the norm in both the commercial and public sectors of the economy (Balarebe, 2009; Williams, 2010).

In Gambia, many laws have been passed to tackle corruption, tribunals set, and commissions of inquiries have been put in place but still yet bear meaningless fruit. The recent multi-million public finance embezzlement in the Gambia have shaken the business world, International community and the Government of the Gambia (Muhammed & Manneh, 2020). The public and governmental reaction to these events has been enormous. It has triggered congressional action that resulted in legislation (The Gambia Government Whitepaper, 2019) and auditing standards (Statement of Accounting Standard No. 99) that require public establishments and their auditors to be more aggressive in detecting and preventing fraud, which in turn, has elevated the importance of the forensic accounting profession in protecting the integrity of the financial system in order to prevent such fraud and embezzlement. To this effect, serious measures are required to be taken on how forensic accounting practices could aid forensic accounting techniques as a means of mitigating corruption through fraud, bribery and embezzlement of reduction in the public sector accounting perspective of the Gambia. Liodorova and Fursova (2018) added that the Gambia governments are required to encourage the practice of forensic accounting by providing adequate training and resources to forensic accountants such that they become an expert in their particular field of expertise and develop new courses related to forensic accounting.

In Indonesia, fraud has been at an upsurge and it is not only government officials of the judiciary, legislative, and the executives who can partake in corrupt practices, but private individuals as well (Hamdani, Kumalahadi, & Urumsah, 2017). For the fact that most corruption cases happen in public sector sectors, the government mainly concentrates to exterminate fraud cases which perpetrate a financial harm to any country. According to the result of the survey Transparency International (2015), Indonesia gained 36 for the score of the Corruption Perception Index (CPI). It placed the country in the position of 88 out of 168 countries being measured. The score increased 2 points in 2015 and led the country to elevate 19 ranks compared with that was in 2014. As such, the role of a forensic accountant is critical in curbing fraudulent practices. From the empirical test of Sumartono, Urusamah, and Hamdani (2020), it is implied that the involvement and training of forensic accountants will ease the process of revealing and reducing cases of fraud in Indonesia.

Furthermore, in recent times, forensic accounting has been in the spotlight in Ghana and has the role of bridging audit expectation gap relating to fraud prevention, detection, and prosecution of economic and financial crime (Evans, 2017). The Institute of Chartered Accountants of Ghana identified the need to work on the skills of auditors with the intention to offer diploma in Forensic Audit programs Though auditing may uncover some economic and financial crimes, detailed disclosure of these crimes and their prosecution demand special techniques and forensic accounting is perceived to provide these techniques.

In Brazil, forensic accounting practice is observed as a detachment of auditing. This enables it to be categorized as one of the professions that will gain space in time in terms of importance, because corruption is gaining ground in most of the developing countries, be it in the public sector or private businesses. The main elements of the characteristics of the forensic accounting practice in Brazil match with the global practices and empirical results show that, in practice, accounting profession organizations are assisting in consolidating the forensic functions of accounting to eradicate fraudulent accounting practices in Brazil territories (Imoniana, Pompa & Formigoni, 2013).

Fraud has also been one of major contributors to slow growth in public and private sectors in Kenya. Several management teams of the key corporations have been accused of poor corporate governance which has resulted to major corporate scandals which could have been deterred if there was proper use of forensic accounting policy. Some practical examples in Kenya includes collapse of Euro Bank in 2004 and the unfortunate case of National Bank of Kenya. Fraud has led to slow economic growth in Kenya and over reliance in debts notwithstanding many resolutions and regulations by Central bank of Kenya (Oguda, Odhiambo & Byaruhanga, 2015). However, Karuti, Mwaniki and King'oriah (2019) revealed that forensic accounting policies were not perceived by the government employees to be the most effective tools in fighting the threat of fraud until the emergence of some empirical evidence across the globe which necessitated and acted as an eye opener to Kenyan Governments on the importance of forensic accounting policy in control of fraud.

The current increase in corruption and scandals in Turkey have made forensic accountancy profession more popular. In recent times, forensic accounting profession finds itself many application fields and is supported by legal regulations and standards in many countries such as the USA, Canada, the UK and Australia. However, Turkey has not yet developed any standards at a desired level or imposed any laws directly concerning the profession (Karabayir, 2019).

Similarly, in the Jordanian legal system, forensic accounting as a profession is yet to be recognized with a specific job title. Legally speaking, a forensic accountant's responsibilities in Jordan have been covered by a different piece of legislation. In the accounting context, such obligations can be offered by professionals in the financial sector in general and accounting specifically (Alhusban, Haloush, Alshurafat, Al-Msiedeen, Massadeh & Alhmoud, 2020).

LITERATURE REVIEW

The Concept of Forensic Accounting

The understanding of what forensic accounting is and what it entails widely varies. This section attempts to synthesize the understanding of what forensic accounting is as discussed in extant studies.

The phrase "forensic accounting" was developed by Maurice E. Peloubet in his 1946 article "Forensic Accounting: Its Place in Today's Economy". Although forensic accounting had demonstrated its effectiveness during World War II and by the late 1940s, established processes were not used until the 1980s, when important academic papers in the topic were published (Razaee, Crumbley & Elmore, 2006). Since the 1980s, a new profession in accounting and auditing has evolved in various Western nations, primarily the United States. This profession of forensic accounting combines accounting, auditing, and investigative abilities (Ozkul & Pamukc, 2012).

Forensic accounting differs from traditional debit and credit accounting in that it offers an accounting assessment that is tailored to the organization's needs in resolving any disputes that may emerge. Accounting, according to Okoye (2006, pp. 3), is "the process of finding, measuring, and conveying economic information in order for consumers of the information to make educated judgments and decisions." Financial investigation, according to Oladipupo (2005), is a review of an organization's records and finances for a specific reason. Forensic accounting being a specialization that combines accounting, auditing, and investigation is therefore concerned with both the data of economic events and reporting included inside an accounting system, as well as the legal framework that permits such evidence to be utilized to prove responsibility and/or value (Okolo, 2007). Simply described, forensic accounting is accounting that is acceptable for legal scrutiny, provides the greatest degree of confidence, and has the now-accepted connotation of having been reached in a scientific manner (Crumbley, 2006).

According to Howard and Sheetz (2006), forensic accounting is a process of accurately, concisely, and factually analyzing, summarizing, and presenting complicated financial matters in a court of law as an expert. It is focused with the application of accounting principles to assist in the determination of factual problems in commercial disputes (Okunbor & Obaretin, 2010). Forensic accounting is a field with its own models and methodology for conducting investigations to find assurance, attestation, and advisory perspectives to create legal proof. Accounting fraud and forensic auditing; compliance, due diligence, and risk assessment; detection of financial deception and financial statement fraud (Skousen & Wright, 2008); tax evasion; insolvency, value studies; and accounting regulatory violations (Dhar & Sarkar, 2010).

Thus, forensic accounting is a discipline that combines investigative, accounting, and auditing abilities to address legal issues using accounting facts and ideas obtained via auditing methodologies, strategies, and processes (Arokiasamy & Cristal, 2009; Dhar & Sarkar, 2010). Meanwhile, Stanbury and Paley-Menzies (2010) view forensic accounting as the science of obtaining and presenting material in a manner suitable for a court of law in cases involving economic crime offenders. Hopwood, Leiner, and Young (2008) also defined forensic accounting as the use of investigation and analytical abilities for the aim of resolving financial concerns in a manner that fulfills legal criteria. Forensic inquiry is all about determining and establishing facts in support of a legal case. To put it another way, using forensic methods to detect and investigate a crime exposes all the crime's accompanying elements and identifies the perpetrators (Degboro & Olofinsola, 2007).

Razaee *et al.* (2006) further described forensic accounting as the use of accounting skills and an investigation attitude to resolve unsolved situations within the framework of the rules of proof. Sheetz (2006) as well described forensic accounting as the application of accounting principles to assist in the determination of factual concerns in company disputes. Manning (2010) describes forensic accounting as the use of financial accounting and investigation abilities to a quality acceptable to the courts to resolve difficulties in civil and criminal action. Forensic accounting, according to Damilola and Olofinsola (2007), is the use of accounting methodologies, investigation operations, and legal processes to identify and investigate financial crimes and associated economic transgressions. However, Zysman (2006) defines forensic investigation as the use of professional investigative abilities to perform an investigation in such a way that the results may be used in a court of law. Financial competence, fraud knowledge, and a thorough awareness of corporate realities and the workings of the legal system are all part of forensic accounting as a field. Its growth is normally accomplished via on-the-job experience and training with investigators and legal counsel (Coenen, 2008; Tijani, 2006).

While conducting an investigation, forensic accountants employ accounting, auditing, and investigative abilities. They often evaluate, interpret, synthesize, and present data in a difficult, comprehensible, and well-documented way. They are also often engaged in a variety of actions such as researching and evaluating financial evidence, building computerized systems, showing papers, and presenting the evidence gathered (Uche, 2009; Balarebe, 2009). This implies that forensic accounting is a branch of study concerned with the production of data intended for use as evidence, particularly for legal reasons. Since forensic accountants are educated to go beyond the statistics and address the situation's commercial realities (Coenen, 2008; Zysman, 2010), in accordance with the evidence presented in court, analyzing current complex financial activities and occurrences requires a high degree of skill (Razaee *et al,* 2006). This implies that forensic investigations may be used in a variety of industries, including accounting, engineering, medicine, and a few others (Owojori & Asaolu, 2009).

Detecting fraud and illicit activities in business companies, banks, the public sector, or any other organization's financial records is a specialty of forensic accountants. To put it another way, forensic accounting is mostly about the excitement of tracking out and exposing mistakes. The concept that accountants look at the numbers while forensic accountants look beyond them distinguishes forensic accountants from external auditors (Balarebe 2009; Kasum, 2009). Forensic accounting should be detailed and comprehensive enough to be able to produce findings on accounts, inventories, or their presentation in such a way that they may be used in legal proceedings or administrative or judicial assessment (Oladipupo, 2005; Grazoli, Janals & Johnson, 2006; Williams 2010).

A common theme across the understandings of forensic accounting is the collection and analysis of financial and non-financial data to investigate incidences of disputes or frauds and generate evidence suitable to resolve the disputes in court or out-of-court. A forensic accountant therefore is one who employs a plethora of skills cutting across accounting, analytical skills, and investigations to solve cases of financial discrepancies either in a court of law or outside of it.

Relationship between Forensic Accounting and Fraud Detection

In this section, discussions about the possibility and plausibility of forensic accounting being suitable for fraud detection is presented.

The signs of fraud may not always indicate fraud since they might be produced by human error (Albrecht, 2005). Also, fraud is difficult to establish because fraudsters put themselves in a position where they are protected (Modugu & Anyaduba, 2013). There is therefore a need for in-depth knowledge of how fraudulent acts are perpetrated. Without continual public engagement and advancements in forensic accounting, fraud cases will be difficult to identify, leading to higher success in financial fraud and a failure to satisfy the expectations of the public, shareholders, or even other stakeholders.

According to Ramaswamy (2005), a key reason for the occurrence and prevalence of fraud is inadequate corporate governance and accounting failure. This is due to a lack of corporate governance, which permits a single person or a group of people with similar interests to commit fraud inside the company. He further says that the challenges with the corporate reporting system are due to a lack of well-implemented corporate governance regulations. This is emphasized by the fact that top management should follow the business's regulations, which will help the organization function better. The problem arises from the fact that certain firm leaders are critical of the policies. Consequently, another concern in financial statement reporting is lack of honesty and transparency. It's understood that an auditor does not have to establish fraud in every case, but they should report fairly and honestly to ensure that the public's and employees' interests are protected. By applying forensic accounting principles, auditors may serve as forensic accountants in cases of suspected fraud or criminal behavior in a business. According to the Ramaswamy (2005), a bad management system cannot be transformed by an ineffective and inefficient internal control mechanism. Even if a company's internal control measures are effective, management will have the largest influence on adoption. Companies should be open to new approaches rather than sticking to old ones since forensic accounting could be the next best choice for resolving problems.

Okoye and Gbegi (2013) conducted research on the use of forensic accountants in the planning and detection of fraud risk. They found that when the risk of management fraud is high, forensic accountants effectively modify the scope and nature of audit tests; forensic accountants propose unique procedures not proposed by auditors; when the risk of fraudulent activity is high, forensic accountants can make to the efficiency of an audit plan; and involving forensic accountants in the risk of management fraud assessment process leads to better forensic accounting. Boritz, Kotchetova, and Robinson (2008) found that forensic accountants could identify a considerably larger number of frauds than traditional auditors. Similarly, Srivastava, Mock, and Turner (2003) found that forensic audit processes dramatically reduced fraud risks.

Further, accountants' perceptions of fraud detection and prevention procedures were investigated in some studies which showed that proactive forensic data analysis utilizing computer-based advanced analytical procedures may discover fraud that could otherwise go undetected for years (Bierstaker *et al*, 2006; Brown, Aiken, & Visser 2007). With reference to KPMG's Fraud Survey (2003), more organizations are: recently suffering fraud occurrences than in previous years; implementing antifraud measures; and initiating new antifraud initiatives and programs in response to the Sarbanes-Oxley Act of 2002. (KPMG 2003). According to PricewaterhouseCoopers' (PWC) 2003 Global Crime Survey, 37% of respondents in 50 countries experienced substantial economic crimes, with an average loss per firm of $2,199, 930. (PWC 2003). These survey findings highlight the significance of forensic accounting practice and education.

According to the US General Accounting Office (GAO) (1996), there is currently a strong emphasis on fraud prevention and detection during statutory audits. In actuality, the US and worldwide standard setters have strengthened auditors' responsibility to consider fraud concerns in financial statement audits. There is also a need that those conducting these audits have superior forensic ability. Enyi (2009) in agreement to this suggests that all regular statutory audits should contain forensic investigative components since evidence of fraudulent conduct may be easily identified if the internal control system's adequacy and compliance are fully reviewed. All of these efforts are aimed at identifying and combating fraud. An auditor, on the other hand, may not be able to achieve this without some understanding of forensic accounting procedures (Efiong, 2012). Meanwhile, Ramazani and Refiie (2010) investigated accountants' perceptions of fraud prevention techniques and forensic accounting, and found that accountants had little exposure to forensic accounting.

The foregoing shows that empirical evidence has been documented on the possibility and effectiveness of forensic accounting to detect and resolve financial frauds more effectively and efficiently than traditional audit however the exposure and development of forensic accounting is limited, particularly in the developing countries around the world where the incidence of fraud and corruption looms larger for the development of the countries.

An Empirical Review in Developing Nations

This section discusses the findings of extant studies regarding the use of forensic accounting for fraud detection in developing countries.

Numerous studies by various researchers have sought to analyze various factors surrounding forensic accounting in numerous developing nations. For example, Hamdan (2018) studied the role of forensic accounting in detecting financial crime in Jordan. The findings revealed that forensic accounting is indeed a useful technique for detecting fraud provided the standard prerequisites for skilled forensic accountants are met. Likewise, Enofe, Okpako, and Atube (2013) document evidence that the use of forensic accounting services by businesses has an impact on reducing the amount of fraud. Evans (2017) assessed the efficacy of forensic accounting and the combatting of economic and financial crimes in Ghana and found that forensic accounting plays a significant role in Ghana's fight against economic and financial crime.

In the Indonesian public sector, Fury and Eka (2013) investigated forensic accounting and fraud prevention examining the role of forensic accounting as a technique for detecting and preventing fraud in the public sector. They found that the application of forensic accounting decreases the frequency of fraud cases in the public sector by a substantial amount. In the Nigerian public sector, Dada and Jimoh (2020) examined forensic accounting and financial crimes and observed that litigation support services in the Nigerian public sector had a substantial negative influence decrease on financial crimes. Owojori and Asaolu (2009) as well concluded that forensic accountants would be extremely valuable in public accounting.

In Kenya, Oyier (2013) investigated the influence of forensic accounting services on fraud detection and prevention in commercial banks. They found that banks use of forensic accounting services resulted in greater fraud prevention in commercial banks, with the biggest application being on improving financial reporting quality. Organizational usage of forensic accountants was the least often utilized anti-fraud approach, but it had the greatest effectiveness rating, according to the research. This is consistent with the results of Ernst & Young's (2003) global fraud study, which found that just 20% of firms used forensic accountants' services, even with the greatest level of satisfaction with the service at 88%. Similar findings were documented by Okafor and Agbiogwu (2016) who examined the influence of forensic accounting skills on the management of bank fraud in Nigeria. They concluded that having basic forensic abilities decreases the frequency of fraud cases in the banking industry by a substantial amount. Furthermore, there is a substantial difference between the services of forensic accountants and those of external auditors and having forensic accountants on staff at banks may help reduce fraud instances.

Ogundana, Okere, Ogunleye, and Oladapo (2018) in a research on forensic accounting and fraud detection in the Nigerian banking business as well found that forensic accounting has a beneficial influence on fraud detection. Onuorah and Ebimobowei (2012) likewise observed that the use of forensic accounting services has an impact on the degree of bank fraud. Meanwhile, In Zimbabwe, Kosmas, Thulani, and Mashanye (2009) found that the forensic auditing section lacked both material resources and technological expertise. It was also discovered that forensic auditing faces managerial influence and that the profession lacks unambiguous recognition.

Modugu and Anyaduba (2013) looked at forensic accounting and financial fraud in Nigeria for their current empirical research and discovered that stakeholder agreement on the efficacy of forensic accounting in fraud control, financial reporting, and internal control quality is significant. Adegbie and Fakile (2012) observed that forensic accounting is a financial method for preventing and resolving economic and financial crimes in Nigeria. Asare and Wright (2004) discovered that forensic accountants may successfully adjust the scope and character of audit tests. They also discovered that rather than contacting forensic accountants, they should be engaged in the risk of management fraud assessment process. Bressler (2011) investigated what can improve knowledge of the function of forensic accountants in fraud investigation among attorneys and judges in the court system. Using conceptual analysis, the researcher discovered that forensic accountants must be well-versed in evidence rules, financial data, accounting information systems, software, and communication skills.

Contrary to the foregoing, Okunbor and Obaretin (2010) found that using forensic accounting services by businesses in Nigeria is ineffective in detecting fraud. While the majority of the studies as discussed above effectively show the potential of forensic accounting to aid in the fight against fraud and corruption in developing countries, majority of the studies have collected data from interviews and questionnaires which are largely dependent on the opinions of practitioners who may or may not themselves be a part of the problem of fraud. Therefore, it is important to have empirical studies examining the archival data relating to the use of forensic accounting in the incidence of fraud to examine the actual effect (if any) of forensic accounting on fraud detection in developing countries.

METHODOLOGY

The main objective of this review paper is to provide an overview on the purpose and prospects of forensic accounting based on the literature in this area. In line with the research objective, this study has taken two steps in the search for relevant forensic accounting articles. The first step encompasses a search for keywords and keywords strings that were encompassed [forensic] and [accounting]; [forensic accounting]; [forensic accounting and expert witness]; [forensic accounting and fraud detection]; [forensic accounting relevance] and [forensic accounting roles].

Using a descriptive research approach which aims to gather data that indicates the characteristics or qualities of an existent phenomena, information about forensic accounting and its use in developing countries is collected from top quality databases which were reviewed in order to lay hands on the past studies that were conducted in the area of Forensic Accounting. The population comprises of all the Forensic Accounting studies that could be obtained. Accordingly, the search for the studies was thoroughly conducted in the following recognized electronic databases which are; Elsevier, Scopus, JSTOR, Proquest, EBSCO host, Emerald Insight, ISI Web of Science, Taylor & Francis Group, OXFORD University Press, SSRN; Springer Link, SAGE Journals Online, Wiley Online Library, and Education Resources Information Center (Eric). These databases were selected because they are known to only consist of research papers with top quality and duplicate research studies are not considered for publications in these databases.

The second step had to do with snowballing search for the reference list of all identified articles in the first step. The search was limited to articles published in English. The selected articles were scattered over 11 years (2009–2020), this period was selected with the aim of analyzing the progress of literature in this area. From the search, the relevant studies were identified and critically analyzed. The selected studies for the review were those that discussed forensic accounting education and profession.

THE NEEDS AND PROSPECTS OF FORENSIC ACCOUNTING

Over the last 52 years, a string of embarrassing audit failures has spurred a paradigm change in accounting. Interestingly, while the upsurge of fraud detection was at its peak in the mid-twentieth century, a few analysts anticipated that in the future, the auditor's general obligation to run tests to detect material defalcations and mistakes, if they exist, would be accepted (Brown et al, 2007). In reaction to some developing fraud-related incidents, forensic accounting is believed to have emerged. The recent corporate scandals, with classic examples being the oft-mentioned Enron and WorldCom instances, have also pushed the area of forensic accounting to the forefront. In the investigation of financial fraud, forensic accounting is considered as encompassing all other investigation-related fields. Because financial fraud is becoming more sophisticated, forensic accounting must be added to the tools needed to conduct a prosperous independent inquiry and presentation of those involved in criminal activity (Moduga & Anyaduba, 2013). The prevailing assumption would be that forensic accounting will provide some relief from the traditional accounting and auditing systems' apparent susceptibility to financial fraud.

According to Crumbley (2009), no matter how hopeful we wish to be about the coming years, the recession has spawned more criminals than ever before, with so many more fraudulent activities yet to be revealed. As a result, there will always clamor for forensic accountants as long as there are fraudulent corporations, criminal gangs, and terrorists wobbling money among us. Since January 2008, over $100 million in fraud has been through the courts in the United States of America (USA), according to the published KPMG fraud barometer (Bolgna & Linqvist, 2010; Rumaswamy, 2009). Financial crimes have gotten more ubiquitous (Okolo, 2007), and the possibility of corporate fraud has increased. According to Kapmag (2008), fraud and abuse cost businesses in the United States more than $84 billion per year, and the average company loses 6% of its total revenue due to corruption and theft committed by its own employees.

In Nigeria, N273.9 billion pension fund fraud was described by Senate Committee on Public Service Chairman Aloysius Etok as syndicated and institutionalized embezzlement in the management of the country's pension fund (Aderibigbe, 2013). The Ex-Vice President of the World Bank, Oby Ezekwesili, has said that since Nigeria's independence in 1960, an estimated $400 billion in oil income had been stolen or misappropriated (The Citizen, 2014). In 2012, 3380 incidents of fraud totaling N17.97 billion were detected in Nigerian banks, according to Lamido Sanusi, the past governor of the Central Bank of Nigeria (CBN). In 2011, 2352 cases totaling N28.40 billion were reported (CBN, 2013). These staggering figures all demonstrate the high level of prevalence of fraud in the society and for a country like Nigeria, these corrupt practices directly hinder the development of the country.

In emerging countries, the rate at which public officials commit financial fraud is frightening. Leaders in third-world countries, in particular, pilfer public funds, oblivious to the effects of their actions on the country's population and its image in the international community when their evil crimes are revealed (Adefila, Kasum & Olaniyi, 2006). Several high-profile embezzlement cases involving leaders of developing nations have been reported in the last forty years. According to Transparency International (2019), the Past President of the Philippines was allegedly discovered to have embezzled up to US$ 78 to 80 million, Former President of Indonesia; US$ 15 to 35 billion, Past President of Zaire (Congo DR); US$ 5 billion, Ex-President of Serbia Yugoslavia; US$1 billion, Former Prime Minister of Ukraine; US$ 114 to 200.

Whichever the justification, an increasing number of forensic accountants are being called upon to meticulously search through documents, discover new information, and assist in attempting to put together all irregular pieces of the economic financial mystery to solve the perplexing issues of embezzlement, corruption, fraud, and mismanagement practice (Damilola & Olinfinsola, 2007). According to experts in the industry, with the tremendous economic pressure and more firms facing bankruptcy, many jobs are at stake, and workers who feel pushed to preserve the status quo are obliged to participate in corrupt behavior. Sophisticated accounting approaches are therefore required to discover, track, and resolve it, particularly when the outcome may have a negative effect on the financial statement (Mojeed, 2007; Owojori & Asaolu, 2009; Tijani, 2006).

The strengths of forensic accounting are its benefits to students and accounting professionals, the significant need and increasing demand, the new career channels and the reduction of fraud (Alshurafat, AlShbail & Mansour, 2021). Furthermore, the limitation of internal audit and audit committee as part of the management function to shed light on the various facts and other hidden aspects of corporate fraud; rotation of the statutory audit in addressing the issues as the method of selecting the statutory auditors' brooks complicity and lobbying all contribute to the need for forensic accounting (Okunbor & Obaretin, 2010). The auditors' certifications are seldom scrutinized, particularly when the reports are dirty and qualified, and the internal audit department may discover what transpired, but they are rarely in a position to take appropriate action (Okunbor & Obaretin, 2010). All of these weaken the effectiveness of the traditional audit function and begs for the introduction of the forensic accounting approaches to address the problems associated with the status quo.

The role of a forensic accountant entails providing preliminary advice on the level of destruction based on an initial interview of the pleading and the evidence available at the start of the proceedings, identifying the key documents that should be made available as evidence in court, and arranging a comprehensive balance report written in a language easily understood by a non-accountant. Other obligations include dealing with all issues, whether or not they are favorable to the client, evaluating professional accounting reports submitted by the other side, as well as reports from other experts on both sides, and advising lawyers on the consequences of these reports, advising lawyers during trials, especially as it relates to cross-examination of all the other side's document, and offering oral evidence at the trial if no act of court settles the case (Aderibigbe, 2013; Mojeed, 2007)

The emphasis of forensic accounting, according to Gottschalk (2010), is on evidence disclosed by financial document scrutiny. A forensic accountant's testimony may be used in a variety of circumstances. According to Curtis (2008), forensic accountants are critical to the legal system because they provide professional services such as phony invoicing values, suspicious bankruptcy valuations, and fraud document analysis. By critically analyzing financial data, these forensic accountants calculate values, draw conclusions, and spot unusual patterns or suspicious transactions (Arokiasamy & Cristal, 2009). In certain cases, it provides an accounting analysis to the court for dispute resolution, as well as an explanation of the fraud committed. As a result, forensic accounting may be useful in detecting and preventing accounting fraud in the business world. In this concept, forensic accountants conduct an account analysis to determine the facts needed to resolve a dispute before it is taken to court or the litigation process begins (Ozkul & Pamukc, 2012).

According to Bhasin (2007), forensic accounting aims to calculate asset values in a split-up proceeding, assessing damages caused by an auditor's negligence, fact-finding to determine whether an embezzlement occurred, in what amount, and whether criminal proceedings should be pursued, gathering evidence in a criminal proceeding, and determining damages caused by an auditor's negligence. The essential direction of forensic accounting, according to him, is the explanatory analysis (cause and effect) of events, including the discovery of deception (if any) and its repercussions in the accounting arena. Bhasin (2007) also claimed forensic accountants are trained to look beyond the numbers and deal with the business realities of situations. Analyzing, interpreting, summarizing, and presenting complex financial and commercial matters is a big part of the job. He went on to say that forensic accountants' duties include investigating and analyzing financial evidence, developing computerized applications to aid in the analysis and presentation of financial evidence, communicating their findings in the form of reports, exhibits, and collections of documents, and assisting in legal proceedings, including testifying in courts, acting as an expert witness, and preparing visual aids to support trial evidence. Therefore, forensic accountants' role is to find the perpetrators of fraud that occurs in businesses every year. This includes tracing money laundering, identity theft, and tax evasion activities. Forensic accountants are used by insurance companies to discover insurance frauds such as arson, and by legal firms to identify marital assets in divorce disputes.

Following the financial reporting difficulties that happened in a number of corporations throughout the globe, forensic accounting has grown in importance on the corporate agenda. These crises resulted in both a loss of public confidence and considerable financial damages. Several organizations made considerable measures to upgrade the architecture of their internal control and accounting systems in order to minimize fraud and theft and regain much-needed public trust. Forensic accounting, according to Baird and Zelin (2009), is a crucial investigative technique for fraud detection. As a consequence of this evolution, the value of accountants who have decided to specialize in forensic accounting and are hence referred to as forensic accountants has expanded.

THE RESPONSIBILITIES AND EXPERTISE NEEDED BY FORENSIC ACCOUNTANTS TO TACKLE FRAUDULENT ACTIVITIES

The specifications and talents necessary for the fulfillment of these tasks stem from the requirement for the forensic accountant. A forensic accountant's profession involves a high degree of skill, probity, integrity, and honesty. To become a member of a recognized accounting organization, a forensic accountant must be adequately trained and demonstrate his competence by completing all applicable examinations (Oladipupo, 2005). Patience and an analytical attitude are crucial since forensic accountants must investigate apparently innocuous records and seek for discrepancies. They should be proactive, suspicious in their examination of the books, and make no assumptions about the management's honesty (Manning, 2010; Tijani, 2006).

Forensic accountants must also have an investigative mentality which needs a critical approach in identifying, pursuing, analyzing, and evaluating information relevant to every engagement, thinking that it may be biased, inaccurate, or incomplete (Aderibigbe, 2013; Kasum 2009). To be a skilled forensic accountant, one must have a sense of utmost discretion and be open-minded to evaluate all options, analyze the minute details, and perceive the large picture all at the same time. According to (Damilola & Olinfinsola, 2007; Oladipupo, 2005), professional accounting abilities necessary by forensic accountants include but are not limited to; an understanding of how business activity is documented, recorded, reported, managed, and controlled; the ability to identify, obtain, examine, and evaluate relevant information; the ability to quantify the financial impact of actual or anticipated transactions or events; the ability to perform and interpret relevant information analyses; the ability to document and explain business information and the results of financial analyses for decision-making purposes; and the ability to perform and interpret relevant information analyses for decision-making purposes. They further went on to say that forensic accountants must have the following investigative skills: an understanding of the context in which the engagement is to be conducted; the ability to identify, obtain, examine, and assess information relevant to the engagement; the ability to analyze and compare various types and sources of information; an understanding of the types of information that would assist in establishing a purpose.

Additionally, Sheetz and Howard (2006) also listed the following as a minimum requirement for a forensic accountant: the ability to quickly extract the key issues from a large volume of documentation ranging from accounting records and management information systems to memos, correspondence, and other less obvious financial data. A thorough awareness of the differences between different business strategies, as well as a feeling of urgency and dedication, will enable rapid responses when needed and adherence to a rigorous time schedule, even if it means working longer hours to achieve the deadline. The capacity to express difficult theoretical concepts in layman's terms, to back up facts and numbers without seeming superior, and, most importantly, to look neutral and professional without participating in the court's inherent politicized process.

According to Grazoli *et al,* (2006) and Kasum (2009), a forensic accountant should be a good interviewer, which is needed to access relevant information; be able to examine and pinpoint relevant documents; be able to decipher financial transactions using information received from third parties; understand the legal implications of information found; know how to uphold chain of custody. Skill to scrutinize records for validity, alterations, forgery, or counterfeiting, as well as the ability to create fraud scenarios by thinking like a fraudster to identify situations where internal controls could be subverted or where controls are not enforced and thus exploited by employees.

Finally, Crumbley (2006) metaphorically summed up the forensic accountant's skills as follows a three-layer wedding cake with the bigger bottom layer being the accounting foundation, a deeper background in investigative auditing is the smaller second layer and the top layer is made up of understanding of legal principles. Effective communication is the cherry on top. Finally, a thorough understanding of computer procedures and interviewing abilities is required throughout the cake.

WHY FORENSIC ACCOUNTANTS?

As highlighted by Owojori and Asaolu (2009), the relevance of forensic accountants may be easily appreciated in the context of failure in statutory audits to identify and prevent fraud. A forensic accountant is useful in the following situations:

- **Assist in the Detection of Fraud**

A forensic accountant may readily discover financial fraud performed by management using analytical and technical abilities, averting organizational collapse. According to Clearing and Thibodeous (2005), a forensic accountant understands how to use Benford law to identify and prevent company fraud (a fraud analytical digital tools). As a result, it may be claimed that a forensic accountant's assistance in detecting and preventing fraudulent actions has aided businesses in minimizing financial fraud, which has often resulted in company failure.

- **Assisting the Police in Investigations**

A forensic accountant works with the police department in criminal investigations, and his report is written with the goal of presenting evidence in a professional and succinct way (Eiya & Otalor, 2013).

- **Increase the Independence of Auditors**

External auditors are hesitant to disclose examples of management fraud to stakeholders, even when the crime is blatant. This compromises the auditor independence, who is frightened of losing his job since most auditors are selected by management, which produces the audited accounts (Albrecht & Denn, 2001). According to Albrecht (2001), strengthening the independence of external auditors by upgrading financial reporting systems with expertise knowledge and ability in both financial concerns and the forensic financial reporting system via use of proactive fraud detection methods.

- **Increase the Accountability of Management**

According to Ramaswany (2009), the financial world has realized that there is a critical need for qualified individuals who can detect, disclose, and prevent vulnerabilities in three important areas: inadequate corporate governance, defective internal controls, and falsified financial statements. Within a corporate reporting structure that stresses its obligation to stakeholders, forensic accounting abilities are becoming more important. According to the preceding statement, a forensic accountant will use his specialist understanding of crime to assist management in improving the corporate reporting system, exposing and preventing bad governance, defective internal control, and false financial statements.

- **Support Members of the Audit Committee**

Forensic accountants help audit committee members perform their oversight tasks by offering improved tools that verify the external auditor has generated a quality assurance audit report. According to Zimbleman and Albrecht (2012), a forensic accountant uses a data-driven fraud detection tool to carry out his responsibilities of controlling fraudulent activities, which is proactive rather than the traditional reactive approach used by the external auditor in performing statutory audit functions.

FUTURE RESEARCH DIRECTIONS

This study examined the essence and prospects of forensic accounting in developing countries by providing a systematic review of the literature on forensic accounting to prove the importance and prospects of forensic accounting especially in the developing nations. It is observed that there is need for more research into the practice of forensic accounting particularly in developing countries which is characterized by high level of corruption and incidence of fraud both in the public and private sector. There is scope for forensic accounting to develop into a tool that can aid the development of such countries if successfully implemented to detect and prevent further frauds in these areas. To encourage widespread adoption, researchers need to explore the practice in more details and provide more evidence on the potential benefits that may serve as motivation for the future adoption of forensic accounting.

CONCLUSION AND RECOMMENDATIONS

According to the extant literature and the discussions presented in this article, forensic accounting is a broad area with several applications. Because of its interdisciplinary character and origins in the professions of accounting and auditing, forensic accounting integrates financial, technical, adjudicative, and investigative expertise (Hegazy, Sangster, & Kotb, 2017; Howieson, 2018). Students in forensic accounting courses get comprehensive knowledge and abilities that enable them to be more insightful in areas that a regular accounting course would not address. When forensic accounting expertise is combined with auditing and accounting knowledge, the value of the service that can be provided to clients is increased. As a result, the growing need and desire for forensic accounting services is justified by the added value that forensic accounting provides to the accounting profession and students. In today's world, the function of forensic accountants is undeniably crucial since they assist attorneys, courts, police, regulatory organizations, and other organizations in detecting and recording crimes. The growing prevalence of fraud in today's corporate climate necessitates the use of forensic accountants to uncover fraudulent activity both within and outside a firm.

As a result, professional groups, such as the Institute of Chartered Accountants, the Association of National Accountants, and the National Universities Commission in Nigeria are encouraged to promote the formalization and specialization of forensic accounting. Furthermore, as indicated by the instances previously provided, the government should take a keen interest in forensic accounting for the sake of monitoring and pursuing potential fraud culprits. Also, to assure acceptance of evidence in a law court for criminal charge of civil and criminal cases, national laws should be updated with the newest technological advancements. The government should have a solid strategy in place with other nations to extradite fleeing fraudsters from all over the world. Finally, it is suggested that the government reduce the costs associated with retaining forensic accountants' services. It is anticipated that if these suggestions are followed and the perpetrators are prosecuted fairly, the incidence of fraud in the developing countries would decrease dramatically, which will have a positive influence on the universal transparency status.

REFERENCES

Adefila, J. J., Kasum, A. S., & Olaniyi, T. A. (2006). The Global Endemic Nature of Financial Malpractices: An Analytical Appraisal. *Africa Journal of Management*, *6*(1), 11–20.

Adegbie, F.F., & Fakile, A.S. (2012). Economic and Financial Crime in Nigeria: Forensic Accounting as Antidote. *Journal of Arts and Social Sciences*, *6*(78), 37-50.

Aderibigbe, P. (2013). *Auditors Independence and Corporate Fraud in Nigeria. Journal of Research and Development in Higher Education.*

Albrecht, C.C., & Denn, J.G. (2001). *Can Auditor Detect Fraud?* Academic Press.

Albrecht, W. S. (2005). Identifying fraudulent financial transactions: A framework for detecting financial statement fraud. Brigham Young University.

Alhusban, A. A. A., Haloush, H. A., Alshurafat, H., Al-Msiedeen, J. M., Massadeh, A. A. M., & Alhmoud, R. J. (2020). The regulatory structure and governance of forensic accountancy in the emerging market: Challenges and opportunities. *Journal of Governance & Regulation*, *9*(4), 149–161. doi:10.22495/jgrv9i4art13

Alshurafat, H., AlShbail, M. O., & Mansour, E. (2021). Strengths and Weaknesses of Forensic Accounting: An Implication on the Socio-Economic Development. *Journal of Business and Socio-economic Development*, *1*(2), 135–148. doi:10.1108/JBSED-03-2021-0026

Apostolou, B., Hassel, J. M., & Webber, S. A. (2002). Forensic Expert Classification of Management Fraud Risk Factors. *Journal of Forensic Accounting*, *10*(1), 181–192.

Arokiasamy, L., & Cristal-Lee, S. (2009). Forensic accounting: Public acceptance towards occurrence of fraud detection. *International Journal of Business and Management*, 145–160.

Asare, S. K., & Wright, A. M. (2004). The Effectiveness of Alternative Risk Assessment and Programme Planning Tools in a Fraud Setting. *Contemporary Accounting Research Journal*, *21*(2), 325–352. doi:10.1506/L20L-7FUM-FPCB-7BE2

Baird, J.E., & Zelin, R. C. (2009). An examination of the impact of obedience pressure on perceptions of fraudulent acts and the likelihood of committing occupational fraud. *Journal of Forensic Studies, Accounting Business.*

Balarebe, I. (2009). *Economic Financial Crimes Commission (EFCC) and the Law*. www.efccnigeria.org

Bhasin, M. (2007). Forensic accounting: A new paradigm for niche consulting. *The Chartered Accountant, Country,* 1000-1010.

Bierstaker, J. L., Brody, R. G., & Pacini, C. (2006). Accountants' perceptions regarding fraud detection and prevention methods. *Managerial Auditing Journal, 21*(5), 520–535. doi:10.1108/02686900610667283

Bolgna, J., & Lindquist, R. J. (1987). *Fraud auditing and forensic accounting: New tools and techniques*. Wiley.

Boritz, J. E., Kotchetova, N., & Robinson, L. A. (2008). Planning fraud detection procedures: Forensic accountant's vs auditors. *IFA Conference*. Available at http://aaahq.org/meetings/AUD2009/PlanningFraudDetectionProcedures.pdf

Bressler, L. (2011). the Role of Forensic Accountants in Fraud Investigations: Importance of Attorney and Judge's Perceptions. *Journal of Finance and Accountancy, 11*(27), 1–9.

Brown, A., Aiken, P., & Visser, L. (2007). Reducing fraud: A programme that will deliver benefits on the bottom line. *Accountancy Ireland, 39*(6), 28–30.

Central Bank of Nigeria (CBN). (2013). *Statistical Report*. Government Printing Press Abuja.

Clearing, R., & Thibodeous, C. (2005). Applying Digital Analysis Using Benfords Law to Detect Fraud. *Auditing*, 77–81.

Coenen, T.L. (2008). *Forensic Accounting, A New Twist of Accounting Profession*. Academic Press.

Crumbley, D.L. (2006). *Forensic Accountants Appearing in the Literature*. Academic Press.

Crumbley, D. L. (2009). Forensic Accounting: Older than you Think. *Journal of Forensic Accounting, 2*(2), 181.

Crumbley, D. L., Heitger, L. E., & Smith, G. S. (2005). *Forensic and Investigative Accounting*. CCH Group.

Curtis, G. E. (2008). Legal and regulatory environments and ethics: Essential components of fraud and forensic accounting curriculum. *Issues in Accounting Education, 23*(4), 535–543. doi:10.2308/iace.2008.23.4.535

Dada, S. O., & Jimoh, F. B. (2020). Forensic accounting and financial crimes in Nigerian public sector. *Journal of Accounting and Taxation, 12*(4), 118–125. doi:10.5897/JAT2020.0417

Damilola, D., & Olinfinsola, J. (2007). Forensic Accountants and the Litigation Support Engagement. *The Nigerian Accountant, 39*(4), 49–52.

Degboro, D., & Olofinsola, J. (2007). Forensic accountants and the litigation support engagement. *The Nigerian Accountant, 40*(2), 49–52.

Dhar, P., & Sarkar, A. (2010). Forensic accounting: An accountant's vision. *Vidyasagar University Journal of Commerce, 15*(3), 93–104.

Efiong, E. J. (2012). Forensic accounting education: An exploration of level of awareness in developing economies -Nigeria as a case study. *International Journal of Business and Management, 7*(4). Advance online publication. doi:10.5539/ijbm.v7n4p26

Eiya, O., & Otalor, J. I. (2013). Forensic Accounting as a Tool for Fighting Financial Crime in Nigeria. *Research Journal of Finance and Accounting, 4*(6), 18–25.

Enofe, A. O., Okpako, P. O., & Atube, E. N. (2013). The Impact of Forensic Accounting on Fraud Detection. *European Journal of Business and Management, 5*(26), 61–72.

EnyiE. P. (2009). Detecting causes of variances in operational outputs of manufacturing organization: A forensic accounting investigation approach. Retrieved from http://ssrn.com/abstract=1144783

Ernst & Young. (2003). Fraud: Unmanaged risk. 8th global survey. Global Investigations Dispute Advisory Services, South Africa. Author.

Evans, O. N. D. (2017). Forensic Accounting and the Combating of Economic and Financial Crimes in Ghana. *European Scientific Journal, 13*(31), 379–393. doi:10.19044/esj.2017.v13n31p379

Fury, K. F., & Eka, A. (2013). Forensic Accounting and fraud Prevention in Indonesia Public Sector. *Journal of Modern Science, 4*(13), 421–433.

General Accounting Office. (1996). *The accounting profession major issues: progress and concerns*. GAO.

Gottschalk, P. (2010). Prevention of white collar crime: The role of accounting. *Journal of Forensic and Investigative Accounting, 3*(1), 23–48.

Grazoli, S., Janal, K., & Johnson, P. E. (2006). A Cognitive Approach to Fraud Detection. *Journal of Forensic Accounting, 7*(2), 65–88.

Hamdan, M. W. (2018). The Role of Forensic Accounting in Discovering Financial Fraud. *International Journal of Accounting Research., 6*(2), 2–6.

Hamdani, R., Kumalahadi, & Urumsah, D. (2017). The Classification of Corruption in Indonesia: A Behavioral Perspective. *SHS Web of Conferences, 10002*(34). 10.1051hsconf/20173410002

Hegazy, S., Sangster, A., & Kotb, A. (2017). Mapping forensic accounting in the UK. *Journal of International Accounting, Auditing & Taxation, 28*(1), 43–56. doi:10.1016/j.intaccaudtax.2016.12.004

Hopwood, W. S., Leiner, J. J., & Young, G. R. (2008). *Forensic Accounting*. McGraw-Hill/Irwin.

Howard, S., & Sheetz, M. (2006). *Forensic accounting and fraud investigation for non-experts*. John Wiley and Sons Inc.

Howieson, B. (2018). What is the good forensic accountant? A virtue ethics perspective. *Pacific Accounting Review, 30*(2), 155–167. doi:10.1108/PAR-01-2017-0005

Imoniana, J. O., Pompa, M. T., & Formigoni, A. H. (2013). The Forensic Accounting and Corporate Fraud. *Journal of Information Systems and Technology Management, 10*(1), 119–144. doi:10.4301/S1807-17752013000100007

Joshi, M. S. (2008). *Definition of Forensic Accounting*. www.forensicaccounting.com

Kapmag, D. J. (2008). Fraud Survey. *Journal of Forensic Accounting*, *4*(36), 9–22.

Karabayir, M. E. (2019). Forensic Accounting: Development and Practices Around the World. Kafkas University, Department of Business.

Kasum, A. S. (2009). *The Relevance of Forensic Accounting to Financial Crimes and Public Sectors of Third World Economies: A Study from Nigeria* [Thesis]. Department of Accounting and Finance, University of Ilorin, Nigeria.

Kosmas, N., Thulani, D., & Mashanye, E. (2009). The Effective of Forensic Auditing in Detecting, Investigating and Preventing Bank Frauds. *Journal of Sustainable Development in Africa*, *10*(4), 405–425.

KPMG. (2003). *Forensic and Fraud Survey*. KPMG.

Liodorova, J., & Fursova, V. (2018). Forensic accounting in the world: Past and present. *Forensic Accounting in The World: Past and Present Journal of Economics and Management Research.*, *7*(30), 84–100. doi:10.22364/jemr.7.06

Manning, G. A. (2010). *Financial Investigation and Forensic Accounting*. CRC Press.

Modugu, K. P., & Anyaduba, J. O. (2013). Forensic Accounting and Financial Fraud in Nigeria. An Empirical Approach. *International Journal of Business and Social Science*, *4*(7).

Mojeed, M. (2007). *Economic and Financial Crime Commission to Probe Babangida's Assets in France*. www.efccnig.org

Muhammed & Manneh. (2020). Forensic Accounting Practices - A Means of Mitigating Corruption: A Case Study of the Gambia Public Sector Perspective. *Journal of Research and Development (Srinagar)*, *5*(2), 41–46.

Oguda, N. J., Odhiambo, A., & Byaruhanga, J. (2015). Effect of Internal Control on Fraud Detection and Prevention in District Treasuries of Kakamega County. *International Journal of Business and Management Invention*, *4*(1), 47–57.

Ogundana, O., Okere, W., Ogunleye, O., & Oladapo, I. (2018). Forensic Accounting and Fraud Prevention and Detection in Nigerian Banking Industry. *COJ Reviews and Research*, *1*(1), 1–8.

Okafor, M. C., & Agbiogwo, A. A. (2016). Effects of forensic accounting skills on the management of bank fraud in Nigeria. *European Journal of Accounting, Auditing and Finance Research*, *4*(6), 70–80.

Okolo, M. N. (2007). Internal Audit and Incidence of Fraud in Nigeria. *The Nigerian Accountant*, *2*(25), 80–85.

Okoye, A. E. (2006). *Financial Accounting for Students and Managers, Mindex*. Publishing Limited Benin City.

Okoye, E. I., & Gbegi, D. O. (2013). An Evaluation of Forensic Accountants to Planning Management Fraud Risk Detection Procedures. *Global Journal of Management and Business Research*, *13*(1), 1–17.

Okunbor, J. A., & Obaretin, O. (2010). Effectiveness of the application of forensic accounting services in Nigerian organizations. *Journal of Management Sciences*, *1*(1), 171–184.

Oladipupo, A. O. (2005). *Principles and Practices of Auditing*. Mindex Publishing Co. Ltd.

Onuorah, A. S., & Ebimobowei, A. (2012). Fraudulent Activities and Forensic Accounting Services of Banks in Port Harcourt Nigeria. *Asian Journal of Business Management*, *4*(2), 124–129.

Owojori, A. A., & Asaolu, T. O. (2009). The Role of Forensic Accounting in Solving the Vexed Problem of Corporate World. *European Journal of Scientific Research*, *29*(2), 183–187.

Oyier, O. E. (2013). *The impact of forensic accounting services on fraud detection and prevention among commercial bank in Kenya* [Unpublished MBA Thesis]. University of Nairobi, Kenya.

Ozkul, F. U., & Pamukc¸, A. (2012). Fraud detection and Forensic Accounting. Academic Press.

Peterson, B. K., & Reider, B. P. (2001). An examination of forensic accounting courses: Content and learning activities. *Journal of Forensic Accounting*, *2*(1), 25–42.

PricewaterhouseCoopers. (2003). *Global economic crime survey*. Retrieved from https://www.pwc.com/extweb/ncsurvers.nsf

Ramaswamy, V. (2005). *Corporate governance and the forensic accountant*. Retrieved from: http://www.nysscpa.org/cpajournal/2005/305/essentials/p68.htm

Ramaswany, V. (2009). *Corporate Governance and the Forensic Accountant. The Certified Public Accountant (CPA) Journal.*

Ramazani, M., & Rafiei, A. H. (2010). Iranian accountant's conception of the prevention methods of fraud and offering some recommendations to reduce fraud in Iran. *Global Journal of Management and Business Research*, *10*(6), 31–45.

Razaee, Z. (2006). Forensic Accounting Education. A survey of Academicians and Practitioners. *Journal of Forensic Accounting*, *10*(3), 48–59.

Sheetz, M., & Howard, S. (2006). *Forensic Accounting and Financial Investigations for Non-Experts*. John Wiley and Sons Inc.

Skousen, C. J., & Wright, C. J. (2008). Contemporaneous risk factors and the prediction of financial statement fraud. *Journal of Forensic Accounting*, *9*, 37–62.

Srivastava, R. P., Mock, T. J., & Turner, J. L. (2003). *The effects of Integrity, opportunity, incentives, mitigating factors and forensic audit procedures on fraud risk*. Business and Information Management Auditing Research Workshop, Australian National University.

Stanbury, J., & Paley-Menzies, C. (2010). *Forensic Futurama: Why Forensic Accounting Is Evolving*. Retrieved from: http://www.aicpa.org/Publications/Newsletters/AICPACPAInsider/2010/jun28/Pages/ForensicFuturmaWhyForensicAccountingIsEvolving.aspx

Sumartono, U. D., & Hamdani, R. (2020). Skills of the Forensic Accountants in Public Sector Reveal Fraud in Indonesia: An Empirical Investigation. *Journal of Accounting and Investment*, *21*(1), 180–194.

The Citizen. (2014). *Financial Crime*. Retrieved from: www.thecitizenng.com

Tijani, K. (2006). *Accounting Role in the Crusade against Corruption in a Corrupt Society*. Paper Presented at a Workshop on Integrity in a Corrupt Society, Organized by the Professionals League, Lagos, Nigeria.

Transparency International. (2019). *Transparency International Report*. Retrieved from: www.transparency.org

Uche, S.O. (2009, Mar. 2). Financial Malpractice: Forensic Accountants to the Rescue. *The Nation Newspaper*.

Williams, I. (2010). Corrupt Practices: Implications for Economic Growth and Development of Nigeria. *The Nigerian Accountant, 38*(4), 44–50.

Zimbleman, M. K., Albrecht, C. C., Albrecht, S. W., & Albrecht, C. O. (2012). Forensic Accounting. Cengage Learning.

Zysman, A. (2006). *World Investigators Networks Standard Practice for Investigative and Forensic Accounting Engagement*. Canadian Institute of Chartered Accountant Journal.

ADDITIONAL READING

Bhasin, M. L. (2016). Contribution of forensic accounting to corporate governance: An exploratory study of an Asian country. *International Business Management, 10*(4), 479–492.

Crumbley, D. L., Heitger, L. E., & Smith, G. S. (2007). *Forensic and investigative accounting*. CCH.

Golden, T. W. (2011). *A guide to forensic accounting investigation* (2nd ed.). Wiley.

Hopwood, W. S., Leiner, J. J., & Young, G. R. D. (2008). Forensic accounting. McGraw-Hill/Irwin.

Ozili, P. (2015). Forensic accounting and fraud: A review of literature and policy implications. *International Journal of Accounting and Economics Studies, 3*(1), 63–68. doi:10.14419/ijaes.v3i1.4541

Pedneault, S., Rudewicz, F., Sheetz, M., & Silverstone, H. (2012). *Forensic Accounting and Fraud Investigation*. John Wiley & Sons, Inc.

Ramamoorti, S. (2008). The psychology and sociology of fraud: Integrating the behavioral sciences component into fraud and forensic accounting curricula. *Issues in Accounting Education, 23*(4), 521–533. doi:10.2308/iace.2008.23.4.521

Seda, M., & Kramer, B. (2014). An examination of the availability and composition of forensic accounting education in the United States and other countries. *Journal of Forensic & Investigative Accounting, 6*(1), 1–46.

Taylor, J. F. (2011). *Forensic accounting*. Financial Times/ Prentice Hall.

KEY TERMS AND DEFINITIONS

Audit: The examination and verification of the financial statements of a company by an independent third party to ascertain whether it presents a true and fair view of the company as at the given date.

Audit Committee: The audit committee is a committee of a company's board of directors responsible for exercising oversight over the financial reporting process of the company. Their functions include managing the internal and external audit process including appointment of auditors, internal controls, and risk management.

Financial Statement: This is a statement of record showing the financial status of a company over a given period of time, usually a year. It will usually include a statement of financial position, income statement, cashflow statement, statement of changes in equity, and notes to the accounts.

Financial Statement Fraud: This refers to the willful misrepresentation of facts on the company's financial statement to convey a different status about the company relative to its actual status.

Forensic Accountant: A forensic accountant is a skilled professional that investigates incidences of financial related crimes such as fraud, bribery, embezzlement, and money laundering.

Investigation: The process of making a formal inquiry into an event, a person, or a company usually in a bid to uncover missing details.

Litigation: The process of taking legal action or filing a lawsuit.

Chapter 12
With the Mediation of Internal Audit, Can Artificial Intelligence Eliminate and Mitigate Fraud?

Ali Rehman
https://orcid.org/0000-0002-6166-7242
A'Sharqiyah University, Oman

ABSTRACT

The purpose of this study is to determine artificial intelligence (AI)-supported Omani publicly listed organisations' attitudes towards fraud elimination and mitigation (FEM) concerns from the lens of agency theory with internal audit (IAF) serving as the mediator. A descriptive cross-sectional survey was conducted by involving Omani publicly listed companies as the unit of analysis. Data were gathered using an internet-based tool and analysed via PLS-SEM and SPSS. For results, AI displayed an insignificant but direct impact on FEM, whereas IAF exhibited a significant and direct effect on FEM. Apparently, AI exerted a significant and direct impact on IAF, while IAF mediated the correlation between AI and FEM. This study serves as a guidance to regulators, professional bodies, and organisations in amending their codes of corporate governance and organisational policies by initiating AI as a governance agent working for the principal, as well as operating towards eradicating fraud and fraudulent practices.

INTRODUCTION

Regulators and authorities have issued several guidelines to ascertain transparency, eliminate fraud, and provide better quality of financial statements. Despite the deployment of laws and regulations, fraudulent cases in organisations have continued to escalate (ACFE, 2020; Rehman & Hashim, 2019; Roszkowska, 2020). Approximately 47% of organisations had reported fraud cases in the past two years - the second-highest for fraud occurrences since the past two decades (PWC, 2020). Fraud not only shatters the confidence among shareholders, but also raises doubt on organizational commitment to continue its business operations. Obviously, the manually-driven laws and regulations are ineffective, while in-

DOI: 10.4018/978-1-7998-8754-6.ch012

Table 1. Reported fraud cases in Oman

Name of Company	Amount of Fraud	Source
Oman Arab Bank	USD 15 million	Observer (2020)
Ministry of Education	USD 41 million	Hamrani & Mahmoud (2021)
Bank Muscat	USD 39 million	Reuters (2013)
Dhofar Cattle Feed Company	USD 0.6 million	MSM (2020)
National Biscuit	USD 0.3 million	Mendoza (2020)
Oman and Emirates Investment Holding Company	USD 0.3 million	MSM-a (2020)

Note: MSM refers to Muscat Stock Exchange

novation is required for fraud elimination and mitigation (FEM). An instance of this innovation refers to artificial intelligence (AI) (Goertzel, 2014; Zeljko, et al., 2019), which can assist organisations in FEM.

In this present business setting, AI has been well integrated into the fabric of all corporate sectors and organisational operations. The AI can be applied in separate but related areas, including regulatory compliances, fraud prevention, and internal audit (Ammanath, et al., 2020; Lamboglia, et al., 2021). A number of ways have been proposed in which AI can reinforce fraud mitigation controls and concurrently assist in enhancing internal controls. When applied to organisational data, AI increases transparency, enhances trust, reduces fraud, and diminishes non-compliance with regulations. The link between AI and fraud prevention practices places the audit profession at the centre of an exciting new era (Govil, 2020; Valkanov, 2019; Aziz & Dowling, 2019).

Despite the mandatory requirement that organisations should update themselves more frequently, as well as maintain the pace of rapid and continuous change; many organisations have disregarded AI due to several implementation obstructions (Ammanath et al., 2020). More than 80% of the organisational board of directors failed to recognise the technological advancements and changing dynamics related to their business (Sarrazin & Willmott, 2016). The nature of businesses turns complex with technological advancements, and it is becoming challenging for CEOs to make accurate and intelligent decision in the absence of AI (Libert et al., 2017). Although AI can enhance business decisions functionality and be part of governance management, the adaptation of AI is occurring at a very slow pace (Sage, 2019) while some business leaders fail to see AI can benefit their organisations (Sage, 2019; Beck & Libert, 2018).

Several frauds could have been avoided if AI was implemented as a governance function working towards eradicating fraud. However, most organisations implement AI for their working operations but not as part of their FEM tool. Recently, more than USD 2 billion fraud was reported in WireCard as AI was implemented for their regular operations (Reuters, 2020) but not for FEM. Table 1 lists the few recent and prominent fraud cases reported in Oman:

The fraud cases tabulated in Table 1 could be easily prevented if AI was utilised in these companies towards FEM. Fraud prevention and detection with AI facilitates in completing data analysis within milliseconds and detecting complex patterns in the most efficient way that can be difficult for the internal audit to detect. On top of that, Omani companies dismiss the use of internationally available guidelines and principles related to AI (Office, 2020). These guidelines and codes serve as the initial guiding principle that can be tailored to the local needs of both the market and the industry. It is timely for organisations to place importance on the integration of AI with effective governance strategies for FEM (Lamboglia, et al., 2021).

The internal audit function (IAF) in Oman has been well regulated for public listed companies. Many amendments have been made in the regulations towards the assurance of IAF independence and legitimacy of their objectivity. In fact, IAF functionally and administratively report to the audit and risk committees, that prevents the interference of organisational management in IAF operations and functionality (CMA, 2018). Despite the authorities and privileges granted to IAF in Oman, 47% of IAF did not utilise the transformation technology and from this 47%, about 56% had no plan to use technology in the near future (Rehman & Mughairy, 2020). Despite the significances and benefits that AI has to offer to auditing function, technological issues related to IAF remain untapped. Although the vast literature depicts digital technologies in the medical and engineering domains, studies on AI related to IAF are in scarcity (Issa, et al., 2016; Lamboglia, et al., 2021).

The AI can assist and augment IAF intelligence, while simultaneously contributing to the governance management system of any organisation (Gonzalez, et al., 2020). The AI can enhance and support both strategic and operational decisions, besides providing competitive advantage to organisations (Beck & Libert, 2018) and serving as an agent from the lens of agency theory. Agency theory upholds the relationship between the principal and its hired agents (Gaaya, et al., 2017). There is always the possibility for agency problems to arise when agents start working for their benefits and neglect both the interest and benefits of the principal (Rashid, 2016). One of such agency problem refers to agency cost that happens due to information irregularity and moral hazard, poor monitoring, conflicting risk investment preferences, and diffused ownership (Panda & Leepsa, 2017; Kılıç & Kuzey, 2018). Issues related to information irregularity, investment preferences, and moral hazard may be resolved easily through proper AI deployment (Agrawal, et al., 2018).

Public listed companies in Oman are regulated under the capital market authority's issued codes of corporate governance, Commercial Companies Law, and other related regulations. The revised codes of corporate governance were issued in 2016 and are updated on regular basis (CMA, 2018). Nevertheless, implementation of AI is stipulated neither in the codes nor in the laws. It is noteworthy to mention that local authorities in Oman have recently signed a memorandum of understanding with several AI platform providers (Observer, 2020). This initiative can create potential towards inclusion of AI as a governance element for organisational functionality in facilitating FEM.

This present study proposes that FEM (dependent variable) is directly and significantly affected by AI (independent variable). Besides, this study implies that IAF mediates the relationship between AI and FEM. This mediation effect is assessed due to the possibility that the AI-FEM correlation may be indirect. By incorporating relevant empirical research and literature, this study extends the intended potentials of AI on IAF and FEM, in which AI serves as an agent for the principal of agency theory.

To the best of the researchers' knowledge, this study is unique because none has identified AI as an agent for the agency theory or determined its impact on FEM with IAF mediation. Past studies verified AI only as an IT support function, but not as a governance management system in facilitating the board of directors, the related committees, and IAF towards FEM. Hence, this study serves as guidance to regulators, professional bodies, and organisations in amending codes of corporate governance and organisational policies by embedding AI as a compulsory element in the governance codes, aside from supporting the board and its related committees.

BACKGROUND AND MAIN FOCUS OF THE CHAPTER

This section discusses the definition, concepts, past studies, hypotheses development, and related theory.

Artificial Intelligence

Artificial intelligence (AI) is the stronger and advanced modern technology that has the capability of transforming the world. The AI assists organisations in executing cognitive functions, including comprehending, recognising, observing, perceiving, learning, and interacting (Ergen, 2019). The AI acts as a business problem solver due to its increasing computational power, storage at low cost, massive data processing, and advancement in algorithms (Agrawal, et al., 2018; Ergen, 2019). The AI can operate in unstructured and uncertain physical or information environments, besides effectively managing unexpected internal and external threats (Powell, 2020; Burns & Steele, 2020) such as fraud, gross mismanagement or third party risks.

Another aspect of AI refers to its capability of fulfilling all organisational requirements (Ammanath, et al., 2020), including corporate governance obligations and satisfying the demands of shareholders. The AI can be best utilised by auditors by providing more predictive and strategic services to identify potential issues before they arise (Burns & Steele, 2020). Moreover, AI can be defined as machine-based activity and system that makes predictions, recommendations, and decisions that influence real, virtual, and foresight environments (Nilsson, 2010; OECD, 2019).

In order to remain competitive, organisations should embrace digitalisation and adopt technology (Tiron-Tudor, et al., 2021; Ghanoum & Alaba, 2020). By offering analytical activities, AI has an impact on business models and future forecast (Huang & Rust, 2018). The latest technology combined with AI and accompanied by statistics and numerical mathematics can be deployed to develop new and effective approaches towards risk assessment and information support (Chornous & Ursulenko, 2013). AI is also effective in making decisions, eliminating fraud, measuring disclosures in financial statements, and enhancing transparency in operations (Grüning, 2011; Lamboglia, et al., 2021). Notably, all Big Four accounting and auditing firms have implemented AI for tax and accounting practices (Zhou, 2017).

Being the third line of control (Babinchak, 2020) and when amalgamated with AI, IAF has the potential to offer vast benefits. The AI has a significant impact on the role of IAF (Ghanoum & Alaba, 2020). The IAF, with the assistance of AI, can perform audit on the whole population instead of merely providing assurance to sample data (Kozlowski, 2018).

Internal Audit Function

Internal audit function (IAF) is an independent and objective assurance activity, which is available in organisations (MacRae & Gils, 2010). The IAF ensures that all needs of shareholders are met in the interest of organisational operations and governance (Florea & Florea, 2016). The IAF is a mandatory constituent of the codes of corporate governance (CMA, 2018) that assists in achieving good corporate governance (Cioban, 2016; Waweru & Prot, 2018). Along with local laws and regulations, IAF is governed by international professional practice framework issued by the Institute of Internal Auditors (Turetken, et al., 2020).

The audit profession has changed as it was a decade ago. Auditors must be agile and up to date with technology, as AI imposes serious changes in the functionality and requirements of IAF (Kozlowski,

Table 2. The impact of artificial intelligence on internal audit function

Impact on Internal Audit Function	Description
Scope of audit assignments	The agility of IAF planning and the desired digital knowledge are expected to enhance, while cybersecurity risks gain importance
Consulting activities	Due to the overall knowledge and enhanced functionality of AI, demand for consulting activities increases
Continuous monitoring	Working practice of IAF modifies from day to day tasks (routine task) towards more focused and risk averse tasks

Source: Betti and Sarens (2020)

2018). The focus of IAF has shifted from compliance and sample-based audits to more detailed, substantive, systematic, predictive, problem solving, and fraud detecting audits (Ghanoum & Alaba, 2020). More importantly, IAF assesses smart controls and lists recommendations towards control improvement (Lamboglia, et al., 2021; Oussii & Taktak, 2018). Table 2 presents the influence of AI on IAF in three different aspects:

The AI obliges IAF to acquire technological knowledge, interpersonal skills, emotional intelligence, project management skills, and critical thinking (Aslan, 2021). The use of AI and its related automation enhances the efficacy and efficiency of IAF as it supports real-time assurance (Chan & Vasarhelyi, 2018; Ghanoum & Alaba, 2020) and assists in achieving the true meaning of corporate governance (MacRae & Gils, 2010).

Fraud

One of the biggest threats an organisation faces refers to fraud and its related activities (PWC, 2020; Siregar & Tenoyo, 2015). All kinds of fraud are a menace, in which organisations not only suffer monetarily but also get their reputation tarnished. Fraud is defined as a deceitful and intentional act that impacts an organisation. Fraud is conducted by the organisation or on the organisation for the benefit of the fraudster (ACFE, 2020).

Following a recent survey, 47% of organisations had experienced fraud since the past two years. In fact, the last two decades saw the second-highest reported level of fraudulent cases. Nevertheless, the battle against fraud is evolving as new technology offers tools such as AI that can hinder and detect fraud (PWC, 2020). Some of the major reasons for the organisations to suffer from fraud are poor fraud risk management, poor internal control, lack of ethical values, and management overriding of control (Siregar & Tenoyo, 2015). With its self-learning capability, AI provides more proactive solutions to organisations in preventing real-time fraud.

In accordance with ACFE (2020), IA is considered as the top function responsible towards detection of fraud. IA with its skills and sceptical mind frame can prevent the fraud by developing controls and implementing them via AI. IA defined controls are based on the past audits and related risk assessments. These controls can be embedded in to the AI enabling it to identify the red flags. These red flags are then tested again by IA to ensure that fraud is prevented and AI is performing as per the desired requirement.

Table 3. Number of companies listed in the Muscat Stock Exchange

Sector	Number of Companies
Financial Sector	36
Financial Sector – Preferred Share	3
Industrial Sector	40
Services Sector	39
Total	118

Source: MSM (2021)

Public Listed Companies in Oman

Public listed companies in Oman operate under Commercial Companies Law and are regulated by the codes of corporate governance issued by Capital Market Authority and Muscat Stock Exchange (MSM) rules. Revised codes of corporate governance were issued in 2016, while the first codes were issued in 2002 (Rehman & Hashim, 2019). Although the codes are amended on regular basis to cater to the needs of the current dynamic market; however, till date there is no provision available in codes for AI and its related utilization. Notably, IAF, as well as audit and risk committees, is given special consideration in the codes (CMA, 2018) with a specific intent to provide transparent information to shareholders and to have proper controls within the organisation. Nonetheless, auditors face challenges in terms of delay in updating their accounting or auditing standards and adopting change in the department (Arrowsmith, 2020; Gauthier & Brender, 2021) that can cause overlook of fraud risk. Problems of delays and updates faced by IAF can be easily rectified by AI. As of March 2021, 118 organisations were listed in MSM (2021), including three preferred shares. These 118 organizations are divided into three sectors, that is, the financial, industrial, and services sectors (see Table 3).

Agency Theory

Agency theory denotes shareholders delegating several responsibilities, including decision making authorities to a group of experts with the perception that they will attain success for their organisations (Afza & Nazir, 2014). Agents are hired by principal(s) and these agents act on behalf of the principal(s). The agency theory is deployed to support the dominant role of agents in corporate governance (Rehman & Hashim, 2020; Earnest & Sofian, 2013).

In light of the agency theory, the delegation of authority can create problems when agents dismiss the concerns of their principals, give importance to their self-interests, and start gathering private benefits via immoral acts such as transcended bonuses, inappropriate increments, and kickbacks. These immoral acts are executed by developing inflated/fake revenues, unsupported receivable balances, and irregular accounting practices. One reason behind such fraudulent thinking is that the entire task is performed by the agents and they do not want to share any benefit with the principals as they only invest money and are not involved in organisational operations (Adrian, Lawrence & Lee, 2009). Such behaviour demands protection and monitoring, which can certainly be provided by AI.

The AI has become a necessary tool for the development and implementation of business strategies and organisational policies. Investment in AI is a strategic cost instead of an operational cost, as AI mi-

Figure 1. Theoretical framework

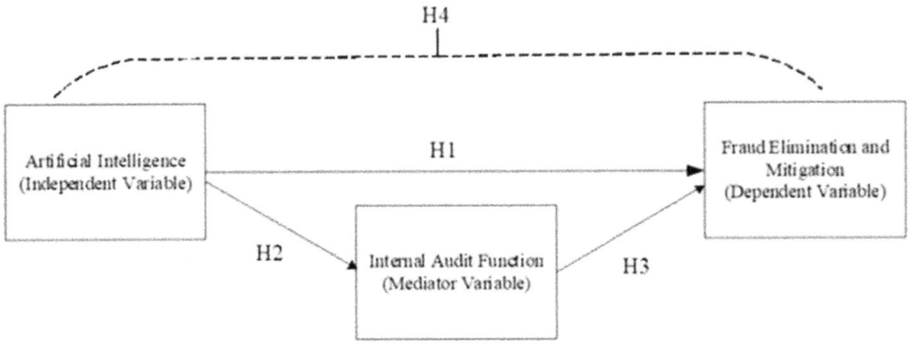

nimises uncertainties and provides a practical framework for internal controls and FEM (Agrawal, et al., 2018). Investment in AI is similar to hiring an agent and providing benefits to that agent, moreover, AI is capable of handling daily tasks with accuracy and precision that can serve the true purpose of corporate governance (Libert, et al., 2017), while concurrently satisfying the principal. If AI serves as an agent for the agency theory, agency cost (costs arise due to agency conflicts) can be avoided or eliminated. Moreover, AI built from current strategic strength can provide digital transformation strategies. These strategies can assist in reimagining work and decision making around distinctively human or artificial capabilities (Moloi & Marwala, 2020).

The AI can be the subset of stakeholders (OECD, 2021). The AI can enhance strategic controls and provide satisfaction to shareholders by tracking capital distribution patterns, accentuate red flags, and incorporate itself in the practices of corporate governance (Else & Pileggi, 2019; Libert, et al., 2017), in which AI acts as an agent for the principal. The definition of personhood in agency theory can change due to AI (LoPucki, 2018). In agency theory, principal and agents are required to be persons with legal rights and legal claims. The AI can be a person formed by an algorithmic entity (Powell, 2020). An algorithmic entity denotes "*advanced autonomous systems paired with limited liability companies that have no individual members*" (LoPucki, 2018). The notion reflects an appropriate development that enables AI to attain legal personhood in agency theory and become agent for the principal.

Theoretical Framework

The framework developed in this study is based on the literature review and applied theory. In this study, AI, IAF, and FEM are the independent, mediating, and dependent variables, respectively. Figure 1 illustrates the theoretical framework:

Hypotheses Development

Following the literature review, this present study formulated a set of hypotheses to examine the effect of AI on FEM mediated by IAF.

Table 4. AI vs. traditional approach for fraud prevention

AI Approach	Traditional Approach
Relies on past experience and considers emerging activities, behaviour, trends, and transactions anomalies	Relies on rules by using Excel to analyse past fraud patterns with no insight to the future
Capable of detecting fraud in real-time	Minimum identification time is 6-8 weeks
Possible to prevent sophisticated abuse attacks	Difficulty to identify customer abuse of identification or collusion
Provides fraud analyst with immediate risk scores and perceptiveness to minimise fraud	No such report or analysis exists. Analysts must develop their own working and with one market at a time
Enables greater controls over charge back rates and operational cost	Requires tremendous effort to identify additional or hidden cost
Provides greater compliance process with policies and regulations	Difficult to identify non-compliances in real-time

Source: Columbus (2019)

Artificial Intelligence and Fraud Elimination and Mitigation

The AI assists organisational management to provide more predictive and strategic services based on available data to identify potential issues before they occur (Aziz & Dowling, 2019). The AI detects and prevents anomalies, besides AI also assign accounting transactions to the correct categories so that the organisation records remain relevant for its business. The overall business process can be enhanced if automated anti-fraud procedures are deployed (Agrawal, et al., 2018). Table 4 lists the variances in preventing fraud between AI and traditional/ conventional approach (Columbus, 2019):

The AI can prevent and detect fraud in real-time (Verver, 2020). Moreover, AI is best suited to provide much needed satisfaction to shareholders and strategic decision makers (Davenport & Kirby, 2016), which is lacking in the present business environment. The AI serves as an accelerator or antidote of fraud and fraudulent activities (Yeoh, 2019). Notably, AI enhances information reliability for financial statements, including the way transactions are initiated, processed, and authorised with the capability to make the system incorruptible (Deloitte, 2016). Based on the discussion above and the ability of AI to be an agent in agency theory, the first hypothesis is as follows:

H1: Artificial Intelligence has a significantly positive impact on fraud elimination and mitigation.

Artificial Intelligence and Internal Audit Function

Initial input data in AI such as historical data that raised the red flags are identified by IAF. Based on these data, a framework is developed, which is again tried and tested to enable AI to detect red flags and potential frauds in newly fed data (Ghahramani, 2015). Such practice introduces more accurate data and less human intervention, thus enabling IAF to investigate further for any potential fraud and develop more preventive controls (Smith, 2017).

In the modern business era, if IAF is not impacted by AI then it would be difficult to detect fraud and impossible to prevent it in real time (Goodman, 2015; Haapamäki & Sihvonen, 2019). The AI can strengthen IAF by enabling solutions, fixing challenges, and reducing the number of issues that historically led to serious frauds and financial scandals (Simon, et al., 2017; Roszkowska, 2020). As such, the following is hypothesised:

H2: Artificial Intelligence has a significantly positive impact on Internal Audit Function.

Internal Audit Function and Fraud Elimination and Mitigation

Fraud prevention, detection, and mitigation are some of the utmost responsibilities of the IAF (Drogalasa, et al., 2017). Among the governance management, IAF is highly effective in detecting fraud (ACFE, 2020) and plays an important role in providing satisfaction to the shareholders, the board, and other related committees (Roussy, et al., 2020).

The IAF provides constant review and appraisal of the controls and procedures intending to assist the organisation in performing tasks free from fraud environment, besides IA also ensures that all organisational resources are properly utilised (Ojo, 2019). The IAF reinforces the internal control environment and ensures the efficacy of internal control system in evaluating fraud risk in a regular manner (WenM, et al., 2019; Kabuye, et al., 2018). The IAF also provides annual assurance for the controls implemented by the organisation (CMA, 2018).

The IAF, along with its independence, objectivity, and knowledge, can completely mitigate fraud and enhance controls to hinder fraud. Accordingly, the third hypothesis of this study is as follows:

H3: Internal Audit Function has a significantly positive impact on fraud elimination and mitigation.

The Mediating Role of Internal Audit Function on the link of Artificial Intelligence with Fraud Elimination and Mitigation

Mediator or intervening variable describes the relationship between independent and dependent variables (Sabir, 2014). The reason behind assessing the mediating role is to determine if the relationship between AI and FEM is not exclusively direct.

With AI, IAF can strengthen the organisational control environment as AI facilitates in executing and recording transactions with minimal human intervention, validate and record non-changeable transactions with opportunities to avoid human error, as well as combat transactional and reporting fraud. The AI-enabled audit tools can increase transparency and detect deviations from standards in timely manner. Moreover, AI facilitates the removal of management's manual intervention from processes, while simultaneously assisting FEM.

Similar to the mediating relationship defined by Popoola et al., (2015) and as stated in hypotheses H1, H2, and H3; there are significant and direct relationships between AI and FEM, between AI and IAF, as well as between IAF and FEM. Hence, this present study assessed the mediation effect of IAF on AI-FEM correlation. Hence, the fourth hypothesis is as follows:

H4: Internal audit function mediates the relationship between artificial intelligence and fraud elimination and mitigation.

METHODOLOGY

This study examined the relationship between AI and FEM, along with IAF as the mediator, among Omani public listed companies. As such, the unit of analysis refers to Omani public listed organisations listed in MSM. The respondents of this study were those who could respond on behalf of the organisations, including the board of director, audit and risk committee members, senior/executive management, and chief internal auditors. The quantitative approach was adopted by executing the descriptive cross-sectional survey method. Both five-point Likert scale and multiple choice questions of 'yes' and 'no' were used for this study. The five-point Likert scale ranged from strongly agree to strongly disagree. The questionnaire comprised of sections pertaining to AI, IAF, and FEM. Each section is explained with the definition and research purpose.

Adapted from previous studies, Table 5 presents the questions used for this study. By adapting questions, studies can be linked to all the other studies connected with the topic (Rehman & Hashim, 2019). G*Power3 was used to identify the required sample size, which led to 76 participants being the most appropriate size for 118 MSM listed companies. Using the one-tailed random-effects model, multiple linear regression was used to determine sample size. With an effect size of 0.15 (small), the G*Power3 sample size was calculated with an independent variable. G*Power3 showed that 76 participants were sufficient for power = 0.95 and $\alpha = 0.05$.

The questions listed above were circulated to respondents along with general demographic items. For data collection, an online tool was used. PLS-SEM and Statistical Package for Social Science (SPSS) were used to analyze data.

A measurement model assessment was conducted according to the directions provided by Ramayah et al., (2016) and Henseler et al., (2015). The guidelines for an acceptable measurement model are presented in table 6.

After the measurement model assessment, the structural model in PLS-SEM was examined. Table 7 presents the acceptable values of the assessment model in PLS-SEM measurement:

RESULTS AND ANALYSIS

In order to obtain the required sample size of 76 organisations, the questionnaires were circulated to all the 118 companies listed in MSM. Responses were received from 102 respondents belonging to 84 organisations. Table 8 presents the demographic profile of the respondents. Notably, more than one response was received from 26 companies and the mean score of their responses was calculated and incorporated into the data analysis. From the 84 organisations, three organisations that did not use any sort of AI in their operations left the questionnaire uncompleted and hence excluded from further analysis. Therefore, data retrieved from the remaining 81 organisations (70% of the total population and exceeded that sample size prescribed by G*Power3) were analysed.

Assessment of Measurement Model

Measurement mode assessment was performed to establish internal consistency and to identify indicator loading. The measurement model ascertains internal consistency and reliability based on the intercorrelations of the observed indicator variables. Convergent and discriminant validity was also measured to determine the correlations, as well as to identify the distinction among the constructs to determine the uniqueness in portraying the phenomena reflected in the model. Table 9 presents the assessment of measurement model:

All requirements listed in Table 6 were met. Referring to Table 9, the AI values of indicators (outer loading) exceeded the threshold value of CR and AVE (0.5) with scores 0.961 and 0.694, respectively. Both CR and AVE values for FEM were 0.933 and 0.585, respectively, while 0.959 and 0.635 respectively for IAF. As for discriminant validity, the HTMT criterion was applied and the retrieved value via PLS-SEM was below 0.85 (see Table 10). Values listed in Table 9 and HTMT values tabulated in Table 10

Table 5. Adapted questions

Code	Question for this survey	Source
	Questions for Artificial Intelligence	
AI1	Artificial Intelligence supports my organisation in strategy formation	Ghanoum and Alaba (2020)
AI2	Artificial Intelligence supports my organisation in objectives development	Ghanoum and Alaba (2020)
AI3	Artificial Intelligence supports my organisation in compliance	Ghanoum and Alaba (2020)
AI4	Artificial Intelligence supports my organisation in regulatory procedures	Ghanoum and Alaba (2020)
AI5	Artificial Intelligence supports my organisation in day to day organisational tasks	Ghanoum and Alaba (2020)
AI6	Artificial Intelligence enhance my organisational process	Ghanoum and Alaba (2020)
AI7	Artificial Intelligence in my organisation is capable to mitigate fraud	Ghanoum and Alaba (2020)
AI8	Artificial Intelligence in my organisation is capable to identify fraud	Ghanoum and Alaba (2020)
AI9	Artificial Intelligence in my organisation is capable to eliminate fraud	Ghanoum and Alaba (2020)
AI10	Over the next three years, my organisation will utilise Artificial Intelligence to help automate all operational tasks	Sage (2019)
AI11	Artificial Intelligence skills are necessary for the new employees joining in my organisation	Sage (2019)
	Questions for Fraud Prevention and Mitigation	
FEM1	My organisation is proactive in dealing with the risk of fraud	Siregar and Tenoyo (2015)
FEM2	My organisation has updated accounting systems to prevent fraud	Siregar and Tenoyo (2015)
FEM3	My organisation has updated internal control systems to prevent fraud	Siregar and Tenoyo (2015)
FEM4	My organisation's external auditors should utilise Artificial Intelligence in their attempt to uncover fraud	Siregar and Tenoyo (2015)
FEM5	My organisation's internal auditors should utilise Artificial Intelligence in their attempt to uncover fraud	Siregar and Tenoyo (2015)
FEM6	My organisation could be threatened by fraud due to poor fraud risk management	Siregar and Tenoyo (2015)
FEM7	My organisation could be threatened by fraud due to poor fraud assessment	Siregar and Tenoyo (2015)
FEM8	My organisation could be threatened by fraud due to poor internal controls	Siregar and Tenoyo (2015)
FEM9	My organisation could be threatened by fraud due to lack of ethical values	Siregar and Tenoyo (2015)
FEM10	My organisation could be threatened by fraud due to frequent management override of control	Siregar and Tenoyo (2015)
	Questions for Internal Audit Function	
IAF1	Internal audit function in my organisation is familiar with the software used for accounting process	Ghanoum and Alaba (2020)
IAF2	In my company, appointment of Internal Auditors is transparent	MacRae and Gils (2010)
IAF3	In my company Internal audit is learning from inside and outside the organisation for continuous improvement	MacRae and Gils (2010)
IAF4	In my company, Internal audit integrates information from across the organisation to improve governance management	MacRae and Gils (2010)
IAF5	In my company, Internal audit integrates information from across the organisation to improve fraud risk management	MacRae and Gils (2010)
IAF6	In my company, Internal audit professional practices are uniformly applied	MacRae and Gils (2010)
IAF7	Internal audit function in my organisation is equipped with advanced technology that can guide in exploring and understanding how the organisation's financial transactions are collected	Ghanoum and Alaba (2020)
IAF8	Internal audit function in my organisation is equipped with advanced technology that can guide in exploring and understanding how the organisation's financial transactions are recorded	Ghanoum and Alaba (2020)
IAF9	Internal audit function in my organisation is equipped with advanced technology that can guide in exploring and understanding how the organisation's financial transactions are processed	Ghanoum and Alaba (2020)
IAF10	Internal audit function in my organisation is equipped with advanced technology that can guide in exploring and understanding how other data in the organisation have been processed	Ghanoum and Alaba (2020)
IAF11	Internal audit function in my organisation is equipped with advanced technology that can guide in exploring and understanding how the entity of other data has been recorded	Ghanoum and Alaba (2020)
IAF12	Internal audit function in my organisation is equipped with advanced technology that can guide in exploring and understanding how the entity of other data has been collected	Ghanoum and Alaba (2020)
IAF13	Internal audit function in my organisation utilises Artificial Intelligence enabled tools	Ghanoum and Alaba (2020)
IAF14	In my organisation, utilisation of Artificial Intelligence for auditing process is effective	Ghanoum and Alaba (2020)

Table 6. Model evaluation using PLS-SEM: acceptable values

Assessment and Name of Index	Description	Guideline
Indicator reliability - Factor loadings	The first step to establish internal consistency is to assess the indicator loading	If other loadings have high scores of loadings to complement AVE and CR, then loading > 0.6, 0.5 or 0.4 is adequate. Otherwise loading of > 0.7 is recommended.
Internal Consistency - Composite reliability (CR)	Based on the intercorrelations of observed variables, internal consistency ensures the reliability of the indicator.	CR ≥0.70 (in exploratory research 0.60 is considered acceptable)
Convergent validity - Average Variance Extracted (AVE)	When a measure correlates positively with another measure of the same construct, then that measure is said to have convergent validity	An AVE of 0.50 or higher is recommended
Discriminant validity - HTMT Criterion	Discriminant validity ascertains the distinction within constructs to determine uniqueness in portraying the phenomena in the model	HTMT below 0.85 is acceptable.

Source: Ramayah et al., (2016)

seemed to satisfy the threshold depicted in Table 6; signifying that all the necessities for the assessment of measurement model were fulfilled, thus enabling the assessment of structural model.

Assessment of Structural Model

The collinearity, path coefficient, and R2 of the structural model must be within the acceptable range defined in Table 7. For collinearity assessment, the value of VIF was below 2. As a result, there is no collinearity issue in the model as the VIF values do not exceed 5 for specific indicators (Garcia-Carbonell, et al., 2015). The values of R^2 for FEM and IAF were 0.522 and 0.424, respectively; signifying acceptance measures. An acceptable R^2 value is between 0.02-0.12 as weak, 0.13-0.25 as moderate, and above 0.26 as substantial (Cohen, 1988). Figure 2 illustrates the values of R^2 and outer loading obtained for this study.

Table 7. Structural model evaluation: acceptable values

Assessment and Name of Index	Description	Guideline	Source
R-square - Coefficient of determination	R^2 value is a measure of predictive accuracy related to model. It is defined as the amount of variance in dependent variables	0.26- Substantial 0.13- Moderate 0.02- Weak	Cohen (1988)
Collinearity - VIF (Variance inflator factor)	When there is a high correlation between independent variables, it may pose a problem for the estimation of weights and statistical significance	In a model, multi-collinearity is present when certain indicators have VIF values of five or more	García-Carbonell, et al., (2015)
Path Coefficient	To determine whether direct effects are significant, path coefficients must be calculated	t value > 2.33 (one tail) p value < 0.01	Hair et al., (2017)

Table 8. Demographic profile of respondents

Demographic Questions	Items	Responses
What is your gender?	Male	95
	Female	7
Which sector does your organisation belong to?	Financial	32
	Industrial	33
	Services	37
What is your highest qualification?	Bachelor	18
	Master	33
	PhD	3
	Professional certification	48
For how many years have you been serving your organisation?	0-1 Year	15
	1-5 Years	37
	5-10 Years	27
	More than 10 Years	23
What is your position in the organisation?	Member Board of Director	15
	Member Audit & Risk Committee	7
	Senior Management	45
	Head of Internal Audit/ Chief Audit Executive	35
Which AI platform does your organisation use?	Machine Learning	7
	Block Chain	10
	Business Intelligence Tools	46
	Business Process Management Software (ERP)	36
	None	3

Significance of Direct Effect

In order to determine the significance of direct effect-path coefficient, bootstrapping was deployed via smart PLS for the 81 samples with 5000 sub-samples. In accordance with Hair et al., (2017) the acceptable values associated to path coefficients for t-values and p-values are >2.33 and <0.01, respectively. The significances of direct effect-path coefficient are presented in Table 11 and Figure 3.

Current study had evaluated the significant effect of the study model. As a result, the mean scores of standard beta (original sample) are as follows: AI and FEM = 0.123, AI and IAF = 0.61, and IAF and FEM = 0.636. The positive beta values demonstrate that the effect is direct. For *t*-value, the correlations of AI-IAF and IAF-FEM emerge as significant as their values exceeded 2.33, whereas the AI-FEM link is insignificant as the value was below 2.33. Similarly, the P values revealed that the relationships of AI-IAF and IAF-FEM are significant with values below 0.01, but insignificant for the relationship between AI and FEM as the P value exceeded 0.01.

The AI, along with its capabilities, displayed a significantly direct impact on IAF, as AI can assist IAF to perform its tasks with better accuracy and to identify red flags based on the data fed by IAF. In

Table 9. Assessment of measurement model

Question Code	Outer-Loading (Indicator Reliability)	Composite Reliability (CR)	Average Variance Extracted (AVE)
Artificial Intelligence			
AI1	0.865	0.961	0.694
AI10	0.726		
AI11	0.699		
AI12	0.91		
AI13	0.916		
AI4	0.895		
AI5	0.831		
AI6	0.862		
AI7	0.86		
AI8	0.827		
AI9	0.737		
Fraud Prevention and Mitigation			
FEM1	0.784	0.933	0.585
FEM 10	0.771		
FEM 2	0.844		
FEM 3	0.842		
FEM 4	0.675		
FEM 5	0.803		
FEM 6	0.708		
FEM 7	0.707		
FEM 8	0.707		
FEM 9	0.785		
Internal Audit Function			
IAF1	0.617	0.959	0.635
IAF 10	0.905		
IAF 11	0.916		
IAF 12	0.88		
IAF 13	0.651		
IAF 14	0.823		
IAF 2	0.608		
IAF 3	0.746		
IAF 4	0.814		
IAF 5	0.817		
IAF 6	0.756		
IAF 7	0.873		
IAF 8	0.884		
IAF 9	0.898		

correlation with FEM, IAF exhibited a significantly direct impact due to IA's fraud combatting ability and IAF is also primarily responsible for FEM within Organization.

Table 10. HTMT values

	AI	FEM	IAF
AI			
FEM	0.537		
IAF	0.668	0.712	

Figure 2. R^2 and outer loading values

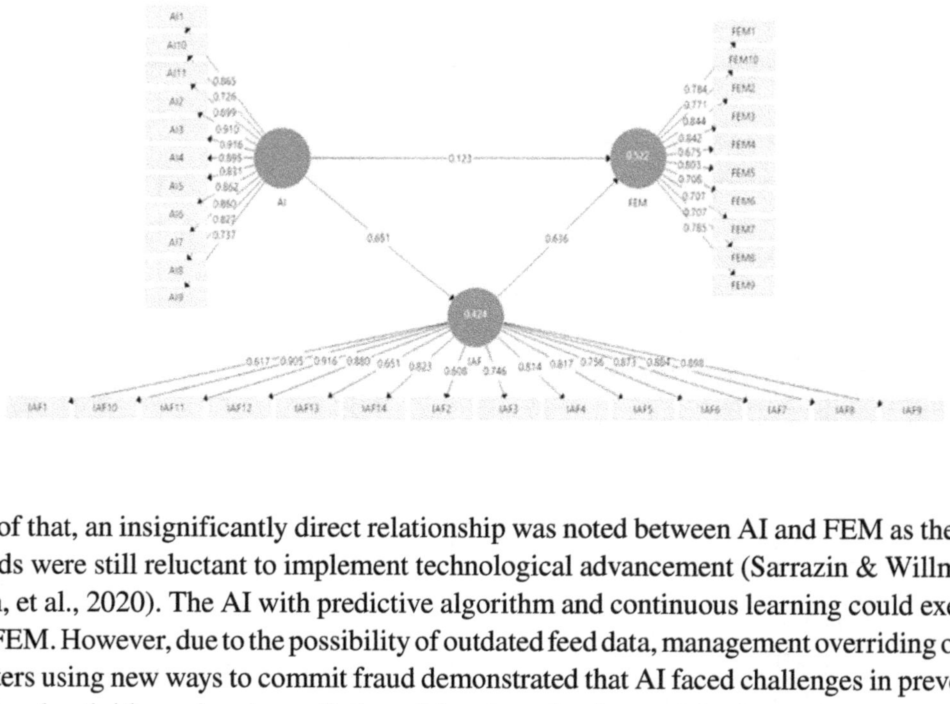

On top of that, an insignificantly direct relationship was noted between AI and FEM as the organisational boards were still reluctant to implement technological advancement (Sarrazin & Willmott, 2016; Ammanath, et al., 2020). The AI with predictive algorithm and continuous learning could exert a direct impact on FEM. However, due to the possibility of outdated feed data, management overriding of controls, and fraudsters using new ways to commit fraud demonstrated that AI faced challenges in preventing and detecting fraud activities, wherein mediation of fraud combatting activity is sought.

Table 11. Significance of direct effect – path coefficient

Hypothesis	Path	Std. Beta (O)	Standard Deviation (STDEV)	T Statistics (|O/STDEV|)	Sig (p<0.01)	Decision
H1	AI → FEM	0.123	0.116	1.057	No	Not Supported
H2	AI → IAF	0.651	0.049	13.376***	Yes	Supported
H3	IA → FEM	0.636	0.101	6.324***	Yes	Supported

Note: ***p<0.01 (t>2.33) (One Tail)

Figure 3. Significance of direct effect – path coefficient (t values)

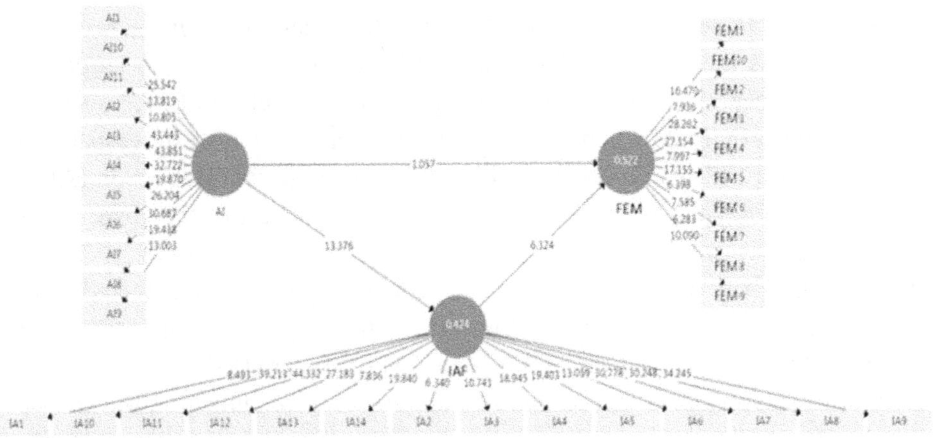

Mediation Analysis - Significance of Indirect Effects-Path Coefficients

For assessing the mediation role of IAF on the AI-FEM correlation, bootstrapping with two-tail test and 5000 sub-samples at a significance level of 0.01 was performed. Table 12 tabulates the significance based on the rules prescribed by Hair et al., (2017) and Ramayah et al., (2016). When the indirect relationship between independent and dependent variables is statistically significant, mediation occurs (Rehman & Hashim, 2020).

Table 12. Significance of the hypothesis path

Hypothesis	Path	Std. Beta Direct Effect	t Value	Sig (p<0.01)	Std.Beta Indirect Effect	t Value	Sig (p<0.01)	Decision
H4	AI→FPM	0.129	1.063	No	0.424	5.428*	Yes	Supported

Note: **p<0.01 (t>2.58) (based on two-tailed test), n=5000-Bootstrapping

Referring to Table 12, the standard beta of direct effect is 0.129, the t-value is 1.063, and the p-value exceeds 0.01; indicating that the relationship between AI and FEM is insignificant. Meanwhile, the standard beta of indirect effect is 0.424 with t-value and p-value being 5.428 and below 0.01, respectively, signify that AI has a significantly indirect effect or entirely indirect effect (full mediation). When a direct or an indirect relationship is significant, it denotes a case of full mediation (Hair et al., 2017).

According to the above-mentioned mediation relationship, AI, with the assistance of IAF, can affect FEM. The continuously learning AI can prevent and mitigate fraud with the mediation of IAF. Internal audit function (IAF) controls and verifies the anomalies, which are later updated on AI for future assistance towards FEM.

DISCUSSION

Purpose of this study was to determine whether AI supports Omani public listed organizations towards FEM with IAF serving as the mediator. This study utilized agency theory in its concept. The study outcome depicts that AI can have a direct but non-significant impact on FEM; however, AI can apply a significant direct impact on FEM when mediated by IAF. The result also suggests that IAF has a significant direct impact on FEM, while concurrently; AI has a significant impact on IAF. The AI serves as an agent in light of agency theory, which can be considered as part of the governance management system and play a crucial role in FEM.

For this study, the majority of the respondents are male having Master degree and working as senior/ executive management in their organizations. Majority of the respondents are utilizing business intelligence tools followed by the business process management software (ERP).

The majority of the respondents agreed that AI supports their organization towards strategy formation, objective developments, regulatory and other compliances and day-to-day organizational task. The majority of respondents also agreed that AI skills are necessary for the new employees joining the organization and organizations will utilize AI to automate their operational tasks in the next three years. It is worth noting that the majority of the respondents do not agree with the fact that AI is capable of identifying, mitigating and eliminating fraud in their organization.

For FEM related questions, the majority responded that their organization is proactive in dealing with the risk of fraud and they have updated accounting and internal control systems to prevent fraud. The majority of the respondents also agreed that their external and internal auditors should utilize AI to uncover fraud. Respondents' majority also agreed to the fact that their organization could be threatened by fraud due to poor fraud risk management, poor internal controls, lack of ethical values and frequent management override of internal controls.

For IAF, the majority of the respondents agreed that IAF is familiar with the software utilized for accounting purposes and hiring of IAF is transparent. The majority of the respondents supported that IAF integrates information across the organization to improve governance management and also to improve fraud risk management. The majority of the respondents also agreed with the fact that IAF is equipped with advanced technology that can guide in exploring and understanding that how the organization's financial transactions and data are collected, recorded and processed. Respondents also consented that IAF is effectively utilizing AI enabled tools.

FUTURE RESEARCH DIRECTIONS

Future research can be conducted on the area where IAF can be compared among those who are utilizing AI and those who are still operating without AI. This comparison can provide understanding about the areas where IAF can demonstrate more competences than those IAF who are not utilizing AI in their operations. Another potential area could be to compare this study of Oman with other GCC countries and identify where Oman can improve and can demonstrate more potential towards utilization of AI and elimination of fraud.

It may also be possible for future Research to adopt institutional theory for AI and IAF, which can help in explaining how structures (such as schemes, rules, norms, and routines) are established as authoritative guidelines for organizational behaviour.

CONCLUSION

In the present business setting, AI has become an inevitable part of daily business life. Despite the deployment of AI, fraud continues to occur within business transactions mainly because AI is still utilised as a support function and not as a tool to mitigate fraud activity or as a governance management system. Given the considerable enhancements in AI capabilities, this study goes beyond this simple vision and advances the notion that AI should be deployed as the agent of the agency theory in facilitating both the board and the management towards FEM.

The study outcome depicts that AI can have a direct impact on FEM, but AI can exert a significantly direct impact on FEM when mediated by IAF. The AI serves as an agent in light of agency theory, which can be considered as part of the governance management system and play a crucial role in FEM. The result suggests that IAF has a significantly direct impact on FEM, while concurrently; AI has a significant impact on IAF.

Notably, this study positions itself in extending past studies on AI to a new perspective by presenting it as an agent of the agency theory, which can enhance governance and assistance in FEM. This study sheds light on an unexplored aspect of AI. This study is beneficial for regulators as they can amend the codes of corporate governance and include AI as a compulsory constituent of the codes.

This study highlighted the fact that AI can change business insights enabling faster and more accurate managerial decision makings. Organizational management can establish the standards that can unify accountability, responsibility and ethics which will eventually assist in the development of modern corporations. AI complements the capabilities of organizational management and can give recommendations based on the analysis of large data that can allow management to make quick decisions in difficult situations. This decision-making can result in amending the policies and procedures which can eventually impact the FEM.

This study may serve as a guide to professional bodies as they can include mandatory utilisation of AI in the process of validation and verification, while enabling management in organisations to amend their policies by introducing AI as the agent working for the benefit of the organisations. It is highly recommended that Omani companies should comply with the available guidelines and codes stipulated by international organisations, which may serve as initial guidelines and tailored to the local needs of both the market and the industry.

REFERENCES

ACFE. (2020). *Report to the nations on occupational fraud and abuse.* Association of Certified Fraud Examiners.

Adrian, N. K., Lawrence, A. & Cristal Lee, A. S. (2009). Forensic Accounting: Public Acceptance towards Occurrence of Fraud Detection. *International Journal of Business Management, 4*(11), 145-149.

Afza, T., & Nazir, M. S. (2014). Theoretical Perspective of Corporate Governance: A Review. *European Journal of Scientific Research, 119*(2), 255–265.

Agrawal, A., Gans, J., & Goldfarb, A. (2018). *Prediction Machines: The Simple Economics of Artificial Intelligence.* Harvard Business Review Press.

Ammanath, B., Jarvis, D. & Hupfer, S. (2020). *Thriving in the era of pervasive AI.* Deloitte Consulting LLP.

Arrowsmith, R. (2020). *Case Studies: AI & data analytics in 2020.* Available at: https://www.accountingtoday.com/news/case-studies-ai-data-analytics-in-2020

Aslan, L. (2021). The Evolving Competencies of the Public Auditor and the Future of Public Sector Auditing. In Contemporary Issues in Public Sector Accounting and Auditing (Contemporary Studies in Economic and Financial Analysis, Vol. 105). Emerald Publishing Limited. doi:10.1108/S1569-375920200000105008

Aziz, S., & Dowling, M. (2019). Machine Learning and AI for Risk Management. In T. Lynn, J. G. Mooney, P. Rosati, & M. Cummins (Eds.), *Disrupting Finance FinTech and Strategy in the 21st Century* (pp. 33–50). Palgrave Studies. doi:10.1007/978-3-030-02330-0_3

Babinchak, J. (2020). *IIA Issues Important Update to Three Lines Model: Modernizing the Widely Used Approach to Governance, Risk.* Available at: https://na.theiia.org/news/Pages/IIA-Issues-Important-Update-to-Three-Lines-Model.aspx

Bauguess, S. W. (2017). *The Role of Big Data, Machine Learning, and AI in Assessing Risks: A Regulatory Perspective.* Available at: https://www.sec.gov/news/speech/bauguess-big-data-ai

Beck, M., & Libert, B. (2018). *How to use AI for strategic decisions.* Available at: https://www.cio.com/article/3271433/how-to-use-ai-for-strategic-decisions.html

Betti, N., & Sarens, G. (2020). *Understanding the internal audit function in a digitalised business environment. Journal of Accounting & Organizational Change.* doi:10.1108/JAOC-11-2019-0114

Bhasin, M. L. (2016). Contribution of Forensic Accounting to Corporate Governance: An Exploratory Study of an Asian Country. *International Business Management, 10*(4), 479–492.

Burns, J., & Steele, A. (2020). *Blockchain and Internal Control The COSO Perspective.* Committee of Sponsoring Organizations of the Treadway Commission.

Burridge, N. (2017). *Artificial intelligence gets a seat in the boardroom.* Available at: https://asia.nikkei.com/Business/Artificial-intelligence-gets-a-seat-in-the-boardroom

Chan, D., & Vasarhelyi, M. (2018). Innovation and Practice of Continuous Auditing. In Continuous Auditing. Emerald Publishing Limited. doi:10.1108/978-1-78743-413-420181013

Chornous, G., & Ursulenko, G. (2013). Risk Management In Banks: New Approaches To Risk Assessment And Information Support. *Ekonomika (Nis), 92*(1), 120–132. doi:10.15388/Ekon.2013.0.1131

Cioban, A. (2016). The Influence of the Corporate Governance Mechanisms and Audit Fees on the Financial Performance Measured with ROA. *Annals of the Constantin Brâncusi. University of Târgu Jiu. Economy Series, 1*(5), 20–31.

CMA. (2018). 10/2018. Muscat: Capital Market Authority.

Columbus, L. (2019). *Top 9 Ways Artificial Intelligence Prevents Fraud.* Available at: https://www.forbes.com/sites/louiscolumbus/2019/07/09/top-9-ways-artificial-intelligence-prevents-fraud/#b398e4514b4f

Deloitte. (2016). *Blockchain technology. A game-changer in accounting.* Available at: www2.deloitte.com/content/dam/Deloitte/de/Documents/Innovation/Blockchain_A-game-changer-in-accounting.pdf

Desk, N. (2008). *Fraud in textile mills capital declaration detected.* Available at: https://fp.brecorder.com/2008/09/20080904803179/

Driel, H. (2019). Financial fraud, scandals, and regulation: A conceptual framework and literature review. *Business History, 61*(8), 1259–1299. doi:10.1080/00076791.2018.1519026

Drogalasa, G., Pazarskis, M., Anagnostopoulou, E., & Papachristou, A. (2017). The effect of internal audit effectiveness, auditor responsibility and training in fraud detection. *Accounting and Management Information Systems, 16*(4), 434–454. doi:10.24818/jamis.2017.04001

Earnest, D. F., & Sofian, S. (2013). The Mediating Role of Corporate Governance on Intellectual Capital and Corporate Performance. *Journal of Economics, Business and Management, 1*(4), 339–342.

Else, S. R., & Pileggi, F. G. (2019). *Corporate Directors Must Consider Impact of Artificial Intelligence for Effective Corporate Governance.* Available at: https://businesslawtoday.org/2019/02/corporate-directors-must-consider-impact-artificial-intelligence-effective-corporate-governance/

Ergen, M. (2019). What is Artificial Intelligence? Technical Considerations and Future Perception. *The Anatolian Journal of Cardiology, 22*, 5–7. doi:10.14744/AnatolJCardiol.2019.79091 PMID:31670719

Fernando, A. (2009). *Corporate Governance: Principles, Policies and Practices.* Pearson.

Flitter, E. 2020. *The Price of Wells Fargo's Fake Account Scandal Grows by $3 Billion.* Available at: https://www.nytimes.com/2020/02/21/business/wells-fargo-settlement.html

Florea, R., & Florea, R. (2016). Internal Audit and Risk Management. ISO 31000 and ERM Approaches. *Economy Transdisciplinarity Cognition, 19*(1), 72–77.

Gaaya, S., Lakhal, N., & Lakhal, F. (2017). Does family ownership reduce corporate tax avoidance? The moderating effect of audit quality. *Managerial Auditing Journal, 33*(7), 731–744. doi:10.1108/MAJ-02-2017-1530

García-Carbonell, N., Martín-Alcázar, F. & Sánchez-Gardey. (2015). Determinants of top management's capability to identify core employees. *BRQ Business Research Quarterly, 18*(2), 69-80.

Gauthier, M. P., & Brender, N. (2021). How do the current auditing standards fit the emergent use of blockchain? *Managerial Auditing Journal, 36*(3), 365–385. doi:10.1108/MAJ-12-2019-2513

Ghahramani, Z. (2015). Probabilistic machine learning and artificial intelligence. *Nature, 521*(7553), 452–459. doi:10.1038/nature14541 PMID:26017444

Ghanoum, S., & Alaba, F. M. (2020). *Integration of Artificial Intelligence in Auditing: The Effect on Auditing Process.* Available at: https://www.diva-portal.org/smash/get/diva2:1446778/FULLTEXT01.pdf

Goertzel, T. (2014). The path to more general artificial intelligence. *Journal of Experimental & Theoretical Artificial Intelligence, 26*(3), 343–354. doi:10.1080/0952813X.2014.895106

Gonzalez, R. A., Ferro, R. E., & Liberona, D. (2020). Government and governance in intelligent cities, smart transportation study case in Bogotá Colombia. *Ain Shams Engineering Journal, 11*(1), 25–34. doi:10.1016/j.asej.2019.05.002

Goodman, M. (2015). *Future Crime*. Doubleday.

Govil, S. (2020). *What AI does for accountants*. Available at: https://www.accountingtoday.com/opinion/what-ai-does-for-accountants

Grüning, M. (2011). Artificial Intelligence Measurement of Disclosure (AIMD). *European Accounting Review, 20*(3), 485–519. doi:10.1080/09638180.2011.585792

Haapamäki, E., & Sihvonen, J. (2019). Cybersecurity in accounting research. *Managerial Auditing Journal, 34*(7), 808–834. doi:10.1108/MAJ-09-2018-2004

Hair, J. F., Hult, G. T., Ringle, C. M., & Sarstedt, M. (2017). A Primer on Partial Least Squares Structural Equation Modeling (PLS-SEM) (2nd ed.). Sage.

Hamrani, K. A., & Mahmoud, W. (2021, Jan 13). *A Green Light to Prosecute: Lessons Learned from the Omani Ministry of Education Embezzlement Case*. Retrieved from https://www.tamimi.com: https://www.tamimi.com/law-update-articles/a-green-light-to-prosecute-lessons-learned-from-the-omani-ministry-of-education-embezzlement-case/

Henning, E., & Kammel, B. (2020). *The Man Who Could Explain the $2 Billion Wirecard Mystery Is Missing*. Available at: https://www.bloombergquint.com/businessweek/jan-marsalek-the-man-who-could-explain-wirecard-s-2-billion-fraud-is-missing

Henseler, J., Ringle, C., & Sarstedt, M. (2015). A new criterion for assessing discriminant validity in variance-based structural equation modelling. *Journal of the Academy of Marketing Science, 43*(1), 115–135. doi:10.100711747-014-0403-8

Huang, M.-H., & Rust, R. T. (2018). Artificial Intelligence in Service. *Journal of Service Research, 21*(2), 155–172. doi:10.1177/1094670517752459

IFA. (2009). *International standard on auditing 240: The auditor's responsibilities relating to fraud in an audit of financial statements*. International Federation of Accountants.

IIA. (2019). *Governance of risk: Three lines of defence*. Available at: https://www.iia.org.uk/resources/audit-committees/governance-of-risk-three-lines-of-defence/

Issa, H., Sun, T., & Vasarhelyi, M. (2016). Research ideas for artificial intelligence in auditing: The formalization of audit and workforce supplementation. *Journal of Emerging Technologies in Accounting, 13*(2), 1–20. doi:10.2308/jeta-10511

Kabuye, F., Nkundabanyanga, S. K., Opiso, J., & Nakabuye, Z. (2018). Internal audit organisational status, competencies, activities and fraud management in the financial services sector. *Managerial Auditing Journal, 32*(9), 924–944. doi:10.1108/MAJ-09-2016-1452

Kılıç, M., & Kuzey, C. (2018). Determinants of forward-looking disclosures in integrated reporting. *Managerial Auditing Journal, 33*(1), 115–144. doi:10.1108/MAJ-12-2016-1498

Kozlowski, S. (2018). *An audit ecosystem to support blockchain-based accounting and assurance. Continuous Auditing: Theory and Application.* doi:10.1108/978-1-78743-413-420181015

Kozlowski, S. (2018). An audit ecosystem to support blockchain-based accounting and assurance. In Continuous Auditing (Rutgers Studies in Accounting Analytics). Emerald Publishing Limited. doi:10.1108/978-1-78743-413-420181015

Lamboglia, R., Lavorato, D., Scornavacca, E., & Za, S. (2021). Exploring the relationship between audit and technology. A bibliometric analysis. Meditari Accountancy Research. doi:10.1108/MEDAR-03-2020-0836

Leonard, W. V. (2010). *The Fraud Audit: Responding to the Risk of Fraud in Core Business Systems.* John Wiley & Sons Ltd.

Libert, B., Beck, M., & Bonchek, M. (2017). *AI in the Boardroom: The Next Realm of Corporate Governance.* Available at: https://sloanreview.mit.edu/article/ai-in-the-boardroom-the-next-realm-of-corporate-governance/

LoPucki, L. M. (2018). Algorithmic Entities. *Washington University Law Review, 95*(4), 887–951.

MacRae, E., & Gils, D. V. (2010). Internal Audit Capabilities and Performance Levels in the Public Sector. The Institute of Internal Auditors Research Foundation (IIARF).

Mendoza, J. (2020, March 11). *National Biscuit scammed out of RO 70K.* Retrieved from https://www.omanobserver.om/national-biscuit-scammed-out-of-ro-70k/#:~:text=Omani%20listed%20firm%20National%20Biscuit,Capital%20Market%20Authority%20(CMA)

Moloi, T., & Marwala, T. (2020). The Agency Theory. In Artificial Intelligence in Economics and Finance Theories. Advanced Information and Knowledge Processing. Springer. doi:10.1007/978-3-030-42962-1_11

MSM. (2020). *Dhofar Cattle Feed (DCFI) Company Fraud Disclosure.* Available at: https://msm.gov.om/MSMDocs/Images/NewsDocs/DCFI-30002020-55.pdf

MSM. (2020a). *Oman & Emirates Investment Holding Company News.* Available at: https://msm.gov.om/snapshot.aspx?s=OEIO&se=4&ni=59066

MSM. (2021). *Number of companies.* Available at: https://www.msm.gov.om/companies.aspx

News, D. (2020). *Wirecard committed 'elaborate and sophisticated fraud' say auditors.* Available at: https://www.dw.com/en/wirecard-committed-elaborate-and-sophisticated-fraud-say-auditors/a-53942273

News, U. (2020). *7 of the Biggest Corporate Frauds in History.* Available at: https://wtop.com/news/2020/07/7-of-the-biggest-corporate-frauds-in-history/

Nilsson, N. (2010). *The Quest for Artificial Intelligence: A History of Ideas and Achievements.* Cambridge University Press.

Observer, O. (2020). *MoU to support Artificial Intelligence projects in Oman.* Available at: https://www.omanobserver.om/mou-to-support-artificial-intelligence-projects-in-oman/

Observer, O. (2020). *Oman Arab Bank reports criminal fraud.* Available at: https://www.omanobserver.om/oman-arab-bank-reports-criminal-fraud/

OECD. (2019). *OECD Principles on AI.* Available at: https://www.oecd.org/going-digital/ai/principles/#:~:text=The%20OECD%20Principles%20on%20Artificial,Council%20Recommendation%20on%20Artificial%20Intelligence

OECD. (2021). *Recommendation of the Council on Artificial Intelligence*. OECD.

Office, S. F. (2020). *The use of Artificial Intelligence to Combat Public Sector Fraud Professional Guidance*. International Public Sector Fraud Forum.

Ojo, A. (2019). Internal Audit And Risk Management In Nigeria's Public Sector. *International Journal of Business & Law Research, 7*(2), 1–15.

Omoteso, K. (2012). The application of artificial intelligence in auditing: Looking back to the future. *Expert Systems with Applications, 39*(9), 8490–8495. doi:10.1016/j.eswa.2012.01.098

Oussii, A. A., & Taktak, N. B. (2018). The impact of internal audit function characteristics on internal control quality. *Managerial Auditing Journal, 33*(5), 450–469. doi:10.1108/MAJ-06-2017-1579

Panda, B., & Leepsa, N. M. (2017). Agency theory: Review of theory and evidence on problems and perspectives. *Indian Journal of Corporate Governance, 10*(1), 74–95. doi:10.1177/0974686217701467

Popoola, O. M., Che-Ahmad, A. B., & Samsudin, R. S. (2015). An empirical investigation of fraud risk assessment and knowledge requirement on fraud related problem representation in Nigeria. *The Journal of Applied Psychology, 88*(5), 879–903.

Powell, D. (2020). Autonomous systems as legal agents: Directly by the recognition of personhood or indirectly by the alchemy of algorithmic entities. *Duke Law & Technology Review, 18*(1), 306–331.

PWC. (2020). *Fighting fraud: A never-ending battle PwC's Global Economic Crime and Fraud Survey*. Price Water House Coopers.

Ramayah, T. (2016). Partial Least Squares Structural Equation Modeling (PLS-SEM) Using SmartPLS 3.0: An Updated Guide and Practical Guide to Statistical Analysis. Pearson.

Rashid, A. (2016). Managerial Ownership and Agency Cost: Evidence from Bangladesh. *Journal of Business Ethics, 137*(3), 609–621. doi:10.100710551-015-2570-z

Rehman, A., & Hashim, F. (2019). Impact of Mature Corporate Governance on Detective Role of Forensic Accounting: Case of Public Listed Companies in Oman. *FGIC 2nd Conference on Governance and Integrity 2019, KnE Social Sciences,* 637-665.

Rehman, A., & Hashim, F. (2020). Is corporate governance maturity measurable? *Corporate Governance, 20*(4), 601–619. doi:10.1108/CG-07-2019-0220

Rehman, A., & Mughairy, M. A. (2020). *2020 Oman Pulse of Internal Audit*. IIA Oman.

Reuters. (2013, Feb 26). *Oman's Bank Muscat hit by $39 mln prepaid card fraud*. Retrieved from https://www.reuters.com/article/oman-bankmuscat-fraud-idUSL6N0BQ1C720130226

Reuters. (2020). *New rules may be needed for payments in wake of Wirecard, BIS boss says.* Available at: https://www.reuters.com/article/us-wirecard-bis/new-rules-may-be-needed-for-payments-in-wake-of-wirecard-bis-boss-says-idUSKBN2411PW

Roszkowska, P. (2020). Fintech in financial reporting and audit for fraud prevention and safeguarding equity investments. *Journal of Accounting & Organizational Change.* . doi:10.1108/JAOC-09-2019-0098

Roussy, M., Barbe, O., & Raimbault, S. (2020). Internal audit: From effectiveness to organizational significance. *Managerial Auditing Journal, 35*(2), 322–342. doi:10.1108/MAJ-01-2019-2162

Sabir, I. (2014). *A Holistic Emotions Measurement Model: Using the Viable System Model to Diagnose Workforce Emotions* (PhD Thesis, University of Hull, UK). Available at: https://www.researchgate.net/publication/299334013_A_Holistic_Emotions_Meas

Sage. (2019). *The Practice of Now*. Sage.

Sarrazin, H., & Willmott, P. (2016). *Adapting your board to the digital age.* Available at: https://www.mckinsey.com/business-functions/mckinsey-digital/our-insights/adapting-your-board-to-the-digital-age

Service, T. N. (2020). *Court of Appeal sentences employee to 10 years in prison.* Available at: https://timesofoman.com/article/3017491/oman/government/court-of-appeal-sentences-employee-to-10-years-in-prison

Simon, A., Kasale, S., & Manish, P. (2017). Blockchain technology in accounting and audit. *IOSR Journal of Business and Management, 6*, 6–9.

Singleton, T., & Singleton, A. (2010). *Fraud Auditing and Forensic Accounting* (4th ed.). John Wiley & Sons. doi:10.1002/9781118269183

Siregar, S. V., & Tenoyo, B. (2015). Fraud awareness survey of private sector in Indonesia. *Journal of Financial Crime, 22*(3), 329–346. doi:10.1108/JFC-03-2014-0016

Smith, S. (2017). *Blockchain, AI, and accounting.* Available at: www.ifac.org/globalknowledge-gateway/practice-management/discussion/blockchain-ai-and-accounting

Tiron-Tudor, A., Deliu, D., Farcane, N., & Dontu, A. (2021). *Managing change with and through blockchain in accountancy organizations: a systematic literature review. Journal of Organizational Change Management.* doi:10.1108/JOCM-10-2020-0302

Turetken, O., Jethefer, S., & Ozkan, B. (2020). Internal audit effectiveness: Operationalization and influencing factors. *Managerial Auditing Journal, 35*(2), 238–271. doi:10.1108/MAJ-08-2018-1980

Valkanov, N. (2019). Mitigation of Regulations Burden in Financial Sector by Application of High Tech Solutions. *Economics and Management, 16*(1), 19–30.

Verver, J. (2020). *Automating Fraud Detection: The Essential Guide.* Galvanize.

Waweru, N. M., & Prot, N. P. (2018). Corporate governance compliance and accrual earnings management in eastern Africa: Evidence from Kenya and Tanzania. *Managerial Auditing Journal, 33*(2), 171–191. doi:10.1108/MAJ-09-2016-1438

Wells, J. T. (2011). *Corporate Fraud Handbook: Prevention and Detection*. Wiley.

Wen, M. C. Y., Ying, S. L. X., & Nair, R. K. (2019). The Responsibility of Internal Auditors in Preventing Fraud in Malaysia Listed Companies. Business, Information Management and Computer Science (EBIMCS2019), 1-5.

Wyk, V. (2015). *Fraud Risk Assessment: A Conceptual Framework for Internal Auditors to Detect Financial Statement Fraud*. Advances in Management, Economics and Social Science.

Yeoh, P. (2019). Artificial intelligence: Accelerator or panacea for financial crime? *Journal of Financial Crime*, *26*(2), 634–646. doi:10.1108/JFC-08-2018-0077

Zeljko, T., Ilija, C. & Branko, K. (2019). Manufacturing and the rise of artificial intelligence: innovation challenges. *30th DAAAM international symposium on intelligent manufacturing and automation, 30*, 192-196.

Zhou, A. (2017). EY, Deloitte and PwC embrace artificial intelligence for tax and accounting. *Forbes*.

ADDITIONAL READING

Sadgali, I., Sael, N., & Benabbou, F. (2019). Performance of machine learning techniques in the detection of financial frauds. *Procedia Computer Science*, *148*, 45–54. doi:10.1016/j.procs.2019.01.007

Zhou, G. (2021). Research on the problems of enterprise internal audit under the background of artificial intelligence. *Journal of Physics: Conference Series*, *1861*, 012051. doi:10.1088/1742-6596/1861/1/012051

KEY TERMS AND DEFINITIONS

Agency Theory: Agency theory defines the relationship between agents and principal. Principal are hired by agents to perform the job and to achieve organizational mission and vision approved by agents.

Artificial Intelligence: Artificial intelligence (AI) can be defined as broad range of computer sciences dedicated to build the smart machines capable of performing task which can be performed by human intelligence. AI enables the task to be performed accurately and in much efficient manner.

Capital Market Authority: Capital market authority (CMA) is the regulator working in Oman. They are responsible for the issuance and updates of codes of corporate governance. They are also responsible for verifying organizations and external auditors' performance with the aim of safeguarding the investors' interest.

Fraud: Fraud can be defined as any act which is conducted for the benefit of one person or organization which is obtained by concealment of facts, theft or by providing misleading/falsifying information.

Fraud Mitigation: Fraud mitigation are the controls and action performed by organizations in order to minimize the risk of fraud.

Fraud Risk Assessment: Fraud risk assessment (FRA) is control tool adopted by organization to access the risk of fraud. With the assistance of (FRA) organizations can identify potential area which is more susceptible to fraud risk and can devise mitigation actions accordingly.

Internal Audit Function: Internal audit function (IAF) is an activity available within organization. They should be independent and objective at the same time. IAF work for the improvement of governance, risk, and controls of the organization.

Regulators: Regulators are the authorities developed by country in order to monitor the progress of companies. Regulators issues orders and notices to organizations (either specific or in general) which is mandatory for all companies to follow.

Chapter 13
Significance of Audit Committees in Corporate Governance

Muhammad Irfan Khan
Jinnah University for Women, Pakistan

Athar Iqbal
Iqra University, Pakistan

Syed Muhammad Salman
Iqra University, Pakistan

ABSTRACT

Corporate governance is considered the backbone of corporations. Audit committee is one of the factors that plays a pivotal role to guide and monitor business-related matters of firms while following the national and international audit standards. The chapter covers the involvement of the audit committee with respect to corporate governance. It ranges from audit committee formations to its importance, composition, significance, and the role in quality financial reporting according to international standards. The chapter generally focuses on the audit committee and not any particular country or firms. The importance of the audit committee has always been recognized, but due to some examples of bad corporate governance practices, it became an important variable of corporate governance.

INTRODUCTION

There are varying systems of corporate governance, representing cultural differences in the growth of the corporate business world. Nonetheless, business professionals and leaders worldwide have raised the concern of accountability not only because of financial scandals that occurred but also due to the dynamic shift in the corporate environment. Several changes were recommended by various eminent members from the business community, including Hilmer in Australia, King in South Africa, McDon-

DOI: 10.4018/978-1-7998-8754-6.ch013

ald's in Canada, Treadway in the United States, Greenbury and Hampel in the United Kingdom, and Vienot in France to improve the quality of financial reporting. The recommendations largely include the increase of non-executive directors within the board and the formation of an audit committee. Although the recommendations are worthwhile, the empirical pieces of evidence to measure the value of protecting shareholders are not only narrower but also unconvincing. Despite the warp debate on the topic, the effect of their recommendations on corporate governance improvement is still in its early stages (Mater, 1997). The definition of corporate governance is still in its evolution phase; however, some main elements include the improvement of corporate performance through supervision and monitoring of performance accountability of management to all stakeholders (Keasey & Wright, 1997).

There are various board roles with respect to corporate governance, differences in the corporate structure, and the board composition bestow with plentiful corporate models in Western countries. Broadly, there are two leading approaches to the organization of corporate boards. Anglo-Saxon One-tier board model was adopted by countries like the US, the UK, and Canada. A two-tier board model exists in continental European countries such as Germany, Finland, and the Netherland.

OBJECTIVES

Indeed, agency cost is present in all walks of life. Agency cost suggests that humans are primarily self-centered in any role of life, especially when working on behalf of someone as an agent. Either employed in any job, the agent will consider his interest before considering what ought to be the principal's best interest. Therefore, the corporate and financial evolution in the last two hundred years is incomplete without proper corporate governance mechanisms! To address agency cost issues, one of the mechanisms inside the organization is the introduction of an audit committee by the Code of Corporate Governance. The objective is to bring transparency accountability and give strength to internal mechanisms that can mitigate the issue of agency cost. The audit committee plays a vital role in the company's internal structure. Stockholders are concerned about the reliability of financial reports presented to them by a company. Of course, external auditors submit their reports, but the code of corporate governance provides another support in the form of an audit committee that oversees the company's financial reporting. Even the audit committee can strengthen external auditors' position in case any dispute arises between management and external auditors. It consists of members that must have sufficient financial knowledge and can assess risk associated with different projects and financial decisions taken by company managers. Many empirical findings support the audit committee to mitigate the issue of agency cost or entrenchment. The internal audit head of companies has access and reports to the chair of the audit committee. From one-tier Board model to two-tier Board models, from the construction of audit committee to expanding its mandate and improving the compositions of the audit committee, the evolution is continued.

We consider that the audit committee plays an essential role in curbing the impact of agency cost, and it is one of the most effective tools of Corporate Governance; hence the purpose of writing this chapter is to go through the evolution and significance of the audit committee with the help of literature review.

LITERATURE REVIEW

One-Tier Board Model

This model allows executive and non-executive directors to work together in one layer of the organization's hierarchy. In some cases, executive directors dominate the board, while boards may also be dominated by non-executive directors. The model may have a board leadership structure that segregates the CEO and chair positions of the board. On the other hand, under this one-tier model, the leadership structure may operate that combines the role of CEO and chairman, called CEO duality. Sheridan & Kendall (1992) suggested a problem exists in one tier model due to the dispersion of tasks and responsibilities of directors. Roles and positions of executive and non-executive directors in the US and UK have no distinction as they face the same legal responsibilities and tackle the same legal liabilities. Further, the majority of the executive directors in the board lead to the potential conflict of interest between management and shareholders. Kesner & Johnson (1990) propose the composition of a corporate board with non-executive directors because of the following reasons:

- their knowledge and experience
- their contacts which may increase the ability of management to secure external resources
- their independence from the CEO

This suggests a negative association between the formal independence of the corporate board and the one-tier board, dominated by executive directors.

Two-Tier Board Model

In organizations' hierarchy, one additional layer has been designed to disengage the executive function of the board from its monitoring function. The non-executive supervisory board enjoys the upper layer of the hierarchy that may represent labor, government, and institutional investors. The lower layer and the management board generally comprise executive managing directors. There is no possibility that directors can have CEO and chairman positions under two-tier board models because CEO does not have any seat in the supervisory board. As practiced in the Netherland and Germany, the corporation's supervisory board does not contain any executive managing directors because they are not entitled to the same. Therefore, CEO duality is not possible. The formal independence of the board in the two-tier board is not disputed in the international corporate governance debate. Further differences in the two boards are depicted in table 1 below.

The Significance of Audit Committee on the Corporate Governance

It has a long history and always remain in the discussion and debate of theorist and professional players working in the corporate sector, the issue of agency problem which was earlier highlighted by Berle in 1932 and later on discussed by Jensen in great detail with comprehensive coverage to a particular issue. The corporate sector is managed by directors who are appointed by stockholders or, in other words, by investors. Fund providers are generally not managing firm operations on a day-to-day basis and neither taking various decisions that impact their wealth; this can be taken as an incomplete contract, as pointed

Table 1. Attributes of one-tier and two-tier corporate boards

Attributes	One-Tier board	Two-tier board
Composition	Executive and non-executive directors in one board	Executive and non-executive directors in a separate board
Committee	Mandatory	Recommended
Organization	Unitary	Binary
CEO duality	Possible	Impossible

out by Jensen. This causes the issue of entrenchment from an investor point of view that might happen when managers take various decisions that are not for the benefit of stockholders. In the finance literature, this is the issue that has been discussed in greater detail as agency cost. There are various mechanisms adopted by companies inside the organization and by regulators outside the company to control, reduce and mitigate this entrenchment issue. An audit committee is one of the mechanisms used inside the company to address this agency cost. Management, independent auditors, and audit committee have a close linkage, but they also have separate responsibilities in monitoring the company's financial matters.

Importance of the Audit Committee

The board of directors makes sure that the company's internal control system is intact and working effectively. This work is also carried out by the audit committee. It reviews the effectiveness of the internal control system. World Bank (2018) observed that the majority of the shareholder's directors review this in most companies. The audit committee also plays its role in the suggestion and appointment of external auditors irrespective of whether external auditors are retiring and reappointed or suggested for the new appointments. Later on in CCG 2017, further weightage was given to the audit committee in the work of external auditors like their recommendations will be considered to decide audit fee, removal of auditors, and if any other task is decided to give to external auditors. On the other hand, during the last three decades' various financial scandals emerged that encouraged policymakers to safeguard the interest of investors, the audit committee is one of the committees that is established to address these issues (Aldamen et. al., 2012; Agyemang-Mintah, & Schadewitz, 2018; Dat et al. 2020). Listed Companies (Code of Corporate Governance) Regulations, 2017 in Pakistan made it mandatory for all listed companies to form an audit committee.

Bansal and Anil (2016) examined the impact on firm performance due to corporate governance, including audit committee Independence. The proxies of a firm's performance were ROA, ROE, Tobin's q, and Market Capitalization. The study found no effect of audit committee independence and meetings on firm performance.

Formation of Audit Committee

To improve the governance mechanism of corporations in Pakistan, SECP issued the Code of Corporate Governance in the year 2002. In this manual practical experiences of other countries were also shared to develop a better understanding of its nature and objective, keeping in view the protection of different stakeholders. This was the first document through which Pakistan's corporate governance may be measured.

As per the Code of Corporate Governance, the audit committee should have at least three members. The majority of them should be non-executive, and the chairman of the audit committee preferably be a non-executive director. In CCG 2002, it was discussed that all related party transactions would be presented to the audit committee, and in case of any transactions, with related part not covered under arm's length, the price will also be presented to the audit committee with proper justification.,

Institute of Chartered Financial Analyst (CFA) argued that the primary objective of the formation of an audit committee in any company is to keep a check on the overall financial reporting mechanism, entire internal audit process, and compliance with all rules and regulations that the company should meet before publishing financial information. The audit committee will also ensure the completion and accuracy of all information published. CFA observed that the audit committee should be independent and not under the influence of insiders and should evaluate external auditors' work as per compliance requirements. The audit committee should disclose to the public in case of any deficiency observed during the entire financial reporting process. Australian Institute of Company Directors also discussed in detail the formation, responsibilities, and key functions of the audit committee and suggested that the audit committee should meet external auditors at least once a year without the presence of management of the company so that committee can discuss without influence with the external auditors.

Birkett (1986) discussed in detail the historical background of the audit committee in his paper. In 1978, New York Stock Exchange (NYSE) decided that the audit committee should be a compulsory part of every company. In 1930, the Securities and Exchange Commission and NYSE planned to form an audit committee after their observations in Mckesson and Robbins case. Mautz, & Neumann (1977) surveyed in 1970 that around 32 percent of companies formed audit committees. In the following survey during 1970, this percentage increased to 87, mainly due to interest taken in forming an audit committee by SEC and Congress.

Composition of Audit Committee

All companies' BOD will appoint an audit committee with at least three members and the chairman. It is also highlighted that the majority of the members should be non-executive, but it is somehow flexible. In the latest CCG 2017, one independent director is required for the composition of the audit committee. World Bank. (2018) observed that around 68% of audit committees in companies are independent that shows substantial compliance. When we compare it with developed countries' practices like in the USA, it is required that all members should be non-executive. However, it is required that all names of audit committee members be disclosed in the company's annual report. Figure 1 shows the practices of companies operating in Pakistan which have corporate board members with their composition.

The audit committee will meet in each quarter before approval of the financial results of that quarter. External auditors may also meet the audit committee at their request. In CCG2017, further clarity was given regarding meetings with external auditors and audit committee like the head of the internal auditor or external auditors may attend the meeting of audit committee where financial matters came under discussion.

An audit committee member should have a good understanding of financial matters and a recognized degree approved by the Higher Education Commission of Pakistan. The BOD prepares terms of reference and provides all the facilities that facilitate the audit committee to carry out their task. All these terms of references will be documented and include major areas of concern like any change in accounting policy, compliance with the regulatory body, and related party transactions. Through their

Figure 1. Board of directors results from the survey of annual reports. Source: Audit Survey

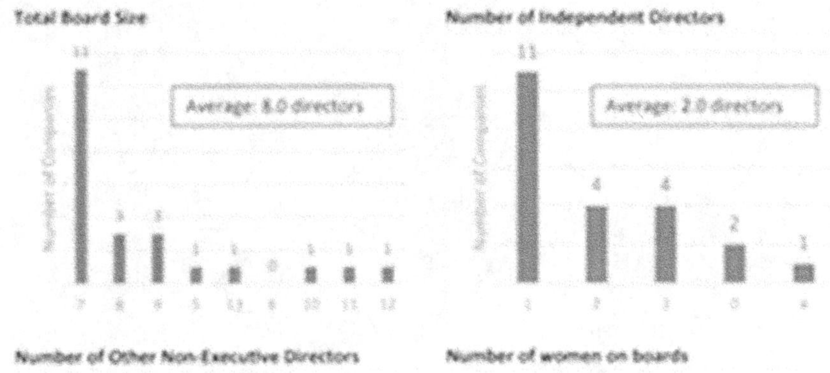

survey, OECD (2017) observed that only Pakistan and Mongolia give importance to audit committees with reference to related party transactions.

EY from 2012 reviewed audit committee proxy statement disclosure by Fortune 100 companies and observed an increasing trend in audit committee disclosure as shown in Figure No.2 above in key areas. Companies are taking more interest in the audit committee's role and responsibilities, even considering the audit committee's role in discussing climate issues. The report also observed that the financial expert's role increased from 58% in 2012 to 66% in 2021, and a number of meetings were on the higher side. Significant female participation was observed in the audit committee, which increased from 18% to 35% in 2021 (Jennifer Lee, 2021).

As Figure 3 pointed out, the specific disclosure that the audit committee's independence increased from 2012 onwards. The audit firm's name is included in an audit committee report, reflecting a higher trend showing that firms are more interested in disclosing this information to stakeholders. It also covers assessment of the external auditor shows that all the factors are improving, including audit committee discussion on external auditor qualification and quality of work, disclosure on the appointment of lead partner, engagement of audit committee in lead partner selection, and statement that external auditor is for the best interest of the company. There is an upward trend in all four factors; nonetheless, the most

Figure 2. Audit committee reporting to shareholders in 2021. Source: Jennifer Lee (2021)

Audit committee attribute	2021	2017	2012
Size	4.3	4.2	4.0
Number of meetings per year	8.4	8.6	8.9
Age	63.0	63.0	62.7
Years served on board	7.3	8.0	8.4
% of designated financial experts	66%	64%	58%
% of female committee members	35%	25%	18%

Figure 3. Audit committee reporting to shareholders in 2021. Source: Jennifer Lee (2021)

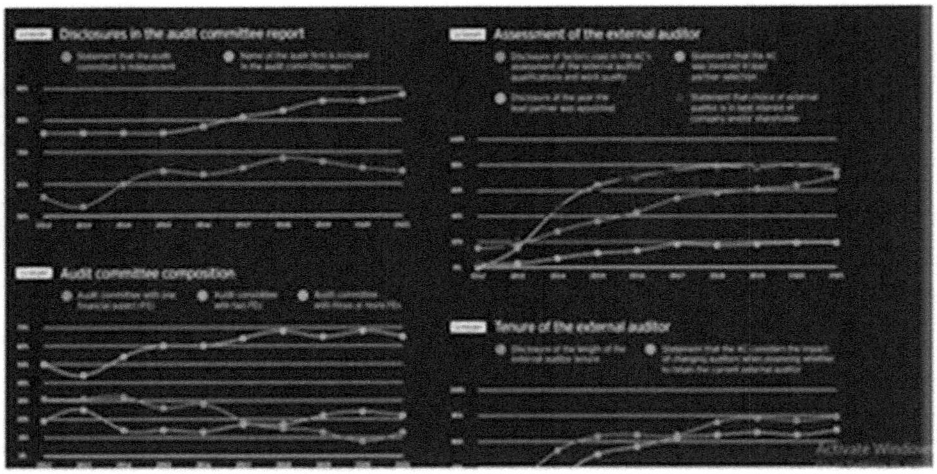

significant shift is observed in external auditor qualification and quality of work, of course, for the benefit of the company and shareholders.

The figure shows the composition of the audit committee with reference to financial experts, highlighting that the majority of firms are keeping more financial experts in their audit committees. The graph indicates the presence of financial experts increasing from one to three with a significant ratio. In effect, a financial expert in an audit committee plays a crucial role in understanding relevant sensitive financial issues and their governance. The figure shows that the importance of the audit committee is continuously increasing, and keeping under consideration even the tenure of the external auditors is critical. They are keeping under review the duration of an external auditor and consider the impact of change of any external auditor.

Council, A. C. G. (2010) discussed all requirements related to the audit committee in their report Corporate Governance principles and Recommendations with 2010 Amendments that All Ordinaries Index should have audit committee during that year. Companies must meet all requirements of the audit committee's formation, procedure, and authority as suggested and outlined by ASX Corporate Governance Council. The ASX Corporate Governance Council mainly gives four recommendations comprehensively covering all critical segments of the audit committee. The board should establish an audit committee; the audit committee should consist of non-executive directors, have a formal charter, and provide all relevant information to complete committee tasks independently and effectively.

Responsibilities and Functions of the Audit Committee

Financial reporting of companies is prepared by management; external auditors provide opinions on the fairness of this financial report. The audit committee should be well aware of control mechanisms and processes and should carefully observe whether the control system is effectively applied or not. The BOD plans a detailed task for the audit committee consisting of many important financial matters and issues that will provide security to the company's assets. BOD provides necessary resources to the audit committee to carry out its responsibilities. All tasks assigned to the audit committee are adequately documented.

During the entire monitoring, the audit committee makes sure that sufficient measures are taken to protect the assets and resources of the company. The audit committee shall review the company's quarterly and annual financial statements before its approval is given by BOD. When the audit committee reviews company financial information, the committee shall focus on any important adjustment arising due to audit, going concern assumption, changes in accounting policies and practices, and any kind of adjustment, as suggested by the management. The audit committee will review whether the company financial statement meets accounting standard requirements or not; regulatory requirements will also be reviewed by the audit committee, specifically related party transactions. World Bank (2018) observed in their report that in the corporate world of Pakistan, audit committees review all related party transactions, but it is not necessary to publicly disclose terms of reference and other directives.

Audit committees shall also discuss with external auditors if any significant observations arise during the audit process. The companies' management letter is issued to the external auditor when they start the audit process. The audit committee also reviews this management letter. External auditors require continuous support from the company to understand the process, operations, and financial structure of the company. Internal auditors provide them support in this regard, and the audit committee performs the role of the coordinator between them. The internal audit's breadth and dimension shall also be reviewed in detail by the audit committee to ensure the smooth functioning of the internal audit. The audit committee's responsibility is to observe that sufficient resources are allocated for internal audit functions. Fraudulent activity and entrenchment of assets will be closely monitored by the audit committee and will point out any such activity for warning on a timely basis. The audit committee makes sure that all assets are properly recorded, and the entire process of internal audit is to ensure the safeguarding of company financial resources.

The charter of the audit committee illustrates the basis of its operations. It explains the responsibilities to be performed by it. As per the charter, the audit committee is assumed to perform the following tasks.

- State the purpose of the audit committee as well as its specific responsibilities.
- State the process of audit committee meetings together with the frequency of the meeting in a year. State also the officers who will attend the meetings.
- Outline the composition of the audit committee.
- Form the authority of audit committee to perform precise responsibilities- recommendation of appointment and setting the compensation of external auditors

Audit committee is an essential area of corporate governance. Past studies have emphasized on the role and existence of audit committee. Likewise, focus has also been placed on the financial reporting quality by audit committee. It is assumed that the audit committee is responsible to monitor the accounting transactions as per international accounting standards. Both of the areas are discussed in detail in the following sections.

The Audit Committee as a Proxy of Corporate Governance

The definitions of the audit committee are available in various research papers and reports and surveys conducted in the studies of Marrian (1988); Peat Marwick McLintock, (1987); Arthur Andersen (1992); Proned (1993); Collier (1993); Keasey and Wright (1993). These definitions focus on subject matter such as who will be part of the audit committee and its key responsibilities assigned by the board:

The Board of directors forms an audit committee; members of this committee are directors who are responsible not for running a business but monitoring how the business is managed, supervised, and reported. Arthur Andersen (1992) states that it is a committee of directors of a firm with the precise responsibility of reviewing the financial activities and related matters. The committee primarily performs as a connection between the board of directors and external auditors, help to determine the scope of the audit, assess the recommendation of the external auditors, review results of the audit, keep a close link with internal audit controls and keep understanding with justification for all financial information that will be published by the company.' (AISG, 1977, quoted in Collier, 1992:2).

The New York Stock Exchange (NYSE) was the first institution that recognized the notion of an audit committee in 1939. Spangler and Braiotta (1990) observed that in the 1970s, the role of the audit committee was encouraged because of concern on corporate accountability and governance of the corporation. This is the era when Jensen & Meckling (1976) address the issue of agency theory and theory of the firm.

In 1972, the United States Securities and Exchange Commission (SEC) initiated their concern and suggested that the corporate sector should form audit committees. These committees should be within the directors but will not be part of routine business management. The American Institute of Certified Public Accountants (AICPA, 1988) observed this issue and developed a guideline in the Statement of Auditing Standards (SAS 61) as "communication with audit Committees" where the linkages were discussed between external auditors, audit committees, and management of the corporate sector.

The role, effectiveness, and compliance monitoring were vital for audit committees and its successful execution. The Blue Ribbon Committee (BRC, 1999) suggested a key rule amendment to improve it. In 2002, the Sarbanes-Oxley Act was approved by U.S. Congress that strengthened the role of audit committees after observing many corporate scandals like Enron and WorldCom. The essential part that encouraged the role of audit committees and gave them more authority and capacity is to monitor disclosure requirements. Sarbanes-Oxley Act 2002 encouraged the role of independent directors in the composition of audit committees together with the financial expertise of members of audit committees that became essential for its design. Contrarily, stock exchanges and Securities and Exchange Commission suggested new rules and regulations to acknowledge the importance of audit committees. Sarbanes-Oxlay Act 2002 strengthened the audit committee's role in the overall audit environment of a company. In developing the audit committee role, local and international laws, rules, code of conduct, and many resolutions were considered that helped improve the objective of better corporate governance in companies. With the help of the audit committee, agents may now be held accountable to stakeholders.

Audit committees are an essential part of corporate governance that helps to discourage financial misconduct in companies and also help to meet compliance requirements of various regulatory bodies. Audit committees not only monitor the internal mechanism of the company in terms of audit quality-related party transactions but also meet and discuss with external auditors to obtain desired results as expected by the shareholders of the companies. Basuony et al. (2014) observed that for effective implementation of corporate governance mechanisms and to ensure smooth functioning of the audit committee, it is required that the audit committee report become part of the company proxy statement where they disclosed this information that they reviewed all significant parts of the financial statement with internal auditors and other management groups.

An audit committee ensures that the financial information and other financial matters published by the company and presented in front of the public are appropriate, thoroughly reviewed, and provide reliable information. All stakeholders can rely on it (BRC, 1999). The report also provided various guidelines for the audit committee to improve the corporate governance of the corporate sector.

Corporate governance and its related issues have been under discussion for many decades, and various mechanisms developed in the literature to address it adequately (Jensen & Meckling, 1976; Fama, 1980; Jensen, 1986; Turnbull, 1997). Two primary mechanisms came under discussion to resolve governance issues, one is internal, and the second is external. There are many areas within the ambit of corporate governance that are considered by researchers for in-depth analysis in different economies. It is so vast that no single report can cover all segments of corporate governance mechanism, and audit committees are one of the internal mechanisms under discussion here. It is observed that there are many ways through which company governance issues are addressed; however, the fundamental structure is somehow similar and concentrates on a few things like directors, auditors' roles, directors' remunerations, audit committees, annual shareholders' meetings.

Cadbury (1992) argued that the main focus should be given to the structure and role of the board of directors, accountability mechanism, transparency, the effectiveness of contracts, and committees that manage the role of the board of directors. To address these issues, emphasis is given to independent directors. The audit committee plays its role in corporate governance. Audit committee expertise, structure, effectiveness, capacity to address financial issues are part of overall corporate governance.

Audit firms in general and the big four, in particular, emphasize audit committee roles and suggest guidelines to overcome various control mechanism issues in corporate governance, strengthening corporate financial disclosure controls with the help of the audit committee. Security and Exchange Commission lays emphasis on the composition of an audit committee where the focus is given to the inclusion of independent directors, disclosure from the company about the formation and function of the audit committee, including the number of meetings held in a financial year.

Significant work has been done in the field of corporate governance by Fraudulent Financial Reporting (Treadway Commission, 1987). They pointed out various factors that can lead to forged and dishonest financial reporting and suggested various measures to reduce these activities. When considering various factors to reduce fraudulent activities, Treadway identifies that audit committees can play an important role in discouraging these activities in the corporate sector. It is pointed out that the audit committee can play a role in supervision on all financial matters of a company by developing linkages among the internal system, the internal audit team, and external auditors. They should be well informed; must have the capacity to identify issues in financial matters and address issues in an effective way.

As discussed earlier, the presence of financial experts in the audit committee strengthens its role to ensure quality work from a corporate governance point of view. Like Defond et al. (2005), many researchers observed a significant positive sentiment in the market when the firm appointed a financial expert in the audit committee. Lee and Mande (2005) found that audit quality may improve when the audit committee plays its given role in the management of the company's financial matters as an overseer and reduces non-audit service that was earlier given to external auditors. Farber (2005) pointed out that firms, where fraudulent activities have been observed, have less number of financial experts in their audit committee. Chan and Li (2008) observed that the presence of independent directors in the audit committee enhanced the firm's value.

Broye and Johannes (2021) studied the audit committee's effectiveness considering the audit committee a key governance mechanism in the process of monitoring financial reporting quality and has the explicit role of addressing any issues regarding the preparation and the overseeing of financial information. The Sarbanes-Oxley Act of 2002 made audit committees obligatory in all US-listed companies.

Nguyen (2021) studied the audit committee and its role in the stability of the banking sector. The study focused on the composition of the audit committee. Raising the question of audit committee effectiveness in the context of ASEAN countries, the study concluded that smaller audit committees with more independent members would be beneficial for bank stability. The study confirms that an effective audit committee enhances the banking sector's stability. The researchers have further given the explanation that audit committee effectiveness principally drives bank stability higher through the reallocation effect for profits and incentives to hold higher capital ratios (Haddad, El Ammari, & Bouri, 2021; Fuller, Joe, & Luippold, 2021). Hence, audit committees play a critical role in minimizing the risk for the banking sector (Fida, & Naveed, 2021; Rodríguez, 2021). Thereby, one cannot ignore the importance of audit committees. This is primarily because of the fact that audit committees play a pivotal role in enhancing the confidence of investors that their money is not going to be wasted. All this happens because the investor deems the presence of the audit committees as the mechanism of check and balance over the firm's management. Once the audit is done, investors think that they have a true picture of the firm's financials, which provides them with confidence in making financial decisions. Contrary to this, the absence of audit committees makes it challenging to analyze the actual financial position of a firm. This, in turn, makes all the financial statements questionable. As a result, investors do not trust these statements. This, in turn, negatively affects the investment decisions of the investors.

Development in Financial Reporting Quality

Academic literature and practitioners both carefully worked on the effectiveness of the audit committee and explored this area further. Birkett (1986) analyzed the role of the audit committee in the US market. The key objective was to analyze the decisions taken by AICPA5, NYSE, and Securities and Exchange Commission as well congress regarding the formation of an audit committee in the corporate sector to work as an overseer of financial matters. The author observed that the audit committees could not achieve their primary objective without better understanding and proper guidelines. Similar kinds of reservations were further observed by other researchers (Millstein, 1999).

After Cadbury Committee, Hampel Committee explored the role of the audit committee and found that the word effectiveness is difficult to measure and implement from both auditors' and directors' perspectives. It is observed that directors and auditors can only ensure that control is effective misstatement avoided, but human error is possible in any case. (Hampel Committee, 1998). Hampel committee suggested removing word effectiveness from Cadbury Code.

Effectiveness may be defined as the improvement of financial reporting quality Cobb's empirical results are still questionable. Cobb's (1993) explained the objective of the formation of an audit committee as minimizing the fraudulent activities in financial reporting. The study also highlighted the effect of various exogenous variables on the performance of the audit committee effectiveness.

The audit committee has many important functions that it can play within the limit defined for an audit committee; the key area is to ensure that internal control provides evidence that the financial report presents a true and fair view. Information is accurate reliable and cannot harm to company reputation when published.

The audit committee's pivotal role in the area of financial reporting during the year 2020 is discussed here. Different stakeholders review company financial reports from their perspective. Stakeholders are not only interested in earning, but they also observe consistency and compliance of accounting standards. Compliance of various regulatory bodies is also important when determining the company's earnings and specific compliance with international accounting standards in this respect.

Non-GAAP information disclosure is always a matter of concern for the Security and Exchange Commission as well as other stakeholders. SEC showed its concern in 2019 again regarding adequate control on non-GAAP disclosure related to financial matters and suggested to audit committees to keep control on the information and make sure whether this non-GAAP information is appropriately covered or not in which earning information is also essential.

Audit committee members should consider and evaluate the implementation of a new accounting system as it is time-consuming and very complex in nature. The audit committee should discuss this with the company's management and external auditors to ensure that all have a sufficient understanding of it and understand its nature and complexity. The audit committee also makes sure that adequate resources are available and it can properly execute in the existing environment of the company. Once the company implements a new system, the audit committee ensures that adequate control is in process and meets all standard requirements as a due process.

The SEC SAB 74 requires companies to disclose financial statements in the footnote before implementing new accounting standards. The preparation of financial statements must explain in the disclosure the Impact that Recently Issued Accounting Standard on the future Financial Statements. It is the responsibility of the audit committee to make sure that the company meets this requirement.

Critical audit matters (CAMs) should be disclosed by the auditors in their audit reports. It is in the best interest of the company that auditors put extra effort into identifying and evaluating matters that require their professional judgment. Auditors can also identify CAMSs that are difficult to assess or obtain sufficient evidence due to the complexity of the matters. The overall objective is to make the audit report more informative and comprehensive. In this respect, the audit committee will be aware of all critical audit matters and keep them under evaluation and discussion when considering CAMs. The audit committee can play a vital role in this regard due to their understanding of all financial matters of the company. They have the required skill to understand financial complexities and their impact on the company's accurate and fair view representation.

There are various areas where the audit committee is not solely responsible for monitoring and keeping under consideration, like social and environmental governance (SEG) activities but can play an essential role in keeping a check on it. These social and environmental issues have become important as ethical considerations have increased in recent times. Since the audit committee is already taking care of various financial and non-financial disclosure, this review will also be attached with other compliances.

The financial team in any company always plays a significant role. Their expertise in managing financial matters and its proper reporting is important for companies in the short term and long term. The financial team, of course, is hired and placed by the human resource department that has appropriate skills to identify and place skilled people in the proper place, but the audit team will look after this work too and ensure quality human, skilled people with expertise in finance, hired to deal with various financial issues in the company. People who are dealing should be familiar with all aspects of reporting and controlling mechanisms. They should be fully equipped and trained when changes occur from an internal control perspective or any instruction reported by a regulatory body.

The main emphasis of stakeholders and regulators has always been related to the significance of oversight of financial reporting by audit committees. The SEC, in December 2019, issued a "Statement on Role of Audit Committees in Financial Reporting and Key Reminders Regarding Oversight Responsibilities." It highlights the opinions of the SEC on the nature of the responsibilities of the audit committee.

Risk Oversight

It is an important area of responsibility of the audit committee. Along with the audit committee, the task of risk oversight has been assigned to some other committees, including the compensation committee and by the Board itself; the responsibility still falls within the preview of the audit committee to see the entire risk process. Organizations are continuously facing risk, which has emerged the importance of risk oversight. The risk may include cyber, geopolitical, technological, cultural, and disruption risks. The audit committee and the Board and management are liable to ponder how to coordinate to oversee these risks. Companies may have risk committees for this purpose, but the impact of these types of risks on financial reporting needs the audit committee's involvement as the key stakeholder.

With all types of risks, cyber risk is the one that may need special attention by the audit committee because it can severely impact several areas of a firm, including the financial reporting disclosure.

Considering the importance of risk oversight, the audit committee must also perform some other tasks that are related to a firm's internal culture, i.e. commitment of the top management with the firm, middle management involvement, and hardworking of lower staff of the firm. Although it is not directly related to the role of the audit committee, culture may have an impact on financial reporting and disclosure, which is why the audit committee should also look into it. This is a culture risk that may encompass communicating with other staff members, understanding employees of the financial reporting and compliance, and inclination towards work. The audit committee is also supposed to control and perform intervallic reviews of a firm's code of conduct.

While modern financial statements its modern reporting framework incorporate all financial and non-financial information, Raimo et al. (2021) brought to light the audit committee's role towards integrated reporting. Although the audit committee influences the disclosure of information as it carries supervision on reporting, the quality of integrated reporting depends on the quality of the audit committee. This study brings out the gap of analyzing the effect of the audit committee attributes on integrated reporting quality (IRQ) from an agency theory perspective. The study sample was 125 international firms, while results conclude the positive effect of size, independence, and meeting frequency of the audit committee on Integrated Reporting Quality (IRQ).

FUTURE OUTLOOK OF THE AUDIT COMMITTEE

Based on the vast literature review and observations, the importance and existence of audit committee cannot be ignored. Out of several proxies of corporate governance, audit committee is an essential one to monitor not only the business activities in accordance with international accounting standards but also suggest the corporate board to make corrective actions that can be fruitful for the company.

CONCLUSION

There is an increased interest in the audit committees. The roles and responsibilities of the audit committee have consistently been recognized as essential in the context of corporate governance. This is because audit committees play a critical role in minimizing the risk for the banking sector. Thereby, one cannot ignore the importance of audit committees. This is primarily because of the fact that audit committees play a pivotal role in enhancing the confidence of investors that their money is not going to be wasted. All this happens because of the fact that investor deems the presence of the audit committees as the mechanism of check and balance over the management of the firm. Once the audit is done, investors think that they have a true picture of the firm's financials, which provides them with confidence in making financial decisions. Contrary to this, the absence of audit committees makes it difficult to analyze a firm's true financial position. This, in turn, makes all the financial statements questionable. As a result, investors do not trust these statements, which subsequently negatively affects the investment decisions of the investors.

Although new challenges have emerged due to malpractices by corporations, it is still assumed to have audit committees' existence in firms. The chapter highlights many aspects of the audit committee, ranging from its composition to its role in quality financial reporting. The chapter is not focused on any country but represents a general view applicable to most developed and developing counties.

Due to the bankruptcy of some corporations, the importance of corporate governance has emerged. The chapter is more focused on the quality of financial reporting by corporations which is an essential part of the responsibilities of audit committees. Policies and Acts of audit committees have also given rise to their importance. The Sarbanes-Oxley Act provides audit committees rights and responsibilities to perform its corporate governance role by having frequent meetings. Codes of Corporate Governance issued by the Security and Exchange Commission of Pakistan gave more responsibilities to the audit committee to monitor firms' business activities.

The chapter also sheds light on firm performance due to the existence of an audit committee. A firm's performance may include firms' internal factors like ROA, ROE, NPM or external factors like market capitalization and Tobin's q.

REFERENCES

Abbott, L. J., Park, Y., & Parker, S. (2000). The Effects of Audit Committee Activity and Independence on Corporate Fraud. *Managerial Finance*, *26*(11), 55–67. doi:10.1108/03074350010766990

Agyemang-Mintah, P., & Schadewitz, H. (2018). Audit committee adoption and firm value: evidence from UK financial institutions. *International Journal of Accounting & Information Management*.

Aldamen, H., Duncan, K., Kelly, S., McNamara, R., & Nagel, S. (2012). Audit committee characteristics and firm performance during the global financial crisis. *Accounting and Finance*, *52*(4), 971–1000. doi:10.1111/j.1467-629X.2011.00447.x

Andersen, A. (1992). *Audit Committees for the 1990s*. Arthur Andersen.

Basuony, M., & Ehab, K. A. (2015). *The Effect of Corporate Governance on Bank Financial Performance: Evidence from the Arabian Peninsula*. Academic Press.

Birkett, B. S. (1986). The Recent History of Corporate Audit Committees. *The Accounting Historians Journal*, *13*(2), 109–124. doi:10.2308/0148-4184.13.2.109

Broye, G., & Johannes, P. (2021). Determinants of audit committee effectiveness: Reviewing a decade of empirical research. *Accounting Auditing Control*, *27*(1), 51–109.

Cadbury Committee. (1992). *Report of the Committee on the Financial Aspects of Corporate Governance*. London: Gee.

Chan, K. C., & Li, J. (2008). Audit committee and firm value: Evidence on outside top executives as expert-independent directors. *Corporate Governance*, *16*(1), 16–31. doi:10.1111/j.1467-8683.2008.00662.x

Collier, P. (1993). Audit Committees in Major UK Companies. *Managerial Auditing Journal*, *8*(3), 25–30.

Collier, P. (1997). Audit Committees in Smaller Listed Companies. In K. Keasey & M. Wright (Eds.), *Corporate Governance: Responsibilities, Risks and Remuneration Chichester*. John Wiley.

Council, A. C. G. (2010). *Corporate governance principles and recommendations with 2010 amendments*. Australian Securities Exchange.

Dat, P. M., Mau, N. D., Loan, B. T. T., & Huy, D. T. N. (2020). Comparative China Corporate Governance Standards after Financial Crises, Corporate Scandals and Manipulation. *Journal of Security & Sustainability Issues*, *9*(3).

DeFond, M. L., Hann, R. N., & Hu, X. (2005). Does the market value financial expertise on audit committees of boards of directors? *Journal of Accounting Research*, *43*(2), 153–193. doi:10.1111/j.1475-679x.2005.00166.x

Fama, E. F. (1980). Agency problems and the theory of the firm. *Journal of Political Economy*, *88*(2), 288–307. doi:10.1086/260866

Farber, D. B. (2005). Restoring trust after fraud: Does corporate governance matter? *The Accounting Review*, *80*(2), 539–561. doi:10.2308/accr.2005.80.2.539

Fida, S., & Naveed, M. (2021). Novel insights into banking risk structure: Empirical evidence from nexus of financial, governance, and industrial landscape through nested tested modeling. *Cogent Business & Management*, *8*(1), 1869362. doi:10.1080/23311975.2020.1869362

Fuller, S. H., Joe, J. R., & Luippold, B. L. (2021). The Effect of Auditor Reporting Choice and Audit Committee Oversight on Management Financial Disclosures. *The Accounting Review*, *96*(6), 239–274. doi:10.2308/TAR-2016-0246

Haddad, A., El Ammari, A., & Bouri, A. (2021). Impact of Audit Committee Quality on the Financial Performance of Conventional and Islamic Banks. *Journal of Risk and Financial Management*, *14*(4), 176. doi:10.3390/jrfm14040176

Hampel Committee. (1998). *Committee on Corporate Governance*. Final Report. London: Gee.

Jensen, M. C. (1986). Agency costs of free cash flow, corporate finance, and takeovers. *The American Economic Review*, *76*(2), 323–329.

Jensen, M. C., & Meckling, W. H. (1976). Theory of the firm: Managerial behavior, agency costs and ownership structure. *Journal of Financial Economics*, *3*(4), 305–360. doi:10.1016/0304-405X(76)90026-X

Keasey, K., Thompson, S., & Wright, M. (Eds.). (1997). *Corporate governance: Economic and financial issues*. OUP Oxford.

Kesner, I. F., & Johnson, R. B. (1990). An investigation of the relationship between board composition and stockholder suits. *Strategic Management Journal, 11*(4), 327–336. doi:10.1002mj.4250110408

Kohler, J. C., & Bowra, A. (2020). Exploring anti-corruption, transparency, and accountability in the World Health Organization, the United Nations Development Programme, the World Bank Group, and the Global Fund to Fight AIDS, Tuberculosis and Malaria. *Globalization and Health, 16*(1), 1–10. doi:10.118612992-020-00629-5 PMID:33081805

Krafft, P. M., Young, M., Katell, M., Lee, J. E., Narayan, S., Epstein, M., ... Barghouti, B. (2021, March). An Action-Oriented AI Policy Toolkit for Technology Audits by Community Advocates and Activists. In *Proceedings of the 2021 ACM Conference on Fairness, Accountability, and Transparency* (pp. 772-781). 10.1145/3442188.3445938

Lee, H. Y., & Mande, V. (2005). The relationship of audit committee characteristics with endogenously determined audit and non-audit fees. *Quarterly Journal of Business and Economics*, 93-112.

Marrian, I. (1988). *Audit Committees*. Institute of Chartered Accountants in Scotland.

Mautz, R. K., & Neumann, F. L. (1977). *Corporate audit committees: Policies and practices*. Ernst & Whinney.

Millstein, I. M. (1999). Introduction to the Report and Recommendations of the Blue Ribbon Committee on Improving the Effectiveness of Corporate Audit Committees. *Business Lawyer, 54*(3), 1057–1066.

Nguyen, Q. K. (2021). Audit committee structure, institutional quality, and bank stability: Evidence from ASEAN countries. *Finance Research Letters*, 102369. doi:10.1016/j.frl.2021.102369

Nidhi, B., & Sharm, A. K. (2016). Audit Committee, Corporate Governance and Firm Performance: Empirical Evidence from India. *International Journal of Economics and Finance, 8*(13), 103–116.

Peat Marwick McLintock. (1987). *The Audit Committee*. Peat Marwick McLintock.

Raimo, N., Vitolla, F., Marrone, A., & Rubino, M. (2021). Do audit committee attributes influence integrated reporting quality? An agency theory viewpoint. *Business Strategy and the Environment, 30*(1), 522–534. doi:10.1002/bse.2635

Rodríguez, P. P. (2021). Accounting and auditing of credit loss estimates: The hard and the soft. *Latin American Journal of Central Banking, 2*(2), 100027. doi:10.1016/j.latcb.2021.100027

Spangler, W. D., & Braiotta, L. Jr. (1990). Leadership and corporate audit committee effectiveness. *Group & Organization Studies, 15*(2), 134–157. doi:10.1177/105960119001500202

Treadway Commission. (1987). *Report of the National Commission on Fraudulent Financial Reporting*. Author.

Turnbull, S. (1997). Corporate governance: Its scope, concerns and theories. *Corporate Governance, 5*(4), 180–205. doi:10.1111/1467-8683.00061

ADDITIONAL READING

Braiotta, L. Jr, Gazzaway, R. T., Colson, R., & Ramamoorti, S. (2010). *The audit committee handbook*. John Wiley & Sons.

Deloitte. (2018). *The Role of the Audit Committee*. Centre for Board Effectiveness.

Endrawes, M., Feng, Z., Lu, M., & Shan, Y. (2020). Audit committee characteristics and financial statement comparability. *Accounting and Finance*, *60*(3), 2361–2395. doi:10.1111/acfi.12354

Eulerich, M., Kremin, J., & Wood, D. A. (2019). Factors that influence the perceived use of the internal audit function's work by executive management and audit committee. *Advances in Accounting*, *45*, 100410. doi:10.1016/j.adiac.2019.01.001

KPMG. (2019). *Keeping pace with disruptive risk and digital transformation. 2019 Audit Committee Pulse Survey*. Audit Committee Institute, Board Leadership Centre.

Murray, T. A., Pearson, E. G., & Plichta, M. T. (2021). *Audit Committee Deskbook*. PLI Press.

See, J. K. P., Pitchay, A. A., Ganesan, Y., Haron, H., & Hendayani, R. (2020). The Effect of Audit Committee Characteristics on Audit Quality: The Moderating Role of Internal Audit Function. *Journal of Governance and Integrity*, *3*(2).

Spira Laura, F. (2002). *The Audit Committee: Performing Corporate Governance*. Oxford Brookes University Business School.

Tai, V. W., Lai, Y. H., & Yang, T. H. (2020). The role of the board and the audit committee in corporate risk management. *The North American Journal of Economics and Finance*, *54*, 100879. doi:10.1016/j.najef.2018.11.008

KEY TERMS AND DEFINITIONS

Accounting Standards: A collection of well-designed practices and procedures applied on bookkeeping and accounting practices across firms and time.

Agency Cost: An internal cost to the firm due to actions of an agent working on behalf of principal. It occurs in the shape of inefficiencies due to conflict of interest between agent and principal.

Audit Committee: A committee constituted by Board of Directors with the mandate to comment on the transparency of accounting practices within firm. The above mandate empowers it to comment on internal and external audits. The Audit committee plays pivotal advisory role in selection of independent external auditors.

Auditing: A set of activities to examine the quality of accounting practices following International Accounting Standards (IAS), International Financial Reporting Standards (IFRS) as well as confirm that financial reports are true representative of the state of affairs of firm.

Board of Directors: A group of agents elected by all the shareholders to represent them in a firm. The mandate of Board is to work in the best interest of shareholders.

Code of Corporate Governance: A set of orientations and training program for Board of Governors which are prerequisite to understand and perform duties efficiently and effectively by Board members in the best interest of Shareholders.

Composition of Audit Committee: A committee which consist of at least three members. The majority of members must be independent but one of the members must be an expert in financial matters hence working as financial advisor for the Audit Committee.

Corporate Governance: A structure of firm designed to give strategic direction as well as establishing control mechanism for smooth, effective and efficient running of operations of firm.

External Audit: It is a detailed examination of firm's books of accounts and its financial records to validate that records are following the International Accounting Standards and display the true picture of events in the firm.

Financial Reporting Quality: The quality of financial reporting depends on how useful the reporting is for the analysts to conclude the firm's performance and its future prospects.

Sarbanes-Oxley Act: It is a law passed by US Congress in July 2002 with the intention to protect investors from fraudulent and misleading financial reporting by firms through major reforms in financial reporting criteria.

Chapter 14
Forensic Accounting Is a Necessity in Today's Corporate World and Not an Extra Option:
A Conceptual Framework

Ali Rehman
https://orcid.org/0000-0002-6166-7242
A'Sharqiyah University, Oman

Fathyah Hashim
Universiti Sains Malaysia, Malaysia

ABSTRACT

In today's business environment, fraud is the main cause of organizational failure, which results in reputational damages and can also lead to the closure of the organizations. Forensic accounting with appropriate skills, knowledge, and mindset can perform proactive tasks towards mitigating fraud risk and can raise red flags even before the occurrence of fraudulent transactions or events. With the utilization of fraud triangle theory and forensic accounting theory, this chapter is focused on the preventive and detective role of forensic accounting which will highlight the importance of this function as a permanent feature in any organization. This chapter will also highlight the problems associated with the non-availability of forensic accounting in the current organizational culture and will also provide related recommendations. This chapter can be beneficial to regulators, organizational governance management, and standard-setting bodies towards drafting or amending the laws and regulations and inclusion of forensic accounting as a permanent element for all organizations.

INTRODUCTION

Global economic activity has never been subject to such rapid and widespread disruptions and frauds as organizations are experiencing today. Such a situation had never occurred before in modern history.

DOI: 10.4018/978-1-7998-8754-6.ch014

It is reasonable to expect a wide range of economic and risk outcomes as the world adjusts to the new normal. It is likely that some organizations will succeed, some will return to pre-pandemic levels of business activity, and some businesses will not be able to recover. Today's risk executives need more than ever to be able to assess fraud risks in real time so that they can make efficient sensible economic decisions while optimizing strategies and preventing fraud (Association, 2021).

Fraud risks which are faced by the organizations are internal and or external. Internal frauds are conducted by the employees of the organization and external fraud are conducted by the external parties such as vendors or other outside parties. These frauds can be managed and mitigated by the control activities available within the organization. However, till date very few organizations have the forensic accounting (FA) function available as a permanent feature of their operation. FA is only called upon as and when required and is treated as outside consultant or expert witness for the court.

In the recent past many external auditors were penalized due to their involvement in fraudulent acts with the organization or they were not able to detect the fraud as they lack the expertise (Browning, 2021; Team, 2011; Nicodemus, 2020). Similar is the situation with the internal audit function where it is stated in International Professional Practicing Framework (IPPF) that internal auditors are not required to have the knowledge and expertise of the fraud expert and it is not the responsibility of internal audit to detect or prevent the fraud (Auditors, 2019). In a recent survey on internal audit function, 41% of internal auditors informed that the effectiveness of fraud risk programs is not good in their organizations and 61% informed that they are not involved in risk management at all or they are slightly involved (Weitz, 2020). Moreover, International Standards of Auditing and other reporting standards label fraud detection and prevention as organizational management responsibility and exclude auditors from such obligations (IFAC, 2009). In this given scenario organizational management can only prevent and detect fraud once they have the capability and knowledge which can be provided only by FA.

Financial fraud investigations and asset misappropriation receive little academic attention (Zagera, Malis, & Novak, 2016) and majority of the available studies/ work is conducted by professional organizations and provide reports on the types of fraud and their related controls. Furthermore; FA is operating without any standards or guidelines which are available for the internal and external auditors. In the absence of these standards or guidelines, FA is considered as part of the audit section and despite FA's capabilities, it is not considered as part of governance or organizational management. The purpose of FA is to prevent fraud by utilizing both accounting and auditing skills to produce productive reports. For the prevention of fraud and for the implementation of fraud risk, FA also utilizes investigative mentalities related to auditing, possesses knowledge of laws and regulations and can be considered as an expert in criminology, communication, victimology, psychology, accounting, and other related matters (Fadilah, Maemunah, Nurrahmawati, Lim, & Sundary, 2019).

Fraud can be defined as an illegal action conducted to earn gains or damage the organizations via disguised actions. Fraud is divided into three major categories namely corruption, asset misappropriation and financial statement fraud (ACFE 2020) Corruption and financial statement frauds can be categorized as internal frauds and asset misappropriation which is also known as occupational fraud can be considered as external and internal fraud. FA performs fraud risk assessment and identifies control weaknesses in the system which enables prevention of these frauds even before they occur. Following are the recent frauds presented in Table 1 that occurred and all of these companies do not have FA in their organizational operations. There is no data available indicating that any organizations having FA functions within their organization have ever committed fraud.

Table 1. Recent frauds in corporate world

Name of Company	Amount in USD	Reference
HM Revenue and Customs	7.46 billion	(Neate, 2021)
NMC Hospital	6 billion	(Ohri, 2020)
M P Border Checkpost Development Co Ltd	22.5million	(Bearu, 2021)
South Florida Addiction Treatment Facility	112 million	(Justice, 2021)

The above mentioned frauds are only few to be mentioned; however, if FA was involved in the organizational operations then these fraud and related damages could have been protected (Moid, 2016).

The purpose of the conceptual paper is to demonstrate the fraud risk is the major reason why organizations suffer, and the only function available to mitigate and prevent the fraud risk is FA. This study can be useful for the regulators, governance management and authorities who can amend the codes of corporate governance, amend organizational policies or introduce standards that can enforce the FA function as a compulsory part of governance or organizational management.

BACKGROUND AND MAIN FOCUS OF THE CHAPTER

This section discusses the definition, concepts, past studies, and related theories.

Fraud

Global cost of fraud is over USD 3 billion with average loss per case of USD 1.5 million (ACFE, 2020). Any organization can be victimized by fraud at any time. In busy organizations or for successful managers, fraud is not usually at the top of the priority list until it strikes. It is easy for fraudsters to succeed because they are able to pay attention to details, exposing weak areas of control and catching the unwary victim by surprise. In fraud, the details are always concealed, and majority of the organizations are reactive instead of proactive and act after the fact of fraud (Comer, 2016). Fraud, contrary to popular belief, isn't primarily the result of dishonest employees, but increasingly involves senior managers, vendors, suppliers, competitors, and can be committed by extensive collusion, deception, bribery, false reporting and technological abuse (Zagera, Malis, & Novak, 2016).

Fraud is defined by International Standards on Auditing (ISA) as "an intentional act by one or more individuals among management, those charged with governance, employees, or third parties, involving the use of deception to obtain an unjust or illegal advantage" (IASB, 2009). Fraud is intentional act as unintentional act can be considered as error or mistake. Fraud can further be categorized as internal fraud (occupational fraud) and external fraud (conducted by outside parties). Occupational fraud is further divided into corruption fraud, asset misappropriation fraud and financial statement fraud and presented in Figure 1 (ACFE, 2020).

A significant number of fraud schemes involved asset misappropriation, where employees stole or misused the employer's assets; however, these schemes tend to cause a relatively small median loss per case. The least frequent, but costliest type of occupational fraud is financial statement fraud, which in-

Figure 1. Fraud tree
Source: *ACFE (2016)*

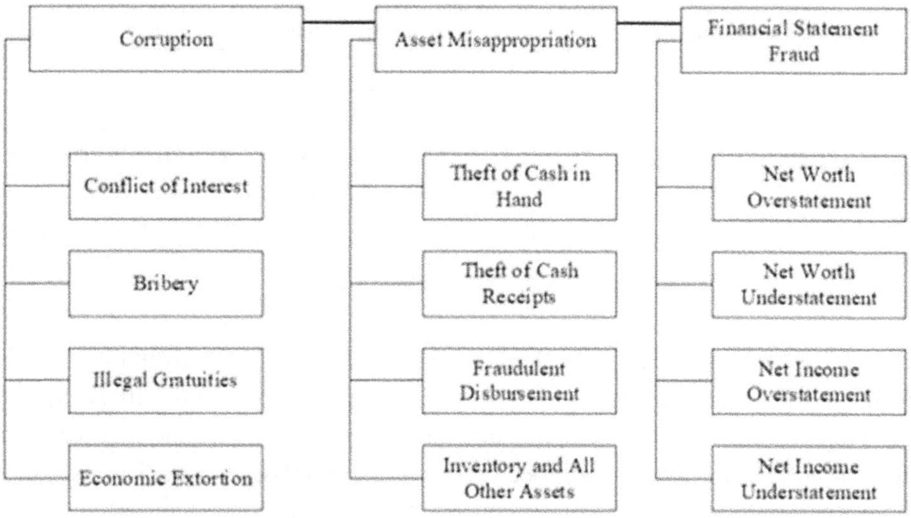

volves intentionally misstating or omitting a company's financial statements. The last category which is corruption includes wrongdoings such as conflicts of interest, bribery and extortion. As far as frequency and financial damages are concerned, corruption is in the middle (ACFE, 2020).

Organizational management requires expertise to combat occupational fraud and this expertise requires continuous monitoring along with the related skills and knowledge which can be surely provided by the FA.

Forensic Accounting

As mentioned by former Prime Minister of the United Kingdom Mr. Gordon Brown, "What the use of fingerprints was to the 19th century, and DNA analysis was to the 20th century, so financial information and forensic accounting has come to be one of today's most powerful investigative and intelligence tools available" (Telegraph, 2006).

We will always remember the first decade of the twenty-first century as a decade of corporate frauds. As a result of the bankruptcies of WorldCom, Enron, Lehman Brothers, the collapse of Arthur Andersen, numerous investigations by the Securities and Investment Banking industry, obliged the accounting profession to identify a need for a new perception to develop an activity that goes beyond corporate governance and statutory auditing compliances (Hegazy, Sangster & Kotb, 2017). This new perception or innovation in the field can be known as forensic accounting (FA). FA goes beyond summarizing and analyzing financial numbers. FA deals with solving complex financial frauds, investigating fraudulent schemes, assessing damages, and resolving other financial disputes.

At the beginning of the 21st century and to cater for financial frauds, the accounting and auditing profession developed multi-skilled forensic teams. Accounting and auditing firms recruited large numbers of non-financial personnel such as former law enforcers, lawyers, computer analysts and private investigators. These personnel all together formed independent and multi-disciplinary forensic units.

Table 2. Forensic accounting and general audit differences

Forensic Accounting	General Auditing
Ensures that fraud actually occurred or not	Based on an opinion of a "True and Fair" presentation
Detail testing	Based on sample testing
No time limit to verify the transactions	Only for specific period of time
Independent verification and utilization of third party records	Opinion and working is based on the documents received from organization
Opinion is accepted in court of law	Opinion is presented to shareholders

Source: Dutta (2021)

Another approach that was involved was to change the name of the activity from FA to forensic services, which signals that forensic services are able to recruit from other professions with additional skills. This was necessitated to ensure that public demands for fraud detection are met and this service extends their offerings to accountants as they are unequipped to handle the fraud detection. However, the fact remains that FA is not a normal part of the accounting profession, is not bound by "international financial reporting standards (IFRS)" or "international auditing standards (IAS)" and accounting profession does not have a domination over FA (Hegazy, Sangster & Kotb, 2017).

As organizations gain a better understanding of why and how fraud crimes occur, organizations can better combat them. The more organizations become vigilant and have appropriate controls, the better organizations will be able to combat fraud. As mentioned earlier, internal and external auditors denied the responsibility of preventing and detecting fraud (Rehman & Hashim, 2018a) and labeled it as organizational management responsibility; in this scenario having forensic accounting (FA) is the only possible activity that can provide proper prevention and detection from fraud. It is worth mentioning that FA is the activity which can be available within the organization and the person who performs it can be defined as forensic accountant.

Detecting and preventing fraud can be seen as one of the top functions of the FA. FA with its skills and skeptical mind frame can prevent fraud by developing controls and implementing policies and procedures (Rehman & Hashim, 2018a). Controls defined by FA are based on past events and risk assessments. Embedding these controls into the organization's framework enables organizational management to identify red flags and anomalies. The FA then tests again for red flags to ensure that fraud is prevented and control lapses are identified and corrected. FA is used to determine whether, in fact, a fraud has been committed and to apply appropriate tactics in order to prevent fraud. The FA activity provides more support to the auditing process by identifying and preventing fraud by collecting evidence of it. Difference between the general audit and FA is defined in Table 2.

The term forensic audit refers to a technique for verifying a legal harmony between accounting transactions, auditing, and legal requirements in order to determine if fraud has occurred. Performing a forensic audit is intended to determine whether fraud has actually taken place or not. In forensic auditing, auditors gather evidence of fraud and use their skills to prevent it (Dutta, 2021). It is worth mentioning that FA or fraud auditors perform the fraud investigations to confirm the existence of fraud and involve several processes and procedures.

In accordance with the recent research conducted by Hegazy, Sangster and Kotb (2017), it was identified that skills and knowledge which can be considered as necessary for FA are written and oral

Table 3. Forensic accounting's required knowledge and skills

Skills and Knowledge	Explanation
Effective presentation, oral and written communication skills	FA is required to be precise and able to communicate clearly. All the reports of FA should be accurate, effective and timely. These reports are required to be presented in front of client and, as the case may be, in front of court as well
Ability to synthesize, analyze and interpret financial information and related fraud discovery	As mentioned, financial statement fraud is low in frequency but higher in monetary values. FA should be able to understand and interpret the financial information and should be skilled enough to identify any fraud within the financial information. FA can utilize many tools and analyses techniques; however, it is all depend upon the skills of FA that how they utilize the information and extract the desired outcome
Analytical, problem solving and fraud investigation skills	FA job is to highlight the existence of fraud, amount of fraud and perpetrator. FA should be skilled in problem solving and it can be achieved in the shape of recommendations. FA is also required to be skilled in fraud investigation skills. These skills are learned over time and are useful in detecting and preventing frauds.
Knowledge of legal laws, court procedure and expert witness skills	Without the knowledge of legal laws and court procedures, FA will not be able to develop a strong case.
Auditing, fraud detection and fraud prevention skills	FA should be able to perform the audits in order to identify the existence of fraud and define its materiality. FA should be able to detect the fraud and provide meaningful recommendations in order to prevent the fraud in future
Critical and strategic thinking skills	FA should be able to think critically and should not deviate from its objectives. FA work and report should be unbiased and only determine the facts
Interview skills	FA should not only able be to analyze the documents but should be able to conduct proper interviews. These interviews are necessary to identify the motive and to know any other information which is not available in the provided/ available documents.
Deductive analysis skills coupled with cross examination ability	FA should be able to deduce the information from the analysis they perform. They should also be able to cross examine multiple people within the organization to identify the fact and to know the real nature of fraud.
Ability to think like a fraudster	Knowledge and skill of thinking about what can go wrong combined with how to perform it creates the ability to think like a fraudster. This skill is useful to identify the gaps within information
Business/asset valuation skills along with asset tracing skills	This skill enables FA to identify the materiality of fraud; furthermore, it also identifies the amount of loss. FA should be capable of identifying the loss amount and its money trail.

Source: Hegazy, Sangster and Kotb (2017)

communication skills, problem solving skills and ability to analyze and understand financial statements. Details of these skills and their desired knowledge is presented in Table 3 below:

Above mentioned required skills and knowledge cannot be available within the profession of accounting and auditing. FA with its unique abilities, capabilities, skills and knowledge can provide the results which goes beyond mere compliance with standards and codes. However, it remains to be seen whether FA can ever be considered a profession. In accordance with Hegazy, Sangster and Kotb (2017) in the foreseeable future, the FA field has little prospects of becoming a recognized profession. Although it is possible that it will eventually be recognized as complete profession but it all depends upon the organizational environment and importance provided by the regulators

FA can be divided into two roles namely preventive role and detective role. The prevention and detection of fraud can be effectually achieved with application of FA with a competent organizational management team and support from the board of directors or regulators. Furthermore, for effective performance of FA, a solid knowledge and understanding of auditing and accounting, suitable information technology knowledge and good communication ability is required. FA can be engage by the management as permanent activity within the organization or by shareholders and regulators (Isa, 2017).

The growing demand for FA is acknowledged by most companies in the world; however, FA as activity is still not visible in many organizations around the globe and still considered as outside/ third party consultants. Fact must be recognized that the services of a FA is necessary as fraud cases have significantly increased in numbers and volumes. FA is the activity with financial and investigative skills required to unsettled issues, conducted within the context of the rules of evidence (Rehman & Hashim, 2018; PWC, 2020). FA preventing and detective role is explained below:

Forensic Accounting Prevention Role

Regardless of any industry or profession, it is universally accepted that "prevention is better than cure" in other words, fraud prevention is always preferable as fraud detection will only identify the lost amount or reputation damage (Isa, 2017); whereas preventing fraud can enable organizations to eliminate or mitigate such an event before its occurrence.

The assurance functions are referred to by three terms namely: forensic accountants, fraud auditors, and financial auditors. Auditors who performs financial audits are usually involved in the assurance activities only which are related to compliances with standards and laws. Fraud auditors are responsible for identifying potential fraud in the form of red flags or other means to indicate it; whereas, forensic accountants can determine the extent of potential fraud, the reason, the amount, and the perpetrator or executor and also recommend controls that can prevent similar fraud in the future. Never ending and ever increasing frauds forced the profession of accounting and auditing to seek out improved and alternative ways to detect and mitigate fraud and the best possible way towards improvement is adoption of FA (Rehman & Hashim, 2018 a).

In accordance with Singleton and Singleton (2010) usually, fraud occurs when organizations are making profit, but it occurs more and with greater intensity when organizations are suffering losses. In such situations, FA is a necessary activity, considering that it can provide assurance that goes beyond the requirements of regulatory compliance. In addition to becoming the fastest growing profession, FA is also becoming a compulsory part of many chartered accounting/ auditing firms (Razak, 2016). In addition to preventing fraud, FA can help in saving legal and litigation costs (Dada, Owolabi, & Okwu, 2013).

FA can be viewed as a preventive activity that identifies fraud before it occurs (Enofe, Ekpulu, & Ajala, 2015). FA possesses skills and capabilities to improve organization's operations and enhancement of fraud risk assessment. In order to enable improvement, FA must be understood for its preventive role and as part of organizational management and also as an unavoidable feature of corporate governance codes (Rehman & Hashim, 2018).

Based on the knowledge and skills, FA can implement anticipatory controls. Integrating these anticipatory controls with organizational goals can help enterprises eliminate and mitigate the fraud and related risk. In accordance with the codes of corporate governance, preventive role is assigned for internal audit function (OECD, 2014); however, several frauds are occurring under watchful management of internal audit as they lack the required skills and knowledge; moreover, in current business environment, their independence is also doubtful (Okoye & Gbegi, 2013). Regulatory audits are ineffective if FA is not included as a team member or auditors do not possess FA's knowledge and skills (Rehman & Hashim, 2018). The board of directors and shareholders should realize the importance of preventive measures and should utilize FA in order to develop these preventive measures (Oh, 2017). FA's preventive role can assist in mitigating fraudulent activity through designing controls and being part of an overall organizational management system.

Compared to the preventive function of FA, the detective function of FA is only responsible for detecting fraud i.e. after the event of fraud (Singleton & Singleton, 2010). Despite the benefits of the preventive role of FA, in the current business environment FA is regarded for its detective role. It is, however, advantageous to have a proactive and preventive role of the FA rather than a detective role, as identifying the fraudster and the reason for fraud will not serve its purpose when capital is lost and reputation is harmed.

Forensic Accounting Detective Role

Accounting scandals in the past and recent ones in organizations have demonstrated that FA expertise is crucial to spotting financial fraud that arises from a firm's financial accounting process. Recently, fraud detection has become a complex process due to new innovations in financial fraud schemes, and changes in accounting methods and policies by companies. In these times, a combination of skill, knowledge, experience, and attention to detail will be the key to success which is only provided by FA (Ozili, 2020)

Detective role of FA is very commonly utilized in many organizations and by several regulating authorities. Detective function of FA is invited as and when required and usually called upon to become the expert witness in the court (Singleton & Singleton, 2010). In the USA, FA role is limited to divorce settlement expert, litigation expert and insurance claim verifier (Rehman & Hashim, 2018) and not considered as the fraud finding expert who can be part of organizational management. It is high time that the board of directors and organizational management accept the risk of fraud and start considering the role of FA as a permanent feature for their organizations.

Detective role of FA performs the work after the occurrence of fraudulent event. These experts perform the task in a way that identifies the money trail, the perpetrator, the affected areas, and the total amount of fraud. When these scenarios have been identified, FA provides a complete report which mentions the reasons for the fraud and also provides recommendations for future use. FA's role is somehow similar to that of internal audit; but it is stated in the International Professional Practicing Framework (IPPF) that internal auditors are not required to have the knowledge and expertise of fraud experts and they are only responsible for identifying fraud risks (Auditors, 2019).

A detective role can be part of an external and internal audit team to ensure financial statements are free of fraud and misrepresentation. Although absolute assurance cannot be provided, but with the availability of technology, FA can provide reasonable assurance in specific areas of financial statements and inform shareholders whether these areas were impacted by fraud or not. (Rehman & Hashim, 2018).

Table 4. Strengths and weaknesses

Description	Strengths	Weakness
Forensic Accounting	• FA add value to work of auditors and accountants when they add some of the fraud related competencies to their assigned task • Accounting, auditing, law, finance, information technology, and criminology are all included in FA, which makes it a vital profession. • While studying FA, students are exposed to a variety of useful skills, abilities, and knowledge which are currently lacking in auditors.	• The lack of regulation and control over profession admission, • There is no consensus on how to teach FA • There are no specialized research journals directly associated with FA • The lack of highly qualified practitioners and the misconception of its purpose • There are no set standards or guidelines available • Lack of public recognition • Reputation of occupation
Preventive role of Forensic Accounting	• Can work as the organizational management • Identify the risk of fraud utilizing the fraud triangle theory and implementing fraud risk assessment • Identify the control weaknesses within the system and develop controls • Proactive in dealing with fraud instead of reactive	• Not able to identify the fraud risk and fraud occurs • Since attention is not provided to this function, preventive role will not be able to function effectively • Many of the academic research is focus on the detective role of FA; therefore, limited literature is available for the preventive role of FA
Detective of Forensic Accounting	• While Investigating fraud, the detective role uses various investigative tools and gather, organize and evaluate evidence. • Able to track the money trail and identify the perpetrator • Identify the reasons for fraud • Develop the recommendations so that similar incident doesn't happen again	• Always calls upon after the act of fraud • Still considered as expert witness in court and not as part of governance management • Perform the investigations and not the regular monitoring of organizational operations • Only involve in financial frauds not in other organizational frauds.

Source: Alshurafat, Al Shbail, and Mansour (2021)

Strength and Weaknesses with Practical Adaptability

Table 4 categorizes the strength and weakness which are related to FA and its preventive and detective role; whereas, Table 5 defines the few cases in which the detective role of FA was utilized.

Research demonstrates that students with anti-fraud knowledge and skills enjoy higher employment opportunities after graduation (Alshurafat, Al Shbail, & Mansour, 2021). The situation can help promote this profession and in the near future organizations and regulators may consider this activity as mandatory. As far as the detective role of FA is concerned, there are several examples and a few of these cases are presented in Table 5 which were detected by FA utilizing their skills and knowledge; however, the researchers was unable to find any study in which FAs' involvement in prevented fraud was evident.

Underlying Theories

Theories which can be associated with forensic accounting are fraud triangle theory and forensic accounting theory. These theories are explained below:

Table 5. Fraud cases detected by forensic accounting

Fraud	Amount of Fraud	Case Summary	Source
Stamp paper fraud	USD 7.9 billion	Forging of stamp papers and selling these to bulk buyers	Mode (2016)
VVIP Chopper deal scam	USD 47 million	Kickbacks and bribery	Modi (2016)
Sino forest spending	USD 2 billion	Illegal spending and money laundering	Kozlov, Hurtado-Guarin and Trakulhoon (2018)
Nigerian stock exchange spending	USD 0.7 million	Illegal spending and gifts	Eliezer and Emmanuel (2015)

Fraud Triangle Theory

Donald Cressey, a criminologist, first examined why people commit fraud in 1950. He studied what motivates people to commit fraud. During the course of five months, he interviewed 250 criminals whose behavior met two criteria:

1. They had to have accepted a position of trust, and
2. They had to have violated that trust.

Donald Cressey found that three factors namely pressure (non-shareable financial problem), rationalization and opportunity to commit the trust violation must be present to breach trust and conduct fraud. Over the years, Cressey's hypothesis becomes a model and is formally known as fraud triangle and is presented in Figure 2:

Committing fraud is usually motivated by the need to meet personal, social, and economic needs. A fraud triangle is a framework widely used to explain why fraud occurs and how fraud is enabled. An individual who commits fraud follows a triangular pattern i.e. there is a pressure that needs to be met, there will be an opportunity to meet the need by means of illegal means, and there is a rationale for the fraud. FA can utilize the fraud triangle to identify any perpetrator before fraud is committed (Ozili, 2020).

Fraud triangle theory provides the understanding of why fraudsters commit fraud (Singleton & Singleton, 2010; ACFE, 2020; AICPA, 2013; Lou & Wang, 2009; Torpey, Walden & Sherrod, 2011). Also, in accordance with Singleton and Singleton (2010) and Leonard (2010) for any anti-fraud profession, no theory has been more successful and useful other than Cressey's triangle as it provides ways to prevent, detect and mitigate fraud and its related risk. Fraud triangle revolves around the motive, opportunity and rationalization of a person who commits fraud. Understanding and adopting fraud triangle theory will assist in developing anti-fraud control and measures such as fraud risk assessment (Abdullahi & Mansor, 2015). Fraud triangle theory defines the reasons behind these individuals to commit fraud. Three constituents of fraud triangle theory are explained below:

Pressure

Pressure can be defined as incentive or motivation. It is related to the fraudster's personal life which generates need beyond a person's reach and motivates him to commit fraud. Mostly pressure to commit fraud is linked towards the financial aspect but there could be other aspects as well such as political and

Figure 2. Fraud triangle
Source*: Kassem and Higson (2012)*

social survival within the organization (Singleton & Singleton, 2010). Employees receive irrelevant targets and bonus incentives coupled with personal needs creates pressure to commit fraud. In accordance with Leonard (2010), this is one the reasons behind financial statement fraud where individuals try to manipulate financial statements by erroneous transactions. FA with its skills and knowledge can either maintain profiling or by personal observation can identify the fraudster and can mitigate its impact over organization. FA plays a major role in identifying such employees or personnel and FA can create control barriers to mitigate any such fraud.

Rationalization

Rationalization can be defined as fraud committed with an intention which fraudster believes is his right (Joseph, 2016). Such rationalization is available in demoralized employees (Singleton & Singleton, 2010). There are many examples mentioned by many scholars however they all point at the same situation that, fraud is committed with self-believe reason which employee considers is better for himself and society (Mintchik & Riley, 2019).

FA cannot account for such behavior but as it is one of the reasons of fraud, therefore controls should be built upon along with level of risk, its likely hood and impact on organization. FA can highlight all the areas where fraud can occur and can also perceive its intensity (Abdullahi & Mansor 2015). As mentioned by Skousen, Smith and Wright (2009), FA can assist organizations in developing control mechanisms to identify the fraud which supports rationalization effect (Mintchik & Riley, 2019).

Opportunity

Fraudster should possess motivation, rationalization and opportunity to commit fraud (Skousen, Smith & Wright, 2009). As pointed out by Abdullahi and Mansor (2015) and Singleton and Singleton (2010), not all employees in organization has the opportunity to commit fraud, thus it can be curtailed down to few personnel that can dominate the system or bypass internal controls. In accordance with COSO (2013) and Leonard (2010) opportunity is only available when there are weak internal controls. Such control lapse can be strengthened and reinforced via fraud risk assessment and only with the assistance of FA.

All three factors of fraud triangle theory are interrelated. Loose control when coupled with motive increases the chances of fraud. Similarly, fraud chances are increased when motive and rationalization are combined. FA is an activity which can be available to identify and mitigate all possible scenarios. FA is best positioned to explore and implement controls keeping aligned with fraud triangle theory (Skousen, Smith & Wright, 2009).

Forensic Accounting Theory

Forensic accounting may become irrelevant and disconnected if there is no theory to explain observed practices. In order to change the mindset of organizations about forensic accounting, a theory relating to forensic accounting is needed.

According to forensic accounting theory, decisions made at the beginning, during, or at the end of an investigation affect how forensic detection methods and techniques are chosen, as well as how forensic findings are interpreted. This theory suggests that forensic investigators use a combination of accounting and non-accounting tools to detect fraud. According to forensic accounting theory, the choice of forensic detection methods depends largely on the forensic investigator's experience, skills, knowledge, as well as the accounting and non-accounting considerations made at the outset, during, or at the end of the fraud investigation process (Ozili, 2020).

Forensic accounting theory utilises materiality hypothesis, ability signalling hypothesis, bonus contract hypothesis, anonymity hypothesis and collapse avoidance hypothesis (Ozili, 2020). These hypotheses are explained below: For this conceptual paper, the authors are emphasising the point that FA can be hired as governance management for organization; however, forensic accounting theory's bonus contract hypothesis can somehow be linked as even FA is the hired employee of organization but additional incentive can be provided for better performance.

Materiality Hypothesis

Materiality hypothesis defines that FA utilizes forensic detection methods to identify whether the amount reported is material or not. This is very necessary as the whistle-blower or anyone who identified the fraud could understate or overstate the amount of fraud. In order to eliminate this assumption forensic accountant utilizes its own detection methods and identify the reported fraud amount is material or immaterial (Ozili, 2020). This decision will lead to further evaluations and testing and will also define the future mode of operation i.e. proceedings need to be reported to court or matter can be solved within the organization.

Ability Signaling Hypothesis

According to the ability signalling hypothesis, forensic investigators will use sophisticated forensic detection methods to demonstrate their superior ability to perform forensic accounting and uncover unresolved issues. Forensic investigators are under pressure to prove their worth when people don't trust investigators or the integrity of their findings. These environments will give investigators strong incentives to use sophisticated techniques to demonstrate their worth and to prove their superior ability to outsiders. Accounting fraud can be revealed by forensic investigators using their knowledge of state-of-the-art FA techniques, their expertise in accounting practice, and their professional experience in the application of accounting standards. As a result of using such sophisticated methods, forensic investigators stand out from their peers and competitors in the crime detection and prevention industry, and they are able to increase their credibility and reputation in the field (Ozili, 2020).

Bonus Contract Hypothesis

Bonus contract hypothesis states that forensic investigators with bonus contracts have a higher likelihood of choosing appropriate forensic detection methods that will uncover unresolved issues, particularly those related to financial crime. In this scenario the client and forensic investigator will both benefit as client will not have to pay if the fraud is not detected; whereas, forensic investigator will make sure that he utilizes all FA techniques to uncover the fraud (Ozili, 2020).

Anonymity Hypothesis

In light of the anonymity hypothesis, when investigators' personal safety is threatened in a forensic investigation, it is in their best interests to use forensic detection methods that obscure their identities, even if this decreases the possibility of solving the case. To adopt this method, questionnaires, text messages, letters, and audio interviews can be conducted. Methods such as these can be particularly useful when investigating financial crimes and fraudulent misstatements committed by criminal gangs, drug cartels, and other groups. The anonymity hypothesis argues that the investigator's safety comes before his need to solve the case. It is a reasonable argument given the long history of associates of fraudsters who have attacked or murdered whistleblowers and investigators (Ozili, 2020).

Collapse Avoidance Hypothesis

Collapse avoidance hypothesis states that forensic investigators have a vested interest in assuring and reassuring the management of the firm that the results of the investigation will only lead to correction of wrongdoing, not company closure. The conclusion from a forensic investigation should avoid implying that the accused firm should be wound up because of their actions as this is the decision of the authorities/ court who can utilize the FA report to form their judgement. It is for this reason that the consequences of committing fraud have both a legal penalty component and a corrective component, and the firm (or individual) involved must maintain a going concern in order to learn how to act ethically in the future (Ozili, 2020).

DISCUSSION AND RECOMMENDATIONS

There is no sector or country that is safe from fraud or fraudulent activities. Despite many ordinances, authorities and codes, fraud still persists. Fraud is increasing every year, and fraudsters are emerging from a wide range of organizational functions. Organizational failure is primarily due to fraud, which raises concerns regarding their ability to continue in business.

As discussed earlier, external and internal auditors both denied the responsibility towards fraud detection, and it is made mandatory by their standards that fraud detection expert services be used in case of fraud. Unfortunately, the organization has already suffered a loss and a fraud expert has been consulted after the damage has already been done. The presence of fraud risk and its related controls in such a situation raises the concept of having another activity available in an organization. That activity is forensic accounting (FA).

It is a standard practice in many organizations and corporate governance codes of many nations to include internal audit as a means of enhancing controls and ensuring compliance. In a similar way, FA can also be part of organizational management and contribute to developing controls, preventing and detecting fraud. FA has been invited several times in the past, across many organizations, to identify fraud and the reasons for it. These frauds could have been prevented if FA had been working as organizational management and not working as out-side/ third party consultant who is invited on the basis of as and when required. FA with its skills, mindset and with highlighted red flags can devise control mechanisms that can not only prevent the fraud but can also enhance the governance culture of the organization.

FUTURE RESEARCH DIRECTIONS

This conceptual paper can be converted to empirical research by identifying the actual need of FA within organizations. Study can be conducted in public listed companies and can also be compared among developed and developing nations.

It may also be possible for future research to consider the education aspect towards FA and research can be conducted on the higher educational institutions. This research may provide insight as to the availability of knowledge among academicians and importance provided by the higher education institutes towards education in FA.

CONCLUSION

This study is to explore how FA can be incorporated into organizational management and work towards enhancing governance and risk management. Several literatures have highlighted the issue of corporate frauds, fraud detection methods, and corporate governance failures. Literature found focuses on FA skills, FA traits, fraud detection techniques, managing corporate governance, as well as FA definitions. However, researchers were able to find limited studies to investigate FA as a preventive and detective constituent for organizations, thus making this paper unique.

FA plays a unique role in achieving a fraud-free environment. Therefore, this indicates that FA must be used in a manner that identifies and optimizes its properties to achieve business goals and eliminate fraud risk. Innovativeness, creativity, skills, and knowledge of FA are potential assets for excellent business operations, well-controlled policies, and eventually a positive impact on profitability, business sustainability, and integrity.

This paper distinguishes itself by incorporating a preventive and detective approach to strengthen organizational operations that extends previous studies on FA. Moreover, utilization of forensic accounting theory for the preventive and detective role is adopted for the first time. This conceptual study is expected to contribute new insights and perspectives on FA that have not been explored before. It should offer many opportunities for future researchers to investigate FA from a variety of perspectives. Additionally, this conceptual paper anticipates that it will be followed by an empirical phase. For regulators, executive management, and standard setting bodies, this paper can be beneficial for integrating FA into the regular operations of organizations.

REFERENCES

Abdullahi, R., & Mansor, N. (2015). Forensic Accounting and Fraud Risk Factors: The Influence of Fraud Diamond Theory. *European Journal of Business and Management, 7*(28).

AICPA. (2013). *Generally Accepted Accounting Standards*. AICPA.

Alshurafat, H., Al Shbail, M., & Mansour, E. (2021). Strengths and weaknesses of forensic accounting: an implication on the socio-economic development. *Journal of Business and Socio-economic Development, 1*(2).

Association, A. B. (2021). *How to Use Internal and External Data to Predict Emerging Risks and Opportunities*. 360 Factors.

Auditors, T. I. (2019). *Fraud and internal audit; Assurance Over Fraud Controls Fundamental to Success*. The Institute of Internal Auditors.

Bearu, E. (2021, Oct 30). Retrieved from Indian Bank reports frauds of over Rs 266 crore in three accounts to RBI: https://economictimes.indiatimes.com/industry/banking/finance/banking/indian-bank-reports-frauds-of-over-rs-266-crore-in-three-accounts-to-rbi/articleshow/87402032.cms

Browning, J. (2021, July 22). Retrieved from EY Accused of Actively Concealing NMC Health Audit Fraud From Investors: https://www.bloomberg.com/news/articles/2021-07-22/ey-accused-of-actively-concealing-nmc-audit-fraud-from-investors

Comer, M. (2016). *Corporate Fraud*. Taylor & Francis.

COSO. (2013). *Enterprise Risk Management: Aliging risk with strategy performance*. Committee of Sponsoring Organizations of the Treadway Commissions.

Dada, O. S., Owolabi, A. S., & Okwu, A. T. (2013). Forensic Accounting a Panacea to Alleviation of Fraudulent Practices in Nigeria. *Int. J. Buss. Mgt. Eco. Res., 4*(5).

Dutta, A. K. (2021). Role Of Forensic Audit As A Tool For Fraud Detection And Prevention In Micro Finance Industry. *The Management Accountant, 56*(10).

Eliezer, O., & Emmanuel, B. (2015). Relevance of Forensic Accounting in the Detection and Prevention *Historical Research Letter, 23*.

Enofe, A., Ekpulu, G., & Ajala, T. O. (2015). Forensic Accounting and Corporate Crime Mitigation. *European Scientific Journal, 11*(7).

Fadilah, S., Maemunah, M., Lim, T. N., & Sundary, R. I. (2019). Forensic accounting: fraud detection skills for external auditors. *Polish Journal of Management Studies*, 168-180.

Hegazy, S., Sangster, A., & Kotb, A. (2017). Mapping Forensic Accounting in the UK. *Journal of International Accounting, Auditing and Taxation, 28.*

IASB. (2009). International Standard On Auditing 240; The Auditor'S Responsibilities Relating To Fraud. In *An Audit of Financial Statements*. IFAC.

IFAC. (2009, Dec 15). Retrieved from International standard on auditing 240; the auditor's responsibilities relating to fraud in an audit of financial statements: https://www.ifac.org/system/files/downloads/a012-2010-iaasb-handbook-isa-240.pdf

Isa, A. A. (2017). The Study of the Effects of Forensic Accounting and Fraud Detection/Prevention for Financial Management Performance in Public Sector in Nigeria: A way forward. *World Wide Journal of Multidisciplinary Research and Development, 3*(12), 197–202.

Joseph, J. (2016). *The Traits and Characteristics of Elite Forensic Accountants.* Retrieved from https://www.accountingweb.com/community/blogs/jessica-joseph/the-traits-and-characteristics-of-elite-forensic-accountants

Justice, D. o. (2021, Nov 4). Retrieved from South Florida Addiction Treatment Facility Operators Convicted in $112 Million Addiction Treatment Fraud Scheme: https://www.justice.gov/opa/pr/south-florida-addiction-treatment-facility-operators-convicted-112-million-addiction

Kassem, R., & Higson, A. (2012). The new fraud triangle model. *Journal of Emerging Trends in Economics and Management Sciences, 3*(3).

Kozlov, M., Hurtado-Guarin, J., & Trakulhoon, P. (2018, Aug 20). *Financial crime has been around as long as corporations have existed. But as perpetrators embrace new scams, regulators are turning to new tools, including machine learning, to nab them.* Retrieved from weareworld quant: https://www.weareworldquant.com/en/thought-leadership/forensic-accounting-detecting-financial-fraud/

Leonard, W. V. (2010). *The Fraud Audit: Responding to the Risk of Fraud in Core Business Systems.* John Wiley and Sons Ltd.

Lou, Y., & Wang, L. (2009). Fraud Risk Factor Of The Fraud Triangle Assessing The Likelihood Of Fraudulent Financial Reporting. *Journal of Business & Economics Research, 7*(2).

Mintchik, N., & Riley, J. (2019, March). Rationalizing Fraud: How Thinking Like a Crook Can Help Prevent Fraud. *The CPA Journal.*

Moid, S. (2016). Application of Forensic Accounting to Investigate Scams in India. *MITS International Journal of Business Research, 3*(1).

Neate, R. (2021, Nov 4). Retrieved from Over £5.5bn of Covid support funds lost to fraud or error: https://www.theguardian.com/world/2021/nov/04/over-55bn-of-covid-support-funds-lost-to-or-error

Nicodemus, A. (2020, Dec 18). Retrieved from EY member firm fined $1.5M for failure to uncover $3B homebuilding fraud: https://www.complianceweek.com/regulatory-enforcement/ey-member-firm-fined-15m-for-failure-to-uncover-3b-homebuilding-fraud/29856.article

OECD. (2014, April 1). *Risk Management and Corporate Governance.* Retrieved from https://www.oecd-ilibrary.org/governance/risk-management-and-corporate-governance_9789264208636-en

Oh, E. (2017, Mar 1). *Against a backdrop of tough economic conditions and growing corporate governance, demand for forensic accountants is increasing, and Malaysia is leading the way.* Retrieved from https://www.accaglobal.com/in/en/member/member/accounting-business/2017/03/practice/forensic-accountants.html

Ohri, R. (2020, Oct 8). Retrieved from BR Shetty seeks probe by CBI, ED into $6 billion 'fraud' in his companies: https://economictimes.indiatimes.com/nri/nris-in-news/br-shetty-seeks-probe-by-cbi-ed-into-6-billion-fraud-in-his-companies/articleshow/78541666.cms?from=mdr

Okoye, E., & Gbegi, D. (2013). Forensic Accounting: A Tool for Fraud Detection and Prevention in the Public Sector (A Study of Selected Ministries in Kogi State). *International Journal of Academic Research in Business and Social Sciences, 3*(3).

Ozili, P. K. (2020). Forensic Accounting Theory. *Finance, Insurance and Risk Management Theory and Practices, 1.*

PWC. (2020). *Fighting fraud: A never-ending battle PwC's Global Economic Crime and Fraud Survey.* Price Water House Coopers.

Razak, A. (2016, January 31). Retrieved from CA Srilanka to Instill Forensic Thinking: https://nation.lk/online/2016/01/30/ca-sri-lanka-to-instill-forensic-thinking.html

Rehman, A., & Hashim, F. (2018). Forensic accounting on corporate governance maturity mediated by internal audit: A conceptual overview. *Forensic Sci Sem, 8*(1).

Rehman, A., & Hashim, F. (2018a). Literature Review: Preventive Role Of Forensic Accounting And Corporate Governance Maturity. *Journal of Governance and Integrity, 1*(2).

Singleton, T., & Singleton, A. (2010). *Fraud Auditing and Forensic Accounting* (4th ed.). John Wiley & Sons. doi:10.1002/9781118269183

Skousen, C., Smith, K., & Wright, C. (2009). Detecting and predicting financial statement fraud: The effectiveness of the fraud triangle and SAS No. 99. In Corporate Governance and Firm Performance (Advances in Financial Economics, Vol. 13) (pp. 53-81). Emerald.

Team, M. D. (2011, April 6). Retrieved from SEC slaps $17.5 million in fines on Satyam, PwC in fraud case: https://www.moneylife.in/article/sec-slaps-175-million-in-fines-on-satyam-pwc-in-fraud-case/15348.html

Telegraph. (2006, Oct 11). *Chancellor throws his forensic accountants into the fray.* Retrieved from https://www.telegraph.co.uk/news/uknews/1531108/Chancellor-throws-his-forensic-accountants-into-the-fray.html

Torpey, D., Walden, V., & Sherrod, M. (2011). *Viewpoint - Breaking the status quo: Moving beyond traditional e-mail review*. Fraud Watch by EY.

Weitz, M. (2020). *Fraud Risk Management*. Internal Audit Foundation.

Zagera, L., Malis, S. S., & Novak, A. (2016). The Role and Responsibility of Auditors in Prevention and Detection of Fraudulent Financial Reporting. In *3rd Global Conference On Business, Economics, Management And Tourism*, (pp. 693-700). Elsevier. 10.1016/S2212-5671(16)30291-X

KEY TERMS AND DEFINITIONS

Detective Role of Forensic Accounting: Role that is responsible for the detection of fraud, money trail, perpetrator and also recommendations to mitigate future fraud risk.

External Audit: Activity which is outside organization and responsible to provide opinion on organization's financial performance. External audit provide opinion based on the compliance with accounting standards and relevant laws.

Forensic Accounting: Combination of accounting and auditing profession with specialized skill of fraud prevention and fraud detection.

Fraud: Fraud is intentional act conducted by individual or organization to obtain financial gain. Fraud is conducted on the organization or by the organization.

Fraud Risk: Risk of fraud which can be existent within organization's operations.

Internal Audit: Activity which is available within the organization and is responsible to improve and add value towards the organization's governance, risk, and control mechanism. Considered as independent activity and reports on organization's operations and financial statements.

Preventive Role of Forensic Accounting: Role which is responsible for devising controls mechanism to prevent fraud.

Risk: Event which can deviate the organization in achieving its objectives.

Chapter 15
Effect of Financial Reporting Fraud on the Performance of Firms in the Nigerian Exchange Group

Ifeoluwapo Adebimpe Oyewobi
Bingham University, Nigeria

ABSTRACT

Financial reporting fraud affects corporate organizations as stakeholders express lack of self-confidence in financial reports. The chapter assessed the effect of financial reporting fraud, improper expense recognition and fictitious revenue on the performance of firms in the Nigerian Exchange Group return on assets (ROA). Secondary data were collected from the firm annual accounts. Correlation and regression analysis were employed. The results revealed that improper expense recognition has a negative significant relationship with ROA. Also, fictitious revenue reflected a positive but insignificant relationship with ROA. The chapter concluded that financial reporting fraud somewhat affects the performance of firms as supported by a positive relationship reflected by fictitious revenue and negative relationships shown by improper expense recognition. The chapter recommended that financial reporting fraud needs to be investigated to reveal the fraud that affects the performance of firms to aid better and easier forensic accounting investigation.

INTRODUCTION

The capital market is central to the fiscal strength, progression and development of any economy including Nigeria. The capital market trading institution in Nigeria is the Nigerian Stock Exchange (NSE). The Nigerian Stock Exchange (NGX), formally Nigerian Exchange Group, is a foremost integrated market in Africa that services the continent's biggest economy. The financial report provided by the firms in the capital market should be reasonable, efficient and clear and must be free from any misleading information (Robert, 2020). Kanu and Okorafor (2013) stated that financial reports are thought to be tools in

DOI: 10.4018/978-1-7998-8754-6.ch015

which users can rely when making investment decisions. However, many firms have suffered a lot in Nigeria nowadays from fraud and untrue deeds in the capital market.

The habitual nature of fraud in firms has posed severe threat to the financial performance of firms and the survival of market in general (Agbaje & Oloruntoba (2018). Fraud methods can be done in many ways which include the reporting of fictitious income, cooking different period accounting information, omission of debts and expenses that is incorrect expense recognition, incorrect reporting, and incorrect examination of the value of properties or inappropriate valuation of asset (Everette, 2012 & Arthur, 2014). The faith of financial reporting on fraud circumstances is brought to questioning by stakeholders (Robert, 2020). Notably, Robert (2020) and Sudaryono (2021) reported that the fictitious revenue, the incorrect asset valuation and the improper recognition of expense constitute major fraud methods in corporate organizations.

Arthur (2014) and Agbaje and Oloruntoba (2018) have opined that the dependence of stakeholders on the information provided in financial report continues to constitute one of the greatest global challenges for businesses as it has always been difficult to stop fraud methods when it takes place. Thus, there is the need to know the direct and indirect link of fraud methods on the performance of businesses in the Nigerian Exchange Group. Generally, the chapter assessed the effect of fraud methods on the performance of firms in the Nigerian Exchange Group. The specific objectives of the chapter were:

1. To examine the effect of improper expense recognition on the performance of firms in the Nigerian Exchange Group.
2. To assess the effect of fictitious revenue on the performance of firms in the Nigerian Exchange Group.

BACKGROUND

Fraud methods is the action or accomplishment intended to deceive others. Fraud is a deliberate deceiving act intended to offer the committer with an illicit gain or to refute a right to a prey. Commonly, the frequent fraud that occur in financial reporting have been observed as the fictitious revenue, the incorrect valuation of asset and the improper recognition of expense (Robert, 2020 & Sudaryono, 2021). Bulk of studies on fraud methods such as Ozondu, Okoye, and Adeniyi (2019), Ibrahim, Mohammed, and Fatima, (2014), AbdulRaheem, Isiaka, and Muhammed, (2012) and Agbaje, and Oloruntoba, (2018) have always been on a particular sector of the economy. The stakeholders want their firms to be accountable, fair and transparent in their everyday activities so as to achieve for operational success (Reurink, 2018). The chapter was specifically inspired by the reason that investors have no self- confidence in the capital market, and also because of the insolvency of large firms which has been evidenced as the result of fraud methods. The chapter therefore sought to examine the effect of fraud methods on the performance of firms in Nigerian Exchange Group using the most capitalized firms, from different sectors, who are the major market players. The chapter investigated the relationship between fraud methods (represented by improper revenue recognition and fictitious revenue variables) and firms' Return on Assets (ROA) taken as a substitution to measure firm performance. The chapter thus addressed the issue relating to the pertinent question of to what extent does fraud methods affect the performance of firms in the Nigerian Exchange Group.

Emphases have not been made to assess fraud methods from different sectors. The chapter embraced Return on Asset (ROA) as proxy for performance. Ogunleye (2009) trusts that, the variable, the Return on Asset (ROA) may establish a good measure of performance of firms listed on the capital market. Undeniably, the chapter exposed the information gap to understand the effect of fraud methods on the performance of firms.

MAIN FOCUS OF THE CHAPTER

In order to establish the understanding of the importance of the chapter, the chapter review related concepts such as financial reporting, fraud methods, improper expense recognition, fictitious revenue, performance measurement and return on asset.

Financial Reporting

Financial reporting is a concept which is defined as the use of financial statements to reveal a firms' financial information and its performance over a particular time, typically on an annual or quarterly basis (Agbaje & Oloruntoba, 2018). According to Sadgali, Sael, and Benabbou, (2019), financial reporting is a standard of accounting practice. Financial reporting can simply be explained as the understanding of how much money a firm has, where the money is coming from, and where the firms' money needs to go. Management is engaged in making informative corporate decisions based on facts that are given by of the firms' business position therefore, financial reporting is important. Normally, prospective investors and banks use the firms' financial report on determining if the investor would want to invest or loan the firm some money.

Fraud Methods

Recently, firms have faced the rising risk of fraud in their diverse and numerous ways. Fraud methods is a concept under forensic accounting. Fraud methods is the deliberate usage of unlawful practices whose motive is to earn monetary advantage (Anan, Hayden, Joshi, Nadeau, & Steitz, 2018). Fraud methods can also be described as the use of someone's job aimed at own enhancement over the thoughtful misappropriation or misuse of the engaging administration's incomes or assets. Fraud methods is any deliberate action of divesting another of belongings or money by sly, trickery or partial acts (Anan, Hayden, Joshi, Nadeau, & Steitz, 2018).

Improper Expense Recognition

Expenses are the outflow of money or any other important items from one person to the other, from firm to firm or from firm to another entity (Egbunike, & Igbinovia, 2018). The disbursement of money is more important to buyers. Theoretically, expenses are said as occasion where a liability is incurred or an asset is used up. In the field of accounting, expenses decrease equity (Reurink, 2018). The term expenses can be referred to as fall in fiscal aids during a particular accounting year (Robert, 2020). In accounting, an important issue is when expenditure is to be recognized. The amount recognized when a business inures expenditure is recorded in its financial records. These expenses will balance the income that is earned in the business which is invariably used to compute the profit of the business. The expenditure and income timing are so essential. According to Everette, (2012) and Arthur (2014) a business firm may abstain from recognizing expenditure which can exaggeratedly make its business appear more lucrative that invariable leads to fraudulent reporting, as a result of improper expense recognition being applied. Improper recognition of expenses is the main type of fraud in accounting. Around 60percent of the actions of Securities and Exchange Commission's (SEC) are on fraud exposed by informers. Such actions involve firms increasing expense identified so as to meet up with earnings benchmark or defer the earnings if target have been met (Robert, 2020). Firms often indulge in portraying healthy financial position as they are always under pressure to show the investors that the firm is growing. Such obligation definitely leads many firms to involve in financial fraud which alter the firms' financial outcomes.

Fictitious Revenue

There are motivations to the misrepresentation of financial reports of firms. One of the deliberate motivations to financial reports is the situational pressures that are bonus calculated based on the performance of the firm (Purnamasari, & Amaliah, 2015). According to Sudaryono (2021), bonus can be manipulated to generate larger bonus. Another motivation is the motive to obtain financial pressure. To achieve this, financial report can be manipulated by either overstating firms' assets or understating the firms' liabilities, so that the firm can appear more solvent. Firms can also falsify on revenue in different ways such as revenue including non-existing sales from non-existing customers. False revenue may include recording of full amount of conditional sales as revenue for particular period Sudaryono (2021). Auditors have always emphasis on cash flows in their attempt to pick fictitious revenues. Also, auditors have always focused on expensive growth and large number of sales to new customer, to expose fictitious revenues. Therefore, fraud will continue to re-occur in financial report every year. Revenue is deliberately increased in some particular year through inventory scheme. This makes the following year profit of the firm to be smaller. If the firm continues the fraudulent act, it will in a long run have negative effect on financial reporting.

It is noticed that fictitious revenue is a major fraudulent practice done in financial reporting. The major cause of fraud methods can be traced to the need for management to meet up with stakeholders numerous expectations. Another reason for fraud methods arises from failure of external auditors such as covering of numerous management mess (Okoye & Alao, 2008). Thus, using profit as basis for measuring performance may not be reliable since variables used to determine the profit are manipulated. Such variables include inventory, asset. Profitability shows the performance level of any organization. If the variables used in determining profitability are manipulated, it may have negative effect on financial reporting (Abgaje & Dare, 2018).

Performance Measurement

Performance is the capability of a firm to make maximum commercial profitability from the material and human resources at its disposal. Based on literature, there are different measures of firm performance such as hard measures which are return on assets, market share, and sales and 'soft' measures. The soft measure includes customer satisfaction, invention, and learning (Gentry & Shen, 2010; Subramanian & Nilakanta, 1996). Also, performance can be measured either objectively or subjectively (Dess & Robinson, 1984). The objective measures of performance rely on financial data while subjective measures of performance depend on managerial assessments. The objective criteria consist of sales growth, return on assets (ROA), return on sales (ROS), and stock price performance (Brews & Tucci, 2004). Subjective measurements comprise ranking by respondent with regards to firm's overall industry, view of current profitability of firms, and quality and social responses (Brews & Hunt, 1999). However, the importance of the objective measurement cannot be ignored because it allows analysis repetition.

Return on Asset

The Return on Assets (ROA) measure is seen as the income of a firm that is gotten from the firms' incomes and assets. The information on return on asset is meaningful to the firm stakeholders. The information represents the effective use of firms' money and assets to make a profit. The Return on Assets is always denoted as the percentage of firms' disposable income and the firm total average assets. The profit measurement such as ROA establishes the efficiency of operation in firms. Growth of sales measures reveal how vulnerable is a firm to new opportunities, in prevailing markets. Return on Asset is the financial measurement adopted in the chapter as performance measure because it provides the most available and fit data. Return on Asset (ROA) measures reveal how much profit a firm (corporation's profitability) generates from its assets (Khatab, Masood, Zaman, Saleem, & Saeed, 2011). Return on Asset is measured by dividing profit after tax by the total assets of a firm.

Nigerian Exchange Group

The Nigerian Exchange Group (NGX) was founded in 1961 in Lagos and started operations formally in 1961 with 19 securities listed on Nigerian Exchange Group for trading (Egbunike, & Igbinovia, 2018). In November 2019, the Nigerian Exchange Group has a total of 161 listed companies. To encourage foreign investment into Nigeria, the government eliminated regulation stopping the movement of foreign capital into the country. This has allowed foreign dealers to register as brokers on the Nigerian Exchange group, and investors are free to invest (Dada, Owolabi, & Okwu, 2013). In a bid to promote transparency and trust in the capital market, the Nigerian Exchange group reconstituted the Investors' Protection Fund in 2012. The Fund is mandated to compensate investors who suffer pecuniary loss arising from the cancellation of the registration of a dealing member; bankruptcy of a dealing member; or defalcation done by a dealing member or any of its directors, or other representatives.

The effect of fictitious revenue and improper expense recognition on market performance is theoretically complex and empirically ambiguous. There have been few different studies examining the effects of fraud methods on performance. A research by Abiloro, Adejuwon, and Folorunso (2020) investigated the effect of inventory fraud reporting on financial performance. Abiloro, Adejuwon, and Folorunso took into consideration some key elements of inventory fraud which include entrusted inventory. Their study exposed that when closing inventory is misstated in the current year it is taken to the next year and it has a negative effect on the next year profit. Therefore, wrong value of inventory is given. It thereby presents a financial reporting that is bias. This is because the financial report is not showing the true state of the firms' businesses. The chapter recommended that there should be frequent changing of staff that handle inventory. Robust internal control system, continuous physical stock taking, electronic surveillance installation and other upright fraud management system on inventory must also be put in place.

Also, Ozondu, Okoye, and Adeniyi (2019) studied corporate fraud and banks financial performance in South-East Nigeria. Ozondu, Okoye, and Adeniyi evaluated the relationship between the two variables.

The chapter used primary data which was taken from institutions financial statement under sample. Fifteen banks were assessed in Nigeria. Emphasis was placed on variables as fraud corrective control (FCCT), fraud occurrence (FRUC), fraud detection (FDTC) and fraud prevention (FPRV), alongside measure of financial performance which was captured by discretionary accruals. It was discovered that corporate fraud has no significant influence on corporate reporting of banks in the nation. And therefore their activities do not influence the earnings quality as displayed in the corporate reporting of the firm especially in banks. It was thus recommended in this light that due to the irrelevance of the corporate fraud on discretionary accruals, banks and organizations at large should prune the size of active auditors and shouldn't compensate quality with quantity.

Again, Odunayo (2014) carried out a study on fraudulent financial reporting: The Nigerian experience. Odunayo used the population consisting of 212 firms that are registered in 2007. The main objective of the chapter was to assess the link between the frail internal control device and the monetary scam communication. The chapter recommended that the internal control arrangement must be reinforced.

Further, Ogbonna and Ebimobowei (2012) observed the effect of ethical funding standard on monetary reports value in the Nigerian economy banking system. Data was analysed in the chapter using the econometrics models, Granger Causality Estimation ADF, and OLS. The chapter showed that standard on ethical funding have significant effect on banking sector monetary reporting in Nigeria. It was recommended in the chapter that financial specialists should abide by the ethics and instructions of the profession.

Moreover, Dabor and Adeyemi (2009) considered the study public organization and monetary report integrity in Nigeria. Both primary and secondary data were used. The secondary data were extracted from the Nigerian quoted firms. It was established in the chapter that the board of directors enhance financial report credibility. Also, the strict compliance with corporate governance again will improve trustworthiness of financial reporting.

Ikpefan (2006) worked on the upsurge of fictitious revenue and its effect on the monetary sector; it was shown in the chapter that fictitious revenue has been increasing in recent time prominent to a substantial increase in financial scam. It was exposed in the chapter that monetary organizations which had declined to accept essential rule and control system that is good which turn to frequent circumstances of financial malpractices. The chapter therefore recommended that financial institutions management should strengthen the operating process by engaging professionals that can give people the confidence on the works of financial sector.

In order to better understand the chapter the author reviewed related theories. The basic theoretical structures of fraud methods include the fraud triangle theory, the routine activities theory, and the legitimacy theory. Thus, the theory of legitimacy forms the theoretical core underpinning the chapter.

Fraud Triangle Theory

As an idea to examine the reasons for fraud, the Fraud Triangle Theory (FTT) was developed. The theory was first coined by Cressey (1950). In 1950, Cressy was bothered with the inquiry of why people oblige fiscal crime. This led to him examining 250 convicts in a period of five months. Fraud Triangle Theory refers to the three elements existing in every state of fraud as perceived pressure, opportunity, and rationalization. Cressey's reveal that all the three components must be present before a cheat could disrupt confidence in an organization (Cressey 2008).

Routine Activities Theory

The Routine Activities Theory observes the ecological setting that misconducts happen (Cohen & Felson, 2014). The theory states that the people we associate with influence the tendency and spread of felonious act. Another which influences the distribution of illegal act is the places people travel to and the events people engage in. Routine activities theory is based on the connections of interested criminals, appropriate goals, as well the lack of clever guards. Under routine activities theory, the crimes are not always unavoidable. Routine activities theory provides propositions on the likelihood of wrong conduct instead of creation assertions about when fraudulent practice may occur. The theory contends that the probability of crime upsurges or reductions is centred on the existence of the three elements.

Successful misconduct or crime entails a crook driven to commit the illegal act and clever to take the drive (Cohen & Felson, 2014). This means ordinary intension is insufficient to take up for a crime. An interested criminal can do his wishes. Routine activities theory assumes that motivation to criminals is constant but the theory does not explain the reason a criminal is motivated to commit a crime. Routine activities theory shows society members can normally be interested to commit crime and they can do it when there are motivations.

Legitimacy Theory

This theory emphasises the way to achieve the firms' projects as to the acknowledgment of the organizations goals. The theory of Legitimacy is built on the firm legacy which links standard and ethics with contemporary beliefs (Burlea & Popa, 2013). The general insight which shows activities are good and suitable in a generally built system of standards and ethics is defined as legitimacy (Suchman, 1995). Van der Laan, Van Ees and Van Witteloostuijn (2008) noted that positive connection among the size of the organization and the organization's drive for legitimacy is needed. Legitimacy theory points on the belief that a firm is influences by the society in which it works, and on the other hand the firm is also socially influenced (Lada & Kozarkiewicz, 2014). The approval to take action means legitimizing from the perspective of a socially responsible firm and it is observed as taking a reasonable influence on internal and external environment. This support the legality to be affected by the properties that the organization possesses and those funds affected indirectly.

According to Burlea and Popa, (2013), legitimacy theory is related to the stakeholder theory, the management theory, and the institutional theory. Legitimacy theory is adopted by several accounting and scientific researches. Legitimacy theory has contributed to the reasons that make management involve in environmental and social events disclosure (O'Donovan, 2002 & Brown & Deegan, 1998). Burlea and Popa, (2013) opined that legitimacy theory is an unused theory that needs further refinements. Very little recent scientific researchers have used legitimacy theory especially relating to management accounting.

SOLUTIONS AND RECOMMENDATIONS

The chapter employed a composite ex post facto research design drawing from previous studies in related areas. It involves the gathering of information about fraud methods and performance of firms quoted on the Nigerian Exchange Group. The population consists of 155 firms listed on the Nigerian Exchange Group. Firms that control above 80% of the Nigerian Exchange Group were selected. A shift in the firms share value constitutes significant effect on the Market (Sudaryono, 2021). Samples of 10 firms were selected on these benchmarks, that is, they must have wider control of the market, larger scale of operation, multinational in nature, and longer years of operation. The following firms satisfy the criteria: Dangote Cement, MTN Nigeria, Access Bank, Nigerian Breweries, BUA Cement, Nestle Nigeria, Zenith Bank, Lafarge Africa, Seplat Petroleum, Dangote Sugar.

The chapter used audited annual report data which spanned from 2011-2020 of the selected firms. The chapter used descriptive statistics to demonstration the processes of tendencies and both correlation and regression analyses were used to examine the connection among fraud methods and firms' performance. The following null hypotheses were tested:

H_{01}: Improper Expense Recognition has no significant effect on the performance of firms in the Nigerian Exchange Group.
H_{02}: Fictitious Revenue has no significant effect on the performance of firms in the Nigerian Exchange Group.

Model Specification

The chapter is anchored on the Beneish and Nichols (2012) and Kajola (2008) theories. As different fraud methods and performance proxies have been employed, the panel data regression analysis model: $PERF_{it} = \beta_0 + \beta_1 IER_{it} + ß_2 FR_{it} + e_{it}$ is thus adapted to assess the linking between fraud methods and the performance of firms in the Nigerian Exchange Group.

Where:

- PERF: represents firm Performance
- IER: represents Improper Expense Recognition
- FR: represents Fictitious Revenue

That is, the regression model for the empirical analysis is

$$PERF_{it} = \beta_0 + \beta_1 IER_{it} + ß_2 FR_{it} + e_{it} \quad (1)$$

Decision Criteria

Accept (H_0) when computed rate falls within the critical positive value of distribution table for whichever degree of freedom that will be computed with 5% significance level. Else, accept the alternative (H_1) by rejecting the null hypothesis.

Return on Asset (ROA), Operating Expense Ratio (OER) and Fictitious Revenue (FR) was presented in the descriptive statistics in table 1, for the dependent and independent variables. The standard deviation of the variables is within the range of 0.1099 to 0.4794. Return on Asset depicts the lowermost standard deviation of 0.1099 to operating expense ratio and fictitious revenue with a standard deviation of 0.1463 and 0.4794 separately. There is relative low standard deviation related with the mean, because all the variables indicate that the residual of the data that was sampled in the chapter is normally distributed.

Table 1. Descriptive statistics

Variable	Obs	Mean	Std. Dev.	Min	Max
Return on Asset (ROA)	100	0.1158	0.1099	-0.15	0.53
Operating Expense Ratio (OER)	100	0.1948	0.1463	0.03	0.72
Fictitious Revenue (FR)	100	0.35	0.4794	0	1

Source: (Stata 13 Results, 2021)

Table 2. Correlation analysis

Variable	ROA OER FR
Return on Asset (ROA)	1.0000
Operating Expense Ratio (OER)	-0.3041 1.0000
Fictitious Revenue (FR)	0.1394 -0.0602 1.0000

Source: (Stata 13 Results, 2021)

Also, table 1 shows the regular value for 0.1158 for Return on Asset. The maximum value of return on asset is 0.53 and the minimum value of return on asset is -0.15. These results mean that all the sampled firms truly have return on asset values in the period of study. Again, table 1 has shown an average value of 0.1948 for operating expense ratio. The minimum and the maximum values of operating expense ratio are 0.03 and 0.72 correspondingly. Fictitious Revenue mean value is 0.35. The Fictitious Revenue has 0 and 1 has its minimum and maximum value.

Table 2 depicts the correlation analysis results of the variables. It is observed that the independent variables are not related to the extent (greater than 0.7) to bring singularity of used data problem. The association between the explanatory variables is thus marginal and insignificant. A weak negative correlation of (-0.3041), and a weak positive correlation of -0.1394 among operating expense ratio, fictitious revenue and return on asset respectively of the firms in the period of study were also revealed. The negative coefficient indicates that operating expense ratio is related with reduction in return on asset of the sampled firms, while a rise in fictitious revenue brings a rise in return on asset.

Table 3. Variance inflation factor (VIF) test result

Variable	VIF	Tolerance (1/VIF)
Operating Expense Ratio (OER)	1.00	0.9964
Fictitious Revenue (FR)	1.00	0.9964
Mean VIF	1.00	

Source: (STATA 13 Results, 2021)

To establish the presence or otherwise of multicollinearity among the variables that are independent, the Variance Inflation Factor (VIF) test was conducted. In table 3, among the independent variables there

Table 4. Heteroskedasticity and normality test

Variable	Chi²	Prob.> chi²
Return on asset (ROA)	13.94	0.0002
Normality test		
Jarque-Bera normality test	33.66	4.9

Source: (STATA 13 Results, 2021)

was nonappearance of perfect multicollinearity. Under operating expense ratio and fictitious revenue, the VIF is less than 10 then the level of tolerance is less than 1. Also, the mean VIF of 1.00 proves the result.

Table 4 showed the results of Breusch–Pagan test, which was conducted to test for Heteroskedasticity. The test was conducted to assess whether error terms variation is stable. The result of Breusch–Pagan test showed that there is Heteroskedasticity because the probability chi square value of 0.0002 for return on asset in models one is less than 0.05. This was corrected by running a robust random outcome regression since it is revealed through the Hausman test that random outcome regression is the suitable test to be used for interpretation. Table 4 also presented the result of Jarque-Bera normality test which has 33.66 chi square and has the probability value of 4.9 that is greater than 0.05. The alternative hypothesis was therefore rejected which means the data is normally distributed.

Table 5. Hausman, Lanrangian multiplier and fixed and random regression tests.

	Model One (ROA)	
	F Sat/Chi-bar ²	Prob.> chi²
Fixed	5.20	0.0073
Random	10.86	0.0044
Hausman	1.08	0.5815
LM test	64.53	0.0000

Source: (STATA 13 Results, 2021)

Table 5 depicts the outcomes of Hausman specification test. The result presented 1.08 as the chi square value with 0.5815 as the probability value. This indicates that the suitable model to be used for the analysis is random effect regression model. To assess among the pooled OLS and random effect regression, the Breusch and Pagan Lanrangian multiplier test was run to select the suitable test to be used. The table results revealed chi bars^2 of 64.53 and conforming prob > chi bar of 0.0000. Hence, the result showed that the random effect regression makes the most appropriate method to be adopted for analysis. Thus, the null hypothesis was rejected. The results of the model were interpreted using random effect regression.

Test of Hypotheses

Table 6 above gives information on the results of the test of hypotheses. The results are interpreted in the following paragraph. The Wald Chi^2 value of 18.24 with a corresponding Prob.> Chi^{2}of 0.0001 and

Table 6. Robust random effect regression results

ROA	Coef.	Robust Std. Err.	z-value	P-value
-Cons	0.1229	0.2305	5.33	0.000
Operating Expense Ratio (OER)	-0.1176	0.4325	-2.72	0.007
Fictitious Revenue (FR)	0.4496	0.2547	1.77	0.078
R^2				0.0843

Prob>Chi^2 0.0001
Wald Chi2 18.24
Source: (STATA 13 Results, 2021)

R^2 of 0.0843 detailed the model fits to clarify the association the chapter articulated. Additionally, the connection between the variables using the z- values and p- values coefficients are described under.

Improper Expense Recognition Hypothesis

In table 6, the regression result showed negative association amid return on asset and improper expense recognition (Operating Expense Ratio) as shown by the coefficient value of -0.1176. It opened that a unit increase in improper expense recognition (proxy with Operating Expense Ratio) leads to 0.1176 unit decrease in ROA. Operating Expense Ratio (OER) with z statistics of -2.72 and a corresponding p-value of 0.007 which is less than 0.05, thus the null hypothesis was rejected. It revealed that improper expense recognition has significant effect on the performance of firms in the Nigerian Exchange Group (proxy by return on asset).

Fictitious Revenue Hypothesis

Fictitious revenue results exposed that positive association exist among fictitious revenue (FR) and return on asset (ROA) during the period of study. It is depicted by a p-value of 0.07 and coefficient value of 0.4496. It showed that a unit increase in fictitious revenue (FR) resulted to 0.4496 unit rise in return on asset. The p-value of 0.078 is greater than 0.05, thus the null hypothesis was accept which states that fictitious revenue has no significant effect on the performance of firms in the Nigerian Exchange Group.

Discussion of Findings

The regression results of the sampled firms showed no statistical significance in the case of fictitious revenue on the performance of firms in the Nigerian Exchange Group but positive link exist with ROA, and a negative significant relationship exist among improper expense recognition and ROA. The chapter findings are in agreement with Agbaje and Dare (2018) which possesses specific features of fraud methods for their results. Agbaje & Dare (2018) analysis revealed a significant association among financial reporting deception and profitability in the manufacturing industry. Similarly, the study of Agbaje and Oloruntoba (2018) supported that improper assets evaluation has a significant positive relationship on profitability. Also, there is significant positive relationship among improper expense recognition and ROA which is a proxy of profitability. The chapter established that by investigating on fraud methods, it would expose and inform on fraudulent practices that forensic investigators should give preference to during the cause of engagement. The chapter recommended that fraud methods needs to be investigated to reveal the fraud that affect the performance of corporate organizations so as to aid better and easier forensic accounting investigation. The chapter also recommended that realistic policy choices should be put in place to efficiently manage revenue recognition and reporting alongside enforcing a robust culture of adherence to internal control system in listed firms in the Nigerian Exchange Group as this will ensure effectiveness in performance management.

FUTURE RESEARCH DIRECTIONS

The chapter examined the effect of fraud methods on the performance of firms in the Nigerian Exchange Group. The chapter revealed that forensic accountants come across a number of fraud methodss in forensic accounting that affects firms' performance. It has been opened in the chapter that most previous researches on forensic accounting have been focused on manufacturing industries. Based on these exposures, the chapter suggests that future researches should be carried out in other sectors in an economy. The chapter also opined more studies on other fraud methods to bring academicians and other researchers to a consensus on the fraud methods that could affect the performance firms. This is knowledge horizon and eye opener on forensic accounting.

CONCLUSION

The chapter focused on the effect of fraud methods on the performance of firms in the Nigerian Exchange Group which was done by examining the effect of improper expense recognition and fictitious revenue on the performance of firms in the Nigeria Exchange Group. The chapter adopted a sample of ten listed firms in the Nigerian Exchange Group using their financial report spanning from 2011 to 2020. The chapter found that fraud methods somewhat affect the performance of firms in the Nigerian Exchange Group as supported by positive relationship reflected by fictitious revenue and negative relationship shown by improper expense recognition. The chapter revealed that the formality of following the regulation regarding financial reporting to deliver positive impacts on the bottom line of a firm are partly supported by the statistics of positive relationship reflected by the chapter of one of the two typical fraud methods, fictitious revenue.

REFERENCES

AbdulRaheem, A, Isiaka, S. B. & Muhammed, A. Y. (2012). Fraud and Its Implications for Bank Performance in Nigeria. *International Journal of Asian Social Science*, *2*(4), 382–387.

Abiloro, T. O., Adejuwon, A. M., & Folorunso, B. E. (2020). Inventory Fraud and Financial Reporting: A Review of Literature. *International Journal of Research and Scientific Innovation*, *7*(10).

Aburime, T. U. (2012). Impact of Corruption on Bank Profitability in Nigeria. *Symposium for Young Researcher, 15*(17), 15-17.

Agbaje, W. H., & Dare, F. (2018). Dynamic Analysis of Financial Statement Fraud on Profitability of Manufacturing Firms in Nigeria. *International Journal of Business and Management Review*, *6*(2), 65–81.

Agbaje, W. H., & Oloruntoba, S. R. (2018). An Assessment of Impact of Financial Statement Fraud on Profit Performance of Manufacturing Firm in Nigeria: A Study of Food and Beverage Firms in Nigeria. *European Journal of Business and Management, 10*(9).

Al-Baidhani, A. M. (2016). The role of audit committee in corporate governance: A descriptive study. *International Journal of Research Methodology in Social Science.*, *2*(2), 45–57.

Anan, L., Hayden, R., Joshi, K., Nadeau, M.-C., & Steitz, J. (2018). Fraud management: Recovering value through next-generation solutions. *McKinsey on Payments*, *11*(27), 30–36.

Archel, P., Husillos, J., Larrinaga, C., & Spence, C. (2009). Social disclosure, legitimacy theory and the role of the state. *Accounting, Auditing & Accountability Journal*, *22*(8), 1284–1307. doi:10.1108/09513570910999319

Arthur, P. (2014). *Detecting Financial Statement Fraud.* Retrieved from: http//www.investopedia.com/article/financial theory/14/08/2015

Beasley, M. S., Carcello, J. V., Hermanson, D.R., & Neal, T.L. (2010). *Fraudulent Financial Reporting 1998-2007: An Analysis of U.S Public Firms*. Research commissioned by the Committee of Sponsoring Organizations of the Treadway Commission.

Beatty, A., Liao, S., & Yu, J. J. (2013). The spillover effect of fraudulent financial reporting on peer firms' investments. *Journal of Accounting and Economics*, *55*(2-3), 183–205. doi:10.1016/j.jacceco.2013.01.003

BeneishM. D.NicholsD. C. (2012). Fraud Detection and Expected Returns. https://ssrn.com/abstract=1998387 doi:10.2139/ssrn.1998387

Bhasin, M. L. (2016). Accounting manipulation Practices in Financial Statement: An Experience of an Asia economy. *International Journal of Economics and Financial Research*, *2*(11), 199–214.

Brews, P., & Hunt, M. (1999). Learning to plan and planning to learn: Resolving the planning school/learning school debate. *Strategic Management Journal*, *20*(10), 889–913. doi:10.1002/(SICI)1097-0266(199910)20:10<889::AID-SMJ60>3.0.CO;2-F

Brews, P., & Tucci, C. (2004). Exploring the structural effects of internetworking. *Strategic Management Journal*, *25*(5), 429–451. doi:10.1002mj.386

Brown, N., & Deegan, C. M. (1998). The public disclosure of environmental performance information – A dual test of media agenda setting theory and legitimacy theory. *Accounting and Business Research*, *29*(1), 21–41. doi:10.1080/00014788.1998.9729564

Burlea, S. A., & Popa, I. (2013). Legitimacy theory. In S.O. Idowu, N. Capaldi, L. Zu, & A.D. Gupta (Eds.), Encyclopedia of Corporate Social Responsibility. Springer-Verlag.

Cohen, L. E., & Felson, M. F. (2014). Social Change and Crime Rate Trends: A Routine Activity Approach. *American Sociological Review*, 44–04.

Cressey, D. R. (2008). *Other peoples' money: A study in the social psychology of embezzlement*. Free Press.

Dabor, E. L., & Adeyemi, S. B. (2009). Corporate governance and credibility of financial statement in Nigeria. *Journal of Business Systems. Governance and Ethics.*, *4*(1), 13–24.

Dada, S. O., Owolabi, S. A., & Okwu, A. T. (2013). Forensic accounting a panacea to alleviation of fraudulent practices in Nigeria. *International Journal of Business Management and Economic Research*, *4*(5), 787–792.

Damage, H. K., & Hanid, O. Y. (2005). *Accountant's Guide to Fraud Detection and Control* (2nd ed.). John Wiley & Sons.

Daniela, P., & Attila, T. (2013). Internal audit versus internal control and coaching. *Procedia Economics and Finance*, *6*(3), 694–702. doi:10.1016/S2212-5671(13)00191-3

Deegan, C. (2007). Organizational legitimacy as a motive for sustainability reporting. In J. Unerman, B. O'Dwyer, & J. Bebbington (Eds.), *Sustainability Accounting and Accountability* (pp. 127–149). Routledge. doi:10.4324/NOE0415384889.ch7

Deegan, C., Rankin, M., & Tobin, J. (2002). An examination of the corporate social and environmental disclosures of BHP from 1983–1997: A test of legitimacy theory. *Accounting, Auditing & Accountability Journal*, *15*(3), 312–343. doi:10.1108/09513570210435861

Dess, G., & Robinson, R. (1984). Measuring organizational performance in the absence of objective measures: The case of the privately-held firm and conglomerate business unit. *Strategic Management Journal*, *5*(3), 265–273. doi:10.1002mj.4250050306

Egbunike, P. A., & Igbinovia, I. M. (2018). Threat of bankruptcy and earnings management in Nigerian listed banks. *Acta Universitatis Danubius*, *14*(3), 238–253.

Eriabie, S., & Odia, J. (2016). Effects of characteristics of audit committee on earnings management in Nigerian quoted companies. *Sokoto Journal of Management Studies*, *10*(1), 139–159.

Everette, E. C. (2012). *Financial Statement Fraud, Part2 and 3. Professional Development Network. The Know How.*

Gentry, R., & Shen, W. (2010). The relationship between accounting and market measures of firm financial performance: How strong is it? *Journal of Managerial Issues*, *22*(4), 514–530.

Githecha, D. K. (2013). The effect of fraud risk management on the financial performance of commercial banks in Kenya [MSC Project]. University of Nairobi.

Ibanichuka, E. A. L. & Oko, I. A. (2019). Electronic fraud and financial performance of quoted commercial banks in Nigeria. *International Journal of Advanced Academic Research Management Practice*, 5(4), 15-35.

Ibrahim, A., Mohammed, D., & Fatima, U. (2014). Managing Bank Fraud and Forgeries through effective control strategies. A case study of Central Bank of Nigeria, Gombe Branch. *International Journal of Business and Management Invention.*, *3*(4), 7–17.

Ikpefan, O. A. (2006). Growth of Bank frauds and the impact on the Nigerian Banking Industry. *Journal of Business*), 106-126.

Kajola, S. O. (2008). Corporate governance and firm performance: the case of Nigerian listed firms. *European Journal of Economics, Finance and Administrative Science, 14*.

Kanu, S. I., & Okorafor, E. O. (2013). The nature, extent and economic impact of fraud on bank deposit in Nigeria. *Interdisciplinary Journal of Contemporary Research in Business*, *4*(9), 253–264.

Khanh, N. (2010). *Financial Statement Fraud: Motives, Methods, Cases and Detection*. Dissertation.com.

Khatab, H., Masood, M., Zaman, K., Saleem, S., & Saeed, B. (2011). Corporate governance and firm performance: A case study of Karachi stock market. *International Journal of Trade, Economics and Finance*, *2*(1), 39–43.

Lada, M., & Kozarkiewicz, A. (2014). Teoria legitymizacji w badaniach z zakresu rachunkowoci. *Zeszyty Teoretyczne Rachunkowoci*, *71*(127), 161–175. doi:10.5604/16414381.1061654

Lang, M., & Wambach, A. (2013). The fog of fraud – Mitigating fraud by strategic ambiguity. *Games and Economic Behavior*, *81*(6), 255–275. doi:10.1016/j.geb.2013.05.009

Mahdi, S., & Zhila, A. (2008). Fraud Detection and Audit Expectation Gap: Empirical Evidence from Iranian Bankers. *International Journal of Business and Management*, *3*(10), 65–77.

Mamo, J., & Aliaj, A. (2014). Accounting manipulation and its effects in the financial statements of Albanian entities. *Interdisplinary Journal of Research and Development*, *1*(2), 55–60.

Mintzer, N. J. (2016). The Bank Internal Auditor as Fraud Buster. *The ICFAI Journal of Audit Practice*, *4*(1), 557–679.

Moses, T. (2019). Corporate Governance and Corporate Fraud: An Examination of Interaction Effects in Nigeria. *Asian Journal of Advanced Research and Reports,* 1-11.

O'Donovan, G. (2002). Environmental disclosures in the annual report: Extending the applicability and predictive power of legitimacy theory. *Accounting, Auditing & Accountability Journal*, *15*(3), 344–371. doi:10.1108/09513570210435870

Obasan, K. A. (2014). Impact of Audit Quality on Organizational Profitability. *Fountain University Journal of Management and Social Sciences*, *3*(2).

Odunayo, B. A. (2014). Fraudulent Financial Reporting: The Nigerian Experience. *The Clute Institute International Conference*, 18-30.

Ogbonna, G. N., & Ebimobowei, A. (2012). Ethical compliance by the Accountant on the Quality of Financial Reporting and Performance of quoted Firms in Nigeria. *Asian Journal of Business Management*, *3*(3), 152–160.

Oghogho, G., Omimi-Ejoor, O. K., Osahenoma, V., & Abusomwan, E. (2013). The role of corporate fraud in enhancing financial reporting in Nigeria. *Journal of Business and Management*, *13*(1), 27–34.

Ogunleye, G. A. (2009). Fraud in the Banking Sector: The Unmanaged Distress Risk. *Journal of Economic Crime.*, *56*(2), 106–126.

Okoye, E. I. & Alao, B. B. (2008). The Ethics of Creative Accounting in Financial Reporting: The Challenges of Regulatory Agencies in Nigeria. *A Quarterly Journal of Association of National Accountants of Nigeria, 16*(1).

Olaoye, C. O., & Dada, R. A. (2014). Analysis of frauds in Banks: Nigeria's Experience. *European Journal of Business and Management, 6*(31), 90–99.

Ozondu, M. E., Okoye, E., & Adeniyi, S. (2019). *Corporate Fraud and Financial Performance of Banks in South-East Nigeria*. https://www.semanticscholar.org/paper/Corporate-Fraud-And-Financial-Performance-Of-Banks-Eberechukwu-Okoye/5c857bfeb0034663e89bf0b738e2ae16cf9c0ed4#related-papers

Paulinus, E. C., & Jones, A. S. (2017). Financial Risk Management And Corporate Performance Of Deposit Money Banks In Nigeria. *Archives of Business Research, 5*(12), 78–87.

Purnamasari, P., & Amaliah, I. (2015). Fraud Prevention: Relevance to Religiosity and Spirituality in the Workplace. *Procedia: Social and Behavioral Sciences, 211*(52), 827–835. doi:10.1016/j.sbspro.2015.11.109

Reurink, A. (2018). Financial fraud: A literature review. *Journal of Economic Surveys, 32*(5), 1292–1325. doi:10.1111/joes.12294

Robert, F. (2020). *Improper revenue recognition tops SEC fraud cases*. https://www.cfodive.com/news/improper-revenue-recognition-sec-fraud-cases/583889/

Ronald, O. O. (2015). *Relationship between fraud risk management practices and financial performance of commercial banks in Kenya* [Master's project]. University of Nairobi.

Sadgali, I., Sael, N., & Benabbou, F. (2019). Performance of machine learning techniques in the detection of financial frauds. *Procedia Computer Science, 148*(65), 45–54. doi:10.1016/j.procs.2019.01.007

Shehu, U. H., & Abubakar, A. (2012). Corporate Governance, Earnings Management and Financial Performance: A case of Nigerian Manufacturing Firms. *American International Journal of Contemporary Research, 2*(7), 214–226.

Span, D. (2015). Fraud analytic: Strategies and method for detection and prevention of fraud. John Wiley & Son Inc.

Subramanian, A., & Nilakanta, S. (1996). Organizational innovativeness: Exploring the relationship between organizational determinants of innovation, types of innovations and measures of organizational performance. *Omega, 24*(6), 631–647. doi:10.1016/S0305-0483(96)00031-X

Suchman, M. C. (1995). Managing legitimacy: Strategic and institutional approaches. *Academy of Management Journal, 20*(3), 571–610.

Sudaryono, D. (2021). Application of Fraud Pentagon for Detecting Symptoms of Shortfall in Financial Statements. *International Journal of Contemporary Accounting, 3*(25).

Sunil, K., Rawat, D. S., & Rajarao, V. (2016). *Financial and corporate frauds, Grant Thornton and the Associated Chambers of Commerce and Industry*. ASSOCHAM.

Umobong, A. A. & Ibanichuka. E. A. L. (2016). *Accounting manipulations and firms financial performance: Evidence from Nigeria*. Academic Press.

Uniamikogbo, E., Ayorinde, B., & Babajide, O. (2014). Fraud preventions and Financial Reporting Quality in Nigeria: An Evaluation of the Interconnectedness using Empirical Evidence. *Mediterranean Journal of Social Sciences*, *5*(20), 628.

Usman, S. (1998). *Comparison of the Nigeria Capital Market with Foreign Capital Markets and the Lessons There From As We Approach 2010. Nigerian Financial Review*, 7 .

Van der Laan, G., Van Ees, H., & Van Witteloostuijn, A. (2008). Corporate social and financial performance: An extended stakeholder theory, and empirical test with accounting measures. *Journal of Business Ethics*, *79*(3), 299–310. doi:10.100710551-007-9398-0

Yusuf, O. T. (2010). Brokers and the control of post contractual opportunism in the Nigerian insurance market. *Journal of Financial Crime*, *17*(2), 223–239. doi:10.1108/13590791011033917

Yusuf, O. T. (2011). Brokers' incentives and conflicts of interest in the control of opportunism. *The Journal of Risk Finance*, *12*(3), 168–18. doi:10.1108/15265941111136923

ADDITIONAL READING

Abdullahi, R., & Mansor, N. (2015). Forensic Accounting and Fraud Risk Factors: The Influence of Fraud Diamond Theory. *The American Journal of Innovative Research and Applied Sciences*, *1*(5), 186–192.

Adeusi, S. O., Akeke, N. I., Aribaba, F. O., & Adebisi, O. S. (2013). Audit Quality and Firm Financial Performance: Do Ownership and Board Size Matter? *Academic Journal of Interdisciplinary Studies*, *2*(3), 251.

Akpa, A. (2007). Advance auditing theory lecture material for accounting doctoral student. Benue State University.

Ene, E. E., & Bello, A. I. E. (2016). The effect of corporate governance on banks' financial performance in Nigeria. *Journal of Business and Management*, *18*(11), 99–107.

Gbegi, D. O., & Adebisi, J. F. (2014). Forensic skills and techniques in fraud investigations in the Nigerian public sector. *Mediterranean Journal of Social Sciences*, *5*(3), 243–252. doi:10.5901/mjss.2014.v5n3p243

Ilaboya, O. J., & Ohiokha, F. I. (2014). Audit firm characteristics and audit quality in Nigeria. *International Journal of Business and Economics Research*, *3*(5), 187–195. doi:10.11648/j.ijber.20140305.14

Imoniana, J. O., Antunes, M. T. P., & Formgoni, H. (2013). Forensic accounting and corporate fraud. *Journal of Information Systems and Technology Management*, *10*(1), 66–93. doi:10.4301/S1807-17752013000100007

Lang, M., & Wambach, A. (2013). The fog of fraud – Mitigating fraud by strategic ambiguity. *Games and Economic Behavior*, *81*(6), 255–275. doi:10.1016/j.geb.2013.05.009

KEY TERMS AND DEFINITIONS

Capital Market: Is a market where buyers and sellers involve in trade of financial securities like bonds and stocks.

Detection: The act of discovering a fraud.

Fictitious Revenue: It is the sale of goods and services that never occur.

Financial Fraud: When someone harms your financial health through ambiguous, deceptive, or other unlawful practices. This includes identity theft or investment fraud.

Improper Expense Recognition: When revenue is incorrectly moved from one period to another.

Investigation: Detailed search for facts of an important situation.

Legitimacy Theory: The theory that a social contract occurs between business and society.

Return on Asset: An indicator of how profitable a company is relative to its total assets. ROA gives an idea as to how efficient a firm's management is at using its assets to generate earnings.

Stock Exchange Group (NGX): The authorized market for trading publicly quoted shares.

Chapter 16
A Proposed Framework for the Disclosure of Credit Risk According to the Basel Agreement and Its Impact on the Financial Reports and the Stability of Banks

Zeinab Kassem
Ain Sham University, Egypt

ABSTRACT

This study aims to develop a proposed framework to explain the impact of disclosure of credit risks on financial reports to achieve bank stability in accordance with the requirements of the decisions of the Basel Committee. The results of the study showed there are specific criteria that can be relied upon in order to measure bank credit risk, create a provision, classify customers and creditworthiness. It is possible to incorrectly classify the merit of a customer to improve his image in front of investors and stakeholders and thus the value and the stability of the bank. The framework proposed by the researcher aids in the disclosure of bank credit risk of commercial banks to obtain more efficiency, competition, stability.

INTRODUCTION

Banks are the cornerstone of the economy.The financial reports are the available indicator and measure ofbanking processes because they reflect banks'work in a clear, comprehensive, and transparent manner.This is "The Disclosure". Which plays an important and pivotal role in the published accounting statements,which have been prepared according to the principle.It is necessary to determine what information should be disclosed and how is disclosed by the authorities.

DOI: 10.4018/978-1-7998-8754-6.ch016

The disclosure of credit risks is necessary as a part of the nature of banking activity, hence the need for the important disclosure in the banks' annual financial reports, which include all banking activities and include lending, cash and liquidity management, and asset management. To reduce potential risks and thus lead to better performance of the bank in the future assessment, (Moumen, Othman, Hussainey., 2015).Several studies at the global and local levels have shown that the availability of complete and accurate information about the bank's position and the risks it may be exposed to, has a direct impact on determining the prices of its shares, as well as predicting the returns of those shares, thus directing investors towards a good investment.

THE PROBLEM OF THE STUDY

The problem appears in the credit risk gap in the banks. Banks must provide the minimum amount of information required in the annual reports, and this has led to a lack of disclosure of credit risks in the annual reports of Egyptian banks. Research has indicated that current risk reports are not complete because they do not convey the full and useful meaning, as stakeholders need good information for the quality of decisions taken, and as a result, the cost of information is not required promptly, which may constitute an obstacle to rational decision-makers in making appropriate decisions that build on the integrity of the financial system in banks.

So, I Succumbed to a Major Question:

Does disclosure of credit risk have an impact on the quality of banks' financial reports?

Sub-questions:

- Is disclosure of credit risk on the impact of bank growth?
- Does the Basel Accord has an impact on the level of credit risk disclosure on banks?
- Will increasing disclosure of credit risks lead to the stability of the bank and increase the market share of the bank?

PREVIOUS STUDIES

Section One: Studies Related to Bank Credit Risks and Disclosure of Those Risks

Study:(González, Gil, López, Sara, Búa,, 2012)

The study aimed to: Find out the reasons why European banks use credit derivatives and analyze to what extent it can be expected to use credit derivatives using hedging theories. The data was obtained from the information contained in the annual reports and disclosure reports.

The results of the study concluded that the use of credit derivatives in most cases agrees with the predictions of hedging theories and is positively associated with the probability of using credit derivatives on the size and costs of the bank and the use of other derivatives, and negatively with capital risks and the level of credit risks.

Study: (Lefcaditis, Tsamis, Leventides,, 2014)

This study aimed to: Determine the minimum capital requirements of Basel II and whereby the bank maintains from its portfolio to cover current risks. The main risk that many banks face is credit risk, and Basel II provides an approach to calculating capital requirements.

The results of the study reached: that the Basel I capital requirements model does not include a focus on risk in the name, as the calculations of the value at risk of credit that were conducted in the current study seem to have gaps with the capital requirements of Basel II. These gaps were more evident when it was there is a high level of risk in credit portfolios.

Study:(Maffei, Aria, Fiondella, Span, Zagaria,, 2014)

The study aimed to: What is the best mandatory way to disclose the categories of risks and to provide a better understanding of the reasons that seem less useful than the disclosure of risks should be. The study analyzed banks that provide risk information by their characteristics to find out any differences between notes on the financial statements and a public report, both of which were prepared following the instructions of the Bank of Italy.

The results of the study reached: that Italian banks formally comply with the instructions, but there is discretion in choosing the characteristics of the information provided. Although the risk categories to be disclosed are different in each report, the form of disclosure is completely uniform, although banks tend to provide more information Density in the notes of the financial statements and the difference in economic signals between two reports decreases while the level of risk increases.

Section Two: Studies Related to the Quality of Financial Reports in Banks

Study: (LIPUNGA, 2014)

The study aimed to: measure the level of risk disclosure in the financial reports of Malawian banks and its impact on profitability. The study used the risk disclosure indicator that was established based on Basel II requirements, the bank governance guidelines issued by the Central Bank of Malawi, and International Accounting Standard No. 7. The disclosure indicator consists of 34 disclosure units. It is divided into six categories, namely: board of directors and management structure related to risk management, market risk, credit risk, liquidity risk, capital management, operational risk, and others.

The results of the study concluded that the level of risk disclosure showed that on average 82% of the items disclosed were the financial reports of the sample. The degrees of disclosure also varied according to the risk disclosure categories. The lowest score was the board of directors and the management structure related to risk management, then operational and other risks. Credit risk, liquidity risk, and market risk were the most significant risks by value.

Study: (Gizaw, Million, Matewos, 2015)

The study aimed to: Study the impact of credit risk on the profitability of commercial banks in Ethiopia for secondary purpose data collected for commercial banks from the reports of the concerned banks and the National Bank of Ethiopia.

The results of the study concluded that: Credit risk measures: non-performing loans, loan loss provisions, and capital adequacy have a significant impact on the profitability of commercial banks in Ethiopia.

The study points to the need to strengthen credit risk management to maintain the prevailing profitability of commercial banks in Ethiopia.

Section Three: Studies Related to Disclosure of Credit Risks and the Quality of Financial Reports

Study: (Oliveira, Rodrigues, cia Lima, 2011)

The study aimed to: evaluate risk disclosure practices in 190 Portuguese credit institutions. The study was based on an analysis of the content of individual annual reports. It found that risk-related disclosures lacked comparability due to the difference in maturity at the time of credit risk, market risk, and liquidity risk. As the VAR differs in the assumptions, sensitivity analysis, and different practices for disclosing capital structure and adequacy.

The results of the study reached: The study evaluates the extent of reform in risk disclosure practices in light of International Financial Reporting Standards and the Basel Convention (II) to address all the identified shortcomings. The study highlights areas in need of further reform and recommended that Portuguese supervisory authorities adopt more effective enforcement mechanisms in brokering compliance with mandatory minimum risk disclosure requirements.

Study: (Akins, 2011)

The study aimed to: prove that the quality of financial reports solves doubts about credit risk and how it affects the difference between rating agencies. Where it was found that classifications have the most important role in solving this problem.

The results of the study concluded that the quality of financial reports has become more important in reducing the discrepancy in the information about the classification. As doubts about credit risk increased the uncertainty among rating agencies. The study contributes to the role of information quality in loan markets, brokers, and reports.

Study: (Desouky, 2014)

The study aimed to study and analyze the impact of the relationship between accounting disclosure of financial risks in annual reports and stock returns. This goal was achieved through studying and analyzing previous research and writings in the accounting literature related to the study problem and determining its variables, with an applied study.

The results of the study reached: There is a disclosure of financial risks in the annual reports of companies listed on the Egyptian stock market, and the most variables affecting stock returns in the Egyptian stock market as a whole are the quick liquidity ratio, the cash ratio, the ratio of networking capital to total Assets, leverage ratio, and long-term debt-to-equity ratio. As for sectors, the ratios affecting stock returns for companies listed on the Egyptian stock market varied.

Study: (Altunba, Polizzi, Scannella, Thornton, 2021)

The study aimed to present the impact of the European Bank Union and its supervisory mechanism on the risk disclosure practices of European banks. The associated rules come as a shock to the availability of an analysis of the effects of the new supervision on the risk disclosure practices of banks.

The results of the study concluded that there was an increase in risk disclosure in banks in general after the European Bank Union, but there was a weakness in the disclosure by banks that are under the supervision of foreign banks about the banks that are supervised by government authorities. The results also showed that the positive impact is stronger for less profitable banks, while the negative impact on centrally supervised banks is stronger if bank CEOs also act as bosses (CEO duplication). The results also show that the new institutional arrangements for banking supervision under which the ECB relies on local supervisors to gather information needed for business leaders to inefficiencies regarding the speed and completeness of information flow between SSM supervised banks and the ECB, which is reflected in banking disclosure practices.

The Current Study Differs from Other Previous Studies in:

These studies did not cover in any of them a proposed framework for disclosure of credit risk and its impact on the quality of financial reports in banks in commercial banks, and No study has dealt with the role of Basel on the financial statements and the stability of the Bank. And knowing the extent of the impact of the increase and quality of risk disclosure. The credit quality of the financial reports on the one hand and the profitability performance of the bank on the other hand, to assess the quality of the information provided.

The Importance of Studying

- Demonstrate the role played by the disclosure of credit risks in banks to increase the bank's value, enhance the competitive advantage, achieve a stable financial position for banks' risks, increase the value of accounting information, the reliability of the private bank, objectivity and the quality of financial statements.
- Show the types of information disclosure, which positively affects the bank's performance to increase transparency and increase information symmetry in the financial statements of commercial banks and to support this sector of services for users of these financial statements.

The Objectives of the Study

The study aims to verify risk disclosure and its effectiveness on financial reports in banks. In light of the study problem, the main objective is represented in the following.

- Knowing and clarifying the disclosure of credit risks in commercial banks through what is stated in international accounting standards, and in particular what is stated in the decisions of the Basel Committee (2 and 3).
- Proposing a framework for disclosing credit risks in commercial banks.
- Contribute to the knowledge of improving the quality of financial information on credit risks and its dissemination to ensure the stability of a bank by the financial accounting system derived from international standards and the level of regulatory authorities.

THE THEORETICAL FRAMEWORK FOR THE STUDY

Credit Risk

Credit risk is the most dangerous type of financial risk in banks. These risks appear due to the possibility of bank customers defaulting on their obligations, which leads to their failure to pay the principal amount of the loan as well as the interest due within the terms specified in the contract.(Natalia, Jurij,, 2020)

The methodology for measuring credit risk (the financial ratios that measure both profitability, leverage, and liquidity ratios) are the most commonly used metrics for analyzing creditworthiness. Whereas the use of large-scale credit scoring models (97% of banks use creditworthiness to approve credit card applications, and 70% of banks use creditworthiness for their small business loans), creditworthiness models are relatively inexpensive to implement. (Allen, Linda, DeLong, Gayle,, 2004)

Credit risk arises through loans and the provision of lending-related services (such as factoring, leasing, etc.), and can also manifest itself in correspondent relationships between banks, carrying out operations with securities, issuing bank guarantees, working with letters of credit, etc. Therefore, credit risk is produced, and there are fears of it, therefore, credit risk can be defined as an opportunity to cause a loss if the debtor of the bank is unable or unwilling to fulfill the obligations that he or she has to the bank, according to the terms of the contract that was agreed upon by. When customers default on interest payments, banks lose a portion of their income; whereas, on failure to pay the principal amount of the loan, the banks will have to write off the bad and bad loans from the expenses and thus bear the losses. There are a variety of factors affecting credit risk among which one can distinguish external factors (macroeconomic factors) as well as internal factors (microeconomic factors). (Natalia, Jurij,, 2020)

The customer's creditworthiness decreases, the more likely he will default, and therefore the changes in returns represent the risks to which the credit facilities portfolio is exposed. Credit risk arises due to non-payment of principal or interest or delay in repayment, and credit risk is affected by macroeconomic, social, and political conditions. (Manual of Banking Risk Management Policies and Procedures), for the credit risk measurement methods in Basel (1), the risk weights were determined by Basel and used as one size fits all, while Basel (2) provided three methods or methods for calculating credit risk, which isthe typical method. Or a standard, the basic internal evaluation method, and the advanced internal rating method. The Bank has the right to choose one of these methods.(Hashad, 2004)

The Impact of Disclosure of Credit Risk on the Financial Reports

Disclosure plays an important role in financial reports for the symmetry of information between the bank and its investors, improving the stability of the bank, and increasing the quality of banks' financial reports, thus reducing the disparity of information between managers and stakeholders, as lenders are increasingly reliant on financial reports in the credit decision. (Balakrishnan, 2009)

The first task of financial reports is to provide stakeholders with appropriate accounting information at the right time and in the fairest manner. However, the preparer of these reports can use what he has of experience and accounting skills to deceive the users of financial statements by using profit mechanisms, especially In the field of the banking industry, and scientific practices have proven that the management of banks, in general, does not find better than credit risks in managing their profits, and the management can use optimistic estimates when classifying debts and credit facilities granted, allowing the room to reduce the provisions made to meet doubtful debts and thus inflate profits and manipulate the timing of proof Profits related to the sale of assets such as securities and fixed assets, which leads to Impact on earnings figures. (Al-Rashidi, 2012)

Manipulating the value of financial estimates on which accounting depends on the accrual basis and the formation of some reserves and provisions at less or more than their real value allowed by accounting standards, which results in what is known as an exaggeration in the formation of reserves, which are later used to enhance revenues or reduce as needed.

Manipulating the classification of the contents of the statement of cash flows, as management can resort to focusing on the items of the first group of that list that are related to operating activities by classifying some items that are related to investment or financing activities as related to operating activities and vice versa, which will not affect at the end On the final balance of cash flows aimed at generating a false impression of the earning ability of the enterprise, which is reflected in the actual operating activities.And then an appropriate trade-off is made between the accounting profit and some of the variables associated with it, which ultimately leads to the disclosure of false profits and manipulation of the disclosed profit. This may be done by reducing loan provisions, which are the basis of a burden on revenue, so the value of profits rises to the level that may satisfy the ambitions of the campaign. Shares and does not expose the value of the facility to decline in the business market, which is a scientific fact because the value of the facility may change up to or down and the value of the share on the stock exchange changes to live up to the owners' ambitions, but it will entail tax burdens or large dividends. The management in this case resorts to the second alternative, which is to increase the value of loan provisions. Where researchers believe that loan provisions are the preferred method of bank managers in managing profits and to prevent the excess that can be resorted to by some bank departments through the excessive use of loan and advances provisions as a profit management tool in a way that reduces the quality of financial reports.

Therefore, the Central Bank of Egypt periodically tries to evaluate the behavior of the management of these banks whenever necessary. This assertion is confirmed by the observation that the Bank took advantage of the opportunity to amend the Egyptian accounting standards, which have come to a large extent under International Financial Reporting Standards, as it issued binding rules from the Central Bank. The Central Bank stressed the need to fully comply with these rules. Among the amendments approved by these rules is what is related to the foundations for the formation of provisions for loans and advances, as its name was changed to the burden of amortization for credit losses instead of provisions for loans and advances. (Hassan, 2016), that risk disclosure is affected by many systemic factors, including (size, profitability, and financial leverage) of the bank. (Jado, 2012)

The fourteenth International Accounting Standard related to segmental financial reporting aims to establish principles for reporting information on information by sector and geographical areas in the banking services provided by the bank and the various in which it operates to assist users of financial statements in a better understanding of the entity's past performance, a better assessment of the bank's risks and returns, and to help form judgments. About the bank as a whole is better supported by information and to provide a complete picture of credit exposure, a bank should disclose the components of the loan portfolio and the total unsecured credit exposure. The credit exposure balance after the guarantees must also be disclosed, including the current and potential exposure based on the broad categories of those in terms of (Rizk, 2011).

The main categories and types of lenders and counterparties.

- Business lines such as commercial, industrial, real estate, construction, credit cards, delay, mortgage, and residential.
- Broad categories of borrowers such as commercial and consumer loans and related parties
- Type of activity/credit exposure (eg commercial, industrial, real estate, credit cards, and financial leasing).
- Geographical areas: such as local and international credit exposures, which show country exposures. Geographical areas may include specific countries or a group of countries or regions within the country.
- Type of Warranty
- Items inside and outside the statement of financial position, including foreign and local governments, foreign and local companies, and other financial institutions.
- How to allocate loans to geographical areas
- Geographical areas including domestic and international credit exposure.
- Total exposure to credit risk plus average total exposure during the period broken down by major types of credit exposure
- Divide the maturity periods used for the entire portfolio according to the main types of exposures credit.

Disclosure Of Risks Following The Decisions Of The Basel Committee (LI) And (LII)

Banking Risks and Requirements of Basel (I), (II) and (III)

The Basel Committee has built a solid foundation for regulation and control over capital adequacy and the adoption of transparency and disclosure in the market and an additional improvement in risk management methods and thus to financial stability by placing a classification of risks to which most financial institutions are exposed. This committee relied on special criteria for classifying risks for each financial institution separately,for example, it classified the risks faced by banks into three main types: credit risk, market risk, and operational risk. (Qader, 2009)

The disclosure rules provide information that is emphasized by the principles of the Basel agreement in the disclosure requirements of banks. The two disclosures enable market participants to take action to monitor operations and make decisions. Transparency may allow shareholders or stakeholders to reduce high-risk behavior, thus reducing more risk of IBs in a short period compared to central banks. However, the disclosure framework and details of the Basel rules have not been developed, and relying on disclosure of regulatory changes only in the disclosure reforms of the Basel principles may not be sufficient to control effectively. (Hafiz Hoque, Heng, 2021)

Disclosure of Risks in with the Decisions of the Basel (II)

1. The decisions of Basel (ll) required the need to disclose the credit risks of all banks, and the disclosure is as follows: (El-Meligy, 2012)
2. Qualitative Disclosure: Disclosure is made about how repayment deadlines are determined, how weak loans are identified, a description of the methods used for specific loan allowances and credit

risk allowances in general, a description of statistical methods, and finally the bank's policy for credit risk management.

3. Quantitative disclosure: The VAR is disclosed according to geographic distribution, industry, or maturity periods, each divided according to the main types of credit exposure (eg loans, off-balance sheet items that are not derivatives, derivatives, securities, etc.). The third pillar required disclosure of private and general allowances and expenses related to allowances, with disclosure of adjustment of changes in allowances for weak loans.

Disclosure of Risks in the Decisions of the Basel (III)

The third pillar of Basel (lll) decisions made it clear that market discipline is achieved by disclosing the bank's risk assessments and the adequacy of its capital. The Basel Committee clarified that the interest in banks' disclosure is due to the legal powers of bank supervisors and the seriousness of the lack of accounting disclosure. The committee stressed the need for banks to explain the differences between accounting disclosure and disclosure by the requirements of the supervisory authorities. The committee also clarified that the data published as additional reports are subject to the review of the external auditor and that the administration is responsible for the accuracy of the data published on the Internet unless otherwise stipulated by accounting and auditing standards. The committee has set several criteria for those in charge of managing the bank to determine what data can be disclosed as follows: (El-Meligy, 2012).

Materiality: The bank decides which information is important when users make their decisions.

- Periodicity: The accounting disclosure shall be semi-annual, except for the qualitative disclosure, which provides a summary of the objectives and policies of risks and definitions, and is published in the annual report.
- Ownership and confidential information: In exceptional cases, the accounting disclosure of certain items may affect the ownership of the bank (such as the software used or the confidentiality of customers). In those cases, the subject is disclosed in general.
- It should be noted that the decisions of the Basel (lll) emphasized the necessity of using the market value method only to measure and evaluate the bank's financial assets and provided objective measures to measure those assets, and they were accepted at the level of the Bank, the supervisory and supervisory authorities, and international rating institutions. (Al-Mihi, 2015)
- From the above, the researcher concludes that the decisions of the Basel Convention (ll) and (lll) did not differ much from what was stated in international standards and international financial reporting standards (30), (39), (7), and (9) in the way, presentation and disclosure in the financial statements. For banks. Where international standards did not differentiate between large or small banks, nor between government banks and private banks, but the decisions of the Basel Agreement, which recognize that the largest active banks globally with the most sensitive risks in the capital markets, demanded that they disclose the first tranche of capital and the total capital adequacy ratios and their components every quarter. Also, if the accounting disclosure of risks or any other items is subject to rapid change, the bank must disclose it every quarter.

Transparency and Disclosure of Credit Risks and Their Relationship to Confidence, Profitability Performance, and Stability of the Bank

Transparency and disclosure are some of the main channels through which banks'financial reports can affect the stability of the banking system by increasing publicly available information about banks' exposure to real economic conditions.(Viralv, Acharya, Stepheng, ryan,, 2016), and that transparency, disclosure, and trust are an integral part of corporate governance, which in turn can provide improved performance and financial stability in the banking system. Whereas, present and potential financial performance is an indicator of investment. Surveys show that institutional investors are paying as much as 28% or more in stocks of well-regulated companies in emerging markets. The vast majority of investors are willing to pay 20% with superior corporate governance practices. (Rogers, 2008), as well as in banks, investors are willing to keep their money in stable and highly competitive banks.

It is assumed that the value of loans and provisions announced in the reports submitted to the management of the bank differs from the value declared in the financial statements used by investors. That is, the bank's management is working on forming a secret reserve through the loan loss allowance, and therefore there is doubt about the correctness of the numbers contained in these lists, which loses confidence in the reports and the bank, which leads to the withdrawal of investments from it instead of attracting new investments, and this is the reaction of the money market and current shareholders and potential investors towards the value of the loan loss provision and the market value of the name of the bank. Investors are willing to pay a high price to buy the bank's shares if the announced losses are few, and on the contrary, they sell the shares even if at a lower price than they bought it to avoid future losses. Disclosure of loans and their provisions helps the investor to (Mohammed, 2006)

- Evaluating the performance of the bank's management.
- Predicting its profitability.
- Forecasting the extent of his ability to fulfill his obligations.

Where loan loss provisions are an important item for the bank's financial reporting in general, and studies have been recently conducted on how financial reporting affects the bank's stability. As banks can record sufficient provisions for loan losses during good economic times, and thus the bank records large provisions during recessions. This entails reducing the regulatory capital of banks. There must be an effective framework for disclosing credit risks based on decisive control policies to ensure its implementation, forcing the bank to disclose the reality of loans (regular and non-performing) and their allocations, which increases confidence between the bank and its customers on the one hand and between the bank and supervisory authorities on the other, because the provision for losses Loans affect the bank's net income, so its disclosure has an impact on investors' decisions, in addition to the fact that the development of disclosure in the financial statements of commercial banks increases the understanding and benefit of the users of these statements, correcting credit operations, reducing non-performing loans, increasing confidence in the bank and its management, which attracts new investments and higher competitiveness.

By reviewing previous research and studies, the researcher found that the return on shareholders' equity and the return on assets is the most widely used to measure the efficiency of profits or economic performance in financial institutions. The researcher studied the variables ("non-performing loans", "non-performing loans ratio", "Loan loss allowance", "Liquidity ratio", "Capital adequacy ratio", "Financial leverage" and "Bank size"), And the impact of these variables and their relationship to profitability performance, which is measured by the following indicators: ("return on shareholders' equity", "return on assets").

Where profitability performance indicators: They are indicators that measure the ability of banks to take risks and/or increase their capital. They refer to the competitiveness of banks and measure the quality of management. This is due to the elements of credit risk and its impact on the net profit. Because the profitability of commercial banks is critical, and credit is the most profitable activity, so the measurement and disclosure of credit risk is through non-performing loans and provision for credit losses (impairment).

The researcher will discuss the determinants of profitability, which are the two indicators: (return on shareholders' equity and return on assets), as it refers to a theory that explains the behavior of managers' estimations to disclose credit risk, which results in information about shares in the market for the bank to avoid any devaluation of its shares because the value of the stock As a result of the bank's realized profits, as non-performing loans and the loan loss allowance are among the main factors for measuring and disclosing credit risk, but most studies have found that managers use the loan loss allowance for different purposes such as profit management study. (Khamis., 2016),

The loan loss allowance ratio is used to identify the level of expectations of bank managers about the quality of assets in the banking sector. Where when the loan loss provision increases, it affects the asset quality by decreasing and vice versa. The basic assumption behind choosing the loan loss provisioning ratio (impairment) is that bank managers reflect their belief in the quality of the bank's assets. (Gizaw, Million, Matewos, 2015), where some studies have confirmed that highly profitable banks have a greater incentive to indicate the quality of their performance and their ability to successfully manage credit risks.

Managers tend to communicate information related to credit risks in a good manner to improve the image of the bank and increase the incentive, therefore, disclosure of credit risks with transparency contributes to presenting the real financial position of the bank in a realistic way to investors, thus contributing to the investors making a correct decision about investing in the bank or not. Good financial performance, disclosure of credit risk reduce uncertainty about current and future cash flows, and has a positive impact on the bank's shares, ensuring investors about the bank's expectations and avoiding the negative impact of future credit risks. Among the previous studies that supported the idea (Fredrick, 2012) and (Kaaya, Indiael, Dickson, 2013), and other previous studies that were referred to in previous studies in the general framework of the study.

The Proposed Framework for Disclosure of Credit Risk

In this part of the chapter, the researcher seeks to propose a framework for credit risk disclosureby the Basel Committee agreement and its impact on financial reporting and the stability of the bank. Their occurrence and control with the highest level of transparency and accuracy to reach the acceptable level from the point of view of the Board of Directors, senior management, investors, and stakeholders. And standards that are generally accepted, where the framework consists of three steps, and in the third step, some reports, procedures, and goals are clarified, which will be clarified as follows:

The Objective of the Proposed Framework for Disclosing Credit Risks in Financial Reports

The framework aims at an integrated and applicable methodological process that can be used periodically and regularly to disclose credit risks in financial reports regarding disclosure and measurement of credit risks to facilitate decision-making, dealing with and managing them, and taking control decisions on those risks and mitigating their effects by taking appropriate measures before they occur.

The Foundations on Which the Proposed Framework for Disclosing Credit Risks is Based

Implementation of the proposed framework requires a set of basic criteria to activate it, which are summarized as follows:

- Compliance with international and Egyptian accounting standards, the rules of the Central Bank, and the Basel Convention.
- Existence of a clear organizational structure, policies, and procedures for credit risk management.
- Availability of a set of policies and procedures for recording and evaluating credit risks, guarantees, and loan portfolios
- A clear strategy for the bank in managing credit risks.
- An information system for extracting reports on risks.
- Segregation of functions and tasks between departments in recording, auditing, and risk management.
- Approval of the framework by the supervisory authority, senior management, and the Central Bank of Egypt.
- The commitment of the organizational and administrative structure to the framework.
- Periodic review regularly to the competent authorities and amendment to improve the level of quality.

Components of the Proposed Framework for Disclosing Credit Risks in Financial Reports

This framework is based on a set of basic elements through which each element of credit risk can be measured and evaluated. As the specific disclosures for each bank will vary in scope and content according to the level and type of activities, all banks should provide sufficient information in a timely and detailed manner. This is to allow market participants to develop a complete and accurate picture of the credit risk of the bank. Moreover, the bank's disclosure should be consistent with the bank's information that is used internally in the management and control of credit risks for the continuation of management information systems to develop and improve financial reports, and to disclose thempromptly. There must be evidence for the disclosure of credit risks to assess disclosure in the bank, in addition to compliance with international standards, Egyptian accounting standards, and decisions of the Central Bank related to disclosure requirements in banks, which provide sufficient guidelines to achieve transparency in the disclosure of information related to credit risks.

The Proposed Framework for Credit Risk Disclosure Consists of the Following Elements

Figure 1. Prepared by the researcher, "A proposed framework for credit risk disclosure to improve the quality of financial reporting and the bank's stability".

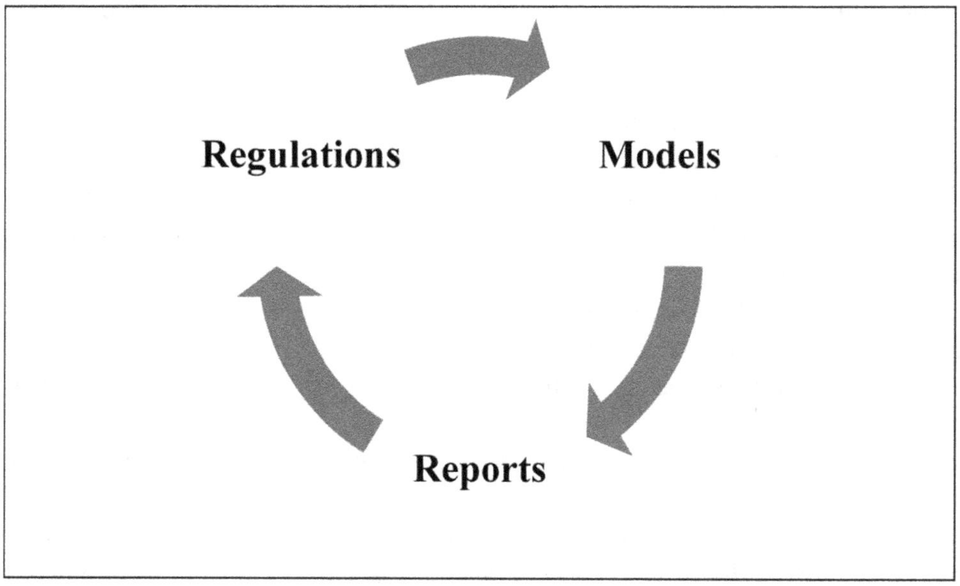

Regulations of the Proposed Framework:

- Defining the credit risks facing the bank and their causes.
- A list of the policies used to determine the provision for loan losses, the burden of loan impairment, and the decision to write off debts for the types of loans.
- A list of qualitative information for credit risk management policies and procedures and the credit rating system.
- A list of the policies and procedures followed in evaluating collateral.
- A model of fixed and clear indicators for calculating non-performing loans and loan loss provisions.

Models of the Proposed Framework:

- Loan classification model and risk assessment method according to the degree of risks associated with loans quantitatively and descriptively.
- Form for classifying collateral according to their maturity dates.

Reports of the Proposed Framework:

- Reports related to credit facility operations and any practices that do not comply with the policies and procedures to be followed.

- A report on the loan portfolio is divided according to its different types and also according to the types of guarantees.
- A report on the movement of the provision for doubtful debts and the volume of bad debts in them compared to the previous period.
- Reports to be prepared to inform the concerned parties of non-interest-bearing and non-interest-bearing debts.
- Annual report on information on risk management and internal control.
- An annual report that determines the extent to which the principles of corporate governance have been adhered to or not adhered to, with reasons given.

RESULTS AND RECOMMENDATIONS OF THE STUDY

- Banks still face severe deficiencies in the current disclosure of credit risk and do not provide a clear picture of bank credit and the risks of allocated components.
- Failure to fully disclose current credit risk and allocate a volume to it to the bank and abide by the rules of the Central Bank to publish in its lists and not to determine the size of the component to face bad (bad) debts.
- The specific criteria that can be relied upon to measure bank credit risk and customize the composition and classification of customers and the creditworthiness of each customer, if used, will improve the bank's image and stability in front of investors and stakeholders.
- The use of a sound fixed model for bank credit risk, under strict supervision by the Central Bank, and the form in which it meets the needs of banks and users' financial statements, depends as being the best.
- Adequate disclosure of credit risk improves financial reports and thus provides an appropriate and reliable feature and the reliability of the information contained therein, thus making good decisions by all parties and thus its stability.

RECOMMENDATIONS OF THE STUDY

Through the results that the researcher reached, she found some recommendations, which are:

- Most of the indicators used to measure credit risk in commercial banks are an objective basis for measuring this risk.
- It is possible to rely on the results of measuring credit risks in the proposed framework for the formation of credit allocations so that these allocations are more objective, more stable, and safer for the bank.
- The necessity of increasing the supervisory role, as well as the audit committees in banks, to reduce credit and audit the creditworthiness of the bank and thus achieve the best quality of accounting information.
- Banks operating in a transparent environment, credit quality is an effective incentive to reduce risky behavior in credit.
- The quality of the information enables users to understand and compare banks.

FUTURE RESEARCH DIRECTIONS

In this chapter, the researcher presented a study and the concept of credit risk in banks, and that it is one of the most important types of risks facing the banking sector and its various types, and given the serious impact of this type of banking risk on the occurrence of financial crises, the banking supervisory authorities, both governmental and international, paid the most attention to the stability of The banking sector and thus the economic sector.

The researcher dealt with the Basel Committee Agreement, (II,III), and reviewed the disclosure and transparency that allow external parties and beneficiaries to obtain information. They lead to improving the quality of information for the various parties, reducing heterogeneous information in the financial markets, and achieving standardization and coordination in the financial statements to help all parties. Taking into account all the surrounding environmental conditions, it was found that the decisions of the Basel Convention (2) and (3) did not lag far behind what was stated in the international financial reporting standards in the way, presentation and disclosure of risks in general and credit risks in particular, credit in the financial statements of banks. At the end of the chapter, the researcher presented a proposed framework for disclosing credit risks (objective, foundations, and elements).

The chapter concluded that the application of the rules of governance is concerned with examining and evaluating the extent of compliance with the policies and procedures for the banking system that would raise the efficiency of the banking system and increase the confidence of users of the financial statements, and it will reflect on strengthening the positive role of supervision. Therefore, accuracy and objectivity in financial reports, as well as compliance with the laws and legislation issued by the state and specialized professional associations, have a clear impact on revitalizing the stock market movement, increasing circulation, stock prices, and the efficiency and stability of banks.

CONCLUSION

This study aimed to demonstrate the role of disclosure of credit risks realistically on the quality of financial reports for commercial banks through the value of the provision for loan losses and the percentage of non-performing loans and the extent of the impact of various aspects in evaluating the efficiency and profitability of the bank to reduce credit risks and the role of the Basel Committee agreement in increasing disclosures and indicating their importance, as well To increase the quality of the financial reports of its users and to prevent fraud in the financial reports, such information must be disclosed lawfully among all shareholders and stakeholders and the very important role BASAL committee for stability banks.

REFERENCES

Akins, B. (2011). *Financial Reporting Quality and Uncertainty about Credit Risk among the Ratings Agencies*. MIT Sloan School of Management.

Al-Mihi, R. A.-H. (2015). Measurement and disclosure of bank liquidity risk in light of the decisions of Basel llll and International Financial Reporting Standards IFRS. *Journal of Accounting Thought, Ain Shams University, 3*.

Al-Rashidi, M. S. (2012). An Analytical Study of Methods for Evaluating the Quality of Financial Reports. *Journal of Contemporary Business Research, Faculty of Commerce, Sohag University, 26*(2), 32-37.

Allen, L., & DeLong, G. (2004). Issues in the credit risk modeling of retail markets. *Journal of Banking & Finance. VOL., 28*, PP736–PP739.

Altunba, P., & Scannella, T. (2021). European Banking Union and bank risk disclosure: The effects of the Single Supervisory Mechanism. *Review of Quantitative Finance and Accounting*, 1–20. doi:10.100711156-021

Balakrishnan, K. (2009). *Credit Market Conditions and Economy-wide Consequences of Financial Reporting Quality*. New York University.

Desouky, A. R. (2014). *Accounting disclosure of financial risks in the annual reports of companies listed on the stock market and its impact on stock returns: an applied study* (Unpublished Master's thesis). Cairo University.

El-Meligy, H. H. (2012). *The Adequacy of Accounting Disclosure of Liquidity Risks in Commercial Banks for the Decisions of the Basel III Committee. The Scientific Journal of Economics and Commerce, Ain Shams.*

Fredrick, O. (2012). The Impact of Credit Risk Management on Financial Performance of Commercial Banks in Kenya. *DBA Africa Management Review, 3*(1), 22–37.

Gizaw, M. (2015). The impact of credit risk on profitability performance of commercial banks in Ethiopia. *African Journal of Business Management, 9*(2), 59–66. doi:10.5897/AJBM2013.7171

González, G., & López, S. B. (2012). Determinants of Credit Risk Derivatives use by the European Banking Industry. *Journal of Money, Investment and Banking,* 1-30.

Hashad, N. (2004). *Basel Convention*. Academic Press.

Hoque, Hafiz, H. (2021). Impact of bank regulation on risk of Islamic and conventional banks. *International Journal of Finance & Economics, 2021*, 1–38. doi:10.1002/ijfe

Jado, S. K. (2012). The impact of risk disclosure in accordance with the requirements of International Financial Reporting Standard No. 7 (IFRS7) on achieving the appropriate value of accounting information (field study). *Journal of Financial and Commercial Studies, 1,* 620-624, 634-638.

Kaaya, I. D. (2013). Credit Risk and Commercial Banks Performance in Tanzania: a Panel Data Analysis. *Research Journal of Finance and Accounting, 4*(16), 1-9.

Khamis., H. K. (2016). The extent to which loan allocations are used in profit management in private commercial banks (practical analysis) before and after the application of the foundations of measurement and accounting recognition issued by the Central Bank. *Journal of Accounting Thought, 3*(1), 393-394.

Lefcaditis, T., Tsamis, A., & Leventides, J. (2014). Concentration risk model for Greek bank's credit portfolio. *The Journal of Risk Finance, 15*(1), 71–93. doi:10.1108/JRF-06-2013-0043

Lipunga, A. M. (2014). Risk Disclosure Practices Of Malawian Commercial Banks. *Journal of Contemporary Issues in Business Research, 3*(3), 154–167.

Maffei, A., & Fiondella, S. (2014). (Un)useful risk disclosure: Explanations from the Italian banks. *Managerial Auditing Journal, 29*(7), 621–648. doi:10.1108/MAJ-11-2013-0964

Mohammed, H. A. (2006). *A proposed framework for measuring and disclosing the provision for loan losses in commercial banks (with an applied study)* [Unpublished Master's thesis]. Mansoura University.

Moumen, O., Ben Othman, H., & Hussainey, K. (2015). The Value Relevance of Risk Disclosure in Annual Reports: Evidence from MENA Emerging Markets. *Research in International Business and Finance, 34*, 2–3. doi:10.1016/j.ribaf.2015.02.004

Natalia, J. (2020). Approaches to credit risk assessment and measurement: Economic and legal aspects. *6th International Scientific Symposium "Economics, Business & Finance" 3rd. International Multidisciplinary Academic Confer*, 5.

Oliveira, R., Rodrigues, L. L., & Craig, R. (2011). Risk-related disclosure practices in the annual reports of Portuguese credit institutions: An exploratory study. *Journal of Banking Regulation, 12*(2), 100–118. doi:10.1057/jbr.2010.20

Qader, O. A. (2009). The Importance of Building Systems for Crisis Risk Management in Financial Institutions. In *International Scientific Forum*. Setif, Algeria: Farhat Abbas University.

Rizk, M. I. (2011). *A proposed framework for the measurement and accounting disclosure of banking risks to assess the extent of sustainability - an applied theoretical study* [Unpublished Ph.D. thesis]. Benha University.

Rogers, M. (2008). *Corporate Governance and Financial Performance of Selected Commercial Banks in Uganda.* Queen's University Belfast. http://www.crrconference.org

Viralv, A., & Stepheng, R. (2016). Banks' Financial Reporting and Financial System Stability. *Journal of Accounting Research, 54*(2), 293.

ADDITIONAL READING

Aras, G., & Aslan, L. (2011). Capital structure and credit risk management: Evidence from Turkey. *International Journal of Accounting and Finance, 3*(1), 1–20. doi:10.1504/IJAF.2011.042217

Bhat, G., Ryan, S. G., & Vyas, D. (2019). The implications of credit risk modeling for banks' loan loss provisions and loan-origination procyclicality. *Management Science, 65*(5), 2116–2141.

Finkelstein, D., Strzodka, A., & Vickery, J. I. (2018). Credit risk transfer and de facto GSE reform. *Economic Policy Review, 24*(3).

Okafor, A., & Fadul, J. (2019). Bank Risks, Regulatory Interventions and Deconstructing the Focus on Credit Risk. *Research Journal of Finance and Accounting, 10*(8).

Oliveira, J., Rodrigues, L. L., & Craig, R. (2011). Risk-related disclosure practices in the annual reports of Portuguese credit institutions: An exploratory study. *Journal of Banking Regulation, 12*(2), 100–118. doi:10.1057/jbr.2010.20

Young, K. L. (2012). Transnational regulatory capture? An empirical examination of the transnational lobbying of the Basel Committee on Banking Supervision. *Review of International Political Economy*, *19*(4), 663–688. doi:10.1080/09692290.2011.624976

KEY TERMS AND DEFINITIONS

Banking Competition: Is struggle for consumer of banking services and creation of such conditions for other participants, which do now allow them having decisive influence upon the market.

Credit Portfolio: Is any collection of credit exposures that is formed as part of financial intermediation activities (e.g., regular Lending products or derivative contracts) or as an investment in Credit Risk sensitive securities (such as corporate bonds).

Efficiency Banks: Are defined as the difference between observed. Quantity of input and output variables with respect to optimal quantity of input and output variables. An efficient bank can achieve a maximum value of one in comparison to an inefficient bank, which can reduce to the level of zero.

Governance: Is the system by which entities are directed and controlled. It is concerned with structure and processes for decision making, accountability, control and behavior at the top of an entity.

International Financial Reporting Standards (IFRS): Are a set of accounting rules for the financial statements of public companies that are intended to make them consistent, transparent, and easily comparable around the world.

Non-Performing Loans (NPL): Are loans in which the borrower is in default due to the fact that they have not made the scheduled payments for a specified period.

Risk Disclosure: Is the communication of information concerning firm's strategies, operations, and other external factors that have the potential to affect expected results.

Transparency: Is the extent to which investors have ready access to required financial information about a company, such as price levels, market depth, and audited financial reports.

Chapter 17
Deep-Auto Encoders for Detecting Credit Card Fraud

Sudarshana Kerenalli
https://orcid.org/0000-0001-9581-6835
Gitam University, India

Mylara C. Reddy
GST Bengaluru, India

A. Usha Ruby
GST Bengaluru, India

ABSTRACT

Internet-based payment methods in recent times are rapidly growing both in developing and developed economies. Credit card-based payment systems are among the prominent cashless payment methods in all economies. Credit card frauds by cyber-criminals are increasing in spite of several precautionary measures. Thus, fraud detection in real-time is a challenging task. Several machine learning tasks have attempted to solve the problem. This chapter proposes a two-step method to detect credit card fraud by coupling the deep learning-machine learning approaches. In the first stage, the dimensionality of the data set is reduced to 50% by a deep auto-encoder. A machine learning classifier classifies the instances in the second stage. Among the machine learning algorithms, the CatBoost and Random Forest achieved better performance. Their performance aligned with the state-of-the-art approaches. The proposed method is robust against the labor-intensive feature selection and imbalanced class problems.

INTRODUCTION

Internet-based payment methods in recent times are growing at a rapid pace in developed and developing economies. The credit card industry players are losing billions of dollars despite an adequate level of security measures. Fear of losing the public and customer trust, credit card firms are typically reluctant to declare such information. Therefore it is difficult to approximate the losses incisively. This kind of

DOI: 10.4018/978-1-7998-8754-6.ch017

Figure 1. Fraud loss forecast till 2027. (Source:https://www.statista.com).

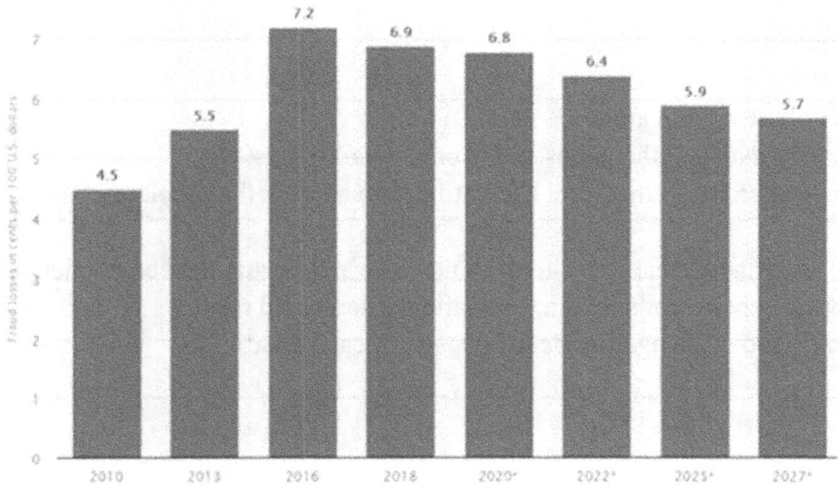

information hiding had resulted in the incapability to precisely audit such losses. From 2010 to 2018, the number of fraud losses per $100 of card transactions is shown in Figure 1 (Szmigiera, 2021). The fraud loss forecasts for 2027 are also documented. The leading global card and mobile payments trade publication Nilson Reports (Nilson Report, 2019) published that 27.85 billion U.S. dollars were lost due to frauds worldwide in 2018. Accordingly, the loss is projected to increase to 35.67 billion U.S. dollars in next five years and 40.63 billion U.S. dollars in ten years.

Most researchers have attempted to use classification or clustering methods in the automated detection of such frauds. In reality, the number of such fraud transactions is lesser than the original or regular transactions. Thus, this skewed nature of the data set made the detection of credit card fraud transactions a more meaningful and exciting problem to be solved. Detection of these small numbers of fraudulent card transactions would save a considerable amount of money for the credit card firm and the credit cardholder. Thus, there is an increasing research trend on detection methods for credit card fraud detection. Application (Phua, Gayler, Lee, & Smith-Miles, 2009) and behavior frauds (Bolton & Hand, 2002) are the most commonly found credit card frauds. Application fraud is carried out by using Identity theft. In this type of fraud, the fraudster applies to the issuer for a credit card with false documents. The banks take several protection actions in curbing such occurrences. It includes knowing the customer (KYC) document verification, calling the employer frequently, and so on. Behavioral fraud happens when the correctly issued credit card is fraudulently used in a transaction.

The proposed approach uses a two-step approach that employs a deep autoencoder (DAE) and a classifier. This approach uses a reduced size input vector to classify the type of transaction as genuine or fake. The main contribution of the proposed work is the use of the Deep-Auto-Encoder for reduced dimensions or attributes. The proposed algorithm improved the classification performance significantly. The proposed model was evaluated for efficacy using European credit card data set.

Chapter Objectives

Objectives of this chapter are enlisted below.

1. A brief overview of the credit card.
2. Types of credit card fraud and the losses due to credit card frauds,
3. Examine the many approaches that have been utilized to address the problem of automated fraud detection,
4. introduce a two-step fraud detection system's innovative architecture and components,
5. A description of the experiment's design, evaluation criteria, and results,
6. Examine the trends and challenges in identifying credit card fraud.

BACKGROUND

A payment or credit card is given to the cardholder by a designated financial firm. The cardholder can pay an amount electronically to the merchandiser for goods and services obtained using the credit card. The card issuer affirms that the cardholder will pay the due amount. The amount is paid along with the fixed charge within the due date as agreed upon. Consumers build a continued financial obligation balance using credit cards under the specific interest rate, duration, etc. The third-party entity pays an amount to the seller typically. The customer returns the spent amount later to this third-party entity.

Different Components of a Credit Card

The major components of a credit card are:

1. Bank emblem
2. A security chip
3. A 16 digit card number
4. Date of expiry or issue
5. Name of the cardholder
6. User details on the magnetic tape
7. Signature of the authorized user
8. A 4 digit card verification value
9. Card issuer hologram.

The credit card size is 85.60X53.98 mm, having rounded corners with a 2.88 to 3.48 mm radius. The ISO/IEC 7810 ID-1 is the commonly accepted card standard and ISO/IEC 7812 numbering standard. The first six digits represent card type, followed by nine digits unique account number and last digit for validation to check the validity code of the card. The magnetic stripe on the credit cards conforms to an ISO/IEC 7813 standard. Recent cards use a well-secured chip-based smart card technology. Apart from credit card numbers, it also includes expiration dates, extra codes such as card verification value (CVV), and security codes, as in Figure 2 (wikipedia.org, 23 April 2021 12:59 UTC).

Figure 2. Different components of credit cards. (Source: (Jiang & HAURY, 2020)).

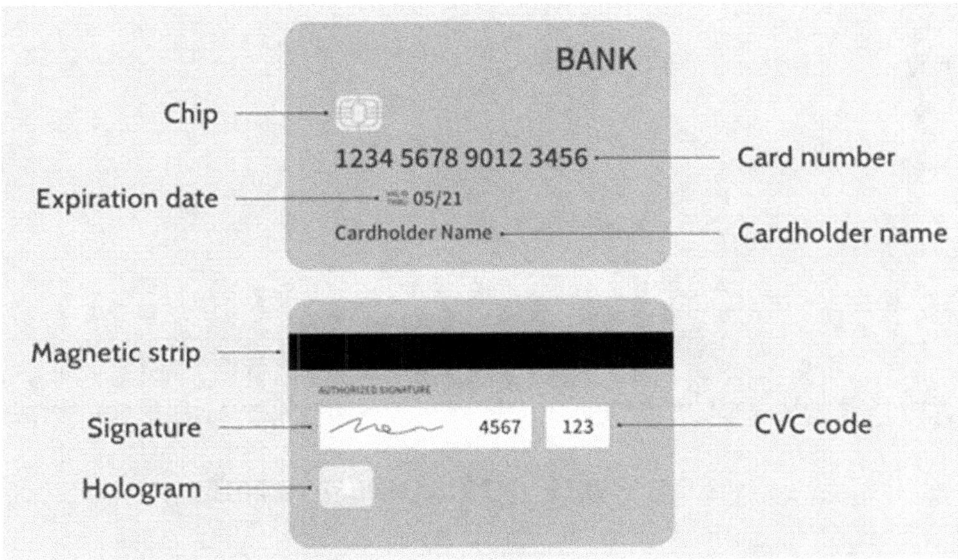

Credit Card Register

A credit card register (CCR) is a ledger of executed transactions. It is used to assure that the outstanding balance of credit card usage is below the credit limit. It also allows searching past transactions for easier coordination and budgeting.

Losses Due to Credit Card Frauds

Credit bureaus, banks, vehicles, debt collection, and credit card fraud were the most common kinds of fraud, according to the Federal Trade Commission's Consumer Sentinel Network's 2020 data book. Credit card fraud was the most prevalent payment method, with debit cards, payment apps, wire transfers, and bank transfers trailing far behind (IC3, 2021). Credit card fraud is a category of cyber-crimes in which someone other than an authorized person uses their credit card or account details to make an unlawful transaction. The fraudster uses the card to buy goods and services or transfer an amount to another account controlled by a criminal. The data security standards were created to secure card payments and reduce card fraud. Because of collaborative efforts from investigators, regulators, card providers, and banks, credit cards are more secure in the current context. The money of the cardholder is usually protected from scam attacks by card issuers and bank account rules. Credit card technology and security measures are becoming increasingly sophisticated, making it harder for fraudsters to steal money.

The Internet Crime Complaint (IC3) center published the complaint and the accompanying data in 2020. The image portrays annual and aggregate statistics for complaints and losses from 2016 through 2020. During that period, IC3 received 2,211,396 complaints, resulting in a $13.3 billion loss (IC3, 2021).

The top five classes of crimes, according to this survey, are:

1. Phishing based crimes

Figure 3. Top five cybercrime types and their comparison. Source: (IC3, 2021)

2. Nonpayment or non-delivery
3. Extortion
4. Breach of personal data
5. Identity fraud.

Types of Card Fraud

Credit card fraud can occur as a consequence of a stolen, lost, or cloned card. Moreover, the emergence of internet shopping has increased the occurrence of card-not-present fraud or the use of a credit card number in an e-commerce purchase. Here is a list of some common types of payment card frauds:

1. Application fraud
2. Account takeover fraud
3. Social engineering fraud
4. Skimming fraud

Application Fraud

I.D. Analytics (2004) states that 88 percent of fraudulent accounts were established using identity fraud strategies based on 300 million fraudulent account applications. According to the same report, identity fraud accounts for three-quarters of the damage caused by identity theft crime. Application fraud is a kind of identity crime that happens when an application form contains credible and synthetic or real but stolen documentation, i.e., the fraudster furnishes false information of the individual to apply for a credit card or other bank account in the name (Phua, Gayler, Lee, & Smith-Miles, 2009).

Account Takeover Fraud

Account takeover is a sort of cyber-attack in which a person obtains the passwords of another user in order to gain access to their online bank account. It is a type of identity theft fraud using data breaches, malware, or phishing attacks by the fraudster. The fraudster is allowed access to a victim's bank or credit card accounts and utilizes them to perform illegal transactions. Deduce, a cyber security organization has released some crucial results (Security.orgTeam, 2021).

1. Account takeovers have affected 22% of individuals in the United States, resulting in over 24 million homes being affected.
2. Financial losses from account takeovers are estimated to be worth approximately $12,000 on average.
3. 60% of account takeover victims have several accounts with the same password as the stolen account.
4. Within the last year, 58 percent of reported account takeovers took place. Accounts taken over on social media accounted for 51% of all accounts taken over, with banking accounts accounting for 32%.
5. The account takeover market has expanded by 250 percent from 2019 to 2020, with 22 percent of U.S. individuals reporting having accounts taken over.

Social Engineering Fraud

According to Marsh, a worldwide professional services corporation and a part of Marsh McLennan's Risk & Insurance Services business unit, the top three cyber threats in 2016 were social engineering with 52 percent, insider threats with 40 percent, and sophisticated, persistent assaults accounting to 39 percent, respectively. The term "social engineering fraud" includes several strategies used by spammers to mislead and manipulate victims into knowingly undertaking acts that result in disclosing personal information or the transfer of funds. Emails purporting to be sent by workers, partners, clients, consumers, or other organizations; phone calls, SMS messages, or even placing a malware-infected USB stick hanging about a workplace are all examples of techniques. Fraudsters tried to piece together information from various sources, including social media and recorded email, to look believable and trustworthy while committing the crime.

Social engineering is an attack by that victim deceived by furnishing confidential information. Due to the highly complex nature of such scams, detecting the fraud before it is too late is exceptionally difficult. Targets range from tiny enterprises to major corporations, and they come from various sectors and locations. Fraudsters are not discriminating, and they will frequently use a chain gun strategy to see what kind of response they can elicit from a fake message. Between October 2013 and May 2016, a wide variety of customers worldwide lost more than US$3.1 billion due to social engineering fraud (Services, PETROS, & MORTLOCK, 2016). Examples of fraud attacks

1. In June 2014, Scoular Co's controller was persuaded to conduct a series of wire transactions totaling $17.2 million to a bank in China using well-targeted emails. Scoular was buying a company in China, according to emails purportedly from the CEO, who directed a controller to obtain wire instructions from an accounting firm employee. This "spearphishing" attempt cost Scoular $17 million.

2. Scrap processor Mega Metals Inc. transferred $100,000 to a German vendor in April 2015 to pay for titanium shavings, but the seller did not receive payment. To obtain money, the hacker faked wire-transfer instructions. As a consequence, Mega Metals Inc. was duped out of $100,000.
3. An outside organization utilized false requests again in June 2015, targeting Ubiquiti Networks' finance department. An attacker utilized a "CEO scam," leading an employee to transfer US$46.7 million stored by a Hong Kong-based firm subsidiary. A US$17 million social engineering campaign was launched against Ubiquitous Networks.

Skimming Fraud

Skimming is the simplest form of an "off-book" white-collar crime. Since the money is stolen before it is recorded in the accounting system or a corporation's books, this scam may also affect individuals. ATM, debit card, or credit card skimming are all possibilities. *Defalcation* is the technical word used for skimming fraud. Skimming is often caught by chance, and hence, skimming seems to be the most challenging credit card fraud to detect. Since no audit traces are left behind the event, such traces may lead to the theft's origin. However, in other instances, firms may anticipate theft if they see revenue below projected. Skimming frauds can be classified as *business frauds,* including direct theft, tax evasion, bribery, and *personal frauds* include ATM frauds or Credit card frauds (Corporate Finance Institute, 2020).

ISSUES AND CHALLENGES

The issues and challenges related to credit card fraud detection are discussed in this section.

Issues

Identification of credit card fraud is complicated by issues (Abdallah, Maarof, & Zainal, 2016) such as

1. *Concept drift:* The phenomenon of concept drift refers to the fact that the underlying model (or notion) evolves with time. The fraud recognition models operate in rapidly changing settings where the activities of real users and cybercriminals are constantly changing.
2. *Imbalanced class distribution*: A class imbalance arises when the final dataset has fewer records of one type and more. There are many fewer samples of fraudulent cases in the University of California San Diego Data Mining Contest (UCSD) than genuine instances. Typical fraud cases (majority class) account for around 97:3 percent of all fraud cases (minority class). The learning and performance of classifiers are seriously skewed in favor of the dominant class due to the above factor.
3. *Finding the minimized set of features*: The large-scale and high-dimensionality of the fraud data set and the existence of numerous features or input variables make data analysis and detection highly complex and complicated. This also slows down the detecting process. As a result, generating a small model size may be advantageous in terms of real-time processing. Small data reduces the size of the model, lowering computing time and resulting in more interpretability.

4. *Detection of real-time frauds*: Online payment or auction applications demand quick detection and response in the credit card business. As a result, a fraud detection system must cope with limited resources (time and memory) to ensure successful identification.

Challenges

The credit card fraud recognition models must be

1. Able to accurately distinguish and categorize fraudulent and valid transactions,
2. Capable of recording and adapting cardholder drifting behavior over time by gradually updating the model to that behavior,
3. Address the skewed distribution of data effectively,
4. Reduce the amount of time, complexity, and cost associated with transaction execution,
5. Capture a sufficient number of characteristics for classification,
6. Provide a reliable method for real-time fraud detection.

SOLUTION AND RECOMMENDATIONS

Earlier Solutions

Automatic fraud detection is carried out either in a supervised or unsupervised mechanism (J. O., A. O., & S. A., 2017). The supervised learning methods attempt to predict the transaction's nature as fraud or authentic using the predictive model. Commonly used methods in this category are Random forests (R.F.), Decision trees (D.T.), Genetic algorithms (G.A.), Logistic regression (L.R.), Support vector machines (SVM), Probabilistic neural networks (PNN), Bayesian classifiers (NBC). The Ensemble classifiers are used, and the effects are more precise. Deep learning algorithms have recently piqued the interest of researchers due to their impressive performance.

The unsupervised methods used are k-Means (Bhati & Sharma, 2018), DBSCAN (H. N, Bastikar, Gavade, & Samota, 2018), and self-organizing map (SOM) to generate a fraud detection model (Olszewski, 2014). The random forest algorithm were used on the Chinese e-commerce company data set. They achieved an accuracy of 96.77% and a precision of 89.46% (Xuan,, et al., 2018).

Supervised machine learning algorithms such as random forest, logistic regression, support vector machines, decision tree induction, and k-Nearest neighbors were used to identify whether a credit card transaction was fake or genuine in a real-world data set. They developed ensemble classifiers and ensemble algorithms. The Precision of the ensemble classifier was higher than that of the random forest system (S, E, & B, 2018).

The European cardholder data collection used a selection of machine learning algorithms such as random forest, support vector machine, linear regression, and SMOTE. They discovered that the random forest outperformed the others when it came to static learning. The linear regression performed higher for gradual learning (M & L., 2019). The Linear regression, Random forest, Naive Bayesian Classifier, multi-level perceptron were used to detect fraud on the European card data set. They achieved higher accuracy and Precision than the benchmark methods (D., M., S., M., & A., 2019).

Random forest algorithm used for fraud detection. The random forest algorithm was found to be less vulnerable to noise results. The training time for the random forest algorithm was longer. They discovered that the Precision was between 90 and 95 percent (Suresh, Soundarya, V, Kavitha, S, E, & E.S., 2019).

A real-time dataset for fraud detection using several machine learning algorithms on the F.I. card dataset was used by (A, C, S, %, & N, 2019). SVM achieved the highest accuracy-91% and k-NN given the lowest accuracy of 77%. The k-nearest neighbor algorithm and other machine learning techniques were used on the European dataset, and k-NN achieved 97.56% accuracy by (Dighe, Patil, & Kokate, 2018).

A comparative study on various machine learning algorithms for fraud detection was carried out by (Y, Dubey,, & Sarika, 2019). They observed that the k-NN, Support vector machine algorithms worked well on the minor data set. Logical regression, Fuzzy logic algorithms worked well on the raw and un-sampled datasets. (K, C K, M, C P, & A K, 2018), successfully used an ensemble of classifiers to identify credit card fraud. AdaBoost and the majority voting ensemble method have shown better results than the single classifier.

The *Donut-* a variational auto-encoder method applied with F-scores ranging from 0.75 to 0.9 for the learn KPIs. They used Restricted Boltzmann machines to learn the distribution and predict the fraud transaction (Apapan & L, 2018).

Using association rule mining (K R & Masoumeh, 2014), succeeded in extracting the underlying relationship among the attributes of the transactions. For highly imbalanced and anonymous data sets, they used an intelligent model. To deal with the issue of class imbalance, they used frequent item-set mining. To detect incoming card purchase trends, the association rules were discovered. For pattern recognition, all attributes from the anonymous dataset existence are given equal weight. For performance assessment, the UCSD 2009 data collection was used. Their proposed model had a high fraud identification rate, a healthy classification rate, and Matthews' correlation coefficient (K R & Masoumeh, 2014).

In 2017, a k-NN based classification method was used to identify the fraud transaction as an outlier. The achieved accuracy of the model was 72% on the outlier detection. It was not easy to tune the system. This method was not applied to real-time fraud detection. The proposed approach lessened the false alarm rates and escalated the fraud detection rate (N & M, 2017).

A hybrid approach is used to combine the Naive Bayesian Classifier, k-Nearest Neighbor, and Logistic Regression approaches (J. O., A. O., & S. A., 2017). On the skewed dataset, they used under-sampling and over-sampling. For the implementation, they used Python. The accuracy, sensitivity, specificity, Precision, Matthews's correlation coefficient, and balanced classification rate were used to assess the technique's success. According to their findings, the most accurate classifiers were Naive Bayes, k-nearest Neighbor, and logistic regression. 97.92 percent, 97.69 percent, and 54.86 percent accuracy were recorded, respectively. The comparison of results revealed that Naive Bayes and k-nearest neighbor classifiers outperform each other.

NBC, logistic regression, J48, and Ada-Boost were used for comparative study. They concluded that the AdaBoost algorithm performed better than the Logistic regression on a customized fraud dataset (Heta & Prashasti, 2019).

The Synthetic minority oversampling technique (SMOTE) to handle the class imbalance problem and whale optimization techniques (WOT) was used (Sahayasakila.V, June 2019). They aimed to detect the fraud credit card transactions on the Kaggle data set. They used the three operators: search for prey, encircle it, and humpback the whales' behavior using the bubble net. They claim that they were able to solve the class imbalance problem, reliability, data optimization. Also, they claimed that they enhanced the convergence speed.

Applied decision tree, random forest, SVM, and Linear regression for fraud detection on skewed European cardholder dataset. The logical regression, decision tree, random forest, and SVM resulted in 97.7%, 95.55%, 98.6%, and 97.5%, respectively. Even though the random forest performed better than the others, the speed was a matter of concern. Also, SVM was unable to perform better due to the skewed nature of the dataset (Sait, & Yunus, 2018).

The fraud discovery problem as an ordered classification task was articulated by (Johannes, et al., 2018). They used feature aggregation strategies and Long Short-Term Memory (LSTM) networks to identify the transactions. Their study revealed that the LSTM worked better than their baseline model-random forest (R.F.) - classifier. They observed that the offline transactions detection improved with the LSTM. They suggested combining both sequential and non-sequential methods to detect the different kinds of frauds.

To generate artificial examples (Ugo, Alfredo, Francesca, Paolo, & Francesco, 2019) have developed Generative Adversarial Networks (GANs) and solved the imbalanced class data set issue. The aim was to improve the performance of the credit card fraud detection method.

An under complete auto-encoder network was proposed for dimensionality reduction and supervised learning method for fraud detection(Sumit, Soumyadeep, Manosij, & Sanjoy Kumar, 2020). Their proposed model performed well to achieve the accuracy of 99.94%, Precision of 85.34%, Recall of 80.15%, and an F1-score of 82.65%.

Proposed Solution

The deep-learning methods gained momentum due to improvements and familiarity with frameworks such as Pytorch (https://pytorch.org/tutorials/, 2021), Tensorflow in recent days. The tensor-flow framework (https://www.tensorflow.org/, 2020) is used to implement the system discussed in the proposed model.

Fraud Detection System: Architecture

The block diagram of the fraud detection scheme is as shown in Figure 4. A transaction is sent to the credit card company as an authorized demand. This transaction is entered into the *online fraud detection module* first; then, the related suspicion score is produced using the historical transaction data of the linked accounts. The transactions' corresponding (transaction, suspicion score) are input into the authorization decision-*making* module. The authorization decision is based on the acceptance verification result and level of fraud risk. Mainly acceptance verification process is concerned about the adequacy of the open-to-buy balance for the transaction of this linked account. It randomly validates the identity details of the authorized user. A "high risk" alert for the transaction is generated if the suspicion score exceeds the specified threshold. The cut-off value is generally defined by the model's tolerance for false positives (Zhang, Han, Xu, & Wang, 2021).

The similarly higher cut-off value is used to identify the exceptional high-risk transactions. During the authorization phase, a valid transaction with verification results has a higher fraud risk score, and the transaction with an inaccurate verification result is rejected. Only those transactions having valid verification results and low fraud risk scores are allowed. Alert management module sends notifications to the transaction monitoring department on High-risk transactions. The credit card holders are alerted of these high fraud risk transactions by the transaction monitoring department via SMS, email, or mobile applications. Also, they occasionally conduct a transaction investigation over the phone. The

Figure 4. The overall process in fraud detection. Source: (Zhang, Han, Xu, & Wang, 2021)

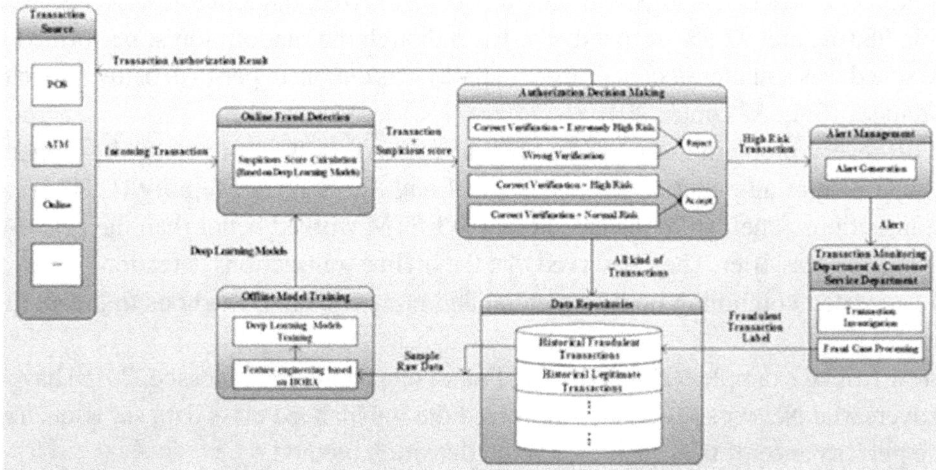

fraud incidents detected by the transactions and customer support departments are gathered, and the associated transactions in the system are tagged as fraud cases.

A training dataset is derived from past occurrences of the data during a specific time-frame. To get the feature variables for the classification model, feature engineering based on the autoencoder is performed. A machine-learning algorithm then determines the nature of the credit card transaction. Following training, the model is evaluated on a test set to get real-time credit card transaction ratings. Here, we take a Kaggle data set as input.

Input

Credit card features are utilized to figure out account holders' buying habits, which are strongly linked to their attributes, such as income, age, profession, number of cards possessed, type of the card, Credit grade and line, Book balance, frequency of usage, overdraft, bad debts, overdrafts but not bad debts, Time bracket, average daily card spending, overdraft rate, spending progress rate, and so on (Abdallah, Maarof, & Zainal, 2016). The details on credit card purchases can be found at "https://www.kaggle.com/mlg-ulb/creditcardfraud" (Machine Learning Group - ULB, 2018). It is used as an input data set in the present study. It includes credit card purchases made by European Union cardholders in 2013. The information gathered is biased against genuine card purchases. There are 284,807 documents in all. There are 2, 84,315 valid transactions and 492 fake transactions in all. Each transaction record has a total of 30 attributes. Fraudulent transactions are unfavorable, whereas legal ones are positive (Sumit, Soumyadeep, Manosij, & Sanjoy Kumar, 2020).

The Autoencoder

An Auto-encoder is a form of unsupervised deep learning technique. An auto-encoder, shown in figure 4, aims to learn to approximate the identity function that maps x to x$^{/}$. An auto-encoder can recreate the exact in-sample input if an extensive and deep neural network is used. There are two types of autoencoders based on the size of the encoding output. They are under complete (UAE) and over-complete auto-encoders (OAE). A UAE is usually not deeper and reduces the size of the input's dimension as an output. An OAE is deeper and produces an encoding output's dimension that is larger than the input's dimension. Auto-encoders that use the fully-connected layers are classified as either fully-connected (FAE) or Convolutional Auto-encoders (CAE). In an FAE, fully connected feed-forward neural networks are used. In CAE, convolutional layers are used (Chollet, 2016).

Encoder

Given X, input data is mapped into latent vector representation 'Z' using an encoder architecture. Here, the nonlinear activation function is $f_E(.)$. Weight vector '$W\varphi$.'is the set of weights, and $B\varphi$ .is the set of biases for the encoder network. The latent vector form, Z, is represented as in Equation (1).

$$Z = f_E\left(W_\varphi \times X + B_\varphi\right). \tag{1}$$

Decoder

The decoder transforms the latent vector Z to reconstruct the approximation of the original data X' .from it. In Equation (2), the nonlinear activation function is represented as $f_D(.)$. The weights vector is W_θ, and the set of biases is B_θ for the decoder network. The approximation of X from Z is represented as X':

$$X' = f_D D\left(W_\theta \times Z + B_\theta\right). \tag{2}$$

Reconstruction Error

The reconstruction error is denoted by the letter 'Δ'. It calculates the difference between an autoencoder's input 'X′' and the initial input 'X.' Overfitting can be avoided when using the regularizer. The reconstruction error is calculated using the Euclidean interval between X and X' .in this configuration. i.e

$$\Delta(X, X') = \|X - X'\|^2. \tag{3}$$

The nonlinear activation functions retain the randomness of the output result. Hence, the activation functions $f_E(.)$ and $f_D(.)$ in this case are leakyReLU.

Method

The network architecture consists of three parts: an encoder, a bottleneck and a decoder. An Encoder in the proposed model has three layers of the feed-forward network. There are 30 nodes in the input layer.

Figure 5. Latent feature extraction and reconstruction of the original data.

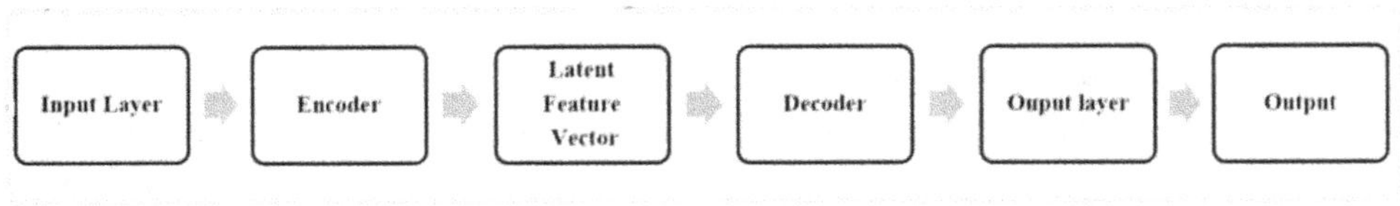

The outcome is fed forwarded to the bottleneck layer. The bottleneck layer reduces the total number of attributes to 15. The decoder has a three-layer feed-forward network. The record is reconstructed at the end of the decoder network. It outputs 30 dimensions as available in the input using the hidden representation. It is as shown in Figure 5.

After training the deep auto-encoder network end to end, its corresponding decoder network is discarded. To this compressed version of this autoencoder network, a classification model- such as CatBoost or Light gradient boosting machines- is attached at the end of the bottleneck layer. This configuration is shown in Figure 6.

Classification Models

Machine learning algorithm models such as CatBoost and Random Forest are attached with the deep auto-encoder in the proposed work. The experiments were carried out on the European credit card dataset. The following algorithms are discussed in this section.

1. Support vector machine
2. Logistic regression
3. CatBoost
4. Random Forest
5. XGBoost

Support Vector Machines (SVM)

In the SVM method (Cherkassky & Ma, 2004) margin between the training examples is maximized with the decision boundary by building a hyperplane. This separates the true and false class instances with the maximum possible margin. The kernel approach tackles the problem of quadratic rise by not mapping the data into the higher dimensional feature space in memory without compromising the features and runtime necessary to calculate the classifier's predictions. Equation (4) defines the hyperplane for the dataset consisting of pairs of D = {(xi, yj) | x_i ε R^P, y_i ε {+1,-1, i = {1, 2, 3…}}, and 'β' is a unit vector.

Figure 6. Classification using the latent features.

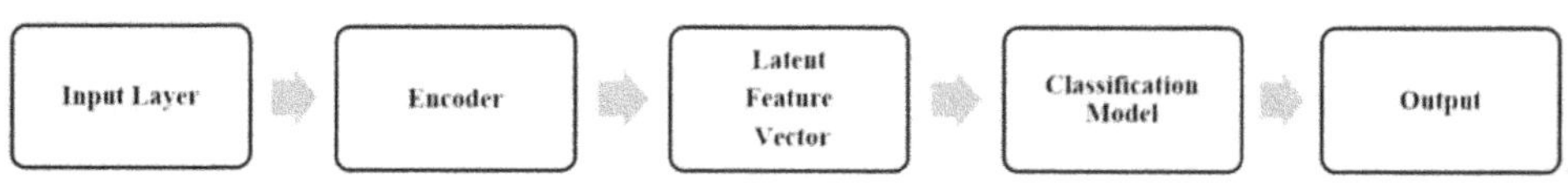

In the case of separable classes, the function is $y_i f(x) > 0$ for all I values. The hyperplane with maximum width separating the samples of {+1, -1} is found. The formula for optimizing the quadratic problem is in Equation (5). (Masetic & Subasi, 2016). As a result, the margin is 'M' unit far from the hyperplane separating examples of both sides.

$$\{x : f(x) = X^T * \beta + \beta_0 = 0\}. \tag{4}$$

$$\text{Maximize } M_{\beta,\beta_0,\beta=1}. \text{ subject to } y_i \begin{matrix} (X^T * \beta + \beta_0) \geq M, \\ i = 1,2,3,\ldots N \end{matrix} \tag{5}$$

CatBoost

The CatBoost (Prokhorenkova, Gusev, Vorobev, Dorogush, & Gulin, 2017) is a gradient-boost algorithm on decision trees. The researchers at Yandex incorp developed it. Ordering principle is the basis for the CatBoost algorithm (Tal, 2018). CatBoost introduced two critical algorithmic advances - ordered boosting and Categorical attribute processor. The ordered boosting is a permutation-driven boosting algorithm. A categorical attribute processor is an innovative processing algorithm for categorical features. They use random permutations obtained from the training examples. These permutations avoid the prediction shift commonly seen in gradient boosting algorithms.

CatBoost is based on the ordering principle. Online learning algorithms have inspired the CatBoost method. These algorithms acquire timestamped training examples sequentially. The value of each Target Statistic (S.T.) relies on the ascertained history. CatBoost introduces an artificial "time" for each training record. To compute the target, static available history is used. CatBoost exercises various permutations for different steps of gradient boosting. For all features, Catboost uses a one-hot encoding with a default value of 2.

There are two modes for selecting the tree structure in CatBoost. They are Ordered and Plain. The basic mode combines ordered target statistics with the standard Gradient Boosting Decision Tree (GBDT) algorithm.

Ordered Boosting

By keeping 'n' supporting templates, a random permutation of training examples is carried out in this method of boosting. The template M_{j1} is used to estimate the residual for the jth sample. It is as given in figure 8. As it requires more computational resources, it is not feasible for practical tasks. A modified version of this algorithm is implemented in CatBoost. In CatBoost, a tweaked variant of this algorithm is used. CatBoost requires all models to share a single tree structure that uses permutations such as $\sigma_1 = \sigma_2$. This ensures that the discrepancy between the expected and real mark is not used in training M_i, nor in calculating the Target Statistic or estimating the gradient.

Figure 7. Ordered boosting

Algorithm 1: Ordered boosting

input : $\{(\mathbf{x}_k, y_k)\}_{k=1}^{n}, I$;

$\sigma \leftarrow$ random permutation of $[1, n]$;
$M_i \leftarrow 0$ for $i = 1..n$;
for $t \leftarrow 1$ **to** I **do**
  for $i \leftarrow 1$ **to** n **do**
    $r_i \leftarrow y_i - M_{\sigma(i)-1}(i)$;
  for $i \leftarrow 1$ **to** n **do**
    $\Delta M \leftarrow LearnModel((\mathbf{x}_j, r_j) : \sigma(j) \leq i)$;
    $M_i \leftarrow M_i + \Delta M$;
return M_n

Building a Tree

Base predictors in CatBoost are oblivious decision trees. They're often referred to as decision tables. The term oblivious refers to the use of the same splitting rule at every level of the tree. The end result is balanced, less resistant to overfitting, and quicker decision trees. Algorithm 2 describes the process of creating a tree in CatBoost. Figure 7 depicts this. Supporting models $M_{r,j}$ are retained throughout the learning phase of the ordered boosting mode, where $M_{r,j}(I)$ is the current forecast for the ith example based on the first j examples in the permutation σ_r. At each iteration t of the algorithm, a random permutation r is sampled from 1,..., s, and a tree Tt is built from it. This permutation is used to calculate all T.S. for categorical functions, and it affects the learning process.

Random Forest Classifier

Random Forest Classifier (Suresh, Soundarya, V, Kavitha, S, E, & E.S., 2019) is a supervised ensemble classifier. It is a scalable, flexible, and accurate classification method. By combining the predictions

Figure 8. Building a tree in CatBoost.

Algorithm 2: Building a tree in CatBoost

input : $M, \{y_i\}_{i=1}^{n}, \alpha, L, \{\sigma_i\}_{i=1}^{s}, Mode$

$grad \leftarrow CaclGradient(L, M, y)$;
$r \leftarrow random(1, s)$;
$G \leftarrow (grad_r(1), \ldots, grad_r(n))$ for $Plain$;
$G \leftarrow (grad_{r,\sigma_r(1)-1}(i)$ for $i = 1$ to $n)$ for $Ordered$;
$T \leftarrow$ empty tree;
foreach *step of top-down procedure* **do**
  foreach *candidate split c* **do**
    $T_c \leftarrow$ add split c to T;
    if $Mode == Plain$ **then**
      $\Delta(i) \leftarrow \text{avg}(grad_r(p)$ for
      $p: leaf(p) = leaf(i))$ for all i;
    if $Mode == Ordered$ **then**
      $\Delta(i) \leftarrow \text{avg}(grad_{r,\sigma_r(i)-1}(p)$ for
      $p: leaf(p) = leaf(i), \sigma_r(p) < \sigma_r(i))\ \forall i$;
    $loss(T_c) \leftarrow \|\Delta - G\|_2$
  $T \leftarrow \text{argmin}_{T_c}(loss(T_c))$
if $Mode == Plain$ **then**
  $M_{r'}(i) \leftarrow M_{r'}(i) - \alpha\, \text{avg}(grad_{r'}(p)$ for
  $p: leaf(p) = leaf(i))$ for all r', i;
if $Mode == Ordered$ **then**
  $M_{r',j}(i) \leftarrow M_{r',j}(i) - \alpha\, \text{avg}(grad_{r',j}(p)$ for
  $p: leaf(p) = leaf(i), \sigma_{r'}(p) \leq j$ for all r', j, i;
return T, M

from the different trees, random forests avoid the over-fitting problem. Random forests are complex, slower, and require more computational resources. The following steps are used in implementing the random forest algorithm and are as in Figure 9.

1. From the given data set, random samples are selected.
2. Construct the decision trees from these selected samples to obtain the prediction results.

3. Apply the voting mechanism to all the predicted results.
4. Consider the most voted prediction result as a final prediction result.

Random forest is a classification method that integrates several tree classifiers. Each tree is based on a randomly generated vector value that is spread equally across all trees in the forest. So, in the random forest algorithm, a random vector θ_k is developed that is independent of the initial random vectors and is scattered to all trees, and each tree is managed to grow using the training dataset and the random vector θ_k, resulting in a collection of tree-structured classifiers {h(x, θ_k), k = 1,... at input vector x.

The generalization error, PE_* .is given by equation (6), where x and y are random vectors indicating the probability over the X, Y space. The margin function 'mg' measures the amount to which the average number of votes at random vectors for the appropriate output that exceeds the average vote for any other output. The I(·) is the indicator function, and $mg(x, y)$ .is the margin function defined in Equation (7). The influence and correlation are two factors that compute the accuracy of an individual classifier and its reliance. A random forest with subjective characteristics is generated by randomly selecting a trivial set of variables on each input node.

$$PE_* = P_{x,y}\left(mg(x,y) < 0\right). \quad (6)$$

$$mg(x,y) = av_k * I\left((h_k(X) = y\right) - max_{j!=y} av_k * I\left((h_k(X) = j\right). \quad (7)$$

Linear Regression

Linear Regression is an approach to establish a linear relationship between the independent variable 'x' and dependent variable 'y'. As indicated in Equation (8), the model fits the best line for estimating the value of y for a given value of x. The model obtains the best regression fit line by identifying the right values of intercept 'm' and coefficient 'c'. Equation (8) describes the linear regression hypothesis function.

$$y = m * x + c. \quad (8)$$

The cost function, J (.) tries to reduce the 'Root Mean Squared Error (RMSE)' between the valid values of y, y_act . and the estimated value, y_est .

$$J = \frac{1}{n}\sum_{i=1}^{n}\left(y\_est - y\_act\right)^2. \quad (9)$$

Figure 9. Basic architecture of Random Forest algorithm

The LightGBM algorithm
Input:
Training data: D = {(χ1, y1), (χ2, y2), ..., (χN, yN)}, χi ∈χ, χ ⊆ R, yi∈{−1,+1}; loss function: L(y, θ (χ));
Iterations:
M; Big gradient data sampling ratio: a; slight gradient data sampling ratio: b;
1: Combine features that are mutually exclusive (i.e., features never simultaneously accept nonzero values) of χi, i = {1, ...,N} by the exclusive feature bundling (EFB) technique;
2: Set $\theta_0(\chi) = arg\ min_c \sum_i^N L(y_i, c)$;
3: For m = 1 to M do
4: Calculate gradient absolute values:

$$r_i = \left|\frac{\partial L(y_i, \theta(x_i))}{\partial \theta(x_i)}\right|_{\theta(x)=\theta_{m-1}(x)}, i = \{1, \dots, N\}$$

5: Resample data set using gradient-based one-side sampling (GOSS) process:
topN = *a* × *len(D)*; *randN* = *b* × *len(D)*;
sorted = *GetSortedIndices(abs(r))*;
A = *sorted*[1 : *topN*]; *B* = *RandomPick(sorted*[*topN* : *len(D)*] , *randN)*;
$\acute{D} = A + B$;
6: Calculate information gains:

$$V_j(d) = \frac{1}{n}\left(\frac{\left(\sum_{x_i \in A_l} r_i + \frac{1-a}{b}\sum_{x_i \in B_l} r_i\right)^2}{n_l^j(d)} + \frac{\left(\sum_{x_i \in A_r} r_i + \frac{1-a}{b}\sum_{x_i \in B_r} r_i\right)^2}{n_r^j(d)}\right)$$

7: Develop a new decision tree $\theta_m(x)'$ on set D'
8: Update $\theta_m(\chi) = \theta_{m-1}(\chi) + \theta_m(\chi)$
9: End for
10: Return $\tilde{\theta}(x) = \theta_M(x)$

The eXtreme Gradient Boosting

XGB is an intelligent algorithm that can manage a wide range of data abnormalities. A gradient boosting technique first uses weaker models to estimate the target variable for a simple data set. These results are then pooled to provide an accurate approximation of the target variable. The XGBoost method is an efficient version of such a gradient boosting technique. It is distributed as open-source software. Equation (10) describes the process of minimizing the objective function of XGB method.

$$L^t = \sum_{i=1}^{n} l(y_{act}, y_{pred,i}^{(t-1)} + f_t(x_i)) + \Omega(f_t). \quad (10)$$

The function $l(.)$.is a differentiable convex loss function. The difference is measured between the prediction $\mathrm{y}_{\mathrm{pred}}$.and the target, $\mathrm{y}_{\mathrm{act}}$. The prediction of the ith instance, $y_{pred,i}^{(t-1)}$. at the tth iteration, f_t.corresponds to an independent tree structure and the leaf weight. To minimize the objective function, L^t. add f_t.greedily to $l(.)$.as shown in the equation $\Omega(f_t)$.is a penalty function. At each iteration the objective function L^t.is minimized as shown in the following Equation (11). The simplified objective function to minimize at step t is,

$$\widehat{L^t} = \sum_{i=1}^{n} \left[g_i f_t(x_i) + \frac{1}{2} h_i f^2_t(x_i) \right] + \Omega(f_t). \quad (11)$$

Using the known techniques, this sum of simple quadratic functions with a single parameter $\widehat{L^t}$ .is minimized. The next step is to build the learner. The simple approach here is, start with a single root containing all the training examples. Iterate over all features and values per feature, and evaluate each possible split loss reduction:

$$\text{Gain} = loss_{parent} - \left(loss_{Left\,child} + loss_{Right\,Child} \right). \quad (12)$$

Gain, Equation (12), of this best split must be positive and more significant than the *min_split_gain* parameter, otherwise halt growing the branch. This "Exact Greedy Algorithm" has a complexity of $O(n*m)$. with a training set of size 'n' and the features set of 'm'.

Light Gradient Boosting Machine

The Light Gradient Boosting Machine (LightGBM) is a variant of the classic Gradient Boosted Decision Tree (GBDT) approach that can speed up Classifier model training without sacrificing accuracy. LightGBM uses the Gradient algorithm and a leaf-by-leaf growth technique to accomplish this effect. The Gradient algorithm works by converting continuous floating-point eigenvalues to discrete values (k) and then creating a distribution with width k. The training data is next scanned, and cumulative statistic is calculated for each discrete value in the distribution.

LightGBM replaces most GBDT's level-wise decision tree development approach with a leaf-wise technique with height limits. In reality, level-wise is an inefficient approach since it handles the leaves of the same layer indiscriminately, resulting in a significant amount of extra overhead. Each time, the leaf-wise method identifies the leaf with the largest split gain from all of the existing leaves, then splits, and so on. As a result, leaf-wise can decrease more mistakes and achieve higher accuracy for the same splitting times when compared to level-wise. Taking into account the over-fitting induced leaf-wise, LightGBM incorporates a factor-the maximum depth limit-into the model. As a result, over-fitting may be

Figure 10. Light gradient boosting machines algorithm (Taha & Malebary, 2020).

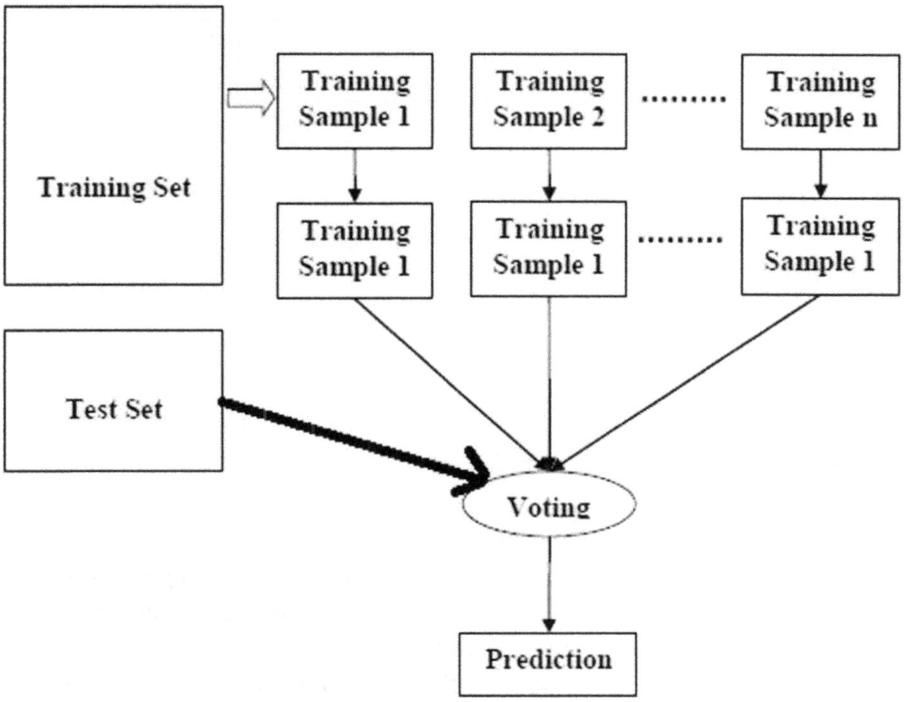

avoided, yet optimum performance can be ensured. LGBM enhances the capability for category features that may be entered directly without the need for further 0/1 augmentation (Taha & Malebary, 2020).

RESULTS AND DISCUSSIONS

In this section, we discuss the details of experiments and results.

Experimental Details

The proposed credit card fraud detection experiment was executed using an Intel Core i3-7000 CPU working at a 3.90GHz processor. An installed memory of 8GB RAM. The experiments were conducted on a 64 bit Windows X64 based operating system. The autoencoder algorithm was implemented using the TensorFlow framework, and the machine learning techniques were implemented and tested using the sci-kit learn package using the Python programming language.

Evaluation Metrics

Various evaluation metrics considered in this work are:

Table 1. Confusion matrix

True **Class**	**Predicted Class**		
	--------	**Normal**	**Fraud**
	Normal	True Positive (T.P.)	False Negative (F.N.)
	Fraud	False Positives (F.P.)	True Negatives (T.N.)

1. Accuracy
2. Precision or Sensitivity
3. Recall
4. F-1 Score
5. ROC AUC curves

Confusion Matrix

The confusion matrix entries are used to quantify the critical performance indicators. The number of true positives (T.P.), true negatives (T.N.), false positives (F.P.), and false negatives (F.N.) are the entries of the confusion matrix. For evaluating the results, the accuracy, Recall, Precision, and F-1 Score were computed. The terms mentioned above are defined as follows:

There are four different ways to determine whether or not the forecasts are correct:

1. True Positive (T.P.): This metric lists the number of positive cases accurately predicted.
2. False Positive: This metric lists the number of negative records that were incorrectly predicted to be positive.
3. True Negative (T.N.): This metric lists the number of negative cases that were accurately expected as such.
4. False Negative (F.N.) counts how many positive records are supposed to be negative.

Accuracy

Precision

The ratio of true positive counts to the number of true positive and false-positive counts is Precision. The Precision is written in Equation (14).

$$Precision = p = \frac{(True\,Positive)}{(True\,Posiitive + False\,Positive)}. \tag{14}$$

Recall

True positive counts divided by the sum of true positive and false negative counts is called Recall. The following Equation (15) explains it.

$$Recall = r = \frac{(True\,Positive)}{(True\,Positive + False\,Negative)}. \quad (15)$$

F1-Score

The ratio of true positive counts to the sum of true positive and false-positive counts is known as the F1-Score. It is given in the below Equation (16).

$$F1 - Score = \frac{2 * precision * recall}{(precision + recall)}. \quad (16)$$

Precision and Recall are essential in an imbalanced data collection. Precision is a metric that assesses the accuracy of the resulting scale and its similarity to the intended solution. The Recall is used to determine the relevance of the findings. The smaller the recall value, higher the false-negative rates, and the higher the accuracy, the lower the false-positive rates. The lower false-negative rates result in higher recall value. Higher Precision results when the false positive rates are lower. Hence the proximity and suitability of the resulting scale are correctly indicated by the Precision. Also, recall score measures the relevant number of results.

Result Analysis

Through the experiments, the model was trained with 1,82,276 training examples. The model has committed no misclassification during the training, and hence the training error achieved was 100 percent. Also, the Precision, Recall, and F-1 scores were 100 each, respectively. However, once the model presented with the test set of 56962 test examples, the accuracy achieved was 99.95 percent. It indicates that the model is correctly predicting both the positive and negative class examples. Precision for the positive class is 99.96, and negative class precision is 94.93 percent. The Recall for the positive class is 99.9, but for the negative class examples, the classifier predicts 35.4 percentage of fraud transactions as authentic. However, the 99.90 percent positive class examples were correctly classified. When the overall predictions are taken into account, the positive class has a 99.97 percent F-1 score, but the negative class has an 84.75 percent F-1 score. Hence, we need to search for a mechanism to reduce the negative class results. The results of the obtained model are shown below in Figure 11.

Figure 11. Snapshot for the deep auto-encoder with CatBoost classifier

```
Train Result:
================================================
Accuracy Score: 100.00%
_______________________________________________
Classification Report:
                  0      1  accuracy  macro avg  weighted avg
precision       1.0    1.0       1.0        1.0           1.0
recall          1.0    1.0       1.0        1.0           1.0
f1-score        1.0    1.0       1.0        1.0           1.0
support    181946.0  330.0       1.0   182276.0      182276.0
_______________________________________________
Confusion Matrix:
 [[181946      0]
 [     0    330]]

Test Result:
================================================
Accuracy Score: 99.95%
_______________________________________________
Classification Report:
                      0          1  accuracy     macro avg  weighted avg
precision      0.999596   0.949367  0.999526      0.974481      0.999509
recall         0.999930   0.765306  0.999526      0.882618      0.999526
f1-score       0.999763   0.847458  0.999526      0.923610      0.999501
support    56864.000000  98.000000  0.999526  56962.000000  56962.000000
_______________________________________________
Confusion Matrix:
 [[56860     4]
 [   23    75]]
```

FUTURE RESEARCH DIRECTIONS

In this section, we discuss the generic issues and challenges in credit card fraud identification.

Trends in Fraud Preventative Measures

Fraud affects many stakeholders- *Financial Services Institutions, Retail and Consumer, and Technology*- in different ways (Vamsi Gullapalli, Sireeshkumar Kalli, Ajay Vijay, 2020). Therefore following trends can be observed in the realm of research:

1. Trends in financial services institutions are,
    a. Organizing the fraud management operations in a centralized location.
    b. Making more use of real-time external data.
    c. Transferring from in-house to commercial enterprise fraud management (EFM) products,
    d. Improve the web fraud detection systems to the next generation.
2. Trends in retail and consumer include:
    a. Merchants are addressing the rising identity frauds
    b. Merchants are increasingly accepting secured mobile payments, and
    c. Consumers use network-branded credit cards to reduce fraud expenses.
3. Trends technology developers: What to Expect in the future?
    a. As mobile devices become more commonly used, new fraud concerns are emerging,

b. Adopting to the increasing tendency of self-learning predictive models from rule-based systems,
c. Better business user interface for alert management.
d. Small and mid-sized enterprises are seeking solutions that are simple to use and maintain.

Prerequisites for Fraud Prevention

Essential preconditions for adequate fraud prevention include

1. Reducing the false-positive rates,
2. Support for the real-time transactions,
3. Analyzing the entity-relationship,
4. Covering the specific channels and items,
5. Automated and intelligent fraud analysis.

CONCLUSION

Banking based on Internet technology has become a vital part of modern life. As technology advances, more secure, quicker, and real-time security against malicious actions is needed. Academic and company analysts have made several attempts to forecast credit card fraud in the past. Since the approaches were centered on the whole array of dimensions, they suffered from the curse of dimensionality. A deep auto-encoder lowers the dimensionality of the dataset by fifty percent in this proposed work. For the prediction, the encoded latent vector is used as an input to the classifier. The findings of the proposed model were compared to those of previous research. The results proved that the proposed architecture is more effective than the existing methods. Even our approach has a limitation; in the future, we shall investigate the ways to increase the recall rate and the F-1 score for the negative class in turn. Finally, a discussion on the recent trends and research issues is shared for future research.

REFERENCES

A, T., C, B., S, P., & N, K. (2019). Real-time Credit Card Fraud Detection Using Machine Learning. *2019 9th International Conference on Cloud Computing, Data Science Engineering (Confluence), 1*(1), 488-493. Retrieved from https://ieeexplore.ieee.org/document/8776942/

Abdallah, A., Maarof, M. A., & Zainal, A. (2016). Fraud detection system: A survey. *Journal of Network and Computer Applications, 68*, 90–113. doi:10.1016/j.jnca.2016.04.007

Apapan, P., & L, Y. (2018). Credit Card Fraud Detection using Deep Learning based on Auto-Encoder and Restricted Boltzmann Machine. *International Journal of Advanced Computer Science and Applications, 9*(1).

Bhati, P., & Sharma, M. (2018). Credit Card Number Fraud Detection Using K-Means with Hidden Markov Method. *International Journal of Mobile Computing and Application*, *2*(2), 15–18. http://www.internationaljournalssrg.org/IJMCA/paper-details?Id=20

Bolton, R. J., & Hand, D. J. (2002). Statistical fraud detection: A review. *Quality Engineering*, *49*, 313–314.

Cherkassky, V., & Ma, Y. (2004). Practical selection of SVM parameters and noise estimation for SVM regression. *Neural Networks*, *17*(1), 113–126. doi:10.1016/S0893-6080(03)00169-2

Chollet, F. (2016, 14 May). *Building Autoencoders in Keras.* Retrieved from The Keras Blog: https://blog.keras.io/building-autoencoders-in-keras.html

Corporate Finance Institute. (2020). *Skimming Fraud*. Retrieved from https://corporatefinanceinstitute.com/resources/knowledge/other/skimming-fraud/

D., V., M., K., S., S., M., A., & A., A. (2019). Credit Card Fraud Detection - Machine Learning methods. *2019 18th International Symposium INFOTEH-JAHORINA (INFOTEH), 1*(1), 1-5. Retrieved from https://ieeexplore.ieee.org/document/8717766

Dighe, D., Patil, S., & Kokate, S. (2018). Detection of Credit Card Fraud Transactions Using Machine Learning Algorithms and Neural Networks: A Comparative Study. *2018 Fourth International Conference on Computing Communication Control and Automation (ICCUBEA)*, 1-6. 10.1109/ICCUBEA.2018.8697799

Gullapalli, V., Kalli, S., & Vijay, A. (2020). *Credit Card Transaction.* https://www.capgemini.com/industry/banking-and-capital-markets/

H. N., B., Bastikar, S., Gavade, M., & Samota, S. (2018). Credit Card Fraud Detection Using HMM and DBSCAN. *International Journal of Science and Research, 7*(10), 1086-1090. Retrieved from https://www.ijsr.net/archive/v7i10/ART20192099.pdf

Heta, N., & Prashasti, K. (2019). Credit card Fraud Detection based on Machine Learning Algorithms. *International Journal of Computers and Applications*, *188*(44), 8–12. https://www.ijcaonline.org/archives/volume182/number44/naik-2019-ijca-918521.pdf

IC3. (2021). *IC3 Releases 2020 Internet Crime Report*. Retrieved from https://www.fbi.gov/news/pressrel/press-releases/fbi-releases-the-internet-crime-complaint-center-2020-internet-crime-report-including-covid-19-scam-statistics

J. O., A., A. O., A., & S. A., O. (2017). Credit card fraud detection using machine learning techniques: A comparative analysis. *2017 International Conference on Computing Networking and Informatics (ICCNI)*, 1-9. Retrieved from 10.1109/ICCNI.2017.8123782

Jiang, S., & Haury, A. C. (2020). *What Happens When Your Credit Card Expires?* Retrieved from https://www.investopedia.com/financial-edge/0712/what-happens-when-your-credit-card-expires.aspx

Johannes, J., Michael Ziegler, G., Calabretto, K., Portier, S., & Edouard, P., & He-Guelton, O. L. (2018). Sequence classification for credit-card fraud detection. *Expert Systems with Applications*, *100*(1), 234.

K, R. S., & Masoumeh, Z. (2014). FraudMiner: A Novel Credit Card Fraud Detection Model Based on Frequent Itemset Mining. *The Scientific World Journal, 2014*(1). Retrieved from https://www.hindawi.com/journals/tswj/2014/252797/

K, R., C K, L., M, S., C P, L., & A K, N. (2018). Credit Card Fraud Detection Using AdaBoost and Majority Voting. *IEEE Access, 6*(1), 14277-14284. Retrieved from https://ieeexplore.ieee.org/document/8292883/

M, P., & L., B. (2019). Detecting Credit Card Fraud Using Selected Machine Learning Algorithms. *2019 42nd International Convention on Information and Communication Technology, Electronics and Microelectronics (MIPRO), 1*(1), 1250-1255. Retrieved from https://ieeexplore.ieee.org/document/8757212

Machine Learning Group - ULB. (2018). *Credit Card Fraud Detection.* Retrieved from https://www.kaggle.com/mlg-ulb/creditcardfraud

Masetic, Z., & Subasi, A. (2016). Congestive heart failure detection using random forest classifier. *Computer Methods and Programs in Biomedicine, 130*, 54–64.

N, M., & M, P. (2017). Analysis on credit card fraud identification techniques based on KNN and outlier detection. *2017 Third International Conference on Advances in Electrical, Electronics, Information, Communication and Bio-Informatics (AEEICB), 255-258*(1), 1. Retrieved from https://ieeexplore.ieee.org/document/7972424/

Olszewski, D. (2014). Fraud detection using self-organizing map visualizing the user profiles. *Knowledge-Based Systems, 70*(1), 324–334. https://www.sciencedirect.com/science/article/pii/S0950705114002652

Phua, C., Gayler, R., Lee, V., & Smith-Miles, K. (2009). 6). On the communal analysis suspicion scoring for identity crime in streaming credit applications. *European Journal of Operational Research, 195*, 595–612. doi:10.1016/j.ejor.2008.02.015

Prokhorenkova, L., Gusev, G., Vorobev, A., Dorogush, A. V., & Gulin, A. (2017). *CatBoost: unbiased boosting with categorical features.* arXiv preprint arXiv:1706.09516.

Protect your users. Be their hero. (n.d.). Retrieved from https://www.deduce.com/

Report, N. (2019). *Card Fraud Losses Reach $27.85 Billion.* Nilson Publisher. Retrieved from https://nilsonreport.com/mention/407/1link/

S, D., E, M., & B, F. (2018). Supervised Machine Learning Algorithms for Credit Card Fraudulent Transaction Detection: A Comparative Study. *2018 IEEE International Conference on Information Reuse and Integration (IRI), 1*(1), 122-125. Retrieved from doi:10.1109/IRI.2018.00025

Sahayasakila.V, D. K. (2019). Credit Card Fraud Detection System using Smote Technique and Whale Optimization. *International Journal of Engineering and Advanced.*

Sait, K. N., & Yunus, S. (2018). Credit Card Fraud Detection Using Machine Learning Models and Collating Machine Learning Models. *International Journal of Pure and Applied Mathematics, 118*(1), 825–838.

Security.org Team. (2021). Account Takeover 2021 Annual Report: Prevalence, Awareness and Prevention. *Account Takeover 2021 Annual Report: Prevalence, Awareness and Prevention*. Retrieved from https://www.security.org/digital-safety/account-takeover-annual-report/

Services, M. M., Petros, E. L., & Mortlock, H. O. (2016). *Social engineering fraud – Recommendations and solutions*. Marsh McLennan's Risk & Insurance Services. Retrieved from https://www.marsh.com/content/dam/marsh/Documents/PDF/UK-en/Social%20Engineering%20Fraud.pdf

Sumit, M., Soumyadeep, T., Manosij, G., & Sanjoy Kumar, S. (2020). An Autoencoder Based Model for Detecting Fraudulent Credit Card Transaction. *Procedia Computer Science*, *167*(1), 254–262. https://linkinghub.elsevier.com/retrieve/pii/S1877050920306840

Suresh, K. M., Soundarya, V., Kavitha, S., E, A., & E.S., K. (2019). Credit Card Fraud Detection Using Random Forest Algorithm. *2019 3rd International Conference on Computing and Communications Technologies (ICCCT), 1*(1), 149-153. Retrieved from https://ieeexplore.ieee.org/document/8824930/

Szmigiera, M. (2021). *Global card fraud losses*. Statista. Retrieved from https://www.statista.com/statistics/1080685/global-card-fraud-losses-forecast/

Taha, A. A., & Malebary, S. J. (2020). An Intelligent Approach to Credit Card Fraud Detection Using an Optimized Light Gradient Boosting Machine. *IEEE Access: Practical Innovations, Open Solutions*, *8*, 25579–25587. doi:10.1109/ACCESS.2020.2971354

TensorFlow: Large-scale machine learning on heterogeneous systems. (2020). Retrieved from An end-to-end open source machine learning platform: https://www.tensorflow.org/

Ugo, F., Alfredo, D., Francesca, P., Paolo, Z., & Francesco, P. (2019). Using generative adversarial networks for improving classification effectiveness in credit card fraud detection. *Information Sciences*, *479*(1), 448–455. https://linkinghub.elsevier.com/retrieve/pii/S0020025517311519

Welcome to pytorch tutorials. (2021). Retrieved from https://pytorch.org: https://pytorch.org/tutorials/

wikipedia.org. (2021). *Credit card fraud*. Wikipedia, The Free Encyclopedia. Retrieved from https://en.wikipedia.org/w/index.php?title=Credit_card_fraud&oldid=1019457467

Xuan, S., Liu, G., Li, Z. L. Z., Wang, S., & Jiang, C. (2018). Random forest for credit card fraud detection. *2018 IEEE 15th International Conference on Networking, Sensing and Control (ICNSC), 2018*(1), 1-6. Retrieved from 10.1109/ICNSC.2018.8361343

Y., C., & X., H. (2021). CatBoost for Fraud Detection in Financial Transactions. *International Conference on Consumer Electronics and Computer Engineering (ICCECE)*, 176-179. Retrieved from https://ieeexplore.ieee.org/document/9342475

Y, J., Dubey, T. N., & Sarika, S. (2019). A comparative analysis of various credit card fraud detection techniques. *International Journal of Recent Technology and Engineering, 7*(5), 402-407.

Zhang, X., Han, Y., Xu, W., & Wang, Q. (2021). HOBA: A novel feature engineering methodology for credit card fraud detection with a deep learning architecture. *Information Sciences*, *557*, 302–316.

ADDITIONAL READING

Chuprina, R. (2021, October 18). Credit Card Fraud Detection: Top ML Solutions in 2021. Technology Partner for Innovative Companies. Retrieved October 10, 2021, from https://spd.group/machine-learning/credit-card-fraud-detection/#:%7E:text=What%20is%20Credit%20Card%20Fraud%20Detection%3F&text=Credit%20Card%20Fraud%20Detection%20with,revealing%20and%20preventing%20fraudulent%20transactions.

Experian.com. (n.d.). Steps to Take if You Are a Victim of Credit Card Fraud. Retrieved November 7, 2021, from https://www.experian.com/blogs/ask-experian/credit-education/preventing-fraud/credit-card-fraud-what-to-do-if-you-are-a-victim/

GraphGists. (n.d.). Credit Card Fraud Detection - graphgists. Neo4j Graph Database Platform. Retrieved October 11, 2021, from https://neo4j.com/graphgists/credit-card-fraud-detection/

K. (2018, January 9). Credit Card Fraud Detection Techniques. StaySafe.Org. https://staysafe.org/credit-card-fraud-detection-techniques/

Karthik, V. S. S., Mishra, A., & Reddy, U. S. (2021). *Credit Card Fraud Detection by Modelling Behaviour Pattern using Hybrid Ensemble Model.* Arabian Journal for Science and Engineering. doi:10.100713369-021-06147-9

Lin, P., & Kattamuri, P. (2021, March 3). How to build a serverless real-time credit card fraud detection solution. Retrieved April 1, 2021, from https://cloud.google.com/blog/products/data-analytics/how-to-build-a-fraud-detection-solution

Mekterović, I., Karan, M., Pintar, D., & Brkić, L. (2021). Credit Card Fraud Detection in Card-Not-Present Transactions: Where to Invest? *Applied Sciences (Basel, Switzerland)*, *11*(15), 6766. doi:10.3390/app11156766

NCR.COM. (2021, March 10). Credit card transaction fraud continues to climb to new heights. NCR. Retrieved November 1, 2021, from https://www.ncr.com/blogs/payments/credit-card-fraud-detection

Singh, A., Ranjan, R. K., & Tiwari, A. (2021). Credit Card Fraud Detection under Extreme Imbalanced Data: A Comparative Study of Data-level Algorithms. *Journal of Experimental & Theoretical Artificial Intelligence*, 1–28. doi:10.1080/0952813X.2021.1907795

Venkata Suryanarayana, S., & Balaji, N., G., & Venkateswara Rao, G. (2018). Machine Learning Approaches for Credit Card Fraud Detection. *IACSIT International Journal of Engineering and Technology*, 7(2), 917. doi:10.14419/ijet.v7i2.9356

Worldpay Editorial Team. (2019, July 30). 6 Things to Look for in a Credit Card Fraud Detection Solution - Insights | Worldpay from FIS. FIS Global. Retrieved November 1, 2021, from https://www.fisglobal.com/en/insights/merchant-solutions-worldpay/article/6-things-to-look-for-in-a-credit-card-fraud-detection-solution

KEY TERMS AND DEFINITIONS

Activation Function: It generates a numeric output from a node that received a given input or set of information in an artificial neural network.

Artificial Neural Network: Artificial neural networks (ANNs) are computer systems that imitate an animal's biological neural networks.

Autoencoder: Autoencoder is a kind of artificial neural network. It is used to learn unsupervised efficient data encoding.

Batch Normalization: Batch normalization is a deep neural network training strategy that quantifies the inputs per layer of each mini-batch. It serves to maintain the learning process in place. It also reduces the number of epochs required to train deeper networks.

Classification: A data mining task that builds a predictive model to predict the target label of an unknown test record.

Clustering: Clustering is an unsupervised learning technique wherein the intragroup similarity is the maximum, and inter-group similarity is the minimum.

Credit Card: A credit card is a financial tool that enables cardholders to carry out a credit-based transaction.

Curse of Dimensionality: Difficulty in analyzing the dataset becomes increasingly complicated as the number of dimensions rises. It is known as the curse of dimensionality.

Decision Trees: It is a supervised learning model. It learns the decision rules from the training data to classify an unknown test example.

Dimensionality: The number of qualities considered for evaluation while studying an object is called dimensionality.

Compilation of References

International Conference of Information Science and Management Engineering, ISME 2013, Volume 2. (2014). *WIT Transactions on Information and Communication Technologies, 46*(2).

International Conference of Information Science and Management Engineering, ISME 2013, Volume 3. (2014). *WIT Transactions on Information and Communication Technologies, 46*(3).

A, T., C, B., S, P., & N, K. (2019). Real-time Credit Card Fraud Detection Using Machine Learning. *2019 9th International Conference on Cloud Computing, Data Science Engineering (Confluence), 1*(1), 488-493. Retrieved from https://ieeexplore.ieee.org/document/8776942/

Abbasi, A., Albrecht, C., Vance, A., & Hansen, J. (2012). Metafraud: A meta-learning framework for detecting financial fraud. *MIS Quarterly: Management Information Systems, 36*(4), 1293-1327. doi:10.2307/41703508

Abbott, L. J., Park, Y., & Parker, S. (2000). The Effects of Audit Committee Activity and Independence on Corporate Fraud. *Managerial Finance, 26*(11), 55–67. doi:10.1108/03074350010766990

Abdallah, A., Maarof, M. A., & Zainal, A. (2016). Fraud detection system: A survey. *Journal of Network and Computer Applications, 68*, 90–113. doi:10.1016/j.jnca.2016.04.007

Abdul Malak, S. S. D., & Wan Hussin, W. N. B. (2019). AirAsia Berhad's accounting in the spotlight. *Emerald Emerging Markets Case Studies, 9*(1), 1–26. doi:10.1108/EEMCS-06-2018-0115

Abdullah. (2015). Transparency and Reliability in Financial Statement: Do They Exist? Evidence from Malaysia. *Open Journal of Accounting, 4*, 29-43.

Abdullahi, R., & Mansor, N. (2015). Forensic Accounting and Fraud Risk Factors: The Influence of Fraud Diamond Theory. *European Journal of Business and Management, 7*(28).

Abdullahi, R., & Mansor, N. (2015). Concomitant debacle of fraud incidences in the Nigeria public sector: Understanding the power of fraud triangle theory. *International Journal of Academic Research in Business & Social Sciences, 5*(9), 2222–6990. doi:10.6007/IJARBSS/v5-i9/1833

Abdullahi, R., & Mansor, N. (2018). Fraud prevention initiatives in the Nigerian public sector: Understanding the relationship of fraud incidences and the elements of fraud triangle theory. *Journal of Financial Crime, 25*(2), 527–544. doi:10.1108/JFC-02-2015-0008

AbdulRaheem, A, Isiaka, S. B. & Muhammed, A. Y. (2012). Fraud and Its Implications for Bank Performance in Nigeria. *International Journal of Asian Social Science, 2*(4), 382–387.

Abdulrahman, S. (2019). Forensic accounting and fraud prevention in Nigerian public sector: A conceptual paper. *International Journal of Accounting & Finance Review, 4*(2), 13–21. doi:10.46281/ijafr.v4i2.389

Abiloro, T. O., Adejuwon, A. M., & Folorunso, B. E. (2020). Inventory Fraud and Financial Reporting: A Review of Literature. *International Journal of Research and Scientific Innovation*, *7*(10).

Aburime, T. U. (2012). Impact of Corruption on Bank Profitability in Nigeria. *Symposium for Young Researcher, 15*(17), 15-17.

Abu-Tapanjeh, A. M., & Al-Sarairah, T. M. K. (2021). The Availability of Forensic Accounting Application Factors to Enhance the Auditors Efficiency in Jordan. *Journal of Asian Finance, Economics and Business*, *8*(3), 807–819. doi:10.13106/jafeb.2021.vol8.no3.0807

ACFE. (2014). *Report To the Nations on Occupational Fraud and Abuse. Global Fraud Study* (Vol. 15). Association of Certified Fraud Examiners.

ACFE. (2016). *Report to the nations on Ocupational Fraud and Abuse*. Association of Certified Fraud Examiners. Retrieved from https://www.acfe.com

ACFE. (2018). *Portal da Association of Certified Fraud Examiners*. http://www.acfe.com

ACFE. (2020). *Report to the nation*. Retrieved from https://www.acfe.com/surveys-and-statistics.aspx

ACFE. (2020). *Report to the nations – 2020 global study on occupational fraud and abuse*. https://acfepublic.s3-us-west-2.amazonaws.com/2020-Report-to-the-Nations.pdf

ACFE. (2020). *Report to the Nations 2020 Global Study on Occupational Fraud and Abuse*. ACFE.

ACFE. (2020). *Report to the nations on occupational fraud and abuse*. Association of Certified Fraud Examiners.

ACFE. (2020). *Report to the nations on Ocupational - 2020 Global Study on Occupational Fraud and Abuse*. Association of Certified Fraud Examiners. https://www.acfe.com

ACFE. (n.d.). *Membership and Certification*. Retrieved from https://www.acfe.com/

Adebisi, J. F., & Gbegi, D. O. (2015). Fraud and the Nigerian public sector performance: The need for forensic accounting. *International Journal of Business Human Technology*, *5*(5), 67–78.

Adefila, J. J., Kasum, A. S., & Olaniyi, T. A. (2006). The Global Endemic Nature of Financial Malpractices: An Analytical Appraisal. *Africa Journal of Management*, *6*(1), 11–20.

Adegbie, F.F., & Fakile, A.S. (2012). Economic and Financial Crime in Nigeria: Forensic Accounting as Antidote. *Journal of Arts and Social Sciences*, *6*(78), 37-50.

Adegbie, F. E., & Fakile, A. S. (2012). Economic and financial crime in Nigeria: Forensic accounting as antidote. *British Journal of Arts and Social Science*, *6*(10), 37–50.

Adegbie, F. F., & Fakile, A. S. (2012). Economic and financial crime in Nigeria: Forensic accounting as an antidote. *British Journal of Arts and Social Sciences*, *6*(1), 37–50.

Ademola, L. S., Ch-Ahmad, A. B., & Popoola, O. J. M. (2017). The forensic accountants' skills and ethics on fraud prevention in the Nigerian public sector. *Academic Journal of Economic Studies*, *3*(4), 77–85.

Adeniyi, A. A. (2004). *Auditing and Investigation*. El-Toda Ventures Limited.

Aderibigbe, P. (2013). *Auditors Independence and Corporate Fraud in Nigeria. Journal of Research and Development in Higher Education.*

Adrian, N. K., Lawrence, A. & Cristal Lee, A. S. (2009). Forensic Accounting: Public Acceptance towards Occurrence of Fraud Detection. *International Journal of Business Management, 4*(11), 145-149.

Adrian, N. K., Lawrence, A., & Cristal Lee, A. S. (2009). Forensic Accounting: Public Acceptance towards Occurrence of Fraud Detection. *International Journal of Business and Management*, *4*(11), 145–150.

Afza, T., & Nazir, M. S. (2014). Theoretical Perspective of Corporate Governance: A Review. *European Journal of Scientific Research*, *119*(2), 255–265.

Agbaje, W. H., & Oloruntoba, S. R. (2018). An Assessment of Impact of Financial Statement Fraud on Profit Performance of Manufacturing Firm in Nigeria: A Study of Food and Beverage Firms in Nigeria. *European Journal of Business and Management*, *10*(9).

Agbaje, W. H., & Dare, F. (2018). Dynamic Analysis of Financial Statement Fraud on Profitability of Manufacturing Firms in Nigeria. *International Journal of Business and Management Review*, *6*(2), 65–81.

Agrawal, A., Gans, J., & Goldfarb, A. (2018). *Prediction Machines: The Simple Economics of Artificial Intelligence*. Harvard Business Review Press.

Agyemang-Mintah, P., & Schadewitz, H. (2018). Audit committee adoption and firm value: evidence from UK financial institutions. *International Journal of Accounting & Information Management*.

Ahlin, C., Kim, I. K., & Kim, K. I. (2021). Who commits fraud? evidence from korean gas stations. *International Journal of Industrial Organization*. https://www.scopus.com/inward/record.uri?eid=2-s2.0-85102045798&doi=10.1016%2Fj.ijindorg.2021.102719&partnerID=40&md5=21cfbb2fc7e1a1465354e13078ca68f0

Ahmadu, B. U., Zayyad, A. B., & Rasak, A. I. (2013). An empirical examination of the role of forensic audit in enhancing financial investigations in Nigeria. *ICAN Journal of Accounting and Finance*, *2*(1), 145–159.

Ahmed, A., McAnally, M., Rasmussen, S., & Weaver, C. (2010). How costly is the Sarbanes Oxley Act? Evidence on the effects of the Act on corporate profitability. *Journal of Corporate Finance*, *16*(3), 352–369. doi:10.1016/j.jcorpfin.2009.11.003

AICP. (2017). *Audit Data Analytics Guide*. Retrieved from AICPA: https://www.aicpa.org/interestareas/frc/assuranceadvisoryservices/auditdataanalyticsguide.html

AICPA. (2013). *Generally Accepted Accounting Standards*. AICPA.

Akinbowale, O. E., Klingelhöfer, H. E., & Zerihun, M. F. (2021). The integration of forensic accounting and the management control system as tools for combating cyberfraud. *Academy of Accounting and Financial Studies Journal*. https://www.scopus.com/inward/record.uri?eid=2-s2.0-85104067180&partnerID=40&md5=8b7e6a6124bc8e0c7ac0a7f06f8185ce

Akinbowale, O. E., Klingelhöfer, E. H., & Zerihun, M. F. (2020). An innovative approach in combating economic crime using forensic accounting techniques. *Combating Economic Crime*, *27*(4), 1253–1271. doi:10.1108/JFC-04-2020-0053

Akinlo, A. E. (2013). Government spending and national income nexus for Nigeria. *Global Journal of Business Research*, *7*(1), 33–41.

Akins, B. (2011). *Financial Reporting Quality and Uncertainty about Credit Risk among the Ratings Agencies*. MIT Sloan School of Management.

Al-Abbadi, H. M., Alrawashdeh, B., Dabaghia, M. N., & Darwazeh, R. N. (2021a). The challenges of application of forensic accounting in Jordan. *Academy of Strategic Management Journal*, *20*(2), 1–10.

Al-Abbadi, H., Alrawashdeh, B., Dabaghia, M. N., & Darwazeh, R. (2021b). The Role of Courts and Universities in Activating the Forensic Accounting to Discover Financial Fraud. *Academy of Accounting and Financial Studies Journal, 25*(2), 1–9.

Alaoubi, A., & Almomani, M. A. (2021). The Moderating Effect for Forensic Accounting on the Relationship between corporate Governance and Quality of Accounting Information in The Jordanian Public Shareholding Companies. *International Journal of Academic Research in Accounting Finance and Management Sciences, 11*(2), 47–61.

Al-Baidhani, A. M. (2016). The role of audit committee in corporate governance: A descriptive study. *International Journal of Research Methodology in Social Science., 2*(2), 45–57.

Albanese, J. S., Artello, K., & Nguyen, L. T. (2019). Distinguishing Corruption in Law and Practice: Empirically Separating Conviction Charges from Underlying Behaviors. *Public Integrity*. https://www.scopus.com/inward/record.uri?eid=2-s2.0-85052105879&doi=10.1080%2F10999922.2018.1423859&partnerID=40&md5=76d67089fff4e497f0c92633e0c304af

Albrecht, C.C., & Denn, J.G. (2001). *Can Auditor Detect Fraud?* Academic Press.

Albrecht, W. S. (2005). Identifying fraudulent financial transactions: A framework for detecting financial statement fraud. Brigham Young University.

Albrecht, W., Albrecht, C., & Albrecht, C. C. (2008). Current Trends in Fraud and its Detection. *Information Security Journal: A Global Perspective, 17*(1), 2–12.

Albrecht, C., Holland, D., Malagueño, R., Dolan, S., & Tzafrir, S. (2015). The Role of Power in Financial Statement Fraud Schemes. *Journal of Business Ethics, 131*(4), 803–813. doi:10.100710551-013-2019-1

Aldamen, H., Duncan, K., Kelly, S., McNamara, R., & Nagel, S. (2012). Audit committee characteristics and firm performance during the global financial crisis. *Accounting and Finance, 52*(4), 971–1000. doi:10.1111/j.1467-629X.2011.00447.x

Alhusban, A. A. A., Haloush, H. A., Alshurafat, H., Al-Msiedeen, J. M., Massadeh, A. A. M., & Alhmoud, R. J. (2020). The regulatory structure and governance of forensic accountancy in the emerging market: Challenges and opportunities. *Journal of Governance & Regulation, 9*(4), 149–161. doi:10.22495/jgrv9i4art13

Ali, M., & Oseni, A. (2010). Corporate Governance, Transparency and Shareholders' Rights: The Role of The Forensic Accountants in Propelling Economic Growth. *Multidisciplinary Journal of Research Development, 15*(1), 1–9.

Alkhafaji, A. (2007). Corporate governance: The evolution of the Sarbanes- Oxley Act and its impact on corporate America. *Competitiveness Review, 17*(3), 193–202. doi:10.1108/10595420710833598

Allen, L., & DeLong, G. (2004). Issues in the credit risk modeling of retail markets. *Journal of Banking & Finance. VOL., 28*, PP736–PP739.

Almeida, F. (2014). *Custos e Benefícios da Lei Sarbanes-Oxley O Caso BPN* [Unpublished master dissertation] Universidade Católica Portuguesa, Portugal.

Almeida, M. (2015). *A fraude de relato financeiro e a indepenência dos auditores* [Unpublished master dissertation] Universidade Autónoma de Lisboa, Portugal.

Al-Mihi, R. A.-H. (2015). Measurement and disclosure of bank liquidity risk in light of the decisions of Basel llll and International Financial Reporting Standards IFRS. *Journal of Accounting Thought, Ain Shams University, 3*.

Almutairi, A. R. (2021). Earnings management and the role of MOSAL in co-ops. *Journal of Co-Operative Organization and Management*. https://www.scopus.com/inward/record.uri?eid=2-s2.0-85103615322&doi=10.1016%2Fj.jcom.2021.100131&partnerID=40&md5=6f69ee5f8e318dd4217e6fec547050ce

Alqirem, R., Abu Afifa, M., Saleh, I., & Haniah, F. (2020). Ownership Structure, Earnings Manipulation, and Organizational Performance: The Case of Jordanian Insurance Organizations. *Journal of Asian Finance, Economics and Business.* https://www.scopus.com/inward/record.uri?eid=2-s2.0-85098487789&doi=10.13106%2FJAFEB.2020.VOL7.NO12.293&partnerID=40&md5=3ac142432343b9a5574a8608f21622ff

Al-Rashidi, M. S. (2012). An Analytical Study of Methods for Evaluating the Quality of Financial Reports. *Journal of Contemporary Business Research, Faculty of Commerce, Sohag University, 26*(2), 32-37.

Alsaadi, A. (2021). Can Inclusion in Religious Index Membership Mitigate Earnings Management? *Journal of Business Ethics.* https://www.scopus.com/inward/record.uri?eid=2-s2.0-85073994888&doi=10.1007%2Fs10551-019-04280-y&partnerID=40&md5=b3464c5aa65ec0dbce2ff8dc2c55b036

Al-Shattarat, B. (2021). The consequence of earnings management through discretionary accruals on the value relevance in Saudi Arabia. *Cogent Business and Management.* https://www.scopus.com/inward/record.uri?eid=2-s2.0-85101147598&doi=10.1080%2F23311975.2021.1886473&partnerID=40&md5=367058ea5b81f0eaead97587cbe97118

Alshurafat, H., Al Shbail, M., & Mansour, E. (2021). Strengths and weaknesses of forensic accounting: an implication on the socio-economic development. *Journal of Business and Socio-economic Development, 1*(2).

Alshurafat, H., Al Shbail, M. O., & Mansour, E. (2021). Strengths and weaknesses of forensic accounting: An implication on the socio-economic development. *Journal of Business and Socio-economic Development, 1*(2), 135–148. doi:10.1108/JBSED-03-2021-0026

Altunba, P., & Scannella, T. (2021). European Banking Union and bank risk disclosure: The effects of the Single Supervisory Mechanism. *Review of Quantitative Finance and Accounting*, 1–20. doi:10.100711156-021

Amahalu, N. (2017). Effect of Forensic Accounting Application on Financial Crime Detection in Deposit Money Banks in Anambra State. *International Journal of Advanced Engineering and Management Research, 2*(6).

Amake, C. C., & Ikhatua, J. O. (2016). Forensic accounting and fraud detection in Nigerian public sector. *Igbinedion University Journal of Accounting, 2*, 148–173.

Ammanath, B., Jarvis, D. & Hupfer, S. (2020). *Thriving in the era of pervasive AI.* Deloitte Consulting LLP.

Anand, S. (2007). *Essentials of Sarbanes-Oxley.* John Wiley & Sons. doi:10.1002/9781118384596

Anan, L., Hayden, R., Joshi, K., Nadeau, M.-C., & Steitz, J. (2018). Fraud management: Recovering value through next-generation solutions. *McKinsey on Payments, 11*(27), 30–36.

Andersen, A. (1992). *Audit Committees for the 1990s.* Arthur Andersen.

Anh, V. D. (2016, August 3). *Integration of Vietnam human resources for accounting in the AEC* [Conference presentation]. National Conference for Brexit and the Asean Economic Community from a perspective of integration, Van Hien University.

Anuolam, O. M., Onyema, T. E., & Ekeke, U. (2016). Forensic Accounting and Financial Crisis in Nigeria. *West African Journal of Industrial and Academic Research, 17*(1), 120–125.

Anyanwu, J. C. (1993). *Monetary economics: Theory, policy and institution.* Hybrid.

Apapan, P., & L, Y. (2018). Credit Card Fraud Detection using Deep Learning based on Auto-Encoder and Restricted Boltzmann Machine. *International Journal of Advanced Computer Science and Applications, 9*(1).

Apostolou, B., Hassel, J. M., & Webber, S. A. (2002). Forensic Expert Classification of Management Fraud Risk Factors. *Journal of Forensic Accounting, 10*(1), 181–192.

Apostolou, Hassell, J. M., Webber, S. A., & Sumners, G. E. (2001). The relative importance of management fraud risk factors. *Behavioral Research in Accounting*, *13*(1), 1–24. doi:10.2308/bria.2001.13.1.1

Apostolou, N., & Crumbley, D. L. (2005). Fraud survey: Lessons for forensic accountants. *Journal of Forensic Accounting*, *6*(1), 103–118.

Archel, P., Husillos, J., Larrinaga, C., & Spence, C. (2009). Social disclosure, legitimacy theory and the role of the state. *Accounting, Auditing & Accountability Journal*, *22*(8), 1284–1307. doi:10.1108/09513570910999319

Aregbeyen, O., & Kolawole, B. O. (2015). Oil revenue, public spending and economic growth relationships in Nigeria. *Journal of Sustainable Development*, *8*(3), 113. doi:10.5539/jsd.v8n3p113

Arokiasamy, L., & Cristal-Lee, S. (2009). Forensic accounting: Public acceptance towards occurrence of fraud detection. *International Journal of Business and Management*, 145–160.

Arrowsmith, R. (2020). *Case Studies: AI & data analytics in 2020.* Available at: https://www.accountingtoday.com/news/case-studies-ai-data-analytics-in-2020

Arthur, P. (2014). *Detecting Financial Statement Fraud.* Retrieved from: http//www.investopedia.com/article/financial theory/14/08/2015

Asare, S. K., & Wright, A. M. (2004). The Effectiveness of Alternative Risk Assessment and Programme Planning Tools in a Fraud Setting. *Contemporary Accounting Research Journal*, *21*(2), 325–352. doi:10.1506/L20L-7FUM-FPCB-7BE2

Aslan, L. (2021). The Evolving Competencies of the Public Auditor and the Future of Public Sector Auditing. In Contemporary Issues in Public Sector Accounting and Auditing (Contemporary Studies in Economic and Financial Analysis, Vol. 105). Emerald Publishing Limited. doi:10.1108/S1569-375920200000105008

Assad, M. J. (2011). Fraud at the central bank of tanzania (A). *Emerald Emerging Markets Case Studies*, *1*(1), 1–12. doi:10.1108/20450621111110492

Association of Certified Fraud Examiners. (2020). *Report to the Nations. Global Study of occupational fraud and abuse.* Author.

Association, A. B. (2021). *How to Use Internal and External Data to Predict Emerging Risks and Opportunities.* 360 Factors.

Attig, N., Chen, R., El Ghoul, S., Guedhami, O., Kwok, C., & Pittman, J. (2020). Are insiders equal? Evidence from earnings management in closely held East Asian firms. *Research in International Business and Finance*. https://www.scopus.com/inward/record.uri?eid=2-s2.0-85087213864&doi=10.1016%2Fj.ribaf.2020.101243&partnerID=40&md5=cbcb35eb6565e98a11fe507d582b3b7d

Auditors, T. I. (2019). *Fraud and internal audit; Assurance Over Fraud Controls Fundamental to Success.* The Institute of Internal Auditors.

Awolowo, I. F. (2016). Financial statement fraud: The need for a paradigm shift to forensic accounting. World Academy of Science, Engineering and Technology. *International Journal of Economics and Management Engineering*, *10*(3), 987–991.

Aziz, S., & Dowling, M. (2019). Machine Learning and AI for Risk Management. In T. Lynn, J. G. Mooney, P. Rosati, & M. Cummins (Eds.), *Disrupting Finance FinTech and Strategy in the 21st Century* (pp. 33–50). Palgrave Studies. doi:10.1007/978-3-030-02330-0_3

Babinchak, J. (2020). *IIA Issues Important Update to Three Lines Model: Modernizing the Widely Used Approach to Governance, Risk.* Available at: https://na.theiia.org/news/Pages/IIA-Issues-Important-Update-to-Three-Lines-Model.aspx

Bac Van. (2019). *Lesson from acquiring AVG's shares.* https://nhandan.vn/tin-tuc-su-kien/bai-hoc-tu-vu-an-mua-co-phan-avg-445948

Baird, J. E., & Zelin, R. C. (2009). An examination of the impact of obedience pressure on perceptions of fraudulent acts and the likelihood of committing occupational fraud. *Journal of Forensic Studies, Accounting Business, 1*(1).

Baird, J.E., & Zelin, R. C. (2009). An examination of the impact of obedience pressure on perceptions of fraudulent acts and the likelihood of committing occupational fraud. *Journal of Forensic Studies, Accounting Business.*

Bala, H., Amran, N. A., & Shaari, H. (2019). Audit committee attributes and cosmetic accounting in Nigeria: The moderating effect of audit price. *Managerial Auditing Journal.* https://www.scopus.com/inward/record.uri?eid=2-s2.0-85076140390&doi=10.1108%2FMAJ-06-2018-1897&partnerID=40&md5=a5f5e05da4e89e826d69570874e90dfa

Balakrishnan, K. (2009). *Credit Market Conditions and Economy-wide Consequences of Financial Reporting Quality.* New York University.

Balarebe, I. (2009). *Economic Financial Crimes Commission (EFCC) and the Law.* www.efccnigeria.org

Banco de Portugal. (2015). *Comunicado do Banco de Portugal: Recomendações do Grupo de Trabalho sobre os Modelos e as Práticas de Governo, de Controlo e de Auditoria das Instituições Financeiras.* Banco de Portugal Eurosistema.

Bansal, N., & Sharma, A. K. (2016). Audit Committee, Corporate sector and Firm Performance: Empirical Evidence from India. *International Journal of Economics and Finance, 8*(13), 103–116. doi:10.5539/ijef.v8n3p103

Bardhan, P. (1997). Corruption and development: A review of issues. *Journal of Economic Literature, 35*(3), 1320–1346. https://www.jstor.org/stable/2729979

Bassey, E. B., (2018) Effect of Forensic Accounting on the Management of Fraud in Micro-Finance Institutions in Cross River State. *IOSR Journal of Economics and Finance, 9*(4), 79-89.

Basuony, M., & Ehab, K. A. (2015). *The Effect of Corporate Governance on Bank Financial Performance: Evidence from the Arabian Peninsula.* Academic Press.

Baten, M. A. (2021). Corporate Governance And Creative Accounting From Bangladesh Experience. *Accounting, Organization & Economics, 1*(1), 12-25. Retrieved from https://fortunepublishing.org/index.php/aoe/article/view/43

Bauguess, S. W. (2017). *The Role of Big Data, Machine Learning, and AI in Assessing Risks: A Regulatory Perspective.* Available at: https://www.sec.gov/news/speech/bauguess-big-data-ai

Bearu, E. (2021, Oct 30). Retrieved from Indian Bank reports frauds of over Rs 266 crore in three accounts to RBI: https://economictimes.indiatimes.com/industry/banking/finance/banking/indian-bank-reports-frauds-of-over-rs-266-crore-in-three-accounts-to-rbi/articleshow/87402032.cms

Beasley, J. V. (2021). Top 10 Audit Deficiencies. *Journal of Accountancy.*

Beasley, M. S., Carcello, J. V., Hermanson, D.R., & Neal, T.L. (2010). *Fraudulent Financial Reporting 1998-2007: An Analysis of U.S Public Firms.* Research commissioned by the Committee of Sponsoring Organizations of the Treadway Commission.

Beatty, A., Liao, S., & Yu, J. J. (2013). The spillover effect of fraudulent financial reporting on peer firms' investments. *Journal of Accounting and Economics, 55*(2-3), 183–205. doi:10.1016/j.jacceco.2013.01.003

Beck, M., & Libert, B. (2018). *How to use AI for strategic decisions.* Available at: https://www.cio.com/article/3271433/how-to-use-ai-for-strategic-decisions.html

Beneish. (2012). Fraud Detection and Expected Returns. *SRRN*, 53.

Beneish. (2013, March). Earnings Manipulation and Expected Returns. *Financial Analysts Journal.*

Beneish, M. (1997). Detecting GAAP violation: Implications for assessing earnings management among firms with extreme financial performance. *Journal of Accounting and Public Policy, 16*(3), 271–309.

BeneishM. D.NicholsD. C. (2012). Fraud Detection and Expected Returns. https://ssrn.com/abstract=1998387 doi:10.2139/ssrn.1998387

Bernardo, R., Lima, N., Medeiros, C., & Miranda, G. (2017). Fraudes corporativas e a formação de contadores: Uma análise dos currículos dos cursos de ciências contábeis. *Revista Ambiente Contábil, 9*(1), 97–116.

Betti, N., & Sarens, G. (2020). *Understanding the internal audit function in a digitalised business environment. Journal of Accounting & Organizational Change.* doi:10.1108/JAOC-11-2019-0114

Bhasin, M. (2007). Forensic Accounting: A New Paradigm For Niche Consulting. *The Chartered Accountant*, (January), 1000-1010.

Bhasin, M. (2007). Forensic accounting: A new paradigm for niche consulting. *The Chartered Accountant, Country,* 1000-1010.

Bhasin, M. (2007). Forensic Accounting: A New Paradigm Niche Consulting. *The Chartered Accountant Country*, 1000.

Bhasin, M. L. (2013b). Corporate governance and forensic accountants: An exploratory study. *Journal of Accounting – Business and Management, 20*(2), 55–83.

Bhasin, D. M. (2017, January). Integrating Corporate Governance and Forensic Accounting: A Study of an Asian Country. *International Journal of Management Sciences and Business Research, 6*(1), 31–52.

Bhasin, M. L. (2013). Corporate governance and forensic accountant: An exploratory study. *Journal Accounting Business and Management-International, 20*(2), 55–83.

Bhasin, M. L. (2013a). Corporate governance and forensic accountants' role: Global regulatory action scenario. *International Journal of Accounting Research, 1*(1), 1–19. doi:10.12816/0001124

Bhasin, M. L. (2013c). An empirical investigation of the relevant skills of forensic accountants: Experience of a developing economy. *European Journal of Accounting Auditing and Finance Research, 1*(2), 11–52.

BhasinM. L. (2015). An empirical investigation of the relevant skills of forensic accountants: experience of a developing economy. *Available at* SSRN 2676519.

Bhasin, M. L. (2016). Accounting manipulation Practices in Financial Statement: An Experience of an Asia economy. *International Journal of Economics and Financial Research, 2*(11), 199–214.

Bhasin, M. L. (2016). Contribution of Forensic Accounting to Corporate Governance: An Exploratory Study of an Asian Country. *International Business Management, 10*(4), 479–492.

Bhasin, M. L. (2016). Contribution of forensic accounting to corporate governance: An exploratory study of an asian country. *International Business Management, 10*(4), 479–492. doi:10.3923/ibm.2016.479.492

Bhasin, M. L. (2016). Contribution of Forensic Accounting to Corporate sector: An Exploratory Study of an Asian Country. *International Business Management Journal, 10*(4), 479–492.

Bhasin, M. L. (2016a). Forensic accounting in Asia: Perspectives and prospects. *International Journal of Management and Social Sciences Research, 5*(7), 25–38.

Bhasin, M. L. (2016b). Contribution of forensic accounting to corporate governance: An exploratory study of an Asian country. *International Business Management, 10*(4), 479–492.

Bhasin, M. L. (2017). Integrating corporate sector & Forensic Accounting: A Study of an Asian Country. *International Journal of Management Sciences & Business Research, 6*(1), 32–52.

Bhati, P., & Sharma, M. (2018). Credit Card Number Fraud Detection Using K-Means with Hidden Markov Method. *International Journal of Mobile Computing and Application, 2*(2), 15–18. http://www.internationaljournalssrg.org/IJMCA/paper-details?Id=20

Bierstaker, J. L., Brody, R. G., & Pacini, C. (2006). Accountants' perceptions regarding fraud detection and prevention methods. *Managerial Auditing Journal, 21*(5), 520–535. doi:10.1108/02686900610667283

Birkett, B. S. (1986). The Recent History of Corporate Audit Committees. *The Accounting Historians Journal, 13*(2), 109–124. doi:10.2308/0148-4184.13.2.109

Biswas, M., Hiremath, K. G., & Shalini, R. (2013). *Forensic Accounting In Indian Perspective* [Paper presentation]. The 5th International Conference on Financial Criminology (ICFC) 2013 on 'Global Trends in Financial Crimes in the New Economies.

Board, A. S. (1997). *Recently Issued Statement of Auditing Standards (SAS) No. 82 and Its Potential Effect on Fidelity Claims*. The Fraud Task Force.

Bologna, G. J., & Lindquist, R. J. (1995). *Fraud auditing and forensic accounting: New tools and techniques* (2nd ed.). John Wiley and Sons, Inc.

Bolton, R. J., & Hand, D. J. (2002). Statistical fraud detection: A review. *Quality Engineering, 49*, 313–314.

Bonotto, P. (2010). *As Fraudes Contábeis da Enron e Worldcom e seus efeitos nos Estados Unidos* [Unpublished final academic course work]. Universidade Federal do Rio Grande do Sul.

Boritz, J. E., Kotchetova, N., & Robinson, L. A. (2008). Planning fraud detection procedures: Forensic accountant's vs auditors. *IFA Conference*. Available at http://aaahq.org/meetings/AUD2009/PlanningFraudDetectionProcedures.pdf

Boritz, J. E., Kotchetova, N., & Robinson, L. A. (2008). Planning fraud detection procedures: Forensic accountants vs auditors. IFA Conference.

Botes, V., & Saadeh, A. (2018). Exploring evidence to develop a nomenclature for forensic accounting. *Pacific Accounting Review, 30*(2), 135–154. doi:10.1108/PAR-12-2016-0117

Brennan, D. (2011). *Corporate social responsibility: The corporate governance of the 21st century*. Kluwer Law International BV.

Brennan, N. M. (2014). Forensic accounting in a constitutional parliamentary democracy: the case of Ireland. *Journal of Forensic and Investigative Accounting, 6*(3), 62-97.

Bressler, L. (2011). the Role of Forensic Accountants in Fraud Investigations: Importance of Attorney and Judge's Perceptions. *Journal of Finance and Accountancy, 11*(27), 1–9.

Brews, P., & Hunt, M. (1999). Learning to plan and planning to learn: Resolving the planning school/learning school debate. *Strategic Management Journal, 20*(10), 889–913. doi:10.1002/(SICI)1097-0266(199910)20:10<889::AID-SMJ60>3.0.CO;2-F

Brews, P., & Tucci, C. (2004). Exploring the structural effects of internetworking. *Strategic Management Journal, 25*(5), 429–451. doi:10.1002mj.386

Brown, M. (2008). *Forensic Accounting-Past, Present, & Future. It's All About Money.* http://www.envoynews.com/rwcpas/e_article001108198.cfm

Brown, A., Aiken, P., & Visser, L. (2007). Reducing fraud: A programme that will deliver benefits on the bottom line. *Accountancy Ireland, 39*(6), 28–30.

Brown, A., Aiken, P., & Visser, L. (2007). Reducing Fraud: A Programme that will Deliver Benefits on the Bottom Line. *Accountancy Ireland, 39*(6), 28–30.

Browning, J. (2021, July 22). Retrieved from EY Accused of Actively Concealing NMC Health Audit Fraud From Investors: https://www.bloomberg.com/news/articles/2021-07-22/ey-accused-of-actively-concealing-nmc-audit-fraud-from-investors

Brown, N., & Deegan, C. M. (1998). The public disclosure of environmental performance information – A dual test of media agenda setting theory and legitimacy theory. *Accounting and Business Research, 29*(1), 21–41. doi:10.1080/00014788.1998.9729564

Brown, R., & Smith, R. G. (2018). Exploring the relationship between organised crime and volume crime. *Trends and Issues in Crime and Criminal Justice, 565*, 1–14.

Broye, G., & Johannes, P. (2021). Determinants of audit committee effectiveness: Reviewing a decade of empirical research. *Accounting Auditing Control, 27*(1), 51–109.

Bruce. (2020). *Coronavirus Pandemic Is a Perfect Storm for Fraud.* Retrieved from Associate of certified fraud examiners: https://www.acfe.com/press-release.aspx?id=4295010491

Buckhoff, T. A., & Schrader, R. W. (2000). The Teaching of Forensic Accounting. *Journal of Forensic Accounting, 1*(1), 135–146.

Burlea, S. A., & Popa, I. (2013). Legitimacy theory. In S.O. Idowu, N. Capaldi, L. Zu, & A.D. Gupta (Eds.), Encyclopedia of Corporate Social Responsibility. Springer-Verlag.

Burns, J., & Steele, A. (2020). *Blockchain and Internal Control The COSO Perspective.* Committee of Sponsoring Organizations of the Treadway Commission.

Burridge, N. (2017). *Artificial intelligence gets a seat in the boardroom.* Available at: https://asia.nikkei.com/Business/Artificial-intelligence-gets-a-seat-in-the-boardroom

Cadbury Committee. (1992). *Report of the Committee on the Financial Aspects of Corporate Governance.* London: Gee.

Cahlik, T. (2000). Comparison of the maps of science. *Scientometrics, 49*(3), 373–387. doi:10.1023/A:1010581421990

Callon, M., Courtial, J. P., Turner, W. A., & Bauin, S. (1983). *From translations to problematic networks an introduction to co-word analysis.pdf.* Academic Press.

Callon, M., Courtial, J.-P., & Laville, F. (1991). Co-word analysis as a tool for describing the network of interactions between basic and technological research: The case of polymer chemsitry. *Scientometrics, 22*(1), 155–205. doi:10.1007/BF02019280

Campos, J. E., Lien, D. & Pradhan, S. (1999). The impact of corruption on investment: Predictability matters. *World Development, 27*(6), 1059–1067. doi:10.1016/s0305-750x(99)00040-6

Cantoria, C. S. (2010). *Financial Statement Audit vs. Forensic Accounting.* https://www.brighthub.com/office/finance/articles/81471.aspx

Carney, W. (2006). The cost of being public after Sarbanes-Oxley: The irony of "going private." *Emory Law Journal*, 51.

Cassim, F. (2015). Protecting personal information in the era of identity theft: Just how safe is our personal information from identity thieves? *Potchefstroom Electronic Law Journal*, *18*(2), 69–110. doi:10.4314/pelj.v18i2.02

Castellano, J., & Lightle, S. (2005). Using Cultural Audits to Assess Tone at the Top. *The CPA Journal*, *75*(2).

Central Bank of Nigeria (CBN). (2013). *Statistical Report*. Government Printing Press Abuja.

CFI. (2016). *Fraud Triangle A framework used to explain the motivation behind an individual's decision to commit fraud*. Retrieved from Corporate financial institute: https://corporatefinanceinstitute.com/resources/knowledge/accounting/fraud-triangle/

Chakrabarty, S. (2015). The Influence of Unrelated and Related Diversification on Fraudulent Reporting. *Journal of Business Ethics*. https://www.scopus.com/inward/record.uri?eid=2-s2.0-84948387956&doi=10.1007%2Fs10551-013-2023-5&partnerID=40&md5=a7316538ac4117d860cbc0fdd3d640df

Chakrabarty, B., Duellman, S., & Hyman, M. A. (2020). A new approach to estimating the relation between audit fees and financial misconduct. *Accounting Horizons*, *34*(2), 41–61. doi:10.2308/horizons-19-042

Chan, D., & Vasarhelyi, M. (2018). Innovation and Practice of Continuous Auditing. In Continuous Auditing. Emerald Publishing Limited. doi:10.1108/978-1-78743-413-420181013

Chan, K. C., & Li, J. (2008). Audit committee and firm value: Evidence on outside top executives as expert-independent directors. *Corporate Governance*, *16*(1), 16–31. doi:10.1111/j.1467-8683.2008.00662.x

Chen, P., & Redner, S. (2010). Community structure of the physical review citation network. *Journal of Informetrics*, *4*(3), 278–290. doi:10.1016/j.joi.2010.01.001

Chen, X., & Cai, D. (2011). Large scale spectral clustering with landmark-based representation. *Twenty-Fifth AAAI Conference on Artificial Intelligence*.

Cherkassky, V., & Ma, Y. (2004). Practical selection of SVM parameters and noise estimation for SVM regression. *Neural Networks*, *17*(1), 113–126. doi:10.1016/S0893-6080(03)00169-2

Chollet, F. (2016, 14 May). *Building Autoencoders in Keras*. Retrieved from The Keras Blog: https://blog.keras.io/building-autoencoders-in-keras.html

Chornous, G., & Ursulenko, G. (2013). Risk Management In Banks: New Approaches To Risk Assessment And Information Support. *Ekonomika (Nis)*, *92*(1), 120–132. doi:10.15388/Ekon.2013.0.1131

Chris, E., & Hogan, Z. R. (2008, November). Financial Statement Fraud: Insights from the Academic Literature. *Auditing*, *27*(2), 231–252.

Cioban, A. (2016). The Influence of the Corporate Governance Mechanisms and Audit Fees on the Financial Performance Measured with ROA. *Annals of the Constantin Brâncusi. University of Târgu Jiu. Economy Series*, *1*(5), 20–31.

Clearing, R., & Thibodeous, C. (2005). Applying Digital Analysis Using Benfords Law to Detect Fraud. *Auditing*, 77–81.

CMA. (2018). 10/2018. Muscat: Capital Market Authority.

CMVM. (n.d.). *Portal da Comissão do Mercado de Valores Mobiliários*. http://www.cmvm.pt

Coates, J. IV. (2007). The goals and promise of the Sarbanes–Oxley Act. *The Journal of Economic Perspectives*, *21*(1), 91–116. doi:10.1257/jep.21.1.91

Coates, J., & Srinivasan, S. (2014). SOX after ten years: A multidisciplinary review. *Accounting Horizons*, *28*(3), 627–671. doi:10.2308/acch-50759

Coelho, S. (2014). CMVM investiga venda de ações do BES no último dia: grandes investidores venderam a correr. *Observador*. http://observador.pt

Coenen, T.L. (2008). *Forensic Accounting, A New Twist of Accounting Profession*. Academic Press.

Coenen, T. (2008). *Essentials of Corporate Fraud*. Wiley. doi:10.1002/9781118386156

Coffee, J. (2004). What Caused Enron-A Capsule Social and Economic History of the 1990s. *Cornell Law Review*, *89*(2), 269–309.

Coffee, J. (2005). A Theory of Corporate Scandals: Why the USA and Europe Differ. *Oxford Review of Economic Policy*, *21*(2), 198–211. doi:10.1093/oxrep/gri012

Cohen, D. A., & Zarowin, P. (2010). Accrual-based and real earnings management activities around seasoned equity offerings. *Journal of Accounting and Economics*. https://www.scopus.com/inward/record.uri?eid=2-s2.0-77950950399&doi=10.1016%2Fj.jacceco.2010.01.002&partnerID=40&md5=4e52610cd23c687d0091eceda8f72f75

Cohen, J., Ding, Y., Lesage, C., & Stolowy, H. (2010). Corporate Fraud and Managers' Behavior: Evidence from the Press. *Journal of Business Ethics*, *95*(S2), 271–315. doi:10.100710551-011-0857-2

Cohen, L. E., & Felson, M. F. (2014). Social Change and Crime Rate Trends: A Routine Activity Approach. *American Sociological Review*, 44–04.

Cole, R., Johan, S., & Schweizer, D. (2021). Corporate failures: Declines, collapses, and scandals. *Journal of Corporate Finance*. https://www.scopus.com/inward/record.uri?eid=2-s2.0-85099838795&doi=10.1016%2Fj.jcorpfin.2020.101872&partnerID=40&md5=81aa80e1e264fd7314ae354d07079bef

Cole, S. (2009). *Suspect identities: A history of fingerprinting and criminal identification*. Harvard University Press.

Collier, P. (1993). Audit Committees in Major UK Companies. *Managerial Auditing Journal*, *8*(3), 25–30.

Collier, P. (1997). Audit Committees in Smaller Listed Companies. In K. Keasey & M. Wright (Eds.), *Corporate Governance: Responsibilities, Risks and Remuneration Chichester*. John Wiley.

Columbus, L. (2019). *Top 9 Ways Artificial Intelligence Prevents Fraud*. Available at: https://www.forbes.com/sites/louiscolumbus/2019/07/09/top-9-ways-artificial-intelligence-prevents-fraud/#b398e4514b4f

Comer, M. (2016). *Corporate Fraud*. Taylor & Francis.

Comissão das Comunidades Europeias. (1996). *Livro verde: Papel, estatuto responsabilidade do revisor oficial de contas na União Europeia*. Bruxelas: Comissão das Comunidades Europeias.

Comissão das Comunidades Europeias. (2003). *Comunicação da Comissão ao Conselho e ao Parlamento Europeu: Modernizar o direito das sociedades e reforçar o governo das sociedades na União Europeia - Uma estratégia para o futuro*. https://eur-lex.europa.eu/

Comissão Europeia. (2003). *Comunicação da Comissão ao Conselho e ao Parlamento Europeu sobre reforçar a revisão oficial de contas na UE*. https://eur-lex.europa.eu

Comissão Parlamentar de Inquérito à Gestão do BES e do GES (CPI). (2015). *Relatório Final da Comissão Parlamentar de Inquérito à gestão do BES e do GES*. Lisboa: Assembleia da República. http://app.parlamento.pt

Communist Party of Vietnam. (2013). *End of a trial of Vinalines case: Duong Chi Dung and Mai Van Phuc were sentenced to death*. Communist Party of Vietnam Newspapers Online. https://dangcongsan.vn/thoi-su/ket-thuc-xet-xu-vu-vinalines-duong-chi-dung-va-mai-van-phuc-linh-an-tu-hinh-222936.html

Comprix, J., & Huang, H. (2015). Does auditor size matter? Evidence from small audit firms. *Advances in Accounting*. https://www.scopus.com/inward/record.uri?eid=2-s2.0-84929953630&doi=10.1016%2Fj.adiac.2015.03.007&partnerID=40&md5=e5dd2da87aca3a47bba08305181b1572

Corporate Finance Institute (CFI). (2021). *Forensic Accounting*. https://corporatefinanceinstitute.com/resources/knowledge/accounting/forensic-accounting-litigation/

Corporate Finance Institute. (2020). *Skimming Fraud*. Retrieved from https://corporatefinanceinstitute.com/resources/knowledge/other/skimming-fraud/

COSO. (2013). *Enterprise Risk Management: Aliging risk with strategy performance*. Committee of Sponsoring Organizations of the Treadway Commissions.

Costa, C. A. (2017). *Salgado permitiu empréstimos de 463 milhões a empresa da família. Sem garantias*. https://www.sabado.pt/

Costa, C. B. (2019). Auditoria Financeira - Teoria & Prática (12.a ed.). Lisboa: Rei dos Livros.

Coulter, N., Monarch, I., & Konda, S. (1998). Software engineering as seen through its research literature: A study in co-word analysis. *Journal of the American Society for Information Science*, *49*(13), 1206–1223. doi:10.1002/(SICI)1097-4571(1998)49:13<1206::AID-ASI7>3.0.CO;2-F

Council, A. C. G. (2010). *Corporate governance principles and recommendations with 2010 amendments*. Australian Securities Exchange.

Craja, P., Kim, A., & Lessmann, S. (2020). Deep learning for detecting financial statement fraud. *Decision Support Systems*, *139*, 113421. Advance online publication. doi:10.1016/j.dss.2020.113421

Cressey, D. R. (1953). *Other people's money; a study of the social psychology of embezzlement*. Academic Press.

Cressey, D. (1953). *Other People's Money: A Study in the Social Psychology of Embezzlement*. Free press.

Cressey, D. R. (1950). The Criminal Violation of Financial Trust. *American Sociological Review*, *15*(6), 738–743. doi:10.2307/2086606

Cressey, D. R. (2008). *Other peoples' money: A study in the social psychology of embezzlement*. Free Press.

Crifo, P., Escrig-Olmedo, E., & Mottis, N. (2019). Corporate governance as a key driver of corporate sustainability in France: The role of board members and investor relations. *Journal of Business Ethics*, *159*(4), 1127–1146. doi:10.100710551-018-3866-6

Crumbley, D.L. (2006). *Forensic Accountants Appearing in the Literature*. Academic Press.

Crumbley, D. L. (2001). Forensic accounting: Older than you think. *Journal of Forensic Accounting*, *2*(2), 181–202.

Crumbley, D. L. (2009). Forensic Accounting: Older than you Think. *Journal of Forensic Accounting*, *2*(2), 181.

Crumbley, D. L., Heitger, L. E., & Smith, G. S. (2005). *Forensic and Investigative Accounting*. CCH Group.

Cunhal. (2018). Determinants of Structure of Corporate Governance Disclosure in Portugal. *RBGN*, 338.

Curtis, G. E. (2008). Legal and regulatory environments and ethics: Essential components of fraud and forensic accounting curriculum. *Issues in Accounting Education*, *23*(4), 535–543. doi:10.2308/iace.2008.23.4.535

D., V., M., K., S., S., M., A., & A., A. (2019). Credit Card Fraud Detection - Machine Learning methods. *2019 18th International Symposium INFOTEH-JAHORINA (INFOTEH), 1*(1), 1-5. Retrieved from https://ieeexplore.ieee.org/document/8717766

Dabor, A. O., Aggreh, M., & Eruse, U. (2017). Forensic accounting and fraud control in the Nigerian banking sectors. *Journal of Global Accounting, 5*(1), 165–174.

Dabor, E. L., & Adeyemi, S. B. (2009). Corporate governance and credibility of financial statement in Nigeria. *Journal of Business Systems. Governance and Ethics., 4*(1), 13–24.

Dada, O. S., Owolabi, A. S., & Okwu, A. T. (2013). Forensic Accounting a Panacea to Alleviation of Fraudulent Practices in Nigeria. *Int. J. Buss. Mgt. Eco. Res., 4*(5).

Dada, S. O., & Jimoh, F. B. (2020). Forensic accounting and financial crimes in Nigerian public sector. *Journal of Accounting and Taxation, 12*(4), 118–125. doi:10.5897/JAT2020.0417

Dada, S. O., Owolabi, S. A., & Okwu, A. T. (2013). Forensic accounting a panacea to alleviation of fraudulent practices in Nigeria. *International Journal of Business Management and Economic Research, 4*(5), 787–792.

Dada, S. O., Owolabi, S. A., & Okwu, A. T. (2013). Forensic accounting a Panacea to alleviation of fraudulent practices in Nigeria. *International Journal of Business Management and Economic Research, 4*(5), 787–792.

Dada, S. O., Owolabi, S. A., & Okwu, A. T. (2013). Forensic accounting is a panacea to the alleviation of fraudulent practices in Nigeria. *International Journal of Business Management and Economic Research, 4*(5), 787–792.

Damage, H. K., & Hanid, O. Y. (2005). *Accountant's Guide to Fraud Detection and Control* (2nd ed.). John Wiley & Sons.

Damilola, D., & Olinfinsola, J. (2007). Forensic Accountants and the Litigation Support Engagement. *The Nigerian Accountant, 39*(4), 49–52.

Daniela, P., & Attila, T. (2013). Internal audit versus internal control and coaching. *Procedia Economics and Finance, 6*(3), 694–702. doi:10.1016/S2212-5671(13)00191-3

Dat, P. M., Mau, N. D., Loan, B. T. T., & Huy, D. T. N. (2020). Comparative China Corporate Governance Standards after Financial Crises, Corporate Scandals and Manipulation. *Journal of Security & Sustainability Issues, 9*(3).

David, A. (2005). *Low level fraud is a high level issue, supply management.* Retrieved from: http://www.highbeam.com/doc/1P3-821992191.html

Davis, C., Farrell, R., & Ogilby, S. (2010). *Characteristics and Skills of the Forensic Accountant.* American Institute of Certified Public Accountants.

Dechow, P. M., & Sloan, R. G. (1995). Detecting Earnings Management. *The Accounting Review, 70*(2), 193–225.

Dechow, P. M., Sloan, R. G., & Sweeney, A. P. (1996). Causes and Consequences of Earnings Manipulation: An Analysis of Firms Subject to Enforcement Actions by the SEC. *Contemporary Accounting Research, 13*(1), 1–36. doi:10.1111/j.1911-3846.1996.tb00489.x

Deegan, C. (2007). Organizational legitimacy as a motive for sustainability reporting. In J. Unerman, B. O'Dwyer, & J. Bebbington (Eds.), *Sustainability Accounting and Accountability* (pp. 127–149). Routledge. doi:10.4324/NOE0415384889.ch7

Deegan, C., Rankin, M., & Tobin, J. (2002). An examination of the corporate social and environmental disclosures of BHP from 1983–1997: A test of legitimacy theory. *Accounting, Auditing & Accountability Journal, 15*(3), 312–343. doi:10.1108/09513570210435861

DeFond, M. L., Hann, R. N., & Hu, X. (2005). Does the market value financial expertise on audit committees of boards of directors? *Journal of Accounting Research*, *43*(2), 153–193. doi:10.1111/j.1475-679x.2005.00166.x

Degboro, D. & Olofinsola. (2007). Forensic accountant and litigate support engagement. *The Nigerian Accountant*, *40*(2), 49–52.

Degboro, D., & Olofinsola, J. (2007). Forensic accountants and the litigation support engagement. *The Nigerian Accountant*, *40*(2), 49–52.

Deloitte. (2016). *Blockchain technology. A game-changer in accounting.* Available at: www2.deloitte.com/content/dam/Deloitte/de/Documents/Innovation/Blockchain_A-game-changer-in-accounting.pdf

Desk, N. (2008). *Fraud in textile mills capital declaration detected.* Available at: https://fp.brecorder.com/2008/09/20080904803179/

Desouky, A. R. (2014). *Accounting disclosure of financial risks in the annual reports of companies listed on the stock market and its impact on stock returns: an applied study* (Unpublished Master's thesis). Cairo University.

Dess, G., & Robinson, R. (1984). Measuring organizational performance in the absence of objective measures: The case of the privately-held firm and conglomerate business unit. *Strategic Management Journal*, *5*(3), 265–273. doi:10.1002mj.4250050306

Dewi, K., & Anisykurlillah, I. (2021). Analysis of the Effect of Fraud Pentagon Factors on Fraudulent Financial Statement with Audit Committee as Moderating Variable. *Accounting Analysis Journal.*, *10*(1), 39–46. doi:10.15294/aaj.v10i1.44520

Dhar, P., & Sarkar, A. (2010). Forensic accounting: An accountant's vision. *Vidyasagar University Journal of Commerce*, *15*(3), 93–104.

Dhiaf, M. M., Atayah, O. F., Nasrallah, N., & Frederico, G. F. (2021). *Thirteen years of Operations Management Research (OMR) journal: a bibliometric analysis and future research directions.* Operations Management Research. doi:10.100712063-021-00199-8

Dichev, I. D., Graham, J. R., Harvey, C. R., & Rajgopal, S. (2012). Earnings quality: Evidence from the field. *Journal of Accounting and Economics.* https://www.scopus.com/inward/record.uri?eid=2-s2.0-84890151024&doi=10.1016%2Fj.jacceco.2013.05.004&partnerID=40&md5=3d337b47fd462c1a8d90c73ab0aae393

Diep, T. N. (2018). An overview of forensic accounting and the need for research on forensic accounting. *Journal of Accounting and Auditing, 9.* https://www.hoiketoanhcm.org.vn/vn/trao-doi/khai-quat-ve-ke-toan-dieu-tra-va-su-can-thiet-nghien-cuu-ve-ke-toan-dieu-tra/

Diep, T. N. (2020). Theoretical concepts of forensic accounting in Vietnam. *Finance Journal, 2*(9). https://tapchitaichinh.vn/tai-chinh-kinh-doanh/mot-so-van-de-ly-luan-ve-ke-toan-dieu-tra-tai-viet-nam-330750.html

DiGabriele, J. (2008). An empirical investigation of the relevant skills of forensic accountants. *Journal of Education for Business*, *83*(6), 331–340. doi:10.3200/JOEB.83.6.331-338

DiGabriele, J. (2009a). Fishbowl the forensic accountant: A closer look at the skills forensic accounting education should emphasize. *Forensic Examiner*, *18*(2), 77–79.

DiGabriele, J. (2009b). Implications of regulatory prescriptions and audit standards on the evolution of forensic accounting in the audit process. *Journal of Applied Accounting Research*, *10*(2), 109–121. doi:10.1108/09675420910984673

DiGabriele, J. A. (2009). Fishbowl the Forensic Accountant: A Closer Look at the Skills of Forensic Accounting Education should emphasize. *Forensic Examiner*, *18*(2), 77–79.

DiGabriele, J. A., & Huber, W. (2015). Topics and methods in forensic accounting research. *Accounting Research Journal, 28*(1), 98–114. doi:10.1108/ARJ-08-2014-0071

Dighe, D., Patil, S., & Kokate, S. (2018). Detection of Credit Card Fraud Transactions Using Machine Learning Algorithms and Neural Networks: A Comparative Study. *2018 Fourth International Conference on Computing Communication Control and Automation (ICCUBEA)*, 1-6. 10.1109/ICCUBEA.2018.8697799

Dimitras, G. I. (2013). Financial crisis and accounting quality: Evidence from five European countries. *Elsevier, 29*(1), 154-160.

Directiva 2003/6/CE do Parlamento Europeu e do Conselho de 28 de Janeiro de 2003 relativa ao abuso de informação privilegiada e à manipulação de mercado (abuso de mercado) (2003). https://eur-lex.europa.eu

Directiva 2006/43/CE do Parlamento Europeu e do Conselho de 17 de Maio de 2006 relativa à revisão legal das contas anuais e consolidadas (2006). https://eur-lex.europa.eu

Diretiva 2014/56/UE do Parlamento Europeu e do Conselho de 16 de abril de 2014 que altera a Diretiva 2006/43/CE relativa à revisão legal das contas anuais e consolidadas (2014). https://eur-lex.europa.eu

Dolmanbateman Chartered Accountants Australia. (2019). *The Role of Forensic Accountants.* https://dolmanbateman.com.au/the-role-of-forensic-accountants/

Dorminey, J., Fleming, A. S., Kranacher, M.-J., & Jr, R. A. R. (2012). The Evolution of Fraud Theory. *Issues in Accounting Education, 27*(2), 555–579. doi:10.2308/iace-50131

Dowd, K. (2016). *A Comparison of Accounting Fraud Before and After Sarbanes-Oxley* (Bridgewater State University Honors Program Theses and Projects). https://vc.bridgew.edu/honors_proj/165

Dreyer, K. (2014). *A History of Forensic Accounting* [Honours Project, Grand Valley State University]. https://scholarworks.gvsu.edu/honorsprojects/296

Driel, H. (2019). Financial fraud, scandals, and regulation: A conceptual framework and literature review. *Business History, 61*(8), 1259–1299. doi:10.1080/00076791.2018.1519026

Driskell, F. D. (2019, Autumn). Conducting Forensic Accounting and Internal Investigations. Forensic Accounting and Special Investigations Thought Leadership. *Insights*, 3-10. http://www.willamette.com/insights_journal/19/autumn_2019_1.pdf

Drogalasa, G., Pazarskis, M., Anagnostopoulou, E., & Papachristou, A. (2017). The effect of internal audit effectiveness, auditor responsibility and training in fraud detection. *Accounting and Management Information Systems, 16*(4), 434–454. doi:10.24818/jamis.2017.04001

Dutta, A. K. (2021). Role Of Forensic Audit As A Tool For Fraud Detection And Prevention In Micro Finance Industry. *The Management Accountant, 56*(10).

Dutta, S. K., Caplan, D. H., & Marcinko, D. J. (2014). Blurred vision, perilous future: Management fraud at olympus. *Issues in Accounting Education, 29*(3), 459–480. doi:10.2308/iace-50787

Dzikrullah, A. D., Harymawan, I., & Ratri, M. C. (2020). Internal audit functions and audit outcomes: Evidence from Indonesia. *Cogent Business and Management, 7*(1), 1750331. Advance online publication. doi:10.1080/23311975.2020.1750331

Earnest, D. F., & Sofian, S. (2013). The Mediating Role of Corporate Governance on Intellectual Capital and Corporate Performance. *Journal of Economics, Business and Management, 1*(4), 339–342.

Efiong, E. J. (2012). Forensic accounting education: An exploration of level of awareness in developing economies -Nigeria as a case study. *International Journal of Business and Management*, *7*(4). Advance online publication. doi:10.5539/ijbm.v7n4p26

Egbunike, P. A., & Igbinovia, I. M. (2018). Threat of bankruptcy and earnings management in Nigerian listed banks. *Acta Universitatis Danubius*, *14*(3), 238–253.

Ehioghiren, E. E., & Atu, O. O. K. (2016). Forensic accounting and fraud management: Evidence from Nigeria. *Igbinedion University Journal of Accounting*, *2*, 245–308.

Eiya, O., & Otalor, J. I. (2013). Forensic Accounting as a Tool for Fighting Financial Crime in Nigeria. *Research Journal of Finance and Accounting*, *4*(6), 18–25.

Elbling, P. (2015). *Fraude e suas implicações em auditoria* [Unpublished master dissertation] Instituto Superior de Contabilidade e Adminsitração de Lisboa, Portugal.

Eliezer, O., & Emmanuel, B. (2015). Relevance of Forensic Accounting in the Detection and Prevention *Historical Research Letter, 23*.

El-Meligy, H. H. (2012). *The Adequacy of Accounting Disclosure of Liquidity Risks in Commercial Banks for the Decisions of the Basel III Committee. The Scientific Journal of Economics and Commerce, Ain Shams.*

Else, S. R., & Pileggi, F. G. (2019). *Corporate Directors Must Consider Impact of Artificial Intelligence for Effective Corporate Governance.* Available at: https://businesslawtoday.org/2019/02/corporate-directors-must-consider-impact-artificial-intelligence-effective-corporate-governance/

Emeh, Y., & Obi, J. O. (2013). An empirical analysis of forensic accounting and financial fraud in Nigeria. *African Journal of Social Sciences*, *4*, 112–121.

Enofe, A., Ekpulu, G., & Ajala, T. O. (2015). Forensic Accounting and Corporate Crime Mitigation. *European Scientific Journal*, *11*(7).

Enofe. (2016). Forensic Accounting and Fraudulent Financial Reporting in Nigeria. *Journal of Accounting and Financial Management,* *2*(1), 21-34.

Enofe, A. O., Mgbame, C. O., Ayodele, F. O., & Okunbo, O. (2013). Forensic accounting: A tool for detecting fraud in Nigeria's business environment. *ESUT Journal of Accountancy*, *4*(1), 194–199.

Enofe, A. O., Okpako, P. O., & Atube, E. N. (2013). The Impact of Forensic Accounting on Fraud Detection. *European Journal of Business and Management*, *5*(26), 61–72.

Enofe, Ao, M. O. (2016). Forensic accounting and fraudulent financial reporting in Nigeria. *Journal of Accounting and Financial Management*, *2*(1), 21–34.

EnyiE. P. (2009). Detecting causes of variances in operational outputs of manufacturing organization: A forensic accounting investigation approach. Retrieved from http://ssrn.com/abstract=1144783

Ergen, M. (2019). What is Artificial Intelligence? Technical Considerations and Future Perception. *The Anatolian Journal of Cardiology*, *22*, 5–7. doi:10.14744/AnatolJCardiol.2019.79091 PMID:31670719

Eriabie, S., & Odia, J. (2016). Effects of characteristics of audit committee on earnings management in Nigerian quoted companies. *Sokoto Journal of Management Studies*, *10*(1), 139–159.

Ernst & Young. (2003). Fraud: Unmanaged risk. 8th global survey. Global Investigations Dispute Advisory Services, South Africa. Author.

Ernst & Young. (2016). *14th Global Fraud Survey: Corporate misconduct — individual consequences: Global enforcement focuses the spotlight on executive integrity*. EY. https://www.ey.com/

Ernst & Young. (2016). *Corporate Misconduct - Individual Consequences*. 14th Global Fraud Survey.

Ernst & Young. (2017). *Human instinct, Machine logic. Which do you trust most in the fight against fraud and corruption?* Europe, Middle East, India and Africa Fraud Survey.

Everette, E. C. (2012). *Financial Statement Fraud, Part2 and 3. Professional Development Network. The Know How.*

Eyisi, E. (2014). The Impact of Forensic Auditors in Corporate Governance. *Research Journal of Finance and Accounting*, *5*(8), 31–39.

Ezuwore, E. a. (2014). The Impact of Forensic Auditors in Corporate Governance. *Research Journal of Finance and Accounting, 5*(8).

Fadilah, S., Maemunah, M., Lim, T. N., & Sundary, R. I. (2019). Forensic accounting: fraud detection skills for external auditors. *Polish Journal of Management Studies*, 168-180.

Fama, E. F. (1980). Agency problems and the theory of the firm. *Journal of Political Economy*, *88*(2), 288–307. doi:10.1086/260866

Fan, J. P., & Wong, T. J. (2005). Do External Auditors Perform a Corporate Governance Role in Emerging Markets? Evidence from East Asia. *Journal of Accounting Research*, *43*(1), 35–72. doi:10.1111/j.1475-679x.2004.00162.x

Farber, D. B. (2005). Restoring trust after fraud: Does corporate governance matter? *The Accounting Review*, *80*(2), 539–561. doi:10.2308/accr.2005.80.2.539

Fernandes, L. (2010). *Alterações normativas na auditoria após SOX: efeitos na opinião do auditor* [Unpublished master dissertation] Instituto Superior de Contabilidade e Administração da Universidade de Aveiro, Portugal.

Fernando, A. (2009). *Corporate Governance: Principles, Policies and Practices*. Pearson.

Fialho, V. (2015). *(Un)Ethical Leadership, Organizational Identification and Sensemaking: the BES case and its impact on employees* [Unpublished work project as part of the requirements for the Award of a Masters Degree in Management]. NOVA School of Business and Economics.

Fida, S., & Naveed, M. (2021). Novel insights into banking risk structure: Empirical evidence from nexus of financial, governance, and industrial landscape through nested tested modeling. *Cogent Business & Management*, *8*(1), 1869362. doi:10.1080/23311975.2020.1869362

Financial Sector Conduct Authority (FSCA). (2021). *Anti-Money Laundering and Counter-Terrorism*. https://www.fsca.co.za/Regulatory%20Frameworks/Pages/AMLCFT.aspx#:~:text=Money%20Laundering%20is%20the%20process,anyone%20has%20in%20such%20proceeds

Financial Services and Markets Act. (2000). https://www.legislation.gov.uk/ukpga/2000/8/contents

Flitter, E. 2020. *The Price of Wells Fargo's Fake Account Scandal Grows by $3 Billion*. Available at: https://www.nytimes.com/2020/02/21/business/wells-fargo-settlement.html

Florea, R., & Florea, R. (2016). Internal Audit and Risk Management. ISO 31000 and ERM Approaches. *Economy Transdisciplinarity Cognition*, *19*(1), 72–77.

Forensic Accounting Standards. (n.d.). *Forensic Accounting Demystified*. https://www.forensicaccounting.com/standards.html#:~:text=1%20provides%20standards%20in%20professional,to%20the%20ultimate%20conclusion%20of

Fortune. (2020). *The biggest business scandals of 2020*. https://fortune.com/2020/12/27/biggest-business-scandals-of-2020-nikola-wirecard-luckin-coffee-twitter-security-hack-tesla-spx-mcdonalds-ceo-ppp-fraud-wells-fargo-ebay-carlos-ghosn/

Fredrick, O. (2012). The Impact of Credit Risk Management on Financial Performance of Commercial Banks in Kenya. *DBA Africa Management Review*, *3*(1), 22–37.

Free, C. (2015). Looking Through the Fraud Triangle: A Review and Call for New Directions. SSRN *Electronic Journal*. doi:10.2139/ssrn.2590952

Free, C., Macintosh, N., & Stein, M. (2007). The organizational fraud triangle: Leadership, culture and control within Enron. *Ivey Business Journal*, *32*(1), 18–54.

Fuller, S. H., Joe, J. R., & Luippold, B. L. (2021). The Effect of Auditor Reporting Choice and Audit Committee Oversight on Management Financial Disclosures. *The Accounting Review*, *96*(6), 239–274. doi:10.2308/TAR-2016-0246

Fury, K. F., & Eka, A. (2013). Forensic Accounting and fraud Prevention in Indonesia Public Sector. *Journal of Modern Science*, *4*(13), 421–433.

Gaaya, S., Lakhal, N., & Lakhal, F. (2017). Does family ownership reduce corporate tax avoidance? The moderating effect of audit quality. *Managerial Auditing Journal*, *33*(7), 731–744. doi:10.1108/MAJ-02-2017-1530

Gallagher, J., & Schiavone, J. (2019, July 10). *AICPA Issues New Professional Standards for Forensic Accounting Service Providers*. https://www.aicpa.org/news/article/aicpa-issues-new-professional-standards-for-forensic-accounting-service

García-Carbonell, N., Martín-Alcázar, F. & Sánchez-Gardey. (2015). Determinants of top management's capability to identify core employees. *BRQ Business Research Quarterly*, *18*(2), 69-80.

Gates, S., Prachyl, C., & Sullivan, C. (2016). Using Report To the Nations on Occupational Fraud and Abuse To Stimulate Discussion of Fraud in Accounting and Business Classes. *Journal of Business and Behavior Sciences*, *28*(1), 106–115.

Gauthier, M. P., & Brender, N. (2021). How do the current auditing standards fit the emergent use of blockchain? *Managerial Auditing Journal*, *36*(3), 365–385. doi:10.1108/MAJ-12-2019-2513

Gbegi, D. O., & Adebisi, J. F. (2014). Forensic Accounting Skills and Techniques in Fraud Investigation in the Nigerian Public Sector. *Mediterranean Journal of Social Sciences*, *5*(3), 243–252. doi:10.5901/mjss.2014.v5n3p243

Gebrayel, E., Jarrar, H., Salloum, C., & Lefebvre, Q. (2018). Effective association between audit committees and the internal audit function and its impact on financial reporting quality: Empirical evidence from Omani listed firms. *International Journal of Auditing*. https://www.scopus.com/inward/record.uri?eid=2-s2.0-85043695901&doi=10.1111%2Fijau.12113&partnerID=40&md5=99cff6d3411d5b36cc6237eca6c86167

Geis, G. (2007). *White-Collar and Corporate Crime*. Pearson.

General Accounting Office. (1996). *The accounting profession major issues: progress and concerns*. GAO.

Gentry, R., & Shen, W. (2010). The relationship between accounting and market measures of firm financial performance: How strong is it? *Journal of Managerial Issues*, *22*(4), 514–530.

Ghahramani, Z. (2015). Probabilistic machine learning and artificial intelligence. *Nature*, *521*(7553), 452–459. doi:10.1038/nature14541 PMID:26017444

Ghanoum, S., & Alaba, F. M. (2020). *Integration of Artificial Intelligence in Auditing: The Effect on Auditing Process*. Available at: https://www.diva-portal.org/smash/get/diva2:1446778/FULLTEXT01.pdf

Giese, G., Nagy, Z., & Lee, L.-E. (2021). Deconstructing ESG ratings performance: Risk and return for E, S, and G by time horizon, sector, and weighting. *Journal of Portfolio Management*. https://www.scopus.com/inward/record.uri?eid=2-s2.0-85101927608&doi=10.3905%2FJPM.2020.1.198&partnerID=40&md5=5d4227b8dc01f23e2e0ccb4c32d145bc

Githecha, D. K. (2013). The effect of fraud risk management on the financial performance of commercial banks in Kenya [MSC Project]. University of Nairobi.

Gizaw, M. (2015). The impact of credit risk on profitability performance of commercial banks in Ethiopia. *African Journal of Business Management*, *9*(2), 59–66. doi:10.5897/AJBM2013.7171

Glover & Prawit. (2003). A Test of Changes in Auditors' Fraud-Related Planning Judgments since the Issuance of SAS No. 82. *Auditing: A Journal of Practice & Theory*, *22*(2), 237–251.

Goertzel, T. (2014). The path to more general artificial intelligence. *Journal of Experimental & Theoretical Artificial Intelligence*, *26*(3), 343–354. doi:10.1080/0952813X.2014.895106

Golden, T. H., Skalak, S. L., & Clayton, M. M. (2006). *A Guide to forensic accounting investigation*. John Wiley & Sons, Inc.

Golden, T. W., & Dyer, M. T. (2006). In T. W. Golden, S. L. Skalak, & M. M. Clayton (Eds.), *The art of the interview, A Guide to Forensic Accounting Investigation* (pp. 349–364). John Wiley and Sons.

Golden, T. W., Skalak, S. L., & Clayton, M. M. (2006). *A guide to forensic accounting investigation*. Wiley.

Gomes, M. (2017). *Corporate Governance at BES: Would new recommendations have avoided the failure?* [Unpublished work project as part of the requirements for the Award of a Masters Degree in Finance]. NOVA – School of Business and Economics.

González, G., & López, S. B. (2012). Determinants of Credit Risk Derivatives use by the European Banking Industry. *Journal of Money, Investment and Banking*, 1-30.

Gonzalez, R. A., Ferro, R. E., & Liberona, D. (2020). Government and governance in intelligent cities, smart transportation study case in Bogotá Colombia. *Ain Shams Engineering Journal*, *11*(1), 25–34. doi:10.1016/j.asej.2019.05.002

Goodman, M. (2015). *Future Crime*. Doubleday.

Gottschalk, P. (2010). Prevention of white collar crime: The role of accounting. *Journal of Forensic and Investigative Accounting*, *3*(1), 23–48.

Gottschalk, P., & Benson, M. L. (2020). *The Evolution of Corporate Accounts of Scandals From Exposure to Investigation*. Oxford University Press. doi:10.1093/bjc/azaa001

Govil, S. (2020). *What AI does for accountants*. Available at: https://www.accountingtoday.com/opinion/what-ai-does-for-accountants

Goyal, S., & Dhamija, S. (2018). Corporate governance failure at Ricoh India: Rebuilding lost trust. *Emerald Emerging Markets Case Studies*, *8*(4), 1–20. doi:10.1108/EEMCS-06-2017-0166

Grant, R., & Visconti, M. (2006). The Strategic Background to Corporate Accounting Scandals. *Long Range Planning*, *39*(4), 361–383. doi:10.1016/j.lrp.2006.09.003

Gray, D. (2008). Forensic accounting and auditing: Compared and contrasted to traditional accounting and auditing. *American Journal of Business Education-Fourth Quarter*, *1*(2), 115–126. doi:10.19030/ajbe.v1i2.4630

Gray, O. R., & Moussalli, S. D. (2006). Forensic accounting and auditing united again: A historical perspective. *Journal of Business Issues*, (2), 15–25.

Grazoli, S., Janal, K., & Johnson, P. E. (2006). A Cognitive Approach to Fraud Detection. *Journal of Forensic Accounting*, *7*(2), 65–88.

Grubor, G., Ristić, N., & Simeunović, N. (2013). Integrated forensic accounting investigative process model in the digital environment. *International Journal of Scientific and Research Publications*, *3*(12), 1–9.

Grüning, M. (2011). Artificial Intelligence Measurement of Disclosure (AIMD). *European Accounting Review*, *20*(3), 485–519. doi:10.1080/09638180.2011.585792

Gullapalli, V., Kalli, S., & Vijay, A. (2020). *Credit Card Transaction.* https://www.capgemini.com/industry/banking-and-capital-markets/

Guo, J., Huang, P., Zhang, Y., & Zhou, N. (2015). Foreign ownership and real earnings management: Evidence from Japan. *Journal of International Accounting Research.* https://www.scopus.com/inward/record.uri?eid=2-s2.0-84956875166&doi=10.2308%2Fjiar-51274&partnerID=40&md5=31fcd005420bda14068534b400cf9649

Gupta, R., & Vij, S. (2021). Financial Frauds and Forensic Accounting: Empirical Evidence from the Indian Corporate Sector. *International Journal of Creative Research Thoughts*, *9*(2), 1611–1619.

H. N., B., Bastikar, S., Gavade, M., & Samota, S. (2018). Credit Card Fraud Detection Using HMM and DBSCAN. *International Journal of Science and Research, 7*(10), 1086-1090. Retrieved from https://www.ijsr.net/archive/v7i10/ART20192099.pdf

Ha, T. (2018). *Around Nguyen Kim Company's arrears of personal income tax.* Public Security News Online. https://cand.com.vn/Kinh-te/Xung-quanh-viec-Cong-ty-Nguyen-Kim-bi-truy-thu-thue-thu-nhap-ca-nhan-501809/

Haapamäki, E., & Sihvonen, J. (2019). Cybersecurity in accounting research. *Managerial Auditing Journal*, *34*(7), 808–834. doi:10.1108/MAJ-09-2018-2004

Haddad, A., El Ammari, A., & Bouri, A. (2021). Impact of Audit Committee Quality on the Financial Performance of Conventional and Islamic Banks. *Journal of Risk and Financial Management*, *14*(4), 176. doi:10.3390/jrfm14040176

Hadian, D. T. (2013). Detection fraud of financial statement with fraud triangle. *Proceeding of 23rd International Business Research Conference.*

Hair, J. F., Hult, G. T., Ringle, C. M., & Sarstedt, M. (2017). A Primer on Partial Least Squares Structural Equation Modeling (PLS-SEM) (2nd ed.). Sage.

Hamdani, R., Kumalahadi, & Urumsah, D. (2017). The Classification of Corruption in Indonesia: A Behavioral Perspective. *SHS Web of Conferences, 10002*(34). 10.1051hsconf/20173410002

Hamdan, M. W. (2018). The Role of Forensic Accounting in Discovering Financial Fraud. *International Journal of Accounting Research.*, *6*(2), 2–6.

Hamilton, S., & Micklethwait, A. (2006). *Greed and Corporate Failure: The Lessons from Recent Disasters.* Palgrave Macmillan UK. doi:10.1057/9780230502758

Hampel Committee. (1998). *Committee on Corporate Governance.* Final Report. London: Gee.

Hamrani, K. A., & Mahmoud, W. (2021, Jan 13). *A Green Light to Prosecute: Lessons Learned from the Omani Ministry of Education Embezzlement Case.* Retrieved from https://www.tamimi.com: https://www.tamimi.com/law-update-articles/a-green-light-to-prosecute-lessons-learned-from-the-omani-ministry-of-education-embezzlement-case/

Handayani, S., & Kawedar, W. (2021). Could the minimization of opportunity prevent fraud? An empirical study in the auditors' perspective. *Accounting*, *7*(5), 1157–1166. doi:10.5267/j.ac.2021.2.023

Hao, X. (2010). Analysis of the necessity to develop the forensic accounting in China. *International Journal of Business and Management*, *5*(5), 185–188. doi:10.5539/ijbm.v5n5p185

Harris, C. K., & Brown, A. M. (2000). The qualities of a forensic accountant. *Pennsylvania CPA Journal*, *71*(1), 6–8.

Harris, C. K., & Brown, A. M. (2000). The Qualities of a Forensic Accountant. Pennsylvania. *The CPA Journal*, *71*, 2–3.

Haruna Abubakar, A., Mansor, N., & Adilah Wan-Mohamad, W. I. (2021). Corporate tax avoidance, free cash flow and real earnings management: Evidence from Nigeria. *Universal Journal of Accounting and Finance*. https://www.scopus.com/inward/record.uri?eid=2-s2.0-85101872498&doi=10.13189%2Fujaf.2021.090109&partnerID=40&md5=4321320ced3149ba01c0556e4e69cf1f

Hashad, N. (2004). *Basel Convention*. Academic Press.

Hashem, F. (2021). The role of forensic accounting techniques in reducing cloud based accounting risks in the Jordanian five stars hotels. *WSEAS Transactions on Business and Economics*, *18*, 434–443. doi:10.37394/23207.2021.18.44

Hegazy, S., Sangster, A., & Kotb, A. (2017). Mapping Forensic Accounting in the UK. *Journal of International Accounting, Auditing and Taxation*, *28*.

Hegazy, S., Sangster, A., & Kotb, A. (2017). Mapping forensic accounting in the UK. *Journal of International Accounting, Auditing & Taxation*, *28*, 43–56. doi:10.1016/j.intaccaudtax.2016.12.004

Helmore, E. (2019). Anna Sorokin: fake German heiress sentenced to up to 12 years in prison. *New York and Agencies*. https://www.theguardian.com/us-news/2019/may/09/anna-sorokin-sentence-fake-heiress-scammer-delvey-jail-time-latest-news-new-york-trial

Henning, E., & Kammel, B. (2020). *The Man Who Could Explain the $2 Billion Wirecard Mystery Is Missing*. Available at: https://www.bloombergquint.com/businessweek/jan-marsalek-the-man-who-could-explain-wirecard-s-2-billion-fraud-is-missing

Henseler, J., Ringle, C., & Sarstedt, M. (2015). A new criterion for assessing discriminant validity in variance-based structural equation modelling. *Journal of the Academy of Marketing Science*, *43*(1), 115–135. doi:10.100711747-014-0403-8

Herbert, W. E., Tsegba, I. N., Ene, E. E., & Onyilo, F. (2017). The rise of fraud examination and forensic accounting in Africa: The Nigerian experience. *Archives of Business Research*, *5*(4). Advance online publication. doi:10.14738/abr.54.3013

Heritage Foundation. (2021). 2021 Index of Economic Freedom. *Vietnam Section*, 436–437. https://www.heritage.org/index/pdf/2021/countries/2021_IndexofEconomicFreedom-Vietnam.pdf

Heta, N., & Prashasti, K. (2019). Credit card Fraud Detection based on Machine Learning Algorithms. *International Journal of Computers and Applications*, *188*(44), 8–12. https://www.ijcaonline.org/archives/volume182/number44/naik-2019-ijca-918521.pdf

Hickman, L. E., Iyer, S. R., & Jadiyappa, N. (2021). The effect of voluntary and mandatory corporate social responsibility on earnings management: Evidence from India and the 2% rule. *Emerging Markets Review*. https://www.scopus.com/inward/record.uri?eid=2-s2.0-85095772108&doi=10.1016%2Fj.ememar.2020.100750&partnerID=40&md5=7584a931ef7ab0c2247f2fc5c4bec42b

Hill, G. N., & Hill, K. T. (2009). *Expert witness*. http://legaldictionary.thefreedictionary.com/Expert+witnesses

Hobeika, A. (2017). *Understanding the impact of technology in audit and finance*. ICAEW and DFSA.

Hogan. (2008, November). Financial Statement Fraud: Insights from the Academic Literature. *Auditing: A Journal of Practice & Theory, 27*(2), 231–252.

Hołda, A. (2020, December 22). Using the Beneish M-score model: Evidence from non-financial. *Investment Management and Financial Innovations*.

Hopwood, W. S., Leiner, J. J., & Young, G. R. (2008). *Forensic Accounting*. McGraw-Hill/Irwin.

Hoque, Hafiz, H. (2021). Impact of bank regulation on risk of Islamic and conventional banks. *International Journal of Finance & Economics*, *2021*, 1–38. doi:10.1002/ijfe

Howard, S., & Sheetz, M. (2006). *Forensic accounting and fraud investigation for non-experts*. John Wiley and Sons Inc.

Howieson, B. (2018). What is the 'good' forensic accountant? A virtue ethics perspective. *Pacific Accounting Review*, *30*(2), 155–167. doi:10.1108/PAR-01-2017-0005

Huang, M.-H., & Rust, R. T. (2018). Artificial Intelligence in Service. *Journal of Service Research*, *21*(2), 155–172. doi:10.1177/1094670517752459

Huber, W. (2014). What is the value of multiple certifications in forensic accounting? *Journal of Forensic and Investigative Accounting*, *7*(2), 113–143.

Huu, N. D. (2005). *Theory and practice of applying forensic audit in current status of State Audit* [Research project]. Vietnam State Audit.

Huy, A. (2018). *Huynh Thi Huyen Nhu was sentenced to life in prison*. Public Security News Online. https://cand.com.vn/Phap-luat/Huynh-Thi-Huyen-Nhu-bi-tuyen-an-chung-than-478435/

IASB. (2009). International Standard On Auditing 240; The Auditor'S Responsibilities Relating To Fraud. In *An Audit of Financial Statements*. IFAC.

Ibanichuka, E. A. L. & Oko, I. A. (2019). Electronic fraud and financial performance of quoted commercial banks in Nigeria. *International Journal of Advanced Academic Research Management Practice,* 5(4), 15-35.

Ibrahim, A., Mohammed, D., & Fatima, U. (2014). Managing Bank Fraud and Forgeries through effective control strategies. A case study of Central Bank of Nigeria, Gombe Branch. *International Journal of Business and Management Invention.*, *3*(4), 7–17.

IC3. (2021). *IC3 Releases 2020 Internet Crime Report*. Retrieved from https://www.fbi.gov/news/pressrel/press-releases/fbi-releases-the-internet-crime-complaint-center-2020-internet-crime-report-including-covid-19-scam-statistics

ICAEW. (2021). *What is corporate governance?* https://www.icaew.com/technical/corporate-governance/principles/principles-articles/does-corporate-governance-matter

IFA. (2009). *International standard on auditing 240: The auditor's responsibilities relating to fraud in an audit of financial statements.* International Federation of Accountants.

IFAC. (2009, Dec 15). Retrieved from International standard on auditing 240; the auditor's responsibilities relating to fraud in an audit of financial statements: https://www.ifac.org/system/files/downloads/a012-2010-iaasb-handbook-isa-240.pdf

IIA. (2019). *Governance of risk: Three lines of defence*. Available at: https://www.iia.org.uk/resources/audit-committees/governance-of-risk-three-lines-of-defence/

Ikpefan, O. A. (2006). Growth of Bank frauds and the impact on the Nigerian Banking Industry. *Journal of Business*), 106-126.

IMF. (2021). *Index 2021: Vietnam section*. https://www.imf.org/en/Countries/VNM

Imoniana, J. O. (2013). The forensic accounting and corporate fraud. *Journal of Information Systems and Technology Management, 10*(1), 119–144.

Imoniana, J. O., Pompa, M. T., & Formigoni, A. H. (2013). The Forensic Accounting and Corporate Fraud. *Journal of Information Systems and Technology Management, 10*(1), 119–144. doi:10.4301/S1807-17752013000100007

Institute of Forensic Commercial Practitioners. (2016). Everything you should know about South Africa's commercial forensic industry. *The Forensic Practitioner*, (3). https://www.icfp.co.za/sites/default/files/articles/2714_icfp_ezine_issue_3_nov_2016.pdf

International Auditing and Assurance Standards Board (IAASB). (2020). *Handbook of International Quality Control, Auditing, Review, Other Assurance, and Related Services Pronouncements*. Academic Press.

International Monetary Fund. (2001). *Financial System Abuse, Financial Crime and Money Laundering-Background Paper*. https://www.imf.org/external/np/ml/2001/eng/021201.htm

Isa, A. A. (2017). The Study of the Effects of Forensic Accounting and Fraud Detection/Prevention for Financial Management Performance in Public Sector in Nigeria: A way forward. *World Wide Journal of Multidisciplinary Research and Development, 3*(12), 197–202.

Ismajli, H., Perjuci, E., Prenaj, V., & Braha, M. (2019). The Importance of External Audit in Detecting Abnormalities and Fraud in the Financial Statements of Public Enterprises in Kosovo. *Ekonomika (Nis), 98*(1), 124–134. doi:10.15388/Ekon.2019.1.8

Issa, H., Sun, T., & Vasarhelyi, M. (2016). Research ideas for artificial intelligence in auditing: The formalization of audit and workforce supplementation. *Journal of Emerging Technologies in Accounting, 13*(2), 1–20. doi:10.2308/jeta-10511

J. O., A., A. O., A., & S. A., O. (2017). Credit card fraud detection using machine learning techniques: A comparative analysis. *2017 International Conference on Computing Networking and Informatics (ICCNI)*, 1-9. Retrieved from 10.1109/ICCNI.2017.8123782

Jadhap, A., & Agarwal, A. (2016). Digital forensics investigation model for social networking site. *Proceedings of the Second International Conference on Information and Communication Technology for Competitive Strategies.*

Jado, S. K. (2012). The impact of risk disclosure in accordance with the requirements of International Financial Reporting Standard No. 7 (IFRS7) on achieving the appropriate value of accounting information (field study). *Journal of Financial and Commercial Studies, 1*, 620-624, 634-638.

Jahmani, Y., & Dowling, W. (2008). The Impact Of Sarbanes-Oxley Act. *Journal of Business & Economics Research, 6*(10), 57–66.

Jain, D. E., & Lamba, J. (2020). Forensic Accounting: A Way To Fight, Deter And Detect Fraud. *International Research Journal. Vic. Australia, 10*(1). Advance online publication. doi:10.51611/iars.irj.v10i1.2020.106

Jensen, M. C. (1986). Agency costs of free cash flow, corporate finance, and takeovers. *The American Economic Review, 76*(2), 323–329.

Jensen, M. C., & Meckling, W. H. (1976). Theory of Firm – Managerial behavior, agency costs, and ownership structure. *Journal of Financial Economics, 3*(4), 305–360. doi:10.1016/0304-405X(76)90026-X

Jiang, S., & Haury, A. C. (2020). *What Happens When Your Credit Card Expires?* Retrieved from https://www.investopedia.com/financial-edge/0712/what-happens-when-your-credit-card-expires.aspx

Johannes, J., Michael Ziegler, G., Calabretto, K., Portier, S., & Edouard, P., & He-Guelton, O. L. (2018). Sequence classification for credit-card fraud detection. *Expert Systems with Applications, 100*(1), 234.

Jones, M. (n.d.). *Creative accounting, fraud and international accounting standards.* University of Bristol. https://pdfs.semanticscholar.org/1c0b/be6f34709bb824586ee3b0b79bfb3105ef65.pdf

Joseph, J. (2016). *The Traits and Characteristics of Elite Forensic Accountants.* Retrieved from https://www.accountingweb.com/community/blogs/jessica-joseph/the-traits-and-characteristics-of-elite-forensic-accountants

Joshi, M. S. (2008). *Definition of Forensic Accounting.* www.forensicaccounting.com

Juárez, F. (2016). Chaos theory and financial statements. Nova Science Publishers, Inc.

Jugurnath, B., Bissessur, R., Ramjattan, Y., Soondrum, H., & Seedoyal, A. (2017). Forensic Accounting and Fraud Investigation: An Empirical Study from Malaysia. *International Journal of Management and Applied Science, 3*(7), 20–24.

Jung, J., & Lee, J. (2017). Contemporary Financial Crime. *Journal of Public Administration and Governance, 7*(2), 88–97. doi:10.5296/jpag.v7i2.11219

Justice, D. o. (2021, Nov 4). Retrieved from South Florida Addiction Treatment Facility Operators Convicted in $112 Million Addiction Treatment Fraud Scheme: https://www.justice.gov/opa/pr/south-florida-addiction-treatment-facility-operators-convicted-112-million-addiction

K, R. S., & Masoumeh, Z. (2014). FraudMiner: A Novel Credit Card Fraud Detection Model Based on Frequent Itemset Mining. *The Scientific World Journal, 2014*(1). Retrieved from https://www.hindawi.com/journals/tswj/2014/252797/

K, R., C K, L., M, S., C P, L., & A K, N. (2018). Credit Card Fraud Detection Using AdaBoost and Majority Voting. *IEEE Access, 6*(1), 14277-14284. Retrieved from https://ieeexplore.ieee.org/document/8292883/

Kaaya, I. D. (2013). Credit Risk and Commercial Banks Performance in Tanzania: a Panel Data Analysis. *Research Journal of Finance and Accounting, 4*(16), 1-9.

Kabuye, F., Nkundabanyanga, S. K., Opiso, J., & Nakabuye, Z. (2018). Internal audit organisational status, competencies, activities and fraud management in the financial services sector. *Managerial Auditing Journal, 32*(9), 924–944. doi:10.1108/MAJ-09-2016-1452

Kacharava, A. (2016, June). *O IC-online é o Repositório Institucional de Informação Científica do Instituto Politécnico de Leiria.* Retrieved from Instituto Politécnico de Leiria: https://iconline.ipleiria.pt/bitstream/10400.8/2139/1/Aleksandre%20Kacharava.pdf

Kajola, S. O. (2008). Corporate governance and firm performance: the case of Nigerian listed firms. *European Journal of Economics, Finance and Administrative Science, 14.*

Kaminski. (2004, Jan 1). Can financial ratios detect fraudulent financial reporting? *Managerial Auditing Journal.*

Kandylas, V., Upham, S. P., & Ungar, L. H. (2010). Analyzing knowledge communities using foreground and background clusters. *ACM Transactions on Knowledge Discovery from Data, 4*(2), 1–35. doi:10.1145/1754428.1754430

Kanu, S. I., & Okorafor, E. O. (2013). The nature, extent and economic impact of fraud on bank deposit in Nigeria. *Interdisciplinary Journal of Contemporary Research in Business, 4*(9), 253–264.

Kao, L., Chen, A., & Lu, C.-S. (2018). Ex ante and ex post overvalued equities: The roles of corporate governance and product market competition. *Asia Pacific Management Review*. https://www.scopus.com/inward/record.uri?eid=2-s2.0-85026657065&doi=10.1016%2Fj.apmrv.2017.07.002&partnerID=40&md5=dfde7f1eaad43e8fb8da6a616e13c35d

Kapmag, D. J. (2008). Fraud Survey. *Journal of Forensic Accounting*, *4*(36), 9–22.

Karabayir, M. E. (2019). Forensic Accounting: Development and Practices Around the World. Kafkas University, Department of Business.

Karwai, S. A. (2002). Bank Fraud: Can Shari'ah prevent it? *Journal of Business Administration*, *2*(1), 62–78.

Kassem, R., & Higson, A. (2012). The new fraud triangle model. *Journal of Emerging Trends in Economics and Management Sciences*, *3*(3).

Kassem, R., & Higson, A. (2012). The new fraud triangle model. *Journal of Emerging Trends in Economics and Management Science*, *3*(3), 191–195.

Kasum, A. S. (2009). *The Relevance of Forensic Accounting to Financial Crimes and Public Sectors of Third World Economies: A Study from Nigeria* [Thesis]. Department of Accounting and Finance, University of Ilorin, Nigeria.

Kasum, A. S. (2009, June). The Relevance of Forensic Accounting to Financial Crimes in Private and Public Sectors of Third World Economies: A Study from Nigeria. *Proceedings of the 1st International Conference on Governance Fraud Ethics and Social Responsibility*. 10.2139srn.1384242

Keasey, K., Thompson, S., & Wright, M. (Eds.). (1997). *Corporate governance: Economic and financial issues*. OUP Oxford.

Kesner, I. F., & Johnson, R. B. (1990). An investigation of the relationship between board composition and stockholder suits. *Strategic Management Journal*, *11*(4), 327–336. doi:10.1002mj.4250110408

Khamis., H. K. (2016). The extent to which loan allocations are used in profit management in private commercial banks (practical analysis) before and after the application of the foundations of measurement and accounting recognition issued by the Central Bank. *Journal of Accounting Thought, 3*(1), 393-394.

Khanh, N. (2010). *Financial Statement Fraud: Motives, Methods, Cases and Detection*. Dissertation.com.

Khatab, H., Masood, M., Zaman, K., Saleem, S., & Saeed, B. (2011). Corporate governance and firm performance: A case study of Karachi stock market. *International Journal of Trade, Economics and Finance*, *2*(1), 39–43.

Khatwani, R. K., & Goyal, V. (2019). Predictor of financial dishonesty: Self control, opportunity, attitudes. *Academy of Accounting and Financial Studies Journal*. https://www.scopus.com/inward/record.uri?eid=2-s2.0-85081894874&partnerID=40&md5=9ce60b2912d6ed1525cc0126f0d35015

Kılıç, M., & Kuzey, C. (2018). Determinants of forward-looking disclosures in integrated reporting. *Managerial Auditing Journal*, *33*(1), 115–144. doi:10.1108/MAJ-12-2016-1498

Kljajić, M., Đurić, L., & Arežina, N. (2017). The purpose of forensic accounting in detecting occupational fraud in contemporary corporate governance. *FINIZ, 78-82*. Advance online publication. doi:10.15308/finiz-2017-78-82

Kohler, J. C., & Bowra, A. (2020). Exploring anti-corruption, transparency, and accountability in the World Health Organization, the United Nations Development Programme, the World Bank Group, and the Global Fund to Fight AIDS, Tuberculosis and Malaria. *Globalization and Health*, *16*(1), 1–10. doi:10.118612992-020-00629-5 PMID:33081805

Kosmas, N., Thulani, D., & Mashanye, E. (2009). The Effective of Forensic Auditing in Detecting, Investigating and Preventing Bank Frauds. *Journal of Sustainable Development in Africa*, *10*(4), 405–425.

Kouki, M., Elkhaldi, A., Atri, H., & Souid, S. (2011). Does corporate governance constrain earnings management? Evidence from U.S. firms. *European Journal of Economics, Finance and Administrative Sciences*. https://www.scopus.com/inward/record.uri?eid=2-s2.0-84860420479&partnerID=40&md5=e7947bb7f8010d890ea7e2faccf2a5fa

Kountur, R., Djohanputro, B., & Sari, M. R. (2021). Past performance and earning management: The moderating effect of employee relative earning. *Accounting*. https://www.scopus.com/inward/record.uri?eid=2-s2.0-85097960334&doi=10.5267%2Fj.ac.2020.11.018&partnerID=40&md5=67cbd80897fa6c1407250365e1abac79

Kozlov, M., Hurtado-Guarin, J., & Trakulhoon, P. (2018, Aug 20). *Financial crime has been around as long as corporations have existed. But as perpetrators embrace new scams, regulators are turning to new tools, including machine learning, to nab them.* Retrieved from weareworld quant: https://www.weareworldquant.com/en/thought-leadership/forensic-accounting-detecting-financial-fraud/

Kozlowski, S. (2018). *An audit ecosystem to support blockchain-based accounting and assurance. Continuous Auditing: Theory and Application*. doi:10.1108/978-1-78743-413-420181015

KPMG International. (2016). *Global profiles of the fraudster: technology enables and weak controls fuel the fraud.* KPMG International.

KPMG. (2003). *Forensic and Fraud Survey*. KPMG.

Krafft, P. M., Young, M., Katell, M., Lee, J. E., Narayan, S., Epstein, M., ... Barghouti, B. (2021, March). An Action-Oriented AI Policy Toolkit for Technology Audits by Community Advocates and Activists. In *Proceedings of the 2021 ACM Conference on Fairness, Accountability, and Transparency* (pp. 772-781). 10.1145/3442188.3445938

Kramer, B., Seda, M., & Bobashev, G. (2017). Current opinions on forensic accounting education. *Accounting Research Journal, 30*(3), 249–264. doi:10.1108/ARJ-06-2015-0082

Kresse, W. J. (2008). The Saint Xavier University graduate program in financial fraud examination and management. *Issues in Accounting Education, 23*(4), 601–608. doi:10.2308/iace.2008.23.4.601

Kumar, S., & Venkataraman, R. (2019). An Empirical Study on Forensic Accounting for Corporate Fraud Management. *Adalya Journal*.

Kumar, A. A. (2018). Forensic Accounting – A Vision for Fraud Detection. *International Journal of Engineering Technology Science and Research, 5*(1), 694–707.

Kumar, D. S. (2012). Forensic Accounting: A Tool of Detecting White Collar Crimes in Corporate World. *Indian Journal of Research, 1*(2), 1–3.

Kumar, M. B., Nandeesh, G., Ayyappa, R., & Jayakumar, K. (2018). Role of Forensic Accounting - An Analysis. *International Journal of Research and Analytical Reviews, 5*(4).

Lada, M., & Kozarkiewicz, A. (2014). Teoria legitymizacji w badaniach z zakresu rachunkowoci. *Zeszyty Teoretyczne Rachunkowoci, 71*(127), 161–175. doi:10.5604/16414381.1061654

Ladda, R. L. (2014). *Introduction: Basic concepts of accounting* (1st ed.). Laxmi Book Publication. https://books.google.com.vn/books?id=q5q2BgAAQBAJ&printsec=frontcover#v=onepage&q&f=false

Lama, P., & Chaudhari, B. (2018). *Forensic Accounting: A Study of its role in Investigating Corporate Frauds and Scams in India* [Paper presentation]. 11th international conference on Science, Technology and Management (ICSTM-18).

Lamboglia, R., Lavorato, D., Scornavacca, E., & Za, S. (2021). Exploring the relationship between audit and technology. A bibliometric analysis. Meditari Accountancy Research. doi:10.1108/MEDAR-03-2020-0836

Lambsdorff, J. G. (2003). How corruption affects productivity. *Kyklos*, *56*(4), 457–474. doi:10.1046/j.0023-5962.2003.00233.x

Lan, D. T., & Phong, P. T. (2021). *Application of forensic accounting techniques at the District 10 Inspection Office*. Vietnam Club of Chief Accountants. https://www.clbketoantruong.com/ung-dung-ky-thuat-ke-toan-dieu-tra-tai-phong-thanh-tra-quan-10-tphcm/

Lang, M., & Wambach, A. (2013). The fog of fraud – Mitigating fraud by strategic ambiguity. *Games and Economic Behavior*, *81*(6), 255–275. doi:10.1016/j.geb.2013.05.009

Lassou, P. J. C., Hopper, T., & Soobaroyen, T. (2021). Financial controls to control corruption in an African country: Insider experts within an enabling environment. *Financial Accountability and Management*. https://www.scopus.com/inward/record.uri?eid=2-s2.0-85082423108&doi=10.1111%2Ffaam.12240&partnerID=40&md5=8627825723b9c3629471b9584fc6f752

Latan, H., Chiappetta Jabbour, C. J., & de Sousa Jabbour, A. B. (2019). 'Whistleblowing Triangle': Framework and Empirical Evidence. *Journal of Business Ethics*, *160*(1), 189–204. doi:10.100710551-018-3862-x

Lee, H. Y., & Mande, V. (2005). The relationship of audit committee characteristics with endogenously determined audit and non-audit fees. *Quarterly Journal of Business and Economics*, 93-112.

Lefcaditis, T., Tsamis, A., & Leventides, J. (2014). Concentration risk model for Greek bank's credit portfolio. *The Journal of Risk Finance*, *15*(1), 71–93. doi:10.1108/JRF-06-2013-0043

Leonard, W. V. (2010). *The Fraud Audit: Responding to the Risk of Fraud in Core Business Systems*. John Wiley & Sons Ltd.

Leuz, C. (2007). Was the Sarbanes–Oxley Act of 2002 really this costly? A discussion of evidence from event returns and going-private decisions. *Journal of Accounting and Economics*, *44*(1–2), 146–145. doi:10.1016/j.jacceco.2007.06.001

Liao, P., Wan, Y., Tang, P., Wu, C., Hu, Y., & Zhang, S. (2019). Applying crowdsourcing techniques in urban planning: A bibliometric analysis of research and practice prospects. *Cities (London, England)*, *94*, 33–43. doi:10.1016/j.cities.2019.05.024

Libert, B., Beck, M., & Bonchek, M. (2017). *AI in the Boardroom: The Next Realm of Corporate Governance*. Available at: https://sloanreview.mit.edu/article/ai-in-the-boardroom-the-next-realm-of-corporate-governance/

Linck, J., Netter, J., & Yang, T. (2009). The effects and unintended consequences of the sarbanes-oxley act on the supply and demand for directors. *Review of Financial Studies*, *22*(8), 3287–3328. doi:10.1093/rfs/hhn084

Liodorova, J., & Fursova, V. (2018). Forensic accounting in the world: Past and present. *Forensic Accounting in The World: Past and Present Journal of Economics and Management Research.*, *7*(30), 84–100. doi:10.22364/jemr.7.06

Lipunga, A. M. (2014). Risk Disclosure Practices Of Malawian Commercial Banks. *Journal of Contemporary Issues in Business Research*, *3*(3), 154–167.

Lohana, P. M. (2013). Forensic Accounting at Nascent Stage in India. *Voice of Research*, *2*(1).

Lokanan, M. E. (2015). Challenges to the fraud triangle: Questions on its usefulness. *Accounting Forum*, *39*(3), 201–224. doi:10.1016/j.accfor.2015.05.002

LoPucki, L. M. (2018). Algorithmic Entities. *Washington University Law Review*, *95*(4), 887–951.

Lou, Y., & Wang, L. (2009). Fraud Risk Factor Of The Fraud Triangle Assessing The Likelihood Of Fraudulent Financial Reporting. *Journal of Business & Economics Research*, *7*(2).

Louwers, T. J. (2015). The past, present, and future (?) of crime-related forensic accounting methodology. *Accounting Research Journal, 28*(1), 4–9. doi:10.1108/ARJ-04-2015-0047

Luong, S. (2018). *Company in US$392 million investment scandal in Vietnam had profile doctored: State inspector.* Tuoi Tre News Online. https://tuoitrenews.vn/news/business/20180316/company-in-362mn-investment-scandal-in-vietnam-had-profile-doctored-state-inspector/44564.html

M, P., & L., B. (2019). Detecting Credit Card Fraud Using Selected Machine Learning Algorithms. *2019 42nd International Convention on Information and Communication Technology, Electronics and Microelectronics (MIPRO), 1*(1), 1250-1255. Retrieved from https://ieeexplore.ieee.org/document/8757212

Machine Learning Group - ULB. (2018). *Credit Card Fraud Detection.* Retrieved from https://www.kaggle.com/mlg-ulb/creditcardfraud

MacRae, E., & Gils, D. V. (2010). Internal Audit Capabilities and Performance Levels in the Public Sector. The Institute of Internal Auditors Research Foundation (IIARF).

Madrueño, R., & Tezanos, S. (2018). The contemporary development discourse: Analysing the influence of development studies' journals. *World Development, 109*, 334–345. doi:10.1016/j.worlddev.2018.05.005

Maffei, A., & Fiondella, S. (2014). (Un)useful risk disclosure: Explanations from the Italian banks. *Managerial Auditing Journal, 29*(7), 621–648. doi:10.1108/MAJ-11-2013-0964

Mahdi, S., & Zhila, A. (2008). Fraud Detection and Audit Expectation Gap: Empirical Evidence from Iranian Bankers. *International Journal of Business and Management, 3*(10), 65–77.

Makarem, N., & Roberts, C. (2020). Earnings management to avoid earnings boosts. *Journal of Applied Accounting Research.* https://www.scopus.com/inward/record.uri?eid=2-s2.0-85091466628&doi=10.1108%2FJAAR-01-2019-0012&partnerID=40&md5=b6a4f42012afb7f2aab28201c8f2e4c3

Mamo, J., & Aliaj, A. (2014). Accounting manipulation and its effects in the financial statements of Albanian entities. *Interdisplinary Journal of Research and Development, 1*(2), 55–60.

Manning, G. A. (2011). Financial Investigation and Forensic Accounting (3rd ed.). Routledge.

Manning, G. A., & CFE, E. A. (1999). *Financial investigation and forensic accounting.* CRC Press.

Manning, G. A. (2010). *Financial Investigation and Forensic Accounting.* CRC Press.

Marrian, I. (1988). *Audit Committees.* Institute of Chartered Accountants in Scotland.

Martini, M. (2012). *Overview of corruption and anti-corruption in Vietnam. U4 expert answer.* A4 - Anti-Corruption Resources Centre. https://www.transparency.org/files/content/corruptionqas/315_Overview_of_corruption_and_anti-corruption_in_Vietnam.pdf

Maruichi, D., & Abe, M. (2019). Corruption and the business environment in Vietnam: Implications from an empirical study. *Asian and the Pacific Policies Studies, 6*(2), 222–245. doi:10.1002/app5.275

Masetic, Z., & Subasi, A. (2016). Congestive heart failure detection using random forest classifier. *Computer Methods and Programs in Biomedicine, 130*, 54–64.

Matson, J. V. (1999). *Effective expert witnessing* (3rd ed.). CRC Press.

Mautz, R. K., & Neumann, F. L. (1977). *Corporate audit committees: Policies and practices.* Ernst & Whinney.

Mayhew, B. W., & Murphy, P. R. (2014). The impact of authority on reporting behavior, rationalization and affect. *Contemporary Accounting Research, 31*(2), 420–443. doi:10.1111/1911-3846.12037

McGuire, M., & Dowling, S. (2013). *Cybercrime: A review of the evidence. Summary of key findings and implications* (Home Office Research Report, 75). Home Office. https://assets.publishing.service.gov.uk/government/uploads/system/uploads/attachment_data/file/246754/horr75-chap3.pdf

McMullen, D. A., & Sanchez, M. H. (2010). A preliminary investigation of the necessary skills, education requirements, and training requirements for forensic accountants. *Journal of Forensic & Investigative Accounting*, 2(2), 30–48.

Meier, R. F. (2001). Geis, Sutherland and white-collar crime. In H. N. Pontell & D. Shichor (Eds.), *contemporary issues in crime and criminal justice*. Prentice Hall.

Meintjes-Van Der Walt, L. (2003). The proof of the pudding: The presentation and proof of expert evidence in South Africa. *Journal of African Law*, *47*(1), 88–106. doi:10.1017/S0221855303001998

Meiryani, F., Susanto, A., & Warganegara, D. L. (2019). The effect of accounting information systems performance and unthetic behavior on accounting fraud. *International Journal of Recent Technology and Engineering*. https://www.scopus.com/inward/record.uri?eid=2-s2.0-85073496595&doi=10.35940%2Fijrte.C4966.098319&partnerID=40&md5=3ed88275c72684e024ea89ef098bebf3

Mendoza, J. (2020, March 11). *National Biscuit scammed out of RO 70K*. Retrieved from https://www.omanobserver.om/national-biscuit-scammed-out-of-ro-70k/#:~:text=Omani%20listed%20firm%20National%20Biscuit,Capital%20Market%20Authority%20(CMA)

Millstein, I. M. (1999). Introduction to the Report and Recommendations of the Blue Ribbon Committee on Improving the Effectiveness of Corporate Audit Committees. *Business Lawyer*, *54*(3), 1057–1066.

Minh, An. (2021). *The scandals that "evaporate" billions of USD in 2020*. https://laodong.vn/kinh-te/nhung-vu-gian-lan-lam-boc-hoi-hang-ti-usd-trong-nam-2020-875852.ldo

Mintchik, N., & Riley, J. (2019, March). Rationalizing Fraud: How Thinking Like a Crook Can Help Prevent Fraud. *The CPA Journal*.

Mintzer, N. J. (2016). The Bank Internal Auditor as Fraud Buster. *The ICFAI Journal of Audit Practice*, *4*(1), 557–679.

Moche Halman, R. (2013). Equity agency costs in payouts, pension plan manipulation and firm performance. *Managerial Finance*. https://www.scopus.com/inward/record.uri?eid=2-s2.0-85015645884&doi=10.1108%2FMF-09-2011-0218&partnerID=40&md5=e4774675540dc5aed39b6673584d2b19

Modugu, K. P., & Anyaduba, J. O. (2013). Forensic Accounting and Financial Fraud in Nigeria. An Empirical Approach. *International Journal of Business and Social Science*, *4*(7), 281–289.

Modugu, K. P., & Anyaduba, J. O. (2013). Forensic Accounting and Financial Fraud in Nigeria. An Empirical Approach. *International Journal of Business and Social Science*, *4*(7).

Mohammed, H. A. (2006). *A proposed framework for measuring and disclosing the provision for loan losses in commercial banks (with an applied study)* [Unpublished Master's thesis]. Mansoura University.

Mohd, S. I., & Mazni, A. (2007, July 10–13). *An overview of forensic accounting in Malaysia* [Conference presentation]. International Conference on Business and Information, Tokyo, Japan. http://eprints.um.edu.my/8616/1/All.pdf

Moid, S. (2016). Application of Forensic Accounting to Investigate Scams in India. *MITS International Journal of Business Research, 3*(1).

Mojeed, M. (2007). *Economic and Financial Crime Commission to Probe Babangida's Assets in France*. www.efccnig.org

Moloi, T., & Marwala, T. (2020). The Agency Theory. In Artificial Intelligence in Economics and Finance Theories. Advanced Information and Knowledge Processing. Springer. doi:10.1007/978-3-030-42962-1_11

Montesdeoca, M., Medina, A., & Santana, F. (2019). Research Topics in Accounting Fraud in the 21st Century: A State of the Art. *Sustainability*, *11*(6), 1570. doi:10.3390u11061570

Morais, L. (2014). *The Good, the Bad and the Ugly - The fall and resolution of Banco Espírito Santo* [Unpublished work project as part of the requirements for the Award of a Masters Degree in Finance]. NOVA School of Business and Economics.

Morales, J. (2005). La Ley Sarbanes-Oxley y la auditoria. *Partida Doble*, *169*, 105–109.

Moses, T. (2019). Corporate Governance and Corporate Fraud: An Examination of Interaction Effects in Nigeria. *Asian Journal of Advanced Research and Reports,* 1-11.

Motsoeneng, T., & Rumney, E. (2019). *PwC investigation finds $7.4 billion accounting fraud at Steinhoff, company says*. https://www.reuters.com/article/us-steinhoff-intln-accounts/pwc-investigation-finds-74-billion-accounting-fraud-at-steinhoff-company-says-idUSKCN1QW2C2

Moumen, O., Ben Othman, H., & Hussainey, K. (2015). The Value Relevance of Risk Disclosure in Annual Reports: Evidence from MENA Emerging Markets. *Research in International Business and Finance*, *34*, 2–3. doi:10.1016/j.ribaf.2015.02.004

MSM. (2020). *Dhofar Cattle Feed (DCFI) Company Fraud Disclosure*. Available at: https://msm.gov.om/MSMDocs/Images/NewsDocs/DCFI-30002020-55.pdf

MSM. (2020a). *Oman & Emirates Investment Holding Company News*. Available at: https://msm.gov.om/snapshot.aspx?s=OEIO&se=4&ni=59066

MSM. (2021). *Number of companies*. Available at: https://www.msm.gov.om/companies.aspx

Muehlmann, B. W., Burnaby, P. A., & Howe, M. A. (2012). The use of forensic accounting experts in tax cases as identified in court opinions. *Journal of Forensic and Investigative Accounting*, *4*(2), 1–34.

Muhammed & Manneh. (2020). Forensic Accounting Practices - A Means of Mitigating Corruption: A Case Study of the Gambia Public Sector Perspective. *Journal of Research and Development (Srinagar)*, *5*(2), 41–46.

Murphy, P. R. (2012). Attitude, Machiavellianism and the rationalization of misreporting. *Accounting, Organizations and Society*, *37*(4), 242–259. doi:10.1016/j.aos.2012.04.002

Mustafa, S. T., & Meier, H. H. (2006). CAP forum on forensic accounting in the post-enron world audit committees and misappropriation of assets: Publicly held companies in the United States [Les comités de vérification et le détournement de biens: les sociétés ouvertes aux États-Unis]. *Canadian Accounting Perspectives*, *5*(2), 307–333. doi:10.1506/CCWW-JRWB-ECUE-YMM

Muzurura, J. (2019). Causes, dissemination channels, and consequences of corruption in Zimbabwe: Searching for a kryptonite solution. *Humanities and Social Sciences Letters*. https://www.scopus.com/inward/record.uri?eid=2-s2.0-85071653198&doi=10.18488%2Fjournal.73.2019.72.105.122&partnerID=40&md5=254654870a65d9f071761ed04a63bce8

N, E. A. (2014). The Impact of Forensic Auditors in Corporate Governance. *Research Journal of Finance and Accounting, 5*(8).

N, M., & M, P. (2017). Analysis on credit card fraud identification techniques based on KNN and outlier detection. *2017 Third International Conference on Advances in Electrical, Electronics, Information, Communication and Bio-Informatics (AEEICB), 255-258*(1), 1. Retrieved from https://ieeexplore.ieee.org/document/7972424/

Naik, M. (2019). Challenges and Scope of Forensic Accounting in India. *International Journal for Research in Engineering Application & Management*, (Special issue), 24–25.

Nam-Anh. (2011). *Former General Director of Vien Dong Pharmaceutical, Le Van Dung was sentenced to 4 years in prison.* Cafef.vn News Online. https://s.cafef.vn/dvd-73453/cuu-tong-giam-doc-duoc-vien-dong-le-van-dung-linh-an-4-nam-tu.chn

Nandini, N. S., & Ajay, R. (2021). A Study on impact of Forensic Audit towards Investigation and Prevention of Frauds. *Asian Journal of Management*, *12*(2), 186–2. doi:10.52711/2321-5763.2021.00028

Nasrallah, N., & El Khoury, R. (2021). Is corporate governance a good predictor of SMEs financial performance? Evidence from developing countries (the case of Lebanon). *Journal of Sustainable Finance and Investment*, *0*(0), 1–31. do i:10.1080/20430795.2021.1874213

Natalia, J. (2020). Approaches to credit risk assessment and measurement: Economic and legal aspects. *6th International Scientific Symposium "Economics, Business & Finance" 3rd. International Multidisciplinary Academic Confer*, 5.

National Commission on Fraudulent Financial Reporting. (1987). *Report of the National Commission on Fraudulent Financial Reporting*.

Neate, R. (2021, Nov 4). Retrieved from Over £5.5bn of Covid support funds lost to fraud or error: https://www.theguardian.com/world/2021/nov/04/over-55bn-of-covid-support-funds-lost-to-or-error

Nena, S. (2015). An Overview of Forensic Accounting. *International Journal of Advance Research in Computer Science and Management Studies*, *3*(8), 170–175.

News, D. (2020). *Wirecard committed 'elaborate and sophisticated fraud' say auditors.* Available at: https://www.dw.com/en/wirecard-committed-elaborate-and-sophisticated-fraud-say-auditors/a-53942273

News, U. (2020). *7 of the Biggest Corporate Frauds in History.* Available at: https://wtop.com/news/2020/07/7-of-the-biggest-corporate-frauds-in-history/

Nguyen, Q. K. (2021). Audit committee structure, institutional quality, and bank stability: Evidence from ASEAN countries. *Finance Research Letters*, 102369. doi:10.1016/j.frl.2021.102369

Ngwube, A., & Okoli, C. (2013). The role of the economic financial crime commission in the fight against corruption in Nigeria. *Journal of Studies in Social Sciences*, *4*(1), 92–107.

Nicodemus, A. (2020, Dec 18). Retrieved from EY member firm fined $1.5M for failure to uncover $3B homebuilding fraud: https://www.complianceweek.com/regulatory-enforcement/ey-member-firm-fined-15m-for-failure-to-uncover-3b-homebuilding-fraud/29856.article

Nidhi, B., & Sharm, A. K. (2016). Audit Committee, Corporate Governance and Firm Performance: Empirical Evidence from India. *International Journal of Economics and Finance*, *8*(13), 103–116.

Nielsen, L. (2011). *Classifications of countries based on their level of development: How it is done and how it could be done.* IMF Working Paper. https://www.imf.org/external/pubs/ft/wp/2011/wp1131.pdf

Nigrini, M. J. (2011). Forensic Analytics. In Forensic Analytics: Methods and Techniques for Forensic Accounting Investigations (2nd ed.). John Wiley & Sons.

Nilsson, N. (2010). *The Quest for Artificial Intelligence: A History of Ideas and Achievements*. Cambridge University Press.

Norad. (2011). *Joint evaluation of support to anti-corruption efforts Viet Nam country report.* Evaluation Department of the Norwegian Agency for Development Cooperation. https://www.oecd.org/countries/tanzania/48912883.pdf

Nwankwo, O. F. (2014). Impact of corruption on economic growth in Nigeria. *Mediterranean Journal of Social Sciences*, *5*(6), 41–41. doi:10.5901/mjss.2014.v5n6p41

O'Donovan, G. (2002). Environmental disclosures in the annual report: Extending the applicability and predictive power of legitimacy theory. *Accounting, Auditing & Accountability Journal*, *15*(3), 344–371. doi:10.1108/09513570210435870

Obasan, K. A. (2014). Impact of Audit Quality on Organizational Profitability. *Fountain University Journal of Management and Social Sciences*, *3*(2).

Observer, O. (2020). *MoU to support Artificial Intelligence projects in Oman.* Available at: https://www.omanobserver.om/mou-to-support-artificial-intelligence-projects-in-oman/

Observer, O. (2020). *Oman Arab Bank reports criminal fraud.* Available at: https://www.omanobserver.om/oman-arab-bank-reports-criminal-fraud/

Ocansey, E. O. N. D. (2017). Forensic Accounting and the Combating of Economic and Financial Crimes in Ghana. *European Scientific Journal*, *13*(31), 379. doi:10.19044/esj.2017.v13n31p379

Odunayo, B. A. (2014). Fraudulent Financial Reporting: The Nigerian Experience. *The Clute Institute International Conference*, 18-30.

OECD. (1993). Accounting reform in Estonia, Latvia and Lithuania. Paris: OECD.

OECD. (2004). *White paper on corporate governance in Latin America.* Organization for Economic Co-operation and Development. Retrieved from www.oecd.org

OECD. (2009). *Corporate Governance and the Financial Crisis: Key Findings and Main Messages.* OECD Steering Group on Corporate Governance. https://www.oecd.org/

OECD. (2014, April 1). *Risk Management and Corporate Governance.* Retrieved from https://www.oecd-ilibrary.org/governance/risk-management-and-corporate-governance_9789264208636-en

OECD. (2017). *Internal Control and Risk Management for Public Integrity in the Middle East and North Africa*. OECD.

OECD. (2019). *OECD Principles on AI.* Available at: https://www.oecd.org/going-digital/ai/principles/#:~:text=The%20OECD%20Principles%20on%20Artificial,Council%20Recommendation%20on%20Artificial%20Intelligence

OECD. (2021). *Recommendation of the Council on Artificial Intelligence*. OECD.

Office, S. F. (2020). *The use of Artificial Intelligence to Combat Public Sector Fraud Professional Guidance.* International Public Sector Fraud Forum.

Ogbonna, G. N., & Ebimobowei, A. (2012). Ethical compliance by the Accountant on the Quality of Financial Reporting and Performance of quoted Firms in Nigeria. *Asian Journal of Business Management*, *3*(3), 152–160.

Oghogho, G., Omimi-Ejoor, O. K., Osahenoma, V., & Abusomwan, E. (2013). The role of corporate fraud in enhancing financial reporting in Nigeria. *Journal of Business and Management*, *13*(1), 27–34.

Oguda, N. J., Odhiambo, A., & Byaruhanga, J. (2015). Effect of Internal Control on Fraud Detection and Prevention in District Treasuries of Kakamega County. *International Journal of Business and Management Invention*, *4*(1), 47–57.

Ogundana, O., Okere, W., Ogunleye, O., & Oladapo, I. (2018). Forensic Accounting and Fraud Prevention and Detection in Nigerian Banking Industry. *COJ Reviews & Research*, *1*(1), 1–8.

Ogundana, O., Okere, W., Ogunleye, O., & Oladapo, I. (2018). Forensic Accounting and Fraud Prevention and Detection in Nigerian Banking Industry. *COJ Reviews and Research*, *1*(1), 1–8.

Ogunleye, G. A. (2009). Fraud in the Banking Sector: The Unmanaged Distress Risk. *Journal of Economic Crime.*, *56*(2), 106–126.

Oh, E. (2017, Mar 1). *Against a backdrop of tough economic conditions and growing corporate governance, demand for forensic accountants is increasing, and Malaysia is leading the way.* Retrieved from https://www.accaglobal.com/in/en/member/member/accounting-business/2017/03/practice/forensic-accountants.html

Ohri, R. (2020, Oct 8). Retrieved from BR Shetty seeks probe by CBI, ED into $6 billion 'fraud' in his companies: https://economictimes.indiatimes.com/nri/nris-in-news/br-shetty-seeks-probe-by-cbi-ed-into-6-billion-fraud-in-his-companies/articleshow/78541666.cms?from=mdr

Ojo, A. (2019). Internal Audit And Risk Management In Nigeria's Public Sector. *International Journal of Business & Law Research*, *7*(2), 1–15.

Okafor, B. (2004). Strategic approach to reduction of employee, theft fraud and embezzlement. *Nigerian Accountant*, *37*(4), 3–5.

Okafor, M. C., & Agbiogwo, A. A. (2016). Effects of forensic accounting skills on the management of bank fraud in Nigeria. *European Journal of Accounting, Auditing and Finance Research*, *4*(6), 70–80.

Okolo, M. N. (2007). Internal Audit and Incidence of Fraud in Nigeria. *The Nigerian Accountant*, *2*(25), 80–85.

Okoye, E. I. & Alao, B. B. (2008). The Ethics of Creative Accounting in Financial Reporting: The Challenges of Regulatory Agencies in Nigeria. *A Quarterly Journal of Association of National Accountants of Nigeria, 16*(1).

Okoye, E., & Gbegi, D. (2013). Forensic Accounting: A Tool for Fraud Detection and Prevention in the Public Sector (A Study of Selected Ministries in Kogi State). *International Journal of Academic Research in Business and Social Sciences*, *3*(3).

Okoye, A. E. (2006). *Financial Accounting for Students and Managers, Mindex.* Publishing Limited Benin City.

Okoye, E. I., & Akenbor, C. O. (2009). Forensic accounting in developing economies - problems and prospects. *The University Advanced Research Journal*, *1*, 1–13.

Okoye, E. I., & Gbegi, D. O. (2013). An Evaluation of Forensic Accountants to Planning Management Fraud Risk Detection Procedures. *Global Journal of Management and Business Research*, *13*(1), 1–17.

Okoye, E. I., & Gbegi, D. O. (2013). Forensic accounting: A tool for fraud detection and prevention in the public sector (A study of selected ministries in Kogi state). *International Journal of Academic Research in Business & Social Sciences*, *3*(3), 1–19.

Okpako, A. E. P., & Atube, E. N. (2013). The impact of forensic accounting on fraud detection. *European Journal of Business and Management*, *5*(26), 61–70.

Okunbor, J. A., & Obaretin, O. (2010). Effectiveness of the application of forensic accounting services in Nigerian organizations. *Journal of Management Sciences*, *1*(1), 171–184.

Oladipupo, A. O. (2005). *Principles and Practices of Auditing*. Mindex Publishing Co. Ltd.

Olaoye, C. O., & Dada, R. A. (2014). Analysis of frauds in Banks: Nigeria's Experience. *European Journal of Business and Management*, *6*(31), 90–99.

Olaoye, C. O., & Olanipekun, C. T. (2018). Impact of Forensic Accounting and Investigation on Corporate Governance in Ekiti State. *Journal of Accounting, Business and Finance Research*, *4*(1), 28–36.

Oliveira, E., & Ferreira, P. (2014). *Métodos de Investigação - Da Interrogação à Descoberta Científica*. Vida Económica.

Oliveira, R., Rodrigues, L. L., & Craig, R. (2011). Risk-related disclosure practices in the annual reports of Portuguese credit institutions: An exploratory study. *Journal of Banking Regulation*, *12*(2), 100–118. doi:10.1057/jbr.2010.20

Olojede, P. (2020). *Audit expectation gap: an empirical analysis*. Future Business Journal.

Olszewski, D. (2014). Fraud detection using self-organizing map visualizing the user profiles. *Knowledge-Based Systems*, *70*(1), 324–334. https://www.sciencedirect.com/science/article/pii/S0950705114002652

Omondi, E. O. (2013, November). *The impact of forensic accounting services on fraud detection and prevention among Commercial Banks in Kenya*. University of Nairobi.

Omoteso, K. (2012). The application of artificial intelligence in auditing: Looking back to the future. *Expert Systems with Applications*, *39*(9), 8490–8495. doi:10.1016/j.eswa.2012.01.098

Onuorah, A. S., & Ebimobowei, A. (2012). Fraudulent Activities and Forensic Accounting Services of Banks in Port Harcourt Nigeria. *Asian Journal of Business Management*, *4*(2), 124–129.

Oseni, A. I. (2017). Forensic accounting and financial fraud in Nigeria: Problems and prospects. *Journal of Accounting and Financial Management*, *3*(1), 23–33.

Oussii, A. A., & Taktak, N. B. (2018). The impact of internal audit function characteristics on internal control quality. *Managerial Auditing Journal*, *33*(5), 450–469. doi:10.1108/MAJ-06-2017-1579

Owojori, A. A., & Asaolu, T. O. (2009). The Role of Forensic Accounting in Solving the Vexed Problem of Corporate World. *European Journal of Scientific Research*, *29*(2), 183–187.

Owojori, A. A., & Asaolu, T. O. (2009). The role of forensic accounting in solving the vexed problem of corporate world. *European Journal of Scientific Research*, *29*(2), 183–187. www.scopus.com

Oyerogba, E. O. (2021). Forensic auditing mechanism and fraud detection: The case of Nigerian public sector. *Journal of Accounting in Emerging Economies*, *11*(5), 752–755. doi:10.1108/JAEE-04-2020-0072

Oyier, O. E. (2013). *The impact of forensic accounting services on fraud detection and prevention among commercial bank in Kenya* [Unpublished MBA Thesis]. University of Nairobi, Kenya.

Ozili, P. K. (2020). Forensic accounting theory. *Finance, Insurance and Risk Management Theory and Practices* (Vol. 1). Emerald. https://mpra.ub.uni-muenchen.de/102566/

Ozili, P. K. (2020). Forensic Accounting Theory. *Finance, Insurance and Risk Management Theory and Practices*, *1*.

Ozili, P. K. (2015). Forensic Accounting and Fraud: A Review of Literature and Policy Implications. *International Journal of Accounting and Economics Studies*, *3*(1), 63–68. doi:10.14419/ijaes.v3i1.4541

Ozkul, F. U., & Pamukc¸, A. (2012). Fraud detection and Forensic Accounting. Academic Press.

Ozondu, M. E., Okoye, E., & Adeniyi, S. (2019). *Corporate Fraud and Financial Performance of Banks in South-East Nigeria*. https://www.semanticscholar.org/paper/Corporate-Fraud-And-Financial-Performance-Of-Banks-Eberechukwu-Okoye/5c857bfeb0034663e89bf0b738e2ae16cf9c0ed4#related-papers

Ozuomba, C.N., Ofor, T.N., & Okoye, P.V.C. (2016). Forensic Accounting and Fraud in the Public Sector (A Case of Imo State Ministry of Finance). *Research Journal of Management Science,* 1-6.

Pagano, W. J., & Buckhoff, T. A. (2005). Expert witnessing in forensic accounting. Academic Press.

Page, M. T. (2018). *A new taxonomy for corruption in Nigeria*. Carnegie Endowment for International Peace.

Pamungkas, I. D., Ghozali, I., & Achmad, T. (2018). A pilot study of corporate governance and accounting fraud: The fraud diamond model. *The Journal of Business and Retail Management Research, 12*(2), 253–261. doi:10.24052/JBRMR/V12IS02/APSOCGAAFTFDM

Panda, B., & Leepsa, N. M. (2017). Agency theory: Review of theory and evidence on problems and perspectives. *Indian Journal of Corporate Governance, 10*(1), 74–95. doi:10.1177/0974686217701467

Parodi, L. (2008). Manual das fraudes (2.ª edição). Rio de Janeiro: Brasport.

Patterson, E., Smith, J., & Patterson, R. (2007). The Effects of Sarbanes-Oxley on and Internal Control Auditing Strength. *The Accounting Review, 82*(2), 427–455. doi:10.2308/accr.2007.82.2.427

Paulinus, E. C., & Jones, A. S. (2017). Financial Risk Management And Corporate Performance Of Deposit Money Banks In Nigeria. *Archives of Business Research, 5*(12), 78–87.

Peat Marwick McLintock. (1987). *The Audit Committee*. Peat Marwick McLintock.

Pedneault, S., Rudewicz, F., Sheetz, M., & Slilverstone, H. (2012). *Forensic accounting and fraud investigation* (CPE Edition). John Wiley & Sons. www.cpestore.com

Perduv. (2018). The role of forensic accounting in corporate governance for economic societies. *Poslovnestudije.com, 10*(19-20), 119-131.

Peterson, B. K., & Reider, B. P. (2001). An examination of forensic accounting courses: Content and learning activities. *Journal of Forensic Accounting, 2*(1), 25–42.

Phua, C., Gayler, R., Lee, V., & Smith-Miles, K. (2009). 6). On the communal analysis suspicion scoring for identity crime in streaming credit applications. *European Journal of Operational Research, 195*, 595–612. doi:10.1016/j.ejor.2008.02.015

Phuc, L. (2020). *The 5 crimes and 26 defendants prosecuted in Nhat Cuong case*. Doanh Tri Newspaper Online. http://www.doanhtri.net/tin-5-toi-danh-va-26-bi-can-bi-khoi-to-trong-vu-an-nhat-cuong-d66510.html

Phuoc, N. T. (2020). Forensic audit – A new type of auditing. *Industry and Trade Magazine Online*. https://tapchicongthuong.vn/bai-viet/kiem-toan-dieu-tra-mot-loai-hinh-kiem-toan-moi-71273.htm

Pickett, K. H. S., & Pickett, J. M. (2002). *Financial Crime Investigation and Control*. Wiley.

Popoola, O. M., Che-Ahmad, A. B., & Samsudin, R. S. (2015). An empirical investigation of fraud risk assessment and knowledge requirement on fraud related problem representation in Nigeria. *The Journal of Applied Psychology, 88*(5), 879–903.

Powell, D. (2020). Autonomous systems as legal agents: Directly by the recognition of personhood or indirectly by the alchemy of algorithmic entities. *Duke Law & Technology Review, 18*(1), 306–331.

Power, M. (2012). The managerialization of security. *Securitization, Accountability and Risk Management: Transforming the Public Security Domain*, 70-87.

Prabowo, H. Y. (2013). Better, faster, smarter: Developing a blueprint for creating forensic accountants. *Journal of Money Laundering Control, 16*(4), 353–378. doi:10.1108/JMLC-05-2013-0017

Prayudi, Y., Ashari, A., & Priyambodo, T. (2015). A proposed digital forensic business model to support cybercrime investigation in Indonesia. *International Journal of Computer Network and Information Security*, *7*(11), 1–8. doi:10.5815/ijcnis.2015.11.01

PricewaterhouseCoopers (PwC). (2018). *Global Economic Crime and Fraud Survey: Pulling fraud out of the shadows.* PwC. https://www.pwc.com

PricewaterhouseCoopers. (2003). *Global economic crime survey.* Retrieved from https://www.pwc.com/extweb/ncsurvers.nsf

Primeaux, E. (2020). *5 most scandalous fraud cases of 2019.* https://www.fraud-magazine.com/recap-article19.aspx?id=4295009428

Prokhorenkova, L., Gusev, G., Vorobev, A., Dorogush, A. V., & Gulin, A. (2017). *CatBoost: unbiased boosting with categorical features.* arXiv preprint arXiv:1706.09516.

Protect your users. Be their hero. (n.d.). Retrieved from https://www.deduce.com/

Purnamasari, P., & Amaliah, I. (2015). Fraud Prevention: Relevance to Religiosity and Spirituality in the Workplace. *Procedia: Social and Behavioral Sciences*, *211*(52), 827–835. doi:10.1016/j.sbspro.2015.11.109

PWC. (2018). *Pulling fraud out of the shadows -Global Economic Crime and Fraud Survey 2018: Vietnam Perspectives.* https://www.pwc.com/vn/en/publications/vietnam-publications/economic-crime-fraud-survey-2018.html

PWC. (2020). *Fighting fraud: A never-ending battle PwC's Global Economic Crime and Fraud Survey.* Price Water House Coopers.

Qader, O. A. (2009). The Importance of Building Systems for Crisis Risk Management in Financial Institutions. In *International Scientific Forum.* Setif, Algeria: Farhat Abbas University.

Quan, H. (2019). *How did the two former presidents of Da Nang and Phan Van Anh Vu caused a loss of 22,000 billion VND?* Ho Chi Minh City Police Newspaper Online. https://congan.com.vn/an-ninh-kinh-te/cuu-chu-tich-da-nang-va-vu-nhom-gay-that-thoat-22000-ty-dong-ra-sao_84392.html

Rafael. (1998, December). Law and Finance. *Journal of Political Economy, 106*(6), 1113-1155.

Rahim, S. A. A., Nawawi, A., & Salin, A. S. A. P. (2017). Internal control weaknesses in a cooperative body: Malaysian experience. *International Journal of Management Practice.* https://www.scopus.com/inward/record.uri?eid=2-s2.0-85015886071&doi=10.1504%2FIJMP.2017.083082&partnerID=40&md5=4c5b97c0acf352ee760e64874fea6d1a

Raimo, N., Vitolla, F., Marrone, A., & Rubino, M. (2021). Do audit committee attributes influence integrated reporting quality? An agency theory viewpoint. *Business Strategy and the Environment*, *30*(1), 522–534. doi:10.1002/bse.2635

Ramaswamy, V. (2005). *Corporate governance and the forensic accountant.* Retrieved from: http://www.nysscpa.org/cpajournal/2005/305/essentials/p68.htm

Ramaswamy, V. (2005). Corporate governance and the forensic accountant. *The CPA Journal.* http://archives.cpajournal.com/2005/305/essentials/p68.htm

Ramaswamy, V. (2007, September 1). New frontiers: Training forensic accountants within the accounting program. *Journal of College Teaching and Learning*, *4*(9), 31–38.

Ramaswany, V. (2009). *Corporate Governance and the Forensic Accountant. The Certified Public Accountant (CPA) Journal.*

Ramayah, T. (2016). Partial Least Squares Structural Equation Modeling (PLS-SEM) Using SmartPLS 3.0: An Updated Guide and Practical Guide to Statistical Analysis. Pearson.

Ramazani, M., & Rafiei, A. H. (2010). Iranian accountant's conception of the prevention methods of fraud and offering some recommendations to reduce fraud in Iran. *Global Journal of Management and Business Research, 10*(6), 31–45.

Ramos-Rodrígue, A.-R., & Ruíz-Navarro, J. (2004). Changes in the intellectual structure of strategic management research: A bibliometric study of the Strategic Management Journal, 1980-2000. *Strategic Management Journal, 25*(10), 981–1004. doi:10.1002mj.397

Randal, J. E., Mark, S. B., Chris, E. H., & Alvin, A. A. (2019). *Auditing and Assurance Services - International Perspective*. Pearson.

Rashid, A. (2016). Managerial Ownership and Agency Cost: Evidence from Bangladesh. *Journal of Business Ethics, 137*(3), 609–621. doi:10.100710551-015-2570-z

Raymond, N. (2016). *Vivendi loses U.S. appeal in long-running investor lawsuit.* Reuters. https://www.reuters.com

Razaee, Z. (2006). Forensic Accounting Education. A survey of Academicians and Practitioners. *Journal of Forensic Accounting, 10*(3), 48–59.

Razak, A. (2016, January 31). Retrieved from CA Srilanka to Instill Forensic Thinking: https://nation.lk/online/2016/01/30/ca-sri-lanka-to-instill-forensic-thinking.html

Rechtman, Y. (2020). The Past, Present, and Future of Forensic Accounting. *The CPA Journal.* https://www.cpajournal.com/2020/04/10/the-past-present-and-future-of-forensic-accounting/

Regulamento (CE) n.° 1606/2002 do Parlamento Europeu e do Conselho de 19 de Julho de 2002 relativo à aplicação das normas internacionais de contabilidade (2002). https://eur-lex.europa.eu

Regulamento (UE) n.° 537/2014 do Parlamento Europeu e do Conselho de 16 de abril de 2014 relativo aos requisitos específicos para a revisão legal de contas das entidades de interesse público (2014). https://publications.europa.eu

Rehman, A., & Hashim, F. (2018). Forensic accounting on corporate governance maturity mediated by internal audit: A conceptual overview. *Forensic Sci Sem, 8*(1).

Rehman, A., & Hashim, F. (2018a). Literature Review: Preventive Role Of Forensic Accounting And Corporate Governance Maturity. *Journal of Governance and Integrity, 1*(2).

Rehman, A., & Hashim, F. (2019). Impact of Mature Corporate Governance on Detective Role of Forensic Accounting: Case of Public Listed Companies in Oman. *FGIC 2nd Conference on Governance and Integrity 2019, KnE Social Sciences,* 637-665.

Rehman, A., & Hashim, F. (2019). Impact of mature corporate governance on detective role of forensic accounting: case of public listed companies in Oman. *FGIC 2nd Conference on Governance and Integrity 2019, KnE Social Sciences,* 637-665. 10.18502/kss.v3i22.5080

Rehman, A., & Hashim, F. (2018). Forensic Accounting on Corporate Governance Maturity mediated by Internal Audit: A Conceptual Overview. *Advances in Economics, Business and Management Research, 46,* 161–168.

Rehman, A., & Hashim, F. (2020). A Conceptual Framework: Forensic Accounting and Corporate Governance Maturity. *International Journal of Accounting Finance and Business, 5*(30), 52–63.

Rehman, A., & Hashim, F. (2020). Is corporate governance maturity measurable? *Corporate Governance, 20*(4), 601–619. doi:10.1108/CG-07-2019-0220

Rehman, A., & Hashim, F. (2021). Can forensic accounting impact sustainable corporate governance? *Corporate Governance (Bingley), 21*(1), 212–227. doi:10.1108/CG-06-2020-0269

Rehman, A., & Mughairy, M. A. (2020). *2020 Oman Pulse of Internal Audit*. IIA Oman.

Reinstein, A., & Taylor, E. Z. (2017). Fences as Controls to Reduce Accountants' Rationalization. *Journal of Business Ethics*. https://www.scopus.com/inward/record.uri?eid=2-s2.0-84930157585&doi=10.1007%2Fs10551-015-2701-6&partnerID=40&md5=8d4292750a411f3f29d8be9a256e33bc

Reinstein, A., Moehrle, S. R., & Reynolds-Moehrle, J. (2006). Crime and punishment in the marketplace: Accountants and business executives repeating history. *Managerial Auditing Journal, 21*(4), 420–435. doi:10.1108/02686900610661423

Renzhou, D. (2011). Research on Legal Procedural Functions of Forensic Accounting. *Energy Procedia, 5*, 2147–2151. doi:10.1016/j.egypro.2011.03.371

Report, N. (2019). *Card Fraud Losses Reach $27.85 Billion*. Nilson Publisher. Retrieved from https://nilsonreport.com/mention/407/1link/

Reurink, A. (2018). Financial fraud: A literature review. *Journal of Economic Surveys, 32*(5), 1292–1325. doi:10.1111/joes.12294

Reuters. (2013, Feb 26). *Oman's Bank Muscat hit by $39 mln prepaid card fraud*. Retrieved from https://www.reuters.com/article/oman-bankmuscat-fraud-idUSL6N0BQ1C720130226

Reuters. (2020). *New rules may be needed for payments in wake of Wirecard, BIS boss says*. Available at: https://www.reuters.com/article/us-wirecard-bis/new-rules-may-be-needed-for-payments-in-wake-of-wirecard-bis-boss-says-idUSKBN2411PW

Rezaee, Z. (2005). Causes, consequences, and deterence of financial statement fraud. *Critical Perspectives on Accounting, 16*(3), 277–298. doi:10.1016/S1045-2354(03)00072-8

Rezaee, Z., Crumbley, D. L., & Elmore, R. C. (2006). Forensic accounting education; A survey of academicians & practitioners. *Journal of Forensic Accounting, 10*(3), 48–59.

Rizk, M. I. (2011). *A proposed framework for the measurement and accounting disclosure of banking risks to assess the extent of sustainability - an applied theoretical study* [Unpublished Ph.D. thesis]. Benha University.

Robert, F. (2020). *Improper revenue recognition tops SEC fraud cases*. https://www.cfodive.com/news/improper-revenue-recognition-sec-fraud-cases/583889/

Rodríguez, P. P. (2021). Accounting and auditing of credit loss estimates: The hard and the soft. *Latin American Journal of Central Banking, 2*(2), 100027. doi:10.1016/j.latcb.2021.100027

Rogers, M. (2008). *Corporate Governance and Financial Performance of Selected Commercial Banks in Uganda*. Queen's University Belfast. http://www.crrconference.org

Ronald, O. O. (2015). *Relationship between fraud risk management practices and financial performance of commercial banks in Kenya* [Master's project]. University of Nairobi.

Rosa, L., & Porto, R. (2018). *Os documentos do 'saco azul' do GES: 20 milhões a mais de 50 altos funcionários. Observador*. https://observador.pt/

Ross, E. A. (1907). *Sine and Society*. Houghton Mifflin.

Rosvall, M., & Bergstrom, C. T. (2010). Mapping change in large networks. *PLoS One*, *5*(1), e8694. doi:10.1371/journal.pone.0008694 PMID:20111700

Roszkowska, P. (2020). Fintech in financial reporting and audit for fraud prevention and safeguarding equity investments. *Journal of Accounting & Organizational Change*. . doi:10.1108/JAOC-09-2019-0098

Roussy, M., Barbe, O., & Raimbault, S. (2020). Internal audit: From effectiveness to organizational significance. *Managerial Auditing Journal*, *35*(2), 322–342. doi:10.1108/MAJ-01-2019-2162

S, D., E, M., & B, F. (2018). Supervised Machine Learning Algorithms for Credit Card Fraudulent Transaction Detection: A Comparative Study. *2018 IEEE International Conference on Information Reuse and Integration (IRI)*, *1*(1), 122-125. Retrieved from doi:10.1109/IRI.2018.00025

Sabir, I. (2014). *A Holistic Emotions Measurement Model: Using the Viable System Model to Diagnose Workforce Emotions* (PhD Thesis, University of Hull, UK). Available at: https://www.researchgate.net/publication/299334013_A_Holistic_Emotions_Meas

Sadgali, I., Sael, N., & Benabbou, F. (2019). Performance of machine learning techniques in the detection of financial frauds. *Procedia Computer Science*, *148*(65), 45–54. doi:10.1016/j.procs.2019.01.007

Sage. (2019). *The Practice of Now*. Sage.

Sahayasakila.V, D. K. (2019). Credit Card Fraud Detection System using Smote Technique and Whale Optimization. *International Journal of Engineering and Advanced*.

Sait, K. N., & Yunus, S. (2018). Credit Card Fraud Detection Using Machine Learning Models and Collating Machine Learning Models. *International Journal of Pure and Applied Mathematics*, *118*(1), 825–838.

Salem, R. I. A., Ezeani, E., Gerged, A. M., Usman, M., & Alqatamin, R. M. (2020). Does the quality of voluntary disclosure constrain earnings management in emerging economies? Evidence from Middle Eastern and North African banks. *International Journal of Accounting and Information Management*. https://www.scopus.com/inward/record.uri?eid=2-s2.0-85090935141&doi=10.1108%2FIJAIM-07-2020-0109&partnerID=40&md5=73f58289a72c2b79d8fa4d3161bc255f

Santos, C. (2017). *Ex-administradores do BES arrasados. Jornal I.* https://ionline.sapo.pt/

Sarbanes-Oxley Act of 2002. (2002). *Exchange Organizational Behavior Teaching Journal*. https://news.findlaw.com/

Sari, M. R., Djohanputro, B., & Kountur, R. (2021). Past Performance and Earnings Management: The Effect of Free Cash Flow. *Journal of Asian Finance, Economics and Business*. https://www.scopus.com/inward/record.uri?eid=2-s2.0-85099637578&doi=10.13106%2Fjafeb.2021.vol8.no1.037&partnerID=40&md5=a11c09379fc61ada4780f669773e12e5

Sarrazin, H., & Willmott, P. (2016). *Adapting your board to the digital age*. Available at: https://www.mckinsey.com/business-functions/mckinsey-digital/our-insights/adapting-your-board-to-the-digital-age

Schiavone, A.-J. (2012). *And The Survey Says... Increasing Demand for Forensic Accounting*. AICPA.

Schmidt, C. W. H., & Rademeyer, H. (2000). *Law of evidence*. LexisNexis.

Schoenefeld, J. J. (2020). Interest Groups, NGOs or Civil Society Organisations? The Framing of Non-State Actors in the EU. *Voluntas*. Advance online publication. doi:10.100711266-020-00283-w

Schwikkard, P. J., & Van Der Merwe, S. E. (2016). *Principles of evidence* (4th ed.). Juta Legal and Academic Publishers.

SEC. (n.d.). *Portal da U.S. Securities and Exchange Comission*. http://www.sec.gov

Security.org Team. (2021). Account Takeover 2021 Annual Report: Prevalence, Awareness and Prevention. *Account Takeover 2021 Annual Report: Prevalence, Awareness and Prevention.* Retrieved from https://www.security.org/digital-safety/account-takeover-annual-report/

Service, T. N. (2020). *Court of Appeal sentences employee to 10 years in prison.* Available at: https://timesofoman.com/article/3017491/oman/government/court-of-appeal-sentences-employee-to-10-years-in-prison

Services, M. M., Petros, E. L., & Mortlock, H. O. (2016). *Social engineering fraud – Recommendations and solutions.* Marsh McLennan's Risk & Insurance Services. Retrieved from https://www.marsh.com/content/dam/marsh/Documents/PDF/UK-en/Social%20Engineering%20Fraud.pdf

Shah, M. K. (2018). Will implementation of forensic accounting identify the sense of financial fraud? *Journal of Commerce & Accounting Research, 7*(4), 47–50.

Shair, P. (2017). Prospects and Techniques of Forensic Accounting in India. *International Journal of Research in Economics and Social Sciences, 7*(8), 604–614.

Shapiro, D. M. (2015, September 2). *Forensic Accounting: Beyond the Courtroom.* https://sfmagazine.com/post-entry/september-2015-forensic-accounting-beyond-the-courtroom/

Sharma, A. (2014). Frauds in India and Forensic Accounting. *International Journal of Research & Development in Technology and Management Science, 21*(5).

Shayan-Nia, M., Sinnadurai, P., Mohd-Sanusi, Z., & Hermawan, A.-N. A. (2017). How efficient ownership structure monitors income manipulation? Evidence of real earnings management among Malaysian firms. *Research in International Business and Finance.* https://www.scopus.com/inward/record.uri?eid=2-s2.0-85018729713&doi=10.1016%2Fj.ribaf.2017.04.013&partnerID=40&md5=858da065c490e22a3c1e8a734d564353

Sheetz, M., & Howard, S. (2006). *Forensic Accounting and Financial Investigations for Non-Experts.* John Wiley and Sons Inc.

Shehu, U. H., & Abubakar, A. (2012). Corporate Governance, Earnings Management and Financial Performance: A case of Nigerian Manufacturing Firms. *American International Journal of Contemporary Research, 2*(7), 214–226.

Shelton. (2001, March). Auditing Firms' Fraud Risk Assessment Practices. *Accounting Horizon, 15*(1).

Silva, T. (2015). *As 21 infrações detetadas na auditoria da Deloitte ao BES. Dinheiro Vivo.* https://www.dinheirovivo.pt

Silveira, A. (2015). *Corporate Scandals of the 21st Century: limitations of mainstream corporate governance literature and the need for a new behavioral approach.* Working paper. doi:10.2139/ssrn.2181705

Silveira, A. (2013). The Enron Scandal a decade later: Lessons Learned? *Homo Oeconomicus, 30*(3), 315–347.

Simões, S. (2014). *Ex-administrador do BES: "Eu sabia tanto de bancos como de calceteiro."* Observador. https://observador.pt/

Simon, A., Kasale, S., & Manish, P. (2017). Blockchain technology in accounting and audit. *IOSR Journal of Business and Management, 6*, 6–9.

Singleton, T., & Singleton, A. (2010). *Fraud Auditing and Forensic Accounting* (4th ed.). John Wiley & Sons. doi:10.1002/9781118269183

Sinha, R. (2020). *Financial Forensics-An overview.* Preprint. doi:10.2139srn.3599703

Siregar, S. V., & Tenoyo, B. (2015). Fraud awareness survey of private sector in Indonesia. *Journal of Financial Crime*, *22*(3), 329–346. doi:10.1108/JFC-03-2014-0016

Skills, P. B. (2021). *Managing a Business*. Retrieved from Practical Business Skills: https://www.practicalbusinessskills.com/managing-a-business/record-keeping

Skousen, C., Smith, K., & Wright, C. (2009). Detecting and predicting financial statement fraud: The effectiveness of the fraud triangle and SAS No. 99. In Corporate Governance and Firm Performance (Advances in Financial Economics, Vol. 13) (pp. 53-81). Emerald.

Skousen, C. J., & Wright, C. J. (2008). Contemporaneous risk factors and the prediction of financial statement fraud. *Journal of Forensic Accounting*, *9*, 37–62.

Slot, J. (2012). *An evaluation of the forensic accountant's role in criminal law proceedings* [Master's Dissertation, North-West University, South Africa]. https://repository.nwu.ac.za/bitstream/handle/10394/9839/Slot_J.pdf?sequence=1

Smith, S. (2017). *Blockchain, AI, and accounting*. Available at: www.ifac.org/globalknowledge-gateway/practice-management/discussion/blockchain-ai-and-accounting

Smith, G. S. (2015). The past, present, and future of forensic accounting. *The CPA Journal*, *85*(3), 16.

Smith, G. S., & Crumbley, D. L. (2009). How divergent are pedagogical views toward the fraud/ forensic accounting curriculum? *Global Perspectives on Accounting Education*, *6*, 1–24.

Soltani, B. (2014). The Anatomy of Corporate Fraud: A Comparative Analysis of High Profile American and European Corporate Scandals. *Journal of Business Ethics*, *120*(2), 251–274. doi:10.100710551-013-1660-z

Soltani, B., & Maupetit, C. (2015). Importance of core values of ethics, integrity, and accountability in the European corporate governance codes. *The Journal of Management and Governance*, *19*(2), 259–284. doi:10.100710997-013-9259-4

Souza, J. L. (2017). Using the classroom to assist students to find their fit in the forensic accounting profession. *Journal of Forensic and Investigative Accounting*, *9*(1), 724–735.

Span, D. (2015). Fraud analytic: Strategies and method for detection and prevention of fraud. John Wiley & Son Inc.

Spangler, W. D., & Braiotta, L. Jr. (1990). Leadership and corporate audit committee effectiveness. *Group & Organization Studies*, *15*(2), 134–157. doi:10.1177/105960119001500202

Srivastava, R. P., Mock, T. J., & Turner, J. L. (2003). *The effects of Integrity, opportunity, incentives, mitigating factors and forensic audit procedures on fraud risk*. Business and Information Management Auditing Research Workshop, Australian National University.

Srivastava, R. P., Mock, T. J., & Turner, J. L. (2003). *The Effects of Integrity, Opportunity, Incentives, Militating factors and Forensic Audit Procedures on Fraud Risk* [paper presentation]. *Business and Information Management Auditing Research Workshop, Australian National Universities.*

Stanbury, J., & Paley-Menzies, C. (2010). *Forensic Futurama: Why Forensic Accounting Is Evolving*. Retrieved from: http://www.aicpa.org/Publications/Newsletters/AICPACPAInsider/2010/jun28/Pages/ForensicFuturmaWhyForensicAccountingIsEvolving.aspx

Statista. (2021). *Number of accountants and auditors employed in the U.S. 2012-2020*. Statista Research Department. https://www.statista.com/statistics/317587/number-of-accountants-and-auditors-employed-us/

Statistic, U. S. B. (2020). *Occupational outlook handbook*. Retrieved from Accountant and Auditors: https://www.bls.gov/ooh/business-and-financial/accountants-and-auditors.htm

Subash, T. (2015). Forensic accounting and Corporate Governance. *EXCEL International Journal of Multidisciplinary Management Studies*, *5*(11), 49–54.

Subramanian, A., & Nilakanta, S. (1996). Organizational innovativeness: Exploring the relationship between organizational determinants of innovation, types of innovations and measures of organizational performance. *Omega*, *24*(6), 631–647. doi:10.1016/S0305-0483(96)00031-X

Suchman, M. C. (1995). Managing legitimacy: Strategic and institutional approaches. *Academy of Management Journal*, *20*(3), 571–610.

Sudaryono, D. (2021). Application of Fraud Pentagon for Detecting Symptoms of Shortfall in Financial Statements. *International Journal of Contemporary Accounting*, *3*(25).

Sule, S., Ibrahim, S., & Sani, A. (2019). The Effect of Forensic Accounting Investigation in Detecting Financial Fraud: A Study in Nigeria. *International Journal of Academic Research in Business and Social Sciences*, *9*(2), 545–553. doi:10.6007/IJARBSS/v9-i2/5590

Sumartono, U. D., & Hamdani, R. (2020). Skills of the Forensic Accountants in Public Sector Reveal Fraud in Indonesia: An Empirical Investigation. *Journal of Accounting and Investment*, *21*(1), 180–194.

Sumit, M., Soumyadeep, T., Manosij, G., & Sanjoy Kumar, S. (2020). An Autoencoder Based Model for Detecting Fraudulent Credit Card Transaction. *Procedia Computer Science*, *167*(1), 254–262. https://linkinghub.elsevier.com/retrieve/pii/S1877050920306840

Sun, E. Y. (2021). The Differential Role of R&D and SG&A for Earnings Management and Stock Price Manipulation. *Contemporary Accounting Research*. https://www.scopus.com/inward/record.uri?eid=2-s2.0-85099405498&doi=10.1111%2F1911-3846.12634&partnerID=40&md5=977fef5faee3f0d38cec19be8623b3e3

Sun, J., Kent, P., Qi, B., & Wang, J. (2019). Chief financial officer demographic characteristics and fraudulent financial reporting in China. *Accounting and Finance*. https://www.scopus.com/inward/record.uri?eid=2-s2.0-85026315834&doi=10.1111%2Facfi.12286&partnerID=40&md5=c9962c7814b0a9c2aa2bf8cd3e010630

Sunil, K., Rawat, D. S., & Rajarao, V. (2016). *Financial and corporate frauds, Grant Thornton and the Associated Chambers of Commerce and Industry*. ASSOCHAM.

Suresh, K. M., Soundarya, V., Kavitha, S., E, A., & E.S., K. (2019). Credit Card Fraud Detection Using Random Forest Algorithm. *2019 3rd International Conference on Computing and Communications Technologies (ICCCT)*, *1*(1), 149-153. Retrieved from https://ieeexplore.ieee.org/document/8824930/

Sutherland, E. H. (1940). White-Collar Criminality. *The Sociological Review*, *5*(1), 1–12.

Sutherland, E. H. (1949). *White-Collar Crime*. Holt, Rirehart and Winston.

Sutherland, E. H. (1983). *White collar crime*. Yale University Press.

Szmigiera, M. (2021). *Global card fraud losses*. Statista. Retrieved from https://www.statista.com/statistics/1080685/global-card-fraud-losses-forecast/

Taha, A. A., & Malebary, S. J. (2020). An Intelligent Approach to Credit Card Fraud Detection Using an Optimized Light Gradient Boosting Machine. *IEEE Access: Practical Innovations, Open Solutions*, *8*, 25579–25587. doi:10.1109/ACCESS.2020.2971354

Taleatu, T. A., Adetula, D. T., & Iyoha, F. O. (2020). Moderating effect of governance quality on the relationship between CFOs' narcissism and corporate earnings management in Nigeria. *Journal of Management Information and Decision Science*. https://www.scopus.com/inward/record.uri?eid=2-s2.0-85099143260&partnerID=40&md5=ca2f8249beb76a5b11ab5cf73e3be5f5

Taminiau, Y., Heusinkveld, S., & Cramer, L. (2019). Colonization contests: How both accounting and law firms gain legitimacy in the market for forensic accounting. *Journal of Professions and Organization*. https://www.scopus.com/inward/record.uri?eid=2-s2.0-85070185712&doi=10.1093%2Fjpo%2Fjoz001&partnerID=40&md5=81c8178d9c0e5aeacc0f3c8f9b3568e2

Team, M. D. (2011, April 6). Retrieved from SEC slaps $17.5 million in fines on Satyam, PwC in fraud case: https://www.moneylife.in/article/sec-slaps-175-million-in-fines-on-satyam-pwc-in-fraud-case/15348.html

Telegraph. (2006, Oct 11). *Chancellor throws his forensic accountants into the fray*. Retrieved from https://www.telegraph.co.uk/news/uknews/1531108/Chancellor-throws-his-forensic-accountants-into-the-fray.html

TensorFlow: Large-scale machine learning on heterogeneous systems. (2020). Retrieved from An end-to-end open source machine learning platform: https://www.tensorflow.org/

Teodósi. (2021). Corporate Governance in Portugal: A Literature Review. In *Comparative Research on Earnings Management, Corporate Governance, and Economic Value* (p. 21). IGI Global.

Terziev. (2020, October). *Libraries and tourism – possibilities for integration and new directions for sustainable social development*. Academic Press.

Thao, L.P. & Hang, N.T.T. (2014). *Factors that Affect Accounting Information System Quality in Small Medium Enterprises in Vietnam*. Summary report of research funded by Vietnam National University of Agriculture.

The Citizen. (2014). *Financial Crime*. Retrieved from: www.thecitizenng.com

Thuong, N. T. (2017). Corruption in Vietnam: The current situation and proposed solutions. In *The changing face of corruption in the Asia Pacific: Current perspectives and future challenges* (pp. 221–230). Elsevier. https://www.researchgate.net/publication/319310522_Corruption_in_Vietnam_the_current_situation_and_proposed_solutions

Tijani, K. (2006). *Accounting Role in the Crusade against Corruption in a Corrupt Society*. Paper Presented at a Workshop on Integrity in a Corrupt Society, Organized by the Professionals League, Lagos, Nigeria.

Tiron-Tudor, A., Deliu, D., Farcane, N., & Dontu, A. (2021). *Managing change with and through blockchain in accountancy organizations: a systematic literature review. Journal of Organizational Change Management*. doi:10.1108/JOCM-10-2020-0302

Tiwari, R. K. & Debnath, J. (2017). Forensic Accounting: A blend of knowledge. *Journal of financial Regulation and Compliance*, *25*(1), 73-85.

Todd Dezoort, F., Harrison, P. D., & Schnee, E. J. (2012). Tax professionals' responsibility for fraud detection: The effects of engagement type and audit status. *Accounting Horizons*, *26*(2), 289–306. doi:10.2308/acch-50137

Torpey, D., Walden, V., & Sherrod, M. (2011). *Viewpoint - Breaking the status quo: Moving beyond traditional e-mail review*. Fraud Watch by EY.

Trang, B. T. (2017). *The death sentences with Giang Kim Dat and Tran Van Liem*. Vietnam Investment Reviews Online. https://tinnhanhchungkhoan.vn/y-an-tu-hinh-voi-giang-kim-dat-va-tran-van-liem-post166006.html

Transparency International. (2019). *Transparency International Report*. Retrieved from: www.transparency.org

Treadway Commission. (1987). *Report of the National Commission on Fraudulent Financial Reporting.* Author.

Trompeter, G. M., Carpenter, T. D., Desai, N., Jones, K. L., & Jr, R. A. R. (2012). A synthesis of fraud-related research. *Auditing, 32*(sp1), 287–321. doi:10.2308/ajpt-50360

Tuan Mansor, T. M., Mohamad Ariff, A., & Hashim, H. A. (2020). Whistleblowing by auditors: The role of professional commitment and independence commitment. *Managerial Auditing Journal, 35*(8), 1033–1055. doi:10.1108/MAJ-11-2019-2484

Turetken, O., Jethefer, S., & Ozkan, B. (2020). Internal audit effectiveness: Operationalization and influencing factors. *Managerial Auditing Journal, 35*(2), 238–271. doi:10.1108/MAJ-08-2018-1980

Turnbull, S. (1997). Corporate governance: Its scope, concerns and theories. *Corporate Governance, 5*(4), 180–205. doi:10.1111/1467-8683.00061

Tuyen, P. (2021). *Who did Phan Van Anh Vu give bribes to?* Ho Chinh Minh City Legal Newspaper Online. https://plo.vn/phap-luat/phan-van-anh-vu-dua-hoi-lo-cho-ai-980489.html

Uche, S.O. (2009, Mar. 2). Financial Malpractice: Forensic Accountants to the Rescue. *The Nation Newspaper.*

Ugo, F., Alfredo, D., Francesca, P., Paolo, Z., & Francesco, P. (2019). Using generative adversarial networks for improving classification effectiveness in credit card fraud detection. *Information Sciences, 479*(1), 448–455. https://linkinghub.elsevier.com/retrieve/pii/S0020025517311519

Umar, S., & Nada, H. (2020). *New World Bank country classifications by income level: 2020-2021.* https://blogs.worldbank.org/opendata/new-world-bank-country-classifications-income-level-2020-2021

Umar, M., Sitorus, S., Surya, R., Shauki, E., & Diyanti, V. (2017). Pressure, Dysfunctional Behavior, Fraud Detection and Role of Information Technology in the Audit Process. *Australasian Accounting. Business and Finance Journal, 11*(4), 102–115.

Umobong, A. A. & Ibanichuka. E. A. L. (2016). *Accounting manipulations and firms financial performance: Evidence from Nigeria.* Academic Press.

UNDP. (2020). *Human development reports.* http://hdr.undp.org/en/content/latest-human-development-index-ranking, http://hdr.undp.org/en/content/developing-regions

Uniamikogbo, E., Ayorinde, B., & Babajide, O. (2014). Fraud preventions and Financial Reporting Quality in Nigeria: An Evaluation of the Interconnectedness using Empirical Evidence. *Mediterranean Journal of Social Sciences, 5*(20), 628.

Usman, S. (1998). *Comparison of the Nigeria Capital Market with Foreign Capital Markets and the Lessons There From As We Approach 2010. Nigerian Financial Review,* 7 .

Valkanov, N. (2019). Mitigation of Regulations Burden in Financial Sector by Application of High Tech Solutions. *Economics and Management, 16*(1), 19–30.

Van Akkeren, J., & Buckby, S. (2017). Perceptions on the causes of individual and fraudulent co-offending: Views of forensic accountants. *Journal of Business Ethics, 146*(2), 383–404. doi:10.100710551-015-2881-0

Van Akkeren, J., Buckby, S., & MacKenzie, K. (2013). A metamorphosis of the traditional accountant: An insight into forensic accounting services in Australia. *Pacific Accounting Review, 25*(2), 188–216. doi:10.1108/PAR-06-2012-0023

Van der Laan, G., Van Ees, H., & Van Witteloostuijn, A. (2008). Corporate social and financial performance: An extended stakeholder theory, and empirical test with accounting measures. *Journal of Business Ethics, 79*(3), 299–310. doi:10.100710551-007-9398-0

Van, N. T. H. (2015). *Developing orientation of forensic accounting in Vietnam* [Master thesis, Ho Chi Minh Economic University]. https://digital.lib.ueh.edu.vn/handle/UEH/44025

Vedrana, J. (2018). The role of forensic accounting in corporate governance for economic societies. *Business Studies*, 119-131.

Vedrana. (2018). The role of forensic accounting in corporate governance for economic socieites. *Poslovne studije/ Business Studies, 10*(19-20), 119-131.

Venkataraman, R., & Kumar, S. (2019). An Empirical Study on Forensic Accounting for Corporate Fraud Management. *Adalya Journal*, *8*(10), 20–35.

Verver, J. (2020). *Automating Fraud Detection: The Essential Guide*. Galvanize.

Vieira & Neiva. (2019). Corporate governance board of directors and firm performance in Portugal. In *Board of Directors and Company Performance: An International Outlook* (p. 121). Virtus Interpress.

Vieira, E., & Neiva, J. (2019). Corporate Governance Board of Directors and Firm Performance in Portugal. In Handbook of Board of Directors and Company Performance: An International Outlook. VirtusInterpress.

Vilelas, J. (2009). *Investigação: O Processo de Construção do Conhecimento*. Edições Sílabo, Lda.

Villaescusa, N., & Amat, O. (2021). When collusion meets the fraud triangle: A case study approach. *Journal of Financial Crime*. Advance online publication. doi:10.1108/JFC-05-2021-0111

Vinh-Duong. (2011). *Nearly 2,000 shareholders of Vien Dong Pharmaceutical are at risk of losing their hands*. Dan Tri News Online. https://dantri.com.vn/kinh-doanh/gan-2000-co-dong-duoc-vien-dong-nguy-co-trang-tay-1316301396.htm

Vinita, R. (2005). Corporate governance and the forensic accountant. *The CPA Journal*, *75*(3), 68–78.

Viralv, A., & Stepheng, R. (2016). Banks' Financial Reporting and Financial System Stability. *Journal of Accounting Research, 54*(2), 293.

Vitez, O. (2021). *What are the Different Kinds of Corporate Governance Mechanisms?* Retrieved from wise-geek.com: https://www.wise-geek.com/what-are-the-different-kinds-of-corporate-governance-mechanisms.htm

Wahyuni-TD, I. S., Haron, H., & Fernando, Y. (2021). The effects of good governance and fraud prevention on performance of the zakat institutions in Indonesia: A Sharīʿah forensic accounting perspective. *International Journal of Islamic and Middle Eastern Finance and Management*, *14*(4), 692–712. https://doi.org/10.1108/IMEFM-03-2019-0089

Wall, D. (2007). Cybercrime: The Transformation of Crime in the Information Age. Cambridge University Press.

Wang, J., Lee, G., & Crumbley, D. L. (2016). Current availability of forensic accounting education and state of forensic accounting services in Hong Kong and mainland China. *Journal of Forensic and Investigative Accounting*, *8*(3), 515–534.

Waweru, N. M., & Prot, N. P. (2018). Corporate governance compliance and accrual earnings management in eastern Africa: Evidence from Kenya and Tanzania. *Managerial Auditing Journal*, *33*(2), 171–191. doi:10.1108/MAJ-09-2016-1438

Wecht, B. E. (2006). *Forensic science and law: Investigative applications in criminal, civil and family justice*. CRC Press.

Weitz, M. (2020). *Fraud Risk Management*. Internal Audit Foundation.

Welcome to pytorch tutorials. (2021). Retrieved from https://pytorch.org: https://pytorch.org/tutorials/

Wells, J. T. (2011). *Corporate Fraud Handbook: Prevention and Detection*. Wiley.

Wen, M. C. Y., Ying, S. L. X., & Nair, R. K. (2019). The Responsibility of Internal Auditors in Preventing Fraud in Malaysia Listed Companies. Business, Information Management and Computer Science (EBIMCS2019), 1-5.

West Virginia University. (2007). *NIJ special report: Education and training in fraud and forensic accounting: A guide for educational institutions, stakeholder organizations, Faculty and Students*. West Virginia University - Forensic Science Initiative Cooperative Argument. https://www.ojp.gov/pdffiles1/nij/grants/217589.pdf

Wijerathna, A. G. H. S. K., & Perera, H. A. P. L. (2020). A Systematic Literature Review on Forensic Accounting. *Proceedings of the 11th International Conference on Business and Information (ICBI 2020)*. https://www.researchgate.net/publication/351710923_A_Systematic_Literature_Review_on_Forensic_Accounting

wikipedia.org. (2021). *Credit card fraud*. Wikipedia, The Free Encyclopedia. Retrieved from https://en.wikipedia.org/w/index.php?title=Credit_card_fraud&oldid=1019457467

Williams, T. (2018). Role of Management, Corporate Governance, and Sarbanes-Oxley in Fraud: A Focus on the Precious Metals Industry. *Accounting, Finance, Sustainability, Governance and Fraud*, 391-409.

Williams, T. (2018). *Role of management, corporate governance, and sarbanes-oxley in fraud: A focus on the precious metals industry*. Retrieved from www.scopus.com

Williams, I. (2010). Corrupt Practices: Implications for Economic Growth and Development of Nigeria. *The Nigerian Accountant*, *38*(4), 44–50.

Williams, J. W. (2005). Governability matters: The private policing of economic crime and the challenge of democratic governance. *Policing and Society*, *15*(2), 187–211. doi:10.1080/10439460500071671

Williams, J. W. (2005). Reflections on the private versus public policing of economic crime. *British Journal of Criminology*, *45*(3), 316–339. doi:10.1093/bjc/azh083

Williams, J. W. (2006). Private legal orders: Professional markets and the commodification of financial governance. *Social & Legal Studies*, *15*(2), 209–235. doi:10.1177/0964663906063575

Wolfe, D. T., & Hermanson, D. R. (2004). The Fraud Diamond: Considering the Four Elements of Fraud: Certified Public Accountant. *The CPA Journal*, *74*(12), 38–42.

Wolfe, D., & Hermanson, D. (2004). The Fraud Diamond : Considering the Four Elements of Fraud. *The CPA Journal*, *74*(12), 38–42.

World Bank and Ministry of Planning and Investment of Vietnam. (2016). *Vietnam 2035: Toward prosperity, creativity, equity, and democracy*. The World Bank Group. https://openknowledge.worldbank.org/handle/10986/23724

World Bank. (2014). *Skilling up Vietnam: Preparing the workforce for a modern market economy*. Vietnam Development Report. https://documents1.worldbank.org/curated/en/283651468321297015/pdf/888950PUB0Box30lso0829400June172014.pdf

World Bank. (2016). *Vietnam report on the observance of standards and codes (ROSC) – Accounting and auditing module*. https://documents1.worldbank.org/curated/en/220021512482581847/pdf/121901-ROSC-PUBLIC-FinalROSCEN.pdf

World Bank. (2019). *Vietnam corporate accounting education in universities*. https://openknowledge.worldbank.org/bitstream/handle/10986/33469/Vietnam-Corporate-Accounting-Education-in-Universities.pdf?sequence=1&isAllowed=y

World Bank. (2020). *Economic profile of Vietnam: Doing business 2020, comparing business regulations in 190 countries*. https://openknowledge.worldbank.org/handle/10986/32436#:~:text=Doing%20Business%202020%20is%20the,business%20environment%20in%20190%20economies

World Economic Forum. (2016). *Insight Report: The Global Competitiveness Report 2016 - 2017.* Geneva: World Economic Forum. https://www3.weforum.org/docs/GCR2016-2017/05FullReport/TheGlobalCompetitivenessReport2016-2017_FINAL.pdf

Wyk, V. (2015). *Fraud Risk Assessment: A Conceptual Framework for Internal Auditors to Detect Financial Statement Fraud.* Advances in Management, Economics and Social Science.

Xu, H., Dao, M., & Wu, J. (2019). The effect of local political corruption on earnings quality. *Review of Quantitative Finance and Accounting.* https://www.scopus.com/inward/record.uri?eid=2-s2.0-85053195338&doi=10.1007%2Fs11156-018-0758-x&partnerID=40&md5=048b681de68277ce67d67e14d2c8f407

Xuan, S., Liu, G., Li, Z. L. Z., Wang, S., & Jiang, C. (2018). Random forest for credit card fraud detection. *2018 IEEE 15th International Conference on Networking, Sensing and Control (ICNSC), 2018*(1), 1-6. Retrieved from 10.1109/ICNSC.2018.8361343

Y, J., Dubey, T. N., & Sarika, S. (2019). A comparative analysis of various credit card fraud detection techniques. *International Journal of Recent Technology and Engineering, 7*(5), 402-407.

Y., C., & X., H. (2021). CatBoost for Fraud Detection in Financial Transactions. *International Conference on Consumer Electronics and Computer Engineering (ICCECE)*, 176-179. Retrieved from https://ieeexplore.ieee.org/document/9342475

Yadav, S., & Yadav, S. (2013). Forensic accounting: A new dynamic approach to investigate fraud cases. *Excel International Journal of Multidisciplinary Management Studies, 3*(7), 1-9.

Yale, G., Grove, H., & Clouse, M. (2013). Risk management lessons learned: Countrywide report. *Corporate Ownership and Control, 11*(1H), 33-46.

Yale, G., Grove, H., & Clouse, M. (2013). Risk management lessons learned: Countrywide report. *Corporate Ownership and Control, 11*(1H), 33-46. doi:10.22495/cocv11i1conf1p4

Yamada, A., Sakurai, Y., & Ishida, R. (2020). Influence of geographic distribution on real activities manipulation within consolidated companies: Evidence from Japan. *Research in International Business and Finance.* https://www.scopus.com/inward/record.uri?eid=2-s2.0-85089901554&doi=10.1016%2Fj.ribaf.2020.101306&partnerID=40&md5=64a2b8249def4ae41d06a4271c1f2dbf

Yang, C., & Lee, K. (2020). Developing a strategy map for forensic accounting with fraud risk management: An integrated balanced scorecard-based decision model. *Evaluation and Program Planning, 80.* Advance online publication. doi:10.1016/j.evalprogplan.2020.101780

Yasser, Q. R., & Mamun, A. A. (2015). The impact of CEO duality attributes on earnings management in the East. *Corporate Governance (Bingley).* https://www.scopus.com/inward/record.uri?eid=2-s2.0-84942770012&doi=10.1108%2FCG-04-2015-0041&partnerID=40&md5=dee41da152434b8c74c812876115c772

Yeoh, P. (2019). Artificial intelligence: Accelerator or panacea for financial crime? *Journal of Financial Crime, 26*(2), 634–646. doi:10.1108/JFC-08-2018-0077

Yin, R. (1994). *Case Study Research: Design and Methods* (2nd ed.). Sage Publications, Lda.

Yu, S., & Rha, J. (2021). Research trends in accounting fraud using network analysis. *Sustainability (Switzerland), 13*(10). Advance online publication. doi:10.3390u13105579

Yusuf, O. T. (2010). Brokers and the control of post contractual opportunism in the Nigerian insurance market. *Journal of Financial Crime, 17*(2), 223–239. doi:10.1108/13590791011033917

Yusuf, O. T. (2011). Brokers' incentives and conflicts of interest in the control of opportunism. *The Journal of Risk Finance*, *12*(3), 168–18. doi:10.1108/15265941111136923

Zagera, L., Malis, S. S., & Novak, A. (2016). The Role and Responsibility of Auditors in Prevention and Detection of Fraudulent Financial Reporting. In *3rd Global Conference On Business, Economics, Management And Tourism*, (pp. 693-700). Elsevier. 10.1016/S2212-5671(16)30291-X

Zang, A. Y. (2012). Evidence on the trade-off between real activities manipulation and accrual-based earnings management. *Accounting Review*. https://www.scopus.com/inward/record.uri?eid=2-s2.0-80155175155&doi=10.2308%2Faccr-10196&partnerID=40&md5=36a3f07a5e0186426d834341805eb3fb

Zeljko, T., Ilija, C. & Branko, K. (2019). Manufacturing and the rise of artificial intelligence: innovation challenges. *30th DAAAM international symposium on intelligent manufacturing and automation, 30*, 192-196.

Zhang, X., Han, Y., Xu, W., & Wang, Q. (2021). HOBA: A novel feature engineering methodology for credit card fraud detection with a deep learning architecture. *Information Sciences*, *557*, 302–316.

Zhou, A. (2017). EY, Deloitte and PwC embrace artificial intelligence for tax and accounting. *Forbes*.

Zimbleman, M. K., Albrecht, C. C., Albrecht, S. W., & Albrecht, C. O. (2012). Forensic Accounting. Cengage Learning.

Zysman, A. (2004), Forensic accounting demystified. *World Investigation Network Standard Practice for Investigative and Forensic Accounting*, 1-28.

Zysman, A. (2006). *Forensic accounting demystified*. http://www.forensicaccounting.com/home.html#one

Zysman, A. (2006). *World Investigators Networks Standard Practice for Investigative and Forensic Accounting Engagement*. Canadian Institute of Chartered Accountant Journal.

About the Contributors

Suleman Sherali Kamwani is a membership associate CPA Australia & Master of professional Accounting from Australia has several years expertise in corporate sector related to the financial accounting issues and thorough understanding of corporate governance, besides around the world more than one decade teaching experiences in advance accounting & audit courses, presented couple of research papers in seminars; related to significance of corporate governance in related party transactions and significance of forensic accounting techniques in corporate governance, besides author of a chapter about why Malaysians are involved in related party transactions in the context of corporate governance.

Elisabete S. Vieira is Coordinator Professor, ISCA-UA, University of Aveiro. She is researcher at the Research Unit on Governance, Competitiveness and Public Policies (GOVCOPP), being Vice Coordinator of the Competitiveness, Innovation and Sustainability (CIS) Research Group. She has a Ph.D. in Finance from the ISCTE, Lisbon. Her research topics include corporate finance, corporate behavior finance, and corporate governance.

Mara Madaleno is Assistant Professor of Finance and Economics at the Department of Economics, Management, Industrial Engineering and Tourist at the University of Aveiro. Finished her Ph.D. in 2011 at the University of Aveiro in Economics. Director of the Master in Economics – Branches: Finance + Business Economics. Full researcher at the GOV.COPP – Research Unit on Governance, Competitiveness and Public Policies, and Vice-Coordinator of the research line SAD – Systems for Decision Support at GOVCOPP. She is also Vice-Director of the Master in Data Science for Social Sciences and Vice-Coordinator of Continua-UA . Her research interests include financial markets, financial economics, financial energy markets, environmental economics, energy and environment, sustainability. Participates in several research projects.

Graça Azevedo has a PhD in Management (scientific field: Accounting) at the Institute of Higher Labor and Enterprise – ISCTE. She has published and presented several articles in national and international journals and conferences as well. She is a member of the Editorial Board of international journal "Accounting and Finance Research". She currently teaches courses in scientific field of Financial Accounting at the Institute of Higher Learning in Accounting and Administration of the University of Aveiro. Her research interests are related to financial reporting, impression management strategies and international accounting standards.

* * *

Abdulkadri Toyin Alabi holds a BSc and MSc in accounting from Kwara State University. Abdulkadri is an associate member of professional bodies like the Institute of Chartered Accountants of Nigeria and the Chartered Institute of Taxation of Nigeria. As a dedicated and detail-oriented chartered accountant, he has been meeting the accounting needs of end users in the practical field of accounting in addition to in the academic setting. He currently works as a senior accountant for the Kwara State Government and as a researcher affiliated with Kwara State University. His research interests lie in the broad areas of financial and corporate reporting as well as forensic accounting and auditing. His recent publication features in Global Journal of Accounting.

Maria Anunciação Bastos holds a PhD Accounting from the joint doctoral program between the University of Aveiro and the University of Minho. She holds a Master Degree in Accounting and Auditing from the University of Aveiro and a Degree in Accounting and Administration, with a major in Accounting and Auditing, from the University of Aveiro - Institute of Accounting and Administration (ISCA-UA). She is an Adjunct Professor at ISCA-UA. She teaches several courses in the area of Accounting Sciences, such as Introduction to Accounting and Financial Accounting. She is member of the research unit on Governance, Competitiveness and Public Policies (GOVCOPP), participating in the research group of Decision Support Systems.

Hawal Olayiwola Dalegan holds a Masters in Financial Management from American Trinity University (ATU), California, USA, Masters in Policy and Strategies Studies from Kwara State University, Nigeria, Masters in Accounting and Finance from IAEC University, Togo, Masters in Business Administration from National Open University, Nigeria, Masters in Accounting and an Advanced Diploma in Forensic Accounting and Fraud Investigation from Niger Delta University, Nigeria. He is currently pursuing his PhD in Professional Accounting at American Trinity University (ATU), California, USA. He is an Associate of the Institute of Professional Financial Managers, London, a Chartered Fraud Manager at the Chartered Institute of Management and Leadership, USA and a Certified Forensic Investigation Professional of International Institute of Certified Forensic Investigation Professional, USA. He is currently an assistant lecturer at College of Islamic Finance and Management Science where he teaches a range of accounting and finance modules.

Varaidzo Denhere is a holder of a PhD in Auditing, MCom (Accounting), BCom Accounting (Hons), BSC Geography & Environmental Studies, and a Diploma in Education (Secondary). She is a versatile, results-oriented professional with strong interpersonal communication skills and an excellent team player. She is currently a Postdoctoral Research Fellow at the University of Johannesburg. In 2020 Varaidzo co-developed content material for an online Short Learning Program for Professional Accountants in the field of Artificial Intelligence at the University of Johannesburg. In 2020-2021 she participated as a research assistant in an ETDP SETA Project on "Implications of the fourth industrial revolution in the Education, Training and Development Sector", chaired by her Host Professor. She was also the organising secretary for the International Conference of Accounting and Business (I-CAB) 2021 hosted by the University of Johannesburg. Currently she is a research assistant for the Namibia 4IR Task Force. She has published in the area of risk management, green banking, sustainability, and the fourth industrial revolution.

Giam Do is an Associate Professor, Dean of the Faculty of Accounting and Business Management, and Chaiman of Department of Managerial Accounting and Auditing at Vietnam National University of Agriculture, Gia Lam, Hanoi, Vietnam. He earned his Ph.D in Economics major in Finance from Chiangmai University, Thailand in 2010. Prof. Giam Do has long years of teaching experience in Analytical Business, Managerial Accounting, Cost Accounting, Financial Report Analysis and other related courses. His research interests are financial economics, accounting and business management.

Ankur Goel is a committed, passionate and motivated academician, researcher, reviewer and speaker. A PhD (Management), UGC NET (Commerce, Management), MA, LLB, M.Com, PGDM, 05 NPTEL certifications. Having over 10 yrs of education industry experience along with 09 years in corporate world. Published many research papers (UGC-Care, Scopus, ABDC), attended various FDP's, participated in numerous conferences, published national & international patent as well and reviewer for many highly indexed journals. Well aware of NAAC/IQAC processes, BOS member, Resource Person, Keynote Speaker, Magazine editor etc and served a position as an 'OSD to VC' at IIMT University, Meerut.

Etienne Harb is currently Assistant Professor of Finance at the Faculty of Business Administration and Economics at Notre Dame University, Lebanon, and Research Fellow at ESSCA School of Management. She holds a Ph.D. in Economics – Financial Markets from Panthéon-Assas University in 2011, a Master's degree in International Economics from Nanterre University in 2005, and a second Master's degree in Finance and Econometrics from Panthéon-Assas University in 2006. Prior to joining NDU, Dr. Harb served as an Assistant Professor of Finance at ESSCA School of Management, and as a Research and Teaching Fellow at Panthéon-Assas University where she taught several courses of Accounting, Corporate Finance and Financial Markets such as Managerial Accounting, Financial Management, Portfolio Management, Derivatives, Credit Risk Management, and International Finance. She published several books and peer-reviewed articles in top-ranked academic journals. Her research activity focuses on Financial Risk Management, High-Frequency Trading, and Financial Markets' Microstructure and Regulation.

Helena Coelho Inácio has a PhD in Accounting and Management from the University Autonoma the Madrid, a MSc in Economy by the University of Coimbra and a degree in Accounting and Audit by the University of Aveiro. She is Professor in the University of Aveiro, at the Institute of Accounting and Administration. She lectures under graduated and graduated courses of accounting and audit. She has a book of Internal Control, communications and publications in audit area. She is a member of the research unit on Competitiveness, Governance and Public Policies (GOVCOPP).

Athar Iqbal is an Associate Professor at Iqra University. He is also an Associate member of the Institute of Cost and Management Accountants of Pakistan. He earned his PhD degree in Finance. He has published more than 20 research papers in different areas of finance. Main area of interest is corporate governance and related issues.

Abdullahi Ishola is an Assistant Lecturer in accounting at Essex Business School, University of Essex, UK where he is currently completing his PhD in Accounting and Finance researching on integrated reporting. His research interests lie in areas of corporate and financial reporting, auditing and assurance and climate change issues. His recent publication appears in Business Strategy and Environment. He is a Fellow of the Higher Education Academy, UK and teaches a wide range of accounting and finance modules. He is also a chartered accountant and a chartered tax practitioner with ample experience as an auditor.

Sudarshana Kerenalli had pursued his graduation and post graduation from VTU Belagavi. His research interests include Machine Learning, Deep Learning and Data Science, IoT applications in Agriculture, and Data Security. He is currently a research scholar at GITAM University, India.

Muhammad Irfan Khan is an Associate Professor and Chairperson, Department of Business Administration at Jinnah University for Women. He earned his PhD degree in Finance from the Iqra University, Pakistan. He has 14 years of work experience in Academia and 6 years experience in corporate sector. He has participated in international research conference as paper presenter and Session Chair. Currently he is serving as Reviewer in various nationally recognized as well as International Impact Factor Research Journals. He has published several research papers in national as well international research journals. He has also got publication of ONE book on the topic of Development Finance, and ONE book chapter titled as" The New Face of Global Trade in a Post-Pandemic World".

Rim Khoury is currently an Associate Professor of Finance at the Faculty of Business Administration and Economics at Notre Dame University, Lebanon. She holds a PhD in International Finance from Sogang University, South Korea, in 2009 and a Master degree of Business Administration (MBA) from University of Balamand in 2004. Prior to joining NDU, Dr. Khoury taught several courses in Accounting, Finance, and Economics at Hanyang University (South Korea). She has also taught as a part-time faculty member at American University of Technology (AUT). She is the recipient of several awards such as Outstanding Doctoral Thesis Award (2009), Grand winner for Korea Times Magazine Economic Contest (2007), and The Academic Excellence Award from the Korean Government (2006). She published numerous peer-reviewed articles in top-ranked academic journals. Her research activity focuses on ESG and Financial Performance, Corporate Governance, Volatility Modeling, Capital Structure and Market Timing, Corporate Finance and Banking, Investments and Asset Pricing, and Bibliometric Studies.

Thao Lai is a senior lecturer and formal researcher of the Department of Management Accounting and Auditing, the Faculty of Accounting and Business Management, Vietnam National University of Agriculture (VNUA), Gia Lam, Hanoi, Vietnam. She holds the following degree: Ph.D. in Accounting - Auditing at the Department of Auditing, Academy of Finance, Vietnam (2020), MS Business Management at the College of Economics and Management, University of the Philippines at Los Banos (2013). At the Department of Management Accounting and Auditing, she taught/teaches the following courses: Auditing and Assurance, Accounting Reports Analysis, Financial Statements Auditing, Performance Auditing, Internal Auditing, Accounting - Auditing Standards. She is a member of the Vietnam Federation of Accountants and Auditors (VAA). The author has written several papers in the field of Auditing and Accounting. She had written the Ph.D. thesis dealing on auditing national target program for new rural development conducted by the state audit office: "Completing the process of auditing national target program for new rural development conducted by the state audit office". She served as a consultant (Auditing and Accounting) for the Vietnam Association of Certified Public Accountants, the Ministry of Finance of Vietnam to amend and supplement the system of Vietnamese accounting and auditing standards.

Nohade Nasrallah earned her PhD in Business administration – Finance from the Lebanese University in 2018 and a Master's degree of Business Administration (MBA) with high distinction from Notre Dame University in 2008. She is an Assistant Professor of Finance and Accounting at the Faculty of Business Administration and Economics at Notre Dame University, Lebanon. She taught at The Lebanese University and La Sagesse University, Lebanon before joining NDU. She is an experienced professor with demonstrated history of working in the Higher Education. She taught many courses: Financial Management, Investments, International Finance, Financial and Managerial Accounting, Taxation and Audit. She published several peer-reviewed articles in top-ranked academic journals. Her research interests include Corporate Governance, ESG, Corporate Finance, Financial Markets, Digital Transformation, Digital Technology and Artificial Intelligence in Accounting and Finance.

Ifeoluwapo Adebimpe Oyewobi grew up in Nigeria Ifeoluwapo is a lecturer at Bingham University. Ifeoluwapo is a Doctor of Public Sector Accounting and Quality Financial Reporting. She is a co-editor of USBED which is an International Journal of Social and Educational Science, Turkey. Ifeoluwapo is currently writing some books about guide to writing your thesis, auditing practices and International Public Sector Accounting Practices. Before devoting her work fulltime to Bingham University, Ifeoluwapo served as operational manager at VICBIM Multi-concepts. At this stage, Ifeoluwapo has established herself and happiest with husband growing their family.

Hong Phi is a senior lecturer and formal researcher of the Faculty of Accounting and Business Management, Vietnam National University of Agriculture (VNUA), Gia Lam, Hanoi, Vietnam. She graduated the doctoral program in Accounting major of Commerce sector at Komazawa University, Tokyo, Japan. Her topic focused on the Accounting for Vietnam Economic Groups. Moreover, she got significant times researching and studying in value chain at Humboldt University in Berlin, Germany from December, 2009 to August, 2010. Recently, she strongly concentrates on researching the international integration of Vietnam in accounting as well as cooperative sector or rural economic development. Particularly, she has also worked as a chief accountant and accounting consultant at Vietnamese Enterprises in many years before being a lecturer or researcher in VNUA.

Mylara Reddy is an Assistant Professor at Department of Computer Science and Engineering, GITAM University, Bangalore, Karnataka, India. He received M. Tech. degree and Ph. D. from Visvesraya Technological University in 2006 and 2019 respectively. His research interest include cloud computing, fault tolerance, Computer networks, and file structures.

A. Usha Ruby is an Associate Professor at Department of Computer Science and Engineering, GITAM University, Bangalore, Karnataka, India. She received M. Tech. degree from Anna University Chennai and Ph. D. from Bharath Institute of Higher Education and Research, Chennai in 2008 and 2017 respectively. Her research interest include Computer Networks, Digital Image Processing.

Syed Muhammad Salman is a PhD scholar, doing PhD in Finance at Iqra University, Pakistan. He has published various research papers in national and international research journals. His main area of interest is corporate finance.

Núria Villaescusa is an assistant professor at Universitat Internacional de Catalunya and senior lecturer in the Accounting and Control Department at IESE Business School. She holds a PhD in Accounting from the Universitat Politècnica de Catalunya and an MBA from IESE Business School. She started her professional career at KPMG Audit. Later, she has worked as a financial manager and as a consultant. Her consulting work focus on the implementation of management control systems, including the specific areas of financial accounting, cost accounting, and business risk management in both large and small and medium-sized companies. She has also worked as an expert witness on issues related to accounting fraud. Her areas of research interest are earnings management, its consequences and how to detect them and forensic accounting.

Index

A

B

C

D

E

F

G

I

L

Recommended Reference Books

IGI Global's reference books are available in three unique pricing formats: Print Only, E-Book Only, or Print + E-Book.

Shipping fees may apply.

www.igi-global.com

ISBN: 978-1-7998-1048-3
EISBN: 978-1-7998-1049-0
© 2020; 605 pp.
List Price: US$ **285**

ISBN: 978-1-5225-8933-4
EISBN: 978-1-5225-8934-1
© 2020; 667 pp.
List Price: US$ **295**

ISBN: 978-1-7998-0357-7
EISBN: 978-1-7998-0359-1
© 2020; 451 pp.
List Price: US$ **235**

ISBN: 978-1-7998-0070-5
EISBN: 978-1-7998-0071-2
© 2020; 144 pp.
List Price: US$ **175**

ISBN: 978-1-5225-6980-0
EISBN: 978-1-5225-6981-7
© 2019; 339 pp.
List Price: US$ **235**

ISBN: 978-1-5225-5390-8
EISBN: 978-1-5225-5391-5
© 2018; 125 pp.
List Price: US$ **165**

Do you want to stay current on the latest research trends, product announcements, news, and special offers?
Join IGI Global's mailing list to receive customized recommendations, exclusive discounts, and more.
Sign up at: **www.igi-global.com/newsletters.**

Publisher of Peer-Reviewed, Timely, and Innovative Academic Research

IGI Global
PUBLISHER of TIMELY KNOWLEDGE

www.ingramcontent.com/pod-product-compliance
Lightning Source LLC
LaVergne TN
LVHW062112300926
849161LV00010B/2442